Classical Social Theory

Classical
Social
Theory

Ian Craib

OXFORD UNIVERSITY PRESS
1997

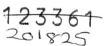

Oxford University Press, Great Clarendon Street, Oxford OX2 6DP

Oxford New York

*Auckland Bangkok Buenos Aires Cape Town Chennai
Dar es Salaam Delhi Hong Kong Istanbul Karachi Kolkata
Kuala Lumpur Madrid Melbourne Mexico City Mumbai Nairobi
São Paulo Shanghai Taipei Tokyo Toronto*

*Oxford is a registered trade mark of Oxford University Press
in the UK and in certain other countries*

*Published in the United States
by Oxford University Press Inc., New York*

British Library Cataloguing in Publication Data

Data available

Library of Congress Cataloging in Publication Data

*Craib, Ian, 1945– .
Classical social theory / Ian Craib.
Includes bibliographical references.
1. Sociology—Philosophy. 2. Social sciences—Philosophy.
I. Title.
HM24.C698 1997 301'.01—dc21 96–24111*

*ISBN-13: 978–0–19–878117–2
ISBN-10: 0–19–878117–2*

10 9

*Printed in Great Britain
on acid-free paper by
Biddles Ltd,
King's Lynn, Norfolk*

Preface

In this book, Ian Craib compellingly shows the value of studying such classic thinkers as Marx, Weber, Durkheim, and Simmel alongside the more popular contemporary questions of sociology. Providing an account of the key ideas of classical social theory, Dr Craib establishes their relevance today, their enduring significance, and their contribution to understanding contemporary problems.

Written in a direct, personal style, *Classical Social Theory*'s thematic structure helps the reader compare the theorists systematically, and the book-by-book approach pays close attention to each of thinkers' key texts, quoting the most important passages and analysing them in a clear, straightforward way.

Other student-friendly features include:

- Biographical details and an elementary overview of the work of Marx, Weber, Durkheim, and Simmel
- *Dramatis personae* at the end of the book, with brief details of the life and thought of other relevant thinkers
- Glossary covering important terms and phrases used in the text

How to use this book

Classical Social Theory is divided up into three parts, covering methodology (ways of thinking about thinking), conceptions of social structure (answers to the question 'what is society?'), and explanations of the nature of social change and historical development.

Each part contains a chapter on each theorist, so that you can either read the book from beginning to end to develop a comparative understanding of all four thinkers, or you can read the chapters on one individual thinker throughout, concentrating on the development of that thinker's theory.

Before you get to the three main parts, there are introductory chapters about this book and on the biographies and social and intellectual backgrounds of the individual thinkers.

Each chapter has suggestions for further reading at the end. Throughout the book you will find summary boxes, outlining the ideas just discussed and consolidating the different thinkers' views of them.

At the end of the book, there are various resources that you may wish to refer to as you go through. There is a list of other relevant thinkers of the time (the *Dramatis personae*), a Glossary, and the complete references for all the books mentioned in the text. Throughout the text, you'll see that the original publication dates are given for the classical texts along with the dates of current editions, so that you can see the development of the ideas as well as being able to get hold of complete versions of the relevant texts.

Acknowledgements

This book has emerged from several decades of discussion and argument with students and colleagues and I can thank only the most recent contributors to an ongoing process. I would like to thank in particular Ted Benton, David Lee, and John Scott, all of the Essex Sociology Department, for reading and commenting on sections of the manuscript. It would be nice to blame them for the book's deficiencies, but sadly I alone am responsible for those.

Contents

Chapter summaries

1. What's the point?

The purpose of the book: the continuing importance of the founding thinkers—the necessity of general theories—sociology's relationship to the Enlightenment; the two-sided nature of Enlightenment thought and of social theory; the basic dualisms of social theory; the structure of the book and how to read it. *How to think about the thinkers*.

2. The main characters and the main ideas

Brief biographies of the classical theorists (*Marx, Durkheim, Simmel,* and *Weber*), together with an elementary introduction to their ideas and intellectual background. *The social and intellectual background* to the rise of sociology.

PART 1. WHAT IS SOCIETY AND HOW DO WE STUDY IT?

Introduction to Part 1

3. Emile Durkheim: the discovery of social facts

Introduction: background; Comte and positivism. *Durkheim's rules*: the objectivity of social facts; considering social facts as things; the use of statistics to identify social facts; the normal and the pathological—the normality of crime. *Suicide as a social fact*: its underlying causes. *What can we take from Durkheim*: criticisms of Durkheim's methodology and discussion.

4. Karl Marx: the primacy of production

Introduction: the problems set by political misinterpretations of Marx; Marx and Darwin. *Marx's methods: the starting point*: the ideology of individualism; the importance of practical, everyday life; the action/structure dualism in Marx; comparison of Marx with Durkheim; dialectical thinking and the separation of analysis and history.

5. Max Weber: the primacy of social action

Introduction: comparison with Marx and Durkheim; Kantian background and the differences between the natural and the human sciences. *The proper object of sociology*: sociology's concern with the individual event and Weber's debate with Marx's ghost; the society/individual dualism; behaviour and action; meaningful social action; further comparison of Marx and Durkheim. *Different types of meaningful action. Understanding social action*: observational and explanatory understanding; causal adequacy and meaning adequacy. *The ideal type*: Weber's individualism and further comparison with Marx and Durkheim; scientific and common-sense knowledge. *Values and value-freedom.*

6. Georg Simmel: society as form and process—the outsider's view

Introduction: Simmel as a herald of postmodernism. *Society and the social*: his conception of society—comparison with Weber and Lukacs; social forms and the life process and the protection of individuality. *The social forms*: society, social relationships, social institutions, and play forms; his methods and organizational principles.

Conclusion to Part 1: the first basic dualism of social theory

---

PART 2. CONCEPTIONS OF SOCIAL STRUCTURE

Introduction to Part 2

7. Durkheim: drunk and orderly

Introduction

Social integration and system integration

Types of solidarity: *The Division of Labour*

Mechanical and organic solidarity: repressive law and the *conscience collective*; the function of the division of labour; Durkheim's functionalism; organic solidarity and restitutive law; individualism and dependency in modern societies; Durkheim and modern politics; the use of the organic analogy. *Abnormal forms of the division of labour*: understanding social conflict; industrialism and capitalism; the forced division of labour; managerial deficiencies.

The sociology of religion and knowledge

The nature of religion: the sacred/profane distinction; totemism; religious beliefs as representations of the social; comparison of Durkheim and Marx on religion. *The arguments in Elementary Forms*: Durkheim's causal, interpretive, and functional analyses of religion. Durkheimian analyses of contemporary societies. *The sociology of knowledge*: Durkheim's attempt at a sociological explanation of Kant's categories; the link between social structure and the structure of thought, the problems with Durkheim's sociology of knowledge and comparison with Marx's theory of ideology.

The sociology of morality and education

The conservative and radical Durkheim; the relation of morality to the social; morality in a period of change; sociology and morality; moral education and its aim; spontaneous education and direct teaching; discipline, authority, and power; the rational justification of moral rules; dignity, self-determination, and attachment to society; the humanistic goals of education and the balance of individual and society.

The sociology of the law, state, and politics

The evolution of punishment towards humanist ideals; the developing sympathy for the criminal; the power of the state; the distinction between governor and governed and the definition of the state; the governing of secondary groupings; the state as defender of individual rights; Durkheim and contemporary political debates.

Conclusion

The importance of Durkheim's insights; his contributions to understanding the basic dualisms of sociology.

8. Was Marx a Marxist?

Introduction

Marxism and popular prejudice and simplistic arguments; relationship between Marx's earlier and later works; his starting point in human action; comparison with Durkheim.

Human powers 1: the theory of alienation

Underlying conception of human nature—distinction from a theory of needs; human nature as a transformative power—humans change themselves through changing their environment. The alienation of the worker from the product, from work, and from co-workers and his/her own nature. Marxist idealism and its problems; the empirical study of alienation; the distinction between economic analysis and the analysis of ideas and action.

Human powers 2: commodity fetishism

The continuity between Marx's earlier and later work; commodity fetishism as the alienation of human relationships; the 'free' market.

Marxist economics: a brief and simple introduction

Classical and marginalist economics; the labour theory of value; use value and exchange value; labour power as a commodity with a use and exchange value; exploitation; surface appearances and underlying reality; capitalism as a system of regular crises; the central contradiction of capitalism—the forces and relations of production; Marx's sociological economics.

Social class

The place of class in Marxist theory; class-in-itself and class-for-itself. The peasantry and its need for strong leadership. The bourgeoisie and its different fractions. The petty bourgeoisie, traditional and new. The proletariat—working-class identity and shared experience; divisions in the proletariat and contemporary attempts to understand them. The lumpenproletariat and the underclass. The contemporary relevance of social class.

The state

Marx's political and analytic writings; the conspiracy theory of the state; the state as alienated human power and revolutionary democracy; comparison with Durkheim; economic explanations of the state and the possibility of its autonomy; the peaceful or violent transformation of the state; the class nature of the modern state; class and citizenship.

Ideology

Ideology as false consciousness and as non-science; ideology and social integration; ideas and the life process—parallels with modern sociology and psychology; ideology as alienation; economic determinist conceptions of ideology; ideology as illusion; ideology as imagination; ideology as the accurate perception of one level of reality; ideology and commodity fetishism; representation as ideology—the link with postmodernism; conclusion—the difficulties with deterministic notions.

Marxism and the family

Primitive communism; private property and the development of the pairing family; the linking of people and property; the social organization of sexuality and love; assessment of Engel's work.

Conclusion

Comparison with Durkheim; further development of the basic dualisms.

9. The liberal Weber

Introduction

Weber's complexity; Weber and Marx.

The fundamental concepts of sociology

Legitimacy; conflict; Weber's cautious evolutionism; communal relations based on identity; associative relations based on interest; corporate groups and different forms of control; the nature of politics and the state; power as an end in itself.

Weber's economic sociology

Weber's concern with the sociological preconditions of the capitalist economy; the advantages of the market; formal and substantive rationality; the stability offered by the market to precarious social and political institutions; free disposal over goods and free labour and other preconditions of the development of formally rational accounting in productive enterprises; different types of capitalism and the peculiarity of western capitalism.

Class, status, and party

Weber and a theory of social structure; comparison of Marx and Weber on social class; class situation as market situation and life chances; the possibility of solidary class relations; the complexity of class structure seen in Weberian terms; the possibility of combining Marxist and Weberian conceptions; status as social esteem and lifestyle and the ambiguity of Weber's concept; the relationships between class and status in Weber's and Marx's sense; status groups in contemporary society; status groups and educational qualifications; professional groups and self-interest—comparison with Durkheim; parties and their ineffectiveness—Weber's determinism.

Power, domination, and authority

Types of domination; charismatic leadership—comparison with Durkheim; the routinization of charisma; traditional patriarchal domination and its development into patrimonialism; feudalism and its development; legal-rational domination and the characteristics of the modern state; the absence of any absolute basis for authority; the basis of legitimacy in legal-rational domination; Weber's ideal type of bureaucracy.

Conclusion

The fragility of the social order.

10. Simmel: the social and the personal

Introduction

Simmel's originality; the mutual implications of Simmel and Durkheim.

Society and the individual

The evolution of the individual/group relation from a starting point of near merging; individuation and the development of individual norms; the paradox of the emergence of the individual and the growing power of the group; the development of multiple and conflict roles; similarities between Simmel and Parsons; Simmel's radical critique of universal institutions; the significance of the size of social groups; the dyad and its internal fragility; the move from the dyad to larger groups.

The Philosophy of Money

Value and exchange; human beings as valuing creatures; Simmel and existentialism; the objectification of subjective value; comparison with Marx; the exchange of value and the exchange of representations—Simmel and postmodernism; money as the extension of freedom and its psychological consequences; the growth of objective culture and the decreasing importance of the personality; Simmel's theory of alienation; the ambivalent implications of the division of labour; the decreasing ability to love objects; conclusion—Simmel and Marxism, Simmel and Weber.

Simmel's sociology

Simmel as a sociological impressionist. *Simmel on relationships*: faithfulness in the maintenance of relationships; the renegade; the distinctive nature of Simmel's notion of the life process; Simmel and Freud; gratitude as a cement for and generator of relationships; Simmel and Kleinian psychoanalysis; sociability as a play form and an example of formal sociology; domination as a form of interaction; domination by an individual, by a plurality, and by principle or law; comparison with Weber; conflict as a contribution to integration; the importance of secrecy; the secret society. *Simmel on social types*: the notion of type in literature and social theory; the miser as a seeker of total control; the miser's similarity to the spendthrift; the adventurer as an artist; the stranger as a newcomer and/or outsider; the objectivity of the outsider; objectivity as participation. *Simmel on modernity*: The psychological effects of urban living; the head ruling the heart; the sophistication of the town-dweller; the standardization of social life; the individual's conflicting needs for identification and separation and fashion as satisfying both; the psychological satisfactions of science; class and status differences in fashion. *Simmel on social groups*: the poor; different obligations and duties; the emergence of the poor as a group in modern societies through state welfare systems; modern developments of Simmel—the social construction of poverty; comparison with Marx; the aristocracy—united by the highest status honour; in-group marriage; the possibility of decadent emptiness; women, love, and sexuality: the masculine nature of objective culture; the psychological differences between men and women and comparison with modern gender theorists; the possibility of gender equality in relation to the objective culture; male and female sexuality; flirtation as a play form; Simmel's essentialism; comparison with Engels.

Conclusion

Simmel's compatibility with other theorists; further development of the basic dualisms.

Conclusion to Part 2: The theorists contrasted

PART 3. HISTORY AND SOCIAL CHANGE

Introduction to Part 3

11. Durkheim's organic analogy

Introduction

Durkheim on history and politics.

The organic analogy and Durkheim's theory of history

The explanation of change in the *Division of Labour*; change through population growth; primary and secondary factors in the division of labour; increasing universality of the *conscience collective* and the growing freedom of the individual; the importance of organic and psychological factors in the division of labour; Durkheim's materialism and his increasing concern with cultural patterns. The explanation of change in *The Rules of Sociological Method*; the classification of social types; the primitive horde and more complex combinations; societies as species; the distinction between society and civilization; critique of the species analogy; Durkheim and modern evolutionary theory.

Durkheim's conservatism and Durkheim's socialism

The debate about Durkheim's politics; the importance of placing limits on human nature; his critique of modernity and his critique of socialism as an ideological reaction to industrialization compared to sociology as a scientific reaction—comparison with Engels. Durkheim's liberal/left sympathies; the emphasis on the importance of professional groupings which would control the state (his syndicalism); his support for the Dreyfusards and his individualism—the sacredness of the individual in general; the importance of freedom of thought and the cognitive role of the state; the problem of politics and analysis in Durkheim; his conservative views on divorce and women.

Conclusion

The continuing importance of Durkheim as a theorist of society and social cohesion; the *conscience collective* in the modern world; the importance of his conception of the state as protector of the individual and civil society; his lack of a theory of action; criticism of his theory of history.

12. Marx and the meaning of history

Introduction

Marx's conception of history; Marx and Hegel; dialectical materialism and historical inevitability.

Historical laws and laws of history

Historical laws; Marx's originality; Marx's suggestions as explanation sketches.

Types of society/modes of production

Primitive communism: possible paths of social development starting from the priority of the community over the individual; forms of distributing the surplus; Marx's theoretical ordering of levels of development in terms of the development of individuality. *The Asiatic mode of production*: dominance of communal property and the despot; important role of the state and religion. *The Germanic mode of production*: the inevitable production of traditional relations. *The ancient mode of production*: dominated by the city; development of individual proprietorship; the emergence of the state; transformation brought about by the reproduction of the system. *Feudalism and the development of capitalism*: the ancient and the feudal modes; the town/country division and the division of labour; the development of the towns—the craft guilds—the merchant class—the bourgeoisie; machine production; the money economy; international markets. *Evolution from feudalism to capitalism*: a theoretical understanding of the development; comparison with Durkheim. *The complexities of class analysis of history*: the English Civil War as an example.

Theory and history

Theoretical and empirical distinctions: modern elaborations of the concept of mode of production. *Contemporary notions of evolution*: The nature of historical progress; open-ended conceptions of evolution.

The dynamics of capitalism

The tendency of the rate of profit to fall: living and dead labour and the increasing importance of the latter; countervailing tendencies; the increasing rate of technological change; the expansionist dynamic of capitalism. *Changes at other levels: transformations of the crisis*: Habermas on the evolution of modern capitalism; economic crisis—rationality crisis—legitimation crisis—motivation crisis.

Communism

The importance of the French Revolution; the proletariat as a revolution class; violence and revolution; the concept of overdetermination; the state and revolution; earlier and later phases of communism; the importance of utopian ideas; comparison with reality.

Conclusion

13. Weber as a tragic liberal: the rise of the West

Introduction

Weber's ghostly evolutionism.

The sociology of religion

Choices between tradition and progress/differentiation; prophecy and the growth of universality; a class analysis of religions, the latter producing action to change the world.

Chinese religion: Confucianism and Taoism

The power of the family giving power to the countryside over the town; the power of the central government; conflict between central government, its local officials, and local kin groups; the growth of capitalism restricted by the power of the family and the Confucian ethic which devalued economic activity; Taoism as a mystical alternative; comparison of Confucianism and Puritanism.

Indian religion: Hinduism and Buddhism

The caste system; distinction between sects and churches in relation to Hinduism; the Brahmins; the absence of a universal ethic, and of the possibility of social criticism in an eternal order; status conflict in the wider social order; the Brahmin ascetic ideal; the absence of a rationalized pursuit of wealth.

Palestine: ancient Judaism

The importance of positive ethical action and unintended consequences; the history of Israel and its special relationship to Jahwe; the emergence of new ideas on the edge of centres of civilization; prophecy and the prophets; Jahwe as a universal God.

The Protestant ethic and the spirit of capitalism

Introduction: the descriptive and analytic in Weber's work; the 'elective affinity' as an explanation; the work ethic in Weber's history. *The spirit of capitalism*: capitalism based on rational accounting; protestantism not originally associated with the accumulation of wealth association; Benjamin Franklin as the source of the ideal type of the spirit of capitalism; accumulation as the supreme good; the notion of a calling; moralized money-making versus traditionalism. *The Protestant ethic*: Protestantism as the origin of the rationality of European capitalism; Luther's notion of a calling; different forms of ascetic Protestantism; Calvin and predestination; worldly success as a sign of salvation; Calvinism as an ideal type; capitalism as an unintended consequence.

Conclusion

Weber's importance to modern sociology; Weber as a theorist of modernity; his view of socialism; the contribution of his religious studies to the basic dualisms; his theoretical ambivalence; his views on German politics.

14. Simmel: countering an overdose of history?

The decreasing importance of history in Simmel's work; his inversion of Marx; Simmel and Nietzsche; his critique of historicism; history as a genre; Simmel's place in differing existential traditions; his aesthetic perspective.

15. Conclusion: the framework of social theory

A discussion of the dualisms of social theory and what happens when they are ignored or when theorists attempt to transcend them; the necessary problems of social theory.

List of boxes

1 | What's the point?

The purpose of the book: the continuing importance of the founding thinkers—the necessity of general theories—sociology's relationship to the Enlightenment; the two-sided nature of Enlightenment thought and of social theory; the basic dualisms of social theory; *the structure of the book* and how to read it; *how to think about the thinkers.*

The purpose of the book

This is an introduction to the classical social theorists—primarily Karl Marx, Emile Durkheim, Max Weber, and Georg Simmel. There are two ways of treating such a text: it can be a historical survey, a history of ideas, or it can be a contribution to contemporary debates about society and about social theory itself: its aims, its scope, and its intentions. I hope this book will be more of the latter, and that it will introduce the reader as much to contemporary arguments about theory and society as to the nineteenth- and early twentieth-century arguments. We can't help looking at the past from the standpoint of the present, and each generation will see the past in a different way, just as we see our own lives differently as we grow older. It is better that this is explicit, rather than disguised under some attempt to find out what Marx—or whoever—*really* said. Such arguments can be important, but perhaps they do not belong to an introductory book.

A recurrent theme in what I will have to say is the apparently increasing rate of social change, on a technological level as well as in terms of social and geographical mobility and the nature of the labour market. It seems to me that this profoundly affects our sense of history and its meaning and that, at least in contemporary European and North American society, we are finding it increasingly difficult to experience ourselves as the products of what seems to be an irrelevant past. A symptom of this is that in the teaching of sociology at university level thirty years ago there was no question but that the founding thinkers of sociology were important figures and that reading nineteenth- and early twentieth-century sociology was not just a matter of historical interest, but also a way of understanding our own society, in fact a way of understanding all societies. Now this is questioned—there are suggestions that perhaps we don't need to teach the classical theorists any more, that what they say might be of historical interest, but that sociology, social theory, and society itself have developed well beyond the range of their work. It is all different now and the early theorists are of only academic interest.

I will try to make the case for studying them by considering some of the arguments that devalue their importance. It is sometimes argued that society itself has changed and that the old theories are no longer appropriate to changed conditions. This was the impetus behind Anthony Giddens's critique of the classical theorists in *Capitalism and Modern Social Theory* (1971). Such arguments have been around since the Second World War but it has always remained the case that the new 'theories' often reproduced old ideas in partial or disguised form. Many of the ideas that go under the label 'postmodernist' can, for example, be found in the work of Marx in the nineteenth and Simmel in the early twentieth centuries. Unless we are aware of the general theories of society that have framed the development of the social sciences, and profoundly and deeply and unavoidably embedded themselves in our ways of thinking about the social world, we are in danger either of constantly reinventing the wheel or of creating a situation where the wheel needs to be reinvented. It seems to me that this is what Giddens does, but that argument belongs elsewhere.

We should not think that the issues that concern us today have changed beyond recognition since the classical theorists were writing. The ideas that I will be examining are fundamental not only to the sociologist's understanding of society but to our everyday understanding; they have entered into the way we think about our social life and the way we conduct our political arguments, and they are part and parcel of those arguments themselves. I will be referring to many contemporary issues in the course of the book: the role of the state and the extent to which individuals are or should be responsible for their actions and their lives; the issue of crime and punishment; changes in the labour market which create increasing job insecurity; issues of wealth, poverty, and social class; the nature of morality; the modern concern with the 'self' and identity; the fragmentation of contemporary society; modern feminism; issues around multiculturalism; the significance of the market economy—all these will be directly relevant. Just as we cannot but work with some overall theory of society, some way of making moral and epistemological judgements, so we cannot but talk about these issues through the spectacles supplied by these theorists. They must be studied to understand the power that their ideas have over us even when we have not heard of them. They have, as it were, entered the air that we breathe. I will discuss the background of each of these thinkers, but, as I noted earlier, I will be less concerned with the historical development of their ideas than with their structure and meaning and their contemporary relevance.

The early thinkers had very little or absolutely nothing to say about some of the issues that concern us today—the information revolution and the packaging of knowledge and computer technology, for example; they were not fortune tellers. But they have provided us with *ways of understanding* these phenomena, ways of approaching them. This should become clear throughout the book, but especially in Part 1.

Many of the arguments against studying the classical theorists can be found under the label of 'postmodernism', an approach at the centre of modern theoretical debates. One argument is that the classical thinkers, particularly Marx and Durkheim, were offering general or 'totalizing' theories of society, but in fact social life is complex and multidimensional and cannot be grasped by one theory. I will argue in the course of this book that it is true that social life is multidimensional and cannot be grasped by one theory, but at the same time the very process of theoretical thinking pushes us towards general theories and we cannot avoid them. Giddens (1971) is critical of the attempt to see the classical theorists as offering a general theory of society but he spent the next two decades developing his own general theory of society—structuration theory—and the lesson is that we cannot *but* think in terms of a general theory of society; an attempt to explain or understand one social phenomenon will always have implications for understanding others, whether we like it or not. If you think about it, the statement that social life is multidimensional is itself a general theory, applying to all societies, and it raises the general theoretical problem of how different theories might relate to each other. That will be a central concern of this book. We *have* to work with general theory.

Amongst the postmodernist thinkers there is a more radical version of this criticism which has to do with sociology's relationship to the Enlightenment—that period during and around the eighteenth century that saw the growth of modern science and a new faith in the power of reason and the improvement of the human condition. Irving Zeitlin sums up what he calls the 'mind of the Enlightenment' as follows:

For the Enlightenment thinkers, all aspects of man's life and works were subject to critical examination—the various sciences, religious revelation, metaphysics, aesthetics, etc. These thinkers felt and sensed the many mighty forces impelling them along, but they refused to abandon themselves to these forces. Self-examination, an understanding of their own activity, their own society, their own time, was an essential function of thought. By knowing, understanding and recognizing the main forces and tendencies of their epoch, men could determine the direction and control the consequences of these forces. Through reason and science, men could achieve ever greater degrees of freedom, and therefore ever greater degrees of perfection. Intellectual progress, an idea that permeated the thinking of that age, was to serve constantly to further man's general progress. (Zeitlin 1968: 5)

Social theory has always had an ambivalent relationship to the Enlightenment: on the one hand, many would see it as growing out of and extending Enlightenment thought to society as a whole; others have seen it as a conservative reaction to the Enlightenment, emphasizing the power of community and tradition over the power and freedom of the individual (Nisbet 1967). There is an ambivalence in Enlightenment ideas themselves—Zeitlin talks about increased freedom and progress, on the one hand, but also about increased power to determine what happens in society, and therefore increased control over others.

Even the most pessimistic of the four theorists considered here—Weber and Simmel—still followed the Enlightenment course of constant questioning and the search for knowledge as a good thing in its own right. The postmodernist reaction to this questions both the search for scientific knowledge or truth and its relationship to human freedom. A leading postmodernist theorist, Jean-François Lyotard (1984) has argued that all knowledge comes in the form of a narrative—a story—and that there is no such thing as a meta-narrative, a story of stories that we might call Science or Reason. Much nineteenth-century theory, but particularly Marxism, laid claim to being a meta-narrative. The growth in modern communications and the resulting confrontation of alternative stories have finally shown that such theories are no more than further stories, no better or worse than others. This way of thinking is very closely related to a political argument: the Enlightenment, it is argued, was concerned with establishing hierarchies and systems of control over people. The founding thinkers of sociology all assume that there is a clear distinction between knowledge and non-knowledge (the latter category including, for example, the imagination or intuition or feeling), and that the former is more valuable than the latter. Scientific knowledge is continually making distinctions and establishing hierarchies.

These ideas and their sociological import are most clearly worked out in the work of Foucault (especially 1973, 1977, 1979). The Enlightenment thinkers saw a close relationship between knowledge and freedom: the more knowledge we gain the more free we can become. Foucault, drawing on the philosophy of Nietzsche, inverts that relationship. The link is not between knowledge and freedom, but between knowledge and power. The establishment of medical knowledge, or psychiatric knowledge, or knowledge about sexuality, for example, is the means by which those who work with this knowledge—doctors, psychiatrists, sexologists—establish a power over those who are subjects of the knowledge.

In this sense, all the nineteenth-century sociologists were concerned with establishing power, hierarchies of knowledge, and control over the social organization of people. This is most obvious in the case of Marxism, but the postmodernist argument would be that all meta-narratives are concerned with the organization of hierarchies and the exercise of power. Some would go further: the authors or proponents of the meta-theories are white males (some might add middle class to the list) and these theoretical systems exclude women and ethnic and sexual minorities. Against such meta-narratives, people juxtapose the importance of the knowledge of subordinate groups—women or blacks or gays—which is seen as an assertion of the multidimensional nature of truth and of social reality, where all stories are equal, and the old white male meta-stories are no longer tenable. These are sometimes summed up in complaints about having to learn the work of 'dead white men', and dead white men are very much the subject of this book.

There are a number of counter-arguments to such a case, and importantly there are counter-arguments that can accept some of the politics of the post-modernists without accepting their philosophical and epistemological position. There are, I think, two decisive and very similar arguments against the overall position. The first is that the argument against meta-narratives is itself a meta-narrative—it is telling us a general story about knowledge, and making claims about good and bad knowledge; 'good' knowledge on this account recognizes that it is one story amongst others, and it lays claim to do nothing more than enhance our experience of social reality. However, this sets up a hierarchy by excluding knowledge which lays claim to be epistemologically superior; it out-laws the grand narratives. It seems to me that it is the case that, just as we can-not but imply a general theory of society, so we cannot but engage in distinguishing between good and bad knowledge, and so setting up hierarchies. If I say that there can be no grand narrative that is better than all the others, I am proposing a grand narrative which *I* think is better than all the others.

It is possible to argue that this sort of logical argument must take second place to political necessity, that it is most urgent to include within social theory the standpoint of the subordinate and oppressed groups, and in order to do that we have to jettison the epistemological criteria which reinforce their oppression. I can understand such an argument, but I think there is a case that this confuses beyond hope epistemological and political criteria. It would mean that there is no difference between making judgements about knowledge and judgements about politics, whereas it seems to me that, whilst the two are closely related (and the relationship will play an important part throughout the rest of this book), they are not the same thing. There are ways of thinking about society and the social world in which we can claim to offer a general theory of society, together with the criteria which enable us to distinguish between good and bad knowledge, and include the points of view of subordinate groups, even if those groups reject epistemology altogether.

In any theoretical argument, or in any other argument come to that, it is a good rule to be suspicious of either/or alternatives; it is almost invariably the case that reality is made up of shades of grey. Although it is comforting to think of the world in terms of heroes and villains, of unalloyed good facing unalloyed evil, perhaps because it brings back the childhood comfort of fairy stories, it rarely matches any external reality. The postmodernist argument seems to deal in either/or alternatives. The starting point is that the Enlightenment, or science, is seeking an absolute, a certain knowledge; because we cannot obtain such knowledge, it makes the unreasonable claim that all knowledge claims are of equal status. It seems reasonable to me to suggest that we might not be able to find an absolute truth, but we can distinguish between better and worse knowledge claims; nor are we faced with a straightforward choice between closed hierarchies and open equality. Further, it does not follow that being able to distinguish between better and worse knowledge is the same thing as, or necessarily leads towards, distinguishing between better and worse people. The grounds on which we judge knowledge are very different from the grounds on which we judge people; the only indisputable thing is that we judge on every level; it is in the nature of human thought to make distinctions of fact and value, even though at times we might like to pretend to ourselves that we don't.

We have already seen that Enlightenment thought itself is ambivalent. The Enlightenment notion of reason, for example, is double edged. On one reading it *is* exclusive, narrow, instrumental; on another it is open and inclusive.[1] Both possibilities are there and they are engaged in a complex relationship with each other. One way in which the notion of reason, or rationality, may be elaborated is as a universal human property: we are human beings, therefore we are rational beings, or (if this strikes you as unlikely or hopelessly optimistic) we have the capacity for rational thought and action. This and similar notions (such as the idea that knowledge comes from our sense experience) were central to the democratic impulse behind the Enlightenment; such ideas meant that knowledge was something each person could arrive at, assess, and understand for themselves—it no longer had to be handed down and taken on trust from our social superiors.

From this point of view, rationality can be taken as a standard by means of which societies can be judged as good or bad; a society, for example, which excludes some of its members from the political process because they are black, or because they are women, or because they are disabled, is acting irrationally; as is a society which provides differential access to political debate. More positively, it is possible to construct models for participation—Jürgen Habermas (1984, 1987), for example, talks about an 'ideal speech situation' where all participants have equal access to relevant information and equal opportunity to participate in debate. If we follow these ideas then we end up with an ideal which combines knowledge, scientific knowledge, and the sort of participation in public debate desired by the postmodernists. In his work in the philosophy of science, Habermas (1972) suggests that the most developed forms of human science pursue what he calls an 'emancipatory' interest, a desire to free human beings from avoidable physical and material restraints and a desire to cut a way through mutual misunderstanding and the exercise of power through exclusive

---

[1] The complexity of Enlightenment thought and its double-edged nature, as well as the radical interpretation the I am presenting here, has been worked out most clearly over the last fifty years by the school of thought known as 'critical theory'. See in particular Adorno and Horkheimer (1972), Held (1980), Habermas (1990).

possession of knowledge. He uses psychoanalysis as an example of such a science: to begin with the analyst possesses knowledge and the analysand is ignorant; at the end of the process they are able to communicate as equals.

My own view is that these two interpretations of the Enlightenment are two sides of the same coin: we cannot have one without the other, and if we try to leave the Enlightenment behind us, we might get away from hierarchies of knowledge but we also lose the possibility of freedom. My account of the founding thinkers of sociology will employ both interpretations as a framework for understanding the founding thinkers, but my emphasis will be on what I shall call the radical rather than the conservative interpretation of the Enlightenment: the ways in which these ideas are steps towards a knowledge of the social world, and, through such knowledge, steps towards some form of human liberation. It is this side which I think modern social theory risks losing.

The double-edged nature of theory will become apparent in other ways. I will argue that we can look at each of the founding thinkers in terms of his approach to four crucial dualisms—four sets of alternatives. Any social theory has to take account of both sides of each dualism and the choice of one or the other side to start with can move the theorist in very different directions; and any attempt to collapse them into one another means that there will be large ranges of phenomena which cannot be discussed. Unfortunately many modern theorists, most recently Anthony Giddens, but in the middle part of this century Talcott Parsons, try to collapse them into each other and I do not think this can be done—each refers to real and different aspects of the world and we have to take account of all of them. I do not think it is possible to develop one coherent, unified social theory.

The four dualisms which provide an organizing framework for social theory are:

1. *Individual/society*: any social theory must say or imply something about individuals and their relationships to whatever it is we call society and vice versa. The crucial question is which takes priority.

2. *Action/structure*: this is slightly different. Any social theory has to say something about human action, whether it be individual or collective, and about social structure—the *organization* of society. Again the crucial question is which takes priority.

3. *Social integration/system integration*: this is a development of the action/structure dualism. *Social integration* refers to what it is that relates actors or individuals within society; *system integration* refers to what relates different parts of a society. Integration does not mean harmony—individuals and parts of a society may be related through conflict.

4. *Modernity/capitalism–socialism*: the fourth dualism is rather different in that the first three would be relevant whatever society we were studying, but this last is relevant only to modern society since the industrial revolution. It is,

therefore, a secondary dualism. Each of the theorists considered here as well as contemporary theorists has to consider whether the features of contemporary society are the result of one particular form of society—capitalism—and whether they might be transformed by another—socialism—or whether they are the more or less inevitable result of modern society *per se*.

Each of these will become relevant at a different time and I will be elaborating on each of them throughout the book.

The structure of the book

After the introductory chapters, the book will be divided into three parts. Each part will contain a chapter on each theorist. The book can thus be read in two ways: the 'normal' way from beginning to end to develop a comparative understanding of all four thinkers; this will provide the reader with an idea of the scope of classical social theory, its complexity, and the way different ideas interrelate. Or it can be read as an account of one of four different thinkers; the reader could concentrate, say, on the chapters on Durkheim, glossing over the comparisons when they are not relevant and concentrating on the substantive account of the one thinker's theory.

Chapter 2 of the introductory section will tell the story of each of the main thinkers, their biographical details and what we know of their personal lives together with an elementary introduction to their work—this should set the scene for people completely new to the area. There will also be a brief account of the conditions under which sociology developed. This section is complemented by the *Dramatis personae* at the end. Here I offer brief biographies of the other dead white men mentioned in the book, which will give you some further basic historical information. You can refer to this when you come across an unfamiliar name of someone writing in the first part of this century or in the last century.

Part 1 will be concerned with methodology in its broadest sense, on the level not of questionnaire surveys or participant observation, but of ways of thinking about thinking. What is this peculiar thing called theory and how does it relate to what might be called reality? What goes on when we theorize, and how is it different from everyday, 'normal' ways of thinking? Is social theory, in some sense or another, scientific and if so, in what sense? What methodology or methodologies, in the narrower sense, are implied by this particular way of thinking about society? At the end of these chapters it will be possible to map out the levels of social reality and the dualisms with which classical theory was concerned.

Part 2 is concerned with conceptions of social structure—answers to the question: what is society? This is the meat (or, if you're a vegetarian, the nut roast) of sociology. Is society made up only of individual people in different types of relationships, and if so what are these relationships? Are some types of relationship more important than others? Or are social groups, such as classes or status groups, more important than individuals? Or is 'society' something which exists over and above individuals? Who exercises power in society and how? What are the relationships between different parts of society?

Part 3 looks at explanations of the nature of social change and historical development. Is modern society caught in a process of increasing rationalization and bureaucratization, or is it driven forward by economic development or conflict between social classes, or by a process of different social institutions adjusting to each other? Or is it none of these things and is social change a much more haphazard, irrational process than we might suppose? In addition each theorist's work contains a critique of his existing society and a vision of what should be—the society which is possible—and through the way in which each explains social change we can look at how he expected the modern world to develop and what he expected to happen.

How to think about the thinkers

It is tempting to preach about the best attitude to adopt when using this book—so tempting, in fact, that I am going to do it. I suggested earlier that classical social theory has entered into our own way of thinking about issues, whether we know it or not; we cannot *but* look through the spectacles that it has created. If you look at particular areas and particular issues that interest you, you are likely to find a gut reaction: one approach or another will articulate what you are already thinking, or will put into words the way in which you think about society and social relationships. This could be a tenuous toehold on the sheer rock face of social theory—at last something I can understand or get hold of!—or it could be the entrance to a large cave—yes, I can understand and develop this way of looking at things. Either way, this is the starting point for further exploration. If, say, it is Marx's theory of alienation that grabs you first, then you can follow this up by exploring the other sections about Marx, leaving the ones that seem most difficult to the last.

My own way of entering into this immense area when I was a student was to take a partisan attitude: I was a Marxist and later, as my pretensions grew, an Existentialist Marxist—the capital letters give a good idea of how pretentious I was. I know many people who have entered social theory through a similar partisanship, although not necessarily with Marx. This might not be everybody's way of proceeding, but if it becomes important to justify the position you sympathize with, you do an awful lot of thinking about social theory; in fact, you begin to make it a familiar part of the world in which you live.

This stage can be difficult enough, but there is another, more difficult stage. It is sometimes tempting to remain a partisan—and perhaps as a citizen engaged in what passes as a democratic political process it is a good thing to remain partisan—but creative thought in social theory does not come only from partisan arguments. Sometimes sociologists will argue as if the different approaches were contestants in some immense sporting contest which would end with one winner. But theories are not generally eliminated through argument. We still read the nineteenth- and early twentieth-century social theorists, and indeed seventeenth- and eighteenth-century social theorists, because something of what they say corresponds with our experience and our knowledge of contemporary society, and ideas do not survive that long if they are simply wrong. Each of the thinkers we will look at in this text grasps, more or less adequately, some crucial aspect of society and social life; exactly how these aspects are related is another matter, beyond the scope of this introduction and really beyond the scope of this book. Suffice it to say that it is not enough to adopt one thinker and cling to him without moving, however necessary that might be at the beginning. To enter fully into thinking about society, we need to understand and in some way come to terms with the truth of other approaches—we need to spend a lot of time *thinking against ourselves* and changing our ideas. So when you feel comfortable with the thinker who most closely approximates your own prejudices (in the sense of pre-judgements, your gut ways of thinking about the social world), you need to move on to the others—if you are brave, starting with the one furthest away from your gut prejudices.

So when you take up this book, be prepared first for the pleasure of finding out what you already think, and learning to think it, and then for the painful task of changing your mind.

2 | The main characters and the main ideas

Brief biographies of the classical theorists (*Marx, Durkheim, Simmel, and Weber*), together with an elementary introduction to their ideas and intellectual background. *The social and intellectual background* to the rise of sociology.

Introduction

When I start setting out the classical theorists in a systematic way I will begin with Durkheim, perhaps the most sociological of the early sociologists and a useful point of comparison. In this chapter, however, I am interested in the historical background and I will start with the earliest of the four, Karl Marx (1818–83), whose political importance and chronological position means that the others are conventionally seen in relation to him. The other three are almost contemporaries, Emile Durkheim and Georg Simmel were both born in 1858, Durkheim dying in 1917, and Simmel a year later, whilst Max Weber was born in 1864 and died in 1920. These are not the earliest social theorists by any means, but they are the ones who have 'stuck' and whose ideas still form the framework for modern social thought. Their ideas have stuck, I would suggest, because they are more coherent and inclusive than those of other contemporaries.

I will set out both biographical details and an elementary introduction to their ideas and the intellectual traditions they come from, and follow this by talking about the social conditions which gave rise to sociology.

Karl Marx (1818–1883)

Marx was born to a large Jewish family—he had seven brothers and sisters—in Prussia; he came from a long line of rabbis, which ended with his father, who was baptized to avoid persecution. In 1836 he went to study law at the University of Bonn, already secretly engaged to Jenny von Westphalen. He is reputed to have led a riotous existence, spending money, drinking, duelling, and writing poetry. A year later he transferred to Berlin, where he became a reformed character, coming under the influence of a group of radical thinkers and deciding to take up an academic career. However, his association with radical thinkers got in the way and, when he left Berlin in 1841, he embarked on a life of radical journalism. The first paper for which he worked was closed after an attack on the Russian Absolutist monarchy, and after marrying Jenny he moved, in 1843, to Paris, living communally with a group with whom he intended to start a new journal. This ran only to one issue, but whilst in Paris Marx began his critiques of the German idealist philosopher, G. W. F. Hegel, and his studies of the British economists, Adam Smith and David Ricardo, and his confrontations with French socialism. In 1845 he was expelled by the French government, under pressure from Prussia, and moved to Brussels, where he began his lifelong collaboration with Friedrich Engels.

In 1847 Marx and Engels attended the second conference of the Communist League in London, out of which came *The Communist Manifesto* (Marx 1848/1968a).[1] The year 1848 was one first of revolutionary upheavals and then of oppression. As he was being expelled from Brussels for breaking his promise not to engage in political journalism, so he was invited to Paris by the leaders of a popular uprising against King Louis Philippe; he then returned to Prussia, where there were also liberal stirrings. Then later that year a spontaneous uprising in Paris was crushed and the Prussian king reasserted his control and Marx ended up in what was to be a permanent exile in London.

He continued to engage in political organization, writing, and disputes, including the founding of the First International Working Man's Association in 1866 and its demise after he split with the anarchist Bakunin in 1872; and he continued with his scientific work—his research into philosophy and economics, culminating with the three volumes of *Capital*. He earned a living by journalism, which he resented—the 'journalistic muck' which kept him away from his real research. During the 1850s and early 1860s this provided him with an often precarious living. In 1852 his daughter Franziska died and he wrote that he could not afford medicine for his family and they were living on bread and potatoes. In 1855 his son Edgar died. Things slowly improved through inheritance and the support of Engels, who had inherited his father's business in Manchester. During the last ten years of his life he suffered from ill health and he never recovered from Jenny's death in 1881, dying himself two years later.

For present purposes it is most useful to think of Marx's ideas as working on three levels: the philosophical, the economic, and the political, all intimately interconnected. His politics is at the centre. As a young man he was caught up with the ideas of the French Revolution of 1789, which, under its slogan of liberty, equality, and fraternity, had generated a new liberalism, and with exploring the failure of the Revolution to make these ideas reality. The philosophical

---

[1] When I refer to major classical texts I will include the original date of publication or of writing (if they are different) and the date of a recent edition which should be more readily available.

tradition against which he was defining himself was German idealism—particularly the work of Hegel.[2] The simplest—rather, the crudest—definition of 'idealism' is the view that the social world is the product of ideas, that we develop ideas and then make them actual, and that history is the steady realization of thought, of Reason. Marx's critique of Hegel was, famously, to turn him on his head—to argue that ideas grew out of human life, the material basis of society.

It was the attempt to understand the material basis which led to Marx's study of economics. His argument concerned itself with a number of levels. Technology is important—the growth of machine production in large factories, for example, brought together large numbers of workers in one place and enabled the formation of trade unions. The experience of day-to-day production, whether in a factory, in a small workshop, or in the fields, shaped the way people thought about the world and politics. Also important were what Marx called the 'relations of production', property relationships: whether people owned or did not own machines and land, whether they earned their living by selling their ability to labour, whether they employed or did not employ workers. These property relationships allocated people to social classes, and their work experience gave them a shared view of the world. These ideas were developed through a critique of the classical economists, primarily Adam Smith and David Ricardo, and Marx came to argue that the failure of the French Revolution had to do with the level of economic development of French society.

The life of the state and the political life of a society, Marx argued, was a result of the struggle for power which occurred between these classes. The state was the means by which the ruling class established its power over subordinate classes. The most radical class, the class that would be able to realize the liberty, equality, and fraternity that could not be realized by the French Revolution, was the new working class. They could achieve a real equality because there was nobody below them in the social order—they had nothing to lose but their chains.

At the centre of Marx's theory, then, is the idea that the economic organization of society is the most important level of social organization, and the major influence on the political, social, and intellectual life of the society. Economically based social classes are the major forces which push societies forward to an ideal state of communism. All this will be explained in more detail, and with a lot more precision, later.

Emile Durkheim (1858–1917)

Durkheim, too, was born into a Jewish, rabbinical family and was initially expected to follow his father into the priesthood. Biographers seem to agree

[2] You need to be fairly enthusiastic to follow up Hegel's work; the best introduction I know is Charles Taylor (1977); the best starting-point for Hegel himself is *The Phenomenology of Spirit* (1977) but you should approach it with a commentary.

that, although he broke away from the faith and called himself an agnostic, the work habits he learnt at the beginning of his training as a rabbi stayed with him for the rest of his life. Whereas Marx had a comparatively adventurous life, often beset by poverty and chased round Europe by reactionary governments whilst trying to organize revolutionary movements, Durkheim seems to have led the life of a quiet but hard-working and productive academic, touched by tragedy when his only son was killed in the First World War, an event which seemed to hasten his own death a couple of years later.

His academic career was distinguished, although in 1876 it began with two failures to gain entrance into the élite *École Normale Supérieure*, but when he did get there he was recognized as brilliant. He concerned himself with social and political philosophy, in particular Auguste Comte's attempt to develop sociology (although, according to Anthony Giddens (1978), he thought the term was a 'barbarous neologism') and Kantian philosophy, another strand of German idealism. After graduation he taught philosophy in schools and spent a year studying in Germany. On his return in 1887 he took up a post in the University of Bordeaux, marrying in the same year. In 1902 he moved to a chair of education, later education and sociology, at the Sorbonne, where he remained until his death. Soon after his son's death, he suffered a stroke from which he never fully recovered.

He is often wrongly characterized as sociology's conservative thinker, an opposite to Marx. Whilst he seems to have had little time for revolutionary socialism, he was nevertheless a reforming liberal or socialist in political terms. His one public political intervention was in defence of Alfred Dreyfus—a famous case of a Jewish army officer unjustly scapegoated for the misdeeds of the army establishment—and took the form of a liberal defence of individualism. His immediate intellectual background was the work of Comte, who was concerned with the development of social science as the final stage in the triumph of the sciences over metaphysical thought and he thought that sociology in particular would put an end to political debates about how society should be organized. For Durkheim this was a matter of showing that sociology had its own proper object, distinct from the objects, say, of psychology and biology, and that it could be studied by accepted scientific methods. This was the aim of two major works: *The Rules of Sociological Method* (1895/1964) and *Suicide* (1897/1952), where he argued that the job of sociology is to study *social facts*, regularities, which are often identifiable statistically—as, for example, in official suicide and crime figures—and which can be shown to depend not on the will of individuals but on the type of society in which individuals live. His attempt to establish sociology as an independent science was not just an intellectual enterprise but also a practical one. In the same year that *Suicide* was published, he founded *L'Année sociologique*—a famous journal intended to bring together the latest research in the area, and which contributed towards the establishment of his own sociological approach as a school.

A second intellectual focus was on the evolutionary change in society from one form of social cohesion to another and in particular the role of individualism in modern societies. This was the centre of attention in *The Division of Labour in Society* (1893/1984). He argued that, despite the apparent collapse of traditional communities and the growth of individualism, modern society was not falling apart. It was being held together not by shared beliefs, as were traditional societies, but by the division of labour, our economic dependence on each other. However, a shared moral basis was necessary to the social order, and Durkheim saw the religion that provided this in traditional societies being replaced by a philosophy of individualism. His concern with religion, with shared beliefs, produced his last major work, *The Elementary Forms of the Religious Life,* (1912/1915), and guided his concerns with education and moral philosophy as well.

Although the division of labour was important for Durkheim, it was not at the basis of his social theory. Unlike Marx, he did not see the economic level of social organization as providing the basis for all others, and he was much more concerned with shared beliefs. He thought that class conflict was a temporary abnormality in social development, and far from seeing the state as Marx did as the way in which one social class established its role over another, he saw it as a mediator, ensuring smooth development during modernization. In this sense he was not the political opposite of Marx but his theoretical opposite. The Kantian idealist tradition in which he worked, when it is taken into the social sciences, is concerned with the ways in which our thought, our ideas, and our ways of thinking organize the social world.

Georg Simmel (1858–1918)

Georg Simmel was neither a political revolutionary nor a successful career academic—it was only near the end of his life that he was offered the chair of philosophy at the University of Strasbourg, which was not regarded as a major university. He was born in Berlin and directly and indirectly he was the theorist of metropolitan life, attributing much of his achievement to living most of his life in that city. He maintained that nobody in his house possessed an intellectual culture and he put one together for himself at Berlin University. His first doctorate was rejected in 1880. According to Frisby (1984), the examiners were not even impressed with his empirical survey of yodelling. A dissertation on Immanuel Kant gained him his doctorate a year later, and from 1885 he was qualified to teach in Berlin at a level roughly approximate to junior lecturer, and he continued at this level until 1900.

Simmel, to the best of my knowledge, was the only one of the founding thinkers of sociology to have an attempt made on his life (Frisby 1984). He is reputed to have been a brilliant lecturer, thinking spontaneously and on the spot. One of his hearers described him as not a teacher but an 'inciter', (Simmel 1950), and he seemed to have evoked a similar response in his reputation as a thinker. He was proud of the number of students he could attract to his courses and he allowed women to attend as 'guest' students long before they were entitled to become full students. It was, according to Frisby, a combination of this sort of action, plus the fact that he attracted students from eastern Europe, and associated with socialists in the early part of his career, that held back his academic progress. But all commentators seem to agree that above all he was held back by anti-Semitism, by his colleagues' jealousy of his popularity, and by a suspicion of the new discipline of sociology. When he got his chair at Strasbourg he was not terribly impressed with his new colleagues—'a half-witted bunch'. In Berlin he had built up a network of artists and intellectuals, including Max Weber, the philosopher Henri Bergson, the poets Stefan Georg and Rainer Maria Rilke, and the sculptor Auguste Rodin. Amongst his students were the sociologist Karl Mannheim and the Marxist philosophers Georg Lukacs and Ernst Bloch. Compared with such central figures it is not surprising that Simmel found his new colleagues dull.

It is difficult to sum up Simmel's theory in the same way as one can that of Marx and Durkheim. In one sense, one could say that he didn't have a theory, although he had an awful lot of interesting theoretical things to say. He had a highly individual way of looking at the world and he is often compared with Goffman in this respect. However, his range of interests and his knowledge were much wider that Goffman's. In the earlier part of his career his focus seemed primarily to be on psychology and social psychology, then moving on to sociology, but throughout there was an interest in philosophy. His doctoral dissertation was on Kant, but he later developed an important interest in Schopenhauer and Nietzsche. Towards the end of his career, he turned to art and aesthetics.

He developed what he called a formal sociology, coming from his interest in Kant; an investigation into how human beings imposed forms on the world of experience, organizing and making sense of it. This is idealist, in the sense that it sees the world not so much as a product of thought, as did Hegel, but as organized by thought. The particular forms which interested Simmel were those of relationships between individuals and groups. His books were largely collections of essays, but the titles of the translations give a good idea of his subject matter: *Conflict and the Web of Group Affiliations* (1955); *On Individuality and Social Forms* (1971); *The Conflict in Modern Culture and Other Essays* (1968). The comparison with Goffman is often extended to link these aspects of Simmel's work with the development in America of symbolic interactionism.

But at the same time there were Simmel's socialist connections, particularly in the early stages of his career and one of his major books, *The Philosophy of Money* (1900/1990), is much closer to Marxism—particularly the Marx of the *Economic and Philosophic Manuscripts of 1844* and the section of *Capital* on commodity fetishism, of which more later. It is here that Simmel links his ideas of the ways in which relationships between people, and individual psychologies, change with the development of modernity and the money economy. In this book he often seems to come closer to a materialist explanation than to a philosophical understanding of the forms of human relationships and the developments of individual psychology.

Simmel is increasingly seen as a forerunner of postmodernism. I shall argue later that there is a degree of truth in this, but there is also a sense in which Simmel goes beyond postmodernism—but he certainly identified one important process which is often regarded as a recent sociological insight. This is the way in which the development of social forms moulds individual lives into socially acceptable behaviour. It is his response to this which takes him to his concern with aesthetics—it is as if ithe only way in which the individual can save his or her spontaneity is by living life as if it were an art form. Many of these ideas link Simmel to existentialist philosophy as well as to later sociological traditions. I was thinking especially of Simmel's sociology when I warned of the danger of reinventing the wheel in our ignorance that it had already been invented.

Max Weber (1864–1920)

Weber's life, and his psyche, have proved a happy hunting ground for amateur psychoanalysts, since for many of his fifty-six years he struggled with what has variously been called a breakdown or melancholia or what would probably be called depression. He was born in Erfurt in what until recently was East Germany, but the family soon moved to Berlin. The root of his trouble was the contrast between his mother and his father, and it was as if he were trying to mediate between the two, and bring them together in his person, his life, and his theory. His father was a lawyer and liberal parliamentarian and a man of action. According to R. Bendix (1966: 1), 'his mother was a woman of culture and piety whose humanitarian and religious interests were not shared by her husband'. It seems that Weber would occasionally try to become, or think about becoming, the man of action and rapidly retreat. He grew up in an environment of political and academic discussion—the society of professors and politicians.

In 1882 he went to study jurisprudence—the law—at the University of Heidelberg and, like Marx, went through his spell of spending, drinking, carousing, and duelling. After military service, he studied at the universities of Berlin and Göttingen. His academic work began with legal studies, but at the same time, while he was trying to qualify for the bar, he showed an interest in the problems of agrarian societies. In 1893 he married. After a couple of years of teaching in Berlin, he moved to Freiburg in 1895 and then back to Heidelberg in 1896. The following year his difficulties began. Frank Parkin (1982) describes him as spending the rest of his life as though on a kind of prolonged sabbatical, although I am not sure that this is entirely fair. However, Parkin's account of the onset of the problem is worth quoting in full:

His illness occurred soon after the death of his father. Weber senior was by all accounts a bad caricature of the Victorian paterfamilias—a martinet to his children, overbearing and insensitive towards his wife. Shortly before his death, he and Max had quarrelled violently. It was something to do with the son's insistence that his mother be allowed to visit him unaccompanied by his father, whom he regarded as a bit of a lout. The row culminated in Weber junior doing the unthinkable and ordering his father from the house. Max never saw his father alive again. On learning of the old man's sudden death he was consumed by guilt and remorse. He then became virtually catatonic.   (Parkin 1982: 14)

He tried, with some success, to deal with his difficulties by running away from them, travelling around Europe and then to the USA, where he began to return to studying and writing, and then, despite recurrent depressions, he became immensely productive. Parkin suggests that today no one could ever master the fields of law, history, and social sciences in the way that he did. He pursued his studies and his arguments with a care and determination that is rarely matched, and he infused his work with a passion that was also present in his lectures.

During the First World War he directed army hospitals in Heidelberg and served on various government committees. Towards the end of his life he accepted a chair at Munich, but this seemed to throw him back into psychological turmoil. At the same time he longed to be a man of action, and he was a dedicated nationalist, to the extent that he is sometimes accused—at least by left-wing students—of being a forerunner of the Nazis. It will become apparent later that I think that this accusation is mistaken. Of course his political activity was ineffective; when he sought nomination as a candidate for the new German Democratic Party at the end of war, he did not canvass support and was very upset when he did not get the nomination. He seemed to share a fantasy with his wife that the nation would call on him in its hour of need.

Bendix sums up the contradiction of Weber's personality neatly: 'he continuously engaged in the simultaneous effort to be a man of science with the strenuous vigour more common in a man of action, and to be a man of action with all the ethical rigor and personal detachment more common in a man of science' (Bendix 1966: 6).

If Weber's personality and his life were full of paradoxes, then so was his work. It will become apparent that there is a sense in which he does not have a conception of 'society' as a social system at all, although he famously talks about the 'iron cage' of capitalism in which we all become caught. It is certainly true that he had a heightened sense of the precariousness of the social order. His starting point was a variant of Kantian philosophy, which argued that the basis of the human sciences was different from that of the natural sciences. Thus sociology would not be a science in the same sense of physics or chemistry. The social sciences were sciences because people behaved rationally and it was possible to construct rational explanations of their actions. The social order produced in such a way was shaky, not least because of the struggle for power between different groups at the heart of politics, and the market economy was particularly important because it acted as a source of stability, holding people in relationships with each other.

In this respect Weber is the founding sociologist at the liberal end of the political spectrum, and much of what he has to say about politics and social life is still familiar today in the mouth of the proponents of the free market, and there is an important sense in which it imposes rational action upon people. The origin of this type of rational action—Weber sometimes calls it rational calculability and others call it instrumental rationality—is of central interest to Weber the sociologist. He saw such rationality and the development of capitalism itself as a specifically European phenomenon. In a series of massive studies of the world religions he tried to demonstrate that what was specific to Europe was a particular development of Christian belief—Protestantism—and its effects on economic behaviour. An equivalent to Protestantism did not exist in the other world religions, even where the other preconditions of capitalist development did exist.

It is often said that Weber was always arguing against Marx's ghost, and one might think from the above account that he was arguing that it was ideas and not economic relationships that determined social development. In fact he was at great pains to point out that social developments had many causes and some aspects of his studies of the world religions could have come just as well from the pen of a sophisticated Marxist. And, in so far as he developed a theory of social structure, he saw it not as dominated by social classes, but as a combination of multiple social classes, status groups, and political parties vying for power. He was not a man to espouse simple causal processes.

There was inevitably a paradox in the way he regarded all this; again Bendix sums it up well: 'He left no doubt that his profound personal commitment to the cause of reason and freedom had guided his choice to subject matter; and his research left no doubt that reason and freedom in the Western world were in jeopardy' (Bendix 1966: 9). Bendix goes on to suggest that Weber's commitment to German nationalism must be understood not in the terms that we might see it after the rise of the Nazis but as a commitment to Germany's mission to protect the reason and freedom set in motion by the Enlightenment. He was ambivalent even about the triumph of reason; the triumph of bureaucratic organization was not something to be welcomed and, with the process of rationalization, contributed to the 'disenchantment' of the world. Throughout, I will emphasize the paradoxes of Weber's thought: from individualism to the iron cage; from the free market to political struggles for power between different social groups; from rationality to disenchantment.

The social and intellectual background

Any attempt to divide history into periods can only be very approximate; it is next to impossible to find a beginning to anything and the history of social theory could be said to begin with Greek philosophy; a good, short history can be found in the first couple of chapters of Swingewood (1991). We can say with reasonable certainty that there were important changes in the way that people thought about the world that emerged in the Enlightenment and continued through the eighteenth century, and that the emergence of social theory through the nineteenth and twentieth centuries is the fruition of these changes. We can also say that these changes are parallel to radical changes in the everyday life of people living in Europe, particularly northern Europe, and that these changes are still continuing and have spread throughout the world. The four thinkers discussed here set the framework for making sense of these changes and do so within the framework set for them by the Enlightenment. The division of philosophy into empiricist and rationalist traditions—that knowledge must be based on sense experience or on reason—provides a frame for the divisions and oppositions in social theory.

However, here I want to concentrate on the social changes that transformed so many people's lives. They too go back over the centuries, beginning in northwest Europe and particularly in Britain. The economy had begun to change as early as the thirteenth century, when the Black Death—bubonic plague—had laid waste the labour force, and the habit of paying workers developed as a way of attracting labour. Over a long period the growth of sheep farming, which needs little labour, and the wool trade, set the conditions for a capitalist agriculture to develop—agricultural wage labourers replaced peasants and a developing market system encouraged farming for profit rather than subsistence. By the eighteenth century, the growth of capitalist farming encouraged new very productive technological changes in farming and fed a process of rapid technological change which we now take for granted. Capitalist agriculture produced profits which financed the new forms of production made possible by technological developments; workers were forced off the land and wandered around often in large unemployed groups until they were absorbed into the new factories in the growing towns.

The first change, then, is the growth of capitalism and the primacy of the money economy, which was especially important for Marx and Simmel. The industrial revolution, which was at its height in Britain from 1750 to 1850, was the second change, bringing people together into large groups—larger than ever before, forcing them into closer contact than ever before, and sharing similar living conditions—in the case of the workers, often appalling living conditions. The third change is now known to sociologists as urbanization—the growth of larger and larger towns, eventually into huge conurbations which dominate the way of life of those who remain in the country.

These changes may have taken centuries to develop, but the speed with which they came to fruition and changed lives was new and dramatic, and beyond the understanding of more traditional ways of looking at the world. They demanded new forms of thinking, new ways of seeing the world. To begin with, there was the experience of people moving together into large groups, sharing common conditions. This was most evident in the case of the poor and the new workers, who were often the source of social unrest. People trying to make sense of all this started in the course of the nineteenth century to talk in terms of 'class' and 'social class', a way of looking at the world which was to be developed furthest by Marx and later Marxists.

The process of industrialization brought immense increases in productive capacity, not least through the division of labour that became possible through large-scale factory production. The nature of people's lives was changed in this respect as well. The family lost its status as a productive unit, and work became something which happened outside the home; traditional communities and ways of life were often washed away. Whereas Durkheim was concerned with this change in his elaboration of the way in which the division of labour itself provided a new source of social cohesion, Marx was critical of its alienating potential, and Weber of the rationalizing dynamic behind it all. The division of labour and the market economy produced an individualizing effect as well which paralleled the opposite tendency to grouping people into classes. This is something which Durkheim in particular identified and gave a central place to in his work. Factory production also brought a new discipline to people, who came to be dominated by the clock and the organization of the workplace. For thinkers like Weber, this growing individualism and rationalization provided not only the central topic for social theory but also its methodology.

Living in towns also placed new demands on the individual personality: it demanded the development of a sort of shell to protect against the constant bombardment of new stimuli, and it replaced traditional forms of relationship, few in number and comparatively deep in nature, with a new way of living involving possibly larger numbers of comparatively shallow, surface relationships. This, coupled with the new and increasing interest in the individual, drove the development of psychology and towards the end of the nineteenth century gave birth to psychoanalysis. Of the thinkers discussed here, Simmel was most concerned with this area.

The middle of the nineteenth century saw one further major development in intellectual life that was to add to the framework of sociology and social theory. Rapid change had by itself already opened the way to historical thinking, to seeing social life in terms of a development, at least from the past to the present, if not on into the future. The publication of Darwin's theory of evolution early in the second half of the century saw his ideas immediately and more or less crudely transposed into social theory. All four thinkers work with some idea of social evolution from some primitive state to some more complex and presumably civilized state; however, as well as the benefits of social change, they were able, in their different ways, to see the drawbacks and dangers—the breakdown of traditional life and the loss of community, the increasing organization and control of everyday life to which people were subjected, and the danger of fragmentation—and each developed his own form of social criticism. We shall see that the political debates that their thought generated are still raging today.

Further reading

David McLennan, *The Thought of Karl Marx* (1971), divides Marx's life up into its important periods and gives an excellent account of his activities during each of them, as well as a clear account of his writings over the same period.

For further details about Durkheim's life, see S. Lukes, *Emile Durkheim* (1973), and for Simmel, see D. Frisby, *Georg Simmel* (1984), chapter 2.

The best account of Weber's life, including a psychoanalytic account of his depression, can be found in A. Mitzman, *The Iron Cage: An Historical Interpretation of Max Weber* (1971).

Part 1

What is society and how do we study it?

Introduction to Part 1

Any social theory worth its salt is difficult, for the self-evident reason that it tries to understand a complex object; there is no easy understanding of social structures or social processes, and—in order to make life even more difficult— I am going to start at the hardest end of social theory, that of methodology in the broadest sense. By this I mean the general ways in which we think about what we are doing, the way in which we decide on and define what we are going to study; the way in which we might map out our task as we proceed with our investigations; and the assumptions we make about what we are doing and why we are doing it. Part of this is the question of what we might mean by a sociological understanding or a sociological explanation of what we study.

Each of the thinkers we will be looking at has a different answer to each of these problems, but what they share in common, explicitly or implicitly, is a concern with something called *society* as a proper object of scientific investigation—even though the meaning of scientific is different for each, as is the meaning of society. My intention is to elaborate what each means by the investigation of society and how each envisages society and sociology in the most general terms. Generally these methods are seen as ways of understanding all societies and also of classifying different types of society.

'Ways of looking at' is important: by using the phrase, I do not think that each of the views I will be discussing is of equal worth to the others, or to those I do not discuss. Rather I think it is arguable that one of the reasons that these theories have survived and these thinkers are still read, discussed, and developed is that each manages to delineate and begin to explore and develop an understanding of an essential aspect of the social, without which we could have no understanding of society. These theories sometimes complement each other, sometimes contradict each other, and are sometimes talking about such radically different things that there can be no contact.

I will begin this part by looking at Durkheim, who on one level offers the simplest conception of what a society is and how we should understand it. I will then move on to Marx, who offers a more complicated way of conceptualizing a society and investigating it. These approaches share one important feature: they both see a scientific understanding of society as penetrating below the surface level of appearances and showing us something which we could not otherwise see. In other words, social science is surprising: it gives us news, it tells us things that we do not know simply by looking around us; as Marx points out on one occasion, there would be no need for a science if we could tell what the world was like simply by looking at it. This means that for Marx and Durkheim there is a gap between the language of social theory and sociological understanding and the everyday language in which we think and talk about our actions. It means also that we do not necessarily know what we are doing—we think we are doing one thing and 'in reality', seen in terms of our relationship to society, we are doing another. I might marry out of love but I also reproduce the family; I might feel desperate and suicidal because my marriage has broken up, but I will also be responding to a form of social integration of which I am unlikely to be conscious.

In the case of Weber, we start with our common-sense notions of the world and we elaborate on these—our understanding of society comes from our interpretation of the ideas that govern peoples' actions; central to his approach is a conception of rationality—we can think of social science as scientific because it presents us with a rational understanding not of society but of social action, of the way people act in relation to each other. Simmel presents yet another model, concerned with the formal structures of relationships.

By the end of Part 1 you should have a preliminary idea of the different approaches outlined by the classical thinkers, of how they think about sociology and sociological investigation. This will be developed over the following chapters. I said earlier that this is the difficult end of social theory but it is also the end which presents the best overview. You should have a good sense of the possibilities of social theory, and, if you are aware of contemporary debates and alternatives in sociology, you will realize that what is set out here covers most of the options open to modern sociology.

3 | Durkheim: the discovery of social facts

Introduction: background; Comte and positivism. *Durkheim's rules*: the objectivity of social facts; considering social facts as things; the use of statistics to identify social facts; the normal and the pathological—the normality of crime. *Suicide as a social fact*: its underlying causes. *What can we take from Durkheim*: criticisms of Durkheim's methodology and discussion.

Introduction

Durkheim's *Rules of Sociological Method* (1895/1964) is a classic text in the best sense, and for generations of students it has represented their first contact with sociology and provided material for the first essay question they have had to answer: 'Is sociology a science?'. Thirty years ago many sociologists—and many non-sociologists—assumed a fairly simple model of scientific activity and explanation, one which generally goes under the name of positivism, and Durkheim has been taken as the archetypal sociological positivist. There is a degree of truth in this but not the whole truth.

What is positivism? Historically the term is associated with Auguste Comte, the French philosopher who was a central, but not the only influence on Durkheim. Like most nineteenth-century philosophers and social theorists, Comte saw history as progress, in his case through three different stages: the religious, the metaphysical, and the scientific, the last of which he thought we were entering. Each stage rejected and replaced the way of thinking about the world that characterized the previous phase. The religious phase involves, as one might expect, the explanation of the world by the supernatural, and its most developed form is monotheism, the belief in one God as a final cause. The metaphysical stage is a transitional stage—gods are replaced by abstract forces such as nature—and this develops into the positive, scientific stage.

In Comte's view, the problem with the metaphysical stage is that it is negative: it sets itself against the traditional order and leads to a constant questioning of ideas and relations, leading to anarchy, a constant argument about how society should be organized. It is bound up with one strand of Enlightenment thought—that as rational beings we gain our freedom by such constant questioning. It enables us to overcome superstition and irrational oppression. Comte—and much nineteenth-century sociology—can be seen as representing a conservative reaction to this strand of thought, an attempt to stop the process of questioning. Comte argued that there was no solution to the constant argument about what society *should* be like—the negative approach; instead we should find out what it *is* like—the *positive* approach. Hence positivism. There was in Comte the idea that we could gain firm positive knowledge about the world. In the twentieth century the strand of Enlightenment that Comte was arguing against has reasserted itself at the heart of positivist philosophy. The work of Karl Popper (1959) has demonstrated that we cannot positively prove something to be always the case. If, for example, I wished to prove that all swans were white in a 'positive' sense I would have to show that every swan that has existed or does or will exist is white and that of course is impossible. Without such proof, however, it is always possible that we can find a black swan. Popper's response is to argue that science is concerned not with establishing absolute forms of knowledge, but with establishing that knowledge claims are false (in this example by trying to find a black swan). Science should always be questioning knowledge claims.

Comte, however, was unaware of the eventual reversal of his project. His aim, through observation, classification, and analysis, was to find the laws of society. If we know what society *is*, we will no longer need to argue about what it *should be*; knowing the laws of society, like knowing the laws of nature, enables us to predict what will happen and therefore to control what will happen. Then we will be able to restore social order. Although Comte himself can be seen as representing a conservative reaction to Enlightenment thought and to the unrest that followed the French Revolution, such ideas are not *necessarily* conservative: indeed in the nineteenth century they influenced George Eliot and her partner and they can be found at the roots of British reformist socialism through the Fabian Society. I don't think anybody today would go all the way with Comte, but common-sense versions of many of Comte's ideas underlie much bread-and-butter social-policy research—on poverty and crime, for example.

We can also find in Comte's work a notion that became very important to Durkheim, that of society as a *whole*—that no one part of a society can be studied separately from the others but must be seen in the context of its relationships to all other parts.

Durkheim's rules

A social fact is every way of acting, fixed or not, capable of exercising on the individual an external constraint; or again, every way of acting which is general throughout a given society, while at the same time existing in its own right independent of its individual manifestations.

(Durkheim 1964: 13)

SOCIAL FACTS AND OBJECTIVITY

Durkheim sees his first task as stating exactly what it is that sociology is *about*, what it studies. One way of thinking about the social world seems to imply that it includes everything, and many modern approaches that go under the name of 'social constructionism' do precisely this; sociological theories of sexuality or of the emotions, for example, talk as if biology and psychology have no relevance (Craib 1995). This sets in train a sociological imperialism which implicitly makes all other sciences, including the natural sciences, redundant. Durkheim's aims for sociology were much more modest—and rightly so, since when he was writing in 1894, the closest sciences to sociology—psychology and biology—were much more highly developed than the social sciences. We would do well to bear that modesty in mind, because in many ways it is still appropriate. Some modern writers seem to think that sociology must explain everything or it can explain nothing, and that there is no alternative in between.

Durkheim's intention was to distinguish sociology from biology and psychology, particularly the latter. What distinguishes a *social* fact is that it is imposed upon us from the outside, that there is a large degree of compulsion about it. It is worth examining this in some detail. I have often heard people saying things like 'Well, society makes us do this or that, or teaches us to believe this or that.' But if we think about this for a while it clearly is not true—we have some sort of choice. It might be true in one sense that society expects each of us to get married and have children, but lots of people fail to do so or choose not to do so—and they are not excluded from society, and they do not find social life impossible, although they might occasionally feel or be made to feel different or odd. On the other hand, if I decided to speak dog Latin rather than English, I would be unable to continue life as a member of this society for very long. Clearly degrees of constraint and freedom vary and there is always a degree of choice, but there is also a degree of constraint. Social facts exercise a particularly high degree of constraint.

Having defined social facts as the proper concern or object of sociology, Durkheim instructs us to consider social facts as if they were things. By such an instruction, he is trying to distinguish sociological analysis from what we might call speculative theorizing. We all have common-sense ideas about the social world and how it works, and the temptation is to focus our thinking on those and build theories around them. Durkheim's warning here is also a warning to take heed of facts, the reality of the society we are studying which remains independent of our ideas about it. A recent example which struck me is the way in which, for some thirty years, people have argued that living together before marriage is a way of finding our whether a couple are suited to each other, thus avoiding a terrible mistake; yet the most recent available evidence (Buck *et al.* 1994) shows that couples who live together before marriage are much more likely to get divorced than those who don't. It is this sort of simple, but profound, mistake that Durkheim is talking about. He argues that our everyday thinking and speculating about the world are geared to the purpose of making us feel 'in harmony with our environment'. In other words, it is wishful thinking. It is often worthwhile thinking about political arguments in this way, as a means of making people—the speaker and the audience—feel comfortable, protecting them from reality. This is not what sociology is about. Durkheim insists on the difference between scientific concepts and what he calls 'prenotions'—our common-sense ideas and prejudices.

The injunction *to treat social facts as things* is to distinguish them from such ideas, or ideologies. He is not saying that we should treat them objectively, which modern students often assume—thinking of objectivity as a state of mind, a way of looking at what we study. Social facts remain the same, however we look at them; they are objective in the sense that they are like objects, and they do not change if we think of them differently, just as my desk would remain a desk, even if I thought it was a rhinoceros. Objectivity is a quality of objects, not an attitude of mind.

As examples of social facts which are fairly clearly things in this sense, Durkheim cites the law, embodied in codes set out in books, or statistical evidence about, for example, suicide. A social fact cannot be accepted as such until we find some external embodiment or identifying feature; it can only constrain us if it has an existence external to us. A scientific investigation needs to be directed at a limited number of clearly defined facts, and defining facts through our pre-notions does not work. We could, for example, try to define crime by reference to some moral law—a crime is that which runs counter to morality, yet morality varies from society to society, if not from individual to individual. However, all societies have a legal system or at least they have laws, and operate various forms of punishment when those laws are broken. It is here that we find the *external* feature of a crime that enables us to identify it as a social fact—the fact that it is punished. The criminal nature of the act is not some feature inherent in the act itself; it is in the fact that it is punished. The definition meets three of Durkheim's criteria for the identification of social facts. The definition must be clear of common-sense pre-notions—that is why it is surprising; secondly, it must be general: we cannot start from individual manifestations of a phenomenon; and, thirdly, there is external constraint: if I want to kill my grandmother in order to inherit her wealth, I cannot rewrite the law to excuse the action. It is a crime whether I like it or not.

THE NORMAL AND THE PATHOLOGICAL

Even now, a century after Durkheim was writing, I suspect that this way of defining crime is surprising to new students, as it might be surprising to many people who take part in popular arguments about crime and punishment. One implication, for example, is that the same act can be a crime in one society but not in another. A second implication is the idea that crime is normal. When Durkheim goes on to distinguish between the normal and the pathological, his borrowing of an organic analogy from biology becomes most evident. Societies are like organisms, and in this context he talks about types of societies as species, individual members of which can be identified as normal or pathological. Unlike many thinkers of that period, and now, Durkheim took the position that it was possible to argue from *is* to *ought*, that on the basis of an analysis of what exists it is possible to develop an argument about what should exist. Basically something is normal if there is a lot of it about. Of course it is not quite as simple as this. We must take into account the type of society and its stage of development—a social fact is normal when it is 'present in the average society of that species at the corresponding phase of its evolution' (Durkheim 1895/1964: 64). Evidence for this is to be backed up by an analysis which shows how the social fact is bound up with the social life of that type of society.

We can return to the striking idea that crime might be a normal social fact. I say striking because for Durkheim the normal is also the healthy, because it is an important part of a functioning society. The notion that crime might be healthy would not, I suspect, be acceptable to many contemporary political parties who make law and order a central part of their platform. It is normal and healthy because, in the first place, the committing of a crime and its punishment help to mark out and reinforce social boundaries, and so contribute towards a cohesion of a society, and, secondly, because it is a mechanism of social change: it can challenge those same boundaries. A contemporary example would be the public relationship between homosexuals at least one of whom is under the age 18— currently an offence in the United Kingdom, but under a law which, happily, is likely to be changed.

SOCIOLOGICAL EXPLANATION

The purpose of all the life sciences, insists Durkheim, is to describe the normal and the healthy, to distinguish it from the pathological; we discover what the normal body is like and how it works by looking at the bodies around us—there is no point in speculating about what it *should* be like (three legs and two livers, perhaps?). He goes on to discuss, comparatively briefly, how we may classify societies and comes to the conclusion that we should start with the simplest societies—those of one segment, one clan or kinship group; it is as if the simplest society is like a single cell and more complex societies like more complex organisms. The explanation of social facts has two dimensions: we should look for their *efficient cause*, which I would understand as a historical explanation, how and why this education system developed, and for their *function* in relation to the whole of the society, how it contributes to the continuing existence of society. The function of an institution does not explain its appearance—a trap into which modern functionalism too easily falls—but might help account for its continued existence once it has appeared. He outlines a comparative method by means of which the histories of different societies may be studied. In all such comparisons, within or between societies, 'Concomitant variation alone, as long as the variations were serial and systematic rather than isolated and spasmodic, was always sufficient to establish a sociological law' (Jones 1986: 75). For example, if we can establish that the suicide rate varies directly with types of social cohesion (see below), we have a sociological law.

Of course, Durkheim did not always employ his own method of concomitant variation—in fact, much of his later work is concerned with ideas, with a 'collective consciousness', but we shall see that this, too, is a social fact.

Suicide as a social fact

Some of these changes are apparent in Durkheim's study *Suicide* (1897/1952) but with some pushing and shoving it can be used as an example of the methods he outlines in *The Rules*. In the latter, he talks about *social currents* as well as social facts: these are general feelings which can run through a society or a large group. They emerge from the collective and move to individuals rather than the other way around. I suspect that most people have had the experience of being pulled along with the crowd into something they would not otherwise have done—even if it is only into getting drunk at a Christmas party. However, he clearly states all the way through that we must concern ourselves with social *facts*, not wishful thinking, and that social facts must be explained by social facts. Thus in *Suicide* Durkheim sets about showing first that, despite the fact that one might think that suicide is an individual act, it is a social fact. Suicide rates show a remarkable constancy, and they vary in a systematic way over time and from society to society. Here, then, is the first of the criteria by which a social fact can be identified—its externality. One might think that constraint—the second criterion—might be more difficult to establish. How can somebody be constrained to commit suicide, particularly by a society which forbids suicide. It must be remembered that, when Durkheim was writing, it had only recently ceased to be the practice to punish the bodies of suicides. The constraint that Durkheim is talking about here is different from the constraint that, for example, might stop us committing murder; it is the constraint of a 'social current' which pushes the individual towards a particular action. He talks about a 'suicidogenic current' present in each society, to which we are all subjected. The determinant—the social fact—which governs the strength of the suicidogenic current in a society can best be described as the form and strength of the social integration of a society.

He identifies four types of suicide dependent upon different degrees and forms of integration, two pairs at opposite ends of a continuum. The two most virulent suicidogenic currents in European society produced anomic and egoistic suicide. Anomic suicide occurs when the rules that govern social life fail and we are left not knowing how to behave, or what is appropriate; this often happens during periods of rapid social change, which will be reflected in individual lives, perhaps through the sudden gain or loss of wealth. There is nearly always a period of anomie, of greater or shorter length, on the break-up of a long-term intimate relationship, and it is not unknown for suicide to occur in such situations. In any case, the important point is about the comparative absence of social integration, a situation where people do not know what to do because the old rules seem no longer to apply, and there are no obvious new rules. At the opposite end of the continuum we have the situation where the social rules or norms are very powerful and apply rigidly—such as when an Indian widow might be compelled to throw herself on the funeral pyre or her dead husband—the practice of suttee. Durkheim calls this fatalistic suicide.

Egoistic suicide is a matter less of the level of integration than of its type. His argument seems to be that we can be integrated into a society in two ways. In the first we are integrated as individuals who are similar to each other, sharing the same sort of ideas—it is what we share with those around us which is important. An extreme variant of this in modern society—at least in Durkheim's time—would be the army, and it would be here that we would find incidents of what Durkheim called altruistic suicide, putting one's own life at risk to save another.

The alternative form of integration occurs when we are integrated into our society not as sharing common features with others but as individuals, responsible for our own individual fates, our own actions. This is not, as it might appear, a fragmentation of society, but it places greater responsibility for social cohesion on the individual, and Durkheim's argument is that in such societies the individual does not receive the collective support that he or she might receive in others types of society and is more vulnerable to isolation and suicide. The statistics that he looks at in this connection show systematic differences in suicide rates between, for example, Protestant communities, with their emphasis on the individual conscience, and Roman Catholic communities, with their emphasis of confession and forgiveness through the community leader, the priest, and systematic differences between the married and the unmarried.

What can we take from Durkheim?

As Mike Gane (1988) has pointed out, it is customary to dismiss much of Durkheim's methodology in modern texts; from the introductory Lee and

Newby (1983) to the more sophisticated study by Lukes (1973), Durkheim's notion of a social fact is regarded as inadequate, and in the case of suicide his statistical methods have been questioned; through the late 1960s and early 1970s there was a much more systematic attack on Durkheim's whole enterprise, particularly as it was manifested in *Suicide*. It seems to me that these criticisms are well worth looking at, but some of them are too easy.

In the first place it is argued that his criteria for the identification of social facts are vague. The nature of externality, for example, is ambiguous: is language, one of Durkheim's central examples of a social fact, internal or external, and how exactly does it constrain us? I have to speak English if I want most of the people around me to understand me, and there is a sense in which the language limits what I can say, but it also enables me to say things without setting in motion some strict process of determination. I can and do choose the words I put on this page; I might choose them badly, but I am not forced to write them.

There are interesting issues arising around these arguments. First of all, it seems to me that the ambiguity is probably necessary and we need to think about what Durkheim was trying to do and what he was trying to persuade us towards. It is clear, within the context of his general sociology, that one of the things that he was interested in was the way in which a society is reproduced within us or through our actions. In contemporary terms this sort of issue arises in debates about, for example, the way in which the personal is political—in, for example, the feminist argument that the way men and women behave in relation to each other on a personal level reproduces the features of patriarchy, the inequalities of power in the wider society. Society is always both inside and outside—and Durkheim was well able to recognize this, as we shall see later when we look at his conception of the *conscience collective*.

If we turn to modern arguments about *Suicide*, other things emerge. One argument is that suicide statistics do not reflect anything 'real' in the outside world but are themselves a social construction, a result of the procedures by which statistics are collected—the theories which organize them (see Hindess 1973) or the social context in which they are collected. Jack Douglas's *The Social Meanings of Suicide* (1967) pointed out that we might expect lower suicide rates in Roman Catholic communities because suicide is a sin, and officials would be reluctant to identify deaths as suicides. Douglas in fact makes a sweeping critique of Durkheim's methodology, arguing that he appears to be talking about objective phenomena 'out there', but his explanations assume not some simple causal process in which something called 'society' forces itself on individuals but a process of interpretation of shared beliefs—that, if more people commit suicide in an economic crisis, or if more Roman Catholics than Protestants commit suicide, then this is as a result of individuals interpreting the meaning of their situations and beliefs. Douglas is of course quite right, but I think he misses what Durkheim is trying to do: it is not only in respect of statistical regularities that suicide can be seen as a social fact; it is in relation to socially established and shared belief systems—the *conscience collective*. The statistics can be seen as the surface appearance; they are *signs* and, if they show regularities, there might be some underlying social, causal process at work—and that cause could lie in the form of social cohesion and/or in socially established belief systems and/or the construction of the statistics themselves.

What I am suggesting here is that Durkheim is not quite the strict positivist in the modern sense that his critics take him to be. Modern positivism has gone beyond Comte in attempting to root knowledge in sense experience and to establish general laws in a rigorous way. If we read Durkheim as trying to do this, then the criticisms hold, but if we regard him as developing more realist arguments—looking for underlying causes of surface phenomena—he can be defended. In this context, his insistence that social facts should be regarded as things is an insistence on the existence of underlying structures or processes which affect the way in which individuals behave to some degree independently of their will—the structures or processes or beliefs push us in one direction rather than another, limit our choices, and *sometimes* perhaps force us to do things. Not many people can resist the force of, for example, a patriotic war, and not many people become voluntarily unemployed, except in a very limited sense of taking up a redundancy offer. In other words, what is valuable is Durkheim's insistence that there is such a thing as society and that there are various ways in which it imposes itself upon us; it is there and it works on us, whatever we might think about it.

There is something else to be learnt about the nature of argument in social theory: that *precise* definitions are rarely not part of the game and, although we need to be as clear and precise as we can, it is possible to define an idea out of existence. When one writer criticizes another for being imprecise, it is often—but not always—a criticism of somebody for thinking, and there is always a degree of ambiguity in thinking. There are types of theoretical argument which open things up and other types of argument which close things down; it is not always easy to decide which is appropriate, but, in the case of Durkheim's arguments about social facts, the criticism of lack of precision closes down possibilities. The notion of a social fact, in a strong or a weak form, has been at the centre of sociology—even the development of a 'postmodern society' must be explained as a social fact, although not many of its proponents would accept this.

Further reading

From Durkheim's original work, *The Rules of Sociological Method* (1895/1964), chapters 1, 2, and 3 are a good starting point, followed by his preface to the second edition; you should also try to look at *Suicide* (1897/1952)—especially parts 2 and 3—as the classic sociological text.

For an oversimple but important criticism of Durkheim's method, see Jack Douglas, *Social Meanings of Suicide* (1967), and for a more conventional discussion, see S. Lukes, *Emile Durkheim* (1973), chapter 10. For a good modern discussion of positivism in sociology, see C. A. Bryant, *Positivism in Social Theory and Research* (1985).

4 | Karl Marx: the primacy of production

Introduction: the problems set by political misinterpretations of Marx; Marx and Darwin. *Marx's method: the starting point*: the ideology of individualism; the importance of practical, everyday life; the action/structure dualism in Marx; comparison of Marx with Durkheim; dialectical thinking and the separation of analysis and history.

Introduction

> The production of ideas, conceptions, of consciousness, is, to begin with, immediately involved in the material activity and the material interaction of men, the language of real life. Conceiving, thinking—the intellectual interaction of men—still appear here as the direct emanation of their material affairs.
>
> (Marx 1846/1977a: 37)

> In the social production of their life, men enter into definite relations that are indispensable and independent of their will, relations of production which correspond to a definite stage of development of their material productive forces.
>
> The sum total of these relations of production constitutes the economic structure of society, the real foundation, on which rises a legal and political superstructure and to which correspond definite forms of social consciousness. The mode of production of material life conditions the social, political and intellectual life process in general. It is not the consciousness of men that determines their being, but, on the contrary, their social being that determines their consciousness.
>
> (Marx 1859/1968b: 181)

Before going any further it will perhaps be useful to read these quotations carefully and think about whether you can see any differences between them. I will be returning to them shortly, but I will say now that the difference between them represents one of the central dualisms which have to be balanced by any social theory.

Marx is perhaps the most problematic of all the theorists we will be looking at; there are multiple interpretations of Durkheim, Weber, and Simmel but their theories did not provide a motivating force for the political struggles of the twentieth century, nor did they provide the principles of social organization for societies in much of Europe, Asia, Africa, and Central America. It is impossible to think of Marx without thinking of Marxism and the political debates that it brings in its train; in the English-speaking West, Marxism has entered into popular culture in profoundly distorted forms. These debates will not be the focus for what follows and my advice to the reader would be to try, as far as possible, to suspend any knowledge which you already might have of Marx and Marxism.

Writing some fifty or sixty years before Durkheim but around the same time as Comte, Marx too developed the idea of a society which existed *sui generis*, but he conceived of it in a very different way, emphasizing the material conditions of people's lives and the fundamental importance of history. Marx dedicated his great work *Capital* to Charles Darwin, and he saw himself as the scientist of society and the development of social forms, as Darwin was the scientist of the development of living forms. It has become common to talk about modern scientific ideas as involving the steady displacement of humanity from the centre of the stage. With Galileo comes the realization that the earth is not the centre of the universe, but just one planet amongst many in one solar system amongst many; with Darwin comes the realization that humanity is not the centre of creation but one development amongst others in the course of a long process of evolution; with Marx comes the realization that human beings are not the creators of society but are the creatures of society, the product of the social world into which they are born; and finally with Freud comes the understanding that the human individual is the product of unconscious forces, not fully in control of him- or herself.

Marx's method: the starting point

There is a long history of philosophical debate over Marx's methodology, some of it very abstract indeed. Marx himself was a philosopher and well acquainted with the history of European philosophy—he was no simplistic thinker, but was at the forefront of the development of the thought of his time, and just as his name is associated with ideas of political revolutions, so is it associated with intellectual revolution. Like Durkheim, Marx argued against the acceptance of contemporary common-sense ideas about society, what Durkheim called prenotions, but what Marx and Marxists would be more likely to call ideology. Whereas Durkheim based his argument on psychological reasons—to avoid wishful thinking—Marx based his on sociological *and* psychological grounds. Our wishful thinking derives from the fact that we will see the world through the blinkers of our social class—it is the product, crudely, of our material self-interest, not just our desire for peace of mind.

This is at the heart of his criticism of the classical economists and of the liberal philosopher John Start Mill. They start their analyses with the notion of the isolated individual, somebody separate from the individuals surrounding him or her; I suspect that this is still the first, rather naïve, way in which people think about society as they come to maturity. Despite the fact that from the moment of birth we are part of a social unit, we can see only other individuals, coming together and separating, engaging in economic and social activities through choice, just as we seem to organize our own lives—conveniently but profoundly forgetting that we have no choice about the family, the socio-economic class, the geographical area, or the culture into which we are born, and these are the very things that make us what we are. Marx argued that such a conception of individuality—the 'individuated individual'—was the result of the loss of the social ties of feudal societies and the growth of the capitalist systems of production and the market economy. In other words, it was the product of a specific historic period, whereas the thinkers that Marx was criticizing tended to regard such an individual as having existed throughout history. A constant theme of the Marxist criticism of bourgeois or ruling-class thought is the way in which it turns temporary, historically conditioned and produced features of social lives into eternal truths of human nature.

Marx regarded such notions of the human individual as abstract, and his criticism of this way of looking at the world merged with his criticism of German idealist philosophy, and particularly of Hegel, whose philosophy he famously 'stood on its head'. Hegel's idealism sees the world as the product of ideas working themselves out through history. Against such a starting point, Marx posits real people, acting practically in real social relations. In his *Theses on Feuerbach* (Marx 1845/1968*d*), Marx writes of Feuerbach—a German philosopher who had begun to move away from Hegel, but in Marx's view only half succeeded—that: 'Feuerbach, not satisfied with *abstract thought* wants *empirical observation*, but he does not conceive the sensible world as *practical*, human sense activity' (Ibid. 29), and later: 'All social life is essentially *practical*. All the mysteries which lead theory towards mysticism find their rational solution in human practice and in the comprehension of this practice' (ibid. 30).

Hegel had seen human history in terms of the development of ideas and Feuerbach had gone half-way to inverting that understanding, half-way to seeing ideas and their development as the product of human social history. He had argued that our conception of God does not come from our process of thinking; rather it is an alienation of a human essence: something which is part of us is projected onto an omnipotent being. Marx takes this further—the notion of a human essence is abstract; in fact, it is our power as practical beings working together that we project onto our idea of God—our strength as people collectively acting on and changing the world. It is this practical and sensuous activity that forms the basis of everything else. The first quotation at the beginning of this chapter seems to me to emphasize this aspect of his work, and it belongs to what commentators usually call the 'young Marx'.

There has been much debate at various times among interpreters of Marx about the difference between the 'young' and the 'old' Marx; there is a clear shift of emphasis in his thinking from the humanism of the above quotations, his concern with real people engaged in real activities and relationships with each other, to his later concern with the economic structure of capitalism, pushing people and societies through processes over which they have no control and of which they are ignorant—an attitude which stands out clearly from the second quotation at the beginning of the chapter. I do not think of this as a major problem; rather it is a mark of Marx's greatness as a thinker that he was able to work with both sides of a dualism which still haunts and I think inevitably must haunt social theory—that between action and structure. As many have done since, he begins by talking about human action and moves into an analysis of the structure created by human action, and which in turn determines human action; this is often called a dialectical process and the same idea was being pushed by such non-Marxist sociologists as Peter Berger and Thomas Luckman (1967) well into the second half of this century.

I sometimes think that the history of Marxist thought can be seen as an extended elaboration of the second quotation, and much of it can be understood as a debate about the meaning of the last two lines: 'it is not the consciousness of men that determines their being, but, on the contrary, their social being that determines their consciousness.' For the moment, however, I want to contrast Marx with Durkheim.

A crucial difference is the starting point. For Durkheim it is the search for social facts, features of life which impose themselves upon us. For Marx it is our sensuous everyday activity, the ways in which we make our living, grow food, manufacture artefacts. Whereas Durkheim starts off in a realm of determinism, Marx begins in a realm of freedom, even if he then moves to look at the way in which what we produce through this freedom acts back upon us to determine our lives, to impose itself on us from the outside, this time through our being placed in relationships over which we have no control. It is perhaps common for people to think of Marx as the social thinker who held the most rigidly determinist view of human existence, but this starting point in human interaction has sometimes led to him being compared to that least determinist of all sociological approaches, symbolic interactionism (see Goff 1980). This movement from the freedom of human interaction through to the way in which society and social relations impose themselves upon us is summed up, at least as far as capitalism is concerned, in the theory of alienation (see Marx 1844/1973a; Ollman 1971). So Marx adds a dimension to our conception of social life which Durkheim, at least in his methodological writings, ignores. There is also a difference in the way in which each conceives of the society that imposes itself upon us—although their important similarity is that they *do* see society as something which imposes itself upon us.

Marx's conception is of a more complex arrangement, less like an organism and more like a building, to use his own analogy of an infrastructure and super-structure. Most important in such an analogy is the argument that one part of this structure, the economic base, is more important than the others, that it somehow conditions their existence and determines, at least in the sense of lim-its, what goes on there.

In both thinkers we find an idea of an underlying social structure: in Durkheim forms of social cohesion, and in Marx the forces of production which produce the visible effects and actions that make up peoples' lives. They share the idea that the function of science is to penetrate below the surface of social life to reveal features of our life of which we are not immediately aware, but the way in which we search for these underlying features is different. For Durkheim it is a matter of looking for empirical regularities—he is much closer to the conven-tional picture of the natural scientist. For Marx, however, it is a different matter, a process of analytic thinking rather than empirical investigation. It must not be forgotten that Marx was a philosopher and Terrell Carver's judgement is, I think, correct: 'My conclusion is not that Marx was exclusively (or even primarily) a philosopher and logician, but that he applied the techniques of philosophy and logic . . . [to] the criticism of political economy' (Carver 1975: 177).

One part of this philosophical thinking was to differentiate between the process of thinking about a phenomenon and the process by which that phe-nomenon comes into existence. Our understanding of the historical develop-ment of capitalism is not the same thing as our understanding of the way in which capitalism works—thinking in the social sciences is not the same as telling historical stories, just as discovering the workings of a particular cancer cell is not the same thing as knowing why it should have appeared in the first place. Marx in his introduction to the *Grundrisse* discusses two 'moments' of thinking—an analytic moment, and a synthetic moment which begins and ends with what he calls the 'concrete'. The analytic moment breaks down what we are studying (the concrete) into its component simpler parts. We can begin our ana-lysis, he suggests, with the population of a society, the people who are engaged in the productive process. But if we start in such a way, we are dealing with an abstraction: the concept of 'population' needs to be broken down into its com-ponent parts—for example, social classes—and these too need to be further broken down. This moves us away from the abstraction and closer to the con-crete reality we are trying to understand. But not only do these abstractions have to be broken down; they need to be brought together in a synthesis, showing how they are related to each other: 'The concrete is concrete, because it is the sum of many determinations [and] therefore a unity of diversity' (Carver 1975: 72).

The important point here is the separation of the historical development of a society and our way of analysing that society, and Marx provides us with a model for the thinking process that enables us to produce knowledge, a process of breaking down and synthesizing that is generally referred to as dialectical in a rather more sophisticated sense than was used in connection with Berger and Luckman above. This use of the term 'dialectical' suggests three dimensions to thinking: the first is the notion of the whole or the totality—the idea that our knowledge can be judged by its inclusiveness, the extent to which it gives a knowledge of the totality of what we are studying. This is implied in the second part of the last quotation—the concrete is the sum of many determinations, a unity of diversity.

The second dimension is an elaboration of the development of thought which is usually attributed to Hegel. The crude and oversimplified version is that thought (and for Hegel, history itself) progresses through stages: a thesis, an initial proposition, an antithesis—the opposite to the thesis,—and a synthesis—a result of the argument which combines both thesis and antithesis, which in turn becomes the thesis for a new movement. In fact Hegel was never as crude as this, and the process of analysis and synthesis is more complex, involving more complex concepts and developmental paths, producing a more complex conception of reality, of 'society'. The 'unity of diversity' implies an understanding of social reality as the product of many causes, none of which we understand properly until we find its place in the whole process. This is in contrast to Marx's desire to give priority to the economic structure in the causal process, and this tension between a multi-causal model and a mono-causal model has haunted the history of Marxism, as well as provided the basis for many alternative arguments.

The third aspect of the notion of dialectic is that of contradiction and movement: a society is not a simple entity, but a combination of contradictory elements in a permanent (and with capitalism, increasingly rapid) process of change. Contradiction, conflict, and change are seen as normal and inevitable aspects of social development, and, as we shall see, this marks a real difference between Durkheim and Marx. For Marx, the 'individuated individual' of capitalism could not grasp this aspect of history, and the importance which he attributed to dialectical thinking is summed up in William McBride's translation from his 'Afterword' to the German edition of *Capital*:

In its rational form (dialectic) is a scandal and abomination to bourgeoisdom and its doctrinaire professors, because it includes in its comprehension and affirmative recognition of the existing state of things, at the same time also, the recognition of the negation of that state, of its inevitable breaking up; because it regards every historically developed form as in fluid movement, and therefore takes into account its transient nature not less than its momentary existence; because it lets nothing impose upon it, and is in its essence critical and revolutionary.   (McBride 1977: 68)

Finally, returning to the notion of totality itself, some of the more important implications were brought out by later Marxists and I want to look in particular at the contribution of Georg Lukacs, a Hungarian Marxist whose most important work was *History and Class Consciousness* (1923/1971*a*). Lukacs elaborated on these ideas in an interesting way. First he took some of Marx's comments to argue that the analytic moment of thought—the separation of what we are studying into its separate components—is in fact an *ideological* moment; the development of capitalism leads to a way of looking at the world which sees it precisely in terms of separate entities which are *externally* related. By this he means that we think of the world as consisting of separate objects related by simple causal relationships which, in essence, can be measured. Durkheim's instructions on how to identify social facts through concomitant variations would be an example of such analytic thinking.

Marxist thought, in contrast, sees each separate entity as part of a network which comprises a whole, and each separate phenomenon can be understood only in terms of its relationship to the whole. To develop the example of suicide, it is not enough to relate suicide rates to a particular religious belief and what that implies for the form of social integration. The development of Protestantism, for example, would need to be related to certain aspects of the economic development of capitalism and in turn might be related to certain forms of political democracy, and certain types of business organization, a changing education system, and so on. We gain a full knowledge of, in this case, suicide only when we have an understanding of the whole network of relationships within which the suicides take place, and this knowledge is produced by theory as well as by observation and measurement. And Marxist thinking is constantly moving from one level of analysis to the next. This way of thinking, this method of analysis, was for Lukacs of crucial importance—to the point that he argued that, even if all Marx's predictions proved wrong, we would not have to abandon the essence of Marxism: its method.

The same could, of course, be said about Durkheim's more conventional scientific method; there are all sorts of reasons why the knowledge produced by any method might be wrong, without invalidating the method; but these are not the only conceptions of society or of method that can be found in the work of sociology's founders. If both Durkheim and Marx insist on the way in which society imposes itself on its members, Weber, at least in principle, if not always in practice, was concerned to show how people actually created the society they live in.

Further reading

There is no easy reading on these matters; amongst the original texts, Marx's Preface and more important Introduction to the *Critique of Political Economy (The Grundrisse)* (1859/1968*b* and 1859/1973 respectively) are worth looking at, perhaps in conjunction with Terrell Carver's commentary in his *Karl Marx: Texts on Method* (1975).

I first came to understand what was meant by dialectical thinking through reading Lucien Goldmann, *The Human Sciences and Philosophy* (1969), and Henri Lefebvre, *Dialectical Materialism*, (1968), in quick succession. If you want to give yourself a really hard time, try Georg Lukacs, *History and Class Consciousness* (1971*a*).

5 | Max Weber: the primacy of social action

Introduction: Comparison with Marx and Durkheim; Kantian background and the differences between the natural and the human sciences. *The proper object of sociology:* sociology's concern with the individual event and Weber's debate with Marx's ghost; the society/individual dualism; behaviour and action; meaningful social action; further comparison of Marx and Durkheim; *Different types of meaningful action. Understanding social action:* observational and explanatory understanding; causal adequacy and meaning adequacy. *The ideal type:* Weber's individualism and further comparison with Marx and Durkheim; scientific and common-sense knowledge. *Values and value freedom.*

Introduction

Sociology (in the sense in which this highly ambiguous word is used here) is a science which attempts the interpretive understanding of social action in order thereby to arrive at a causal explanation of its course and effects. In 'action' is included all human behaviour when and in so far as the acting individual attaches a subjective meaning to it. Action in this sense may be either overt or purely inward or subjective; it may consist of positive intervention in a situation, or of deliberately refraining from such intervention or passively acquiescing in the situation. Action is social in so far as, by virtue of the subjective meaning attached to it by the acting individual (or individuals), it takes account of the behaviour of others and is thereby oriented in its course.

(Weber 1922/1947: 88)

And now for something completely different. Max Weber's most productive years covered the first two decades of the twentieth century and many would think of him, perhaps together with Simmel, as the most contemporary of the four theorists, even as representing the first signs of postmodernism. He has a very different starting point from both Durkheim and Marx and emerges from a very different philosophical tradition. Whereas Durkheim's work came out of

Comte's concern with the unity of the sciences, and directs itself to the natural sciences, and Marx's model of science is Darwin's theory of evolution and involves a notion of underlying structures of social reality to which we do not have immediate access, Weber comes from a tradition which asserts a radical difference between the natural and human sciences.

This tradition was developed through Rickert (1962; see also Burger 1976), who started with a distinction in Kant's philosophy between the phenomenal world, the world of external objects, and the *nuomenal* world, the world of consciousness. The former exists in time and space and can be known through experience and the methods of the natural sciences. Consciousness, on the other hand, is not an object out there in the world. We cannot see it, it does not exist in any particular space or at any particular time out there. However, we do have an experience of what it is to be conscious. I can look around and distinguish between people and animals and objects. It is possible to construct from such experience an understanding of what consciousness *must be* like in order to have such experiences. We are constantly making judgements about the world—that if I cross the road here, that car in the distance will stop before it hits me, or that moving object over there is a dog and not a flamingo, and we can say that one of the qualities of consciousness is to make judgements, or to distinguish between different types of object. This is known as a *transcendental* argument, an argument which transcends—goes beyond—given, empirical reality. It is a form of argument employed recently by Roy Bhaskar (1978, 1979) in his development of a modern realist philosophy for the social sciences.

I do not want to follow this aspect of Kantian philosophy too far, but it does provide an idea of why Weber should think that the process of thought in itself produces knowledge, in addition to the knowledge produced by observation and experiment. I discussed Marx's version of this in the last chapter, but it must be remembered that neither Marx nor Weber thought we could dispense with observation, or, when possible, experiment (at least thought experiments) or measurement; it is just that they gave a greater role to thought than Durkheim (at least explicitly) recognized. It is also important to know that Kant gave a particular role to moral judgement, which appears in Weber's work as a concern with value and value choice.

Now, whereas both Marx and Durkheim were concerned with establishing social laws or general truths about society, the Kantian tradition thought this was only possible in the natural sciences, which are concerned with what is general and common to different phenomena, with the laws of nature. By contrast, the human sciences are concerned with individuals, individual events, individual actors, and the way people express themselves.

In these senses, then, Weber continues the great tradition of German idealism, the concern with the constitutive nature of ideas, compared with Marx, who half a century before had attempted to stand that tradition on its head. It is often said that Weber was engaged in a lifelong debate with Marx's ghost, and, while there is a degree of truth in this, it is, as ever, not that simple. There are many aspects of Weber's substantive sociology which seem to me to be open-ended Marxist studies, and Weber himself, in *The Protestant Ethic and the Spirit of Capitalism* (1904–5/1976) insisted that he was not setting out to replace a one-sided materialist, Marxist argument with a one-sided idealist argument. One of the factors that has made Weber's work such a rich source of ideas right up to the present time has been that, in practice, Weber was never one-sided about anything, even if, in theory, he appeared to be so. Thus his individualism, as we shall see, is never quite as individualistic as it seems, his relativism is never quite as relativist as it seems, his idealism is never quite as idealist, and his rationalism never quite as rationalist as it seems. And, in the comparison between Weber, on the one hand, and Durkheim and Marx, on the other, we have found another central sociological dualism: that between individual and society. Every sociological theory must deal with both, yet the two are very different and can provide mutually exclusive understandings of the social world.

The proper object of sociology

In his methodological writings, Weber is always drawing distinctions. The social sciences are concerned with individual phenomena, events, and people. But if social organizations—societies—are simply collections of individuals acting randomly, there could be no scientific investigation of society. What makes such an investigation possible is that people act rationally, organizing the world in a coherent way; the aim of the social sciences is to arrive at a rational understanding of human action. But not of all human action. This is where the distinctions begin. First of all there is a distinction between behaviour and action. Behaviour is what we do without attaching a meaning to it. If I sneeze, or cough, or blink, my movements can be understood as the end result of physical processes in the body, as the result of a physical cause rather than as a *meaningful* action. Sociology is concerned with the latter. If we take Freud seriously, much action which we think is meaningless might have an unconscious meaning, and we will find that, in all these distinctions, the edges are constantly blurred, something which Weber himself recognized. They are not meant to be watertight compartments but rather to bring order from chaos, to offer a way of understanding which can begin to make sense of what at first glance seems a muddle—and if we look at the social world as made up of individual actions, then it does appear to be a muddle.

Sociology is concerned with meaningful action—whether meaning is attributed to an action by an individual or to one by a group of individuals, in which case our knowledge of the meaning is more approximate. We must also take account of the meanings attributed to inanimate objects, which, of course, do not have their own subjective meanings—they must be seen in relation to human action as means and ends. But then comes a further distinction: not all meaningful action concerns sociology, only meaningful action which is directed towards or takes account of other people—meaningful *social* action. Weber's own example here is of a distinction between a collision between two cyclists, which we can look at as an event in the natural world, a result of a causal chain of physical events. Although each cyclist is engaged in meaningful action, their collision was not meant by either. What follows, however, whether an argument or an apology or the expression of concern, is meaningful social action in which each is directing his or her action towards the other. It becomes clear here that Weber is concerned with what we might call *intentional acts of meaning*, rational actions that we deliberately or consciously take in relation to and directed towards other people. Actions into which we are pushed—for example, by the influence of crowds—do not count.

This marks an important difference from Marx and Durkheim. They also deal with human action, as must every social theorist. For Marx, however, human action can be affected by forces of which the actors do not necessarily have any knowledge—for example, our actions are constantly conditioned by economic forces which we don't know about or understand, and to which we do not, therefore, attribute a subjective meaning. In Durkheim's case, the notion of social consciousness implies that meaning itself is social—we are socialized into ways of thinking. The modern British philosopher Peter Winch (1958) arrives at the same conclusion via a rather different course. Social action, he argues, is rule-following, and by definition rules are social constructs: to establish a rule we need at least two people. Thus any meaningful action is rule-following and therefore social. I don't think that many modern sociologists would see Weber's distinction as important.

Different types of meaningful action

Weber goes on to distinguish between four types of meaningful social action which vary in the degree of meaningfulness and therefore of rationality. First he talks about *traditional* action, close to the borderline of the rational : 'For it is very often a matter of almost automatic reaction to habitual stimuli which guide behaviour in a course which has been repeatedly followed. The great bulk of all everyday action to which people have become habitually accustomed approaches this type' (Weber 1922/1947: 116). Thus Weber sees as borderline an area of social reality—everyday routine—which modern sociologists from Garfinkel (1967) to Giddens (1984) regard as central to understanding social cohesion.

Weber's second type of action, that based on emotion, the 'purely affectual', is also on the borderline of the rational; it is not meaningful when it is uncontrollable, but the more control that is exercised, the more meaningful it becomes. The crucial issue seems to be whether the action has an aim outside itself. If I am angry and smash something simply to express and relieve the anger, it is not rational; if I smash the plate in order to intimidate the person I am arguing with, it is an angry action but also a meaningful social action. Again, some contemporary theorists might see emotions as part of the central dynamics of social interaction, but Weber was concerned to limit the range of the study of sociology, to define its proper object.

The third type of action is oriented towards an ultimate value in a self-conscious way; like affectual action, it does not necessarily have an end external to itself but is satisfying for its own sake. If I am a Christian and I go into a church to pray, I am not engaging in a rational action to achieve a practical result but rather I am acting in a way that satisfies my belief in my duties to a Christian God. However, there is a difference from affective action: it might not be rational to believe in a Christian God, but, given that I do so believe, then it is rational that I engage in such actions as church-going and praying. When Weber talks about ultimate values, he is thinking of such values as are enshrined in a religious belief, and, by implication, in, say, atheism or agnosticism, humanism or communism, or indeed the pursuit of scientific knowledge itself—if such beliefs govern our action.

Jean-Paul Sartre, the French existentialist philosopher, argued that human beings were always engaged in choosing how they would live; we cannot do otherwise—we have no choice but to choose and we are always responsible for our actions; they are not forced on us. Weber seems to be saying something like this several decades before Sartre and without the latter's concern with responsibility and everyday life. We have to choose between ultimate values and there is no rational basis for that choice. Once the choice has been made, however, the actions that follow on from it can be understood as rational.

The fourth, most rational, type of action:

> is rationally oriented to a system of discrete individual ends, when the end, the means and the secondary results are all taken into account and weighed. This involves rational consideration of alternative means to the end, of the relations of the end to other prospective results of employment of any given means, and finally of the relative importance of different possible ends.   (Weber 1922/1947: 117)

Weber goes on to make a point which is obvious if you have been thinking about the different types of action as you have read through this: that very few actions are oriented in only one way. Think, for example, about the activity of lecturing in a university. There is a traditional element to it—things have always been done this way in universities, even though there is evidence that it is not the most effective way of teaching. It is also an affectual action, in a not very obvious way: it creates a sense of security for students and staff in what might otherwise be an unstructured and therefore anxiety-provoking situation. We can all feel that we are doing something, even if nothing much is happening in the way of education. Then on many occasions it can be an activity oriented to an ultimate value, with both students and staff committed to the value of learning and education, the growth of knowledge. And finally it is a straightforward instrumental activity: I lecture as a way of securing a salary which in turn secures me a roof over my head, food, and other goods that I feel are useful or enjoyable to me; students come perhaps in the hope of learning what it is expected that they shall reproduce in examinations, in order to make sure that they get their piece of paper at the end of the course which in turn will help them secure a job which in turn will supply them with an income, and so on. This might sound a very depressing way of looking at the world, as well as at your own future, and Weber would agree with you. He talked about a process of disenchantment, of the world losing its magic and becoming steadily more rationalized; in fact, he saw this as the major process of change in the modern world.

So, of Weber's four types of action, only one and a half are fully rational, meaningful forms of social action. His conception of rationality has become known as 'instrumental': it involves a strict relationship between means and ends, each step leading on to the next in a necessary way, until the desired end is reached. Marxist critics (and others) think of this conception of rationality as one concerned with domination: the control and manipulation of the natural world, spreading to the control and manipulation of human beings as if they were things. This is juxtaposed to dialectical rationality, the process of analysis and synthesis which I discussed in the previous chapter. Here, too, we can see the contrast I discussed in Chapter 1 between the view that knowledge is a liberation and the view that it is an enslavement; what is often lost in the modern debate is the idea that there are different aspects of knowledge and different types of rationality. Weber's particular conception of rationality represents the analytic moment of understanding, breaking down, and describing the elements of social reality as it exists at the moment; it is the moment of domination. In contrast, the Marxist conception can be seen as the synthetic movement, which brings together these elements and takes us beyond what exists at the moment to what might exist; it is the liberating moment.

Understanding social action

The next question to answer is how we understand meaningful social action. Weber makes a distinction between what he calls *observational* understanding and *explanatory* understanding. If somebody in the room gets up and opens a window, I recognize that 'he or she is opening the window'. This is observational understanding. Explanatory understanding goes further: it involves realizing that, for example, the room is very hot, or full of cigarette smoke or assorted bodily smells, or—if a lecture is in progress—that people are going to sleep, and that opening the window is a way of clearing the air or waking people up. The explanatory understanding sets out the chain of means leading up to an end; Weber talks about this as a context of meaning and the contexts can be elaborated—waking people up in a lecture can be linked into a broader chain of steps which encompasses the purposes of education from the points of view of the teacher and the student.

Weber uses the German term *verstehen* when he talks about understanding. This often seems to have been taken by English-speaking commentators as closer to empathic understanding, a sort of emotional identification with the actors whom we are trying to understand (see e.g. Runciman 1972), and this has provided an easy target for criticism—empathy might be a useful way of arriving at hypotheses about what someone is doing, but by itself it is entirely subjective and cannot possibly be a way of gaining knowledge. However, there is, as it were, another interpretation of interpretation. Talcott Parsons's version in a footnote to his translation of Weber's methodological writings is rather placid but makes the basic point:

Its primary reference in this work is to the observation and theoretical interpretation of the subjective 'states of mind' of actors. But it also extends to the grasp of the meaning of logical and other systems of symbols, a meaning which is usually thought of as in some sense 'intended' by a mind or intelligent being of some sort.   (Weber 1922/1947: 87)

Diana Leat (1972) makes the same point with rather more verve. We could imagine, for example, a statistical correlation between the birth rate and stork population; it would be amusing, but we would not take it seriously as suggesting a causal relationship. On the other hand, if we are told that there is a correlation between the number of days lost through strike action and the level of unemployment, we do think that there is likely to be a causal connection. We are members of the same society, or type of society, to which the statistics apply, and we can therefore follow the likely reasoning of the actors involved. If there is a high level of unemployment and jobs are hard to find, workers will not strike for fear of being sacked and replaced by others; if unemployment is lower and alternative employment can be found, then they are likely to be more adventurous. In other words, we have understood the rationality of the actors and we can regard the statistical correlation as meaningful—not meaningless, as in the first example.

Weber talks about two criteria by which we can judge that our understanding is adequate—adequacy on the level of cause and adequacy on the level of meaning. By adequacy on the level of cause, he means that we must search for similar situations in which the same outcome might be expected, finding confirmation of our understanding if the same outcome does ensue. Or does not ensue— Weber's argument that a certain sort of Protestantism is necessary for the development of capitalism finds evidence for its adequacy if we can find other situations where all the other preconditions for the growth of capitalism exist but there is no equivalent of the Protestant ethic and capitalism does not develop.

Adequacy on the level of meaning is a matter of the account making sense, being intelligible and comprehensible to us; it must be a believable story. There are all sorts of interesting possibilities here, since novelists too tell believable stories, but the sociologist's stories have to meet more rigorous standards of rationality and also to meet the condition of causal adequacy. Weber did not put himself in the position of many contemporary thinkers and argue that all stories were equal; he clearly thought that some were better than others, that his stories of the rise of capitalism were, for example, better than Marx's.

The ideal type

The tool that we use to understand social events and processes using interpretive understanding is the *ideal type*. Although, in the following passage, Weber describes the ideal type as a *utopia*, he does not mean this in the sense that it is a desirable state of affairs at which we should aim—he means it simply in the sense that the ideal type does not exist in reality. We do not construct an ideal type of, say, a bureaucracy by taking the average or typical components of existing bureaucracies or by trying to construct a model of a real bureaucracy. Rather it is the most rational form of the bureaucracy that we can imagine:

The ideal type is formed by the one-sided *accentuation* of one or more points of view, and by the synthesis of a great many diffuse, discrete more or less present and occasionally absent *concrete individual* phenomena which are arranged according to those one-sidedly emphasized viewpoints into a unified *analytical* construct. In its conceptual purity, this mental construct cannot be found anywhere in reality. It is a *utopia*.   (Weber 1904/1949: 90)

Alfred Schutz (1972) glosses Weber's arguments as setting out to construct concepts and types by a process of typification—of using rational criteria to select out common elements of what we are studying and linking them together in a rational way. He suggests that it is a matter of building—in the mind—a rational puppet theatre, and then manipulating the puppets to see how they would act in different situations. This enables the social scientist not only to understand past events but also to predict future events. The following quotation covers the construction of ideal-type concepts and illustrates some further important points about Weberian methodology:

when we inquire as to what corresponds to the idea of the 'state' in empirical reality, we find an infinity of diffuse and discrete human action, both active and passive, factually and legally regulated relationships, partly unique and partly recurrent in character, all bound together by an idea, namely the belief in the actual or normal validity of rules and of the authority of some human beings towards others. This belief is in part consciously, in part dimly felt, and in part passively accepted by persons who, should they think about the 'idea' in a really clearly defined manner, would not first need a 'general theory of the state' which aims to articulate the idea. The scientific conception of the state, however it is formulated, is naturally always a synthesis we construct for certain heuristic purposes. But on the other hand, it is also abstracted from the unclear syntheses which are found in the mind of human beings.   (Schutz 1972: 99)

There are two significant ways here in which Weber differs from the approaches of Marx and Durkheim. In the first place he is saying that what we call the 'state' does not have an existence in its own right over and above the people whose relationships and actions comprise reality—there is a confused network of relationships and actions that comprises reality, and the concept of the state makes some sense of the confusion. This is so for the sociologist but it is also true for the person he or she studies, and if the people we study think there is such a thing as the state, then we can treat it as existing, because it then figures in their action and they take account of it. The second point is that, in order to understand the state, the sociologist elaborates on and clarifies the common-sense ideas of those he or she studies: there is not that radical break between 'pre-notion' or 'ideology' and scientific concept: they develop out of each other.

Finally, Weber argues that sociology is not concerned with totalizing explanations: only individuals have an *ontological* reality, society does not exist in that real sense, and so sociological explanations must be in terms of individual events and processes. Thus, unlike Marx, Weber would not claim to offer a totalizing explanation of the development of capitalism, prioritizing different causal processes, but would rather offer a series of snapshots, taken from different angles and showing different aspects: *The Protestant Ethic and the Spirit of Capitalism* shows, as it were, the 'ideological' preconditions for the growth of capitalism, but one can also find in Weber studies of the economic preconditions of capitalism and of the legal preconditions—but he does not bring them together into some sort of overall explanation which would link them together in causal processes.

Values and value freedom

There is one final point to be made about Weber's methodology: he raises the issues of value in a way different from that which we find in Durkheim and Marx. For Durkheim, value freedom was the result of shedding 'pre-notions' and sticking to social facts; for Marx, social science itself carried the values of human emancipation and provided the basis for political action. Weber produced a subtle and complex argument which contained elements of both positions. For many years English-speaking sociologists interpreted Weber's injunction to 'value freedom' as implying a sort of simple objectivity on the part of the sociologist—the sort of grey neutrality. That interpretation disappeared during the 1960s in favour of one that is much closer to Weber's real intentions. Martin Albrow lists ten points that Weber makes about values. The first four are particularly important:

1. Science is guided by values, such as integrity, rigour, clarity, truth.

2. Human beings are valuing beings. They live lives through and for values.

3. History only makes sense if it is considered from the standpoint of values.

4. Social scientists choose their lines and objects of inquiry by reference to values. (Albrow 1990: 243–4)

So, if Weber saw values as so central to peoples' lives, how could he talk of value freedom? The answer is that sociology is only value-free in a limited and rather sophisticated way. The choice of a scientific career is itself a value choice—the scientist commits him- or herself to the values of integrity, rigour, clarity, and truth; what I choose to study as a scientist is a value choice, as is the method with which I choose to study it. Once these choices have been made, however, the overarching values of science—integrity, and so on—come into play and it is possible to construct—in the social sciences—a shared rational understanding of what we are studying. Value freedom is always value freedom within the limits of the values of our culture and our personal choices; in fact value freedom is itself a value that we choose.

Weber is adding something important here to our understanding not only of social life but of sociology itself; sociology might produce knowledge (Durkheim); it might produce knowledge which becomes a tool or weapon in political emancipation (Marx), but it also involves the choices of some values over and against other values; it involves what are basically moral choices and the implication is that we need to elucidate the moral choice that we make. Very few sociologists embark on that enterprise.

Further reading

The most accessible and intelligible of Weber's methodological writings are the opening sections of *The Theory of Social and Economic Organization* (1922/1947); his account of the ideal type and of value freedom can be found in *The Methodology of the Social Sciences* (1949)—these are more difficult essays and require a lot of concentration.

6 | Georg Simmel: society as form and process—the outsider's view

Introduction: Simmel as a herald of postmodernism. *Society and the social*: his conception of society—comparison with Weber and Lukacs; social forms and the life process and the protection of individuality. *The social forms*: society, social relationships, social institutions, and play forms; his methods and organizational principles.

Introduction

> How does the raw material of immediate experience become the theoretical structure that we call history? The transformation in question is of a more radical sort than common sense usually assumes. To demonstrate this is to develop a critique of historical realism—of the view that the science of history should provide a mirror image of the past 'as it really was'. Such a view commits no less an error than does realism in art, which pretends to copy reality without being aware of how thoroughly this act of 'copying' in fact stylizes the contents of reality.
>
> (Simmel 1907/1971: 3)

Georg Simmel was a contemporary and colleague of Weber, part of an intellectual group which would meet regularly and included the Marxist Georg Lukacs, whom I discussed earlier. He never quite seems to qualify as one of sociology's founding thinkers of equal status with the other three. Yet he is frequently cited as the most original and seminal of the four (e.g. Levine 1971) with a major influence on early American sociology; he is often also cited as the most difficult, an ambivalent attitude that was common to his contemporaries as well. There is little that is systematic about his work and Coser (1991*a*) talks of the 'almost studied disorderliness of his method'. It is perhaps his disorderliness that sometimes gives the impression that he belongs to the contemporary world. The way in which he bridges the gap between the first and the last decades of the twentieth century can be seen in the above quotation. He begins with Weber's problem: how do we make sense of the complex reality of our experience. But he moves immediately towards the novelist's task, comparing it directly with that of the social scientist and presenting us with a very modern idea: that what we think of as reality is in fact a construction, just as the novelist's 'real world' is a construction. He seems to move to and fro between the realist and postmodern constructionist position. Overall perhaps the latter dominates, but there are interesting elements of the former.

Society and the social

Simmel's conception of society is not as clear as Durkheim's or Marx's but it is there, in some ways clearer than Weber's. Sometimes he writes as if society is the combination of relationships between people, a more or less Weberian position, but he seems to give that combination a reality of its own. In a difficult sentence he talks about society being 'the sum of those forms of relationship by virtue of which individuals are transformed, precisely, into "society" in the first sense'— that is, the combination of relationships between individuals. There is in this the notion of a society producing or reproducing itself by socializing its individual members into more or less determinate relationships which together make up the society in question. In other words, there is also the notion here of a society existing over and above its individual members. But there are good reasons why Simmel does not pursue a more systematic analysis of society.

As might be expected from Lewis Coser's comments, it is difficult to give a coherent account of Simmel's conception of society and his sociological method—not because his own accounts are incoherent but rather because they often seem fragmented, and looking through some of the secondary accounts of Simmel one could almost think that each refers to a different thinker. I have already mentioned the links between Lukacs, Weber, and Simmel, and I want first to try to explore these a little further; I hope that this might make more sense of his fragmentary style of working. All three worked within the conceptual context of a fundamental dualism, between human existence and the natural world, with whatever it is we call 'society' coming in between. For Weber, society was only the relationships between individuals; for Lukacs, working with the Marxist notion of alienation, these relationships could become 'solidified' as a 'second nature' which imposes as many restrictions and limitations on us as the natural world, and which seems to us as unchangeable as the natural world. It is precisely this fear of 'solidification', or 'ossification', or alienation that haunts Simmel's conception of modern society, his conception of what sociology ought to be about, and his own style of sociological work.

One clue to Simmel's method comes from an early and comparatively little known work of Lukacs before he embraced Marxism: *Soul and Form* (1910/1971*b*). This has been described as one of the first great works of European existentialism (Goldmann 1977). Lukacs attempts to explore what might be called the fundamental forms of relationship which are possible between the soul, the human spirit, and its surrounding world, arguing that the 'inauthentic' (my word) relationships are those in which the soul becomes stifled, or allows itself to be stifled by what is around it. Simmel in his own work was afraid of this happening on a world scale—that the modern world would 'socialize' the human spirit, limit and standardize it; Simmel wished to preserve the autonomy of spirit, or mind, or—a word I would prefer but I suspect many wouldn't—the soul.

Systematic sociological theorizing threatened just such a socialization or stifling of, in his case, his own soul. He was insistent that sociology was not and should not be some synthesizing queen of the sciences, regarding the whole of what would now be called the 'social' as its province; the objective realm of nature and the realm of the individual were also suitable subjects for other sciences. Not everything was a social construction and, what's more, it was desirable that we should not think that that was the case and that society should not provide the explanatory base of every aspect of human life. Simmel would certainly not have used this term, but he was arguing against a totalitarian sociological vision.

His style can be seen as a defence against such a vision and a defence against his incorporation into such a vision. This is summed up clearly by Charles Axelrod in a passage worth quoting at length:

For Simmel, his style as method cannot be divorced from his experience of theorizing. Rather, by virtue of his topical preoccupation with the theme of individuality, it produces a conception of method as a consequence of the individuality achieved in theorizing. For Simmel, any method imposed on a member by the scientific community binds that member and restricts his ability to articulate his individuality. That is, method imposed by the community is precisely what the individual must attempt to transcend (even as he is participating in the life of the group). . . . Through his writing Simmel can only become the exemplar of individuality within his scientific community.   (Axelrod 1991: 166)

If, in his method, fragmentation was an attempt to preserve his autonomy, he was less sure about fragmentation in the social being a good thing. According to Levine, Simmel (unlike Marx, whose radical vision presented the possibility of a united humanity) saw

the generation of increasingly specialized cultural products ordered in fundamentally discrete and incommensurable worlds. The Gods who rule these worlds are not at war with one another—any more than colours and sounds are in basic conflict—but each tries to move human accomplishment closer to the universal implementation of its basic principle. (Levine 1971: pp. xvii–xviii)

Allowing for difference in style and concepts (jargon ?) this sounds remarkably like Foucault's critique of modernity, but with rather more profundity.

The social forms

The profundity in the way that Simmel talks about these issues lies in his notion of the human spirit which he wishes to protect from extinction by society, and the way in which he develops the notion of different social forms which comprise and emerge from social interaction. Sociology itself can be seen as part of the enemy. The science arose in the course of the nineteenth century as a consequence of the growing power of social groupings, in particular social classes, and from this power came the idea that the social constitution of life is all pervasive and this is then projected back onto history. It is, therefore, as I said earlier, important for Simmel not to allow sociology to be taken as the most important of the social sciences, and he used the distinction between form and content, which coheres with his Kantian background, to try to establish the nature of sociology as one autonomous science amongst others. The 'contents' of sociology are those aspects of human life which push individuals into association with each other, our needs, our drives, and our aims and intentions. Forms are the means by which we synthesize these relationships in social entities which are over and above the individuals who make them up. There are four forms. We have already encountered the most abstract—'society' itself. The least abstract are the social relationships which individuals enter into with each other to satisfy their mutual and individual needs; we can regard these relationships as the elementary form of society, a sort of molecular structure. What is important is the *relationship*:

Strictly speaking, neither hunger not love, work nor religiosity, technology nor the functions and results of intelligence, are social. They are factors in association only when they transform the mere aggregation of isolated individuals into specific forms of being with and for one another, forms that are subsumed under the general concept of interaction. Sociation is the form (realized in innumerably different ways) in which individuals grow together into a unity and within which their interests are realized. And it is on the basis of their interests—sensuous or ideal, momentary or lasting, conscious or unconscious, causal or teleological—that individuals form such unities'   (Simmel 1907/1971: 24)

In between the molecular structure and society, there are two other forms. There are those activities and relationships which solidify into institutions which are effectively visible and goal-oriented—institutions such as the state or trade unions, the church, the university or college. These become autonomous from the flux of interaction and react back on it to organize it. Secondly, there are those forms which develop for, as Levine (1971) puts it, the sake of the forms themselves, not for practical purposes. These are 'play' forms of association: instead of engaging in economic competition I might compete at football or cricket; instead of having affairs and hurting my wife, I flirt. As Levine points out, 'In all these modes of interaction, the emphasis is on *good form*'—in a peculiarly English fashion, it is playing the game that matters, not winning or losing.

It is clear from our contemporary perspective that the latter form has been sub-ordinated to the former, the instrumental form. Simmel is one of the few soci-ologists to take play seriously for its own sake—that is, as an activity in its own right rather than as a part of the much more serious process of socialization, as it was for Mead. It is possible to develop a second string to Simmel's critical soci-ology: not only do certain social developments threaten the imprisonment of the spirit; they also threaten the dominance of instrumentality over play.

Simmel's method is to choose a particular phenomenon from the flux of experience and examine its structure and its history. It is not unlike Weber's ideal-type analysis which I described as producing a series of still snapshots of social reality from different points of view, but Simmel's version is more frag-mentary, lacking the cohesion that Weber finds through his concept of rational-ity. Levine (1971) identifies four principles which underlie all of Simmel's analyses. We have already met the first: each study seeks the form which has imposed a particular order on the world—Simmel sees the form/content dis-tinction as fundamental to human thought. The second is the principle of reci-procity—each phenomenon takes a meaning only through its relationships with others; no event or object has an intrinsic meaning 'in itself'; thirdly, there is the principle of distance—that 'the properties of forms and meanings of things are a function of the relative distances between individuals and other individuals or things' (ibid., p. xxxiv); finally, the world can be understood in terms of dualisms that may involve conflict or may simply be contrasted with each other. Many of Simmel's studies, for example, consist of analyses of different combi-nations of proximity or closeness.

These principles fulfil the same functions as the notion of rationality in Weber's thought—they link together the apparently disparate nature of his studies and, like Weber's conception of rationality, they are important aspects of the development of the modern world. I have already pointed to Simmel's view that modernity leads to fragmentation—there is no sense in his work of the prospect that Lukacs held out, from a not dissimilar viewpoint, of the transcen-dence of the dualisms, the achievement of a unity of form and content in the establishment of socialism

Further reading

Trying to make overall sense of Simmel is rather like trying to catch a fish with your hands—it keeps slipping away. As might be evident from my quotations, I found Donald M. Levine's introduction to *Georg Simmel on Individuality and Social Forms* (1971) very useful; the four essays by Simmel in part 1 of this book are the best of the original texts.

Conclusion to Part 1: the first basic dualism of social theory

What emerges most clearly from the four previous chapters is that Marx and Durkheim have one starting point for sociological analysis—society—and Weber another—the individual—whereas Simmel seems to fall between the two although he gives some priority to the individual. This is the first of the basic dualisms with which social theory has to contend—it is a dualism because the starting point is not sufficient. Each theorist of society also has to take account of the individual and in turn Weber and Simmel also have to take account of something called society. Any theory has to choose one as a starting point, but cannot avoid the other.

Perhaps the most important thing to note at this point is that all four were struggling to come to grips with something called 'society', even if they did so in very different ways. In Durkheim there is the notion of society existing over and above the individual and of social facts, and their discovery and explanation through identifying, measuring, and correlating their external manifestations. There is already here a notion of an *underlying* social structure (forms of solidarity) which has surface effects. The consistency of suicide rates indicates that social forces are at work, and it is not a matter of purely individual whims. Different forms of suicide are traced to different forms of social cohesion, so we can predict that rates will increase when, for whatever reason, the rules and norms of a society lose some of their strength or when too much responsibility is placed on the individual ego rather than on the community.

The other three did not talk about suicide, but it is possible to illustrate how they would differ in their approaches. A Marxist would approach the problem through placing suicide in a wider context of an interaction between the individual and society; whereas Durkheim comes close to seeing a suicide as a result only of society acting on the individual, a Marxist would be concerned with this—in particular with what we will discuss in the Chapter 8 as the alienating effects of the capitalist relations of production—but also with the situation and perceptions which are involved in the individual's decision to commit suicide. I think it is fair to say that there would be a more complex social analysis which would lead on to different distinctions from those found in Durkheim. For example, a Marxist might point out that there is a different wider social meaning to the suicide of a Wall Street banker after the 1929 slump than there is to a Buddhist monk publicly burning himself as a protest against the American presence in Vietnam. Durkheim would see the first as anomic suicide, the second as altruistic, but he would miss or underrate these wider social meanings, whereas the Marxist would see them as primary. In the first case suicide would be symptomatic of the isolating and alienating effects of the market; the second would be part of a significant struggle for national liberation.

Box 6.1. **The first basic dualism of social theory**

THE INDIVIDUAL	SOCIETY
Durkheim: the individual is formed and limited by society.	**Durkheim:** society exists over and above the individual.
Marx: the 'individuated' individual is an idea produced as part of the development of capitalism.	**Marx:** society is created by human action but acts back upon individuals as an external power.
Weber: the individual is the only reality and analysis must start from individual rational action.	**Weber:** society is the rather fragile result of human interaction.
Simmel: the individual life is engaged in a constant dialectic with social forms.	**Simmel:** 'society' is an increasingly important form organizing peoples' lives.

A Weberian study of suicide would concern itself with *the social meanings of suicide*. Jack Douglas's book of that name (1967) might not be technically a 'Weberian' study but it concerns itself with the meaning of a suicide to the actors involved; from this he argues that it is possible to build up a picture of the meanings that a particular society gives to suicide. He or she would direct attention to what we might call suicide as a rational action—to avoid further suffering, to take revenge on another person ('you'll be sorry') , to avoid the humiliation of bankruptcy, or to make a symbolic statement about an occupying army; the structural dimensions, forms of social cohesion, relations of production, and so on would not be considered.

Now, turning to Simmel, there are two options. The first, and the least Simmelian, would be to attempt to apply some of the ideas I discussed in Chapter 6; this could involve seeing suicide as an individual's way of resisting social forms, or in a more Durkheimian sense an individual's reaction to a collapse of established forms. A true 'Simmelian' approach, however, would contain something unexpected—perhaps along the lines of an elaboration of the French psychoanalyst Jacques Lacan's reported comment that a person may be kept alive by the possibility of committing suicide, or looking at suicide as a way of maintaining relationships and social cohesion.

What I find most interesting about this discussion is that none of these approaches seems to be mutually exclusive and none of them is complete by itself; yet they cannot somehow be added together into a total view. Each reveals a different aspect of what we are studying, and the disagreement would come in trying to give priority to one form of explanation or another. This, in turn, leads on to a range of philosophical issues which are beyond the scope of this particular text. Further complications will emerge as we come across the other dualisms in future chapters. At this stage it is possible to sum up the individual/society dualism as shown in Box 6.1.

Part 2

Conceptions of social structure

Introduction to Part 2

Strictly speaking, this part is not about *models* of society, in the sense that we have models of aeroplanes, small-scale versions of the real thing. However, it is a useful metaphor for attempts to think about the crucial aspects or components of a society and the way in which these are related to each other. These theories begin life as attempts to understand changes in late-nineteenth and early twentieth-century European and North American society. Inevitably, however, each theorist produces concepts which have a wider applicability and help us to reach an understanding of very different types of society, including, of course, our own. There will be some overlap between Part 2 and Part 3 on theories of social change, and you should bear in mind that the division is arbitrary. But I think that it is a useful division: Part 2 will describe the various models of society offered by the classical theorists, including the mechanisms which hold them together and keep them working; Part 3 will look at different conceptions of history and of further development—their ideas about where we are all going.

As we proceed it should become clear just how complex these thinkers are and how their explicit methodologies considered in the last chapter do not quite contain their work—it often goes beyond what they say they are doing, and it is often when they go beyond their explicit methodology that they are most interesting.

7 | Durkheim: drunk and orderly

Introduction
Social integration and system integration.

Types of solidarity: *The Division of Labour*

Mechanical and organic solidarity: repressive law and the *conscience collective*; the function of the division of labour; Durkheim's functionalism; organic solidarity and restitutive law; individualism and dependency in modern societies; Durkheim and modern politics; the use of the organic analogy. *Abnormal forms of the division of labour*: understanding social conflict; industrialism and capitalism; the forced division of labour; managerial deficiencies.

The sociology of religion and knowledge

The nature of religion: the sacred/profane distinction; totemism; religious beliefs as representations of the social; comparison of Durkheim and Marx on religion. *The arguments in Elementary Forms*: Durkheim's causal, interpretive, and functional analyses of religion. Durkheimian analyses of contemporary societies. *The sociology of knowledge*: Durkheim's attempt at a sociological explanation of Kant's categories; the link between social structure and the structure of thought; the problems with Durkheim's sociology of knowledge and comparison with Marx's theory of ideology.

The sociology of morality and education

The conservative and radical Durkheim; the relation of morality to the social; morality in a period of change; sociology and morality; moral education and its aim; spontaneous education and direct teaching; discipline, authority, and power; the rational justification of moral rules; dignity, self-determination, and attachment to society; the humanistic goals of education and the balance of individual and society.

Sociology of the law, state, and politics

The evolution of punishment towards humanist ideals; the developing sympathy for the criminal; the power of the state; the distinction between governor and governed and the definition of the state; the governing of secondary groupings; the state as defender of individual rights; Durkheim and contemporary political debates.

> Conclusion
>
> The importance of Durkheim's insights; his contributions to understanding the basic dualisms of sociology.

Introduction

in general 'la société' had an intoxicating effect on his mind.

(Ginsberg 1956: 51)

Durkheim is the most sociological of all four thinkers, in the sense that he saw political, social, and philosophical problems as amenable to sociological analysis and solution. He would often refer to 'society' as an explanation, and a change in society as a solution. However, Ginsberg's point that Durkheim was content to use the term 'society' without further analysis is not quite fair. There is much more to his work than a simplistic notion of the social whole.

Chapter 2 discussed social facts, their discovery, and their explanation. Durkheim generally proceeds in the way he prescribes and gives the impression of identifying a social fact and going on to test various hypothetical explanations. Some of these arguments are useful and some seem to have a mainly rhetorical purpose and I will not always consider all his points. My intention is less to trace the detail of his argument than to present an overall picture. There is a change of emphasis as his work progresses which is perhaps best seen as a move between two levels of social organization (although both are present all the time). In the earlier work he concentrates on the level of practical relationship between people and groups; in the later work he moves to a concern with shared ideals and systems of thought. It is useful here to introduce a distinction from modern sociology which follows on the action/structure dualism, a distinction made by David Lockwood (1964) between social integration and system integration. The latter refers to the way in which institutions are bound together, the former to the way in which individuals are bound together, usually through shared values and beliefs. Lockwood takes Marx as being concerned primarily with system integration and Durkheim, and later Talcott Parsons, with social integration. Of course, the distinction appears within each individual theorist and I shall suggest that in the *Division of Labour* Durkheim is closer to a concern with system integration.

If Durkheim was drunk on the concept of society, he still saw society as orderly, not a chaotic jumble. He was trying to understand how different parts of society were related to each other in a functioning whole and he was increasingly concerned with the place of the individual in modern society, as witnessed in my earlier discussion of *Suicide*.

Types of solidarity: *The Division of Labour*

Mechanical and organic solidarity

In his earliest major work, *The Division of Labour in Society* (1893/1984), we find Durkheim contrasting two very different types of society: those that are held together by *mechanical* solidarity, in which there is very little division of labour, and those held together by *organic* solidarity, where the division of labour is highly developed. The way in which one develops to the other is a matter for the next chapter. For the moment we can regard them as two types of society at opposite ends of a continuum.

We can think of the different forms of solidarity as social facts, like suicido-genic currents, not immediately visible but identifiable through an external phenomenon. The 'visible symbol' of the form of solidarity is the legal system, the organization of social life in 'its most stable form'. Mechanical solidarity is distinguished by *repressive law*, which insists on the punishment of the wrongdoer for those actions which offend against the clearest and most determinate moral sentiments held by a society, or its 'average members'. There are gradations of clarity matched by gradations of punishment—murder is fairly clear and is punished by death or life imprisonment; not being courteous to one's siblings brings only mild disapproval, if that. The totality of such beliefs 'forms a determinate system with a life of its own'—the *conscience collective* of a society. Giddens (1978) points out that neither of the two usual English traditions of this term—collective conscience or collective consciousness—is quite accurate. In fact, Durkheim seems to use the term to cover both. In this context he is using it to refer to the collective values and what modern sociologists would call the norms of a society: the strongest values and norms shared by most people and enforced by repressive law. This is close to the collective-conscience translation. Elsewhere—particularly in *The Elementary Forms of the Religious Life* (1912/1915)—he uses it to refer to very basic ways of seeing the world which we all share: the forms of logic that we use and our conceptions of time and space which impose order and sense on the world. This is closer to the collective-consciousness translation.

In a society held together by mechanical solidarity, the *conscience collective* exists over and above individuals and becomes implanted in them. It is a society in which the division of labour remains at a very basic level—no more, perhaps, than the sexual division of labour implied by the different biological make-up of men and women. Mechanical solidarity implies the similarity of individuals. All share the same basic beliefs about the world and about life, essentially based on religion, and all engage in the same basic activities—often a matter of subsistence hunting and gathering; even physical differences are at a minimum. The individual is absorbed into the *conscience collective*—one is either 'in' a society or 'outside' it; one cannot be an individual in society and members of the society are not mutually dependent. Strictly speaking 'mechanical solidarity' is not itself a form of social structure but it is the form of solidarity found in 'segmented societies'—societies originally clan (kinship) based but later based on locality.

Societies held together by organic solidarity have a well-developed division of labour. It is apparent on a common-sense level that the division of labour has economic advantages—several hundred workers using specific skills and doing specific tasks can build more jumbo jets than one person working by him- or herself in the back garden. But Durkheim suggests it has another function, beyond increasing economic prosperity. Difference acts to bring people together—whether they be men or women in marriage or friendships based on different qualities; the differences involved in the division of labour also bring people together:

> We are therefore led to consider the division of labour in a new light. In this case, indeed, the economic services that it can render are insignificant compared with the moral effect that it produces, and its true function is to create between two or more people a feeling of solidarity.   (Durkheim 1893/1984: 17)

Durkheim makes a particularly important point about his use of the term 'function'—one often forgotten by later sociologists who went under the label of 'functionalism'—that to identify the function of the division of labour does not explain its existence. We need a historical explanation of how something comes into existence; the function of this something might then explain why it continues in existence. The function of the division of labour is not its 'aim' or 'intention'—some modern sociologists might refer to it as an 'unintended consequence'. It remains in existence because it holds society together.

The social structure associated with this type of solidarity is the one we are all used to—highly complex and organized. The *conscience collective* remains but becomes less and less important, covering a smaller proportion of our lives and concentrating on the individual. It is here that the distinction between system integration and social integration becomes important. System integration, the division of labour, is highly organized through markets, the state, and so on; social integration—the shared norms and values of a society—becomes less important. We find ourselves living amongst and working with people with very different sets of beliefs and views. It seems to me that one of the features of our contemporary world is precisely the highly organized social system in which we live—Giddens calls it the 'juggernaut' of late modernity which leaves us dependent on many things beyond our experience—contrasted with the vast space we have in which to be individuals, created by the weakening of social integration through the *conscience collective*. It can come to seem that we have complete control over our lives; that we have a high degree of independence because our dependence on others is so well hidden.

The external manifestation of organic solidarity is restitutive law, which is concerned with the relationships between individuals and groups, aiming less to punish than to restore the *status quo ante*; the situation as it was at the beginning of the relationship. It becomes important to ensure that contracts are kept, that people deal honestly in their relationships with each other, and are compensated for any wrong they might suffer in these relationships. If a builder takes the old roof off my house and then vanishes with my money without putting the new roof on, I might be very angry with him or her but I would not seek through the courts to have the person publicly flogged, sent to jail, or executed. I would concentrate on getting my money back, perhaps with some compensation, so that I can pay somebody else to do the job. Steven Lukes (1973: 158) cites civil, commercial, procedural, administrative, and constitutional law as comprising restitutive law.

The paradox of organic solidarity based on the division of labour is that members of society become both more individuated and more dependent on society at the same time: more individuated because in modern societies people fulfil many different social roles, behave differently in those roles, and work with different, specialized bodies of knowledge. Beliefs and knowledge shared by the whole community are no longer sufficient to enable each individual to fulfil his or her task. We become more dependent on society and more bound into society because we are dependent on everybody else fulfilling their task—vitally dependent. If I were a member of a hunter-gatherer society, I could go off by myself for long periods of time, looking for food, finding my own shelter, and so on. In contemporary society I am dependent on other people—many of whom live on the other side of the world—to grow my food, make my clothes, supply me with warmth and light, print the books I read, service the word processor I write on, and so on. I could have or do none of these things without society.

The *conscience collective* comes to attach, in Lukes's words, 'supreme value to individual dignity, equality of opportunity, work ethic and social justice' (ibid. 158). It is important to remember that the value of individualism is a *collective* value shared by the whole society. One of Durkheim's targets was the utilitarian argument typified by Herbert Spencer, the English sociologist. This is an argument which will be familiar to anyone who has listened to modern right-wing politicians or economists who talk about market forces. If we each pursue our self-interest on the open market, then solidarity will ensue—it will be in each person's self-interest to honour contracts, and so on. Durkheim's point was that there is, in fact, an underlying collective agreement that individuals should pursue their own interest—in fact, individuation and the development of self-interest in the first place depend upon the development of the *conscience collective*. As in the development of the division of labour itself, it is the moral dimension which underpins its continued existence. This is in direct contrast to a Marxist approach, which would see individualism *and* its associated morality as a product rather than a producer of the division of labour.

It is also important to note that these issues, translated into the language of modern politics, are at the very centre of contemporary debates at least in the USA and the UK: arguments about the benefits and the limitations of the free market and its undermining of the stability of social life contend with arguments about the importance of our obligations to society, our sense of community, and so on. One possible Durkheimian interpretation of the contemporary western world might be that the individualism of the *conscience collective* is eating away at its own foundations, the underlying consensus which once supported individualism. Christopher Lasch, for example, has argued that élites no longer identify with the well-being of their society but are concerned *only* with their own well-being (Lasch 1995).

In the term *organic* a whole social theory is hidden: the idea that there is rather more than an analogy between societies and organisms—that societies can actually be considered as living organisms. Rather like the human body, in which the different organs—heart, liver, kidneys, intestines—complement each other and depend upon each other for their continued functioning, while the body as a whole depends upon each and all of them, so society and its separate parts depend upon each other for its continued existence. These ideas recur constantly throughout the history of sociology.

One final point, before moving on from this particular set of issues, has to do with the theoretical usefulness and empirical accuracy of looking at the world in this way. Steven Lukes (1973: 159) makes the point that Durkheim 'vastly understated the degree of interdependence and reciprocity in pre-industrial societies, as well as vastly overstating the role of repressive law' in such societies. Now it seems to me that we do not have to regard these two models of integration as empirically existing realities, but rather as ideal types in the Weberian sense. Perhaps both forms of solidarity are always present, but their comparative weights and relationships differ.

Abnormal forms of the division of labour

The organic analogy implies a high level of system integration and stability and it has always been a criticism of functional theories that they cannot explain, or perhaps even recognize, social conflict. In a society where there is a highly developed division of labour and a balance between system integration and social integration, things would work smoothly. Whether such a state of affairs has ever existed might be debatable, but it certainly did not exist at the time Durkheim was writing and does not exist now. But Durkheim was no fool and could see what was going on around him, as could later functionalists. The accusation that a theory cannot account for something as obvious as a social conflict assumes a stupidity on the part of the theorist which is not credible, and Durkheim's attempt to deal with this came under the heading of 'the abnormal division of labour'. He suggested that there were three forms.

The most obvious form of conflict at the end of the nineteenth century was class conflict. Anthony Giddens (1978) makes the point that we can find in Durkheim's way of dealing with this a division in the history of sociological theory. Whereas, for Marx, class conflict marked the appearance of a new type of society—capitalism—for Durkheim it was a feature of the incomplete development from mechanical to organic solidarity through the development of *industrial* society. It was a product of the *anomic* division of labour. Industrialization had developed too quickly and economic enterprises had not yet developed the values and rules which would enable their smooth functioning; nor had society as a whole yet developed the mechanisms by which competition could be controlled and the markets regulated. Once again we find the arguments of a century ago being rehearsed again in contemporary politics. We also find another dualism at the centre of social theory—that of capitalism/industrialism. I shall refer to this as a secondary dualism—it is not involved directly in the fundamental dilemmas of social theory which we would find in discussing any society, but refers rather to ways of thinking about contemporary society and its comparatively recent history.

The second form of the abnormal division of labour also has echoes in contemporary political arguments. Durkheim called it the *forced* division of labour. The constraint comes from external inequalities which prevent the healthy development of the division of labour. Thus people might be allocated to positions in the division of labour to which they are not suited by their natural talents or their abilities. An example would be somebody who becomes a manager of an enterprise through family connections rather than through managerial ability, or somebody who pursues a menial job because of parental poverty and lack of opportunity to develop talents. A similar misallocation might come through the economic inequality which results from inheritance—if some people start life in a worse economic situation than others, the poorer are necessarily subjected to the rich, and real organic solidarity cannot develop.

Contemporary arguments about equality of opportunity and 'level playing fields' address precisely these issues.

The third abnormal form of the division of labour is a managerial deficiency, where the enterprise is not organized to get the best and most out of its members—the more continuous and coordinated the various functions, the more solidarity grows and the more skilled the worker becomes. Various critics (Friedmann 1961; Lukes 1973) have pointed out that this argument is simply not true—the more developed the division of labour, the less skilled and the less happy the workers. It is as if Durkheim himself was confusing social and system cohesion here, assuming that the latter automatically led to the former rather than undermining it, which I think would be the dominant contemporary view.

This is an appropriate point at which to move on to Durkheim's theory of social cohesion.

The sociology of religion and knowledge

Before all, [religion] is a system of ideas with which the individuals represent to themselves the society of which they are members, and the obscure but intimate relations which they have with it. This is its primary function; and though metaphorical and symbolic, this representation is not unfaithful.

(Durkheim 1912/1915: 225)

Religion is at the centre of Durkheim's sociology; his major work, *The Elementary Forms of the Religious Life* (1912/1915), was published nearly twenty years after *The Division of Labour*. It is the last of the major texts in the Durkheimian canon.

The nature of religion

In the course of his career Durkheim changed his mind about the defining feature of religion. In *The Elementary Forms* we find him abandoning the obligatory nature of beliefs and settling on the distinction between the sacred and the profane. This text is a 'second-hand' study of the religion of Australian aborigines: Durkheim never went to Australia but uses the studies of those who had investigated these tribes first hand, with some extra evidence from studies of native Americans. He assumed that all the essential aspects of religious life would be visible in the simplest religious forms and the most simple was totemism, found in societies closest to 'the beginning of evolution'. Totemism appears in what I referred to earlier as 'segmented societies', or societies based on kinship and divided into clans; the members of each clan believe they are related to each other, not through any definite blood relationship but through the fact that they share the same name—the name of an object, the *totem*, which has a very special—a sacred—significance. In Australian societies this is often if not always something from the natural world—an animal, a fish, or a tree.

The belief in the power attributed to the totem, or, in more complex societies, to the gods or to God or Allah is neither a mistake nor an illusion, nor is it the truth. If religious beliefs were illusions, they would not have lasted throughout human history—they are not simply errors, as some humanist and rationalist thinkers would have us believe. On the other hand, one does not have to accept that these beliefs are literally true—that the Christian God really exists and is all powerful, or that the tortoise that is the clan totem really has special powers. Rather these figures—whether the tortoise or God—stand for something else which really is immortal and possesses special powers, including immense moral power over the individual, and on which the individual depends for his or her continued protection and survival: *society*. Religious beliefs are representations—*collective* representations—of the power a society has over each of its members. When he moves to talking about *collective representations* rather than the *conscience collective*, Durkheim is shifting his focus away from shared norms and beliefs (although they are still important) to shared ways of thinking.

Before going on to explore this, I want to spend some time comparing Durkheim's theory of religion with that of Marx—for whom the topic is of minor importance. The comparison is nevertheless instructive. In a famous comment Marx called religion the 'opium of the people'; a belief in future happiness in the next world which was deployed in this world to justify an acquiescence in suffering. This was a political judgement which, I fear, was often only too correct. His intellectual understanding of religion took up the arguments of the Hegelian philosopher Ludwig Feuerbach: God was a projection of powers that were really human, and progress would involve humanity taking those powers into itself and exercising them itself. Humanity would, as it were, become God, and would establish a proper control over society as a way of gaining its freedom. It seems to me that there is very little difference and all the difference in the world between this view and Durkheim's views—a paradoxical contrast that we will come across time and time again.

The arguments in *Elementary Forms*

Durkheim's argument is subtle and complex; Steven Lukes (1973) provides the best account I have come across and I shall follow him here for a while. He suggests (p. 462) that Durkheim is presenting three 'hypotheses' about religion: the causal, the interpretive, and the functional.

The *causal* explanation of religion is that it is the result of a collective experience; what he called, in a wonderfully evocative phrase, a 'collective effervescence'. It is a fairly common experience that people change when they are caught up in large group processes—we 'get carried away', there is something exciting going on, and we behave differently from the way we behave when we are alone, and this gives us a sense of the power of the collective. Militant trade unionists were once directly aware of this in their preference for shop-floor votes by a show of hands rather than by secret ballots. On the shop floor, amongst one's co-workers, it is possible to sense power; alone, with a voting paper, one can only feel weak against a powerful and wealthy employer. It is this sense of collective strength and excitement which Durkheim sees as the origin of religion.

Lukes (1973: 465–70) is particularly lucid about what he calls the *interpretive* explanation. It is here that we meet again the significant of the word 'representation'. Religion can be seen as an elementary theory of the way the world and society work. The totem is the personification of the clan and its power. This representation enabled the clan to think about itself as well as its social and natural world—for example, the distinction between body and soul can be seen as matching that between sacred and profane, the soul being the representative of the collective, of the totem or the god in the individual. Religion

seeks to translate these [social] realities into an intelligible language which does not differ in nature from that employed by science: the attempt is made by both to connect things with one another, to establish internal relations among them, to classify and systematize them.   (Lukes 1973: 467)

Religion is not only a way of thinking about social realities; it is also a way of dramatizing them. The Christian Mass, particularly in its Roman Catholic or High Anglican manifestations, could be seen as theatre in which the consumption by the congregation of the body and blood of Christ (the bread and wine that some believe are actually transformed into flesh and blood) is a dramatic metaphor of our internalization of society and its rules and prohibitions. We eat our leader, the one who represents us, and we become part of him and of each other: 'We break this bread to share in the body of Christ. Though we are many, we are one body because we all share in one bread' (*The Alternative Service Book* (1980), 142). Those of other denominations or faiths might find it a useful exercise to find equivalent dramatizations from their own experience.

The third hypothesis that Lukes identifies is the *functional* hypothesis—the consequences of religion. This is clearly one of maintaining and reinforcing social cohesion. In the case of totemism, the totem is the permanent reminder to the clan of its unity, and to the individual of his or her membership in the clan; the rituals reinforce this, and in a society where many of its members spend much of the year in small groups foraging for food, the rituals strengthen the individuals who might otherwise feel overpowered by their conditions of life. Durkheim makes much of the way in which the individual feels stronger as a result of the ritual and in fact is stronger.

Durkheim's work has inspired interesting analyses of ritual in modern societies (see especially Lane 1981; Alexander 1988). As a useful exercise it might be worth trying to think about collective effervescences that you might have found yourself involved in—group activities where you became aware of the power of the group—and see if Durkheim offers you any new understanding. In the case of modern societies, however, we can rarely see collective symbols as representing the whole of society. A major danger of Durkheim's thought often pointed out by Marxist and radical critics (e.g. Zeitlin 1968) is that it can hide major divisions in society. They are only to a very limited extent 'wholes' which can be unified around symbols. A Durkheimian analysis of the 1953 British coronation (Shils and Young 1953) offers a rather trite analysis of the symbolism of the service as it illustrates social unity, but I know that there are people to whom that symbolism is powerful. I am a republican, but I found myself—to my surprise—moved almost to tears on the one occasion when I saw the queen. But there were even in the 1950s many people who would not be moved in that way—the amount of petty theft rose dramatically on Coronation Day. And of course in a modern society we cannot assume that participation in ritual celebration is a sign of belief—there are good reasons to go to a street party, even if one is a republican; and even amongst religious believers in the same church there can be huge disagreements on the meaning of the symbols.

The sociology of knowledge

Beyond the analysis of the function of rituals and the relationship between the group and the individual, and whatever faults in his work that have been revealed by later anthropologists, Durkheim's work remains relevant for its contribution to the sociology of knowledge, and it is here that the notion of collective representations really comes into its own. I mentioned earlier that Durkheim thought his theory of religion was able to explain the way in which we perceived the relationship between body and soul, the latter being the internal representation of society. It will become apparent when we come to other substantive areas of Durkheim's sociology that he is concerned with the way in which a potentially vulnerable and dangerous human physical organism is brought into the discipline and power of society—a way of looking at the world which is familiar to us these days through the work of Freud (and latterly Foucault); both Freud and Durkheim are concerned with the way in which humans employ metaphors to think about themselves and their relationships.

Durkheim, however, moved towards philosophy rather than psychology. He thought that sociology could solve the dualism of Kantian thought by rooting it in society—in the social itself. Put as simply as possible, the frameworks which we employ to organize our experience come from experience itself—but from what we might call a different level of experience from that considered by empirical sciences. The experience that we organize is our own day-to-day individual experience of the world; our ability to organize comes from our experience of collective life, the life of our society. Each society, depending on its organization, generates its own conceptions of time and space and of logical connection.

There is a problem here which haunts sociological explanations of our subjective capacities: in order to recognize, for example, the spatial relations suggested to us by our social experience, we must already have a sense of space. Kant's organizing categories belong to the *mind* and without them we would be unable to recognize *any* experience, including social experience. There would also be a problem of relativism: each different society would generate different forms of knowledge, and there would be no basis on which we could choose between them. This would clearly be unacceptable to Durkheim, given the rigour of the scientific method he outlined in *The Rules*, and he got round the problem by placing it in an evolutionary context. Our basic form of thinking is in essence no different from that of Aboriginal societies:

Is not the statement that a man is a kangaroo or the sun a bird, equal to identifying the two with each other? But our manner of thought is not different when we say of heat that it is not a movement, or of light that it is a vibration of the ether etc. Every time that we unite heterogeneous terms by an internal bond, we forcibly identify contraries. Of course the terms we unite are not those which the Australian brings together; we choose them according to different criteria and for different reasons; but the processes by which the mind puts them in connection do not differ essentially.   (Durkheim 1912/1915: 238)

The difference is that we have separated logic and scientific modes of thinking from their original religious basis and they have developed independently. The arguments are now pursued with more precision and rigour. In other words, we are doing the same thing as the aborigines, but better. This argument is pursued in a book written with his nephew, Marcel Mauss, called *Primitive Classification* (1903/1963), and, although I don't think anybody would now accept Durkheim's evolutionary theory, the issues raised in this book were taken up in a rather different way by the French anthropologist Claude Lévi-Strauss, a founder of modern structuralist thought, who argued that totemic classifications can reveal the basic organizing structure of the human mind, something that I think Durkheim was close to saying but managed to lose because, paradoxically, he was concerned with establishing a sociological explanation.

If we take the weak sense of Durkheim's argument, we are on much stronger ground. The weak sense is that of the sociology of knowledge: the idea that the structure of the society in which we live is in one way or another responsible for the structure and the content of our thinking. It is this emphasis on the structure of thinking that is important—if we drop the notion of finding a sociological solution to the problems of western philosophy and think instead simply of the ways in which we think, we can gain interesting insights. We can find in the nineteenth and early twentieth centuries, for example, parallel ways of thinking in the social and the natural sciences which tend towards relativism, and this seems to occur concurrently with changes in class structure that represent not an end to old social divisions but a loosening of them and perhaps an increasing ability to see the world from different points of view. I have put this very simplistically, but I hope the idea gets across.

The strength of Durkheim's link is precisely that it is between the structure of society and the structure of thought—he is not just saying that I learn my ideas from society (although, of course, I do), but I learn how to think about my ideas from society. The form of logic that I use—my understanding of the structure of a rational argument, the process of thinking itself—is a metaphor for the type of society I live in—so that, for example (an oversimplified example), a society based on agriculture and the repetitive cycle of the seasons might understand time as a repetitive movement and see human life as repetition through rebirth, etc., and would perhaps produce self-contained philosophical (religious) images with which to think in a circular fashion, deducing everything from the existence of God in such a way that everything that happens proves

God exists. On the other hand, modern society based on linear processes of production and the development of technology sees time as a linear movement from the past towards the future and thinks employing a linear logic: we start with certain assumptions and a certain amount of knowledge and we can deduce from that starting point; or alternatively we start with our sense of the outside world and we can induce general laws from our knowledge of that world.

The weakest point in Durkheim's sociology of knowledge is again his tendency to talk abut society as a whole when referring to modern complex societies. The sociology of knowledge was not a specifically Durkheimian achievement—Marx before him, and many Marxists after him, as well as Karl Mannheim (1938) grappled with these problems and particularly with the problem of relativism: if all knowledge is produced by specific social circumstances and is relative to those circumstances, then how can we claim that one form of knowledge is better than others? Could we argue that one social position actually grants a particular group of people a privilege in producing knowledge—that from their social position, this group can see more than others? Lukacs (1971a) was to claim that the proletariat, the working class, was such a group, and their advantage came from the structure of thinking to which their class position gave rise. Mannheim (1938) was to argue that intellectuals, because of their 'free-floating' class position, were able to integrate and see beyond more limited points of views. And modern 'feminist-standpoint' epistemology (Harding 1986, 1991) attempts to make a similar claim for women.

Now whether or not these claims work, the point I am making is that Durkheim's theoretical framework tends towards seeing society as essentially unitary, even when organic solidarity predominates. He is therefore blinkered to some of these possibilities. He is also blinkered to the possibility that there might be a sense in which religious belief might be 'the opium of the people'. A religion which, in comparatively undifferentiated societies, can be a metaphor for the whole society might continue to exist as that society becomes more differentiated, but it gets taken up into relations between different groups in society and becomes multi-dimensional, perhaps used as an ideology which can contribute towards maintaining a social order which benefits not the whole of the society but only one part of it. The Marxist theory of ideology suggests that ruling-class ideology masks itself as the way in which everybody looks at the world and Durkheim does rather leave himself open to criticism from this point of view. The important point perhaps is to avoid Durkheim's intoxication and recognize that there is more going on in society than he sometimes recognizes.

It was Durkheim's concern with social cohesion that pushed forward his interests in the sociology of education and morality.

The sociology of morality and education

There are two contrasting sides to Durkheim's work—the arch conservative identified by Zeitlin (1968) and more radical reformer that Pearce (1989) talks about. In his work on morality we see a more conservative Durkheim, whilst in his work on education we come closer to the reformer. His discussions of morality appeared after his death in 1917 (Durkheim 1925/1953, 1926/1962). He agrees with Kant that we cannot call a rule moral without implying some sort of obligation, and by now you should be able to predict that Durkheim saw the obligation as coming from society itself. This idea is reinforced by the argument that we cannot call an action moral if it is in pursuit of individual interests. In public life, for example, a politician who uses his or her political position to pursue his or her own private interests would be open to discipline and eventual punishment in most democratic societies. A *moral* action seeks the common good over and above that of the individual and it is directed towards others in accordance with society's ideals and values. This is another dimension to Durkheim's argument against the utilitarians, and it is an argument against those who in contemporary society argue that a free market eventually brings the common good.

In some of Durkheim's statements about morality and the all-powerfulness of society, we can see the evidence for those who accuse him of conservatism: 'it is never possible to desire a morality other than that required by the social conditions of a given time. To wish for a morality other than that implied in the nature of society is to deny the latter and, consequently, oneself' (Durkheim 1925/1953: 38). Such words would not have sounded strange coming from the mouth of an orthodox communist party hack in Soviet Russia, and perhaps Soviet communism possessed a simplistic notion of society equal to that employed by Durkheim in this quotation. However, he was not always as rigid as this. In his discussion of the abnormal forms of the division of labour, Durkheim talked about the rapid pace of change and the need for business concerns to develop a new morality; he argued that forms of morality could become outdated and new forms might develop as society changed, so that at any one time in modern society the morality implied in the 'nature of society' might be open to debate. The sociologist would be able to demonstrate scientifically which moral rules no longer served society and which ones might replace them. Thus, for example, we can take the law of blasphemy, which in the most straightforward Durkheimian sense is a protection of the sacredness of society itself. In a contemporary multicultural society it could be argued that the essential moral content of the *conscience collective* to which everybody must come to subscribe would be an ethic of mutual tolerance in which all religions or none must be protected by a law of blasphemy. But Durkheim seems to have had a rather touching faith in the ability of sociology to make scientific judgements about morality.

In his work on morality Durkheim returned to the dualism of human nature—its impulsive biologically based side and its 'civilized' socialized side. I have already mentioned the parallel with Freud, but there is a close connection with the work of Talcott Parsons (1951), who dominated mid-century sociology at least in the English-speaking world, and who was accused of working with 'an over-socialised concept of man' (Wrong 1957)—and presumably of woman too. Parsons used a tame version of Freud and the work of G. H. Mead to explain the way in which society moulded the personality to fit in with its requirements. Durkheim's account of socialization is rather more interesting and ambivalent. In contemporary debates about morality, it often seems that there is a desire to return to something that is conceived of as traditional morality—as, for example, in the British prime minister John Major's 'Back to Basics' campaign—but, as he found out when his ministers had to resign over sexual peccadilloes, to demand a return to traditional values is easier said than done. President Clinton learnt the same lesson during the 1996 Democratic Party Conference when his special adviser on family values resigned after a sex scandal. The traditional values that the traditional right seem to desire are usually 'Victorian'—paradoxically, the period during which Durkheim began his work and when he could see perfectly well that traditional morality was already gone for ever.

Durkheim approaches the matter of education through his theory of morality, and his lectures were on the subject of 'moral education' (Durkheim 1979). He saw the education of the young in the widest possible sense as the influence of any adult on children not yet ready to become full members of society, and he also saw education as a lifelong process; it is the means by which we learn how to cope with our physical existence, control our desires and impulses, and adjust to the social environment. The aim of education must be to enable each of us to act willingly in the way that society requires if it is to survive, and not just to conform to what is required. But it must also enable us to make our own decisions within these limits—modern society requires free agents.

He contrasts what he calls 'spontaneous' education with more direct teaching. The former describes a situation in which the child learns simply by being with adults as they go through their normal daily activities. This is the sort of education which has been sufficient for much of human history and it is appropriate to mechanical solidarity. Direct teaching occurs when society becomes too complex for the child to learn essentials in such a way—although spontaneous education continues in the ways that teachers themselves behave. If there is a gap between what they say and what they do, problems occur. Direct teaching is concerned with intellectual concepts and moral ideas. One central aim of education is the formation of character, not in the modern psychological sense but in the sense once used by the English schoolmasters (and it was always a very masculine phenomenon—as was Durkheim's sociology itself, since he had little to say about women) when they said that military discipline, cross-country running, rugby, cold showers, and other deprivations were good for character-building. It meant stability and reliability, an inner consistency, a denial of emotion—at which women were notoriously not very good.

Discipline is central to the teacher's work in two senses; one is the sense of regularity learnt through the school routine, conveying a sense of boundaries and of an authority greater than the child and the teacher. The teacher must teach morality as coming from a powerful source over and above the personalities in the classroom. Now in some respects *these* meanings of discipline are akin to ideas in modern psychoanalytic theories of child-rearing: the need for consistent, routine care which provides a sense of inner security, and the laying-down of boundaries of behaviour enabling the child to gain a firm sense of him- or herself, and his or her limitations. Of course, these boundaries have to be carefully judged so as not to damage the child through being too restrictive or too relaxed. However, there is one very significant difference: for psychoanalysis it is important that the authority in both cases be a personal one (although he/she might represent an impersonal authority) so that the child can introject and use a competent 'internal object'; for Durkheim, the authority is impersonal and external and would, I suspect, seem to modern eyes a distant and hostile authority. Ernest Wallwork takes up this point:

Durkheim denies the widespread assumption in his era, as well as in ours, that discipline is incompatible with self-realization, freedom and happiness. Discipline, by restraining limitless ambitions and by canalizing limited reserves of psychic energy in pursuit of determinate goals, is the indispensable means without which regular realization of human potentialities would be impossible. And, genuine psychological freedom, in Durkheim's view, is only possible though self-mastery of the unlimited power of unrestrained appetites.   (Wallwork 1972: 125)

I think that one of the problems with this sort of issue is that in Durkheim's time it was perhaps a little less difficult than it is now to distinguish between authority and power—in the former case, power is accepted and agreed to; in the latter case, power rests on forcing the other person to do something against his or her will. Durkheim is talking about the use of authority to enable the child to develop his or her own authority. And, on a common-sense level, I imagine that most people are aware of somebody who has limitless ambitions but who can barely organize him- or herself to get up in the morning. As Wallwork also points out, Durkheim was well able to recognize that discipline could turn into oppression and tyranny. Moral rules must be explained so that they become acceptable to the child on rational grounds. A tyrannical teacher would frighten his or her charges into submission. Durkheim opposed corporal punishment: the aim of discipline is to demonstrate to the wrongdoer the error of his or her ways in such a way that the reason behind the rule becomes apparent and is accepted; an essential element of the modern *conscience collective* is a belief in human dignity, and corporal punishment is an offence against human dignity. And human dignity is necessary for the self-determination for which modern society seems to call; we have to bring children to the stage where they do not just simply obey, or just understand the reasoning behind the moral rules that they are taught to follow, but can engage in their own independent moral reasoning. Here we move to the liberal Durkheim.

Moral education also involves the teaching of an attachment to society, and teachers should try to develop the child's nascent ability to empathize with others; there is a conflict within the child between egoism, which for Durkheim is always the enemy of morality, and altruism, which in the child is the weakest side. The purpose of education is not just to develop a child's own natural talents but to try to attach him or her to the social ideal—to create something new that was not there at the beginning.

In one of his more impressive in scope but lesser known works (Durkheim 1938/1977), Durkheim traced the development of French—and European—educational ideals, developing the notion of the whole person and a modern ideal of secular education that combined the natural sciences—which had the moral task of teaching the place of humanity in the world of nature—and the humanities, producing a humanism which would come to replace religion as the way in which society thinks of itself, or perhaps better, thinks itself. The aim of education then should be, in Wallwork's words, 'to honour rules respecting human rights, to appreciate the autonomy that man alone enjoys, and to devote themselves to genuinely humanistic goals' (Wallwork 1972: 145). I think this is the nearest we find in Durkheim to a view of what will or could replace religion at the centre of the *conscience collective* in organic solidarity. God/society is replaced by humanity/society. We also see here Durkheim trying to juggle concepts to arrive at a conception of individualism and autonomy which is not egoistic. He is, I think, trying to describe something much stronger than what proponents of the free market would describe as 'enlightened self-interest', which often amounts to saying: 'be greedy but not so greedy that other people will want to punish you for it' and something much weaker than 'Do as you are told and work for the greater glory of the fatherland (or the revolution or whatever)'. We will see that this is a central issue in contemporary politics and it leads on to Durkheim's political sociology.

The sociology of the law, state, and politics

We have already outlined the basis of Durkheim's sociology of the law in the discussion of *The Division of Labour*—the development from repressive to restitutive law. Connected with this was his work on punishment 'Two Laws of Penal Evolution' (1901/1969). This is particularly interesting because there is an indication that the state plays an independent role. Durkheim argues, first, that the intensity of punishment is greater in less developed societies *and in so far as power is more centralized and absolute*, and, secondly, that with the development of organic solidarity the main form of punishment becomes deprivation of liberty for periods depending on the nature of the crime. I will discuss these two laws briefly before going on to make the connection with the state. Now here Durkheim is talking not about the change from repressive to restitutive law with the increasing division of labour, but about the way repressive law itself changes. The explanation of this change has to do with the change towards humanist ideals that were discussed in relation to education—the focus moves to human dignity and the worth of the individual. This enables us to find a certain pity and fellow-feeling for the perpetrator as well as for the victim. It implies a point which needs to be made as much today as it was in Durkheim's day: that a concern for the *criminal* is a mark of civilization, and, by implication, an exclusive concern for punishment is a mark of less advanced societies. But the decline in the desire for punishment and for the more humane treatment of the criminal is not quite as directly related as that, and it is not simply a matter of growth in human sympathy—that could in some circumstances lead to a desire for greater punishment. It is rather that compassion for the victim is not swamped by anger with the criminal, and the compassion can therefore be spread around more.

Now, to return to the state: a strong central power with no opposition was seen by Durkheim as historically contingent, not as necessarily connected to mechanical solidarity. As Lukes points out in his intelligent discussion of this issue, Durkheim did not take the opportunity to discuss the possibility of authoritarian government in advanced societies, but he suggests that 'The influence of Governmental organisation could neutralise that of social organisation' (Lukes 1973: 258).

Durkheim begins his discussion of the state, *Professional Ethics and Civic Morals* (1957) by saying that the opposition of governing and governed is central in political life. It is likely that in the earliest forms of society such a division did not exist and we can only really talk about politics in a society where it does exist. But the division of a social group into governing and governed does not only exist in states—there is a similar division in the patriarchal *household*, so we need to find something which distinguishes the state from such social organizations. He considers size and control of a determinate territory, but neither is adequate—there are always counter-examples. The crucial feature of a state is that it controls not necessarily large numbers of *people* but a number of different secondary *social groupings*. The state is the organization of officials concerned with governing these secondary groups. It is not an embodiment of society as a whole, as Hegel had argued, but a specialized institution.

Durkheim next takes up the relationship of the state to the individual. This was not an issue in societies where mechanical solidarity dominated—the individual was absorbed into the social whole; however, as organic solidarity develops, so the power of the state develops, together with the rights of the individual. The growth of the state does not threaten but enables the rights of individuals.

Here we find the importance of the distinction between society and the state. 'Every society is despotic, at least if nothing from without supervenes to restrain its despotism' (Durkheim 1957: 61). As societies become more complex, then there is a need for individuals to move from group to group and a need to prevent the secondary groups exercising despotic control over their members; it is the function of the state to provide for this need.

We can identify, through this part of Durkheim's work, some real problems in a clearer way than we can through the other thinkers examined in this book, and there is another link with Freud here which highlights an important dimension to psychoanalytic social criticism. We do not find the distinction between society and state in the work of psychoanalysts, but we do find the argument that the stronger the state control over individual lives, the less strong the individual ego and superego. The state or society can become a sort of external superego which leaves the individual unable to take responsible decisions for him- or herself. Durkheim's argument was that, given that individual members of society felt their commitment to society, the function of the state was to create and protect the space where the individuals could exercise such responsibility:

The planning of the *social milieu* so that the individual may realise himself more fully and the management of the collective apparatus in a way that will bear less hard on the individual; and assure an amicable exchange of goods and services and the co-operation of all men of good will towards an ideal they share without any conflict; in these, surely, we have enough to keep public activity fully employed.   (Durkheim 1957: 71)

I think the problem here *is* Durkheim's tendency to get drunk on the notion of society. Although he presents us with a conceptual framework for looking at one range of contemporary issues, his unitary conception of society still dominates and we get no sense of the possibility central to Marx, for example, that the state may act as an instrument for one section of the population. It is essentially a mediator between secondary groups. These develop as the division of labour becomes more sophisticated, and they mediate between society and the individual just as the state mediates between the individual and the secondary group. The secondary groups develop their own *conscience collective*, as the strength of society itself is reduced by the division of labour. We shall see in Part 2 that the role of such groups is, for Durkheim, central to the development of modern society.

Durkheim made other contributions to social analysis. Wallwork (1972) praises him for the first truly modern sociological study of the family, in which he defined the family not as a group of blood relations nor as a group of people living together but as a group of people united by reciprocal rights and obligations sanctioned by society. This is a model sociological definition different from that offered by biology or psychology. It seems to me that Durkheim's lasting value is that he always points us to society, the force of the social, even if sometimes he goes over the top.

Conclusion

I want to use the conclusions to these chapters in Part 2 to look at the way in which each theorist might approach a cluster of connected contemporary political and social problems. The first involves the changes in the labour markets in the western world, the supposed growth of 'flexibility', and the decline in traditional industrial production which has moved to developing countries; the second is the apparent or alleged decline in morality, and /or traditional values, or community; the third is the development of new forms of political movement that seem to be concerned with identity—ethnic, cultural, or gender—or with the environment. In the conclusion to Part 2, I will compare the different approaches. I must emphasize that there is material here for a couple of dozen books and I will sketch a very general outline; you might think of it as looking at the same landscape through different spectacles—or, perhaps more accurately, through the wrong end of different pairs of binoculars.

The first thing that a Durkheimian sociologist would do would be to establish that these trends are actually happening, that they are not common-sense pre-notions, and he or she would certainly find variations from area to area and social class to social class, but I will assume that it would be found that they are happening to some greater or lesser extent in most areas in the western world. The evidence would come from statistics about employment, crime rates, marriage and divorce rates, and so on, and attempts to relate them to political movements. It would be at this point that the real theoretical work would start.

I do not think that there is much doubt that, from a Durkheimian perspective, the change in the labour markets would be seen as a result of the developing division of labour on an international level, between societies; generally the process requires the development of more and better communications and these in turn encourage further changes. Many of the less pleasant effects of these changes in the West—higher levels of unemployment, higher levels of job insecurity, and the decline of traditional forms of industrial employment—might be seen in Durkheimian terms as involving periods of adjustment during which abnormal forms of the division of labour were dealt with and a new, more universal set of values emerge.

All this would be straightforward, but the apparent decline of community indicates that something else is happening—that perhaps the individualizing thrust of the division of labour is undermining even the individualist *conscience collective*, that the progress of system integration is undermining social integration and the modern state has protected the individual from the tyranny of secondary groups by undermining those groups. Durkheim talks about the way in which the development of the state freed the individual from the tyranny of medieval guilds in much the same way that modern free-market right-wing politicians talk about freeing workers from the tyranny of trade unions and breaking the power of professional groups. We are increasingly left with isolated individuals.

It is in this context that we can place the development of 'communitarianism' particularly in the USA, although it is now beginning to cross the Atlantic. The work of Etzioni (1995, 1996) seems to be suggesting that we should try to build up a *conscience collective* on a local level, developing support and control systems out of existing community relations. Interestingly, when he talks about the development of what he terms 'authentic communities', he discusses them in a very Durkheimian way, arguing for the need to develop ways of allowing individual autonomy without undermining the coherence of the community. In situations where the community is becoming too powerful, individual autonomy must be stressed, and where individual autonomy threatens the community, community power must be stressed.

If it is the case that system integration has been undermining social integration, then it is possible to think about the new political movements as spontaneous attempts to find a necessary form of social integration on some other basis than membership of a particular nation state or society. A sense of belonging does not come automatically in modern societies; it might never have come easily in any society, but Durkheim's theory offers good reasons for supposing that in complex modern societies it is especially difficult. These issues will be taken up again in Part 3, when we will look at Durkheim's politics and his vision of the future. They will also be considered in relation to the other three thinkers in the following chapters.

Box 7.1. **An elaboration of Durkheim on the individual and society**

THE INDIVIDUAL	SOCIETY
Durkheim: the individual is formed and limited by society. He/she becomes more important in complex societies and individualism becomes the focus of the conscience collective, binding people together.	**Durkheim:** society exists over and above the individual, over whom it exercises an immense power, especially in less complex societies.
Marx: the 'individuated' individual is an idea produced as part of the development of capitalism.	**Marx:** society is created by human action but acts back upon individuals as an external power.
Weber: the individual is the only reality and analysis must start from individual rational action.	**Weber:** society is the rather fragile result of human interaction.
Simmel: the individual life is engaged in a constant dialectic with social forms.	**Simmel:** 'society' is an increasingly important form organizing peoples' lives.

It is now possible to elaborate further on what I have called the basic dualisms of social theory, pointing out once again that all theories have to consider both sides and this creates tensions and contradictions at their centre.

In Box 7.1 there is an elaboration of Durkheim's handling of the first basic dualism—that of individual and society; in Box 7.2 an elaboration of his handling of the second basic dualism of action and structure; and in Box 7.3 an elaboration of his handling of the third basic dualism, that of social and system integration.

Box 7.2. Durkheim on action and structure

ACTION	STRUCTURE
Durkheim: there is no real theory of social action in Durkheim; the individual action is always conditioned by the group, and collective action is taken to reinforce the strength of the group.	**Durkheim:** in societies dominated by mechanical solidarity, the social structure consists of networks of kin groups (segmented societies); more complex modern societies consist of secondary groups formed by the division of labour and managed by the state.

Box 7.3. Durkheim on social integration and system integration

SOCIAL INTEGRATION	SYSTEM INTEGRATION
Durkheim: in all societies social integration is achieved through the *conscience collective*—shared ways of thinking (logic, conceptions of space and time, shared beliefs, norms, and values). In societies governed by mechanical solidarity, religion is central. In more complex modern societies, the *conscience collective* covers less of our lives but focuses on the ethics of individual freedom—it becomes a religion of humanity.	**Durkheim:** where mechanical solidarity predominates, system integration *is* social integration, guaranteed by the *conscience collective*. Where organic solidarity predominates, system integration is achieved by the division of labour.

Further reading

It is always a good idea to read as many of the original texts as possible; in terms of this chapter, there are two important texts: *The Division of Labour in Society* (1893/1984) especially the Introduction; book 1, chapters 2, 3, and 7; book 2, chapter 2; book 3, chapters 1, 2, and 3; and *The Elementary Forms of the Religious Life* (1912/1915), especially the Introduction; book 1, chapter 1; book 2, chapters 1 and 2; books 3, chapters 4 and 5, and the Conclusion.

There are a number of short introductions to Durkheim, of which the best are Anthony Giddens, *Durkheim* (1978), and Kenneth Thompson, *Emile Durkheim* (1982). By far the best and most thorough secondary source is Steven Lukes: *Emile Durkheim* (1973). P. Hamilton's four-volume *Emile Durkheim: Critical Assessments* (1990) includes the most important modern discussions, whilst Jeffrey C. Alexander's collection *Durkheimian Sociology: Cultural Studies* (1988) shows the modern use of Durkheim and Alexander's four-volume *Theoretical Logic in Sociology* (1982–4) contains a sympathetic discussion of his work.

8 | Was Marx a Marxist?

Introduction

Marxism and popular prejudice and simplistic arguments; relationship between Marx's earlier and later work; his starting point in human action; comparison with Durkheim.

Human powers 1: the theory of alienation

Underlying conception of human nature—distinction from a theory of needs; human nature as a transformative power—humans change themselves through changing their environment. The alienation of the worker from the product, from work, from co-workers, and from his/her own nature. Marxist idealism and its problems; the empirical study of alienation; the distinction between economic analysis and the analysis of ideas and action.

Human powers 2: commodity fetishism

The continuity between Marx's earlier and later work; commodity fetishism as the alienation of human relationships; the 'free' market.

Marxist economics: A brief and simple introduction

Classical and marginalist economics; the labour theory of value; use value and exchange value; labour power as a commodity with a use and exchange value; exploitation; surface appearances and underlying reality; capitalism as a system of regular crises; the central contradiction of capitalism—the forces and relations of production; Marx's sociological economics.

Social class

The place of class in Marxist theory; class-in-itself and class-for-itself. The peasantry and its need for strong leadership. The bourgeoisie and its different fractions. The petty bourgeoisie, traditional and new. The proletariat—working-class identity and shared experience; divisions in the proletariat and contemporary attempts to understand them. The lumpenproletariat and the underclass. The contemporary relevance of social class.

The state

Marx's political and analytic writings; the conspiracy theory of the state; the state as alienated human power and revolutionary democracy; comparison with Durkheim; economic explanations of the state and the possibility of its autonomy; the peaceful or violent transformation of the state; the class nature of the modern state; class and citizenship.

Ideology

Ideology as false consciousness and as non-science; ideology and social integration; ideas and the life process—parallels with modern sociology and psychology; ideology as alienation; economic determinist conceptions of ideology; ideology as illusion; ideology as imagination; ideology as the accurate perception of one level of reality; ideology and commodity fetishism; representation as ideology—the link with postmodernism; conclusion—the difficulties with deterministic notions.

Marxism and the family

Primitive communism; private property and the development of the pairing family; the linking of people and property; the social organization of sexuality and love; assessment of Engel's work.

Conclusion

Comparison with Durkheim; development of the basic dualisms.

Introduction

The collapse of the communist regimes in eastern Europe has perhaps shown that we cannot use a social theory to produce a blueprint for social organization—and it is arguable that these societies were nothing like what Marx imagined a communist or socialist society would be like anyway. Neither of these facts, however, mean that Marxism does not offer an interesting and tenable understanding of how some societies—or some parts of all societies—work. And whatever theory we are looking at, there is always a link between understanding and changing society.

Compared with Durkheim, Marx had a comparatively sophisticated conception of 'society', which he saw as structured in a more complex way. For long periods since Marx wrote, it has been customary to present very simplistic accounts of his work. This has often been the fault of Marx's followers, who have constructed political arguments that explain everything in crude economic terms—to the point where Marx himself is alleged to have said 'I am not a Marxist'. My account here will try to emphasize, on the one hand, the importance that he gave to the economic level of society, and, on the other, the complexity of his model of society.

A central issue in Marxist scholarship has been the relationship between his earlier and later work. Up until the middle of this century, he was known primarily through his later work, in particular the three volumes of *Capital* and the simplistic *Communist Manifesto*. The second half of the century saw the publication of Marx's earlier work, *The Economic and Philosophic Manuscripts of 1844* ('*The 1844 Manuscripts*') which cast a very different light on his ideas. Whereas the later work seemed to be concerned with the ways in which individuals were the product of economic and social structures, the earlier work showed a Marx concerned with human freedom, and the realization of human powers. It is as if he moved from one side of the dualism to the other via an invisible bridge.

The earlier work is an appropriate place to start, not simply because it comes first chronologically and helps us to understand his later work, but because it provides a significant contrast with Durkheim. We have seen that, for the latter, society is always the centre, even in modern societies where individual autonomy is so important. It is as if society determines that self-determination. For Marx, the human ability to be self-determining is the starting point, not as an individual characteristic but as a quality which belongs to humanity as a whole.

Human powers 1: the theory of alienation

I mentioned earlier that Marx saw religion as the projection of human powers on to an imaginary figure that we call God. His theory of alienation is about the loss of human powers in society, the way in which a particular type of social organization *alienates* us from our world. Underlying this idea is a particular philosophical anthropology. By this I do not mean the social science of anthropology—the study of other societies. A philosophical anthropology is a conception of human nature which underlies explanations of human social behaviour. Interest in such an area has all but disappeared from sociology over recent decades, or it has become redefined in terms of a theory of 'human needs'. It is argued that a philosophical anthropology is 'essentialist', that it assumes that human beings are the same throughout history whereas in fact they are historical products. Now there is at least a weak sense in which human beings *are* the same throughout history—they have always, with some exceptions, walked upright with one head, two lungs, one liver, and so on. Marx was, however, trying to suggest that there is a stronger sense in which we can think of human nature, and this stronger sense not only sees certain features of human nature as constant but also explains why human beings change through history. The argument is that it is human nature to transform human life and this transformation establishes the developments that we call history.

One of the things that distinguishes human beings from other animal species is that we do not simply adjust to our environment, but *change* it—in such a way that it then entails changing ourselves in order to adjust to it. Other species change the environment but in a way that does not entail changing themselves: when rabbits dig their burrows, that is all they need to do—they do not have to change themselves to adjust to the burrows they dig. When human beings build cities, they have to change themselves in order to live in them.[1] We change psychologically and develop new skills and abilities. We can see this work from generation to generation—I have all sorts of possibilities that my parents could not dream of, such as using a computer or regularly travelling abroad. The changes over centuries are even greater, but not so great that we cannot understand what has been left us from earlier centuries or millennia. We might not understand them so clearly or deeply as did contemporaries, but we do find a resonance in the work of, say, Homer and Horace, not to mention Shakespeare.

So it is human nature to change through creating our own environment and then adjusting to and recreating it. My understanding of what Marx means by *species being* in the *1844 Manuscripts* is that this constant process of transformation is a collective enterprise; it is something in which we are all involved, and in which we are all connected to each other. *Alienation* is a state in which the environment we create takes on a real solidity, comes to seem unchangeable—when it takes on the sense of what Lukacs called a second nature. The system we create acts back on us to form and control us, and it alienates us from our own collective nature as beings who work together to transform our world and ourselves.

Marx was concerned with the particular form of alienation brought about by capitalism, and the crucial part of the *1844 Manuscripts* is the section on 'Estranged Labour'. Much of the work is a criticism of classical economic theory, equally applicable to contemporary economic theory, arguing that it takes for granted what it ought to be explaining. In particular Marx argues that it took private property as the starting point of explanation, a sort of natural state, rather than as what has to be explained. His own starting point is the power of the market; in an idea which already encapsulates a crucial section in the first volume of *Capital* (1867/1970), he argues that market labour itself becomes a commodity—a thing bought and sold like any other object—and the paradox is that the more the labourer produces, the cheaper his or her labour becomes: 'With the *increasing value* of the world of things proceeds in direct proportion the *devaluation* of the world of men' (Marx 1844/1974: 107).

The worker is, in the first place, alienated from his or her product. If I work in a factory producing cars, I have no control over what I produce, and it is impossible to distinguish the work I have done from what anybody else has done or could do. Again the same paradox is at work: the more I produce, the less control, the less power I have:

The *alienation* of the worker in his product means not only that his labour becomes an object, an *external* existence, but that it exists *outside him*, independently, as something alien to him, and that it becomes a power on its own confronting him. It means that the life which he has conferred on the object confronts him as something hostile and alien. (ibid. 108)

---

[1] Simmel gives a very clear account of the effects of living in cities; see Chapter 10.

Simply because the worker's labour becomes an external quality, not something which comes from his or her inner life, the worker is alienated from the activity of working itself—it is a matter of fulfilling another's desires. I think you can get an idea of what Marx was talking about by thinking of your own work as a student: if you are interested in a course and you want to learn, writing an essay is work which comes from the inside—you are motivated from the inside; if you are taking a course simply because you have to get the qualification at the end, it is a different matter entirely. There is nothing of yourself in the work. The work becomes a burden. For Marx this is the permanent condition of capitalism:

> As a result, therefore, man (the worker) only feels himself freely active in his animal functions—eating, drinking, procreating, or at most in his dwelling and in dressing up etc.; and in his human functions he no longer feels himself to be anything but an animal. What is animal becomes human and what is human becomes animal.   (ibid. 111)

Finally, since labour—work on and transformation of the natural world—is a definitive aspect of our 'species being', we are alienated from the species and from our co-workers. We cannot recognize ourselves in those around us—we do not see fellow humans but people who might be competing with us for jobs and scarce resources, people who are potential threats.

There is much more in Marx's early work than I have covered here, including some interesting comments about the relationship between human beings and the rest of nature (see Benton 1993), and he develops a substantial critique of private property. I have concentrated on this section because it leads us directly into Marx's later work, and the analysis of commodity fetishism at the start of the first volume of *Capital*, but before moving on to that I want to spend some time talking about these ideas.

My first point is that we can find the origins of Marxist idealism in his work—the vision of a free and unalienated world in which people can work together in cooperation to improve their lives and develop their culture; Marx identifies this with the political and economic emancipation of wage labour. Private property and wages go together and a free society entails the abolition of both. We would work together as cooperative equals. Whether such a world is possible is debatable, but for the moment, however, what I want to point out is that in this vision we find possibly the strongest and most effective political ideal of the western world, an idea which finds its origins in the French Revolution, more than half a century before Marx was writing and which continues in various ways until this day. Such utopian visions should not be dismissed easily. They can lay the basis for terroristic regimes, as did the French Revolution and, closer to our own time, the Russian Revolution, but they can also act as guiding principles for social improvement and social justice and resistance to tyrannical systems. As with everything else, ideals are always double-edged but perhaps they are necessary.

Now there are reasons to doubt this particular conception of human nature.

If we take Freud seriously, not to mention Durkheim, it entails accepting that perhaps this defining human feature of working collectively is not simply given but an achievement which always requires some sacrifice and suffering. Our 'natural' state is to seek immediate satisfaction of our desires, but the world is not that kind or generous and we have to give up that desire for immediate and full satisfaction and work to achieve what satisfaction we can. In other words, work is always a burden. This undermines the more utopian versions of Marxist theory, but it does not undermine the subtlety of his conception of it being human nature to change human nature. We can keep hold of the importance of work, even if it is not as fundamental as Marx thought, and Marx's distinction between working for other people and working collectively for ourselves remains important. Work might always be a burden, but it can be heavier or lighter and we have some control over that.

There have been various attempts to 'operationalize' the notion of alienation (see e.g. Blauner 1964) in empirical studies, but these tend to lose the philosophical dimensions of the concept and they turn into studies of work satisfaction—Blauner, for example, suggests the alienation moves through an inverted U-curve, at its lowest in craft industries and highly automated industries but at its highest in factory production. It is this sort of study which is used to criticize Durkheim's suggestion that the division of labour means a general deepening of satisfaction with work, since the division is at its highest in factory production. However, I am not sure that Marx is talking about work satisfaction in that sense; we can find various ways to be satisfied with our work and still not experience it as an expression of ourselves, of our own inner world. I remember in my youth sweeping streets for a while and gaining immense and rather obsessive satisfaction from looking back along a clean gutter, but I could not claim that it had much to do with the meaning of my life. Marx is talking about a more profound and less comfortable satisfaction.

Finally we have in the *1844 Manuscripts* the division that still haunts Marxism between economic analysis and the analysis of human action and ideas. In the early work the latter was clearly more important and in his later work the analysis of economic and social structures predominates. It has always been difficult to keep these two sides together in all of the schools of social theory—not just Marxism—and Jürgen Habermas (1972), the most prominent contemporary thinker in the Marxist tradition, has separated the analysis of economic production and of social interaction as distinct areas of investigation. The social action/social structure distinction seems to be a necessary one; we can try to understand the relationships between the two, but they remain separate objects of study.

Human powers 2: commodity fetishism

I mentioned earlier debates over the differences between Marx's earlier and later work. Some argue that there was a radical break between the *1844 Manuscripts* and *Capital* (see Althusser 1969), whilst others (McLellan 1971) argue that there is a continuity. This too is about the action/structure dualism. It is always rather silly to see these things in terms of either/or arguments. It seems to me that there is both continuity and change. The continuity lies in the connection between the theory of alienation and that of commodity fetishism; the development lies in the way that the latter comes to form the basis for the development of Marx's economic theory and his structural analysis of society. The notion of commodity fetishism is very close to the analysis of the alienation of the product of labour, but Marx is concerned this time less with the alienation of labour into its product than with the alienation of social relationships in the division of labour into market relationships between commodities:

A commodity is therefore a mysterious thing, simply because in it the social character of men's labour appears to them as an objective character stamped upon the product of labour; because the relation of the producers to the sum total of their own labour is presented to them as a social relation, existing not between themselves, but between the products of their labour. This is why the products of labour become commodities, social things whose qualities are at the same time perceptible and imperceptible by the senses. . . . There is a definite social relation between men that assumes, in their eyes, the fantastic form of a relationship between things. . . . This I call the Fetishism which attaches itself to the products of labour, so soon as they are produced as commodities. (Marx 1867/1970: 76)

The division of labour, the way in which society divides up its workforce to produce the necessities and the luxuries of life, creates social relationships between groups of people. If I am producing cars, somebody else is fishing, and somebody else again is making clothes; we are related to each other, in fact dependent upon each other—even if we never set eyes on each other. But we do not experience this relationship as a social relationship, we experience it as a relationship between the commodities that we produce. I am paid money for the work I do on the conveyor belt which turns out cars, and I use that money to buy a suit, and whoever makes my suit might use the payment he or she receives for the labour to buy a car I make. Somehow or the other, cars get equated to suits get equated to fish and so on.

We need only think about how contemporary politicians talk about the 'free market' to get a good idea of what Marx meant by commodity fetishism. The market is endowed with human powers: people will say 'let the market decide' as if it had powers of thought and judgement; sometimes the market will dictate, or it will demand; it will move in different directions, but usually either up or down. We are led to believe that our livelihood depends on this invisible, powerful, thoughtful entity which nobody has seen but which everybody assumes to be real—we are not even expected to have faith in it; it is simply there and our newspapers write about it every day. The classical economist Adam Smith talks about the 'hidden hand' of the market; it seems to be mystically invested with all the powers of the separate individuals and groups that make it up and at the same time seems to control each of them, each one has to react to the market. To understand this in greater depth we need to look at Marx's economic theory—but don't worry, it won't be at too great a depth.

Marxist economics:
a brief and simple introduction

Marxist economic theory is not simply an economic theory. We have already seen that it is in part philosophical and we shall see that it is also a profoundly sociological theory.

Marx belongs to an earlier and different tradition from the marginalist economics that provides the basis for most of what is taught in schools and universities today. The modern tradition is concerned with price, the classical tradition with *value*: not quite the same thing. It worked with a *labour theory of value*. The idea at its simplest is that the value of a good depends upon the labour expended upon it, but it is not quite so simple as that—to leave it there would mean that, if I took five years to write a book, it would be worth five times a book I took a year to write. Marx talked about *socially necessary labour*—this is the average productivity of labour at one particular time—so if everybody else is producing a book in a year, I will get proportionately less for my five years' work.

The problem faced by the classical economists (Adam Smith, David Ricardo, and others) was to explain the source of profit. If I am, say, working in a shoe factory, and I am paid the value of my labour, and the shoes are sold at the value of the labour expended in their production, there is no space for profit—the two amounts would be the same and value would equal price; profit could occur only through some form of dishonesty or unfair exploitation. The way in which Marx dealt with this problem takes us back to the idea of labour as a commodity and a central distinction between *use* value and *exchange* value. The former is the value of a commodity to the person who uses it—the pleasure, say, of drinking a couple of pints of beer. The exchange value is what that beer would exchange for via the medium of money. The definition of a commodity is that it is produced for the purpose of exchange rather than use by the producer and it is the exchange value which is determined by the amount of socially necessary labour expended on the production of the commodity. Only it is a little more complicated than that, because what I sell if I am a worker is my *labour power*, or my ability to work.

Now, labour power is a *commodity*—it has a use value and an exchange value. The exchange value of labour power is what is needed to ensure its reproduction—that is, it must be sufficient to enable workers to feed, clothe, and house themselves and enable the next generation of workers to be raised, educated, and so on. There are two components to this: an absolute minimum needed to keep the worker alive plus something extra depending on what is acceptable to society at large. Thus over the last fifteen years in British society it has become socially acceptable to pay very low wages at the bottom end of the market, perhaps in some cases close to a subsistence wage, and at the other end to pay very high wages, many many times above subsistence level.

Now, if I were an employer, the only point in employing workers would be if their use value to me—the value of what they produce for me—is greater than what I have to pay them, the exchange value of their labour power. The difference between the two is surplus value, which is appropriated by the employer. This is Marx's definition of exploitation, and it is not the result of the actions of unscrupulous employers; it is built into the wage–labour relationship itself, into the buying and selling of labour power. There is no such thing as a 'fair day's pay for a fair day's work'. At the same time as I work for my own wage, I am working for my employer's profit, I am producing surplus value, and I am being exploited. If this were not the case, I would not be employed. This sets the scene for permanent conflict between workers and employers.

We find here an implicit but absolutely fundamental distinction between the level of appearances and that of underlying reality. In the case of commodity fetishism, what we can see on the surface is the relationship between commodities as they are determined by the market; the underlying reality is the social relations that comprise the division of labour. In the case of the wage relationship, what we can see is the labour I sell and the wage I receive for it; the underlying reality is the difference between the use value and the exchange value of my labour and the surplus value taken by my employer—what is hidden is exploitation. We shall see when we discuss Marx's various theories of ideology that this distinction is particularly important.

Contained in these ideas as well is the argument that capitalism is a system of permanent crises; Marx suggests a number of ways in which crises can occur, but I would suggest that the crucial crises arise from exploitation, and what is revealed by the distinction between use value and exchange value. If I am a worker and I produce £50 worth of goods in a day (the use value of my labour to my employer), and I receive £10 a day in wages (the exchange value of my labour power), then I do not receive in wages sufficient to buy back the value of goods I have produced. This applies right across the system, so that if stocks of unsold goods build up, workers have to be laid off, and the economy enters a crisis, a depression, or slump, until the stocks of goods are used up and firms go

back into production. There is a cycle of growth and slump, something that capitalist economies have been trying to deal with for over a century and a half. A
temporary solution was found by John Maynard Keynes in the 1930s through
public expenditure on work that does not produce commodities or which produces commodities that have a market guaranteed by the state, such as the arms
industries. This circulates money which can then be used to purchase the surplus commodities. But by the late 1970s this policy was seen as responsible for
unacceptably high rates of inflation and it was reversed. The results must be
familiar to everyone.

We find here what Ernest Mandel (1962, 1970) calls the central contradiction
of capitalism between the forces and relations of production. The forces of production are the abilities we possess to create wealth. Capitalism represents a
huge step forward in human productive capacities compared with previous
forms of society. The competition between private entrepreneurs constantly
drives forward the pace of technological change as each capitalist tries to outstrip his rivals (and, of course, in Marx's day, capitalists were only 'he's'). Yet the
full potentiality of the capacities, of the productive forces, cannot be realized
precisely because of the private ownership of productive capacity. Private ownership involves wage labour, which in turn involves exploitation, which produces regular crises, which reduce productive capacity. As Mandel puts it:

this socialisation of production which transforms the labour of all mankind into objectively co-operative labour is not regulated, directed, managed to any conscious plan. It
is governed by blind forces, the 'laws of the market' in fact by the variations in the rate
of profit. . . . This is why the totality of production . . . develops independently of the
human needs it has itself aroused, and is urged onwards only by the capitalists' thirst for
profit.   (Mandel 1962: 171)

This has been a very simplistic account of Marx's economic theory, but I hope
I have shown that it is a *sociological* economic theory at the centre of which are
the social relations entailed by the division of labour and private property. It is
sometimes said that Marx was a technological determinist, arguing that the
stage of technological development determined the form of social organization,
but in fact the important factor is the *social relations* within which technology
develops. The same technology could exist in very different types of society.
Secondly, it is also often argued that Marx was an 'economic determinist'. There
are two replies to this: the first is a repetition of the argument I have just made—
that it is social relations that are important. The second is that there are many
and various links to be made between these social relations of production and
other aspects of social life—far too many for us to interpret Marx as arguing for
some tight causal process.

If we want to move on to Marx's wider social analysis from the point we have
reached, then it can most easily be done through a discussion of social class. The
economic theory as I have presented it here lays the basis for defining two social

classes: the owners and controllers of the means of production and the workers, those who sell their labour power: the bourgeoisie and the proletariat.

Social class

The history of all hitherto existing society is the history of class struggles. Freeman and slave, patrician and plebeian, lord and serf, guildmaster and journeyman, in a word oppressor and oppressed, stood in constant opposition to one another, carried on an uninterrupted, now hidden, now open fight, a fight that each time ended, either in a revolutionary reconstitution of society at large, or in the common ruin of the contending classes.

(Marx 1848/1968a: 35–6)

One might think, rightly, that social class is a central concept in Marx's work, but he had very little to say about it—a famous forty lines at the end of the third volume of *Capital* and scattered comments elsewhere. It always reminds me of a detective story where the victim dies just before he or she can gasp out the murderer's name. The concept of class has the same status in Marx's theory as the murderer in a detective story; it is class which sets the scene and moves things forward—it is guilty not of murder but of creating history.

Sometimes Marx talks about social groups as being classes in a loose common-sense way, but at others he is being more rigorous; at times he talks as if there are only two social classes—as in the first passages of *The Communist Manifesto* quoted above. At other times and in a more realistic way he talks about a number of different classes. The central defining factor in his more rigorous statements has to do with groups of individuals who are united and defined sometimes in very different ways by their relationships to the means of production. But historically they develop in opposition to one another, building up their own culture and practices. The best account of such development is still to be found in E. P. Thompson's *The Making of the English Working Class* (1965), but here I will be concerned with class on a more theoretical level, looking at the classes that Marx and Marxists have talked about and discussing their characteristics.

It is normal to make a distinction between two components in Marx's conception of class: the class-in-itself, as defined by a particular relationship to the means of production, and the class-for-itself, a class whose members have recognized a shared social position and a common interest and opposition to other classes. We can be a member of a class-in-itself without any awareness of the fact, although it might influence our ideas and actions—it is part of an underlying reality, of which we don't necessarily have any direct experience at all. When we do become aware of this underlying reality we begin to see the world in a different way.

THE PEASANTRY

The small-holding peasants form a vast mass, the members of which live in similar conditions but without entering into manifold relations with one another. Their mode of production isolates them from one another instead of bringing them into mutual intercourse. . . . Their field of production, the small holding, admits of no division of labour in its cultivation, no application of science and therefore no diversity of development, no variety of talent, no wealth of social relationships. Each individual peasant family is almost self-sufficient; it itself directly produces a major part of its consumption and thus acquires its means of life more through exchange with nature than in intercourse with society. A small holding, a peasant and his family; alongside them another small holding, another peasant and another family. A few score of these make up a village, a few score of villages make up a Department. In this way the great mass of the French nation is formed by simple addition of homologous magnitudes, much as potatoes in a sack form a sack of potatoes. In so far as millions of families live under economic conditions of existence that separate their mode of life, their interests and their culture from those of the other classes and put them in hostile opposition to the latter, they form a class. In so far as there is merely a local inter-connection among these small-holding peasants, and the identity of their interests begets no community, no national bond and no political organisation among them, they do not form a class. They are consequently incapable of enforcing their class interests in their own name, whether through a parliament or through a convention. They cannot represent themselves, they must be represented. Their representative must at the same time appear as their master, as an authority over them, as an unlimited governmental power that protects them against other classes and sends them rain and sunshine from above. The political influence of the small-holding peasants, therefore, finds its final expression in the executive power subordinating society to itself'.

(Marx 1852/1968c: 170–1)

I have quoted this passage (from *The Eighteenth Brumaire of Louis Bonaparte*, an analysis of political struggles in France from 1848 to 1851 which ended with Bonaparte seizing power in a *coup*) at length, not only because it tells us what Marx thought of the peasantry but also because it provides an illustration of how he thought about social class in general. We can see not only the simple definition of class according to relationship to the means of production, but also the notion of the development of a class for itself and the way in which the material conditions of life condition the development of such consciousness, and, in the case of the French peasantry, prohibit it. Unable to represent themselves, the peasantry respond to a strong leader who promises to do it for them. They are denied the individual richness and variation which might potentially be derived from the division of labour.

In western Europe the peasantry declined with industrialization. The poorer peasants became agricultural labourers and most were forced off the land into the urban working class. Even when it is large, the strength of the peasantry as an independent social force seems to be limited, although, where there is a form of collective organization of the peasant village life under the feudal system, as in China, they might be a stronger force.

THE BOURGEOISIE

The term 'bourgeoisie' originally referred to the French middle classes; its meaning in contemporary society has two dimensions. The first stems from its use by avant-garde artists, referring to the conventional, respectable, narrow, and boring—the supposed lifestyle of lawyers, priests, business men, civil servants, and so on. It is used as a term of abuse and sometimes has the ring of aristocratic arrogance about it—'you're so bourgeois'. The second dimension comes from Marxist theory and refers to capitalists, the owners of the means of production. During the early years of the industrial revolution (from approximately 1750 onwards), the capitalists were the middle class—the group between peasants and workers, on the one hand, and the traditional landed classes, the aristocracy, on the other. At the end of the third volume of *Capital* Marx talks about there being three great classes in society: workers, capitalists, and landowners.

Landowners as a major class were most significant in the period leading up to and into industrialization. Barrington Moore, Jr. (1966) argues that the future development of democracy depended on whether industrialization came from above, from a section of landowners (as in Germany and Japan), or from below, from a bourgeois revolution, as happened in France. After industrialization, the importance of landowners has decreased and they are best seen as what N. Poulantzas (1976)—a modern French Marxist—would describe as a 'fraction' of the bourgeoisie. Another very important fraction of the modern bourgeoisie would be finance capitalists. These groups can in different situations have coinciding or conflicting interests. In Britain for many years industrial capitalists were the dominant section of the bourgeoisie, having achieved important victories over the landed aristocracy in the middle of the nineteenth century, but that place has been taken over by finance capitalists over the course of this century. David Harvey (1989) traces the development of what we call postmodernism to the increasing power of financial capitalists to use modern information technology to move capital to where it is most profitable at short notice. Marx recognized that there were conflicts between these different sections of the bourgeoisie and he suggested that these conflicting interests were managed through the state as a sort of 'central committee' of the bourgeoisie.

There are certainly many points where Marx seems to think that the two main classes of capitalism, bourgeoisie and proletariat, capitalists and workers, will face each other across the barricades with nothing left in between, all other classes having been absorbed into the major blocs. And the bourgeoisie itself would have a comparatively short life—its historical function was to develop capitalism to the point where the working class was sufficiently well developed to take power for itself. In this he was simply wrong, and if anything the intermediate groups have grown in number. One major intermediate group was the petty bourgeoisie.

THE PETTY BOURGEOISIE

This is much closer to what we would today call the middle classes. It would include small business people, who maybe employ a few workers or none at all, and the professionals who have no particular relationship to the means of production; lawyers, small shop keepers, and so on. David McClellan (1971) points out that, in the second volume of *Theories of Surplus Value* (Marx: 1862/1969), Marx censures Ricardo for not recognizing the importance of the growing middle classes. This, however, is only one reference, and it has been left to later Marxists to make up the deficiency. Poulantzas (1976) suggests a distinction between the traditional petty bourgeoisie and the new petty bourgeoisie, the latter including workers in the state system—civil servants, teachers, and so on. The traditional petty bourgeoisie are usually associated with reactionary politics: they cannot see themselves as part of a class, only as individuals, and they feel threatened by the bourgeoisie above them and the more powerful organized workers' movement below them. They do not develop their own political movements but, like the French peasantry, tend to turn to strong leader figures whom they believe will protect them. Poulantzas's argument about the new petty bourgeoisie was that, at times of crisis, it would tend to split politically along the lines of the class of origin of its members. Teachers from working-class backgrounds would move towards the workers' movement whilst those from middle-class backgrounds might move in the opposite direction. At this point I should say that one of the difficulties of Marxist class theory is that the *a priori* reading of likely political behaviour from class position does not always work.

THE PROLETARIAT

> In proportion as the bourgeoisie, i.e. *capital,* is developed, in the same proportion is the proletariat, the modern working class, developed—a class of labourers who live only as long as they find work, and who find work only so long as their labour increases capital. . . . Owing to the extensive use of machinery and to division of labour, the work of the proletarians has lost

all individual character, and consequently all charm for the workman. He becomes an appendage of the machine . . .

(Marx 1848/1968*a*: 41)

To begin with, the working class is geographically scattered and unorganized and reacts to industrialization by attacking the machinery—as did the Luddites in nineteenth-century Britain; but slowly they are brought together into large factories, where they can recognize their identity with each other and their common interest. Their material conditions of work bring them into social relationships with each other, and if labour is dehumanizing it also enables workers to understand their mutual dependence. This sense of solidarity would spread from one factory to a group of factories to the development of nationwide labour organizations and beyond that to international organizations.

Of course, it has not been as simple as this and contemporary Marxists would recognize all sorts of complicating factors, not least the way in which the working class can so easily get caught up in nationalist rather than internationalist movements; but there have also been the major divisions within the working class itself—between skilled and unskilled, white- and blue-collar, men and women, black and white, and so on. Marx himself indicated that he could see such problems, although of course they were different 150 years ago. He talked, for example, of the way in which workers could end up competing with each other for jobs, relevant today in arguments about immigration and gender equality. He also made a distinction in his economic theory between productive and unproductive labour—productive labour being that which produces commodities for sale on the market and unproductive labour that which does not.

In the twentieth century, discussions about the composition of the working class have arisen around the proliferation of divisions—the divisions not only between white- and blue-collar workers but between managers and workers, different levels of managers and workers, and so on. Erik Olin Wright (1978) calculated that, if we were to take the proletariat as consisting only of productive workers in Marx's sense, the working class would comprise a very small part of the population indeed. Wright tried to deal with these problems by talking about 'contradictory class locations', suggesting that the same person can occupy different class positions.

THE LUMPENPROLETARIAT

Here we reach the bottom of the pile. In *The Eighteenth Brumaire* Marx talks about Louis Bonaparte as himself a member of the lumpenproletariat, a bohemian adventurer who organized this particular class into a sort of private militia to back him up in his seizure of power. Marx describes this class vividly:

Alongside decayed roués with dubious means of subsistence and of dubious origins,

alongside ruined and adventurous offshoots of the bourgeoisie, were vagabonds, discharged soldiers, discharged jailbirds, escaped galley slaves, swindlers, mountebanks . . .
pickpockets, tricksters, gamblers . . . brothel keepers, porters, literati, organ-grinders, rag
pickers, knife grinders, tinkers, beggars—in short, the whole indefinite, disintegrated
mass, thrown hither and thither, which the French term *la bohème*. (Marx 1852/1968c:
136–7)

Now what are we to make of this class today? The social level that Marx is talking about has always more readily supplied mercenaries for the right than the
left, and it is doubtless still there, only now there would be less rag pickers and
knife grinders, more permanently unemployed, maybe drug pushers, and so on.
In contemporary society there would be some overlap with what has become
known as an underclass, but I think there is a difference. The underclass if it
exists is a section of the population permanently trapped at or below the poverty
line, not necessarily unemployed or beggars but people who are employed in
low-wage and/or temporary work.

THE CONTINUED SIGNIFICANCE OF CLASS

The significance of social class is still debated both in sociology and in the world
at large (see M. Mann 1995; Lee and Turner 1996) and it is a debate which has
continued since Marx himself and one that was stimulated by and drawn into
Weberian sociology. It has been clear certainly for the second half of the century
that the reality is much more complicated than might be expected from Marx's
analysis and that rarely, if at all, do we find social classes walking across the stage
of history like giant actors, but this does not mean that social class is not a
significant factor that we have to take into account in understanding what is
happening in late capitalism. It is sometimes suggested that class has no relevance to everyday life in contemporary society and it has been replaced by ethnicity or gender or other factors, yet this is demonstrably untrue to anybody
who listens to political debates or looks at the distribution of wealth and illness
or the workings of the education system. On a theoretical level, the postmodernist arguments drag in Marx behind them—they do not offer an alternative
theory to Marxism but rather a counter-theory. One suspects that, if Marxism
did not exist, neither would postmodernism.

My own view is that it is useful to look at Marx's analyses of class and class
structure as representing a sort of underlying skeletal structure, and that he
makes a very good case that we should see capitalist society as inherently contradictory. The problem then becomes to understand why conflict does not
occur in the way that might be expected from Marxist analysis and why history
has not developed in the way that Marx predicted. This has led to the most interesting developments in social theory over the last fifty years. It is difficult to

overestimate the contribution of Marxism to modern social thought, and, if Marxism is necessary to understand class formation, it is also necessary to understand class fragmentation (Harvey 1989; Jameson 1991).

Marx's discussion of class, in particular the bourgeoisie, takes us on to the nature of the state.

The state

Each step in the development of the bourgeoisie was accompanied by a corresponding political advance of that class . . . the bourgeoisie has at last, since the establishment of Modern Industry and the world-market, conquered for itself, in the modern representative State, exclusive political sway. The executive of the modern State is but a committee for managing the common affairs of the whole bourgeoisie.

(Marx and Engels 1968a: 37)

legislation, whether political or civil, never does more than proclaim, express in words, the will of economic relations.

(Marx 1847/1976: 147)

Marx cannot be accused of being afraid of making rash statements—although it is also useful to remember that he is writing not only as a social analyst but also as a political polemicist and agitator. As Richard Miller (1991) points out, it would be easy to conclude that Marx believed the state to be a sort of conspiracy against the working class, or that the wealth of the bourgeoisie could be used to ensure that whoever is in power pursues its interests. Given the contemporary mistrust of politicians, perhaps both possibilities might be more acceptable now than they were twenty years ago, and paradoxically they are not too far away from ideas expressed by right-wing militias in the USA.

Again, Marx defined his own position by arguing against Hegel, who saw the state functioning to producing harmony between the different groups which made it up and bringing them together at a higher level, which it did through the monarchy, representative assemblies, and the state bureaucracy. Now, as McLellan (1971: 180) points out, Marx subjected this view to the same argument to which he subjected Hegel's view of religion: the state in reality is the projection of society's powers, the powers of the men and women who make up society, onto an external body. Against this Marx developed a notion of radical democracy. In undemocratic states, the law and the constitution exists over and above people, but in a truly democratic society they would be the result of the collaboration of all citizens in the political processes that produce the law and the constitution. This vision has become a central part of Marxist political idealism and its latest forms can be found in the work of the German social theorist Jürgen Habermas.

Like Durkheim, Marx also traced the development of the state to the division of labour—as societies become more complex, so some central organizing agency is necessary. If you remember, for Durkheim, the function of the state was to mediate between different interests and in particular to protect the individual against the power of smaller groups. For Marx, it was also an organizing agency, but one which was necessarily involved in the domination of one class over others. Capitalism is an inherently expanding system, and the social class at its helm is carried into political power not because of any deliberate or conscious action, but because that is the way that society develops. For Marx, the concern of the state for individual liberty could be seen as an attempt to enforce the rights of the individual property owner against those without property, whose only power lay in their banding together to take collective action. This involves a political struggle for trade-union rights which was fought in the UK through the nineteenth century up to the present time, and in the USA throughout this century.

If the first quotation suggests conspiracy or corruption, then the second suggests a simple economic determinism, and this would be equally misleading. Marx made various modifications of and reservations about these earlier views. For example, he talks about different sections of the bourgeoisie engaging in political struggles through and over the state—for example, the factory acts and the arguments over the corn laws in the UK in the 1840s can be seen as a struggle between the industrial bourgeoisie and the agricultural bourgeoisie. He also talks about the state being controlled by people who do not belong to the dominant class, but nevertheless exercise power in the interests of the dominant class. Thus in the UK by the end of the nineteenth century it can be argued that the holders of office came from the landowning class but exercised power in the interests of the industrial bourgeoisie. Returning to the *Eighteenth Brumaire*, it can also be seen that Bonaparte's seizure of power seemed to give the state some autonomy for a while. Although Bonaparte came to power on the basis of the peasantry and the lumpenproletariat, the state does not represent them—the logic of economic development meant that his regime had to protect the interests of the dominant class if it were going to survive. In capitalist society the state becomes more powerful as the bourgeoisie becomes more dominant.

The traditional debate on the left was about whether the capitalist state could be transformed through a democratic process or whether it had to be overthrown by violent revolution; over recent years this has become obviously irrelevant. However, there is still a question about the extent to which a radical, left-wing government can bring about reforms that favour the subordinated classes. If we take UK politics as the example, then the advent of a socialist government, even a moderate one, is greeted with warnings of a 'run on the pound', of businesses leaving the country, and so on. The fate of the democratically elected socialist government in Chile in the 1970s is a frightening reminder of the international power of the ruling class.

At the same time left-wing governments have been able to achieve important reforms, more so in Europe than in the USA. The existence of the National Health Service is perhaps the most dramatic example in the UK—a system of national insurance which originally promised health care from cradle to grave. How are we to explain such reforms being introduced by the 'executive committee of the bourgeoisie'? There are in fact two ways of approaching it. The first is a sort of conspiracy theory: the ruling class (or classes) can weigh up their long-term interests balanced against what they can get away with in the present. A more interesting and certainly a more respectable theoretical explanation leads us to a Marxist functionalism. The state does not simply protect the individual and balance group interests, as Durkheim argued, nor does it simply enforce the interests of one class in a direct and conscious way. Rather it rises in response to the basic system needs of the economy. This is an argument most clearly articulated by the French Marxist Louis Althusser in the middle of the twentieth century, but he succeeds as well as anybody in elaborating on Marx's own writings in this matter. If capitalism is to survive, it requires a reasonably healthy workforce, educated to a level necessary to operate at the relevant level of technological development, and it needs to ensure that the next generation is raised in a reasonable way to whatever standards are required. The state develops in order to fulfil these needs. Now this is not an especially satisfactory explanation—even if we can talk about an economic system having needs, it does not follow that these needs will be automatically met, or met in any particular way. But it does make sense of Marx's view of the state as working in the interests of the ruling class because it is working to reproduce the sort of economic and social system that that class rules—it becomes the guarantor of system integration rather than the agent of a particular section of the ruling class.

There is also a way that the development of the democratic state can be seen as undermining class struggle. I mentioned earlier that we could see the state's defence of individual rights as an intervention on behalf of the bourgeoisie. One way of putting this in a more interesting, and less crude, light is through thinking about the development of citizenship rights. This, it seems to me, is essentially what Durkheim was talking about when he saw the state as protecting the rights of the individual. The British sociologist T. H. Marshall (1950/1973), writing in the mid-twentieth century, distinguished three dimensions to citizenship. He saw these as developing one after the other, although I think they are best thought of as coexisting side by side, each providing a focus for social conflict.

The first dimension is that of civil rights which guarantee individual freedom—equality before the law, freedom of speech, etc.; the second dimension is political—the right to vote and to engage in political organization; and the third dimension is socio-economic—the right to a certain level of economic and social security. Some of these rights, particularly the civil rights and the right to vote, are often historically involved in the establishment of capitalist society and the overthrow of the traditional order; however, the right to political organization and welfare rights can actually challenge capitalism, as Giddens (1973: 157) points out. But more important perhaps is the fact that civil and political rights are often individualizing rights, undermining a sense of class, and perhaps, as Marshall himself wondered in passing, compensating for and enabling people to accept considerable degrees of class inequality. Perhaps civil justice and political freedom can compensate for economic injustice and unfreedom, undermining the class dynamics that Marx identified. The development of these rights could also be seen as fulfilling a functional need of the system. My argument over these last sections has been that, even though class struggle has not developed in the way that Marx predicted, the class structure has become more, not less, complicated, and even though the state cannot be understood in terms as simple as those which Marx proposed, we can still talk about class and about the state as a site for class conflict and class rule. In many examples, this means talking about an objective or underlying reality which is not necessarily apparent to those people who belong to the class or who are participating in political activities. In the case of the state, I would suggest that its function of administering the division of labour and ensuring individual rights—which are very important and certainly not illusory—contributed to undermining the awareness of class. This takes us on directly to the area where modern Marxism has been most creative and Marx himself perhaps was under-creative—the area of *ideology*.

Ideology

INTRODUCTION

The term ideology has changed its meaning quite radically since it was coined by Antoine Destutt de Tracy, a philosopher engaged in the French Revolution who used the term to refer to a science of ideas. Today it is a term often used critically, if not disparagingly. In British and North American culture there is often a profound mistrust of intellectuals, and 'ideology' is used to condemn any theoretical discussion. At other times it might be used to describe a general worldview. For Marx, however, the term applies to partial, one-sided ideas—ideas that are misleading because they consciously or unconsciously serve the interests of a powerful group—or to ideas that are wrong, in error for the same reason. This last notion of ideology as a false representation of the world leaves it juxtaposed to truth or to science. In this way it draws us to the philosophy of science and in particular to epistemology—the theory of knowledge. This has been most developed in modern Marxism by Louis Althusser (1969), but without doubt it was present in Marx's work.

These two uses come together in Lukacs's Marxism: the position of the working class in the production process in particular and in society in general enables it to develop an ideology which was *also* a science. It is worth pointing out at this point that there is a radical difference between Lukacs's vision and that of Althusser, and that this ambivalence, as we shall see, haunts Marx's work. In Lukacs's vision it is possible for people to come to understand and control the society in which they live; in Althusser's vision only social scientists and Marxist theorists can understand society; for the rest of us an ideology is necessary. I will be pointing to the different roots of these theories at several points in what follows.

It is in the theory of ideology that Marx comes to grips with the problems of social integration. Sometimes he seems to be arguing that social integration is simply the product of system integration; at other times he seems to be moving in the direction of suggesting that ideas and their development can be to some significant degree independent of the economic base. There is, in fact, a number of different conceptions of ideology to be found in Marx's work. There follows a long series of quotations from his work in which we can find some of his most simplistic and his most complex comments on the issue. Children's comics sometimes contain complicated drawings in which other drawings are hidden and the reader is asked to find the hidden drawings. These quotations can be seen as such a drawing. I will identify a number of different theories which I think are present in these quotations and it might be a useful exercise to see if you can identify the relevant quotations or parts of a quotation—I am not going to give answers, since that tends to stop people thinking!

The fact is, therefore, that definite individuals who are productively active in a definite way enter into these definite social and political relations. Empirical observation must in each separate instance bring out empirically, and without any mystification and speculation, the connection with the social and political structure with production. The social structure and the State are continually evolving out of the life-process of definite individuals, but of individuals not as they may appear in their own or other people's imagination, but as they really are, i.e. as they operate, produce materially, and hence as they work under definite material limits, presuppositions and conditions independent of their will.

The production of ideas, of conceptions, of consciousness, is at first directly interwoven with the material activity and the material intercourse of men, the language of real life. Conceiving, thinking, the mental intercourse of men, appear at this stage as the direct efflux of their material behaviour. The same applies to mental production as expressed in the language of politics, laws, morality, reality, metaphysics etc., of a people. Men are the producers of their conceptions, ideas etc.—real, active men, as they are conditioned by a definite development of their productive forces and of the intercourse corresponding to these, up to its furthest forms. Consciousness can never be anything else but conscious existence, and the existence of men is their actual life-process. If in all ideology men and their circumstances appear as upside-down as in a *camera obscura,* this phenomenon arises just as much from their historical life-process as the inversion of objects on the retina does from their physical life-process.

. . . We do not set out from what men say, imagine, conceive, nor from men as narrated, thought of, imagined, conceived, in order to arrive at men in the flesh. We set out from real active men, and on the basis of their real-life-process we demonstrate the development of the ideological reflexes and echoes of this life-process. The phantoms formed in the human brain are also, necessarily, sublimates of their material life process, which is empirically verifiable and bound to material premises. Morality, religion, metaphysics, all the rest of ideology and their corresponding forms of consciousness, thus no longer retain the semblance of independence. They have no history, no development; but men, developing their material production and their material intercourse, alter, along with their real existence, their thinking and the products of their thinking. Life is not determined by consciousness, but consciousness by life.   (Marx 1846/1977*a*: 164)

. . . the division of labour implies the contradiction between the interest of separate individuals or the individual family and the communal interest of all individuals who have intercourse with one another. And indeed this communal interest does not merely exist in the imagination, as the 'general interest', but first of all in reality, as the mutual interdependence of the individuals among whom the labour is divided. . . .

And out of this very contradiction between the interest of the individual and that of the community the latter takes an independent form as the state, divorced from the real interests of individual and community, and at the same time as an illusory communal life. . . . It follows from this that all struggles within the State, the struggle between democracy, aristocracy and monarchy, the struggle for the franchise, etc., etc., are merely the illusory forms in which the real struggles of the different classes are thought out among one another.   (ibid.)

Everything appears reversed in competition. The final pattern of economic relations as seen on the surface, in their real existence and consequently in the conceptions by which the bearers and agents of these relations seek to understand them, is very much different from, and indeed quite the reverse of, their inner but concealed essential pattern and the conception corresponding to it. (Marx 1865/1972: 209)

This sphere . . . within whose boundaries the sale and purchase of labour power goes on, is in fact a very Eden of the innate rights of man. There alone rule Freedom, Equality, Property, and Bentham. Freedom because both buyer and seller of a commodity, say of labour power, are constrained only by their own free will. They contract as free agents, and the agreement they come to is but the form in which they give legal expression to their common will. Equality, because each enters relation with the other, as with a simple owner of commodities, they exchange equivalent for equivalent. Property because each disposes only of what is his own. And Bentham, because each looks only to himself. The only force that brings them together and puts them in relation with each other is the selfishness, the gain, and the private interests of each. Each looks to himself only, and no one troubles himself about the rest, and just because they do so, do they all, in accordance with the pre-established harmony of things, or under the auspices of an all-shrewd providence, work together to their mutual advantage. For the common weal and in the interest of all.   (Marx 1867/ 1970: 172)

IDEAS AS THE EXPRESSION OF THE LIFE PROCESS

This is not so much a theory of ideology as a theory of thinking: that our ideas do not, as Mao Tse Tung once put it, 'fall from the sky', but that they emerge out of our experience of the world, our relationship to the world and to each other; not in any deterministic way—our ideas are not 'caused' by our daily life and its relationships but are based on it, both as an expression of our experience and an attempt to deal with its problems. This gives a hint of what thinking would be like in a socialist society—a constant flux of ideas and debates centred around our everyday living.

This way of looking at thinking is reflected in contemporary sociology and psychology. In sociology the notion of human interaction as a constant flowing process, giving rise to and constantly redefining ideas, has been at the centre of symbolic interactionism (see Blumer 1969). The notion of ideas being the expression of life experience has moved to the centre of some modern psychoanalysis—but there it is less a matter of ideas emerging from 'material experience'—the experience of production and of daily life—than from earliest physical experience of ourselves and other people (Bion 1976). In fact these two contemporary approaches illustrate both the limitations and the advantages of Marx's position. The first limitation is that Marx and many Marxists pay no attention to childhood, when we learn to think. Jean-Paul Sartre, who became a critical Marxist after the Second World War, talked about Marxists writing as if people were born fully developed onto the factory floor. The second limitation is that work is not the only thing we do in our daily lives: there are the activities of friendship, of family life, play, love, etc., which Marxism often ignores. The great advantage of Marx's position is that it develops an understanding of how these ideas that we build up from our experience can be systematically distorted.

IDEOLOGY AS ALIENATION

I have already mentioned Marx's theory that religion represents a projection of *human* powers into a supernatural being. Similarly, but on a more concrete level, the state is a representation of human communal life—a projection of the real collective powers that belong to our relationships with each other. The end of this sort of alienated ideology comes from practical political action: if we collectively take over the state, 'seize state power', and the state ceases in reality to be an institution counterposed to society, then we have abandoned ideology. McLellan argues that, in his earlier work, Marx 'had set the scene for his conception of ideology. The mistaken conception of religion and politics that he criticized were not merely errors; these inverted conceptions have their basis in a real social world that was so misconstructed as to generate these compensatory illusions' (McLellan 1971: 11). This view of ideology sees it as the alienation of our free and creative thinking.

THE ECONOMIC DETERMINIST CONCEPTION OF IDEOLOGY

Sometimes when Marx is talking about political struggles, he seems to be saying that ideologies are illusory ways of seeing the world that are determined entirely by class position or the economic structure/stage of the development of a society. Thus in *The Eighteenth Brumaire* he argues that the two conflicting monarchist parties represent different sections of the bourgeoisie. It is not a matter of rational justifications of a monarchy and rational and legal argument between the two factions. Rather the whole process is driven by economic interests. But not consciously—each class believes that its own interests are in fact the general interests of the society as a whole.

I want to suggest here that each of Marx's conceptions of ideology is useful and if we play them off against each other we develop a very complex position. Now if we compare the simpler economic-determinist arguments with the theory of alienation and Marx's references to the life process, we can perhaps argue that in trying to make sense of our life processes we transform our own interests into some general belief about the world—in the way my son justifies his demands for pocket money by referring to fairness. A French bourgeois in 1848 would not cynically have chosen one monarchist faction because it would have been to his advantage; rather the arguments of that faction would resonate with him because they shared his life conditions.

IDEOLOGY AS ILLUSION

Next is Marx's frequent insistence on the illusory nature of ideology, ideas as phantoms, inverted impressions of the real world. Many later Marxists talk of false consciousness, although Marx does not usually use the term. It is often attributed to Lukacs, although I am not sure that this is particularly fair either. I think these statements are best read as polemical attacks on more conventional ways of thinking. In particular, Marx is trying to underline that we should not start with ideas since this places us immediately in the world of the imagination, but with the activities out of which ideas are produced. If we start with ideas and simply assume that they are true, then we are likely to be left with illusions. He is also saying that we should not take things at face value. Just as we do not take what an individual might say about him- or herself as necessarily the truth, so we should mistrust the way in which political parties and groups present themselves and the ways in which societies think about themselves.

IDEOLOGY AS IMAGINATION

There is a sense in which, in referring to these ideas as imaginary, Marx is a century ahead of his time; if we can return for a moment to the work of Althusser (1971), part of his rewriting of Marx borrows from contemporary French psychoanalysis (Lacan 1977) to argue that ideology consists not in one particular set of ideas but in a particular imaginary relationship to the world: we *imagine* that we are in charge of ourselves and our lives, that we make free decisions according to rational considerations and open choices. It actually takes very little thought to realize that, however much we might like to hold on to this as an ideal, life is really not like this. We are constantly finding that we are not as aware of ourselves or of what we are doing as we thought we were. Sometimes, in fact, we can find out that what we are doing, especially within the field of political activity, turns out to be the opposite of what we thought we were doing.

To take an example where it seems to me that Marx's analysis is almost precisely right: during the social upheavals of 1960s, the student left developed a slogan 'the personal is political'. At the time it seemed a radical extension of politics to everyday life, and the argument was that political action should not just involve changing governments but should transform the quality of everyday life itself. On the one hand, this can be seen as a radical slogan; it was, for example, important for the genesis of modern feminism. But it seems to me arguable that it also had another effect in opening the way to the political *control* of everyday life, not its political liberation—the opposite of what was intended.

But ideology can never completely be a matter of the imagination. Its imaginary aspect adds another dimension to those I discussed earlier, different from creative thought, thought unconsciously governed by self-interest and the projection of powers involved in alienation. But another thing one learns from modern psychoanalysis is that the imaginary and the real are often mixed together, sometimes inextricably. This moves us on to the core of Marx's later theory of ideology.

IDEOLOGY AS THE ACCURATE PERCEPTION OF ONE LEVEL OF REALITY

If we think about the earlier theories of ideology, there is always some point at which a real perception of the world enters. Marx seemed to assume—even when he was talking about the imagination and phantoms—that there was some real basis for the development of these phantoms, that there is some perception of the reality of the life process, and that it is in fact the nature of the life process which prevents us from grasping the reality of our lives and leads to us creating these phantoms. If we think about the process of alienation, it is a *real* human power that we invest in God, a real communal power that we invest in the state.

We can find in the theory of commodity fetishism the mechanisms that lead to the production of phantoms, and the reality of these phantoms. It is at the level of appearances that ideology is rooted—the appearances that mask the inner reality of the capitalist system and which are built into the system through the sale of labour as a commodity. It is at the level of exchange on the market that the full force of 'bourgeois ideology' lies, because there everything seems to work as the economists and politicians say it works. When I sell work to the university, I get paid for what my work is worth—within limits, and when those limits are breached, it seems the fault of bad management or bad government, or perhaps my own fault for not selling myself sufficiently vigorously. Life seems to be a matter of relationships between individuals, almost always a matter of bargaining and trading. This is not simply true of the world of work; several centuries ago Kant noticed that this way of thinking was penetrating marriage, and that is even clearer today. It is not just that people in the West are beginning to make agreements to protect property before entry into marriage; it is that the market is now providing a model for the emotional connection as well. Anthony Giddens (1991) talks about a process of 'effort-bargaining' between partners which can easily be seen as an economic trade-off, and the American sociologist Arnie Hochschild (1994) has suggested that certain forms of modern feminism have encouraged a commercial model for personal relationships. In the UK it is also easy to see how the market model has eaten away at traditional ideals of public service and a national health service and is also gradually entering the education system, in the development of interchangeable commodities (called modularization) and through the increasing role of student choice and assessment. It has not quite reached the stage where the only courses available are the ones that sell well, but that is the logic of the development.

It is developments such as these which generate the illusions of ideology and the alienated projection of human powers into external structures—and, in the context of what I have just been talking about, the market as an invisible entity is invested with the human power of allocating resources to the best effect and making choices between possible courses of action. We are now back to where started: Marx's economic analysis of capitalism.

REPRESENTATION AS IDEOLOGY

There is one last aspect to Marx's theory of ideology which has emerged only in recent years. It is difficult to explain in simple terms but I will do the best I can. The argument is basically that Marx's analysis of money as the medium of exchanging different goods identifies one stage in a historical development in which signs have become dominant. The sign, in linguistics, can be seen as enabling an exchange between (crudely) concept and reality. The sign 'desk' links my idea of a desk with this wooden construction on which I am writing. In

Marx's economic theory, money is the sign which enables the exchange of two very different objects—for example, £20.00 can equate a hardback book with half a dozen bottles of cheap wine, three haircuts, or half an hour with a psychotherapist. Jean Baudrillard, who has developed this argument furthest, argues that the sign which started full of meaning, as a religious icon, becomes flattened out, losing meaning, and then in contemporary society comes to be able to mean anything and therefore nothing. Contact with 'reality' is lost—we are left only with free-floating signs and signs of signs.

CONCLUSION

If we take ideology to be based on an accurate, but surface, conception of reality, then we can see that the deterministic notions of ideology, the formulations in which it is seen only as epiphenomenal, do not hold water. The liberal ideologies of utilitarianism have been governing economic thought ever since Marx and have developed independently in many different directions. Ideas do seem to have a life of their own; they develop not only as a result of changes at the economic level and developments in the progress of class struggle but also as a result of debate, research, and thought that goes on the basis of those ideas. There is always a degree of original as well as illusory thinking in ideology. What Marx gives us is a number of ways to explore the relationship between our life processes, our everyday activities, and our sensuous experience of the world and each other, which later Marxists have encapsulated under the label *praxis*, and the ways in which systems of ideas grow up and develop is more or less alienated from our *praxis*. And in Marx's work as well we find these ideological forms juxtaposed to a knowledge of the world which can penetrate these surface experiences to underlying structures. Over the last century, these ideas have generated a variety of different critiques of modern society, as well as themselves providing an ongoing and highly relevant critical approach to our own society.

Perhaps it would be more accurate to say that, while Marx has left us with a powerful tool of critical theory, the gaps in his arguments have created even more powerful tools. These gaps have to do with making theoretical sense of the move from the analysis of social structures to the analysis of human experience and action—*praxis*—and then to the analysis of ideas and systems of thought—a set of problems which are still at the centre of social theory.

Marxism and the family

Of the four theorists that I am discussing here only Marx has contributed anything substantial to modern feminism and this owes more to his companion

Friedrich Engels (1968), whose work has inspired a number of analyses of the position of women under capitalism (Zaretsky 1973; Sacks 1984; Hartman 1986).

Engels tries to trace the development of the family from primitive times in an exercise not unlike Durkheim's study of religion, involving the use of ethnographic material provided by others. The basis as always with Marxism is production, a matter of asking who does the work and who owns the tools. He posits a state of primitive communism, in which the tribe collectively owned the resources (although because of this very fact, the question of ownership would have made no sense to them). The tribe only produced what was sufficient for day-to-day life. Engels suggests that sexual relations were promiscuous, and one way of looking at the development of the family is as a process of the steady limitation of those with whom sexual relations are permissible:

the communistic household implies the supremacy of women in the house just as the exclusive recognition of a natural mother, because of the impossibility of determining the natural father with certainty, signifies high esteem for the women, that is for the mothers. That woman was the slave of man at the commencement of society is one of the most absurd notions that have come down to us from the period of Enlightenment in the eighteenth century. Women occupied not only a free but also a highly respected position. (Engels 1884/1968: 481)

Decision-making in these groups involved everybody.

The development of the pairing family was intimately bound up with the development of private property, which in turn is involved in the production of a surplus—or more than the tribe needs to feed itself on a day-to-day basis. This occurs as nomadic groups settle to raise crops and (especially) animals. These formed the basis of private property although, as Sacks (1984) points out, they are not really private property in the modern sense; rather their owners have more power of disposal than hitherto. Looking after domestic animals and the growing of crops were men's activities, outside the family, and consequently it was men who came to own property. As wealth increased, tribes began producing for exchange purposes, thus producing a surplus.

The result of this was, again in Sacks's words, 'that people and property became entwined, and each became part of the definition of the other'. The property that is passed on becomes important, and it becomes important for the man to ensure that his property is passed on to his own children. The primitive form of group or communist family changed: women's work became clearly different from that of men and subordinated to it—their main function came to be the bearing of children who would inherit their father's property and position. This required not only a pairing marriage but also monogamy—at least for the women—since that was the only way the man could be sure that he was passing on property to his own child.

An important concomitant of this was that the social organization of sexuality changed to a system of 'hetaerism'—the practice of sexual intercourse outside marriage alongside monogamy:

With the rise of property differentiation . . . wage labour appears sporadically alongside of slave labour; and simultaneously, as its necessary correlate, the professional prostitution of free women appears side by side with the forced surrender of the female slave. Thus the heritage bequeathed to civilisation by group marriage is double-sided, just as everything engendered by civilisation is double-sided: on the one hand, monogamy, on the other hetaerism, including its most extreme form, prostitution.   (Engels 1884/1968: 495–6)

The contradiction and conflict between men and women carries in embryonic form the antagonisms which split society into different classes. In modern society, marriage is always to some degree a marriage of convenience, determined by the class position of the participants, effectively often only a form of prostitution for the wife. Rather romantically, and I think mistakenly, Engels argues that sexual love can only become the rule amongst the oppressed classes—it is not often possible where property must be taken into account. Even amongst the oppressed classes, brutality towards women has taken root, although, amongst those without property, the woman has in fact the right to leave. Engels talks about the slow movement towards women's legal equality— which I think has probably been a much slower process than even Engels imagined a century ago. However, at the end of this particular part of his discussion we get an idea of what Engels saw as the real basis on which women can achieve social equality—drawing a parallel with the way in which the democratic state does not abolish the inequality between social classes:

In the industrial world . . . the specific character of the economic oppression that weighs down the proletariat stands out in all its sharpness only after all the special legal privileges of the capitalist class have been set aside and the complete juridical equality of both classes is established. The democratic republic does not abolish the antagonism between the two classes; on the contrary, it provides the field on which it was fought out. And, similarly, the peculiar character of man's domination over woman in the modern family, and the necessity as well as the manner, of establishing real social equality between the two, will be brought out into full relief only when both are completely equal before the law. It will then become evident that the first premise for the emancipation of women is the reintroduction of the entire female sex into public industry; and that this again demands that the quality possessed by the individual family of being the economic unit of society be abolished.   (ibid. 504)

If property is returned to common ownership, then the family would lose its economic function—housekeeping and child-rearing would become a social activity, 'a social industry'. However, we would not return to the promiscuous sexuality of primitive communism. The Middle Ages saw the appearance of what we would now call romantic love and Engels calls sexual love; the development of socialism would enable this to come into its own—there would develop a 'true monogamy' in which couples would come together freely through love. Sexual love is spontaneously, naturally monogamous, but this monogamy will not be accompanied by the dominance of the man, and people will be free to leave each other as well as to come together: 'If only marriages that are based on love are moral, then, also only those are moral in which love continues' (ibid.). The antagonism between men and women, the first form of class struggle, will disappear.

The empirical basis of Engels's work, particularly the evidence on which he claimed that early societies are matriarchal, is now generally accepted as inadequate, but the suggested link between women and private property and inheritance is an interesting one. What has become clear is that the market economy tends towards producing a limited equality between men and women, but it is the equality of the 'abstract individual'—not the collective freedom of men and women working together that Engels envisaged. The evidence from the contemporary world, especially from the eastern European societies that called themselves communist, is, whatever the legal and economic status of women, they are still expected to take responsibility for work *in* the home. Again it has been the failure of more orthodox Marxist approaches to such issues that has stimulated so much modern research and argument. One line of argument has moved through Marx's theories of ideology to psychoanalysis and postmodernism, or to more conventional analyses of mothering; others have tried to develop a concept of patriarchy as a system of oppression interwoven with, but different from class oppression. And these debates have been matched by political debates within the feminist movement between liberal, radical, and socialist feminists (Barrett 1980; Barrett and McIntosh 1982; Walby 1990).

Conclusion

I think that perhaps the crucial difference between Marx and Durkheim is that Marx saw industrial society as essentially divided against itself, whereas Durkheim saw it as possessing an essential unity. For Durkheim, it follows that ideas and belief systems express the whole of a society, whereas for Marx they can mask society and its divisions and prevent the conflict that would emerge if people were to become aware of their real interests.

Turning to the contemporary problems that I am considering at the end of these chapters, it would be true to say that a Marxist sociologist would also look for empirical evidence that these processes are actually occurring, but he or she might be interested in different figures (changes in the relative distribution of wealth, relative profit rates, or numbers of days lost through strikes might, for example, be considered more important than, say, the symptoms of anomic or egoistic states), and the same evidence might be interpreted in different ways.

To begin with, a Marxist might focus on the growth of monopoly capitalism and multinational companies, as the capitalist market seems to have permeated nearly every corner of the world and produced organizations that transcend the boundaries of the nation state. This is a process that sociologists have come to term globalization and it has produced conceptions of a 'world system'—an idea not confined to Marxists (Wallerstein 1974; Giddens 1981). One argument is that this process of globalization creates an international labour market and that factory production, for a good part of this century established in the 'developed' world, moves to the developing world, where labour costs are cheaper. The dominance of finance capital and the growth of information technology— encouraged by the globalization process—means that capital can be moved around the world rapidly to wherever the return in greatest. It is this that produces the emphasis on flexibility and change, a 'short-termism'. The best account of this development can be found in Harvey (1989). The class conflicts which occurred in the UK in the late 1970s and early 1980s, in Germany and France more recently, and to a lesser extent in the USA under Reagan are symptoms of these changes.

Contrasted with a Durkheimian approach which might see the 'natural evolution' of the division of labour, the Marxist account would emphasize the mechanisms of competition and conflict and different class interests which drive the process forward. The apparent loss of a shared morality, shared norms, and community life would be seen as the result of these economic changes. Capitalism has always tended to break down traditional communities and beliefs and then to build up new communities and break them down again— first destroying the traditional rural communities and building up working-class communities around the new heavy industries and now breaking them down again. Whereas a Durkheim might see this change as a result of industrial society *per se*, a Marxist would see it as a result of capitalism—an underlying structure of social relationships.

A Marxist might try to explain the rise of new types of political movement less as a result of a modernizing process which eats away at social cohesion than in terms of the decline in class-based politics in the West which follows on the political and industrial battles of the last twenty years. This in turn would be seen as enabling the fragmenting effects of the competitive market to dominate and people would be seen as trying to create communities on the basis of surface factors such a gender or sexuality. It has become harder to see through these surface appearances to the underlying forces that are at work, and even if we can see through the appearances it is more difficult to know what can be done about it. As far as the West is concerned, capitalism has won for the foreseeable future and perhaps the function of Marxism would be seen as the analytical one of pointing to underlying structures and maintaining a critique of modern ideologies. Postmodernism in particular fits very easily with the individualism and fragmentation created by the market economy; it loses sight of the existence of a global system, emphasizing differences and rejecting causal explanations. Whereas postmodernist theory might see many of these changes as a form of liberation, freeing the individual to create him- or herself at will (see especially

Gergen 1991), Marxism would see them as involving a sophisticated form of enslavement—the more we are dominated by a global system, the more we believe we are free individuals. It might be argued that this is the central feature of modern capitalism.

Boxes 8.1–8.3 show Marx's contributions to the central dualisms.

Box 8.1. An elaboration of Marx on the individual and society

THE INDIVIDUAL

Durkheim: the individual is formed and limited by society. He/she becomes more important in complex societies and individualism becomes the focus of the *conscience collective*, binding people together.

Marx: the 'individuated' individual is an idea produced as part of the development of capitalism. The 'natural' state of the individual is as an integral part of the group.

Weber: the individual is the only reality and analysis must start from individual rational action.

Simmel: the individual life is engaged in a constant dialectic with social forms.

SOCIETY

Durkheim: society exists over and above the individual, over whom it exercises an immense power, especially in less complex societies.

Marx: society is created by human action but acts back upon individuals as an external power—a dominant force in all but the most primitive and most advanced (communist) societies.

Weber: society is the rather fragile result of human interaction.

Simmel: 'society' is an increasingly important form organizing peoples' lives.

Box 8.2. Marx on action and structure

ACTION

Durkheim: there is no real theory of social action in Durkheim; the individual action is always conditioned by the group, and collective action is taken to reinforce the strength of the group.

Marx: in capitalist societies, the major agents are social classes—primarily the bourgeoisie and the proletariat. Some classes—the middle classes and the peasantry—do not share the life conditions which enable them to act as collective agents, and they tend to follow a strong leader.

STRUCTURE

Durkheim: in societies dominated by mechanical solidarity, the social structure consists of networks of kin groups (segmented societies); more complex modern societies consist of secondary groups formed by the division of labour and managed by the state.

Marx: different types of society have different forms of social structure. In capitalist societies the economic structure and resultant class structure are most important, and the state and state institutions are central features of social control.

Box 8.3. **Marx on social integration and system integration**

SOCIAL INTEGRATION	SYSTEM INTEGRATION
Durkheim: in all societies social integration is achieved through the *conscience collective*—shared ways of thinking (logic, conceptions of space and time, shared beliefs, norms, and values). In societies governed by mechanical solidarity, religion is central. In more complex modern societies, the *conscience collective* covers less of our lives but focuses on the ethics of individual freedom—it becomes a religion of humanity.	**Durkheim:** where mechanical solidarity predominates, system integration *is* social integration, guaranteed by the *conscience collective*. Where organic solidarity predominates, system integration is achieved through the division of labour.
Marx: a 'false' and rather tenuous integration is achieved through ideologies, and the development of the market constantly threatens whatever integration is achieved. The major contending classes strive towards achieving their own integration in opposition to the others—the proletariat being the class most likely to achieve this.	**Marx:** system integration in capitalism is constantly threatened by class conflict and is supported by the state and by ruling ideologies.

Further reading

From the original works, the best starting point is *The Economic and Philosophical Manuscripts of 1844* (1974)—as much of it as you can but especially the section on alienated labour; much more difficult but also very important is Volume I of *Capital* (1867/1970)—especially part 1. The best of Marx's own political analyses is to be found in *The Eighteenth Brumaire of Louis Bonaparte* (1852/1968c), but it might be an idea to read it in conjunction with a simple textbook on nineteenth-century French history. On ideology, as well as Volume I, part 1 of *Capital*, see David McLellan's selection from *The German Ideology* (1846/1977a).

You should also read *The Communist Manifesto* (Marx 1848/1968a) and Engels, *The Origin of the Family, Private Property and the State* (1884/1968).

The best secondary source for the beginner is David McLellan, *The Thought of Karl Marx* (1971), and, on Marxist economic theory, Ernest Mandel's excellent little *An Introduction to Marxist Economic Theory* (1970). On the family, see Karen Sacks's article 'Engels Revisited' (1984) and Eli Zaretsky, *Capitalism, The Family and Personal Life* (1973).

For accounts of different forms of Marxism since Marx, see Ted Benton, *The Rise and Fall of Structural Marxism* (1984), and Perry Anderson, *Considerations on Western Marxism* (1976). For a Marxist critique of postmodernism, see Fredric Jameson, *Postmodernism or the Cultural Logic of Late Capitalism* (1991) and for postmodernist discussion of Marxism, see Crook, Pakulski, and Waters, *Postmodernization* (1992).

9 | The liberal Weber

Introduction
Weber's complexity; Weber and Marx.

The fundamental concepts of sociology
Legitimacy; conflict; Weber's cautious evolutionism; communal relations based on identity; associative relations based on interest; corporate groups and different forms of control; the nature of politics and the state; power as an end in itself.

Weber's economic sociology
Weber's concern with the sociological preconditions of the capitalist economy; the advantages of the market; formal and substantive rationality; the stability offered by the market to precarious social and political institutions; free disposal over goods and free labour and other preconditions of the development of formally rational accounting in productive enterprises; different types of capitalism and the peculiarity of western capitalism.

Class, status, and party
Weber and a theory of social structure; comparison of Marx and Weber on social class; class situation as market situation and life chances; the possibility of solidary class relations; the complexity of class structure seen in Weberian terms; the possibility of combining Marxist and Weberian conceptions; status as social esteem and lifestyle and the ambiguity of Weber's concept; the relationship between class and status in Weber's and Marx's sense; status groups in contemporary society; status groups and educational qualifications; professional groups and self-interest—comparison with Durkheim; parties and their ineffectiveness—Weber's determinism.

Power, domination, and authority
Types of domination; charismatic leadership—comparison with Durkheim; the routinization of charisma; traditional patriarchal domination and its development into patrimonialism; feudalism and its development; legal–rational domination and the characteristics of the modern state; the absence of any absolute basis for authority; the basis of legitimacy in legal–rational domination; Weber's ideal type of bureaucracy.

Conclusion
The fragility of the social order.

Introduction

> . . . it is, of course, not my aim to substitute for a one-sided materialistic
> and equally one-sided spiritualistic interpretation of culture and of history.
> Each is equally possible, but each, if it does not serve as the preparation,
> but as the conclusion of an investigation, accomplishes equally little in the
> interest of historic truth.
>
> (Weber 1904–5/1930: 184)

These lines, the conclusion to Weber's famous *Protestant Ethic and the Spirit of Capitalism*, show Weber at his best and perhaps explain why he has been the most popular classical theorist in the development of British sociology, displaying the straightforward common sense for which British intellectuals seem to yearn. But Weber is difficult to pin down. I think it is arguable that there are several Webers, although for the purposes of this book I shall concentrate on two. In this chapter I shall focus on the Weber who put the free market at the centre of his work, arguing that it provided a source of fragile social stability; in Part 3 I shall concentrate on the tragic Weber who saw history taking us into an iron cage. The above quotation is often taken as an example of the dictum that Weber was forever conducting a debate with Marx's ghost, and in his religious studies and in his work on class, status, and party we can perhaps see him as an exceptionally sophisticated Marxist. Bendix (1966) describes Weber as holding to a 'complex . . . position in which ideas must be understood within their social context but also as having a power of their own'. The most important starting point for understanding Weber is that, despite the scope of his theory, it is not totalizing; we saw in Part 1 that he works with a conception of multi-causality, and focuses on meanings.

To begin with I will follow Weber's own outline of his work, on which he was working at his death, and which has been translated as *The Theory of Social and Economic Organization* (1925/1947), the opening sections of which I have already discussed in Chapter 5. It is important to remember that at this stage he is not engaging in substantive sociological analysis; rather he is using rational argument to try to set up a number of distinctions and classifications which can then be used as part of a substantive analysis. At one point he feels it necessary to defend himself against the accusation of the 'apparently gratuitous tediousness involved in the elaborate definition of the above concepts'. I have tried to select the most important distinctions.

The fundamental concepts of sociology

Weber here is concerned with the nature of legitimacy, conflict, organization, and the use of force.

LEGITIMACY

After outlining the forms of social action, Weber goes on to discuss the concept of 'legitimate' order. Action may be oriented to a belief in a legitimate order, and the probability that people will actually act in such a way is called the 'validity' of that order. 'Order' has a number of connotations, and the way in which Weber goes on to elaborate the notion pushes it towards what Durkheim meant by a social fact. It is a rule which has to be followed, not out of habit or self-interest, although these might be involved, but also because of a sense of obligation or duty, and indeed he goes on to talk about the law as an example of such order.

The legitimacy of a particular order may stem from either 'disinterested' motives which may be based on emotional allegiance or a belief in ultimate values (such as are involved in religion). If the validity of a particular order is guaranteed by the disapproval that I would incur by going against it, then Weber says it should be called a convention, and he distinguishes this from the law which entails the presence of a group of people specifically devoted to its enforcement. The most important basis for legitimacy in modern society is legality—reached by agreement and/or imposed by what is generally held to be legitimate authority. An understanding of his meaning can be gained by looking at what happens when an authority oversteps its conventional legitimacy—for example, when the Thatcher government imposed a poll tax which was generally considered to be grossly unfair. In the USA there seems to be a constant debate over the legitimacy of the federal government.

CONFLICT

Conflict is defined as a social relationship in which one person or group of people attempt to achieve their will against the resistance of others; this can range from all-out war to well-regulated competition, but Weber here introduces a very crude Darwinism. Conflict cannot be eliminated, and attempts to do so will always result in its reappearance in some other form; its purpose is to sort out those who are best suited to prevailing conditions and eliminate those who are not. Weber recognized the practical and moral difficulties of establishing this sort of argument:

There is, above all, a danger of being primarily concerned with justifying the success of an individual case. Since individual cases are often dependent on highly exceptional circumstances, they may be in a certain sense 'fortuitous'. In recent years there has been more than enough of this kind of argument. The fact that a given specific social relationship has been eliminated for reasons peculiar to a particular situation proves nothing whatever about its 'fitness to survive' in general terms.   (Weber 1922/1947: 135)

COMMUNAL AND ASSOCIATIVE RELATIONSHIPS

Communal relationships occur when a group of social actors see themselves as belonging together and they act accordingly; associative relationships depend on the mutual adjustments of interest—this may be on the basis of the market, or self-interest, or because of adherence to some ultimate value. Thus my relationship to my family is communal, and that to my trade union, my church, and my local shopkeepers are associative. This echoes a distinction made by Ferdinand Tonnies (1957) between 'community' and 'association', *Gemeinschaft* and *Gesellschaft*, which represented for him a major historical change away from homogenous societies characterized by clear status positions and intimate relationships to societies based on calculated self interest and contacts. This clearly mirrors Durkheim's understanding of the move from organic to mechanical solidarity and it also mirrors contemporary debates about the nature of community.

Weber makes the point that the existence of common biological factors, a common language, or any other common qualities does not imply the existence of communal relationships between the people who share these qualities; he has no conception of people belonging to a 'class-in-itself', independently of their consciousness. He regards market relationships as a most important contemporary form of associative relationship, and we shall see that his conception of market-based classes has been very important in the development of sociology.

CORPORATE GROUPS

Today, a corporate group might be called a 'collective actor'. It is a relatively closed group in which order is enforced by a number of individuals whose specific task it is to do just that. Weber distinguishes between 'power', the probability that one individual will have his or her orders carried out, and 'imperative control', the probability that a specific command will be obeyed. The notion of a corporate group does in the end seem to depend on an individual issuing orders which the group then carries out. As we shall see when we discuss Weber's view of political democracy, this places a limit on democracy—the need for some sort of sovereign who personifies the unity of the group.

Out of this discussion comes an interesting and important point. He argues that we cannot define a *political* corporate group from its purpose. Political groups have all sorts of purposes and there is no one purpose which they would all recognize. Thus we cannot achieve any clarity from such a definition: 'Thus it is possible to define the "political" character of a corporate group only in terms of the *means* peculiar to it, the use of force. This means is, however, in the above sense specific, and is indispensable to its character. It is even, under certain circumstances, elevated into an end in itself' (Weber 1922/1947: 155).

This is interesting because it sees power in a way we have not encountered so far, as an autonomous factor over which struggles can take place. For Durkheim, in so far as power was a problem, the exercise of power was a function of the division of labour. For Marx, power was determined by social class and the state of the class struggle. Weber's conception continues through to Parsons and on to postmodernism via the connection to Nietzschean philosophy, the 'will to power' which replaces notions of morality or justice or equality or freedom. This leads Weber on to the state:

The primary formal characteristics of the modern state are as follows: It possesses an administrative and legal order subject to change by legislation, to which the organized corporate activity of the administrative staff, which is also regulated by legislation, is oriented. This system of order claims binding authority, not only over the members of the state, the citizens, most of whom have obtained membership by birth, but also, to a very large extent, over all action taking place in the area of its jurisdiction. It is thus a compulsory association with a territorial basis. Furthermore, today, the use of force is regarded as legitimate only so far as it is permitted by the state or prescribed by it.   (ibid. 156)

This concern with force is unique amongst the founding thinkers of sociology.

Weber's economic sociology

In his introduction to *The Theory of Social and Economic Organization*, T. Parsons makes it clear that Weber is not trying to provide an economic theory but to do something which modern economists generally do not do—that is, offer a theory of the institutions that are involved in the capitalist economy. He points out that Weber assumes first, that social structures are inherently unstable and variable, and, secondly, that the rationalization and the dominance of the 'capitalist spirit' are an ongoing process—crudely, an attitude to life which sees the accumulation of capital *in a rational and systematic way* as the most important value, around which daily life should be systematically organized, at the expense of pleasure and relaxation.

Weber underlines what he saw as the positive aspects of the market economy. The use of money broadens the possibility of exchange and widens the scope for planning, for rational calculation, and for increasing wealth. He makes an important distinction between formal and substantive rationality. Formal rationality points to the extent to which rational calculation is possible—and he seems to be saying that it refers only to calculability. Substantive rationality, however, refers to the extent to which a group is provided with goods which meet its needs, and this is much more difficult, since absolute values enter in. Substantive rationality cannot be understood simply in terms of rational calculation—it concerns the things we value. A high level of formal rationality tends to enter into conflict, or at least tension with a high level of substantive rationality. This is a lesson which contemporary free-market economists are beginning to learn again. Effectively he is pointing out that economic efficiency does not necessarily get us what we want. Weber himself seemed to be doubtful about the possibility of a resolution to this tension. These days one might suggest that a fully developed socialist economy might achieve a high degree of substantive rationality but would be likely to have all sorts of problems in the realm of rational calculability. For a fully developed market economy, the opposite would be the case.

Weber based his arguments on the marginalist economics which replaced classical tradition in which Marx worked and which concentrated on the play of supply and demand, but unlike the economists themselves he was concerned with the social ramifications or preconditions of the processes by which price is determined. He argued that the market had an important stabilizing function in relation to political and social institutions. As one might expect from a theorist whose starting point was a rigorous methodological individualism, he saw such institutions as precarious and inherently unstable, without the power of tradition to anchor them down. They certainly did not have an existence in their own right over and above the individuals who comprised them. In this situation the successful, spontaneous determination of price through the matching of supply and demand provides a fixed point of orientation for a range of activities. If I know what goods and services are available and at what price, and if neither I nor anybody else can influence that price by our individual actions, then the range of rational actions open to me is limited and comparatively stable. In this sense the market can replace tradition as a fixed point in the midst of potential chaos.

There are a number of preconditions for the market to work in such a way: first, the owners of the means of production must have the right to dispose of them as they wish—they must not be bound by laws of inheritance, for example, or, as church-owned land once was, by rules which narrowly stipulate the uses to which it can be put. Political battles over this issue today tend to be fought out in terms of government interference and regulation rather than the abolition of traditional feudal restrictions, with which I think Weber was most often concerned. Secondly, there must be 'formally free' labour—no slavery, no serfdom, only wage labour. Although this enables the development of formal rationality, it is not clear that it enables the development of substantive rationality. Labour has to eat, and this provides the employer with a weapon which perhaps enables him or her to exercise *de facto* appropriation rights over workers—the use of the 'truck' system in nineteenth-century England, where workers were compelled to buy food from their employers' shops, would be an example. Marx made a similar point when he talked about 'wage slaves'. Whether we are talking about land, labour, or capital, however, the modern system of production is, for Weber, inherently unstable. In Weberian terms, value commitments are constantly entering into economic life. Many of his points fit well into contemporary debates about the role of the market, and in this context Weber would most often, I think, be supporting the political right. In the words of Parsons:

Perhaps his most important insight is that there is both a similarity of effect and an intrinsic connection between appropriation of the means of production by workers and appropriation of workers by owners. As to effect, both tend to break down the mobility of economic resources, human and non-human, and to open the door to traditionalistic stereotyping of economic structures.   (Parsons 1947: 64)

This makes sense if we see it in the context of a society emerging from feudalism and where some fall-back into feudal relationships is a major danger; whether it makes sense in a society which has left feudalism well behind is another matter.

Weber's own summary of the necessary preconditions for the full development of the capitalist market is as follows—I have glossed them in square brackets where I think it necessary:

The following are the principle conditions necessary for obtaining a maximum of formal rationality of capital accounting in productive enterprises:

(1) The complete appropriation of all the non-human means of production by owners, and the complete absence of all formal appropriation of opportunities for profit in the market; that is market freedom. [The owners of the means of production should have complete freedom to dispose of their property as they wish and there should be no restriction on who can pursue opportunities for profit.]

(2) Complete autonomy in the selection of management by the owners, thus the complete absence of formal appropriation of rights to managerial functions. [Managers do not own their jobs.]

(3) The complete absence of appropriation of jobs and of opportunities for earning for workers, and, conversely, the absence of appropriation of workers by owners. This involves free labour, freedom of the labour market and freedom in the selection of workers. [The workers don't own their jobs, and employers don't own the workers.]

(4) Complete absence of substantive regulation of consumption, production and prices, or of other forms of regulation which limit freedom of contract or specify conditions of exchange. This may be called substantive freedom of contract. [No government interference.]

(5) The maximum of calculability of the technical conditions of the productive process; that is a mechanically rational technology. [We need to know what things cost.]

(6) Complete calculability of the functioning of public administration and the legal order and a reliable formal guarantee of all contracts by the political. This is formally rational administration and law. [A state apparatus which guarantees the other conditions and the contracts which are agreed within them.]

(7) The most complete separation of the enterprise and its conditions of success and failure, from the household or private budgetary unit and its property interests. It is particularly important that the capital at the disposal of the enterprise should be clearly distinguished from the private wealth of the owners, and should not be subject to division and dispersion through inheritance.   (Weber 1922/1947: 275)

It is only on this last point that Weber perhaps differs from the contemporary political right, who are often to be heard encouraging small family businesses.

Weber makes one more important set of distinctions, this time in connection with types of 'capitalist orientation'; this takes us to the edge of his comparative sociology, which will be considered in greater depth in Chapter 13. He distinguishes between six 'qualitatively different' capitalist orientations to profits, which we can think of as six different types of capitalism. Again I will quote Weber at length and add my own occasional comment in square brackets.

1. Profit-making activity may be oriented to the exploitation of market advantages in a continuous process of purchase and sale on the market where exchange is free; that is, formally not subject to compulsion and materially, at least relatively, free. Or it may be oriented to the maximisation of profit in continuous productive enterprises which make use of capital accounting. [i.e. the system we have just been discussing.]

2. It may be oriented to opportunities for profit by trade and speculation in money, taking over debts of all sorts, and creating means of payment. A closely related type is the professional extension of credit, either for consumption or for profit-making purposes. [Merchant capitalism.]

3. It may be oriented to opportunities for acquiring 'booty' from corporate political groups or persons connected with politics. This includes the financing of wars or revolutions and the financing of party leaders by loans and supplies. [This is the sort of activity that got King John into trouble with the barons in thirteenth-century Britain and led to the Magna Carta.]

4. It may be oriented to opportunities for continuous profit by virtue of domination by force or of a position of power guaranteed by political authority. There are two main sub-types: colonial capitalism, operated through plantations with compulsory payments or compulsory labour and by monopolistic and compulsory trade. On the other hand there is the fiscal type, profit making by farming of taxes and of offices, whether in the home area or in colonies. [I think this is self-explanatory.]

5. The opportunities for orientation to profit opened up by unusual transactions with political bodies. [I think he might mean corruption.]

6. The orientation to opportunities for profit of the following types: (*a*) to purely speculative transactions in standardized commodities or in the securities of an enterprise;

(*b*) by carrying out the continuous financial operations of political bodies; (*c*) by the promotional financing of new enterprises in the form of sale of securities to investors; (*d*) by the speculative financing of capitalist enterprises and of various other types of economic organization with the purpose of a profitable regulation of markets or of attaining power. [Again, the system we have just been talking about.]   (Weber 1922/1947: 276–7)

Weber goes on to point out that types 1 & 6 are peculiar to western Europe whereas the others can usually be found in other places but do not have the same type of consequences that produce modern western societies. The theme of the uniqueness of the West is central to Weber's sociology and his understanding of historical development and we will come across it, in close relationship to his notion of the rationalization of society, time and time again. These issues will be pursued in detail in the Chapter 13 but you should bear them in mind throughout this chapter.

Now, what can we take from Weber's economic sociology. First of all, it is important to note that it is an *economic sociology*—unlike that of Marx, which was a sociological economics. Holton and Turner (1989), who offer an apologia for Weber's work on the economy, argue, I think rightly, that Weber was well aware of the alternatives to capitalism, and Marxist criticisms that he takes the market economy as a natural given (e.g. Clarke 1994) are mistaken. I think the real criticism from a Marxist point of view would be that Weber takes as a basis what is actually the result of complicated underlying processes and structures, and it is in fact his methodological individualism that leads him to do so. For Weber, individuals are taken for granted and come into relation with each other through the market; for Marx, individuals in this sense are a result of the market. For Weber, the free market unifies individuals; for Marx, the free market individualizes social groups.

Turner and Holton look at Weber's conception of the market as a way of overcoming what they call the problem of intersubjectivity—if we start with the individual then how do we explain collectivities, mutual understanding, and so on? In the form known as 'the problem of order', this is sometimes seen as the *raison d'être* of sociology, *the* question that it sets out to solve. However, it is only *the* problem if we start with the individual; if we start—as did Durkheim, and in effect Marx—with society or social facts, then the problem of order arises in a different and much less basic way.

It is probably fairly clear that I am not very enthusiastic about this part of Weber's work. He does seem to me to take too much for granted and he offers us an understanding of the institutions necessary for market capitalism to reach its apogee, but he does not offer more than that. If we read him as giving us a whole truth, I think we are lost; if we look at him as talking about the surface preconditions for a market economy, he becomes interesting.

Class, status, and party

If Weber had a theory of social structure, rather than a theory of individuals act-ing together, then his comparatively short piece on class, status, and party, together with his analysis of the state and bureaucracy, would be at the centre of it. Despite its brevity, it has had a massive influence on American sociology, where status was a concern for structural functionalism, and on British soci-ology, where it has been used to produce a more elaborate analysis of stratification than that offered by Marx.

Each grouping is focused around, or 'oriented towards', power as an independent point of conflict. Each represents an aspect of and a basis for power.

CLASS

There are moments when Weber sounds distinctly Marxist. Class is defined by property. The ownership of property confers a real power on the employer, and lack of ownership of property confers a real powerlessness on the worker—Weber here recognizes that the worker is compelled to work. He does not talk about 'wage slavery' but he does talk about the 'wage whip', but at the same time he did not seem to see the conflict that arose from this, or the worker's lack of property in itself, as having the significance that Marx attached to it. He criti-cized Marx's definition for not being able to take account of divisions, partic-ularly amongst the proletariat—almost anybody who wasn't a property owner could be a worker; as a university teacher I would find myself alongside a coal miner, a computer programmer, and an airline pilot, all of us in the working class, and it is difficult to see how any common interest could result from that. We have already seen that, in fact, Marx's categorization was not quite so simple, but that is by the way.

Weber's definition of class was in terms of a group of people who shared the same 'typical chance for a supply of goods, external living conditions and per-sonal life experiences insofar as this chance is determined by the . . . power to dispose of goods or skill for the sake of income in a given economic order. . . . "Class situation" is, in this sense, ultimately "market situation" ' (Weber 1922/1947: 181–2). One thing that is clear about this definition is that it does not help the basic problem of arriving at a coherent theory of class. Instead of the unlikely collection of people that I listed just now belonging to one class, we would, by Weberian criteria, each belong to separate classes; and it could be argued that there are different classes even within, say, the same occupational group, depending, say, on age or geographical area.

There is one occasion on which Weber tends to move away from this view to a position closer to Marx. In *Economy and Society* (1925/1978) he talks about the classes developing as 'solidary' as opposed to 'associative' organizations, which is closer to the way Marx saw the working class, if not the other classes, as a community. This occurs, he suggests, when a group shares the chances of moving between a limited number of class positions, but moving into a wider range of positions is blocked by power differentials. Thus one might argue that women have a limited number of employment possibilities between which they can move, but major changes are blocked by men and this gives rise to the possibility that women could form themselves into a social class. Perhaps this approximates to what has happened over the last thirty years. The classes defined in this way that Weber saw in the first decades of this century were the working class, the petty bourgeoisie, the intelligentsia and specialists, and classes privileged by property and education.

If Marx leaves us with too simple a model of class structure, then Weber leaves us with a complex and chaotic one. It is a definition of class from surface factors, and that can be useful, but it is not a model of a class *structure*. I think if we return to the notion of there being different levels of reality, then we can make sense of Weber as offering a way of understanding groupings within limits set by an underlying (Marxist) definition and as pointing to the complexity of class groupings. In a classic Weberian text, Rex and Moore (1967) talk about 'housing classes' to refer to empirically defined groupings—council tenants, private tenants, landlords, owner-occupiers, etc.—*within* the major classes, while David Lockwood (1958) used the concept of market position to explain why white-collar workers did not identify with manual workers. These different positions will interrelate with the underlying class position in different ways. Perhaps the right sort of imagery is that Weber offers us a pattern of groups which are always on the edge of collapsing into chaos, whereas, by combining Weber and Marx, the chaos is transformed into a sort of kaleidoscope—changing patterns of groups held in an underlying framework.

An alternative way of thinking about this is that implied by Holton and Turner (1989). They point out that Weber saw the formation of class communities as a contingent, rather than a necessary, feature of capitalism, and one constantly undermined by developments in social mobility. In this context Weber can be seen as describing a stage in the historical disappearance of social class as a significant feature in social life. There are a number of reasons to be careful of such an argument, not least because people have been announcing the disappearance of class for a number of decades and the arguments continue. I think the weightier argument, however, is that, even if social classes do not play the role that Marx thought they would, there is a continuity in the social classes that people identify as important and they seem to coalesce around the underlying framework that Marx identified rather than forming and disappearing purely and simply around market positions.

STATUS

The same sort of ambiguity can be found in the way that Weber deals with status or 'social honour'; on the one hand, he acknowledges that in the long term it goes with the possession of material wealth, but he also wants to maintain that it is an autonomous focus for conflict over power. 'Status situation' refers to that part of a person's life chances which are decided by the social esteem in which he or she is held; such esteem might be positive or negative. An attempt in the UK during the 1970s to form a public-contact group for paedophiles did not do much to improve the life chances of the organizers.

Along with the social esteem, we can often find a specific lifestyle and restrictions on social contact which are not subordinated to economic interest. Thus somebody who joins the Roman Catholic priesthood will wear distinctive clothes, will live according to distinctive rules, and will not marry, however rich his possible bride and however much she might offer to donate her riches to his church. In other status groups marriage might be prescribed within the group—orthodox Jewish communities would be a good example. There is usually a monopoly of ideal or material goods which is part or parcel of stratification by status—thus only the Roman Catholic priesthood can administer the sacraments and once upon a time, when services were in Latin, they might have been the only ones to understand what was happening.

At the time Weber was writing, there was probably a greater distinction—in some respects—between status and class than there is today, especially in Europe. For example, the distinction in British upper-class circles, especially in the nineteenth century, between 'old' and 'new' money meant that the impoverished aristocrat of a renowned and once powerful family might receive much more esteem and respect than the newly rich industrialist; and it is a well-documented fact that the latter would wish their children to marry into the former—although, of course, honour did not rub off as easily as the *nouveau riche* might have hoped.

I have already suggested that we can combine Marx's theory of class with Weber's, and the notion of status groups can add to such a model, as groups within or cutting across several classes. However, Weber's ambivalent relationship to Marxism remains. Bendix points out that:

The distinction between class and status group is directly related to Weber's sociology of religion. On the one hand, he investigated group formation on the basis of shared religious ideas. Here ideas serve as a bulwark of group cohesion, a means of status distinction, and as a basis for monopolizing economic opportunities. On the other hand, he examined given social groups . . . in terms of the religious propensities engendered by their class situation and status interests. Here ideas become a reflection of material interests.   (Bendix 1966: 87)

So status groups of this type are difficult to distinguish from social classes, in Weber's definition at any rate. So far I have talked about Weber defining such groups at the empirical level, rather than in the context of some underlying structure, but another way of putting the same thing is that most of the time class and status are defined by the distribution of goods and services, not (as in Marx) by their production.

There are other types of status group that are perhaps more significant for Marxist theory—these are groups which cut across social-class boundaries but are based on another 'solidary' identity—such as ethnicity or religion. Thus it is arguable the we can understand more about Northern Ireland using the notion of status group than we can using that of social class (although I think both would be necessary), and perhaps the same might be true of the former Yugoslavia; and of course ethnicity has become particularly important, as has gender, in contemporary societies, and it is conflict drawn along these lines as much as class conflicts which divides these societies. Weber thought that status conflict would come to the fore in periods of economic stability, rather than rapid economic change, which would bring class conflict. Frank Parkin, writing in the mid-1980s, shows how oversimple an assumption this is.

This proposition would seem to have a fairly limited historical validity. Class conflict in the nineteenth and early twentieth centuries was no doubt sufficiently acute and absorb- ing as to force most other social questions into the background. Class action during this period was aimed not merely at a more just distribution of goods and opportunities but at the incorporation of the propertyless masses into civil society. When the conflict between classes revolves upon issues as large as the political transformation of society, it might well be that all status group demands pale into insignificance. But when class conflict becomes domesticated and routinized, there is more social leeway for the fur- therance of both class and status ambitions. Under modern capitalism, conflicts on the class and status fronts seem able to co-exist quite happily.   (Parkin 1982: 100)

Weber suggests that ethnic groups in particular offer their members a social esteem that is not available to them in the wider hierarchy—and it is a source of esteem open to everybody in the group; it is worth adding in support of Weber's contention that within the wider social hierarchy it is often amongst the lowest strata of the dominant ethnic group that we can find the most rabid hostility to subordinate groups—here ethnicity becomes the only claim to status and hence vitally important, to be reinforced at every opportunity. Holton and Turner (1989) argue that the notion of status group is particularly important for under- standing modern multicultural societies.

The other important criterion for closure of status groups is educational quali- fication; professional groups such as doctors have a series of educational hurdles to pass, and these arguably become more and more specialized. Groups 'profes- sionalize' by demanding higher qualifications—in the UK over the last decade the professionalisation of psychotherapy has led to increasingly elaborate and strictly governed training and has moved towards insisting on a Master's degree as an entry qualification. This leads to a consistent inflation of qualifications—if everyone has a Master's degree, then advancement will require doctorates.

Here we have a very different conception of the professional group from the one we found in Durkheim. If for Durkheim the professional group was able to develop its own norms and values, its own *conscience collective* which governed the behaviour of its members and provided a source of social solidarity, then for Weber they were groups vigorously pursuing their own self-interest on the market. In reality, both positions have something of the truth and it seems reasonable to suggest that whichever dimension predominates depends upon the state of the wider society: in a free-market economy, which moves closer to Weber's ideal type, the professions will pursue their own interests against others; in a society where the free market is limited, then perhaps the development of a collective morality is more important. But it must not be forgotten that both will go on all the time; human animals are creatures of self-interest *and* they are rule-following, moral beings as well. The difficulty is holding both sides together.

Parkin points out a significant and puzzling lack in Weber's treatment of status groups: the lack of any reference to the state, which can grant legal monopolies. This prevents him, argues Parkin, from developing any analysis of structured inequality. However, I have already suggested it was Weber's overall individualism which tended towards blinding him to the more structured and collective aspects of society, although he did sometimes talk about the state and the state bureaucracy as if it were itself the most important status group. My own point of view is that, if we start from a methodological individualism, then it is very difficult to talk about the state without seeing it as a privileged status group, seeking to pursue its own interests, and we lose sight of notions of the public interest or the common good.

PARTY

With the question of political parties we run into Weber's scepticism about democratic politics and the possibilities of social change. He did not think political parties would be able to drastically to effect social reform or bring about greater economic equality. He distinguishes between patronage parties—which were concerned primarily with gaining power and dividing up the goodies between themselves—and parties of principle—which ended up, through a process of bureaucratization, doing much the same thing. Parties, too, become status groups pursuing their own self-interest. Weber was sympathetic to the view of his contemporary, Robert Michels, who argued (1911/1962) that such ideals inevitably become displaced—that, as the political party is organized, so the maintenance of the organization itself takes priority over the original ends, and an inevitable process of bureaucratization takes place.

So here we find a strange determinism in Weber's position—strange at least if we think of Weber as the theorist who contested Marx's determinism; it is not socialism that is inevitable and the mode of production that determines politics; rather it is the process of rationalization that determines everything. We shall see later what he thought of socialism.

Power, domination, and authority

We have already touched briefly on Weber's political sociology, his theory of the state and of authority in imperatively coordinated associations. I want to turn now to the centre of that political sociology, his more developed theories of power, domination, and the state. The starting point for this is his typology of types of domination: charismatic, traditional, and legal-rational. These are *ideal-typical* in the sense discussed in Chapter 5, and they are also related to his typifications of action, particularly in the case of legal-rational and traditional authority. There is also a possible historical order to them as well—most obvious again in the case of traditional and legal-rational domination, but this will be more significant in Chapter 13. In practice, the three types can coexist in any situation, but it is likely that one or the other will be dominant. Groups competing for power are always trying to transform the means at their disposal and so in modern society in particular there is an inherent instability in the form of domination.

I will follow Bendix's (1966) order of exposition of the different types, which is the opposite to that of Weber himself, and for the same reason: that, in Weber's own discussion, the point he is trying to make gets lost. I will begin with the notion of charisma, which has entered everyday language.

CHARISMATIC LEADERSHIP

> The term 'charisma' will be applied to a certain quality of an individual personality by virtue of which he is set apart from ordinary men and treated as endowed with supernatural, superhuman or at least specifically exceptional powers and qualities. These are such as are not accessible to the ordinary person, but are regarded as of divine origin or as exemplary, and on the basis of them the individual concerned is treated as a leader.
>
> (Weber 1922/1947: 358–9)

This type of power should be distinguished from power on the basis of charismatic authority. Thus Jesus possessed charisma and the disciples obeyed him because they knew him and he was (presumably) a remarkable man; the pope possesses an authority based on that charisma, but without the personal aspect;

people obey the pope, if in fact they obey him, without knowing Jesus except in some metaphorical sense. Charismatic leadership can arise at times of trouble when other forms of domination do not seem to be fulfilling their task; it is a product of a collective enthusiasm which sees in this person a solution to the troubles that plague them, and the leader promises such a solution. There is a dramatic opposition between charismatic leadership and everyday life; the leader must seem to be separate from the concerns of everyday life, and the leader's disciples are themselves special, separating themselves from their own past lives. Bendix quotes Luke's gospel (14: 26): 'If any man come to me and hates not his father, and mother, and wife, and children and brethren and sisters, yea, and his own life also, he cannot be my disciple.' This is the call of the millenarian leader—'leave everything behind, follow me and we will save the world'. The pope, of course, is not noted for encouraging people to abandon their families and this marks an important difference.

Charismatic leadership is of the same sociological type, whether the activity of the movement is legal and illegal, morally good or bad: Jesus Christ, Adolf Hitler, Robin Hood, Mahatma Ghandi all fall into the same category. Under such leadership, well-established rules, whether traditional or legal-rational, are abandoned.

We can get an alternative view of charismatic leadership by returning to Marx's analysis of Bonaparte's *coup*. Bonaparte, according to Marx, came to personify the interests of the peasantry, the lumpenproletariat, and others who could not represent themselves; if we combine this with Durkheim's notion of the sacred and of 'collective effervescence', it is possible to see an alternative understanding of charisma: not as a quality of the leader but as a quality projected on to a leader by virtue of situation, opportunity, and events. Thus, for a few years it appeared that the British prime minister Mrs Thatcher was the most remarkable British leader of the century—she certainly possessed charisma. But it came and went: the first few years of her premiership were not at all successful and her charisma seemed to appear with victory in the war over the Malvinas and then was reinforced for some by a victory in an industrial conflict against the coal miners, and then it disappeared very quickly as she lost power in 1990. Her charismatic power was projected upon her and then retracted. Great leaders are created by their followers.

Charismatic leadership exists in its pure form only for a short period and has to adjust to the reassertion of the demands of everyday life—the opposite problem to the other forms of authority, which are adjusted to everyday life but cannot deal with times of trouble. The need to adjust to everyday life involves the 'routinization of charisma'. In the case of Christ, for example, the disciples became apostles and priests, and they travelled around setting up branches of the church in different places; they created an organization. If non-Christians will forgive me, this is a particularly good example to carry through to illustrate Weber's points.

The first major problem comes with the succession and Weber argues here that there is a special relationship between charismatic and tradition authority, since both are invested in a particular person rather than a set of rules. A new leader has to be designated—possibly on the basis of charismatic properties that he or she is thought to possess, or he or she is appointed by the original leader of the disciples. Thus St Peter became the first pope and his successors have been appointed in unbroken line by the College of Cardinals. The further we get away from the original leader, the further we are from the unique qualities of 'pure charisma—as charisma is passed on but becomes second-hand, less powerful.

Charismatic leadership, once it is established, is in a sort of Catch-22 situation; if it is to be preserved, it must transform itself to the demands of everyday life—a society needs stable families rather than people going off to change the world; on the other hand, when it transforms itself, the charisma begins to fade. Another crucial problem is that the disciples themselves wish to ensure their own power and position, which is threatened by the instability of the charismatic leadership of just one person. This pursuit of self-interest becomes easier if the charisma is somehow lifted from its original leader and attached to a position or to a family. This is effectively what has happened in the Roman Catholic Church and it is also a basis for the British monarchy. Charisma can be inherited (the monarchy), or passed on by ceremony (the Roman Catholic Church) and education. Familial charisma ensures only succession, but institutional charisma takes on a lasting power as an organization which can act as a balance to secular power. The routinization of charisma in an institutional form involves the emergence of priests as a distinct status group, making universalistic claims to dominance, over and above the claims of family and, as time goes on, nation as well. A body of knowledge—theology—grows up and is taught to new entrants. Such churches do not exist everywhere (as we shall see in Chapter 13). Where they do exist they are inevitably conservative; the priesthood hold on to their privilege of interpreting the word of God to their followers and new charismatic leaders are resisted. Monastic orders are often a threat to the church because they embody the way of life of the original charismatic leader, renouncing the world. The monk is a 'model' religious person, perhaps the first proper professional of the western world.

Weber spends a lot of time discussing the relationship between the secular and religious power, a competition which continues today in all sorts of interesting ways. In the USA, charismatic religious leaders offer a challenge to the federal government, particularly when that government is dominated by the Democrats; and in the UK the relationship between the Church of England, an 'established' church supported by the state, has moved from a very close connection with the ruling party in the first part of the century (when it was known as 'the conservative party at prayer') to a situation where it was distancing itself from government policy fairly rapidly during the 1980s, and thus coming under attack for ignoring its spiritual duty and inappropriately engaging in politics.

Weber points out, rightly, that for most of the time a compromise is reached. Each power needs the other: the church can supply ideological justification for the state, whilst the state can protect the church.

It is tempting to read a theory of historical development into Weber's work, perhaps that charismatic leadership pushes forward social change, or that it provides a bridge between traditional and rational-legal forms of domination. Bendix (1966) suggests that this would be mistaken. If the social order is inherently unstable, than charismatic leaders can arise at any time. I think both interpretations are tenable—there are different Webers. Frank Parkin seems to think that Weber underestimated the likelihood of charisma transforming a legal-rational society.

Weber would have been unsurprised at the spectacle of the sons and daughters of the modern bourgeoisie held in thrall by chubby mystics from the East. He might, though, have been more surprised, as well as deeply shocked, at the apparent ease with which a charismatic leader on his own doorstep would revolutionize an entire society and its rational structure to the most devastatingly irrational purposes.   (Parkin 1982: 87)

But, of course, Hitler was not just a product of his own charisma or his own powers, or of the disorder of the Weimar Republic. He was much more the product of the belief that the German people placed in Hitler's offer of an easy target to blame for their troubles and their surrender of their own powers to him.

Weber suggests that, in any form of domination, his three types will exist side by side in different relationships to each other. Charismatic leadership can exist in any historical period, but not its more routinized forms—familial charisma, for example, may not exist in rational-legal forms of domination, although even here one might argue that the existence of a constitutional monarchy belies this.

TRADITIONAL DOMINATION

The pure form of traditional domination is 'patriarchalism'—the domination of the father over the household, the members of whom live together and work together. The women of the household are physically and mentally dependent on the master, the children are helpless or have been trained into dutiful obedience, and the servants, as well as being trained, require the master's protection. The master's will is absolute, and not limited by law; only by tradition. It is as if he has a credit of tradition which he can spend by demanding tributes from his household; but if he should overspend, and demand more than is sanctioned by tradition, then his power could be in trouble. Patriarchalism runs into difficulty first when the master's property grows; his initial reaction is to divide his land up between his dependents, but together they then develop an interest in having their rights and duties clarified—they are no longer so amenable to the master's arbitrary authority. But, once these rights are written down, they become more limited than when the master simply had to ensure the goodwill of his dependents. The problems multiply when large areas of land are involved.

The result of this extension is patrimonialism—which existed in the despotic regimes of Asian and European mediaeval society—where the master's household grows to sometimes an immense size over a large area, in which all his subjects owe him the same loyalty as the immediate members of his household. The administration of the society is bound up closely with the administration of the household. The ruler's domination of a large area enables him to carry out his own trade and to control and profit from that of others in order to maintain his extended household. The further extended these regimes become, the more decentralized they tend to become, perhaps with rights and duties to be determined by independent courts. But on the whole power remains personal, and office-holders become office-holders through 'connections, favours, promises and privileges'.

Such regimes are inherently unstable because of the difficulty of keeping the loyalty of widespread forces, and they can suddenly disappear. Patrimonial domination can develop through the use of military force as a personal instrument. If administrators are appointed, they can help extend the dominated area, but they can come to form a status group that can contest power with a central authority—perhaps rather like the barons who forced King John to sign the Magna Carta—or they can be pawns in struggles between central authorities, particularly when the officials are celibate clergymen who do not have a family interest of their own and who can be kept in order by the promise of a pension.

Weber suggests that feudalism is a second variety of patriarchalism. In a feudal system, the nobility are united by a sense of status honour. He suggests that in England the Norman invasion instituted an essentially patrimonial system which was opposed by an entrenched local baron, and the two systems became entwined, often producing conflict between monarchy and nobility. To balance the power of the nobility, the monarchy created local notables—the yeomanry, which developed a strong sense of its own status honour.

It is the development of a distinct status honour that takes us into feudalism. The paternal authority of the master is replaced by a contractual relationship in which the subordinate owes military service—or whatever—in return for the protection of the master. As Bendix points out, this distinction is really useful only if we remain on the level of theory—on the ground, there were a wide mixture of arrangements. Weber is working at a fairly abstract level of ideal types. The existence of a contractual relationship means that rights and duties are more formalized than in patrimonial systems.

The military becomes important when the feudal lord finds it necessary to raise a cavalry equipped with horse and armour like his own. This becomes a military élite in fief to the lord, which, unlike patrimonial authority, can dispense with the goodwill of its subjects. Whereas education in patrimonial regimes tended towards preparation for administrative service, education under feudalism is for martial skills and aristocratic honour and nonchalance. Frank Parkin points out that the peasantry are a silent witness to all the power struggles between the lords and their officials and knights.

When we come to his understanding of legal-rational authority, it is more difficult to deny that there is a theory of history in Weber's work—it all leads to the modern word, and, in addition to his ideal-type methodology, I think that one of the reasons that he draws a distinction between patrimonialism and feudalism is because the latter is a step towards modernity, via the establishment of formal rights and duties.

LEGAL-RATIONAL DOMINATION

There are, according to Weber, four defining characteristics of the modern state. First, it has a legal and administrative order which is subject to change by legislation—not by the whim of a lord or the dictat of a charismatic leader. Secondly, it has an administration which works in accordance with legislation—civil servants and the judiciary do not make up their own rules but implement those formed by the legislature. The state has binding authority of all its members—membership is usually by birth—and over the acts carried out in its territory. Finally, it can use force if that is legally prescribed or permitted. The modern state is legitimate if people believe in its legitimacy—and as with other forms of domination, this argument is circular and illustrates something important about Weber's work. Laws are legitimate if they are enacted according to the law. Each system justifies itself—traditional domination is justified by tradition, charismatic domination by charisma. There is no overall or superior set of values by means of which we choose better or worse systems. We cannot choose between the three on any rational grounds, and each can be justified only on its own grounds. Weber goes on to discuss the 'natural-law' justification which replaces tradition and the routinization of charisma. The basic principle is the individual's right to acquire or dispose of property, and this freedom is limited only by the fact that it must not impose limits on itself—so, for example, trade-union closed shops or legal monopolies do not accord with natural law. He thought that a conception of positivist law might be replacing that of natural law, but what was important was that in practice there was a general recognition of legitimacy of enacted laws. This implied that any norm could be enacted as a law with the expectation that it would be obeyed; government and government apparatuses are bound by the abstract system that these laws comprise, and justice is the application of these laws. People who hold authority do so by virtue of being temporary office-holders rather than from possessing a personal authority, and people obey the laws rather than the office-holders who enforced them. The state could not interfere with individual rights without the consent of the people through their duly elected representatives.

Generations of students have come to know Weber through his idea type of bureaucracy, the features of which have probably been learnt by heart by more students than any other sets of ideas in sociology. Bureaucracy is the most typical organizational form of legal-rational domination. Under the rule of law, a bureaucracy is governed by the following principles. Again my own comments follow in square brackets.

(1) A continuous organization of official functions bound by rules. [not at the whim of a leader, or an official. We expect government departments, for example, to be open five days a week, excluding public holidays, for a fixed and predictable number of hours a day, and to proceed in a predictable way. They should not be closed when the boss wants a day off or open on a Sunday because he or she wants to get away from the family.]

(2) A specified sphere of competence. This involves (*a*) a sphere of obligation to perform functions which has been marked off as part of a systematic division of labour. (*b*) The provision of the incumbent with the necessary authority to carry out these functions. (*c*) That the necessary means of compulsion are clearly defined and their use is subject to definite conditions. [Thus the Inland Revenue will deal only with taxation, and another agency will deal with social security, yet another health, and so on; there is a systematic organization of the different agencies; the official who assesses my taxes is authorized to do so, and we both know what powers the official has to penalize me—he or she cannot fine me because of bad handwriting, but there might be some sanction if I delay returning my forms for too long after the due date. However, I know that I will not face execution. I am using the state bureaucracy as an example, but Weber points out that such organizations—'administrative organs'—can exist in the armed forces, private organizations, and political parties.]

(3) The organization of offices follows the principle of hierarchy; that is, each lower office is under the control and supervision of a higher one. There is a right of appeal and of statement of grievances from the lower to the higher. Hierarchies differ in respect to whether and in what cases complaints can lead to rulings from an authority at various points higher in the scale, and as to whether changes are imposed from higher up or the responsibility for such changes is left to the lower office, the conduct of which was the subject of complaint. [Different organizations will deal with complaints in a different way, but there will be formal procedures. Although currently hierarchies might be being 'flattened out', what seems to be happening is a reduction of levels rather than a fundamental change in organization. And in some areas—the UK National Health Service, for example—levels of management seem to be increasing.]

(4) The rules which regulate the conduct of an office may be technical rules or norms. In both cases, if their application is to be fully rational, specialized training is necessary. It is thus normally true that only a person who has demonstrated an adequate technical training is qualified to be a member of the administrative staff of such an organized group, and hence only such persons are eligible for appointment to official positions. [Again, there is a contemporary deskilling going on, but I am not sure that it dramatically changes the nature of the bureaucratic organization. There is an argument that in contemporary societies the norms which govern public organiza-

tions are changing and that, for example, notions of public service are declining in favour of self-interest.]

(5) In the rational type it is a matter of principle that the members of the administrative staff should be completely separated from ownership of the means of production and administration. Officials, employees and workers attached to the administrative staff do not themselves own the non-human means of production and administration. These are rather provided for their use in kind or in money, and the official is obligated to render an accounting of their use. There exists, furthermore, in principle complete separation of the property belonging to the organization, which is controlled within the sphere of office, and the personal property of the official, which is available for his own private uses. There is a corresponding separation of the place in which official functions are carried, the 'office' in the sense of premises, from living quarters. [This last distinction is now being blurred by the development of computer technology which enables people to work from home for the office, but the distinction between personal and official property is still quite important. I might sometimes use office envelopes for personal purposes, and sometimes use my personal telephone for office purposes. But if this distinction is blurred too far then it opens the door either to exploitation—I have to supply my own notepaper, use my own telephone, buy my own filing cabinets and desk, or I don't get the job—or corruption—I use the university's property and facilities to run, say, a small estate agency; or I use a research grant to pay off the mortgage of my house. The move towards short-term contract-based employment also blurs some of the boundaries—if I did not own my own computer and have an office at home perhaps I would be unable to work at my job.]

(6) In the rational type case, there is also a complete absence of appropriation of his official position by the incumbent. Where 'rights' to an office exist, as in the case of judges, and recently of an increasing proportion of officials and even of workers, they do not normally serve the purpose of appropriation by the official but of securing the purely objective and independent character of the conduct of the office so that it is oriented only to the relevant norms. [Thus I do not own my position in the university—I can't sell it to the highest bidder, or nominate the person who will take over when I retire, or will it to my son when I die; on the other hand, I did once have tenure—it was not possible to fire me if, for example, the university wanted to cut back on its wages bill, and I could not be fired because I was saying things that people didn't like, or investigating something which presented a threat to those in the organization who were higher up in the hierarchy. This acted as a protection for academic freedom, just as a judge's tenure of office acts as a guarantee of his judicial independence—he cannot be sacked for giving a decision that upsets those in political power. The fact that academic tenure has been eaten away in the return to the values of a market economy is perhaps a matter for some reflection.]

(7) Administrative acts, decisions and rules are formulated and recorded in writing, even in cases where oral discussion is the rule or is even mandatory. This applies at least to preliminary discussions and proposals, to final decisions, and to all sorts of orders and rules. The combination of written documents and a continuous organization of official functions constitutes the 'office' which is the central focus of all types of modern corporate action. [Thus all interaction can be traced in written

records which can be used as evidence in complaints that the rules have been broken, and can be used for reference purposes. This consistent recording of decisions and encounters seems to be on the increase, in the case of the UK at least, as a result of ways of attempting to make public services—the health service and education, for example—'accountable'. The way to establish that we are doing our jobs properly is to write down what we do. One might think that there was a conflict between formal and substantive rationality here.]   (Weber 1922/1947: 330–2)

Weber goes on to mention that he has not mentioned the supreme head of a system of legal authority, which, as we shall see, is important for his understanding of democracy. Pursuing his analysis of bureaucracy, he goes on to talk about the employment of the bureaucrat—only the head of the organization can hold a position through 'appropriation, election or [being] designated for the succession' (ibid. 333); but even then the scope of his or her power is legally limited.

The pure type of bureaucratic employment leaves the office-holder personally free outside his or her professional obligations: my job is delineated more or less clearly, and my boss cannot tell me what to do in my free time outside the organization or call on me to wait at table when he or she has a dinner party—as might happen under patrimonial authority. The employee is part of a clearly organized hierarchy—I know who is superior to me and who is below me in the hierarchy—and each position has a clearly defined 'sphere of competence'—i.e. I know what I can and cannot legitimately do. The official holds office through a contractual relationship for which there is an open and free selection, and office-holders are selected on the basis of technical qualifications—rather than, say, personal friendship or wealth or whatever might have been the basis of selection under patrimonial authority. Officials are paid a salary, often with a pension attached; they can be dismissed only in specified circumstances, although they can resign at any time. Salary is usually graded in accordance with position in the organization, although, Weber adds, interestingly, that account might be taken of the requirements of the official's social status. The office is the primary or sole occupation of the official (again unlike patrimonial authority), and the official has a career where promotion comes through seniority and/or achievement, and is decided upon by superiors in the hierarchy. The official does not own his or her office or means of administration, and is subject to systematic discipline in the way he or she carries out the duties of office.

Bureaucratic domination is unstable in the same way as other systems in that it is constantly open to change through the struggle for power between different status groups, but these changes in modern society tend to be changes in control over bureaucratic organization rather than in the organization itself. All these issues will be taken up in Chapter 13, when we look at Weber's conception of social change; there his sociology of law and of religion will become important.

Conclusion

We do not find in Weber references to societies as a whole, whether in terms of modes of production or the Durkheimian 'society' as something which exists over and above individuals; but nor do we find the individual stories that one might expect from Weber's methodology, and, as I have already mentioned, there is an unexpected determinism in his account of modern societies. The key to all of this is his notion of rationality, which brings together the myriad of individual actions into recognizable patterns and also makes sense at least of modern history as a process of rationalization. Thus the changes in the labour market that we have experienced over the last decades can be seen as a result of the development of capitalism as a system embodying rational calculability. One of the clearest accounts of a Weberian approach to these changes can be found in Holton and Turner (1989) and they point to the way in which Weber, like Marx, saw capitalism as bringing about a process of constant revolution. We can see this process at the root of regular changes in values—it seems that at almost any time over the last 250 years at least we can find notable people lamenting a decline in values. The Weberian approach raises the issues of the dominance of instrumental rationality, a favourite topic of modern critical Marxism, and in the Weberian context the relationship between formal and substantive rationality. A common contemporary debate is about how far formally rational activity on the part of enterprises—'downsizing', 'contracting out', etc.—undermines the community or society in which this occurs together with its more tradition values, creating disillusion and possibly unrest; these actions could be seen as substantially irrational.

To begin with, this constant revolution creates social classes, but then, a Marxist would argue, fragments them—a Weberian would argue destroys them. They point to the evidence about the decline of the traditional urban working class that emerged during the 1970s and 1980s and that has clearly accelerated since then. They follow Parkin in making a distinction between status groups that develop *within* social classes, such as skill groups, and the distinctions say between the industrial and financial bourgeoisie, and status blocs which cut across social classes, and they suggest that modern capitalism, as it undermines the traditional proletariat, creates new status blocs, based perhaps on gender or ethnicity or age. In this context the new political movements can be seen as status-group movements battling in the struggle for political power; it might be possible to see established political parties as losing their traditional connections with social classes but establishing new connections with status blocs. In democratic societies, the value of equality tends to inflate expectations and it provides a central issue for competition between status groups.

Thus a modern Weberian would not see capitalism in terms of some central contradiction or of class struggle; Holton and Turner suggest that there is in fact a particular tension between democracy and the requirements of the market economy. If the principle of equality (democracy) is established, those who find themselves belonging to groups that are underprivileged will take action to correct the situation: 'The very success of democracy produces clientelism which requires greater bureaucratic regulation and state intervention, bringing about further social control within the political sphere and a greater tax burden of the economy' (Holton and Turner 1989: 155). The evidence in support of this can be found in all the equal opportunity and affirmative action legislation that has been established in the West over recent decades. This would include not only women and ethnic minorities but also gays and the disabled, those with learning difficulties, and so on. Underneath a lot of the silliness of 'political correctness', there are some serious issues. The contemporary state ends up administering a system of status blocs—Holton and Turner call these modern political systems 'state-administered status bloc politics'. Referring back to Weber's methodology, we see it as the result of the rational pursuit of a value—that of equality/democracy. We can now turn again to the basic dualisms (see Boxes 9.1–9.3).

Box 9.1. **An elaboration of Weber on the individual and society**

THE INDIVIDUAL	SOCIETY
Durkheim: the individual is formed and limited by society. He/she becomes more important in complex societies and individualism becomes the focus of the *conscience collective*, binding people together.	**Durkheim:** society exists over and above the individual, over whom it exercises an immense power, especially in less complex societies.
Marx: the 'individuated' individual is an idea produced as part of the development of capitalism. The 'natural' state of the individual is as an integral part of the group.	**Marx:** society is created by human action but acts back upon individuals as an external power—a dominant force in all but the most primitive and most advanced (communist) societies.
Weber: the individual is the only reality and analysis must start from individual rational action.	**Weber:** society is the rather fragile result of human interaction and struggles for power between different types of group.
Simmel: the individual life is engaged in a constant dialectic with social forms.	**Simmel:** 'society' is an increasingly important form organizing peoples' lives.

Box 9.2. **Weber on action and structure**

ACTION	STRUCTURE
Durkheim: there is no real theory of social action in Durkheim; the individual action is always conditioned by the group, and collective action is taken to reinforce the strength of the group.	**Durkheim:** in societies dominated by mechanical solidarity, the social structure consists of networks of kin groups (segmented societies); more complex modern societies consist of secondary groups formed by the division of labour and managed by the state.
Marx: in capitalist societies, the major agents are social classes—primarily the bourgeoisie and the proletariat. Some classes—the middle classes and the peasantry—do not share the life conditions which enable them to act as collective agents, and they tend to follow a strong leader.	**Marx:** different types of society have different forms of social structure. In capitalist societies the economic structure and resultant class structure are most important, and the state and state institutions are central features of social control.
Weber: status groups and market-based social classes can become 'collective actors' in the form of communal or more usually associative groups. Such groups exist only if members recognize a common identity or shared interest. The only 'real' actor remains the individual.	**Weber:** social structure is a fragile achievement; in traditional societies it is based on kin and status groups and in modern societies market-based classes enter into play. Bureaucratic organization and the state become more important.

Box 9.3. **Weber on social integration and system integration**

SOCIAL INTEGRATION

Durkheim: in all societies social integration is achieved through the *conscience collective*—shared ways of thinking (logic, conceptions of space and time, shared beliefs, norms, and values). In societies governed by mechanical solidarity, religion is central. In more complex modern societies, the *conscience collective* covers less of our lives but focuses on the ethics of individual freedom—it becomes a religion of humanity.

Marx: a 'false' and rather tenuous integration is achieved through ideologies, and the development of the market constantly threatens whatever integration is achieved. The major contending classes strive towards achieving their own integration in opposition to the others—the proletariat being the class most likely to achieve this.

Weber: at this point there is no real conception of social integration in Weber's work.

SYSTEM INTEGRATION

Durkheim: where mechanical solidarity predominates, system integration *is* social integration, guaranteed by the *conscience collective*. Where organic solidarity predominates, system integration is achieved through the division of labour.

Marx: system integration in capitalism is constantly threatened by class conflict and is supported by the state and by ruling ideologies.

Weber: it is a gross exaggeration to use the word 'system' in connection with the writings we have looked at in Chapter 9. Social structures are held together by different forms of domination and by stability provided by the market.

Further reading

All the relevant original texts for this chapter can be found in Weber, *The Theory of Social and Economic Organisation* (1922/1947), and Parson's introduction is a useful secondary source. Reinhard Bendix, *Max Weber: An Intellectual Portrait* (1966), contains a useful discussion on forms of domination and authority. A liberal interpretation of Weber can be found in R. J. Holton and B. S. Turner, *Max Weber on Economy and Society* (1989). The best brief account of Weber is Frank Parkin, *Max Weber* (1982). For good contemporary discussions, see Bryan S. Turner, *Max Weber: From History to Modernity* (1992), and *For Weber* (1996), and the good, but difficult *Maturity and Modernity: Nietzsche, Weber, Foucault and the Ambivalence of Reason* by David Owen (1994).

10 | Simmel: the social and the personal

Introduction

Simmel's originality; the mutual implications of Simmel and Durkheim.

Society and the individual

The evolution of the individual/group relation from a starting point of near merging; individuation and the development of individual norms; the paradox of the emergence of the individual and the growing power of the group; the development of multiple and conflicting roles; similarities between Simmel and Parsons; Simmel's radical critique of universal institutions; the significance of the size of social groups; the dyad and its internal fragility; the move from the dyad to larger groups.

The Philosophy of money

Value and exchange; human beings as valuing creatures; Simmel and existentialism; the objectification of subjective value; comparison with Marx; the exchange of value and the exchange of representations—Simmel and postmodernism; money as the extension of freedom and its psychological consequences; the growth of objective culture and the decreasing importance of the personality; Simmel's theory of alienation; the ambivalent implications of the division of labour; the decreasing ability to love objects; conclusion—Simmel and Marxism, Simmel and Weber.

Simmel's sociology

Simmel as a sociological impressionist. *Simmel on relationships*: faithfulness in the maintenance of relationships; the renegade; the distinctive nature of Simmel's notion of the life process; Simmel and Freud; gratitude as a cement for and generator of relationships; Simmel and Kleinian psychoanalysis; sociability as a play form and an example of formal sociology; domination as a form of interaction; domination by an individual, by a plurality, and by principle or law; comparison with Weber; conflict as a contribution to integration; the importance of secrecy; the secret society. *Simmel on social types*: the notion of type in literature and social theory; the miser as a seeker of total control; the miser's similarity to the spendthrift; the adventurer as an artist; the stranger as a newcomer and/or outsider; the objectivity of the outsider; objectivity as participation. *Simmel on modernity*: the psychological effects of urban living; the head ruling the heart; the sophistication of the town-dweller; the standardization of social life; the individual's conflicting needs for identification and separation and fashion as satisfying both; the psychological satisfactions of science; class and status differences in fashion. *Simmel on social groups*: the poor; different obligations and duties; the emergence of the poor as a group in modern societies through state welfare systems; modern developments of Simmel—the social construction of poverty; comparison with Marx; the aristocracy—united by the highest status honour; in-group marriage; the possibility of decadent emptiness; women, love, and sexuality: the masculine nature of objective culture; the psychological differences between men and women and comparison with modern gender theorists; the possibility of gender equality in relation to the objective culture; male and female sexuality; flirtation as a play form; Simmel's essentialism; comparison with Engels.

Conclusion

Simmel's compatibility with other theorists; further development of the basic dualisms.

Introduction

Whilst we might talk about Marxist or Weberian or Durkheimian sociologists, it is difficult to talk about 'Simmelians', although perhaps one might call a particular piece of work 'Simmelesque'. The true Simmelian would not be a Simmelian—he or she would be trying to convey an individual grasp of the world. There have been attempts to trace a phenomenological sociology and symbolic interactionism, and other strands in American sociology, back to his work, but a systematic linking is not possible and his most distinctive contribution is, I think, rightly identified by David Frisby (1981) as the idea that we might look at society as an aesthetic object, a work of art. In a remarkably romantic passage also quoted by Frisby, Simmel writes:

For us the essence of aesthetic observation and interpretation lies in the fact that the typical is to be found in what is unique, the lawlike in what is fortuitous, the essence and significance of things in the superficial and transitory. . . . To the adequately trained eye, the total beauty and total meaning of the world as a whole radiates from every single point.   (Simmel 1968: 71–2)

The whole world can exist in a grain of sand.

This imagery, I think, contradicts a strong contrast that Frisby, in this same text, draws between Durkheim and Simmel:

In contrast to Durkheim, who viewed society as a 'system of active forces' operating *upon* individuals, Simmel . . . sees society as constituted by interactional 'forces' *between* individuals. This enables him to reflect upon our experience of society in every single social interrelation in which we engage.   (Frisby 1992: 14)

The problem with this formulation is that each position implies the other. If we conceive of the social world as a web of relationships between individuals, then we can conceive of a *society* which this web comprises as something more solid than Weber suggests; and if we conceive of a society, then we need to consider the web of interaction which that society contains and, therefore, must determine. There is a difference of emphasis, but, in their unthought-out implications, Simmel and Durkheim can possibly be seen as *closer* to each other than either is to Marx or Weber, concentrating on different sides of the same version of the individual/society dualism.

In what follows I have been selective—there is a fair amount of Simmel's work that I do not cover. My criteria in choosing what to include are first that it conveys the most important aspects of his *œuvre* and his way of working, and, second, that it is relevant to the themes of this book.

Society and the individual

Here I want to concentrate on Simmel's analysis of the different forms of relationship which can exist between the individual and society, as it is set out in his early (1890) untranslated work and outlined by Frisby (1984). He begins with a conception of what we might call 'primitive' society, akin to Durkheim's notion of mechanical solidarity. In such societies there are comparatively few ties binding the individual into the group, but they bind him or her very closely. Simmel uses the analogy of an organism very clearly here (1890) and talks about its 'life forces'—its power to resist, its healing power, and its ability to preserve itself—but he insists, that these powers do not exist independently of the individuals in the society but are the expression of their interaction.

At this level there is a merging of the individual and the group in such a way that it is difficult to punish wrongdoing—there is a collective responsibility for actions. As societies become more differentiated, so individuation becomes possible and important. It also becomes more difficult for the individual to achieve his or her desired ends; we have to bargain with other people and this leads to individuals servicing each other's interests in ongoing bargaining—you scratch my back and I'll scratch yours. This, in turn, produces a collective morality which regulates the pursuit of self-interest. The more the individual comes to the fore, the more universal become the norms which govern behaviour. But at the same time the individual is subjected to a much greater range of stimuli and this reaches a stage where it is difficult to deal with. Frisby produces a quotation which could almost come from Durkheim:

The actions of a society, compared to those of the individual, possess an unswerving accuracy and expediency. The individual is pushed hither and thither by contradictory impressions, impulses and thoughts and his mind offers at each moment a multitude of possibilities for action, between which he not always knows how to choose with objective accuracy or even merely with subjective certainty. In contrast, the social group is indeed clear who it holds to be its friend and who its enemy.   (Simmel, quoted in Frisby 1984: 84)

We can already see a number of tensions present in Simmel's work. The larger and the more variegated the social group, the more developed, but also the more confused the individual becomes. Simmel, going back to the organic analogy, also talks about the principle of energy saving, which encourages individuals and the smaller social group to hand over functions to the wider collective. Thus, as the individual comes to the fore, so the society grows stronger. There is a further tension between the vulnerability of the individual arising from movement through incompatible spheres with conflicting interests—an idea which was tamed by later sociologists as role conflict—and the individual's ability to combine membership of widely different groups where he or she can find the support of a range of sympathetic people. Frisby writes:

Hence in the modern world there are other groups outside the family which may also possess a close-knit structure. How far this is the case can be measured by whether and to what extent they have evolved a particular sense of 'honour' which ensures desirable behaviour on the part of their members. Such groups do not require external compulsion to achieve this aim.   (Frisby 1984: 86)

In the light of a further century, we can perhaps see Simmel's suggestion as optimistic; the power of differentiation eats away at any sense of honour that might be developed. It is arguable that in the contemporary world people turn in on themselves in a fantasy that security can be found internally (Craib 1994).

Part of the paradox of Simmel can be found in two very different ideas that Frisby then takes up from his early work. When he talks about the division of labour, the argument is that, to begin with, it creates separate spheres and these come together on a more abstract level and a new social sphere appears. This is identical with Talcott Parsons's theory of social evolution which he developed half a century later—that there is a constant process of differentiation and reintegration at a higher level involving more universal values. This type of functionalist theory is generally considered to be a very conservative conception of social change and of social cohesion, leaving no space for conflict and assuming an inherent tendency to stability. At the same time, as Frisby points out, Simmel comments that it is a 'peculiar manifestation of social life' that 'meaningful, profoundly significant institutions and modes of life are replaced by others which *per se* appear utterly mechanical, external and mindless' (Frisby 1984: 88). This is a far from conservative view of the development of universal institutions.

SIZE MATTERS

Simmel (1908/1950) pays a great deal of attention to the size of social group and again foreshadows Parsons in working up from an analysis of the dyad, a relationship between two people; typically, however, he starts with the isolated individual, pointing out that isolation is itself a *social* relationship, a relationship to other people. It is not necessarily a matter of being alone—one is never more isolated than when in a crowd of strangers—and it is particularly important in relationships whose purpose is to deny isolation. For example, I might marry or live with another person in order to avoid isolation, but as soon as I am engaged in this relationship, periods in which each of us might be alone could be essential for its survival. In this context, isolation implies freedom which, like most things for Simmel, is double-edged. It can be seen as an attempt to avoid being dominated by my partner (or others in my social group) and it can also be seen as an attempt to dominate, to establish power over my partner or colleagues.

The most important thing about the dyad is that, whilst it might appear to be a cohesive unity to outsiders, it is not so to its members. They do not experience the dyad group as a collectivity over and above themselves; each partner sees only him- or herself confronted by the other. As a result the relationship is haunted by death—only one member has to die for the union to end, and this gives the dyad its particular emotional tone, that of an 'authentic sociological tragedy', but also an elegiac and sentimental quality. The dyad involves an irreplaceable individuality on the part of its members and without that (if, for example, all that matters to me is that my wife does the housework) it can disappear; in any case, it can easily go wrong for the same reason that it can generate intimacy: it doesn't 'result in a structure that goes beyond its elements' (Simmel 1950: 126). Intimacy requires sharing things unique to that relationship and the danger is that the two partners do not share the most important part of their personalities, the objective dimensions that they share with others, such as intellectual interests; if these are excluded from the relationship, they can undermine it. If all this sounds as if Simmel is talking about a friendship or an affair rather than marriage, you might be right. Marriage, he argues, is not a typical dyadic relationship, since both members can feel that they are part of a wider whole—the institution of marriage sanctioned by the wider society.

The dyad is also defined negatively, by the absence of features that are present in larger groups such as the delegation of individual powers to the group organization and the loss of individuality that we experience in a crowd. Things change as soon as a third member is added: one new member brings two new relationships—as well as *A–B*, there is *A–C* and *B–C*. This enables factions to form and the role of mediator to develop to protect the continued existence of the group. A third member can create or exploit conflict between the others in pursuit of his or her own interests. Anybody who has lived in a family of more than two should be able to recognize all this.

We can see in this the beginning of what we would now call a role structure, the beginnings of what Simmel calls 'objective culture', as well as the beginnings of *micro-sociology*. Many modern sociologists try to follow through from the discussion of small-scale interactions to large-scale social analysis. Parsons builds his system on the analysis of the dyad, and the most recent attempt can be found in Anthony Giddens's *The Constitution of Society* (1984). Giddens, however, loses the sophistication that comes with Simmel's acknowledgement of the qualitative changes resulting from increased group size. These take the form of emergent properties of the group process: in a group we find features that do not seem to belong to any one individual and the group is more than the sum of individuals who make it up; it has an existence over and above them.

We get a different sense of relationships between individuals when we turn to Simmel's *Philosophy of Money*.

The Philosophy of Money

> The attempt is made to construct a new story beneath materialism such that the explanatory value of the incorporation of economic life into the causes of intellectual culture is preserved, while these economic forms themselves are recognized as the result of more profound valuations and currents of psychological or even metaphysical preconditions.
>
> (Simmel 1900/1990: 56)

The Philosophy of Money was first published in Germany in 1900 and it develops a number of ideas from the earlier work. The quotation opening this section is an invitation to take a Lukacsian approach to Simmel. If economic forms are a product of human psychology combined with metaphysical causes, then it is unlikely that we can do anything about them—they become a fixed, 'second nature'. However, it is, of course, more complex than this.

VALUE AND EXCHANGE

Simmel begins with a discussion of value, defining it in terms which for Marx would limit it to use value. Value is not some quality of the natural world—the natural world is just there, neither good nor bad, valued nor unvalued. 'Value is an addition to the completely determined objective qualities, like light and shade, which are not inherent in it but come from a different source' (Simmel 1900/1990: 60). It comes from my desire: the valued objects I see around me are those I desire, and I, like all other human beings, am a creature of desire and therefore a valuing creature. It is precisely this conception of human beings as meaning- and value-choosing beings that characterized Jean-Paul Sartre's existentialism in the mid-twentieth century, but, whereas Simmel uses this as a starting point for understanding sociation, Sartre (1957) used it as a starting point to emphasize the loneliness and adrift-ness of human existence. But both would agree that values do not come from anywhere else but the valuing subject. Simmel goes on to argue that economic value is the objectification of subjective value. This occurs through the act of exchange: 'The technical form of economic transactions produces a realm of values that is more or less completely detached from the subjective personal substructure' (Simmel 1900/1990: 79). Here Simmel draws on the theory of marginal utility and opportunity cost. Valued objects are bought into relation to each other through exchange—if I want to buy books, then I have to give up something else that I might buy with the money—say food, or furniture. In this way I equate a sociology textbook with two McDonald's meals. Other people making their choices at the same time as I make my own create the objective value relationships between objects. 'The fact that the object has to be exchanged against another object illustrates that it is not only valuable for me, but also valuable independently of me; that is to say, for another person' (ibid. 81).

This is where we move on to sociology. The act of economic exchange is an act of sacrifice: I give up one good in order to gain another, and Simmel argues that this is the basic model for all social interaction—every interaction that we have is an act of exchange, although in most cases without the sacrifice which is peculiar to economic exchange. Simmel makes no distinction between use value and exchange value, and exchange value is seen as the same as price, which is not the case in Marx's theory. And, directly counter to Marx, Simmel is barely interested in production, criticizing the labour theory of value on the ground that mental effort involves an unpaid contribution to production which cannot be adequately measured or paid for—and this makes manual labour an inappropriate measure for measuring labour.

REPRESENTATIONS

The model of exchange is then transformed into a theory of knowledge. Social interaction is seen as an exchange of representations (such as money—something which stands for something else), and truth—like value—is to do with a relation of representations to each other. Society is thus a combination of exchange relations between individuals, it is in constant movement, and money, as it emerges from economic exchange, embodies this constant movement. It is as if money becomes the symbol which represents everything:

The philosophical significance of money is that it represents within the practical world the most certain image and the clearest embodiment of the formula of all being, according to which things receive their meaning through each other, and have their being determined by their mutual relations.   (Simmel 1900/1990: 128–9)

In this sense money is an essential part of and a signifier of progress. It is worth noting here how yet again Simmel foreshadowed contemporary ideas, in this particular case the varieties of postmodernism that talk about the significance of representations and representations of representations. In one respect, perhaps the work of Baudrillard can be regarded as an immensely elaborate philosophy of money: 'The increasingly influential principle of economizing strength and materials leads to more and more extensive experiments with representatives and symbols that have virtually no relation to what they represent' (ibid. 151).

MONEY AS THE EXTENSION OF FREEDOM AND ITS PSYCHOLOGICAL CONSEQUENCES

Large sections of the book unravel the cultural, social, and psychological meanings of money, moving all the time from one level to another and back again. Money takes on an independence: 'The functioning of exchange, as a direct interaction between individuals, becomes crystallized in the form of money as an independent structure' (Simmel 1900/1990: 175) This extends immensely the range of actions open to the individual human:

Primitive man, who has only a limited knowledge of natural causes, is consequently restricted in his purposive action. For him the arc of purposive action will contain as intermediate links little more than his own physical action and the direct effect he can have upon a single object. (ibid. 208)

First of all we develop tools which extend the chain of means and ends and this gives us greater power. I can do more with a hammer than I can with my hand; and I can do more with a wheel, or even better a number of wheels, than I can with a hammer. Money gives me access to an immense number of means—'it is the purest example of the tool'. If I have £10,000 in cash or in the bank, I can do infinitely more than if I have £10,000 worth of coffee beans piled up in the back garden. And money can be used to earn more money through loans and interest. Money becomes an end in itself, particularly for the marginalized, the underprivileged, and the dispossessed. It becomes a means whereby they can work their way back into society.

The move towards money itself as an ultimate end can lead to greed and avarice, or to extravagance, when it is spent on 'non-sensical' goods unsuited to the conditions of the person spending the money; I would be squandering money if I bought a fleet of fast cars if I could not drive and did not want to go anywhere. Simmel also explores ascetic poverty—the positive choice of poverty as a way of life, the right way to live. However, the most important part of this section of the book concerns the subjective underside of the meaning of money—the development of cynicism and a blasé attitude which Simmel describes as 'endemic to the heights of a money culture' (ibid. 255), suggesting that they can be seen as the opposite of avarice and greed.

Whereas the cynics of antiquity pursued strength of mind and indifference as ultimate values, modern cynicism allows no ultimate values, and is concerned with degrading those that others might espouse; it seems to be summed up in the phrase 'everybody has their price'. The blasé attitude involves having no particular reaction to value at all, not even the perverse reaction of the cynic to degrade it. The cure of this is found in the search for excitement. Much later, Simmel suggests that money is the purest example of the tendency in modern culture, particularly in the sciences, to the reduction of the qualitative to the quantitative, almost as if science itself becomes cynical. The concern of many twentieth-century sociologists with small-scale quantitative studies perhaps explains why Simmel has been neglected by later generations of sociologists.

THE GROWTH OF OBJECTIVE CULTURE AND THE STRUCTURE OF SUBJECTIVITY

Simmel engages in a long exploration of the meaning of money for human life in general, developing what might be called a theory of human nature as well as a double-edged approach to modern culture. He constantly reasserts the importance of exchange and its result in creating an objective world. Money extends the range of human freedom, removing personal obligations and duties to others—these can be paid off by money rather than, say, by service. And it enables the production of objective values which can be shared by everybody. This long quotation is typical of his argument:

man has been defined as the political animal, the tool-creating animal, the purposeful animal, the hierarchical animal. . . . Perhaps we might add to this series that man is the exchanging animal, and this is in fact only one side or form of the whole general feature which seems to reflect the specific qualities of man—man is the *objective* animal. Nowhere in the animal world do we find indications of what we call objectivity, of views and treatment of things that lie beyond subjective feeling and volition.

I have already indicated how this reduces the human tragedy of competition . . . more and more contents of life become objectified in supra-individual forms: books, art, ideal concepts, . . . [knowledge] . . . all this may be enjoyed without any one depriving any other.   (Simmel 1900/1990: 290–1)

Some of his most interesting observations concern what happens to the personality in a money economy. Today we are often presented with an argument that the Enlightenment produced a conception of a unified, rational subject which was simply taken for granted by sociology up until the last couple of decades, when poststructuralism and postmodernism showed us how wrong we were. In fact, conceptions of the self have been much more varied, as have, incidentally, conceptions of what rationality might involve. Simmel *starts* from the position (which I would regard as self-evident) that 'Just as the essence of the physical organism lies in the fact that it creates the unity of the life process out of the multitude of material parts, so a man's inner personal unity is based upon the interaction and connection of many elements and determinants' (ibid. 296). He continues a little later in what I regard as a profound passage, which I am therefore quoting at length:

Only the combination and fusion of several traits in one focal point forms a personality which then in its turn imparts to each individual trait a personal-subjective quality. It is not that it is this *or* that trait that makes a unique personality of man, but that he is this *and* that trait. The enigmatic unity of the soul cannot be grasped by the cognitive process directly, but only when it is broken down into a multitude of strands, the resynthesis of which signifies the unique personality.

Such a personality is almost completely destroyed under the conditions of a money economy. The delivery man, the money lender, the worker, upon whom we are dependent, do not operate as personalities because they enter into a relationship only by virtue of a single activity such as the delivery of goods, the lending of money, and because their other qualities, which alone would give them a personality, are missing. . . . The general tendency . . . undoubtedly moves in the direction of making the individual more and more dependent upon the achievements of people, but less and less dependent upon the personalities that lie behind them.   (ibid. 296)

Simmel thinks that socialism is the end state of this process—an interesting comparison with Marx's actual statement of socialist ideals, in which the personalities of people would be more important than ever before. For Simmel, the more people we are dependent upon, the more it seems that personalities are unimportant—any one bus driver is as good as any other and this cultivates 'an inner independence and feeling of individual self-sufficiency'—the qualities now encouraged on an emotional level by contemporary forms of psychotherapy (see Giddens 1991).

Simmel is rightly ambivalent about the increase in human freedom involved in this process. Money adds to the range of possible human relationships, but these relationships do not touch people in any profound way. As well as being freer, we gain what might be called a broader personality, but one which loses its depth—it becomes more fragmented. This process goes hand in hand with a decline in the importance of individual objects and an increasing importance and dependence on classes of objects.

SIMMEL'S THEORY OF ALIENATION

The last chapter of *The Philosophy of Money* brings us close to the theory of alienation in the young Marx and in Lukacs. In fact Simmel's notion of objective culture is similar to Lukacs's notion of a second nature—except that Simmel does not hold out any hope of changing it.

Simmel analyses this in terms of the division between subjective and objective culture—the latter being the objects that a culture produces which are beyond influence by any single person. As society grows larger and objective mind or culture itself grows larger, discrepancies occur between objective and subjective culture. My observations on Simmel will, when they are published, become part of the objective culture. However, they will enter only in a very marginal way to the subjective culture of a few people. A society in which objective and subjective culture coincide—a society in which we all knew as much as it is possible to know—would be a sort of Golden Age.

The growth in objective culture eats away at such a possibility and most important in this process is the division of labour. Simmel argues—referring to Marx—that the product is 'completed at the expense of the development of the producer', recognizing more clearly than Durkheim that the division of labour did not always produce individual satisfaction and contributed to the fragmentation rather than the wholeness of the individual. In this respect, those of us who are engaged in some of the social sciences or the arts are privileged over those studying or practising the natural sciences or a narrower social science such as economics, since our work will tend to flow back into the main purpose, the wholeness of our lives. But, for that to have meaning, the wholeness of the objects on which we work is important. When I discussed Durkheim's conception of the division of labour, I pointed out how many more jumbo jets it enabled us to build, comparing it with each person working away in the back garden on his or her own jet. Simmel's point is that, if it were personal wholeness and satisfaction that we were after, we would choose the back garden every time. The division of labour does not allow us to see our whole selves in what we produce: we are alienated from the product of our labour. The separation of the worker from the means of production works in the same way.

Simmel goes on to look at the implications of this in everyday life. The objectification of culture affects our relationship to objects. In a paragraph which I can imagine will be as resonant to my contemporaries as it might have been to Simmel's, he says:

During the first decades of the nineteenth century, furniture and objects that surrounded us for use and pleasure were of relative simplicity and durability and were in accord with the needs of the lower as well as of the upper strata. This resulted in people's attachment as they grew up to the objects of their surroundings, an attachment that already appears to the younger generation today as an eccentricity on the part of their grandparents. (Simmel 1900/1990: 459–60)

As classes of objects become more important, it is increasingly difficult to endow one object with a special, personal significance. Simmel suggests that there are three reasons why this has happened: the sheer quantity of objects has meant that it is difficult to form a close personal relationship with them, and the objects which people do love—an old jacket or slippers or whatever—are often occasions for poking fun. This is reinforced by the standardization of objects and rapid changes in fashion, of which more later.

CONCLUSION

Now what are we to make of *The Philosophy of Money*? I have presented Simmel as the unsystematic theorist, but in this work we find a general theory of modern society and history and of the way it works which underlies all his essays, which taken as a whole could just about be interpreted as a systematic social theory. In part we are up against the unavoidable paradox that I spoke about in the introduction: that the denial that there can be any general theory of society is itself a general theory of society; buy Simmel is not as crass as that. He is in fact producing a theory of modern society in a quite self-conscious way, although those who might claim him as forerunner of postmodernism might not like seeing it that way. A sign of this is the way it was taken up by Marxists and in particular by Lukacs. Strictly speaking, Simmel is much closer to Weber and the marginal utility theorists—what Simmel had to say about objective culture can be seen as part of the process that Weber saw as rationalization, and both accept the 'givenness' of the market economy rather than seeing it as a product of underlying relationships. I think that what Simmel held on to that Weber did not manage to hold on to is a sense of human experience and the way in which it was transformed and fragmented by modern society. This enables him to start from a position that was similar to Weber's starting point and to end with a position very close to Marx's starting point.

Simmel's sociology

Frisby (1981) uses the helpful metaphor of impressionism to discuss Simmel's sociology. Impressionism was an artistic movement which developed through the latter half of the nineteenth century, breaking with traditional conventions, moving out of studios into the open air, trying to capture variations in light and shade as they actually appear to the eye. The most famous impressionist was Van Gogh. Frisby (1981) points to Lukacs's comment that (Simmel's sociology was the 'conceptual formulation of the impressionist world view'.) Lukacs goes on to argue that, though the impressionists rejected traditional forms because they inhibited or stultified or trapped the multidimensional flux of life, they had themselves to develop a new classical form more appropriate to the complexities of modern life.

The same is true of Simmel and explains his ambivalence about form and the social world that I discussed in Chapter 6. As Lukacs noted, his work contains a real commitment to the individual and the unique—the individual's experience of the play of social light and shade; at the same time, he has a conception of the totality and history which emerges in *The Philosophy of Money*, but he is interested only in particular aspects of that totality. And, just as the impressionists were portraying the same external world as the classicists, so Simmel is portraying the same social world as that described by the other classical theorists. Each of Simmel's sociological essays explores a particular topic from different points of view. I have divided his essays into four groups: first, those where the dominant theme is relationships and the maintenance of relationships in everyday interaction—his *micro*-sociology; secondly, those that deal with a social type which illustrates something important about the social whole—the miser, the spendthrift, the adventurer, etc.; thirdly, the essays which have been most influential on modern sociology and deal with his analysis of what we would now call modernity; and, finally, his discussion of different social groups—including his essays on women, sexuality, and femininity.

Simmel on relationships

FAITHFULNESS AND GRATITUDE

> Without the phenomenon we call faithfulness, society could simply not exist, as it does, for any length of time. The elements which keep it alive—the self-interest of its members, suggestion, coercion, idealism, mechanical habit, sense of duty, love, inertia—could not save it from breaking apart if they were not supported by this factor.
>
> (Simmel 1908/1950: 379)

Here Simmel seems to start from an extreme individualist position as opposed to his earlier evolutionary viewpoint. If we start from individuals, we have to explain why they maintain consistent relationships; if we start from society, this is not a problem.

Faithfulness cannot be measured, it is a quality that keeps a relationship in existence beyond the disappearance of the conditions that originally brought it about. 'Faithfulness might be called the inertia of the soul.' We can go on loving our partner as he or she, in Simmel's straightforward terms, becomes ugly, even if it was beauty which first attracted us. Faithfulness is a psychic state, not a feeling: I can be faithful to my friends or to my country, whatever I feel about them. We become habituated to a relationship, and its mere existence over time produces faithfulness. Faithfulness must exist for society to exist.

This leads Simmel to note that faithfulness can develop where relationships start for non-emotional reasons and it can generate affection and love—

although affection is not necessary for faithfulness, nor *necessarily* entailed by it. A special instance of this occurs with the figure of the *renegade*, the person who changes sides: the convert is characteristically more enthusiastic about and committed to his or her new faith or country or political party than established members. Most members of the Roman Catholic Church will recognize this phenomenon—those born into the church will find all sorts of ways around the pope's ruling on birth control, whereas converts will follow it enthusiastically.

If the original motive remains, then faithfulness itself takes on a more energetic form—this again is often the case with the renegade, who cannot go back. Faithfulness is unlike feelings towards other people, such as love, since it is concerned with maintaining a relationship more than with self-satisfaction:

This specific sociological character is connected with the fact that faithfulness, more than other feelings, is accessible to our moral intentions. Other feelings overcome us like sunshine or rain, and their coming and going cannot be controlled by our will. But *un*faithfulness entails a more severe reproach than does absence of love or social responsibility, beyond their merely obligatory manifestations.   (ibid. 385)

In this essay I think Simmel is embarking on a project which has largely been lost to modern sociology. He talks about habit, but he also talks about many other things, the intra-personal and interpersonal shifting sands of emotional life. He calls this the life process, a constant flux which contrasts with the rigidity of social forms. The forms, the relations we are engaged upon, never bend to fit the flux of our life process—it is as if we are wearing shoes that are just too small for us. Now modern sociologists have reduced this life process to habit, the routine and taken-for-granted *forms* of interaction (see e.g. Giddens 1976, 1984), with no sense of the underlying flux. Simmel in this essay shows a very sophisticated conception of the inner life. He points that this external contrast between life process and form is reproduced internally as we produce formulae and directions of how to live. This is not too far away from the functions which Freud attributes to the ego and superego, different levels of internal control over our drives. Whether internal or external, forms can move either slightly ahead of or slightly behind the life process, rather like children's clothes: they can become clearly too tight and small as the child grows quickly, and the new ones will be too large—deliberately so—in order that the child can grow into them. Faithfulness crosses the boundary between form and life process; it brings some firmness of form to the life process.

Turning to gratitude, Simmel comments that its sociological significance is more obscure than that of faithfulness but is very important. It is obscure because its external manifestations appear insignificant. All contracts rest on the exchange of equivalents, and this is enforced by law; however, there are many other interactions which involve exchange which are not backed up by law, and here gratitude is an important supplement. In another version of a theme from *The Philosophy of Money,* Simmel talks about the objectification of human relationships in the exchange of objects; as this develops, the exchange of objects becomes more important than human interaction. Gratitude also emerges from interaction and Simmel seems to think of it as the internal equivalent of the external process of objectification and it can on its own generate new interactions. Gratitude, like faithfulness, survives the beginning of the interaction: it is one of the feelings that keeps relationships going:

> It is an ideal living-on of a relation which may have ended long ago. . . . Although it is a purely personal affect . . . its thousandfold ramifications throughout society make it one of the most powerful means of social cohesion. It is a fertile emotional soil which grows concrete actions among particular individuals . . . although it is interwoven with innumerable other motivations . . . it gives human actions a unique modification or intensity: it connects them with what has gone before, it enriches them with the element of personality, it gives them the continuity of interactional life. If every grateful action, which lingers on from good turns received in the past, were suddenly eliminated, society (at least as we know it) would break apart.   (ibid. 388–9)

Here Simmel describes in a very common-sense way an aspect of human relationships which was developed as basic to psychoanalytic theory several decades later by Melanie Klein (1957). Klein developed her ideas in a dialectical form which would have delighted Simmel, derived from an account of human drives in which gratitude and reparation are seen as a balance to and development from human destructiveness, usually in a process of unconscious conflict. In this context, gratitude is basic to all human relationships, not just those with the exchange of objects as their base. Simmel's comments about the 'dark' side point out that gratitude can also be experienced as an obligation, a duty, and a lack of freedom.

SOCIABILITY

Simmel (1917/1950) calls his essay on sociability an example of pure or formal sociology. Some forms become removed from what we might call the 'serious' contents of everyday life and become ends in themselves. If *sociation* refers to the way in which we come into contact with each other in the pursuit of our everyday lives, *sociability* is the play form of such activity. Because it lacks the seriousness of everyday life, many people regard it as unimportant—'small talk'—but this is not Simmel's view. Its relationship to the serious world is rather like that of art to reality. When we are not pursuing our own interests, we are governed by *tact*, and this involves suppressing our most personal characteristics. He talks of upper and lower 'sociability thresholds': the upper point is where serious personal interests intrude in a situation (talking social theory at a cocktail party) and the lower point is where personality features intrude (making a pass at the host or hostess). In between, sociability is a sort of sociological art form creating an artificial world, where at the same time everybody is equal and everybody is special; it is done for its own sake, and it is only false if it is a mask for personal interests—if my cocktail sociability is a way of impressing my boss. My talk should be for its own sake, a matter of give and take for mutual pleasure. But, of course, if I could not engage sociably, it might work against my interests. It is not quite as easy to avoid instrumentality as Simmel seems to think.

DOMINATION

As might be expected, Simmel offers a more psychologically sophisticated conception of domination than did Weber. Even the most tyrannical domination is a form of interaction: I impose my will on you so that you give me what I want. My authority might come through my institutional position (I am senior to you, so you should do what you are told), or it might come through the convincing power of my action or ideas. This is different from prestige, which comes simply from the power of my personality, not through the identification of my personality with any objective feature such as knowledge or position.

Simmel distinguishes three types of domination:

(*a*)   Domination by the individual, which might be accepted or opposed by the group. It may have a levelling effect (we're all equal in the face of the leader), or it may be hierarchical. Simmel believes this is the primary form of domination.

(*b*)   Domination by a plurality, as in the British rule of India. The rights of individuals in the dominant group are not necessarily extended to those in the subordinate group. Simmel suggests that Britain has throughout its history been characterized by high standards of justice for individuals and high levels of injustice towards groups. Relationships between groups are characterized by greater objectivity—they are more distant from each other than individuals and therefore fellow feeling does not develop. He also explores different forms of group domination—are the dominant groups opposed to each other, for example, or hierarchically ordered.

(*c*)   Finally there is domination by a principle or law. This is compared at length to individual domination and to the different situations in which one or the other might be preferable to the subordinate, with the interesting conclusion that, in the last analysis, which is preferable 'depends upon decisions of ultimate, indiscussable feelings concerning sociological values' (Simmel 1908/1950).

Simmel makes many more points in this particular essay, which includes a long discussion of subordination, but very little of what he says has much relevance for contemporary sociology. I think we can see why if we compare this discussion to Weber's analysis of domination.

Weber's analysis is profoundly historical, and his characterization of forms of domination comes from historical analysis whereas Simmel confines himself to the formal—logical and therefore abstract—analysis of the individual–group relationship. The historical background is hidden in Simmel—there is just the link between objective culture and the rule of law (or, in Weber's terms, legal-rational authority).

THE SOCIOLOGY OF CONFLICT

Simmel's essay (1908/1971) on conflict was still important in the mid-century dominance of English-speaking sociology by functionalism and the work of Talcott Parsons. Coser's book *The Functions of Social Conflict* (1956) in many ways answers the criticism that functionalism cannot deal with social conflict, and a great deal of the argument is developed from Simmel.

Simmel argues that conflict must be a form of sociation, since it links at least two people; it results from 'dissociating factors' such as hatred and envy and it is an attempt to resolve the resulting divergences and restore unity, even if it is through the elimination of one of the parties. Both divergence (conflict) and convergence (peace) are forms of sociation, the opposite of both being indifference. Conflict itself combines both positive and negative aspects, and society is necessarily a product of convergent and divergent forces, harmony and disharmony. Unity in the widest sense includes conflict, and, whilst conflict might be destructive on an individual level, it is not necessarily so on a social level.

Conflict contributes towards the integration of a social unit. If I regard one of my colleagues as unbearable, awful in every conceivable way, our conflict can be something which enables us to work together. If I could not fight such a person, if I had to suppress my hostility rather than sublimate it, perhaps through competition, then I could find life so difficult I would want to leave. The relationship would be ended. It is a matter of attaining an inner balance; my hostility need not have any external effect at all—it leaves me feeling better, feeling that I am not trapped. We will see later how Simmel sees our hostility to others as one of the ways in which we keep our sanity and our relationships in the flux of urban life. He also talks about limiting cases of conflict where it does not act as a form of sociation—where conflict is desired for its own sake or there is a desire to kill the other person.

SECRECY AND THE SECRET SOCIETY

If two people interact, then they will have a picture of each other; it won't be a complete picture—it will be what is necessary for the interaction to succeed. A complete knowledge of the other person is impossible; we cannot enter each other's heads, and each of us will have a different picture of a friend or acquaintance from everybody else. I see my newsagent when I pay his weekly bill; a regular customer who chats to him every day will know a different character, and his wife will know yet another. To know another person is to know somebody who is capable of hiding his or her inner truth; in fact, since our inner life is such a complex and jumbled flow, it is impossible to present it fully anyway:

> With an instinct automatically preventing us from doing otherwise, we show nobody the course of psychic processes in their purely causal reality and—from the standpoints of logic, objectivity and meaningfulness—complete incoherence and rationality. Always, we show only a section of them, stylized by selection and arrangement. We simply cannot mention any interactions or social relations or society which are *not* based on the teleologically determined non-knowledge of one another.   (Simmel 1908/1971: 312)

One might add to this non-knowledge of ourselves, because we cannot be aware of the constant and multifaceted flow of thoughts when we give priority to our immediate practical purposes. It would not be very far from here to a theory of the unconscious, but that is not the route that Simmel decides to take. Instead he goes on to discuss the sociological significance of lying, which, as always, is double-edged. If I am attracted to another and lie to my wife when she challenges me about it, I might be contributing to keeping the marriage together; on the other hand, if I have a secret affair with that woman and I am discovered, my deceit can break the marriage. If I divulged every passing thought, I doubt if I would keep my friends for very long; by keeping parts of myself secret, I maintain relationships.

The closer one is to a person, the more likely one is to be hurt by that person's lying or secrecy. Simmel suggests that, in more 'primitive' groups, lying is comparatively unimportant, since individuals are leading more or less self-sufficient lives in the group and mutual dependence is at a minimum. Modern societies, in contrast, are 'credit' societies; we are dependent upon large numbers of people to tell the truth about what they are doing, and we can suffer considerably if they let us down—he suggests that in modern societies the lie is the intellectual equivalent of the footpad's club.

Simmel relates secrecy to what he regards as the basic dimensions of human relationships—cooperation and harmony, on the one hand, and distance and competition, on the other—looking at a range of relationships according to the degree of knowledge that participants might have of each other. In a simple interest group—for example, a trade-union branch—all one needs to know is that the others share the same interest. The more we move towards relationships rooted in the total personality, the more we want to know about the other person, and in between my fellow trade unionist and my wife there are any number of possibilities. Simmel places particular social value on acquaintanceship and discretion, and on differentiated friendship, where I look to one friend for intellectual qualities, another for emotional understanding, and so on; these are the relationships that are necessary in a complex society, and they all involve respect for intentional and unintentional secrets. Compared with the childish desire to reveal everything, the ability to hide realities 'is one of man's greatest achievements'. As civilization grows, what was once open becomes secret and what was once secret comes into the open. Public affairs are opened up and individual lives become private.

Secrecy holds a certain fascination: to have a secret marks one off and gives one a special sense of possession; people become jealous if they know you have a secret, and this leads to a great temptation to betray. If I were the only person who knew that my boss was having an affair, the temptation to betray would be immense. The importance of secrecy grows with and reinforces the process of individuation; the possessor of a secret increases his or her social distance from others and comes to rely on that distance. The growth of the money economy enables secrecy to reach new heights—bribery can be hidden indefinitely.

Finally, Simmel turns to the secret society, producing a set of ideas that has recently been used in a discussion of the British Institute of Psychoanalysis (Rustin 1991). The first characteristic of secret society is reciprocal protection and confidence—which Simmel regards as a particularly intense relationship of high moral value. To have a real sociological value, such a society must be an organ of transition, enabling the development of a new sort of life content. Thus the closedness of the Psychoanalytic Institutes perhaps allowed the protection of clients during the treatment and is still necessary for that reason. On the other hand, it protects practitioners when perhaps they should not be protected—as the recent conflict about the training of homosexuals illustrates.

Beyond this the secret society uses ritual to create what Simmel calls a 'life totality', confirming the centrality of the group when separation and fragmentation threaten as people leave to pursue their individual lives (a very Durkheimian insight this). Through its hierarchy it becomes the mirror image of the wider society against which it sets itself, perhaps offering a greater degree of freedom. Paradoxically, the more free the wider society, the more authoritarian the secret society—Simmel quotes as an example the American freemasons. Secret societies are more self-conscious and lay greater claim to self sufficiency than other groups; they rely on secret signs by which members can recognize each other (the notorious masonic handshake). They can emphasize social exclusiveness and superiority, and they can pursue their interests at the expense of other groups. Within the secret society there is a process of deindividuation to protect the group and it is likely to be centrally organized. Because of its secrecy, the central government nearly always sees the society as a threat.

Simmel on social types

I will now turn to the essays on social types. In these essays Simmel outlines a particular type of personality which he regards as embodying something particularly important about modern societies. When Georg Lukacs (1972) developed his literary criticism, he argued that the best form of modern realism is peopled by characters who typify important and conflicting underlying social processes—as in Thomas Mann's *The Magic Mountain* (1961) or Solzhenitsyn's *Cancer Ward* (1968). Simmel's portrayal of social types can be seen as a sociological version of literary realism. His clearest statement of his method comes not in one of his social-type essays but at the end of his discussion of the nobility, which I discuss below. We see here his distinctive ability to combine comparatively abstract analysis with an awareness of individuality and the life process:

Every human being emerges as a combination of predetermination and accident; of received material for, and unique formation of, his life; of social inheritance and the individual administration of it. In each person, we see the stereotypings of his race, his stratum, his traditions, his family, in brief, of everything that makes him a bearer of pre-existing contents and norms; we see these combined with the incalculable and the personal, with free autonomy.   (Simmel 1908/1971: 213)

This is extraordinarily like Jean-Paul Sartre's (1963) description of the 'project' in his attempt to bring together Marxism and his existential philosophy. The 'project' is something we have, whether we like it or not: it is what we do with what we have been given, with the materials with which we are provided at the start of our lives, and which we turn into something else in the course of our lives. For Sartre, the important issue is whether we can go beyond what we are given to start with, and produce something new.

THE MISER AND THE SPENDTHRIFT

Each segment of our conduct and experience bears a twofold meaning: it revolves about its own centre, contains as much breadth and depth, joy and suffering, as the immediate experiencing gives it, and at the same time it is a segment of a course of life—not only a circumscribed entity, but also a component of an organism. Both aspects, in various configurations, characterize everything that occurs in a life. Events which might be widely divergent in their bearing on life as a whole may none the less be quite similar to one another; or they may be incommensurate in their intrinsic meanings but so similar in respect to the roles they play in our total existence as to be interchangeable.

(Simmel 1907/1971: 187)

The miser is the person who hoards money for its own sake and who illustrates in an archetypal way the power of money. The miser enjoys the contemplation of what he or she can do with money:

satisfaction in the complete possession of a potentiality with no thought whatsoever about its realization. At the same time, it exemplifies an attraction akin to the aesthetic, the mastery of both the pure form and the ideal of objects or of behaviour, in respect of which every step towards reality—with its unavoidable obstacles, setbacks and frustrations—could only be a deterioration, and would necessarily constrain the feeling that objects are potentially absolutely to be mastered.   (ibid. 180)

It is as if Simmel is here picking up the earlier signs of cultural narcissism (Lasch 1980), the fear of being found wanting or lacking in some way which would be experienced as the destruction of the personality rather than as a practical problem which could be solved, and which inhibits attempts to come to grips with reality.

The spendthrift might at first sight seem to be the opposite to the miser, yet the spendthrift too has problems with coming to terms with the effects of external reality—he or she is attracted by the instant pleasure of spending, which outweighs the pleasure of hoarding money or of possessing the object. Again it is as if Simmel were identifying what we recognize today as the pleasure of shopping, less for what is bought than for the activity itself, a narcissistic pleasure because it doesn't involve commitment or human contact—perhaps better even than promiscuous sex, because it does not involve even the momentary annoyance of adjusting to another person. Simmel goes on:

At this point, the position of the spendthrift in the instrumental nexus becomes clear. The goal of enjoying the possession of an object is preceded by two steps—first, the possession of money and second, the expenditure of money for the desired object. For the miser, the first of these grows to be a pleasurable end in itself; for the spendthrift, the second.   (ibid. 183)

The lack of concern with money—an indifference towards it—is itself a sign of the dominance of the money economy: it is only because money is valued by everybody that its profligate rejection can be so effective. Money encourages immoderation.

THE ADVENTURER

The adventurer is the person who breaks the continuity of everyday life, 'a foreign body' in our existence which is somehow yet connected to the centre. The adventure has a beginning and an end and it is often difficult to remember the details of an adventure precisely because it is not part of everyday life; it fades as a dream might fade for the same reason—its strangeness. In its separation from everyday life, it is also like a work of art. It is separate from but part of life and consequently it seems that it somehow contains the whole of life within it—there is something special about its meaning. The adventurer thus becomes an eternal figure, someone who has broken free of the past and has no future.

It might be a sign of the times that what Simmel called an adventure might sometimes today be called a trauma. Many traumas have the same features as adventures; they are cut out of everyday life yet they seem to contain special meaning. If we momentarily face death and come away unscathed, for example, we are likely to see something significant in the event, however accidental it might have been: 'There is in us an eternal process playing back and forth between chance and necessity, between the fragmentary materials given us from the outside and the consistent meaning of the life developed from within' (Simmel 1911/1971: 191). It is the combination of these two, the external accident and the internal meaning, which makes the adventure so important.

Simmel goes on to connect these ideas to a metaphysical level, suggesting that, if we believe, for example, in the timeless existence of the soul, then the whole of life can seem like an adventure. The adventure is one of the fundamental categories of life:

A fragmentary incident, it is yet, like a work of art, enclosed by a beginning and an end. Like a dream, it gathers all passions into itself and yet, like a dream, it is destined to be forgotten, like gaming, it contrasts with seriousness, yet like the *va banque* of the gambler, it involves the alternative between the highest gain and destruction.   (ibid. 192)

It combines, as well, activity and passivity, certainty and uncertainty—the adventurer treats the uncertain as if it were certain, involving a form of fatalism. After drawing parallels between love and the adventure, Simmel concludes the adventure is not suited to old age—the old person is less able to be overwhelmed by the force of life.

THE STRANGER

> In the case of the stranger, the union of closeness and remoteness involved in every human relationship is patterned in a way that may be succinctly formulated as follows: the distance within this relation indicates that one who is close by is remote, but his strangeness indicates that one who is remote is near.
>
> (Simmel 1908/1971: 143)

Simmel's essay on the stranger is the most well known of his essays on social types and takes us into the analysis of modernity. His concern with space is echoed by many contemporary sociologists, and the notion of the stranger is often taken as a metaphor for Simmel himself and his own career. The stranger is in a paradoxical position: he or she is geographically near to the group but psychologically and culturally distant, near and far at the same time, and this puts the person in what we might call a privileged position. McLemore (1991) argues that we can find two research traditions that have developed from Simmel's essay. The first comes from his comments on the stranger as trader and is really the sociology of the newcomer. The second refers to the marginal person and can involve the idea that at some point in our existence we are all marginalized, by others or ourselves. Levine (1991) argues that the emphasis on the marginal character is the less faithful to Simmel's essay. In the sense that historically the stranger has usually been a trader, I suspect he is right. However, I also suspect that a reason for the continued popularity of the essay comes, first, from the theme of marginality and its affinity to the Romantic reaction to the Enlightenment, where we find a belief that people on the edge of society have some special insight not available to the rest of us—whether it be Shelley's country dweller or William Burrough's junkie—and, secondly, from the sense in which contemporary society can be said to leave us all in the position of the marginal, the stranger, given the break-up of traditional communities and increasing geographical and social mobility.

The stranger is considered objective: Simmel refers to Italian cities which used to call in their judges from outside because a native would be too entangled with the litigants. The stranger is free with no commitments to local interests and this enables a commitment to objectivity, and the stranger who passes through is often a receptacle of secrets which cannot be shared with the people to whom we are closest. The stranger can see things that the insider cannot see because he or she is too close, and perhaps say things that the insider cannot say because it would be too damaging. In the introductory chapters I talked about the objective existence of social structures—in the sense of their object—such as qualities which remain the same whatever we think about them. We might call this the 'objective sense of objectivity'. I contrasted it with the more common-sense use of the term as denoting a particular attitude—what we might call the *subjective* sense of objectivity. Simmel offers an excellent criticism of this second sense of the term that also redefines it: 'Objectivity is by no means nonparticipation, a condition that is altogether outside the distinction between subjective and objective orientations. It is rather a positive and definite kind of participation' (ibid. 144). It can be defined, he suggests, as freedom, a position which perhaps should belong to the sociologist.

Our relationship with the stranger is through sharing the most abstract human qualities, and perhaps the stranger is more readily seen as the representative of a particular type or group than as an individual. What Simmel does not deal with is the way in which such groups—Jews, blacks, gays—can become scapegoats which serve to generate a sense of community amongst the home culture.

Simmel on modernity

Now we move on to another issue—Simmel's conception of modernity, which, perhaps more than other issues, is beyond his time.

THE METROPOLIS

> The deeper problems of modern life derive from the claim of the individual to preserve the autonomy and individuality of his existence in the face of overwhelming social forces, of historical heritage, of external culture and of the technique of life. The fight with nature that primitive man has to wage for his *bodily* existence attains in this modern form its latest transformation.
>
> (Simmel 1902/1950: 409)

The essay on the metropolis is one of Simmel's best-known pieces, often cited as a foundation of urban sociology. The big urban centres of the modern world bring about a change in human life, requiring different capacities from those required by the country and the small town. In the latter, life is comparatively slow, and it is possible to build up deep emotional connections with others on an unconscious level. In the big city we are constantly bombarded with changing sense impressions, myriads of fast-moving people, heavy traffic, countless activities, shop displays, advertising, all calling on our attention. It is not possible to survive this world without developing the intellect. The city-dweller reacts with the head—'that organ which is least sensitive and quite remote from the depth of the personality'—rather than with the heart, distancing him- or herself from the shocks and changes that urban life brings.

The metropolis and the urban mind are intimately bound up with the money economy. The complexity of urban life forces us into punctuality, calculability, and exactness and transforms the world into an arithmetic problem. The city-dweller becomes a sophisticate, blasé, and protects him- or herself from being overwhelmed with sensations, on the one hand, or with indifference, on the other, by adopting a reserved, even an antipathetic attitude towards others. Fights break out easily in the city.

Whilst physically closer to other people, the individual is psychologically separated from and independent of them. This gives him or her immense freedom, the reverse side of which is loneliness and an increasing sense of meaninglessness: 'The atrophy of individual culture through the hypertrophy of objective culture is one reason for the bitter hatred which the preachers of the most extreme individualism, above all Nietzsche, harbour against the metropolis' (ibid. 422). Charles H. Powers argues that this essay 'heralds the spread of distinctly modern social roles. Narrow, specialized, standardized, interchangeable roles are the defining form and are an inherent feature of modern urban life' (Powers 1991: 354).

It is not simply that Simmel identifies modern role structures; he identifies processes that have been taken up by contemporary thinkers as essential aspects of late modernity or postmodernity (Weinstein and Weinstein 1993). Thinkers as far apart as David Harvey (1989) and Anthony Giddens (1990b) point out that cities are becoming more and more standardized: shopping centres in Europe and North America look increasingly similar—often the shops are the same. The difference between Simmel and the contemporary thinkers is that Simmel was critical. Weinstein and Weinstein comment mildly on the danger of metropolitan life generating a 'mild schizophrenia' but on the whole see it as increasing individual freedom. Simmel's language indicates that he was more aware of the dangers, and, as Fredric Jameson, a Marxist critic of postmodernist thought, points out (1991), 'schizophrenia' has become a defining metaphor for contemporary human life.

FASHION

Simmel (1904/1971) begins by pointing to the contradictory tendency to identify with and separate oneself from society. This contradiction is reflected on different levels—at the biological level it is between heredity and variation. There is no way of living and no form of society which can satisfy urges. In psychological terms, the side of social adjustment is reinforced by the tendency to imitation, which has the advantage of avoiding both the demands of creativity and the responsibility for action, which is passed on to another.

Social institutions such as fashion can be seen as the compromise between the desire for stasis and the desire for change: fashion allows one both to follow others and to mark oneself off from them as a member of a particular class or group. The items that become fashionable have very little or no instrumental use (baseball caps worn backwards in mild weather), and they often come from a distance (the popularity of kaftans in the 1960s, or, again, in Britain, of baseball caps in the 1990s). If fashion fails to supply either the need for union with others, or the need for separation, it disappears. In societies or social classes where there is little differentiation, fashions change slowly; in modern societies, where there is a danger of obliteration of the individual, fashion becomes much more important. The further fashion spreads within a group, the more it heads towards its end—it is necessarily transitory and carries with it a strong feeling of the present. The very fact that we know it will come to an end makes it all the more attractive. It is particularly attractive for dependent individuals, and the fashionable person is both envied and approved of. The person who follows fashion can identify with the group and assert his or her individuality. The dude does this to perfection, always slightly exaggerating the dominant fashion, wearing the baggiest trousers, the shortest skirt, or whatever—employing the fashion in the most individualistic way. This is one of the peculiar paradoxes of fashion—the person who appears to be leading the group is in fact most dominated by it. Simmel sees this as one of the distinctive features of a democratic society.

If following or apparently even leading fashion is a sign of subordination to the group, the explicit and self-conscious rejection of fashion is equally a sign of subordination—the first subordination has a positive sign in front of it, and the second a negative sign. Neither the following nor the rejection of fashion is necessarily an indicator of a strong sense of individuality. Simmel argues that, in the adoption of a fashion, the individual can avoid a feeling of shame that might otherwise attach to his or her action; it is also a means by which we can preserve an inner freedom by following the crowd in matters of external display. Another form of fashion is linguistic—when certain words are applied to all sorts of experiences or objects: 'cool' and 'wicked' seem to be popular now amongst my son's friends—although this can change very quickly, and might be cyclical—I can remember using 'cool' thirty years ago. This sort of fashion treats objects and experiences in a cavalier way, denying their individuality and establishing the control of the individual over the surrounding world. In this sense, it is ego-reinforcing and perhaps exactly what is needed amongst adolescents; in adults, however, I suspect that it is more a matter of avoidance—a way of not thinking about the world.

Simmel goes on to argue that rapid changes in fashion are not likely to be found in the highest classes, since they will be consciously conservative, or in the lowest classes, 'with their dull unconscious conservatism'—a phrase which unfortunately says much about Simmel's own prejudices but very little about the working class, who, as the last century has shown, have developed their own fashions as they have moved above subsistence level and as clothing, in particular, has become mass produced and relatively cheaper. It is a sign of social mobility:

Classes and individuals who demand constant change, because the rapidity of their development gives them the advantage over others, find in fashion something that keeps pace with their own rapid soul-movements. Social advance above all is favourable to the rapid change of fashion, for it capacitates the lower classes so much for imitation of upper ones, and thus the process . . . according to which every higher set throws aside a fashion the moment a lower set adopts it, has acquired a breadth and activity never dreamed of before.   (Simmel 1904/1971: 318)

The development of late modernity has, I think, 'flattened' the sort of status struggles to which Simmel was referring and enabled an even more rapid change in fashions.

Simmel also notes that the spread of changing fashions encourages the production of cheaper goods, and that fashion tends to move in cycles—as soon as an old fashion becomes at least partially forgotten, it can be resurrected.

Simmel on social groups

Finally there is Simmel's discussion of different forms of social groups.

THE POOR

Simmel begins his discussion of the poor by talking about the reciprocities of obligation and duties; if the poor are considered and consider themselves to have a right to sustenance from those better off than themselves either because they are poor or because they belong to the same community as those who are better off, they and society are in a better position than either the situation in which the poor believe that poverty is a cosmic injustice, when they will attack the better-off, or the situation where giving to the poor is motivated by its consequences to the giver. If I give my money to charity because it might enable me to get to heaven, a completely new situation is created—a situation which Simmel clearly thinks is not a good one since it brings about 'the senseless distribution of alms, the demoralization of the proletariat through arbitrary donations which tend to undermine all creative work' (Simmel 1908/1971: 154).

When the welfare of society requires assistance to the poor, either to ward off social disruption or to increase productivity, attention turns away from both the giver and the recipient. This type of help seeks to alleviate individual needs, not the needs of all citizens. Its aim is to mitigate inequalities that would otherwise challenge the society—to reinforce rather than transform the existing society through creating overall equality. It is a process which subordinates the needs of the individual to those of the wider society: 'Within the modern, relatively democratic State public assistance is perhaps the *only* branch of the administration in which the interested parties have no participation whatsoever' (ibid. 157). In this sense, the poor have the same status as a road that the government might decide to build; on the other hand, they are also citizens. Their position is rather like the stranger, outside society and at the same time incorporated into it as part of a larger whole.

Simmel suggests that there is another reciprocal right and duty between the wealthy and the community as a whole, on the one hand, and the poor, on the other, to relieve suffering. In this relationship, the poor are an end in themselves: 'The State assists poverty; private assistance assists the poor' (ibid. 169). In modern societies where the state assists poverty, we can talk about the poor as a group; otherwise we can talk only about poor individuals: this person is poor and unemployed, this one a poor farmer, this one a poor single mother—they become part of *the* poor only when they receive state assistance; the poor, in modern terminology, are socially constructed. This might have a distinctly modern ring to it for some readers, and they would be right in the sense that it has been taken up by the New Right and by centre–left parties as they move to the right.

Lewis Coser (1991*b*), developing Simmel's argument, illustrates the general tendency. There are no absolute measures of poverty; definitions are always relative. This is fair enough: poverty in London or Paris or New York might be very unpleasant but it would often not be regarded as poverty in Rwanda or Somalia or some areas of India. Returning to Simmel's point about the state classification of the poor, Coser goes on to argue that, although the fact that the state takes a measure of responsibility for the poor and recognizes that they are members of society, it also degrades them, assigning them to a stigmatized role—this is perhaps particularly true of the American system even at the time Coser was writing (1965) but the European systems also tend towards degradation—constant checking, surveillance, steady withdrawal of benefit over time, and so on. Not only does the provision of assistance degrade; it also keeps the poor dependent. Coser then makes a leap:

I showed earlier how the core category of the poor arises only when they come to be defined as recipients of assistance. We now see that correlatively the poor will be with us as long as we provide assistance so that the problem of poverty can be solved only through the abolition of unilateral relationship of dependence.   (Coser 1991*b*: 238)

This view produces various schemes intended to push the poor into looking after themselves and thus no longer being poor.

It might be useful to think about this argument in contrast to a Marxist approach. It seems to me that it is possible to accept the argument about the state defining 'the poor' through fixing minimum standards of living and providing assistance to those who fall below it—this is a surface analysis which would involve writing a history of the development of the welfare state. However, this works only on one level. There is a process of the social construction of poverty on another, prior level. The mechanisms of economic competition and the overproduction/underconsumption crises produce systematic social inequalities which leave some people at the bottom of the pile and some people at the top, with those at the bottom suffering distinct physical and environmental disadvantages—higher infant mortality rates, higher levels of disease, lower life expectancy, and so on, as well as the day-to-day absence of many of the goods necessary to become good citizens. The social definition that Simmel and Coser are talking about, then, occurs on the basis of this primary inequality and involves a selection of the point in the hierarchy where we begin using the *word* poor. This defines the poor, but does not create them. This is an example which would support the need for theoretical pluralism, using the different approaches at the same time, and I will return to the relationships between the theoretical approaches in the conclusion to Part 2.

THE NOBILITY

Simmel begins his essay on the nobility by arguing that, like the middle classes, the nobility are between the highest and the lowest classes, but, unlike the middle classes, they are relatively bounded both above and below, and this produces the particular nature of the aristocracy. We expect them to be privileged in respect of people below them, but Simmel points out that historically they have had special responsibilities in relation to those below them. Whilst the lower classes, for example, could be expected to steal and would be subjected to routine punishments, the aristocracy were not expected to engage in such behaviour and would be more severely punished. The invariant social position of the nobility produces a homogeneity: they can make many assumptions in their interactions and can get down to personal details much more quickly than other members of other classes.

In other social strata it is usually the case that what is shared by all members is a sort of lowest common denominator; in the case of the nobility, the opposite is the case—members share in the glory attained by the highest members, not through the possession of externals such as power and property but through internal qualities preserved through the tendency to marry within the class. A person born into the aristocracy automatically shares in its glory:

This recruiting from within conveys the unique insularity and self-sufficiency of this status group which, so to speak, can and may need nothing that lies outside itself; the nobility is, thereby like an island in the world. It is comparable to a work of art, within which each part also takes its meaning from the whole, and which shows through its frame that the world cannot enter, that it is absolutely sufficient unto itself.   (Simmel 1908/1971: 208)

This socially transmitted honour can, however, lead to what Simmel calls a 'decadent emptiness'. Socially transmitted features have to be combined with an inner creativeness on the part of the individual; at its best this can create ideal examples of independence and responsibility, but where that individual component is not there, decay sets in. The aristocrat does not work: the 'substance' of nobility comes from inside the person, and it is not to be transmitted to an object—although Simmel acknowledges that this may be changing. The ideal aristocratic pursuits are warfare and hunting—the subjective factor has importance over the objective factor, and, in this, there is an analogy to the work of the artist.

WOMEN, LOVE, AND SEXUALITY

The man externalizes himself. His energy is discharged into his performance. Thus he 'signifies' something that is in some sense independent of him, either dynamically or ideally, in a creative or a representative fashion.

The constitutive idea of the woman, on the other hand, is the unbroken character of her periphery, the organic finality in the harmony of the aspects of her nature, both in their relationship to one another and in the symmetry of their relationship to their centre. This is precisely what epitomizes the beautiful. In the symbolism of metaphysical concepts, the woman represents being and man represents becoming. This is why the man must establish his significance in a particular substantive area or in an idea, in a historical or cognitive world. However, a woman should be beautiful in the sense that this represents 'bliss in itself'.

(Simmel 1911/1984: 88–9)

In arguments that with a little translation will be very familiar to those who have followed contemporary feminist debates, Simmel (1911/1984) begins by suggesting that the modern women's movement poses two 'value questions'. The first is the access of women to already established 'objective culture'—the sort of issues that would now be seen in terms of equality of access and opportunity; the second is whether the movement can add anything new to the objective culture, qualitatively different from what has gone before. Now objective culture is not asexual; it is masculine, at least in the sense that men have produced it—the artists and scientists and philosophers who have contributed to it have all been men. However, Simmel wants to go beyond this, to establish that there is something about objective culture that is specifically associated with the male personality. In his useful introduction to Simmel's essays on these issues, Guy Oakes (1984) lists a number of basic differences between men and women that Simmel sees as important.

To begin with—and Oakes rightly calls Simmel's reasoning here 'banal and hardly persuasive'—is the fact that the division of labour, as it has developed since the industrial revolution, has moved men out of the home into a separate specialized economic role; women's activity in the home has remained unspecialized. Simmel's conclusion is that men are able to engage in specialized activities without a threat to their sense of self or identity, whereas women cannot be so incorporated. Following on from this, man is able to engage in actions that are *detached* from the centre of his being, whilst woman is only able to engage in actions which are integrated with her self. Men are more able to deal with other people in a depersonalized way, whereas women become more wholly involved in their relationships and so are more vulnerable. They are unable to objectify and free their action from its personal and subjective roots. Women have to express their emotions directly whereas men can express theirs through the mediation of objective culture.

These ideas might sound quaint to modern ears but they are not so different from the more contemporary arguments of Parsons (1951) or Chodorow (1978), except that Simmel is concerned to establish that being male and being female are two irreducible forms of being. For Parsons there is a functional division of labour in which men are assigned to work and women to the home, and for Chodorow the difference has to do with women's mothering role and is passed on by the psychological differences in mother–daughter and mother–son relationships. The characteristics which each thinker assigns to men and women are not the same as those discussed by Simmel, but they belong recognizably to the same families.

Simmel is ambivalent about the possibility of women contributing anything to objective culture. On the one hand, the two forms of being are important and should be maintained as such; if a woman were to try to take on and contribute to objective culture, she would no longer be feminine—feminine culture is entirely subjective. On the other hand, he suggests that there *might* be a feminine objective culture which has not yet been discovered, presumably because of male domination. He hints at a specifically feminine art—rather as, several decades later, Virginia Woolf talked about the feminine sentence that had yet to be written, and several decades after that Carol Gilligan (1982) was to write of women having different conceptions of morality and justice compared with men.

Postmodern feminists would accuse Simmel of reproducing a traditional 'essentialism'—the idea that men and women have essential, different characters, independent of context. A modern form of this sort of argument can be found over whether there is a specifically feminist epistemology (Harding 1986, 1991), which suggests that women have something very important to add to objective culture, at least so far as the philosophy of science is concerned, and this has to do with the subjective side of existence. The paradox is that in these terms Simmel's concern with the subjectivity and relationships can be seen as putting him in the feminine position in relation to the other classical sociological thinkers.

I think that it is probably the case that Simmel was simply reproducing common prejudices. This becomes clearer in his discussion of female sexuality; it follows from the above that sexuality for the man is something that he does, whereas for the woman it is something that she *is*. Her femininity is independent of her relationship to the man—as is evidenced by pregnancy, where the woman is at her most feminine and has no further need of the man: 'she is *intrinsically* sexual. . . . It is as if she has a secret sense of self-possession and a self-contained completeness' (Simmel 1911/1984: 108). Man is always drawn in two directions—towards the sensual and the transcendentally spiritual, on the one hand, and, on the other, towards recognizing autonomy and the desire to control and change. A woman, according to Simmel, stands 'beyond' this dualism; if she does not feel that she is connected with anything, then it does not concern her.

When he discusses flirtation, Simmel seems at first to be saying something different: that in flirting the woman is saying yes and no at the same time, departing from the unitary, 'centralized' nature that he attributes to her; however, he argues that these two apparently contradictory messages actually unite the whole of a woman's relationship to a man—following the biological imperative of nature, the woman chooses the man. Flirtation is the play form of a sexual relationship, in which we can, as it were, all be promiscuous:

> flirtation ensures that in definitive not-having, there is still a sense in which we can have. . . . With the advance of culture . . . increased sensitivity, on the one hand, and the equally large increase in the number of provocative phenomena, on the other, have produced an erotic repression in men. It is simply not possible to possess all the attractive women— whereas in primitive times, such an abundance of attractive phenomena just did not exist. Flirtation is a remedy for this condition. By this means the woman could give herself—potentially, symbolically or by approximation—to a large number of men, and in the same sense, the individual man could possess a large number of women.   (ibid. 150)

In his writings on femininity Simmel is one of the few sociologists who can really be regarded as essentialist, and he seems to be talking about a very mysterious essence, a form of pure self-identity. Men are defined in relation to women but not vice versa, yet the two are also spoken of as comprising two elements of a dichotomy and we would expect each to be defined in terms of the other. Compared with Engels on the family, we could say that Simmel has little contact with mundane reality, although he occasionally notes the similarity between marriage and prostitution and he is perhaps closer to some forms of the subjective experience of sex and gender differences. However, neither Simmel nor Engels is really able to cross the barrier between seeing the relationships between the sexes in social-structural terms and seeing them in experiential terms. Before turning to these issues, I want to bring the discussion of Simmel to an end.

Conclusion

It is perhaps a tribute to the breadth of Simmel's sociological vision that there have been regular attempts to integrate him into widely different sociological traditions. Thus Jonathan H. Turner (1991) argues that if we take Marx and Simmel together we can begin to build a proper conflict theory; in the same volume Jim Faught (1991) argues that there are significant convergences between Weber and Simmel in their discussion of politics and rationalization, and Lawrence Scaff (1991) emphasizes their joint concern with the development of modern culture. In the course of this chapter I have drawn parallels between Simmel and Durkheim, and finally there is Weinstein and Weinstein's (1993) recent attempt to claim Simmel for postmodernism. I think that the reason for this is Simmel's concentration on the individual/society dualism—he is closer to social psychology than sociology, and that is a gap in the other approaches which can be plugged with some of his ideas. Turning to the issues at stake in these conclusions, I think that perhaps a true 'Simmelian', if there could be such a thing, might have given up sociology altogether, seeing it as having become irretrievably part of the objective culture. Paradoxically, I suspect that some of the contemporary ideas that owe most to Simmel would be what would drive him into retirement. In any case, he or she would not be interested in systematizing a method or a theory.

I do not think that Simmel would have a lot to say about the changes in the labour market; the only account of social change that he offers is a comparatively simple, neo-Durkheimian notion of organic evolution in which the individual emerges from the group. His version of globalization would, I think, be in terms of the increasing universalization of objective culture, and this would carry with it the decline in significance of local communities. This was a decline that Simmel had begun to chart in his essay on the metropolis and which he, I think unconsciously, senses when he talks about the stranger, but he is less interested in communities than in the psychological consequences for individuals. The conflict between what I have called the life process and objective culture is at the centre of his work; it is the fact that he sees this as a dialectic rather than a process of socialization or the social construction of subjectivity that makes him more interesting than postmodernism, whilst in other ways he might be taken as a precursor of some postmodernist ideas (Weinstein and Weinstein 1993). I think the important point in this respect is that noted by Powers in the earlier quotation: that Simmel was the one of the first to note the development of a multiplicity of standardized and specialized roles; we can move from there to talking about a multiplicity of techniques for socializing people into these roles—or what Nikolas Rose, developing Foucault, calls the government of conduct (Hall and du Gay 1996). What is lost in all this is precisely the notion of a life process, an individuality which can transform and resist such governance.

It is difficult to think of what a Simmelian would make of the new political movements. Given Simmel's work on poverty, such a sociologist might well follow Holton and Turner and talk about 'state-administered status blocs', and he or she would, I think, certainly be interested in the processes of identification and separation that go in relation to such movements. The basic model for this process could be the church or the traditional far left, which have produced regular splits throughout their existence. What characterizes such movements is that they believe they have answers which draw the individual into identifying with them and push him or her into separating from them. Thus we can find divisions within feminism, within the gay movement, within the green movement, in a constant process of formation and reformation. These political movements are not fashions but they behave like Simmel's description of fashions.

A Simmelian sociologist might alternatively be interested in psychoanalytic social criticism along the lines of Christopher Lasch's (1980) argument about the way in which modern society undermines the possibility of coherence within the individual personality and inhibits the development of individual maturity. One of the results of this is the loss of play forms—such an individual cannot engage in sociable conversation, in flirtation, or in play at sport. Everything is very serious. We can now elaborate on Simmel's views of the basic dualism (see Boxes 10.1–10.3).

Box 10.1. **An elaboration of Simmel on the individual and society**

THE INDIVIDUAL

Durkheim: the individual is formed and limited by society. He/she becomes more important in complex societies and individualism becomes the focus of the *conscience collective*, binding people together.

Marx: the 'individuated' individual is an idea produced as part of the development of capitalism. The 'natural' state of the individual is as an integral part of the group.

Weber: the individual is the only reality and analysis must start from individual rational action.

Simmel: the individual life is engaged in a constant dialectic with social forms and the objective culture. In modern societies, the individual is engaged in a struggle to maintain his or her integrity against the objective culture.

SOCIETY

Durkheim: society exists over and above the individual, over whom it exercises an immense power, especially in less complex societies.

Marx: society is created by human action but acts back upon individuals as an external power—a dominant force in all but the most primitive and most advanced (communist) societies.

Weber: society is the rather fragile result of human interaction and struggles for power between different types of group.

Simmel: 'society' is an increasingly important form organizing peoples' lives. It can be understood as 'objective culture'—increasingly universal shared symbols and beliefs which form our lives.

Box 10.2. **Simmel on action and structure**

ACTION	STRUCTURE
Durkheim: there is no real theory of social action in Durkheim; the individual action is always conditioned by the group, and collective action is taken to reinforce the strength of the group.	**Durkheim:** in societies dominated by mechanical solidarity, the social structure consists of networks of kin groups (segmented societies); more complex modern societies consist of secondary groups formed by the division of labour and managed by the state.
Marx: in capitalist societies, the major agents are social classes—primarily the bourgeoisie and the proletariat. Some classes—the middle classes and the peasantry—do not share the life conditions which enable them to act as collective agents, and they tend to follow a strong leader.	**Marx:** different types of society have different forms of social structure. In capitalist societies the economic structure and resultant class structure are most important, and the state and state institutions are central features of social control.
Weber: status groups and market-based social classes can become 'collective actors' in the form of communal or more usually associative groups. Such groups exist only if members recognize a common identity or shared interest. The only 'real' actor remains the individual.	**Weber:** social structure is a fragile achievement; in traditional societies it is based on kin and status groups and in modern societies market-based classes enter into play. Bureaucratic organization and the state become more important.
Simmel: concerned primarily with individual interactions and their relationship to the wider culture; no concept of collective action.	**Simmel:** no real concept of social structure, except perhaps as relations entailed by economic exchange. Instead of a concept of social structure, he employs a notion of 'objective culture'.

Further reading

It is difficult to pick essays that are central to or typical of Simmel's work; my personal favourites, which include the best-known and most influential are 'The Secret and the Secret Society', especially parts 1, 2, and 3, 'Faithfulness and Gratitude', 'The Stranger', and 'The Metropolis and Mental Life', all of which are in *The Sociology of Georg Simmel*, ed. Kurt H. Wolff (1950), and the essay on 'Conflict' in *Georg Simmel on Individuality and Social Forms*, ed. D. Levine (1971). If I had to select one part of *The Philosophy of Money* (1900/1990), it would be chapter 6, where the theory of alienation is developed.

Amongst the secondary works the most straightforward is David Frisby, *Georg Simmel* (1984), but his *Sociological Impressionism* (1981) and *Simmel and Since* (1992) are also important. For a recent application of Simmel, see Michael Rustin's essay on psychoanalytic institutions in *The Good Society and the Inner World* (1991). Larry Ray (ed.), *Formal Sociology* (1991), is an excellent collection which gives a good sense of Simmel's reception in the USA, and the Weinsteins's *Postmodern(ized) Simmel* (1993) brings Simmel into the centre of contemporary debates.

Box 10.3. Simmel on social integration and system integration

SOCIAL INTEGRATION

Durkheim: in all societies social integration is achieved through the *conscience collective*—shared ways of thinking (logic, conceptions of space and time, shared beliefs, norms, and values). In societies governed by mechanical solidarity, religion is central. In more complex modern societies, the *conscience collective* covers less of our lives but focuses on the ethics of individual freedom—it becomes a religion of humanity.

Marx: a 'false' and rather tenuous integration is achieved through ideologies, and the development of the market constantly threatens whatever integration is achieved. The major contending classes strive towards achieving their own integration in opposition to the others—the proletariat being the class most likely to achieve this.

Weber: at this point there is no real conception of social integration in Weber's work.

Simmel: social integration is achieved through objective culture—the development of universal symbols and meanings that begins with economic exchange. The growth of such a culture extends human freedom but constricts the integrity and depth of the individual life.

SYSTEM INTEGRATION

Durkheim: where mechanical solidarity predominates, system integration *is* social integration, guaranteed by the *conscience collective*. Where organic solidarity predominates, system integration is achieved through the division of labour.

Marx: system integration in capitalism is constantly threatened by class conflict and is supported by the state and by ruling ideologies.

Weber: it is a gross exaggeration to use the word 'system' in connection with the writings we have looked at in Chapter 9. Social structures are held together by different forms of domination and by stability provided by the market.

Simmel: no real concept of system integration, except perhaps through economic exchange.

Conclusion to Part 2: the theorists contrasted

It is difficult to sum up the information contained in the last four chapters and I think the most useful thing at this point is to try and situate the different theoretical approaches in relation to each other. My first point is the obvious one: they are different from each other but they also overlap—by this, I mean that we are not looking at alternative candidates for a total explanation of social reality as a whole—it is not a matter of saying that one theory is better than another overall; we can, in certain circumstances, say that one or the other of the approaches is better for looking at a particular aspect of social reality; we can talk about what a particular social theory does not or cannot see and what it sees more clearly. The notion of basic dualisms that I have developed stems from the idea that social reality is made up of a number of different aspects which are very different from each other but all of which must be taken into account, and each theory will assign one side of the dualism a more important place than the other. In what follows I will try to relate the different theoretical contributions to understanding the issues that I have discussed in the conclusions to the previous four chapters.

When we think about the worldwide changes in the labour market, it is probably Marxism which can give us the clearest conception of a world-system with its own underlying dynamic and underlying structure, and which would explain developments in the division of labour in terms of this underlying structure. The effects of this would be mediated by the class structure of western society and this in turn would explain some of the industrial and political changes in recent decades and the conflicts that they have generated. But I think Marxism is best at the broad picture—it misses the detailed complexities.

Durkheim's contribution to this would be twofold: first he points to the importance of the division of labour in separating and relating people in different ways and he gives us a number of indices through which we can try to examine the form of social cohesion and community life—crime rates, suicide rates, marriage and divorce rates, and so on. Secondly, he directs us towards an understanding of how a society thinks itself—its collective representations—and through these we can also gain an understanding of the form and depth of social cohesion. It can do these tasks rather better than Marxism, but a Durkheimian approach tends to miss or underestimate the divisions of interest which separate social classes.

Through Weber we can make better sense of the complexity of social conflict and the forms of social and political conflict that Marxism has a difficulty in apprehending—this is especially so given that Weber sees the state not just as an instrument of class rule but as the focus of a power struggle between many different groups. In this sense Weber offers probably offers the best available analytic route into understanding the new social movements. A Weberian analysis also adds to our understanding of changes in the way modern society sees itself—especially through his analysis of rationality and rationalization. Weber's idea is quite compatible with the utilitarianism that Durkheim criticized. Remember that Durkheim's point was that the pursuit of self-interest rested on an underlying *collective* value agreement about the boundaries of the pursuit— an agreement, say, that contracts should be honoured. Although I think he was right about this, his emphasis hid from him the power of rationalization and the instrumental advantages bought about by the division of labour—just as, arguably, Weber (or at least the Weber discussed in Chapter 9) might have some difficulty in seeing how a *conscience collective* could mediate the power of rationalization—why, for example, some colonized nations rejected the rationality of colonization.

What all three miss, and what Simmel above all grasps, is the way these various processes affect and transform individual and group psychology, the forms and depth of relationship that are possible between individuals and groups. I think it is probably fair to say that Simmel is the only one of the four who values the individual in a concrete sense. For Marx, the notion of the individual in a modern sense is a product of capitalism, and I think this is true if we are talking about a view which sees the individual as free and self-creating, but often he seemed to see real people only as examples of human nature and of alienated human nature and as members of a social class. They might be all of these, but they are also living beings with difficult internal struggles and Simmel is the one sociologist who offers a possibility of understanding. Durkheim overemphasizes socialization, and sees individuality as possible only through the modern *conscience collective*—what Simmel would regard as the very objective culture which would deny individuality. And Weber seems only to see the individual as already colonized by rationality.

Earlier I commented that a Marxist would be interested in different evidence from a Durkheimian; it should be clear why this is the case, not only for these two approaches but for all four: they are talking about related but different aspects of the social world. It is a matter of finding not the evidence that will enable us to choose between the approaches but the evidence that will enable us to extend the depth of the understanding offered by each theory.

Part 3

History and social change

Introduction to Part 3

I want to turn now to issues that have been implicitly or explicitly present throughout, but have only now come to the fore. My focus now moves to history and social change, and the direction in which that change might be moving. It is as if so far I have described the machinery of society as each thinker sees it, and it is now time to look at that machinery in motion—only here we are dealing with a strange machine that changes its nature as it progresses: it might start off as a crude wheelbarrow, but will develop into a horse-drawn chariot, a wagon, and a model T Ford, and then at some point it will take off and develop jet propulsion.

I am using the word 'history' to indicate a long process stretching back into the mists of time up to the present day. We cannot think about society without in some way or another implying a theory of history. Even if we claim that we have no theory and that history is this vast sense is not amenable to 'a theory', some sort of theory is implicit. We cannot escape a theory of history just as we cannot escape a general theory.

The late nineteenth century was dominated by theories of evolution and on into the mid-twentieth century it was almost automatic to apply some sort of evolutionary framework. Even Weber implies a theory of social evolution. The late twentieth century has seen the development of relativist rather than evolutionary visions of the world, with an emphasis on value choices and chance. The difference is one between a view that the primitive wheelbarrow has some internal quality which will lead to its eventual transformation into a space rocket and a view that it is only through the ingenuity of some character who could easily not have been born that humanity got as far as hitching animals to cart-like structures. My own view here, which will inform the following discussions, is that there is no evidence for a 'hard' evolutionary theory in social science, but there does seem to be some mileage in a looser theory which perhaps sees evolution as a movement from the comparatively small and simple to the comparatively large and complex. Even those theorists such as Anthony Giddens who dismiss evolutionary theory tend to produce classificatory theories that have evolutionary implications (see Wright 1989; Bottomore 1990; Craib 1992a).

By social change I mean less the broad sweep of history than the nature of change in the modern world since the industrial revolution up to the present time and into the foreseeable future. Here the question of whether the modern world is best characterized by what has become known as 'modernity' or 'capitalism' comes to the fore, as well as the significance of imperialism (Marx) and the significance of the history of western Europe (Weber). Both writers seem to imply—for different reasons—that the history of modern society necessarily draws the rest of the world into its orbit. This happens either through the expansionist dynamic of capitalism, which continually seeks new markets, and sources of cheaper raw materials and cheaper labour, or through the dominance of western rationality, which is more practically efficient and pulls everything along behind it. It also raises again the problem of the relationship between the individual and society. One might think, at least in modern society, that the scope of individual freedom is becoming wider and wider, but there are arguments to suggest that this apparent freedom is coupled with an increasing control over our internal psychological processes. As the forces of tradition decline, we are changed internally by the conditions of modern life. We can already see this argument developing in the work of Simmel and Weber, and it is one of the options open in Marx's view of history.

I have already suggested that perhaps we are in a situation where structural cohesion is becoming firmer and beyond the perception and often the understanding of most—if not all—people and this generates a situation in which social cohesion begins to fragment. Each theoretical tradition has different and perhaps contradictory ways of saying the same thing. For Durkheim, it would be the abnormal division of labour eating away at the power of the *conscience collective*; for Marx, it would be the increasing dominance of the capitalist system over those groups which might oppose it; for Weber, it might be the iron cage of rational calculability; for Simmel, the increasing dominance of objective culture. This raises the question of how far modern social structures are open to conscious political change; whereas socialist and communist parties once promised revolutionary change, they now seem to offer only a counter-balance to the more extreme manifestations of the free market. The classical thinkers still set the limits of our thinking around all these issues: it is as if the picture they painted in broad outline has become more and more detailed and less and less clear, but no new outlines have emerged: we are still caught in the same picture.

Now each of these theorists, as well as suggesting what can happen, also explicitly or implicitly says what *should* happen—what the world should be like: they each imply a set of values which can be realized in our social organization and in our individual and collective behaviour. They imply what we might call social moralities and these will turn out to be connected with the dualisms that I have tried to use as a guiding framework for talking about the classical theorists. I think in this respect I would argue a position that is close to Charles Taylor's (1989) in his remarkable study of the development of our moral conceptions of the self. The values which these imply are usually all desirable, but contradictory. This means that, if we choose one value then we have to sacrifice another—that, for example, there might be a choice, in degree, between social cohesion and individual freedom; between freedom and stability in personal relationships; between freedom and equality; between personal autonomy and a welfare state. Part of the social function of social theory should be to explore these alternatives and clarify what would be entailed by different intentions.

11 | Durkheim's organic analogy

Introduction
Durkheim on history and politics.

The organic analogy and Durkheim's theory of history
The explanation of change in the *Division of Labour*; change through population growth; primary and secondary factors in the division of labour; increasing universality of the *conscience collective* and the growing freedom of the individual; the importance of organic and psychological factors in the division of labour; Durkheim's materialism and his increasing concern with cultural patterns. The explanation of change in *The Rules of Sociological Method*; the classification of social types; the primitive horde and more complex combinations; societies as species; the distinction between society and civilization; critique of the species analogy; Durkheim and modern evolutionary theory.

Durkheim's conservatism and Durkheim's socialism
The debate about Durkheim's politics; the importance of placing limits on human nature; his critique of modernity and his critique of socialism as an ideological reaction to industrialization compared to sociology as a scientific reaction—comparison with Engels. Durkheim's liberal/left sympathies; the emphasis on the importance of professional groupings which would control the state (his syndicalism); his support for the Dreyfusards and his individualism—the sacredness of the individual in general; the importance of freedom of thought and the cognitive role of the state; the problem of politics and analysis in Durkheim; his conservative views on divorce and women.

Conclusion
The continuing importance of Durkheim as a theorist of society and social cohesion; the *conscience collective* in the modern world; the importance of his conception of the state as protector of the individual and civil society; his lack of a theory of action; criticism of his theory of history.

Introduction

> The division of labour varies in direct proportion to the volume and density of societies and if it progresses in a continuous manner over the course of social development it is because more societies become regularly more dense and generally more voluminous.
>
> (Durkheim 1893/1984: 205)

This quotation conveys the sense of Durkheim's theory of history as a steady process; generally it seems to me that this is less interesting than what he has to say about modern societies but we cannot fully understand the latter without the former.

The organic analogy and Durkheim's theory of history

Durkheim's use of the organic analogy is at its clearest in his writing on social evolution, particularly in the development from the *Division of Labour* to *The Rules of Sociological Method*.

THE DIVISION OF LABOUR

Durkheim does not present a very elaborate theory of social change in *The Division of Labour*. The basis for the development from mechanical to organic solidarity is mainly a matter of population growth, of social density. In segmented, tribal societies, clans live at a distance from each other and do not necessarily come into much contact; as they grow in numbers and contact between them becomes easier, higher levels of social interaction give rise to competition and conflict for resources. This in turn provides the basis for the differentiation of functions which is the organic division of labour. The development begins with the settlement of nomadic groups into agricultural communities, creating centres of population which can then grow by attracting others to a more settled existence. This leads on to the development of the towns. It is wrong to associate urban growth with decline and decadence; in fact, it is a product of societies of the higher type—France, for example, was never an agricultural society in its pure type. Durkheim predicts, rightly, that the process of urban growth will continue, and Anthony Giddens (1981) argues that the city is now the dominant form of life, so that even comparatively remote country areas are under its sway.

Finally, the improvement of transport and communication brings the settlements closer together.

Darwin's theory placed a lot of emphasis on random variations which might not survive in the struggle for life; Durkheim chooses the struggle for survival as an important impetus for social development, emerging from the competition for scarce resources. The more alike these social groupings are, the fiercer the conflict. On the other hand, if the neighbouring societies belong to different types with different needs, the necessity for conflict abates—this is as true for humans as it is for plants and animals. Within societies, particularly with an urban environment:

different occupations can coexist within being forced into a position where they harm one another, for they are pursuing different objectives. The soldier seeks military glory, the priest moral authority, the statesman power, the industrialist wealth, the scientist professional fame. Each one of these can therefore reach his goal without preventing others from reaching theirs. This is the case even where the functions are less remote from one another. The medical eye specialist does not compete with the one who cares for the mentally ill, the shoe maker does not compete with the hatter, the mason with the cabinet maker, the physician with the chemist etc. As they perform different services they can perform them in harmony.   (Durkheim 1893/1984: 209–10)

Where conflict does result, the loser can deal with it only by going off and doing something else and hence the division of labour progresses. We have seen that, as this process develops, organic solidarity becomes the dominant form of social cohesion and the *conscience collective* both changes in importance—it becomes less important—and moves towards a more individualistic base. The material basis for the increasing division of labour, the growth in population and density, is aided by what Durkheim calls 'secondary factors', what Marxists would refer to as ideological factors, and Weberians perhaps refer to as value choices.

The pressure towards individuation and the division of labour is in fact countered by the strength of the *conscience collective*; for the division of labour to take place and for the external pressure to have its effect, the individual must be free to move in whatever direction is appropriate. The first secondary factor is the autonomy of the individual. On the face of it, this seems to be a tautology: in order for the individual to gain autonomy, the individual must possess autonomy. Durkheim draws on the biological analogy, talking about 'the law of the independence of anatomical elements'. By this I take him to mean that, for example, the hearts and the lungs and the liver do not merge into each other but remain identifiably separate, each carrying out its specific function for the body. In organisms this independence is a primative fact—it just *is*; there never was a stage where hearts, lung, and liver were merged. In societies, it has to be achieved.

As societies grow larger, the experiences of its members begin to vary. The *conscience collective*, if it is going to symbolize all the experiences of all the members of society, must become more inclusive—as Durkheim puts it, 'rising above' local variations and therefore becoming more abstract. This is seen most clearly in the way in which divinity is abstracted from specific objects in particular places to become more and more abstract, until eventually we reach notions of 'the one', God, or Allah who is no longer anywhere specific in this world. The more abstract our symbols become, the more rational they become—universality and rationality necessarily imply each other. And the more universal the *conscience collective* becomes, the more the individual variations it can allow.

There are other factors at work in all this. It takes a long time for the *conscience collective* to change, not least because it comes to us with all the weight of the past behind it. This is especially powerful where segmented societies exist—if I can only live and work in my own particular family, or geographical area, then the power which the group has over me is very strong; when this type of society begins to break down, so that I can move from group to group and area to area, the power of the dead generations fades. I move away from my father, and my father's generation, who taught me their ways, and he cannot keep his power over me on a day-to-day basis. I use the word father deliberately as we are dealing with patriarchal societies, but in modern societies the same goes for the relationship between mother and daughter. With the growth of towns and then large cities, the power of the older generation reaches its lowest point.

It is easy to see the way in which we can be more free in large towns and cities. We become anonymous and can carry on our various sexual, intellectual, and work activities without our families and neighbours knowing anything about them. This also sets up a nostalgia and a conflict—a desire for a return to community life and family values. If Durkheim shows anything, it is that societies and individuals have to face these choices, and, in so far as they have any power over events, make decisions about them.

Mechanical causes ensure the domination of the individual by the collective. Segmentary society exercises a tight grip over its members, limiting their horizons and tying them into tradition; but the same mechanical causes begin to enable the individual to begin to gain some independence. This is part of Durkheim's ongoing argument against the utilitarians—the division of labour does not occur because it is useful (which it is) or because it makes people happy (which it might do) but because it is the natural result of the growth of population and consequent decline of segmented societies. It is the social result of a social process. Professional societies and classes develop to fill the space left by the disappearance of segments (the clan groupings), but their regulations do not restrict the individual in the same way. First they limit only professional life—I might have a code of ethics to follow at work, but at home I can do what I like, within reason of course. The new rules never attain the far-ranging authority of the original *conscience collective* and the same general process of abstraction goes on within the professional groups.

Durkheim goes on to argue that the division of labour is produced by organic and psychological as well as social factors. For example, we each possess at birth natural talents and aptitudes which push us in one direction or another. In very simple societies heredity seems to play no role at all, but with some development it becomes more important. But the power of heredity lessens as the division of labour grows and new modes of activity appear. The things we inherit are static—for example, we inherit our racial characteristics but it is an extraordinarily long time since any new races have arisen; simple and general psychological states may be passed on, but not complex states and specific abilities which are highly individual. The division of labour produces precisely such specific skills, and the place of society, of socialization, becomes much more important than heredity, as do the specific talents of the individual. As we saw in the discussion of the abnormal forms of the division of labour, there is then a question of whether a society can enable individuals to realize these talents.

Perhaps the most interesting feature of the account of social change in *The Division of Labour* is that it is almost a materialist account—it is the material growth of the population and the increased production which comes with settled agricultural communities which pushes the process forward, not via class struggle, as it does in Marxist theories of history, but directly through increasing competition and complexity. This is worth remarking because Durkheim is so often thought of as the theorist of social cohesion through shared norms and ideas. Yet here he is producing an explanation which would differ from but not be foreign to Marxism, as we have seen in Engels's account of the origins of the family. The point to be taken from this—and it is well worth repeating—is that, although the thinkers we are studying are different from each other, what they offer is less a matter of mutually exclusive alternatives than differences of emphasis.

Having said this, it is also true that, as his work progressed, Durkheim was increasingly concerned with the processes by which and forms in which human beings symbolize their lives; nevertheless it must be remembered that they have material lives and an experience of the material world which have to be symbolized. These symbolic systems come to mediate the effect of changes in the external environment. Kenneth Thompson (1982: 97) argues that this ambiguity in his work, the failure to distinguish properly between what Gouldner (1958) calls social structure and cultural patterns of moral beliefs, is responsible for contradictory labels being attached to his position; I would argue that this ambiguity is one of Durkheim's strengths: he raises problems about the relationship which clearly need to be thought about and both the older Marxist crude materialist position and the newer postmodern crude idealist position manage to avoid thinking about such things.

SOCIAL SPECIES

The other work in which Durkheim elaborates his evolutionary theory is *The Rules of Sociological Method*. We saw earlier that for Durkheim it was important to arrive at a classification of social types. He argued that this classification should come through a study of the way in which the different parts of society are bound together:

We know that societies are composed of various parts in combination. Since the nature of the aggregate depends necessarily on the nature and number of the component elements and their mode of combination, these characteristics are evidently what we must take as our basis. (Durkheim 1895/1964: 81–2)

Most conceptions of evolution, strong or weak, see social development as moving from the simple to the complex, and a problem is always the definition of the simple society—what we think of as simple societies have a habit of turning out to be sufficiently complex to be quite different from each other. This was one of Durkheim's criticisms of Herbert Spencer, the British sociologist who is perhaps the major evolutionary sociologist of the nineteenth century. Just to talk about 'simple' societies lumped together very different types of society.

Durkheim's definition of a simple society was one that showed no previous sign of segmentation—an absence of parts: the 'horde'—'the protoplasm of the social realm and consequently, the natural basis of classification' (ibid. 83). Whether such types for society ever existed is, for Durkheim, not very important; what is important is that they provide a basis for classification. Here again there is a theme shared with Freud, who also worked with a notion of a primitive horde, a more or less undifferentiated group under the dominance of the strongest male, who had exclusive access to the women of the group. For Freud, differentiation begins when the younger males in the group overthrow the father and share the women out amongst themselves. Freud called his account a 'scientific myth': its purpose was as a sort of speculative hypothesis which enabled us to think about certain problems (the universality of the incest taboo) connected with human evolution which otherwise we would not be able to think about. Perhaps we can think about Durkheim's idea in the same way—in his case it enables us to develop a way of classifying societies as equivalent to animal species.

We can move from the simple horde to 'simple polysegmental societies'—societies with a number of segments or clans—and then on to polysegmental societies simply compounded—which, as I understand it, is a combination of simple polysegmental societies—and polysegmental societies doubly compounded, compounds of compounds. Durkheim here was holding fast to his biological analogy: animal species do not change very much even over very long periods, and therefore we cannot expect social species to change. If we try to classify societies by historical periodization, it would mean that species were changing all the time:

Since its origin, France has passed through very different forms of civilization; it begins by being agricultural, passed to craft industry and to small commerce then to manufacturing, and finally to large-scale industry. Now it is impossible to admit that the same collective individuality can change its species three or four times. A species must define itself by more constant characteristics. . . . The economic state, technological state etc., present phenomena too unstable and complex to furnish the basis of a classification. It is even very probable that the same industrial, scientific and artistic civilization can be found in societies whose heredity constitution is very different. Japan may in the future borrow our arts, our industry, even our political organization; it will not cease to belong to a different social species from France and Germany.   (ibid. 88)

It is a rather odd view, if you think about it, that France is still essentially the same as it was a number of centuries ago under a feudal regime, and changes such as industrialization are only surface changes. It is a view which one might find among the traditional conservative right: that there is an essential Frenchness or English-ness or, presumably, an American way of life that has existed for centuries and must be defended against dilution and domination by other nations. In British politics, such ideas could be found in the speeches of Enoch Powell and it sometimes emerges in opposition to British involvement in the European Union. For German historians of Durkheim's time and later it would be argued that the 'race' or 'national spirit' remained constant through these changes. The dangers of such positions must be self-evident. However Thompson (1982) does try to save something from these rather odd ideas, suggesting that a cultural inheritance can be inherited across such changes as industrialization.

In fact this is probably as good an example as you are likely to find of an analogy being pushed too far: types of society are *not* animal species, even if the organic analogy is sometimes useful. Durkheim did not try to classify actual societies in the way he proposed and it is difficult to see how useful it could be in this form—as Thompson points out, unless France, Japan, and Germany had surprisingly similar histories, Durkheim would be compelled to think of them as belonging to different species. On the other hand, Durkheim's ideas were developed much later in a different way by Parsons (1966). Instead of conceiving of change as coming from combinations of simple societies, he suggested that societies evolved through their own internal divisions and subdivisions, rather as a cell divides and subdivides (Craib 1992*b*). As Pearce (1989) points out, the earlier book, *The Division of Labour,* enables us to see modern societies in such a way. Once started along the road, the division of labour generates the division of labour.

If, then, we think about Durkheim as offering a theory of history, we do not get that far if we stick to *The Rules of Sociological Method. The Division of Labour* is more helpful and can take us to the comparatively rapid developments of late modernity.

Durkheim's conservatism and Durkheim's socialism

There has been a debate in sociology of recent decades about Durkheim's conservatism. Some of my critical comments have pointed to his conservatism—for example, his difficulty in understanding inbuilt social conflict, as opposed to social conflict which is a result of functional imbalance. Steven Lukes (1973) points to another conservative aspect of Durkheim's thought—his view that human nature is in need of limitation and moral guidance, although why this should necessarily be conservative is not clear. It is perhaps more of a commentary on political change over recent decades than an accurate interpretation of Durkheim. If human nature needs limitation and morality, then that is what it needs, and what makes it conservative or otherwise depends on the morality itself. That Lukes should see this as necessarily conservative seems to be a result of his writing at a time when long-established restrictions on individual morality, particularly sexual morality, had been lifted. What is clear twenty years later is that the values of the market economy seem to have eaten away at many forms of morality and it is the conservative parties which have supported the freeing of the market. To talk of morality now is no longer conservative. It is, as ever, a matter of finding a middle way between the individual freedom and the authority of social morality.

The changes of the last thirty years have also changed the way in which we can read another aspect of Durkheim's work. In *Suicide* Durkheim talks about the threat to society that comes from unrestrained individuality, less from egoism—which, as we saw, can be regarded as a form of social integration—than from anomie. If there are no limits to our ambitions, then we constantly try to outstrip ourselves, building up a constant nervous tension:

Since imagination is hungry for novelty, and ungoverned, it gropes at random. Setbacks necessarily increase with risk and thus crises multiply, just when they are becoming more destructive. Yet these dispositions are so inbred that society has grown to accept them and is accustomed to think them normal. It is everlastingly repeated that it is man's nature to be eternally dissatisfied, constantly to advance, without relief or rest, toward an indefinite goal. The longing for infinity is daily represented as a mark of moral distinction whereas it can only appear within unregulated consciences which elevate to a rule the lack of rule from which they suffer.   (Durkheim 1897/1952: 257)

This is as damning a psychological critique of modern societies as any, again not far from Christopher Lasch's conception of narcissism, against which Lasch (1980) poses not the professional group but more of a populist conception of a community of solid, honest people. John Horton (1990) calls anomie a utopian concept of the radical right, and it is easy to see how it could have seemed so when his article was first published, in 1964, but again, as with Steven Lukes' comments about Durkheim's conception of moral authority, such talk now does not seem necessarily to belong to the right.

For all four classical thinkers socialism is at the centre of the political agenda in the modern world. Although Durkheim's study *Socialism and Saint-Simon* was not published until 1928, it was based on lectures delivered in the mid-1890s. His approach to the subject was based on the sociology of knowledge, the way in which particular social conditions generate particular ideas; it is a pity that Durkheim never got as far as taking on Marx head-on, dealing only with the beginnings of socialism and the ideas of Saint-Simon, a French utopian socialist. Durkheim was never to match his own scientific sociology to Marx's scientific socialism.

Durkheim's definition of socialism, according to K. Thompson (1982: 156), made it an 'inevitable development in social evolution': We denote as socialist every doctrine which demands the connection of all economic functions, or of certain among them, which are at the present time diffuse, to the directing and conscious centres of society' (Durkheim 1962: 54). He writes 'the centre of society' rather than the state because he recognized Marx's hope that the state would vanish once a classless society was established. Durkheim distinguished this version of socialism from utopian versions—just as Engels (1967) had distinguished Marx's scientific socialism from the utopian socialists. For both, utopian ideas are individual inventions, not based on a scientific understanding of social development. But, of course, each has a different conception of social science. Durkheim dismissed what he called communist utopianism, which he saw as opposed to wealth *per se*, whereas he argued that the socialist opposition to private property, as expressed by Saint-Simon in France and Robert Owen in Britain, was based on the modern developments of social structures. For Marx and Engels, both Owen and Saint-Simon were utopians.

Durkheim suggested that there had been three reactions to industrialization at the beginning of the nineteenth century: the first was socialism; the second was an attempt to establish a quasi-religious basis for a new morality, and, finally, there was sociology itself as the new science of society. All three had their origins in the work of Saint-Simon and can still be distinguished in Comte. He argued that the time had come to separate them, and his concern was to protect the growth of a scientific sociology. His central criticism of socialism was its concentration upon economic arguments and answers when moral arguments and answers were also necessary, and he was of course critical of the way socialism claimed to be scientific, on a par with sociology when it was an ideology and a social movement. In this respect Durkheim thought that socialism had in fact contributed more to sociology than vice versa—it had stimulated argument and reflection and research, but it also made claims about areas which went well beyond research and beyond any claims that science could make:

The only attitude that science permits in the face of these problems is reservation and circumspection, and socialism can hardly maintain this without lying to itself. . . . Not even the strongest work—the most systematic, the richest in ideas—that this school has

produced: Marx's *Capital*. What statistical data, what historical comparisons and studies would be indispensable to solve any one of the innumerable questions which are dealt
with there . . . Socialism is not a science . . . it is a cry of grief, sometimes anger.
(Durkheim 1958: 40–1)

Durkheim argues that the same goes for the opponents of socialism—*laissez-
faire* economics makes equally vast but unsubstantiated claims. Socialism offers
a cry of pain but not a diagnosis of the illness.

His own sympathies were to the left, a liberal socialism, and, although he was
not especially active politically, he did show his sympathy with the
Dreyfusards—those who opposed what would now be known as the French
Establishment when Alfred Dreyfus, a Jewish army officer, was scapegoated for
crimes committed by his superiors, and he did develop a number of political
ideas from his analysis of modernity. For example, he argued that territorial
constituencies for elections were a throwback to the days of mechanical solidarity and that the 'natural' constituencies should be functional groups—especially
the professional groups. We have seen earlier that Durkheim saw the state as
protecting the individual against such groups, but these groups would also protect the individual against oppression by the state, and the state against individualist egoism. J. E. S. Hayward (1990) called this a 'reformist syndicalism'—a
system of self-government by groups of workers. Industries and factories and
the professions would be run by those who work in them (rather than by the
state, as happened with the state socialist societies of eastern Europe), and the
state, in so far as it existed, would be governed by the representatives of these
groups. However, Durkheim saw this developing through a process of evolution
rather than violent revolution—the tendency with which the name is most usually associated. Each group would determine wages and working conditions,
pensions and social benefits—modern industrial society was too large and complex for all this to be determined by one central power.

The conservative interpretation of Durkheim is based on his insistence on the
need for moral control, as a restriction on the individual, yet in the essay
'Individualism and the Intellectuals' (Durkheim 1898/1990) we find an elaboration of the liberal principles behind the *Dreyfusard* campaign, which he supported. He points out that the intellectuals' support of Dreyfus (particularly the
novelist Émile Zola, who produced the famous letter *J'accuse*) had been met by
the government and the military with a campaign against individualism. He
makes the point that he would agree with the condemnation of egotistical individualism—the sort of self-interest that is seen as a basic motivation by the utilitarians to whom Durkheim was so consistently opposed: 'it is only too clear
that all social life would be impossible if there did not exist interests superior to
the interests of individuals' (Durkheim 1898/1990: 172).

There is, however, another sort of individualism which Durkheim puts at the
centre of European philosophy and politics which has its roots in the work of
Kant and Rousseau. Beginning with Kant's moral philosophy, this alternative

sees in personal motives the 'very source of evil'. The good is universal, or part of the general will. Moral action involves looking at what we have in common with our fellow human beings. This, in turn, rests on the assumption that it is in relation to the human person that we can distinguish good and evil; the human person is in this sense sacred:

[it] is conceived as being invested with that mysterious property which creates an empty space around holy objects, which keeps them away from profane contacts and which draws them away from ordinary life. And it is exactly this feature which induces the respect of which it is the object. Whoever makes an attempt on a man's life, on a man's liberty, on a man's honour inspires us with a feeling of horror, in every way analogous to that which the believer experiences when he sees his idol profaned. Such a morality is therefore not simply a hygienic discipline or a wise principle of economy. It is a religion of which man is, at the same time, both believer and God.   (ibid. 173)

This religion is an individualistic religion and the philosophers who have developed these ideas are also aware of the rights of the collectivity. This type of individualism involves 'the glorification not of the self but of the individual in general'. It leads on to ideals such as the autonomy of reason and freedom of thought, and here, according to Durkheim, we come across the major conservative objection to individualism: if people think freely and make up their own minds, what is to stop anarchy? This is a reaction not unknown in our own times, particularly when it is a matter of sexual morality. Durkheim's response is that freedom of thought actually carries with it the recognition of the expertise of others: I might at first glance decide that the earth is flat, but if geographers who have greater knowledge of these things tell me it is round, I am, within reason, willing to accept that. But there are also issues which concern people in general which are not matters for experts alone but upon which everyone can express an opinion and this includes the most important political issues. If a doctor diagnoses cancer, I must bow to his opinion; if he argues that everybody with cancer should be painlessly killed, I have something to say about it. The intellectuals who protested against Dreyfus's conviction were not claiming special expertise but were commenting on a matter of common concern. Conservative arguments that what is needed is a return to traditional religion are pointless—the social conditions that produced traditional religion are no longer in existence. The new religion is the religion of humanity.

Giddens (1990a) points out that Durkheim saw the state as having a cognitive as much as an active role in the development of this new way of thinking. It should elaborate on the content of the modern *conscience collective*, and define and implement the principles of moral individualism. It is only through membership of a collective and through recognizing a moral authority that the individual can actually realize him- or herself. Again we find here a parallel with Freud's psychoanalysis where it is only through the discipline imposed by the ego and superego that creativity becomes possible.

Giddens goes on to argue that Durkheim never really tackled the problem of the relationship between sociology and politics; he had a personal disdain for political squabbles, and his concern with the scientific status of sociology left sociology itself aloof from politics. But it also meant that his analytic and prescriptive work tended to blur into each other, since he had no conceptual tools to separate them. The distinction between the normal and the pathological is both analytic and descriptive at the same time. It is certainly true that Durkheim envisaged a classless society, but it would not be classless in Marx's terms; for Durkheim inheritance was the problem, for Marx it was ownership. Nevertheless it is arguable that Durkheim also had what Pearce (1989) calls a radical socialist vision. He points to Durkheim's critique of *laissez-faire* economics in *Professional Ethics and Civil Morals* (1957). Whereas economists argue that the state has no productive function, and in effect only the negative function of protecting individual liberty, Durkheim argues that the state had a positive function. It is, in Pearce's words, 'socially productive'. Pearce uses the following quotation from Durkheim to illustrate that vision. In a complex society, the state must govern economic transactions:

by rules that are more just; it is not simply that everyone should have more access to rich supplies of food and drink. Rather it is that each one should be treated as he deserves, each be freed from an unjust and humiliating tutelage, and that, in holding to his fellows and his group, a man should not sacrifice his individuality. And the agency on which this special responsibility lies is the State. So the State does not inevitably become either simply a spectator of social life (as the economists would have it), in which it intervenes only in a negative way, or (as the socialists would have it) simply a cog in the economic machine. It is above all, supremely the organ of moral discipline.   (ibid. 72)

The basis of Pearce's argument is that if we shed some of Durkheim's assumptions, we can find a picture of a feasible democratic socialist society. He argues that a class society inhibits the development of a truly organic solidarity and Marxism can identify a number of economic and social structural factors that interfere with the development that Durkheim foresaw or desired. At the same time Durkheim can contribute new dimensions to Marxism, eventually replacing a Marxist utopianism with a more realistic sense of what is possible.

Durkheim held what would today be considered some rather conservative ideas about marriage and sexuality, but he does raise some interesting issues. In *Suicide* he points out that, where rules governing divorce are strict there are higher rates of suicide amongst women, where they are easier (conjugal anomie) there is a higher rate amongst men, and generally suicide rates vary directly with divorce. This is a form of anomic suicide.

In the same discussion, he argues that the function of marriage is not simply to control physical desires; in humans the sexual urge has become complicated by moral and aesthetic feelings and social regulation thus becomes necessary— Durkheim is on firm ground here and is explaining an often forgotten reason why we need a sociology of sexuality:

just because these various inclinations . . . do not directly depend upon organic necessities, social regulation becomes necessary. They must be restrained by society since the organism has no means of restraining them. This is the function of marriage. It completely regulates the life of passion, and monogamic marriage more strictly than any other. For by forcing a man to attach himself forever to the same woman it assigns a strictly definite object the need for love, and closes the horizon.   (Durkheim 1897/1952: 270)

Thus it is desire, not the sexual drive itself, which has to be restrained (and I think anyone who has fallen in love has some intimation that the desire for love can be powerful, even addictive). And, if the desire is not controlled, then ambitions rocket and the impact of disappointment grows correspondingly. According to Durkheim, this is true even for the 'humdrum existence of the ordinary bachelor':

New hopes constantly awake only to be deceived, leaving a trail of weariness and disillusionment behind them. How can desire, then, become fixed, being uncertain that it can retain what it attracts; for the anomie is twofold. Just as the person makes no definitive gift of himself, he has definitive title to nothing. The uncertainty of the future plus his own indeterminateness therefore condemns him to constant change. The result of it all is a state of disturbance, agitation and discontent which inevitably increases the possibilities of suicide.   (ibid. 271)

Now for the crunch: women have less need for such regulation because their mental life is less developed; they are more tied to and led by bodily needs and instincts, and have only to follow these to achieve 'calmness and peace'. Marriage for the woman closes off realistic hopes and narrows her horizons, whereas she is protected by divorce—it is a relief for her. One might think it is a relief for her for other reasons that those suggested by Durkheim, but that is for the reader to decide. At any rate, marriage cannot be simultaneously agreeable 'to two persons, one of whom is almost entirely a product of society, while the other has remained to a far greater extent the product of nature' (ibid. 385). But, according to Durkheim, we can imagine a position where women can play a more important social role—although, of course, it would never equal that of men. Women would be given their own specific role in the social division of labour—perhaps, for example, taking a more active role in the aesthetic sphere. Many contemporary readers will, I suspect, read that, with some justification, as saying the women will come to do what we would call 'women's work' and go on to talk about discrimination on the labour market.

But it is worth pointing out that even here there is a radical edge to Durkheim, and, if we allow him to be a (male) child of his time, it is possible to take his ideas as leading somewhere else. He *is* talking about the possibility of increased equality in marriage, even if he does not go as far as talking of a marriage between equals. The course of the division of labour has certainly taken women closer to equality than at Durkheim's time, but the result has been the opposite of stabilizing marriage, which as an institution seems to have been steadily weakened not only by increasingly high divorce rates but by the reluctance of couples to marry in the first place. I think this says something important about Durkheim's political naïvity—at least it is possible to call it naïvity with hindsight. The continued development of the division of labour has not led to the 'religion of humanity' that he thought would be at the centre of the modern *conscience collective*, but to something closer to the unlimited egoism that he feared. The capitalist market which has been the main agent of individualization (as opposed to an organically developing division of labour) reduces people to an abstract individuality and leaves them face to face less with a society than with a global system which has no *conscience collective*.

Conclusion

I want now to try to sum up some of the points I have made about Durkheim in the book as a whole as well as in this chapter. My first point is that Durkheim's value lies most clearly in the fact that, first, he is the theorist of *society* as something which exists over and above individuals, and, secondly, he is the theorist of *social cohesion*, of the way in which a society holds together through shared logics, shared symbolic systems, and shared norms and values. Sometimes he tends towards identifying *society* with the *conscience collective*, when in fact within his framework it would be more accurate to see society as comprising both the *conscience collective* and the division labour and the group relations produced by the division of labour. Another way of putting this in terms of the dualisms I set out at the beginning is that Durkheim tends to merge social cohesion with structural cohesion, rather than examine the possibility that, as the division of labour develops, there might be a conflict, even a contradiction, between the two—that the division of labour might undermine the *conscience collective*.

Yet, even though this might be happening, it is still happening within the framework of something we call society—even if we have to think of that society as existing on a global rather than a national or regional level. It is a society in which individuals are subjected less to collective ideas and more to structural processes. However, the *conscience collective* remains. First, it remains on the deeper level that I discussed earlier—the level of the logical forms (our language, the way in which we conceive of causality, time, and space) are imposed upon us from without, and without them there would be no possibility of communication. Indeed the standardization and universalization of time and space mean that, at this level, we *are* effectively talking about a global *conscience collective*. However, at the levels of norms and values we seem to be looking at a world of infinite variety, a world where the notion of value itself is often challenged, and this provides a focus for political arguments throughout western Europe and North America. We can witness our modern version of the very arguments that Durkheim was discussing in his justification of the Dreyfusard position and his justification of individualism. On the one hand, we find demands for a return to traditional values, against which the forces of chaos and anarchy are ranged, and, on the other, we find demands for individual liberty, minority rights, sexual equality (which perhaps combines both of the foregoing), and a multicultural pluralism.

And again, rather as Durkheim constructed an argument in favour of the *value* of the individual as the centre of the modern *conscience collective*, so we can find arguments in favour of a modern ethic of tolerance. Indeed, some forms of postmodernism seem to elevate tolerance almost to the point of chaos, but that is another matter; certainly this aspect of postmodernism could be regarded as pointing perhaps to a postmodern *conscience collective* of as wide a variety of meanings, ethics, and narratives as possible. From this point of view, it is less the individual *per se* that should be valued, less a religion of humanity, than the multiplicity of internal narratives—not so much the 'me' but the many 'mes' that I am in different situations (see Gergen 1991).

A second alternative focus for the centre of the modern *conscience collective*, arrived at in a very different way, is Habermas's notion of a 'procedural ethics'. Put simply—not to say crudely—the central proposition is that it is not so much the substantive content of a morality that matters; that will vary from culture to culture and even sub-culture to subsubculture; rather it is the way in which decisions about morality are arrived at; our nature as human beings involves us each in rationality and we can set up a social ideal in which we all, by virtue of our rational capacity, participate in decision-making. In other words, it is the democratic nature of decision-making that matters rather than the decision itself. Now, put this simply, there are all sorts of problems with the idea, but I think the basic idea is clear. The 'sacred' element becomes neither individualism, nor tolerance or variety as such, but the democratic process in which everybody is involved in the decisions which affect them.

The important point is that it seems that we cannot think about social life without referring to or implying or arguing for some central 'sacred' value or set of values which comprise a *conscience collective*; even if we are attacking the very idea of a *conscience collective* we are employing some set of values which must stand in its place—just as modern individualism opposing traditional religious forms can be seen as a religion of individualism. It is also the case that these putative contents of the *conscience collective* become more and more abstract—the sort of procedural ethic proposed by Habermas would include cultures with very different moral systems and the movement from content to form is possibly as abstract as one can become where morality is concerned.

Paradoxically, although Durkheim is the theorist of society, he is the only one to talk in any depth about individualism and the difficulties of a society based on individualism. In modern societies the individual is neither a simple product of his or her society nor one of signifying systems—rather he or she is the *user* of signifying systems, of the norms and beliefs of the society, who can argue and judge, accept or reject, what he or she is offered. Durkheim warns us of the importance of preserving the space for these judgements through the setting of moral boundaries, limiting the powers of groups, and encouraging the formation of responsible associations. He offers a conception of civil society which limits both the power of the state and egoism. It seems to me arguable that it is precisely this level of social organization which has diminished in importance with the development of market capitalism—opening the door to the sort of narcissistic and egoistic individualism that contemporary society seems to encourage. He speaks for the middle ground between the free-market individualism of the New Right and the rigid state control of the Old Left. And he leaves us with a greater understanding of the continual and unavoidable dilemma between individual freedom, and on the one hand, and social control, on the other.

It is when we come to look at the modernity/capitalism—socialism dualism that we begin to find the limitation of Durkheim's thought and aspects of what we might regard as a structural determinism. Individual freedom and the development of occupational groups are both the result of the division of labour; they do not themselves bring about any sort of change. There is not a theory of individual or collective action in Durkheim, even though he is not a sociological determinist. This represents a gap, a sort of silence—he does not have much to say about political action, and in particular about class and class conflict. Yet, if we want to explain why the division of labor has not developed in the way that Durkheim thought it would, it is to the theory of capitalism that we must turn; to the development of the free market and of state power. We can perhaps read Durkheim as offering an 'acceptable face' of modernity—a form of socialism that is neither centralized nor simply a matter of limited controls on the free market.

Returning now to the theory of history in the wider sense with which I started this chapter, we can see that, once society develops away from the state of mechanical solidarity, it is not simply a matter of developments in the division of labour but also developments of ownership and the appearance of class divisions which complicate matters. The evolutionary conception of social development is too simple, yet, as we shall see when we turn to Marx, it is not irrelevant to understanding the contemporary world. If Durkheim has difficulty in grasping the importance of the effects of capitalism, then perhaps Marx has difficulty grasping the effects of modernity *per se*.

We can now move to summarizing the different positions around the secondary dualism of modernity and capitalism which I begin in Box 11.1.

Box 11.1. Durkheim on modernity and capitalism/socialism

MODERNITY

Durkheim: a movement towards a balanced society of occupational groups held together by the state and a new humanist 'religion' which emphasized the value of the individual.

CAPITALISM/SOCIALISM

Durkheim: Durkheim's concept of socialism was based on his conception of the development of modernity; although problems arise in the abnormal forms of the division of labour, these would be ironed out in continued historical development. He does not seem to see capitalism as a specific form of modern society responsible for either its problems or its benefits.

Further reading

From Durkheim's own work, see *The Division of Labour in Society* (1893/1984), book 1, chapters 5 and 6; book 2, and book 3, for his account of the development of the division of labour and its abnormal forms in modern society; see also *The Rules of Sociological Method* (1895/1964), chapter 4. For his discussion of socialism, see his *Socialism and Saint-Simon* (1928/1959). His discussion of Dreyfus and individualism can be found in Volume IV of *Emile Durkheim: Critical Assessments*, edited by Peter Hamilton (1990), 62–73.

For more modern discussions of Durkheim's politics, see Steven Lukes, *Emile Durkheim* (1973)—check the index references. Zeitlin, *Ideology and the Development of Sociological Theory* (1968), damns Durkheim for his conservatism, but more recently Frank Pearce, *The Radical Durkheim* (1989), gives a very different point of view. More recent discussions of Durkheim include M. S. Gladis, *A Communitarian Defence of Liberalism* (1992), and W. F. Pickering and H. Martins, *Debating Durkheim* (1994).

12 | Marx and the meaning of history

Introduction

Marx's conception of history; Marx and Hegel; dialectical materialism and historical inevitability.

Historical laws and laws of history

Historical laws; Marx's originality; Marx's suggestions as explanation sketches.

Types of society/modes of production

Primitive communism: possible paths of social development starting from the priority of the community over the individual; forms of distributing the surplus; Marx's theoretical ordering of levels of development in terms of the development of individuality. *The Asiatic mode of production*: dominance of communal property and the despot; important role of the state and religion. *The Germanic mode of production*: the inevitable production of traditional relations. *The ancient mode of production*: dominated by the city; development of individual proprietorship; the emergence of the state; transformation brought about by the reproduction of the system. *Feudalism and the development of capitalism*: the ancient and the feudal modes; the town/country division and the division of labour; the development of the towns—the craft guilds—the merchant class—the bourgeoisie; machine production; the money economy; international markets. *Evolution from feudalism to capitalism*: a theoretical understanding of the development; comparison with Durkheim. *The complexities of class analysis of history*: the English Civil War as an example.

Theory and history

Theoretical and empirical distinctions: modern elaborations of the concept of mode of production. *Contemporary notions of evolution*: the nature of historical progress; open-ended conceptions of evolution.

The dynamics of capitalism

The tendency of the rate of profit to fall: living and dead labour and the increasing importance of the latter; countervailing tendencies; the increasing rate of technological change; the expansionist dynamic of capitalism. *Changes at other levels: transformations of the crisis*: Habermas on the evolution of modern capitalism; economic crisis—rationality crisis—legitimation crisis—motivation crisis.

Communism

The importance of the French Revolution; the proletariat as a revolutionary class; violence and revolution; the concept of overdetermination; the state and revolution; earlier and later phases of communism; the importance of utopian ideas; comparison with reality.

Conclusion

Introduction

If Durkheim's conception of history amounts to a smooth evolutionary process from mechanical to organic solidarity, then Marx's conception, whilst evolutionary in the sense of movement from one stage to another, also involves a conception of conflict and revolutionary transformation, at least at the later stages. Perhaps the most useful interpretation of Marx is as offering a conception of history moving on a number of different levels, not necessarily in conjunction with each other. This is not the case if one starts and ends with Marx the economic determinist, but if we allow his theory to open up a little, a number of interesting possibilities arise.

The term 'history' has a particular importance for Marxism both analytically—it is an important concept—and motivationally—several generations of Marxists have seen themselves as on the side of history, even as agents of a history which, in the none-too-pleasant jargon of some Marxist groups, possesses a dustbin into which their opponents will be thrown. Some forms of Marxism have worked with an overarching theory of history developing according to a particular logic—an inheritance from Hegel. The Marxist 'science of history', *dialectical materialism*, is Marx's inversion of Hegel's conception of history, which he sees as a moving force not of ideas but of material practices—the production of goods.

Engels (1940) attempted to formulate universal laws of the dialectic, arguing that everything in society and nature develops in the same way, through a process of conflicting opposites. As Ted Benton (1977) points out in an intelligent discussion, this claim is rather too vast for comfort. It is not as if natural scientists have themselves developed the idea of the dialectic or its laws out of their work; rather Engels has reinterpreted their results and theories and imposed a dialectical logic upon them. There are two classic examples of eminent men making fools of themselves by insisting that there is a dialectic of nature: the first is Hegel himself, who used the dialectic to predict that there would be a star in a certain place where none was ever found; the second was more serious: in the 1930s the Russian biologist Lysenko developed a 'dialectical method' of growing wheat which led to disastrous crop failures.

However, when we come to human thought and human action, it is perhaps a different matter and we can talk about a dialectical logic. But human action, at least when we think about history, is caught up with the natural world in a complex way, so again even when we talk about history, things are not so simple as we would like them to be. Just how complex they are can be discovered through a brief perusal of Sartre's *Critique of Dialectical Reason*—perhaps *the* major attempt to establish a foundation for a non-determinist dialectical thought and a dialectical philosophy of history.

The simplified version of the dialectic of history—that history progresses through the conflict between opposing forces—works best for capitalism. The growth of the capitalist system itself produces the proletariat, the opposing force which will eventually destroy it and establish a socialist system. But the problem of how capitalism, for example, grows out of the feudal system that preceded it is another matter—it is not the case that it emerges through some central contradiction, nor is it the case that the class conflict between peasants and landlords somehow produces capitalism. I don't think that there is anybody who would propose such an overarching theory of history these days—certainly not a Marxist theory, although occasionally people will play about with Hegelian ideas: Francis Fukuyama (1992), for example, goes back to Hegel to argue that history has come to an end with modern liberalism.

Before outlining a more modest version of Marxist evolutionary theory, I want to look in a little more detail, first, at the notion of historical laws and laws of history, and, secondly, at the variety of modes of production that we can find discussed in the work of Marx and Engels and the work of later Marxists. I will answer negatively the question of whether we can really find a tenable overall theory of history in them. However, I shall argue that, when we get to the modern world, it is another matter—we can find a number of complex but none the less clear ideas about the way in which modern society is developing. I will then go on to talk about Marx's conception of socialism and communism.

Historical laws and laws of history

Nicholas Lobkowicz (1978) draws a number of very useful distinctions around the ideas that are often found in Marx or Marxist writings about 'historical laws' or 'laws of history'. Whilst we might think of laws of nature as eternal, unchanging or at least lasting for very long periods—so that, for example, it is likely to be a long time before the laws of gravity cease to apply—this is not quite the way in which we can think of laws which might apply to social life. Lobkowicz comes to the following conclusions about historical laws. I have broken down the quotation into separate propositions. My explanatory comments are in square brackets. By 'historical laws' Marxists mean:

- first of all that specific empirical social laws are historically limited. [For example, a law might apply to capitalist societies only during certain periods of its development.]
- secondly that general social laws which constitute the framework of social science are historically varying. [i.e. general laws vary in the way in which they work from historical period to historical period—so that, if the law is that the economic level of society is determinant in the last instance, the way it is determinant varies from type of society to type of society—see below, for example, for the difference between feudalism and capitalism.]
- thirdly that some historically limited social laws are tendential. [Under capitalist conditions, the law of the falling rate of profit describes a tendency which can, in certain circumstances, be reversed.]
- fourthly that laws that are neither historically limited nor historically varying nor tendential are of no use in social science. [This has resonances of Weber's argument that general laws are not much use—the only sort of laws that would fall into this fourth category would be along the lines of] 'All societies are made up of people, animals and objects'.   (Lobkowicz 1978: 120)

Lobkowicz points out that various thinkers have suggested that there are laws of history, but only in Marxism do we find the idea of *historical* laws of history. He makes the important point that Marx made very limited claims for his laws—that, for example, when he talked about 'historical inevitability' he is only talking about western Europe. At another time:

in a letter to a Russian newspaper, written in 1877 and first published in Russia in 1886, he explicitly says that he did not intend to advance 'historic-philosophic theory of the general course of development every people is fated to tread' but only the 'inexorable laws' of the capitalist system. And he adds: 'Events strikingly analogous but taking place in different historical surroundings lead to totally different results. By studying each of these developments by itself and then comparing them one can find the clue to the phenomenon, but one will never arrive there by using as one's master key a general historico-philosophical theory, the supreme virtue of which consists in being supra-historical'.   (ibid. 122)

These reservations should be borne in mind whenever you come across claims about Marxist determinism and historical inevitability. As Lobkowicz goes on to argue, there is a sense here in which Marx's claims can be empirically tested and the fact that his predictions have not come true is not so much because the notion of a historical law is misguided *per se* but because this aspect of Marxism produces what the positivist philosopher Carl Hempel calls 'explanation sketches'—outlines of explanations which require filling in. Lobkowicz continues:

Hempel puts great emphasis upon the distinction between explanation sketches, on the one hand, and what he calls psuedo-explanations, on the other. While a scientifically acceptable explanation sketch is incomplete in that it needs to be filled out by more spe-cific statements but at the same time clearly points in the direction where these state-ments are to be found, a psuedo-explanation subsumes the phenomena under some general idea which in principle is not amenable to empirical test and therefore cannot indicate in which direction concrete research should turn. It has often been suggested that the Marxist-historicist theory of society is such a psuedo-explanation rather than an explanation proper. I do not believe that this is the case. Concrete research may not, and in fact did not, corroborate many of the laws by which Marx was trying to explain capi-talist development; but the fact that research is at all relevant to the Marxist theory indi-cates that the latter in not a psuedo-question.   (ibid. 230)

Lobkowicz goes on to suggest that the reason for maintaining Marx's develop-mental theory, despite the fact that his predictions have not come true, is that there is no serious alternative; and I have pointed out elsewhere (Craib 1992*a*) that attempts such as Giddens's to suggest a non-evolutionary theory of the development of capitalism is remarkably similar to Marx's own account.

Lobkowicz's argument is a more conventional and orthodox philosophical version of Lukacs's Hegelian argument that the fact that Marx's predictions were wrong does not disprove his method—in the same way, perhaps, that a wrong weather forecast does not undermine either the attempt to forecast the weather or necessarily the means used to produce that particular forecast; rather like weather forecasting, social prediction is a matter of informed hit-and-miss.

Types of society/modes of production

Marx refers to a number of different types of society. A type of society is not quite a mode of production: the latter refers to relationships of ownership and control of productive goods, whereas a society includes the various classes and institutional forms which develop on the basis of these relationships. The rela-tionships to the means of production form the base, the society includes both base and superstructure.

Primitive communism

It would be wrong to see the pre-capitalist formations as a chain in which each develops out of the other; rather Marx suggests a number of different ways in which societies can change from primitive communism, and it is clear that he does not think that all changes constitute progress. Rather like Durkheim, Marx sees history as beginning with the horde, or the tribal group, the stage of prim-itive communism. The individual is only an individual and only possesses property by virtue of his or her membership of the community—the community is the precondition of everything.

We have already seen Engels's account of the development from primitive communism. One of the problems with his account is that there are always non-labourers, young children, the old, and the sick, so it would be wrong to say that there is no surplus produced. In a book which in many ways represents the worst type of Marxist a priori argument (i.e. forcing the world into a general schema), but which nevertheless does make some useful points, Barry Hindess and Paul Hirst (1975) suggest that primitive communism can be seen as a mode of production with only two levels: the economic and the ideological (where decisions about distribution are made). Drawing on the work of the Marxist anthropologist Claude Meillasoux (1972), they suggest a distinction between those societies—mainly hunting societies—which employ a process of simple redistribution through a network of relations which are temporary, which might last only long enough for the immediate distribution of the kill, and societies with a more complex redistribution system. Complex redistribution involves a permanent network of relationships and this tends to happen in agricultural societies. Kinship units become more important here, and, with the importance of kinship units, so marriage rules have to be developed. It is very dubious whether there is a direct line from this sort of development to capitalism; rather it is a description after the event of a process of social change which might lead to the development of class societies.

We can find in Marx mention of other modes of production which do not seem to follow each other either theoretically or in reality. The ancient mode of production and the Asiatic mode of production are the best known, although he also talks about a Germanic mode of production (which is not confined to Germanic people) and he mentions in passing a Slavic mode. Then we come to feudalism and the transition to capitalism. But perhaps here, before we move on from primitive communism, it is worth raising the possibility that we are not talking about one *world* history but about several histories, perhaps as many histories as there are different modes of production or types of society.

The analysis I am following here is broadly similar to that suggested by Eric Hobsbawm (1964) in his introduction to Marx's *Pre-Capitalist Economic Formations*. In the first place he points out that the different modes of production do not follow each other in chronological order, nor, with the exception of feudalism and capitalism, do they develop out of each other. On the other hand, Marx does talk about historical stages in the evolution of individuality—the division of labour in Durkheim's framework—which, for Marx, are stages in the evolution of private property. But again these are not chronological stages, they are analytic: by this he means that Marx did not see these stages as necessarily following each other in time. Rather there is a logical order to them which perhaps allows us to arrange societies separated, possibly radically separated, by time and space, in relation to each other.

After the general communal ownership of primitive communism we move to a more developed form of direct communal property (the oriental and perhaps Slavic mode of production) where there is still no development of class societies; at the second level there is communal property coexisting with class societies (the ancient and Germanic modes of production). The third level involves the growth of craft manufacture—the independent craftsman (it was at this stage usually men) who exercised personal control over the means of production: the spinner, for example, would own the loom; the blacksmith would own and control his anvil and hammer. Then finally there is class society proper, where we move from the appropriation of people—slaves—to the appropriation of labour as I described earlier. We can regard these as four paths from primitive communism, not all of which lead to capitalism, but all of which involve some change from simple communal property.

The Asiatic mode of production—oriental despotism

In the Asiatic mode of production, communal property is still dominant; there would be a number of small groups, family based, within the society, and Marx suggests that the inhabitants of these societies feel the power of the collective, which gives them their rights over their land, and they project this power into a single source—the despot from whom the land seems held in trust:

The despot here appears as the father of all the numerous lesser communities thus realising the common unity of all. It therefore follows that the surplus product . . . belongs to this highest unity. Oriental despotism, therefore, appears to lead to a legal absence of property. in fact, however, its foundation is tribal or common property . . .   (Marx 1964: 69–70)

Property is created through agriculture and manufacturing, both of which are carried on in small self-sufficient communities, containing within themselves 'all conditions of production and surplus production'—the surplus being handed over to the despot as a form of tribute and a form of celebration of the group's unity. Where large-scale irrigation systems are required for the continuation of agriculture, together with communication networks over long distances—particularly important in Asian societies—these are provided by the 'higher unity', the despotic government. There is, as yet, no clear division between town and country. There is little or no 'push' towards change in such systems. They remain the same until they are broken down from the outside by the expansion of capitalism.

There have been many debates about the existence of oriental despotism, both on empirical and theoretical grounds. Hindess and Hirst (1975) argue that the concept is incoherent, but that is a negative version of Hegel's claim about a star: instead of theoretically deriving a type of society which does not exist, they are arguing that theoretically such a society cannot exist when in fact it might do so. In either case the argument is not very helpful. More interesting is Karl Wittfogel's (1963) development of the notion. He offers a functional analysis of such societies where the despotism arises less from an alienating projection of communal power, the way that Marx describes it, than from the necessity of large-scale irrigation which only the state is able to undertake. This occurs only in very specific conditions—it is not simply a matter of too little water plus state water control. The society must be above the simpler forms of subsistence economy—there must be a surplus, outside the geographical areas where there is heavy rainfall, but without any significant development of private property.

Under these circumstances, only a bureaucratically organized state system can provide water and maintain the means by which it is provided—it is a managerial enterprise. The state maintains order through its control of the irrigation system—it can bring dissident communities into line by threatening not to maintain water supplies—as well as through a large standing army and a highly organized intelligence network. The ideological cement for such a system tends to be religious. Wittfogel set up a gradation of hydraulic societies according to the density of the population, and he was able to include in the category ancient Egypt and Mesopotamia, Rome and Byzantium, the Ottoman Empire, India and China, Muslim Spain, and others. Wittfogel was an early member of the Frankfurt School of Social Research—the group that in the late 1920s and early 1930s began to develop a Marxism which was critical of the Soviet Union. His contribution to this was to suggest that the Stalinist regime grew out of a preceding 'semi-Asiatic' regime—and there are certainly similarities between the pre-revolutionary Tsarist regime and aspects of oriental despotism. Anne Bailey (1981) suggests that post-Wittfogel research has tended towards the argument that the Asiatic mode of production and tribal societies are not as classless as once thought and they are also systems in which exploitation takes place—again, the general drift has been away from unilinear, fixed conceptions of evolution.

The Germanic mode of production

Marx does not say a lot about the Germanic mode of production, and even less about the Slavic mode. The former represents a slightly more developed form of property than, although of course it does not emerge from, the Asiatic mode. According to Hobsbawm, 'the "Germanic system" as such does not form a special socio-economic formation. It forms the socio-economic formation of feudalism in conjunction with the mediaeval town (the locus of the emergence of the autonomous craft production)' (Hobsbawm 1964: 38). Marx says of these earlier modes:

In all these forms the basis of evolution is the *reproduction* of relations between individual and community *assumed as given*—they may be more or less primitive, more or less
the result of history, but fixed into tradition—and a *definite, predetermined objective*
existence, both as regards the relation to the condition of labour, and the relation
between one man and his co-workers, fellow tribesmen, etc. Such evolution is therefore
from the outset *limited*, but once the limits are transcended, decay and disintegration
sets in.   (Marx 1964: 83)

In other words, these societies are comparatively static, and if for some reason
change does set in, they can disintegrate.

The ancient mode of production

When we turn to the ancient mode of production, Marx argues: 'The *community* is here the precondition, but unlike (the Asiatic mode) it is not here the substance of which the individuals are mere accidents or of which they form mere
spontaneously natural parts' (Marx 1964: 71). The basis of the ancient mode is
the city as the centre of the landowners—the cultivated area belongs to the city,
as opposed to the village being an appendage to the land, as it was in the Asiatic
mode.

The relationship between the community and the land can be broken only
from the outside, by being conquered, and therefore being prepared for war is
central to the society's life, 'the all-embracing task, the great communal labour'.
The community of kinship systems must be ordered as a military force. Unlike
the Asiatic mode, the individual peasant is not required to contribute communal
labour to keep the land productive and is in this sense not directly dependent on
the community except in so far as it is a protection against external enemies. The
more this occurs the more the tribe becomes united against the outside world.
This makes it safe for individual members and their families to cultivate their
own particular plots. The peasant is both an individual proprietor *and* a member of the community. Ancient modes of production include the city states:

There is concentration in the city, with the land as its territory; small scale agriculture
producing for immediate consumption; manufacture as the domestic subsidiary, labour
of wives and daughters (spinning and weaving) or achieving independent existence in a
few craft occupations. . . . The precondition for the continued existence of the community is the maintenance of equality among its free self-sustaining peasants, and their
individual labour as the condition of the continued existence of their property. Their
relation to the natural conditions of labour are those of proprietors; but personal labour
must continually establish these conditions as real conditions and objective elements of
the personality of the individual, of his personal labour.   (ibid. 73)

Rome is probably the best example of such a society: 'Property formally
belongs to the Roman citizen, the private owner of land is such only by virtue of
being Roman, but any Roman is also a private landowner.' Marx opposes this to

the Germanic mode where the peasant is only the possessor of land. In the ancient mode, the community has its existence through the city—it is a form of independent organism; in the Germanic mode there is no such organism. Marx seems to suggest that it is with the development of the city that we can begin to think of the state with its officials. There exist side by side both state and private landed property. He draws (ibid. 88) a very modern parallel with language: just as the individual can only speak his or her own mind by virtue of belonging to the community that shares the language, so he can own property only by virtue of belonging to the state, the community which also owns property.

In Rome wealth was not the main purpose of production—this tended to be confined to trading groups; the argument was not about what property earned the most but about what sort of property enabled people to become citizens; humanity was the purpose of production and Marx did not lose the opportunity to point to the contrast between Rome and his and our society: 'The child-like world of the ancients appears to be superior.'

Having said this, however, Marx turns to a less attractive aspect of ancient societies. He goes on to argue that, despite appearances, the ancient mode of production, based on slavery and serfdom, is not an alienated system; people are not separated from the world on which they work, rather the slave is regarded as an inorganic part of the world—like the soil or the cattle.

In Rome, as in other city states, the very process of reproduction changed things—this seems to be something new that did not happen in the other modes. Once Rome was built and the land around it settled, the conditions of the society were different from what they had been before. Reproduction becomes a change in, a destruction of, the old form. The increase in population alone changes the situation. Conquest and colonization become important and lead to slavery. Hence we come back to the understanding that human beings change themselves by changing their situation. And it is here that we find the contradiction that leads to the collapse of the ancient mode of production. Originally every citizen is equal; as the land is used up and the population grows, conquest is necessary; conquest leads to slavery and the original democratic city state disappears. Hobsbawm (1964) points out that there is no reason why the breakdown of the ancient modes should lead to feudalism, and it certainly does not lead to capitalism.

Feudalism and the development of capitalism

It is only with the transition from feudalism to capitalism that we find an evolutionary and revolutionary conception of history, which takes us right through to socialism and communism. Feudalism developed not through any evolutionary course from the ancient mode, but out of the ruins of the ancient mode, in Europe out of the decay of Roman Empire. There had been a decline in the population and therefore in agricultural activity with minimal markets leading to a decline in industry and trade. Marx argues that feudalism started from the country. Ownership remained based on the community, but the producers were not slaves but the small peasantry, the serfs. The nobility exercised their power through a hierarchy of landownership and their armed retainers, their private armies.

This form of agricultural production had its equivalent in the town:

in the feudal organisation of the trades. Here property consisted chiefly in the labour of each individual person. The necessity for organisation against the organised robber-nobility, the need for communal covered markets in an age when the individualist was at the same time a merchant; the growing competition of the escaped serfs swarming into the rising towns, the feudal structure of the whole country: these combined to bring about the gilds. Further, the gradually accumulated capital of individual craftsmen and their stable numbers, as against the growing population, evolved the relation of journeyman and apprentice, which bought into being in the towns a hierarchy similar to that in the country.   (Marx 1964: 126)

There was little division of labour. In the towns the central social divisions were between masters, journeymen, apprentices, and, as time passed, the rabble, and in the country there were distinctions between princes, nobility, clergy, and peasants. There was little division of labour within or between trades.

Marx then moves on to the growth of capitalism. The division between mental and manual labour is most clear in the division between town and country: 'The existence of the town implies, at the same time, the necessity of administration, police, taxes, etc., in short, of the municipality and thus of politics in general' (ibid. 127). The town represents the concentration of population, the country represents isolation; antagonism between the two grows on the basis of private property and the abolition of the conflict between town and country will be one of the first conditions of communist life. The separation between the two marks the beginning of the conflict between landed property and industrial capital.

The serfs, escaping from the land and entering or establishing the towns, had only their labour and the minimal tools of their trade as property; this required the establishment of a police, but it also needed the construction of markets and other material preconditions of trading, and there was also a need to protect skills. All of these contributed to the development of craft guilds. New arrivals had to subject themselves to the guilds if they possessed a skill; if not they became day labourers, part of the urban rabble, unorganized and without power, watched over by an armed force. The journeymen and apprentices were tried to their masters through powerful obligations and possessed an interest in the system in that they could become masters themselves. There was no basis for effective uprisings in the towns, and the great class conflicts of the Middle Ages were peasant rebellions, but the peasantry were isolated and so unsophisticated and ineffective.

Marx's discussion of the craftsman's relationship to his work in the towns is interesting: on the one hand, he describes a situation that on the face of it might seem desirable. There is a minimal division of labour within the guild, so each craftsman must be an expert at every aspect of his work; we can often find in such craftsmen an interest and proficiency which might reach 'narrow' artistic heights. At the same time, however:

every mediaeval craftsman was completely absorbed in his work, to which he had a con-tented, slavish relationship, and to which he was subjected to a far greater extent than the modern worker, whose work is a matter of indifference to him.   (ibid. 130)

Marx describes capital in the town as 'natural', by which he means the basic necessities of work, the house, the tools, and traditional customers—all of which passed from father to son. Unlike modern capital, it was connected to specific persons and things.

The division of labour then evolves through a separating-out of a specific merchant class. This created the possibility of communication and trade beyond the immediate area of the town, but whether this occurred depended upon the state of roads, public safety, and so on, which in turn depended upon political conditions. So to the next stage, and here Marx is reminiscent of Durkheim:

with the extension of trade . . . there immediately appears a reciprocal action between production and commerce. The towns enter into relations *with one another*, new tools are brought from one town into the other, and the separation between production and commerce soon calls forth a new division of production between the individual towns, each of which is soon exploiting a dominant branch of industry.   (ibid. 131)

Out of the growth and interaction of the towns and conflict with the landed nobility there gradually arose the new 'burgher class'—the bourgeoisie. By free-ing themselves from feudal restraints, they came to share common work condi-tions and a common enemy, and these called forth similar customs, similar ways of behaving and thinking. The class develops slowly and splits according to the development of the division of labour, absorbing previous ruling groups into itself and eventually turning the non-possessors of property, as well as some sec-tions of the old possessing classes, into the proletariat—this happens as all prop-erty is transformed into industrial and commercial capital. In a clear account of class formation, Marx writes of the bourgeoisie:

The separate individuals form a class only in so far as they have to carry on a common battle against another class; otherwise they are on hostile terms with each other as com-petitors. On the other hand, the class in its turn achieves an independent existence over against the individuals, so that the latter find their conditions of existence predestined, and hence have their position in life and their personal development assigned to them by their class, become subsumed under it. This is the same phenomenon as the subjection of the separate individuals to the division of labour and can only be removed by the abo-lition of private property and of labour itself. We have already indicated several times how this subsuming of individuals under the class brings with it their subjection to all kinds of ideas etc.   (ibid. 132)

In terms of the development of manufacture, the process can be slow and unsteady and it can go into reverse—a development in an isolated town can be lost through war with nobody else knowing about it.

With the development of the division of labour between towns, manufacture began to outgrow the guild system and, through a sort of natural selection, the work which from the beginning involved machinery—weaving—had the advantage. A new class of weavers arose who worked not only to supply the home market well beyond the immediate locality but also overseas markets. Weaving demanded little skill, and soon divided into many branches, breaking free of the guilds, and the areas where 'guild-free' weaving developed soon grew faster than the traditional towns dominated by the guilds. Merchant capital began to develop, more mobile, more like modern capital, which in turn enabled the peasantry to enter into production without the interference of the guilds. Manufacture also absorbed those who had steadily been driven off the land by the enclosures, as the landed nobility turned to sheep for profit (through the wool trade) and shed their agricultural workers (you need very few people to look after sheep). This process went on for several centuries, as did the change in the nature of international trade. From 'inoffensive exchange', it developed to trade wars and physical wars, a matter of intense competition. The whole process got an immense boost from the discovery of America and the sea route to the East Indies.

In manufacture, money replaced the patriarchal relationship of the guild, and manufacture itself replaced the guild. International markets expanded rapidly and the impetus built up to the industrial revolution in the middle of the eighteenth century. The movement from cottage manufacture to capitalism proper involved the moving of machines which had hitherto been in the home into one location, where economies of scale were rapidly developed. Work and home became separate and we arrive at the fundamental movement of modernity.

Evolution from feudalism to capitalism?

I want now to look back over this last section, the one true evolutionary account of Marx, and ask about its theoretical content. I have presented it, as does Marx himself, as a real historical process, a story in which one thing leads to another. If we work this way, how does theory inform our history? In the first place, it tells us what to look for: Marx's account is in terms of the changes at the economic level of social organization and how these affect other levels, ranging from the individual's experience of work to international relations. There are, of course, other ways in which we could write a history of the same period—in terms, for example, of the actions of kings and major political figures, and how we decide between such explanations is itself a theoretical question, albeit a fairly simple one in these circumstances. Did the economic changes occur because great men took decisions about what they wanted the world to be like, or were the decisions of great men hemmed in and pushed in one direction or another by economic developments over which they had no control? Nobody and no group decided that the guild system should develop or that it should decline, or that the bourgeoisie should become a class; some sociologists would argue that these things happen as the unintentional consequences of human action, and that, of course, is true; but these actions were taken under a range of pressures pushing in a particular direction, and it is these pressures that Marx is talking about.

Comparing Marx's account with Durkheim's, we can see that both are concerned with the progress of the division of labour. Marx is probably superior, because he does not assume that it is an automatic process, whereas for Durkheim that does seem to be the case. For Marx, more is going on than the straightforward division of labour—class formation, for example—and it is in many ways a hit-and-miss process, one not of organic evolution but of chance, though not necessarily on a grand scale; it seems to me likely that something like capitalism would have developed, but there were very wide possibilities as to when, where, and how. However, where the two thinkers are furthest apart, in Durkheim's concentration on the *conscience collective*, it seems Durkheim has more to offer. Marx's analysis works on the level of system integration and has a more sophisticated grasp of the process, whereas Durkheim has a more sophisticated grasp of the process of social integration.

The complexities of the class analysis of history

Perhaps one example of the complexities of this come from debates about the nature of the class conflict that was fought out in the context of the English Civil War. The simple Marxist account would see this as a conflict between the rising bourgeoisie, both industrial and financial, on the parliamentarian side, and the old landed aristocracy on the side of the monarchy. The problem with this is that, at an abstract level, it is probably right—the policies desired by each side would probably have benefited the classes that were supposed to support them. But when we get down to looking at which real persons supported which side, it becomes much more difficult. The wrong people crop up in the wrong place all the time. The way in which we can understand this more concrete level of analysis, why people would fight for the side against their own class interest, is to look more closely at what Marxists would call ideological factors. In this case the important point is the religious divisions that were beginning to appear and the way they become subordinated to sectional interests. These beliefs, as do all symbolic systems, have a dynamic of their own and can carry people in unexpected directions.

Theory and history

Theoretical and empirical distinctions

Theory can do more than simply guide us to look at certain things first and other things later; at a theoretical level we can make much clearer distinctions between modes of productions then we can get through the historical account. If we stick to the latter, it is difficult to say when feudalism ends and capitalism begins, and it is difficult to know what to make of cottage industry—is it a separate mode of production, a transitional stage, or something else. On a theoretical level, we can make finer and firmer distinctions. I will try to show this first and then I will return to the relationship between the theory and the reality.

The theoretical distinctions can be found in the work of Althusser and Balibar (1970), who offer a highly abstract but none the less useful definition of modes of production. A mode of production is defined in terms of a combination of relations and elements. The elements are the means of production—the machines and tools employed in the production process—and the labourers and the non-labourers. The relationships between them are (crudely) those of control and ownership. As we shall see, the elements themselves vary between modes of production, but the relationships are constant.

I will begin with the relationships—of ownership and control of the means of production. Ownership might appear self-evident, but its nature can vary from society to society. It does not necessarily mean modern legal ownership in the Weberian sense, where the owner has complete disposal of his or her property. In the feudal system, for example, the king held land in fief from God, the lords in fief from the king and the peasants in fief from the lord. None had the freedom to dispose of land as he thought fit. Yet, in terms of this model of the mode of production, the lords owned the land and were the non-labourers. Control of the means of production means the ability to decide when the tools are put to work, and in what context. Thus, in feudalism, if ownership was in the hands of the non-labourers, the lords, control was in the hands of the peasants. This was not necessarily any big deal: there was not much choice—to work most daylight hours growing a limited range of crops.

The 'transitional mode' reverses these relationships. The transitional mode is cottage industry. The labourer owns the means of production, the spinning jenny, the loom; but he or she was dependent for the ability to put the machines into operation on the non-labourer, the merchant who supplied raw materials and ordered finished products, deciding when the machines would be used and what was to be produced.

The capitalist mode produces the concentration of both relationships in the hands of the non-labourer. The capitalist, whether an individual or a corporate body, owns the machinery and the factory, and decides what will be produced, the hours that the worker will work, and so on. The non-labourer neither owns nor controls the means of production. The socialist mode of production reverses these relationships: the labourer both owns and controls the means of production.

In logical terms we cannot derive much more than the four modes of production from this schema and it is quite possible that Marxism perhaps does not have much more to say about other types of societies. However, this approach does succeed in clarifying sharply between types of society and enabling us to understand them in terms of the different dynamics of each, the ways in which they are reproduced. For example, in the feudal system the dues, perhaps a proportion of the harvest, which are to be paid to the lord do not automatically reach him—they have to be given or taken. The peasant, bluntly, has to be fooled or beaten into giving the lord his due. In terms of the different levels of society, this means that the ideological level (religion) or the political level, or both together, play an important part in determining what happens. In capitalist systems, as we saw, the surplus is extracted at the same time as the worker works for his or her own living. Consequently the economic level is dominant—at least in early capitalism—determining the major lines of development. These differences are the result of the different relations of control—the peasant controls the means of production, the industrial worker does not. But if we expect these types to exist in pure form, we will be mistaken: the theory enables us to make sense of a complex reality and one might surmise that it underlay Marx's organization of his account of history, but it was not imposed upon it.

Contemporary notions of evolution

Before going on to talk about the development of capitalism through to the contemporary world, I want to elaborate on some modern conceptions of evolution that I began discussing in relation to Durkheim. I said then that evolutionary theories of history were not the most popular amongst contemporary sociologists and I want now to look at some contemporary versions of this process that perhaps capture the central aspects of Marx's arguments. Erik Wright (1989) makes a distinction between 'organic growth models' and evolutionary development, both of which can be found in biology. The first is genetically determined and involves a more or less inevitable process of growth, which in the social sciences would be a deterministic theory, and it seems to me the critics of evolutionary theory in the social sciences direct their fire against such a version. There is also the proper evolutionary model—in which there are random variations, some of which survive for environmental factors white others die out. This is a much more precarious process—societies can move in either direction and go off at different angels and this is much more appropriate to the social sciences. And it is much more in accordance with the sort of process that Marx is portraying in his account of pre-capitalist economic formations: the Asiatic mode does not develop, but awaits transformation from the outside; the ancient mode does develop, but not very far before it falls into decay and the growth of feudalism from that disintegration is not an inevitable process. In feudal societies, progress can be made and lost according to local conditions. Capitalism seems to develop only where machine production can be maintained and where local conditions allow a sufficient volume of trade to develop. And the development of such conditions themselves, of course, must be a matter of a number of other chances; a proper evolutionary conception allows for contingency and random variation.

In a recent paper W. G. Runciman (1995) takes up a defence of evolutionary theory which I think owes much to Marx though disagreeing with him—particularly about the claim that class and class conflict are the 'bearers' of evolutionary development. He suggests it is 'social practices' that matter, and capitalism is defined in Weberian terms as the employment of free labour by competing enterprises. He argues that there are many varieties of capitalism; the nature of the employing agency can vary and the economic system can coexist with a range of different political and ideological systems, and each development requires its own specific explanation. He goes on to distinguish between endogenous and exogenous evolution—the former developing from some internal feature of the society, the latter developing from some external development. What we cannot say is that evolution moves in one direction or that it is necessarily progressive. He is arguing against the idea that capitalism has necessarily triumphed over other forms of production—a view which seems particularly easy to hold since the collapse of the communist regimes in eastern Europe. He argues that these regimes collapsed not because of the failure of their economic practices but because of the collapse of the mode of coercion—the political regime which surrounded the economic practices. He concludes:

The proposition is that social, like natural, evolution proceeds not from stage to stage but from byway to byway. To borrow a metaphor used by Stephen Jay Gould for biological evolution, it must be seen not as a ladder but as a branching bush. It is true that there is a sequence of distinguishable modes of production, persuasion and coercion, but it is not true that the sequence is in any sense progressive. Likewise, it is true that history never repeats itself, but it is not true that social evolution only goes in one direction. The process of social selection not only permits but requires that modes of production, persuasion and coercion will not succeed each other in a uniform manner across the globe. (Runciman 1995: 46)

This is a Weberianized, open-ended Marxism which seems to me fully in the spirit of Marx's explorations of history. Yet, even allowing for Runciman's argument, it seems to me that we can still give a little more than he does to an evolutionary process which on certain levels has a progressive dimension. Erik Wright suggests that, when societies have made advances in knowledge or in their productive forces, they are unlikely to give them up easily. They might be bombed back into the stone age or collapse into the sea but they will not voluntarily give up what they consider as advances. They will not, of course, necessarily be successful in this enterprise but it is this which provides the evolutionary push.

The dynamics of capitalism

If Marx's conception of the development of capitalism from feudalism can be called evolutionary, his conception of the development from capitalism to socialism can be called revolutionary. Socialism does not emerge from the normal development of capitalism, but more from the failure of capitalism to develop. The capitalist system is driven by contradictions which put it in a permanent crisis, and it comes to an end when these contradictions reach breaking point. There are a number of different dynamics at different levels of society that we can identify and pull out of Marx's work, not all of which push towards revolution. What is clear is that the simple model of *The Communist Manifesto*, of capitalism dividing into two huge opposing armies of bourgeoisie and proletariat, with the latter getting stronger and eventually overwhelming the bourgeoisie—this simple model was not really tenable even in Marx's lifetime. Other aspects are, however, much more tenable. I will begin with changes at the economic level, changes which are framed within what Marx saw as the basic contradiction between the forces and relations of production, and I will then move on to developments which occur at other levels. Some of these ideas come from Marx himself and some from later developments—I will be concentrating on the usefulness of these ideas for our understanding of contemporary society.

The tendency of the rate of profit to fall

I tried earlier to show how there are regular cycles of crises—overproduction or under-consumption—which leave stocks of goods building up, workers being laid off, surplus productive capacity (empty factories, etc.) increasing. The forces of production, the capacity to produce, are increasing: the competitive dynamic of capitalism forces enterprises to seek constant changes in production techniques to allow cheaper production, to find new markets, and so on. But these capabilities would periodically outstrip the relations of production, the private ownership of the means of production.

All the classical economists had noticed a tendency of the rate of profit to fall, but they disagreed on its causes. Marx's explanation had to do with the accumulation of capital, of 'dead labour'. Profit could be made only from living labour; it comes from the difference between the exchange value of labour power—what I pay my workers, what is necessary for them to maintain a life which enables them to keep working for me—and its use value, what I can get them to produce for me. As productive capacity increases through the growth of capital goods, I need less labour and I pay out more on machines—'dead labour'—and consequently I make proportionately less surplus value. This is not necessarily less 'profit' in absolute terms but less profit as a proportion of outlay.[1] Critics have argued that there are three counteracting tendencies. First, the growth in the mass of 'dead' or constant capital reduces its value and might counteract the tendency (i.e. proportionately I pay out less on it); secondly, the rate of exploitation can be increased to the point where it counteracts the tendency of the rate of profit to fall (i.e. I cut wages and/or insist on longer hours); and, thirdly, to quote Simon Clarke:

Marx ignores the fact that the capitalist will only introduce a new method of production if it provides an increased rate of profit, so that faced with the prospect of such a fall capitalists will continue to use the old method of production and earn the old rate of profit, at least until such a time as shortage of labour leads to a fall in the rate of profit as a result of rising wages, at which point labour-saving methods might become profitable. (Clarke 1994: 212)

I think it is possible to draw from this a number of themes in our understanding of the development of contemporary society. The first is that the cycle of crises has continued and, as Ernest Mandel notes, the period of the cycle has lessened from round about ten years at the beginning of the century to four or five years now. His explanation of this is that the renewal period for constant capital has become shorter and shorter, not least because of the spin-off of the vast expenditure on arms during the cold war. This was part and parcel of the long-term expansion of capitalism since the end of the Second World War, and Mandel (1970: 57) refers to it as 'a permanent technological revolution'. This is clearly continuing, and the sort of contemporary economic developments that David Harvey (1989) analyses within a Marxist framework are a continuation of such developments—the growth of information technology, the movement of industrial production to low-wage economies, the increasing emphasis on short-term production cycles, and so on.

It is worth underlining the expansionist dynamic of capitalism. I find this a difficult issue; on the one hand, it seems to me that the Runciman argument that I discussed earlier is basically right—there is no necessary development towards the triumph of capitalism, nor, by implication, socialism. And, of course, capitalist relations can exist with very different political and ideological systems. On the other hand, the development of imperialism—the tendency of capitalism to export itself and subordinate if not actually replace other modes of production—is important. And the continuation of this process leads on to the 'world-

---

[1] I am using 'profit' and 'surplus value' here as equivalent, although they are not—one should remember that Marx's economics can become very complex! For a good discussion, see Clarke (1994).

system' analysis of modern sociology, the greater and more consistent degree of system cohesion that seems to exist in contemporary society. Interestingly, Immanual Wallerstein's response (Runciman 1995: 46), as a leading world-system theorist, to Runciman's argument is that capitalism is best defined not by free labour but by the accumulation of capital, and in fact it is not free labour which pushes capitalism to expand but the necessity of accumulation in the competitive market. However, if we take them on their relevant levels, I do not think the arguments are contradictory. We can talk about a capitalist world system which includes within itself different forms of capitalism in relation to other modes of production; or, if we prefer, we could talk about capitalism as being defined by both the accumulation of capital and free labour, and in fact for Marx the two depend on each other: capital can be accumulated only through the exploitation of free labour. This definition takes account of Runciman's objection to Wallerstein—that, if we employ the accumulation of capital as a defining feature, then we would have to take the Roman Empire and the Soviet Union as capitalist; on the other hand, it allows us to recognize the sort of differences between societies that Runciman refers to. However, it would be within the context of an overall capitalist system to which other forms of production could exist in a subordinate position. None of this helps us understand any development towards socialism.

Changes at other levels: transformations of the crisis

The economic dynamics of capitalism—regular crises, the accumulation of capital, an expansionary process, and increasingly rapid transformations in technology—are not, of course, the only ones. The various Marxist attempts to understand the development of capitalism without revolution have, as I remarked earlier, concentrated on ideology. I indicated then the various ways in which the other levels of society were related to the economic level. Habermas (1972, 1974, 1976, 1979) presents an evolutionary model of human society of which the period of early capitalism is only one stage. It is not my intention here to give a full account of Habermas's work, but I do want to look at his attempt to develop an evolutionary theory of modern capitalism which takes us in a rather different direction. He talks about an 'evolutionary learning curve' along which different societies might move in different ways. His model of social evolution is the individual's cognitive evolution—from the perception and grasp of specifics to the perception and grasp of universals: from recognizing that thing in the garden as our tree, to recognizing it as one of a general category of tree. Societies also develop towards universal values and universal standards of rationality, morality, and law, towards the growing independence of the individual, growing ability to make moral decisions, but it is not a simple process of development and in that process economic development is very important.

The stages that interest us here are those that come through the sort of developments in capitalism that we have been discussing. The crises of early capitalism are economic crises—crises in system cohesion. To deal with these, the state intervenes to boost demand in what are seen as under-consumption crises; the state becomes involved in economic regulation and welfare provision. This shifts the crisis to another level: the state has to borrow to fund its activities and this fuels high inflation and a financial crisis. The state becomes unable to reconcile the demands of industrial and financial capitalism, hence Habermas calls it a *rationality* crisis. This is a crisis at the level of system integration, but it also has effects on the level of social integration, where it is a 'legitimation' crisis—the state loses its popular justification. This should be a familiar story to anybody with a knowledge of western politics of the last few decades, and perhaps its latest and most dramatic manifestation is the militant opposition to the federal government in the USA.

If the political system can manage the rationality crisis, it moves on to what traditional Marxists would call the ideological level, but Habermas calls social integration. The new crisis is a *motivation* crisis. This brings us back to a regular thesis of this book: the increase in state power and control needed to deal with the earlier crises undermines motivations for participating in the system. Politics become more centralized, the profit motive is less important, and the work ethic declines in significance. We can see all these issues arising in contemporary political arguments: do welfare payments keep people idle or encourage them to work? Are taxation levels too high to encourage initiative? Why don't politicians take any notice of what people say?

The main point of my argument at this stage has been to suggest that we can identify an evolutionary process—towards the 'world system' and/or universal systems of justice and morality of which Habermas speaks, but there are many ways of getting there and a range of possibilities within the system, not least perhaps that of moving backwards. The next question is what this has to do with socialism.

Communism

Communism (is) the *positive* transcendence of *private property*, as *human self-estrangement*, and therefore as the real *appropriation of the human* essence by and for man; communism therefore (is) the complete return of man to himself as a *social* (i.e. human) being—a return become conscious, and accomplished within the entire wealth of previous development. This communism, as fully developed naturalism, equals humanism, and as fully developed humanism, equals naturalism; it is the *genuine* resolution of the conflict between man and nature and between man and man—the true resolution of the strife between existence and essence, between objectification and self-confirmation, between freedom and necessity, between the individual and the species. Communism is the riddle of history solved, and it knows itself to be this solution.

(Marx 1844/1974: 135)

There are a number of different ways in which we can think about socialism and the way in which it might be achieved. The Marxist social vision is very different from that of Durkheim, who sees it as a matter of evolution into an organic whole, a balance of individualism and collectivism, the state guaranteeing the balance between the two. For Marx, the emphasis is less on balance than on control—not the individual's control over his or her life which has become the centre of so much contemporary concern, but the collective control of our living conditions and activities. Unlike Durkheim, Marx raises questions of radical democracy, of the organization of social life on a collective basis not through professional associations but through an understanding of a shared human condition.

It is 'common-sense' knowledge that Marx saw socialism as coming about through revolution—a seizure of political power which would transform the economic, social, and political conditions of life; less well known is the fact that he thought this would realize once and for all the ideals of the French Revolution: liberty, equality, and fraternity. Popular prejudice would often maintain that socialism or communism is about dictatorial power, the violent seizure of power and wealth by a minority, and it is arguable that this is what eventually happened in the Soviet Union and eastern Europe. However, it is not what Marx had in mind. David McLellan (1971) comments on how Marx was preoccupied for many years with the failure of the French Revolution, and the possible realization of its ideals. Marx argued that the distinctive feature of the proletariat as a revolutionary class was that its particular interests coincided with the interests of society as a whole, and this explained the failure of the French Revolution, a 'partial, purely political revolution' in the interests of one class:

What is the basis of a partial, purely political revolution? It is that a part of civil society emancipates itself and attains to universal domination, that a particular class undertakes the general emancipation of society from its particular situation. This class frees the whole of society, but only under the presupposition that the whole of society is in the same situation as this class, that it possesses, or can easily acquire for example, money and education.   (Marx 1971: 125)

Now in one sense the French bourgeoisie who carried out the revolution liberated the whole of society, breaking the traditional feudal ties and granting each man a right to citizenship. However, this is only a formal political right; it does not affect the material conditions of the citizen's life. The bourgeoisie cannot grant a real equality and a real liberty, since that would involve the abolition of private property; it can grant only an individual—not a collective—freedom, and, of course, the individual by him- or herself is powerless.

The proletariat is in a very different position. It is the *universal* class:

Of all the classes that stand face to face with the bourgeoisie today, the proletariat alone is a really revolutionary class. . . . In the conditions of the proletariat, those of old society at large are already virtually swamped. The proletarian is without property; his relation to his wife and children has no longer anything in common with the bourgeois family relations; modern industrial labour, modern subjection to capital, the same in England as in France, in America as in Germany, has stripped him of every trace of national character. Law, morality, religion, are to him so many bourgeois prejudices, behind which lurk in ambush just as many bourgeois interests.

All the preceding classes that got the upper hand sought to fortify their already acquired status by subjecting society at large to their conditions of appropriation. The proletarians cannot become masters of the productive forces of society, except by abolishing their own previous mode of appropriation. They have nothing of their own to secure and to fortify; their mission is to destroy all previous securities for, and insurances of, individual property.

All previous historical movements were movements of minorities, or in the interests of minorities. The proletarian movement is the self-conscious, independent movement of the immense majority, in the interests of the immense majority. The proletariat, the lowest stratum of our present society, cannot stir, cannot raise itself up without the whole, superincumbent strata of official society being sprung into the air.' (Marx 1848/1968*a*: 44–45)

McLellan (1971) points out that, when Marx talks of violence as part of the revolution, he sees it primarily in terms of a response to the violence of the ruling classes, who will not always be willing to give up their privileges without a physical fight; in some countries it might be possible to win power through the ballot box, and he never expressed any approval of the sort of revolutionary terror that followed the French Revolution. If that were to happen after the socialist revolution, it would mean that the time for the revolution had not come—that the society had not yet reached the stage of development or the intensity of contradiction that would lead to the establishment of socialism without oppression. Marx also commented that, whilst Russia wasn't fully industrialized—and therefore did not have a fully developed industrial proletariat—communism could take a root there because of the communal nature of the Russian peasant village. Paradoxically, it was precisely this structure that Stalin destroyed during forced collectivization of agriculture.

The simple model of a victorious proletariat taking power when its time comes with the support of other classes and with minimal opposition has faded, although more sophisticated conceptions have developed on the basis of the experience of the Russian Revolution. Both Lenin and Trotsky developed analyses which Althusser pursued in a theory of what he called 'overdetermination' (Althusser 1969). The revolution is seen as a result of the conjunction of a number of contradictions, not just that resulting from the contradiction between the forces and relations of production and the consequent conflict between bourgeoisie and proletariat. In Russia in 1917 there were conflicts between native

Russian capitalists and entrepreneurs from western Europe, between both of these and the landed aristocracy, between proletariat and bourgeoisie, peasantry and landlords, financial and industrial bourgeoisie, and so on (see Trotsky 1967). In such a situation, it is not just the strength of the revolutionary forces that matter but the inability of the ruling classes to act against them because of internal divisions. When Althusser develops this sort of analysis he suggests that contradictions can also come together to produce a stalemate. What is clear is that revolutions are more complex and dangerous than Marx imagined in his theory, and that revolutionary parties have not been the democratic creations of the working class that he expected them to be.

McLellan also points out that Marx was wary about making predictions—that was the work of the utopian socialists. In practical terms he seemed to be caught between two stools. On the one hand, he foresaw the disappearance of the state; for Marx, it is not a mediator but an instrument of class oppression, and if social classes disappeared then there would be no need for the state: 'for Marx the abolition of a state based on class distinction involved the abolition of an independent state apparatus in which an irresponsible executive and judiciary insured the invulnerability of the bureaucracy' (McLellan 1971: 213). However, one of the aims of the revolutionary movement was to push towards the centralization of power, so that it would be that much easier to take over the state; but once class society is abolished, the question arises about what functions the state would then have. In the 'Critique of the Gotha Programme' Marx (1875/1977b) says as much as he says anywhere about the future communist society. The Gotha programme was a compromise between two wings of German socialism drawn up in the spring of 1875. Marx argues that the state is always a product of bourgeois society, and it is not, as the Gotha programme assumes, an entity which continues to exist in all forms of society. But the state will not immediately disappear after the socialist revolution—there will be a period of transition:

What we have to deal with here is a communist society, not as it has developed on its own foundations, but, on the contrary, just as it emerges from capitalist society; which is thus in every respect, economically, morally and intellectually, still stamped with the birth marks of the old society from whose womb it emerges.   (ibid. 568)

For example, the worker still has to work and he or she will be paid according to how much time is worked and this will be an act of exchange with 'society', presumably the state, which would supply the worker with a certificate which he or she would then use to withdraw what goods he or she needs from the common stock; so in the period after the revolution there would still be the exchange of commodities. As a consequence of this—one amount of labour exchanged for what has been produced by another equal amount of labour—this transitional society will still maintain the notion of equality basic to bourgeois society. One of the defects of this arrangement is that people are in fact unequal—in terms of strength and stamina and ability to work, or in terms of knowledge or family size—so this system will produce necessary inequalities during the transitional period. The Gotha programme places too much emphasis on equal distribution, when in fact it is production that is important. The notion of equal rights and equality of distribution will steadily disappear as the society moves forward:

In a higher phase of Communist society, after the enslaving and subordination of the individual to the division of labour, and therewith also the antithesis between mental and physical labour, has vanished; after labour has become not only a means to life but one of life's prime wants; after the productive forces have also increased with the all-round development of the individual, and all the springs of co-operative wealth flow more abundantly—only then can the narrow horizon of bourgeois right be crossed in its entirety and society inscribe on its banners: from each according to his ability, to each according to his needs.   (ibid. 569)

Marx goes on to emphasize the primacy of production, and argue in effect that the distribution of wealth and goods is a red herring—or rather an anti-red herring. The distribution of wealth reflects and depends upon the production of wealth.

It is reasonable to ask questions about the possibility of achieving this democratically ordered, stateless society. McLellan points out that when Marx was writing the state was a much less formidable institution than it is now in Europe and North America; it had not yet, for example, taken on any of the welfare functions that we normally associate with it, nor had it taken on many of its contemporary economic functions. It is now unlikely that it would simply wither away, especially if we add to this the fact that a communist party would come to power in times of civil unrest, or that its coming to power, even through elections, might actually *create* civil unrest (as, for example, it did when the Chilean socialist party won power through the ballot box in the early 1970s). In fact, it was already difficult to imagine when Lenin wrote *State and Revolution* (1972), and even in theory the eventual disappearance of the state receded further and further.

The utopia at the end of the process would not necessarily be one in which there is plenty for everybody; the argument is that human beings themselves would change during this period. They would become free, able to cooperate and argue with each other as the occasion demanded and organize their lives in collectively satisfying ways. They would lose the acquisitiveness, the selfishness, and the mutual mistrust engendered by capitalism, and the need for state-administered social control would disappear. The oft-heard right-wing argument that human beings are selfish is clearly not true—not all societies have been based on acquisitive and self drives, although such drives exist in all societies. This should already be clear from Weber's account of traditional attitudes to work and of other forms of capitalism.

However, it is debatable how far personalities can be transformed, and how quickly, and during the last part of the twentieth century the movement has been away from emphasizing collective responsibility towards a steadily greater individualism. This utopian aspect of Marxism is perhaps the best way into the conclusion.

Conclusion

It is perhaps difficult to think of the sort of radical transformation that Marx desired as a real possibility and I suggested earlier that, if we take Freud seriously, we would have to say that human beings would not spontaneously choose to work, however ideal the conditions. Work always involves an internal repression, and human relations are always to some extent hostile and envious. However, it is possible to use psychoanalytic ideas to maintain the importance of these ideals: Freudians often talk about a superego—an internalized social control which can become punitive if we do not do what we think we should do—and an ego-ideal, an idea of the sort of person we would really like to be. The two are closely related: if I do not live up to my ego-ideal, then my superego springs into critical action. They are also different: the ego-ideal carries hope, and the superego has irrational aspects. We have to live with both.

The political utopia offered by Marxism can combine both. Marxist parties and Marxist states have too easily taken over the destructive superego side, whereas the utopia has also acted as an ego-ideal, inspiring those who want to build a better, more equal and humane society. I think it is the universalism of this idea that is important and it is an ideal which comprises a central root of sociology, and which tends still to be carried by modern elaborations of Marxism. In that sense the best parts of Marxism can still contribute hope to sociology.

If Durkheim is primarily the theorist of society, then Marx is the theorist of social structure. I did not make any big deal out of the base/superstructure distinction when I mentioned it before because it can easily become a cliché, but if we can think about a multi-story building with different activities developing on different floors, each depending upon and affecting the others without determining them, its usefulness becomes clearer. In the first place we can see 'society' as a complex *structure*—not a jumble of activities (Weber) or an organism (Durkheim). Some levels of this structure are more important than others and that depends upon the various stages of development of the activities that go on at each level. There are also different rates of development at each level—one could think of the activities as Runciman's evolving bush, but it is an indoor plant, contained within the structure.

Marxism is also the central realist theory of classical sociology—parts of the social structure are not available to our perception, and these are usually the most important parts (perhaps the basement levels of the building). They have to be theorized and understood in order for us to grasp what is going on at a surface level (or the levels about the surface). And, because of this distinction between underlying and surface levels of reality, Marx is also the theorist of *ideology*, the theorist most able to take a critical approach to systems of ideas and beliefs about the social world. From a Marxist point of view, there is always the space to be wrong about what is happening in the world, the space between what we see and what causes what we see. The building is designed to hide its structure—there are no obvious signs, for example, of a basement, no steps leading down from the outside, no lighted windows below ground level, and inside there are multiple split-level floors and unexpected connections. It is by no means always clear how the activities carried on inside are connected.

There are various ways in which the critical role of Marxism can be described: it points to ideas that are caught up only in surface appearances, or it places such ideas in relation to the totality—to other levels of social organization, other developmental processes; it is always the ideas of totality and/or underlying structure and/or process that are important. It is this critical impetus that Marxism has always tended to reflect back upon itself. Whereas the other approaches have developed primarily in relation to external stimuli, Marxism seems to have generated and regenerated its own self-criticism so that, in the mid- and late twentieth century, there have been multiple strands of Marxist thought and it is still at the centre of arguments in social theory. Even the most renowned of the postmodernist philosophers, Jacques Derrida (1995), has recently found it necessary to return to trace a debt to Marx. A much more conventional social theorist, Nicos Mouzelis (1990), has suggested that, rather than Marxism being used as a totalizing theory, it can provide frameworks for analysing specific 'institutional spheres'. Whatever institution we look at—from the economic to the religious—he argues that we always identify technological, political, and ideological levels and we can investigate their interrelationships. And I would repeat again that the best accounts of postmodernism—David Harvey's *The Condition of Postmodernity* (1989) and Fredric Jameson's *Postmodernism or the Cultural Logic of Late Capitalism* (1991)—are both Marxist analyses of the contemporary world. We can now summarize Marx's views on the secondary dualism (see Box 12.1).

Box 12.1. Marx on modernity and capitalism/socialism

MODERNITY

Durkheim: a movement towards a balanced society of occupational groups held together by the state and a new humanist 'religion' which emphasized the value of the individual.

Marx: the modern world was moving towards the realization of the values of the French Revolution—liberty, equality, and fraternity. This was not an inevitable or smooth process and entails conflict and revolution.

CAPITALISM/SOCIALISM

Durkheim: Durkheim's concept of socialism was based on his conception of the development of modernity; although problems arise in the abnormal forms of the division of labour, these would be ironed out in continued historical development. He does not seem to see capitalism as a specific form of modern society responsible for either its problems or its benefits.

Marx: capitalism represented immense progress over previous types of society in terms of the ability to produce wealth, although it is driven by contradictions which do not allow it to realize this ability. The competitive market system produces rapid change and fragmentation—seen by many as defining features of modernity; a socialist revolution would create a collectively organized democratic and more stable society which would realize the ideals of the French Revolution.

Further reading

Marx's own work on pre-capitalist societies can be found in *Pre-Capitalist Economic Formations* (1964); if you read this, together with Eric Hobsbawm's commentary, and then compare them to Barry Hindess and Paul Hirst, *Pre-Capitalist Modes of Production* (1975), you will get a good idea of Marxism at its best and worst. My account of the theory of modes of production comes from Louis Althusser and Étienne Balibar, *Reading Capital* (1970). This is very difficult and it is also the source for Hindess and Hirst—you should read it for ideas and not take it as gospel truth.

In the next chapter you will find Weberian accounts of historical development with which this chapter can be compared; it might be worth looking as well at Giddens's two-volume *Contemporary Critique of Historical Materialism* (1981, 1985) and the discussion of evolutionary theory in T. Bottomore, 'Giddens's View of Historical Materialism' (1990), and E. O. Wright, 'Models of Historical Trajectory' (1989); also look at W. G. Runciman, 'The "Triumph" of Capitalism as a Topic in the Theory of Social Selection' (1995).

For Marx on the revolution and communism, see McLellan, *The Thought of Karl Marx* (1971), and Marx's own 'Critique of the Gotha Programme' (1875/1977b).

13 | Weber as a tragic liberal: the rise of the West

Introduction
Weber's ghostly evolutionism.

The sociology of religion
Choices between tradition and progress/differentiation; prophecy and the growth of universality; a class analysis of religion; humans as seekers of meaning; the tension between immanent and transcendent religions, the latter producing action to change the world.

Chinese religion: Confucianism and Taoism
The power of the family giving power to the countryside over the town; the power of the central government; conflict between central government, its local officials, and local kin groups; the growth of capitalism restricted by the power of the family and the Confucian ethic which devalued economic activity; Taoism as a mystical alternative; comparison of Confucianism and Puritanism.

Indian religion: Hinduism and Buddhism
The caste system; distinction between sects and churches in relation to Hinduism; the Brahmins; the absence of a universal ethic, and of the possibility of social criticism in an eternal order; status conflict in the wider social order; the Brahmin ascetic ideal; the absence of a rationalized pursuit of wealth.

Palestine: ancient Judaism
The importance of positive ethical action and unintended consequences; the history of Israel and its special relationship to Jahwe; the emergence of new ideas on the edge of centres of civilization; prophecy and the prophets; Jahwe as a universal God.

The Protestant ethic and the spirit of capitalism
Introduction: the descriptive and analytic in Weber's work; the 'elective affinity' as an explanation; the work ethic in Weber's history. *The spirit of capitalism*: capitalism based on rational accounting; Protestantism not originally associated with the accumulation of wealth association; Benjamin Franklin as the source of the ideal type of the spirit of capitalism;

accumulation as the supreme good; the notion of a calling; moralized money-making versus traditionalism. *The Protestant ethic*: Protestantism as the origin of the rationality of European capitalism; Luther's notion of a calling; different forms of ascetic Protestantism; Calvin and predestination; worldly success as a sign of salvation; Calvinism as an ideal type; capitalism as an unintended consequence.

Conclusion

Weber's importance to modern sociology; Weber as a theorist of modernity; his view of socialism; the contribution of his religious studies to the basic dualisms; his theoretical ambivalence; his views on German politics.

Introduction

For Weber, history was the product of individual actions, open-ended, and, like social structures, precarious. History, on this view, would be the telling of stories. Yet the stories which he tells, especially in his studies of the world religions, contain a sort of 'ghost' evolutionary theory, one which owes little to Darwin or organic analogies. We have already met it in his discussion of forms of domination; there seems to be steady development of western rationality, from Judaism onwards, which eventually comes to dominate everything. It is this which gives rise to the view of Weber as a tragic liberal—the individualist who ends up by describing the iron cage of modern society. This chapter will concentrate on Weber's sociology of religion—first of all his theoretical framework and then his studies of the major world religions, Confucianism, Hinduism and Buddhism, and Judaism, culminating with his *Protestant Ethic and the Spirit of Capitalism*.

The sociology of religion

Weber starts with the universality of belief in the supernatural and turns his attention to the ways in which this develops, the breakthrough which moves a society beyond a primitive belief. There are important historical points where a society makes choices and he sees these choices in dichotomous terms, between a course of action which will further the differentiation of spheres of life and a course of action which would continue traditional ways of acting.

The first important distinction is between the magician and the priest, or between magic and religion as systems of beliefs. Both mediate between the human and the supernatural, but they do so in different ways. Magic is involved with the demands of everyday life and involves the use of spells or some equivalent to force the supernatural into acting in a particular way on behalf of the magician and/or his or her client. If I am having arguments with my boss, the magical answer is to go and collect some of his or her nail clippings or hair, go home, put these items into a wax model, and stick pins in it in the knowledge that he or she will suffer acute physical pain. Religion, on the other hand, does not work in such an *ad hoc*, immediate way; it is systematically organized and God (or the Gods) cannot be forced into action. The most I can do if I am a Christian is pray to God to give me the patience to deal with my tyrannical boss; there is no guarantee that God will do this, and I might have to wait until the next Sunday before I even get a chance to pray in what I would consider a proper context. Magical forces are not worshipped.

As conceptions of the supernatural order develop, religion gains an autonomy which influences the social order. The importance of the magic/religion appears when he distinguishes between societies based on what he calls 'taboo' and those based on religious ethics. The first are concerned with specific acts: perhaps prohibiting incest or compelling marriages outside the individual's clan. Taboos are not confined to magic but are certainly more primitive than religious ethics, which move away from the specific towards the universal; they work at a higher level of generality and a higher level of personal responsibility, not least because people are no longer subject to magical retribution. The realm of the supernatural always combines both but to different degrees.

The evolutionary process is that of rationalization—increasingly universal and elaborate belief and value systems. This movement to a higher level comes through the appearance of the *prophet*. As far as sociology is concerned, the prophet is the bearer of charisma—he or she might be the founder of a new religion, or somebody breathing new life into the old religion, and, Weber adds, it doesn't matter whether people are more attracted by the person or the doctrine, the sociological point is that the prophet announces a personal revelation. For this reason prophets rarely come from the organized and routinized priesthood. The priest has influence through office, the prophet through 'personal gifts'; unlike the magician, the prophet is concerned with specific revelations and with doctrines, but, like the magician, he is likely to perform some miraculous acts—turning water into wine, raising from the dead, etc. The prophet is also different from the legislator—although the prophets of Israel, unlike those of Buddhism and Hinduism, were concerned with social reform and this might sometimes blur the difference. However, the more concerned they were with social reform, the less prophet-like they were. Ezekiel, 'the real theoretician of social reform . . . was a priestly theorist who can scarcely be categorized as a prophet at all . . . Jesus was not at all interested in social reform as such' (Weber 1922/1965: 51). The messages of Zoroaster, and of Buddha, were also essentially religious. It is worth remembering that there are still debates, at least in the Christian churches, about the relationship between the social and religious duties of the church; interestingly, people who might be considered latter-day prophets, the media evangelists, particularly in the USA, are interested in right-wing social reform.

The founders of schools of philosophy cannot be considered as prophets; they do not usually engage in 'vital emotional preaching', whereas the prophet is closer to the 'popular orator'. There are various other related roles which Weber goes on to separate from the prophet proper, who can be either an 'ethical prophet', preaching God's word as an ethical duty (Muhammad) or an 'exemplary prophet', who shows the way to salvation by personal example (Buddha).

The exemplary prophet tends towards the conception of a God who is somehow present everywhere in this world and the concern is with how to experience the deity, to achieve personal enlightenment, an experiential state very different from the meaning of enlightenment in western philosophy. The ethical God, on the other hand, is transcendent—he, she, or it stands outside the world and demands obedience. Christianity is clearly an ethical religion but the contrast is not an absolute one; there is, for example, a long tradition of Christian mysticism which at times does not seem too far away from Buddhism (see, e.g., *The Cloud of Unknowing* (anon. 1960)).

Weber goes on to suggest that there is a connection between types of religious organization and forms of domination in the wider society; one of the things that makes prophecy important is that it breaks from the established order and the prophet and followers stand in a special relationship to those who do not follow the prophet as a subgroup in the wider society whose special concern is religion. Whereas exemplary prophets tend to generate an élite of the enlightened and a rather indistinct mass of followers, ethical prophets tend to generate a more firmly organized church. The latter favours the development of rationalization—especially if a written tradition is established.

There then follow two chapters which show Weber at his best, in his sophisticated Marxist guise—he presents what can be seen as a class analysis of religion, a way in which different sorts of religion may be carried by different classes. He begins with the peasantry, who, he argues, are dependent on nature and natural cycles; they have little interest in rational systematization and will turn to religion only when they are threatened—either by an external army or by enslavement or by proletarianization—and when such a threat appears, prophetic cults rise in opposition to the established church. Here it is a matter of war or class struggle pushing the development forward. Most of the time, however, the peasantry stay with their magic. The idea of the peasant as the main support of traditional organized religion is, with few exceptions, a modern phenomenon. In early times, urban centres were also centres of religion—from early Christianity right through to the Middle Ages.

The feudal ruling classes were not bearers of religion—the life of the warrior noble had little to do with religious ethics and it would run counter to their honour to submit to the authority of a prophet or a priest. The noble might be drawn in for a while on the upsurge of a prophetic movement—which at the beginning might draw supporters from all classes—but he is likely to drop out, particularly as routinization sets in. The exception is when the religion gives a purpose to the warrior—for example, in the Crusades (on both sides). Religion, he suggests, has more appeal to professional, standing armies with a bureaucratic command structure. It also appealed to some urban officials who were involved in bureaucratic administration. Such social groups will occasionally be attracted to prophetic movements, but usually they carry 'a comprehensive sober rationalism' and an 'ideal of disciplined order'. Irrational religion does not appeal to them. Confucianism represents the distinctive bureaucratic attitude to religion, the absence of emotional needs, and the absence of any transcendental root or justification for an ethics.

The most privileged social strata produce striking contrasts in their attitudes to religion. Prophetic movements have been movements not of the dispossessed, but of the middle classes, who have made economic sacrifices in the process. There are two factors which seem important in determining whether a group is likely to be a 'carrier' of a rationalizing religion: the first is whether that group in its normal life involves generalized rational and responsible procedures, and the second is whether the group is separated in their lives from the traditional order of religion. Amongst the first group, merchants and artisans could be included; amongst the second, subordinate groups of artisans, apprentices, and journeymen.

Next Weber turns to intellectuals as a social group. One might expect them to be at the centre of the process of rationalization but this can be counteracted by their identification with traditional ruling groups—for example, when the intellectuals are priests in an established church. If these groups move towards 'salvation religion', it is often via mysticism, the movement being created by inner rather than social tensions. To seek enlightenment in this way takes one above any concern with social status; this was particularly important in the development of Indian religion. He argues that the intellectualism of relatively deprived groups is particularly important. The notion of relative deprivation has been important in modern sociology (Runciman 1966); the *relative* part is more important than the *deprivation*—it allows comparisons to be made with those in a better and/or worse position and this raises the possibility of change. Where deprivation approaches the absolute, change is inconceivable. The particular groups that Weber thinks were important in this respect were the Jews, the early Christians, and the Puritans.

The process of rationalization within which all this takes place is a process of finding meaning in the world. Human beings for Weber in this context are essentially meaning-finding or rather meaning-hunting beings, and this brings people up against the understanding of the apparently meaningless: of suffering, of death, or whatever—particularly when they afflict those who do not deserve it. There is a discrepancy between what we expect from leading the good life—rewards, justice, success—and what we get—pain, mistreatment, and suffering. This sort of problem seems to me not only still a matter of religion in the contemporary world but one at the centre of every aspect of our lives—it is extraordinarily difficult to accept the contingency and meaningless dimension of the things that happen to us. Whether we are dealing with accidents, natural disasters, death, or illness, we look for somebody to blame.

Attempts to explain such things become ever more abstract and generalized from everyday life. In immanent religions (where God is seen everywhere in this world) we find more radical discountings of the world, whereas in transcendent religions (where God is outside the world) we find the attempt to make the world closer to what is expected or hoped for. Weber calls this the problem of salvation, the area of tension between the real and the ideal, worldly compromise and perfection. There are some who cannot accept compromise and seek salvation according to standards of perfection, and this is at the root of social change:

Our concern is essentially with the quest for salvation, whatever its form, insofar as it produced certain consequences for practical behaviour in the world. It is most likely to acquire such a positive orientation to mundane affairs as the result of a pattern of life which is distinctively determined by religion and given coherence by some central meaning or positive goal . . . a quest for salvation in any religious group has the strongest chance of exerting practical influences when there has arisen, out of religious motivation, a systematization of practical conduct resulting from an orientation to certain integral values.   (Weber 1922/1965: 149)

This systematization can be inhibited by magical features of the search for salvation—the sacramental system of the Roman Catholic Church is offered as an example of this. If the tensions of the world are dealt with by withdrawal, then the process of rationalization, of social evolution, is not helped. If there is an attempt to solve the worldly tension, then the evolutionary process is pushed forward. We do not have to look far back into the history of religion to find examples of this, they are there in the secular and political history of the last three decades. The period of social turmoil that developed to differing degrees across western Europe and in the USA in the 1960s and 1970s, which might have been student-led in some countries but also involved ethnic minorities, women, and workers, shows, at least as far as the student and youth dimensions are concerned, a similar division. There were those who sought an inner enlightenment and retired from the world, and there were those who rejected compromise and sort to change the world to something closer to their ideals, which were often seen in terms of individual freedom, individual rights to self-expression, and so on. It is arguable that the tensions that Weber found are still present, not only in religious life but also in radical political life. The current form on inner resolution is perhaps being sought by those around 'New Age' groups and the this-worldly solutions being sought by the green movement, some forms of feminism, and some ethnic movements, but with a lot of over-lap.

Chinese religion: Confucianism and Taoism

One of the common criticisms of Weber's (1915/1951) study of Chinese religion is that he cited material from the very earliest period up to the beginning of the twentieth century as if he were talking about the same society; Reinhard Bendix (1966) (whose account of Weber's religious studies I would recommend highly) argues that this can be justified—there had, in fact, been comparatively little change in some aspects of Chinese society, Weber was concerned with showing the potentialities of this society, and such an analysis could be developed from different periods of its history.

Weber's prime concern, however, was with the early stages of Chinese history. One feature of Chinese society is that cities, whilst recognizably centres of pop-ulation, craft, and trade as they were in the West, never developed the same autonomy—they did not receive charters or obtain political independence and did not function as corporate bodies. The residents of the towns remained tied to their villages through kinship relations, in which the practice of ancestor wor-ship was particularly important. Relationships to the supernatural were not a direct individual matter as they became in the West, but were mediated through the family. The towns remained subordinate to the countryside, and to the cen-tral authority. Here we find Weber's version of oriental despotism. The central government needs to defend large and open boundaries and defend against flooding as well as regulate irrigation to supply the cities.

However, central power was not absolute and local groups were strong, but they could not organize opposition to the central power. Local rulers derived their power from their ancestral inheritance, but, according to Weber, this also inhibited them coming together in a unified status group to oppose the emperor. Because of the early centralization of power and development of an administrative body, power struggles were about office rather than land. Office-holders could be freely removed from office (whereas in the West they were inherited positions), and any movement towards a more rational form of organ-ization was automatically inhibited by the power of the emperor, who was also the chief priest in the state religion, which had no prophetic tradition.

The emperor kept a fairly strict control over his regional officials; appoint-ment was by educational qualification, not birth, for comparatively short periods and away from the area where the official was born; they were subjected to regular assessments, the results of which were made public. In this way, they were kept on a tight rein. This is a lesson which has been learnt by the contemporary British government and management—regular audits, 'quality assessments', the publication of league tables for hospitals and schools, all establish a very high level of central control.

In China, however, these regional officials were dependent on local translators and officials and this masked the power of the central government—central decrees did not take on the aura of orders from above. The tax system did not boost the central government either. At each stage in the process, an official would have to extract his own salary and expenses and that of his staff, and this encouraged immense pressure on the peasant who actually paid the taxes, but the amount of money paid upwards at each stage becomes less and less. This sets the scene for a three-way struggle between status groups: the central government, its appointees, and the local kinship networks, which were very powerful and organized along a mixture of democratic and what Weber calls 'hereditary charismatic' principles. These networks involved all male members of the family and provided the basis for regular ancestor ceremonies.

Here we come to the central issue for Weber: why did capitalism not develop in China. In terms of the social structure, the strength of the kinship network was important—preventing the development of legal-rational authority necessary for the growth of capitalism. By definition the family is a bastion of traditionalism, especially where ancestors are religiously important; the centrally appointed officials remained dependent on their families' support, and, importantly, no separate class of lawyers developed. The family group was responsible for the law.

This enabled the development of a limited form of commercial capitalism run by 'purveyors to the state and tax farmers'. But it did not enable the development of rational industrial capitalism, which needs the stability of conditions in which rational accounting can develop, and the dominance of the family network does not allow this. Moreover, the 'feud' element of feudalism—struggles between local rulers—did not develop into rational warfare as it did in the West. On the other hand, there was a period of increasing agricultural production and population increase, and considerable personal fortunes were amassed and personal freedom of movement was increasing—all conditions which would favour capitalism. These forces were in turn negated by the absence of a rationally administered and formally guaranteed legal system and by the 'ethos peculiar to a stratum of officials and aspirants to office' (Weber 1915/1951: 104). This was the Confucian ethic by which officials led their lives.

The Chinese official was educated in literature, in proper ways of behaving, in writing instead of speaking; his charisma derived from this and was proved by his 'harmonious' administration. Confucianism is the religion of intellectuals: education can remove human faults and lead to the dominance of the 'heavenly' aspects of human nature over its demonic aspects—the 'gentleman ideal' was that of all-round perfection, 'who had become a "work of art" in the sense of a classical, eternally valid, canon of psychical beauty, which literary tradition implemented in the souls of disciples' (ibid. 131).

It was not appropriate for such a man to engage in economic activity—except insofar as he was concerned with the proper level of consumption, neither too little nor too much. The pursuit of wealth for its own sake was disapproved of because it would involve an imbalance in the development of the self:

Confucian virtue, based upon universality or self-perfection, was greater than the riches to be gained by one-sided thoroughness. Not even in the most influential position could one achieve anything in the world without the virtue derived from education. And vice versa, one could achieve nothing, no matter what one's virtue, without influential position. Hence the 'superior' man coveted such a position, not profit.   (ibid. 161)

This was directly opposed to the western feudal ethic of accumulation for lavish expenditure. However, if the Confucian ethic did not encourage economic activity and rational calculation, what about the more popular religions: Taoism and Buddhism?

Taoism was developed from the same sources as Confucianism. It rejected

Table 13.1 Contrasting Confucianism and Puritanism

Confucianism	Puritanism
Belief in impersonal, cosmic order; tolerance of magic.	Belief in supramundane God; rejection of magic.
Adjustment to the world to maintain harmony of heaven and earth; the ideal of order.	Mastery over the world in unceasing quest for virtue in the eyes of God; the ideal of progressive change.
Vigilant self-control for the sake of dignity and self-perfection.	Vigilant self-control for the sake of controlling man's wicked nature and doing God's will.
Absence of prophecy related to inviolability of tradition; man can avoid the wrath of the spirits and be 'good' if he acts properly.	Prophecy makes tradition and the world as it is appear wicked; man cannot attain goodness by his own efforts.
Familial piety as the principal governing all human relations.	Subordination of all human relations to the service of God.
Kinship relations as the basis for commercial transactions, voluntary associations, law, and public administration.	Rational law and agreement as the basis for commercial transactions, voluntary associations, law, and public administration.
Distrust of all persons outside the extended family.	Trust of all persons who are 'brothers in faith'.
Wealth as the basis for dignity and self-perfection.	Wealth as a temptation and unintended by-product of a virtuous life.

worldly concerns and encouraged the use of magic. Both Taoism and Confucianism, but particularly the latter, were important inhibitions on economic activity in China. Confucianism was able to use Taoism to defend its own interests, although both Taoism and Buddhism were persecuted if they presented a threat; but for most of the time they did not—they emphasized withdrawal from the world and contemplation in the search for salvation, and as part of this a submissive obedience to the external order. Clearly neither could provide the basis for a rational capitalism.

Weber ends his study with a comparison of Confucianism with the Puritanism which he saw as primarily responsible for the growth of capitalism in the West. As we have seen, his analysis of Chinese society is concerned with the economic level and the way in which different status groups form on the basis of economic organization, political and administrative organization, and religious beliefs. There were elements in economic organization which favoured the growth of capitalism as well as inhibited it; the main political inhibition came from the strength of the family and the importance of ancestor worship—a religious belief. But it was the wider religious ethic that was perhaps crucial and here we must begin to look at Puritanism. Bendix (1966: 140–41) produces an excellent table of the differences that Weber identifies when he is comparing the two (see Table 13.1).

Indian religion: Hinduism and Buddhism

Weber's study of Indian religion begins with the caste system, the role of which is as central to the development of Indian society as the relationship between the family and the bureaucracy was to Chinese society. In China the effect of religion on the social structure was indirect—the beliefs of Confucianism had the effect of inhibiting capitalist development, but did not prescribe a particular type of social structure. In India, however, the caste system *was* Indian social structure and was intimately bound up with Hinduism.

He distinguishes first between different sorts of religious groupings: sects (which in the modern West include such groups as the Plymouth Brethren, Jehovah's Witnesses, and so on) and churches (the Anglican Church, the Roman Catholic Church, or the Greek or Russian Orthodox Churches):

A 'sect' in the sociological sense of the word is an exclusive association of religious virtuosos or especially qualified religious persons, recruited through individual admission after establishment of qualification. By contrast a 'church' as a universalistic establishment for the salvation of the masses raises the claim, like the 'state', that everyone, at least each child of a member, must belong by birth. It demands sacramental acts and, possibly, proof of acquaintance with its holy learning as a precondition of its membership rights, but establishes as a duty the observance of the sacraments and the discharge of those obligations which are a condition of its membership rights. The consequence of this is that when the church reaches its full development and has power, it coerces opponents to conform. . . . The individual is normally 'born' into the church, single conversions and admissions occurring only until the time the church has attained its principal goal—the unification of all men in the universal church.   (Weber 1921/1958: 6)

Hinduism possesses properties of both sect and church; membership is by birth to Hindu parents, but it has the sect's exclusiveness; no one can enter from the outside and it has no aspiration to universalism, to convert the whole of humanity. Each caste is recruited from only one social group, who share the same status by virtue of their rituals, and movement between castes is not allowed. They are an exceptionally rigid form of status group—although there is some variation in rigidity brought about through social aspirations and status consciousness.

The family is particularly important. In the West we are familiar with the notion of the 'divine right of kings'—or for that matter queens—which involves a familial charisma which is passed on from generation to generation, even if some generations don't appear to possess as much of it as others. For Weber, Indian society was dependent upon familial charisma, which bound kin groups together into castes, giving religious significance to all sorts of status distinctions. The caste system developed partly due to military conquest, with the invading groups refusing any intermixing with the conquered but claiming the land and a proportion of its product. The subordinate group owed obligatory service to the ruling group as a whole, not to its individual members. This led to a division of labour between rather than within groups.

This was reinforced by the conversion of tribes (already economic units with their internal division of labour) to Hinduism; sometimes this happened because the ruling groups of these tribes saw the chance of gaining a religious justification for their position, or perhaps because a tribe or specialist group had lost its territory, so it took on the status of a pariah group and they formed the lowest castes. Castes would also subdivide—new practices might appear because environmental conditions change. As ever, Weber offers a multi-causal analysis for the predominance of the caste system.

Rather like the Confucian literati, the highest caste—the Brahmins—gained charisma from their knowledge of literature; but, whereas the former were officials, such careers were rare amongst the Brahmins, who comprised 'princely chaplains . . . counselors, theological teachers and jurists, priests and pastors' (ibid. 140). For the Brahmin, the pursuit of a career, the highest Confucian ideal, meant very little. And, in contrast to China, there was a separation between church and state: the kings were not priests, and in fact they were subordinated to priests. Whereas the Confucian officials were concerned with written literature, and relegated magic to the people, the Brahmins cultivated and protected an oral tradition and relied on magic for the maintenance of their position. There was no universal ethic, but different ethics for each caste within an overarching world-view which saw the rank order of castes as a matter of retribution for misdeeds in a previous life. There was no idea of natural right or of fundamental human equality as appeared in the West and there could be no basis for social criticism. Everyone existed in a pluralistic, eternal order. In the wider social structure, patrimonial and feudal organization existed; in the struggle between various groups, no one was able to establish overall power, and there was a fluctuation between the appearance of centrally governed patrimonial empires and fragmentation into small areas of control.

There was a period of competition for popular support between Hinduism and Buddhism, but the latter's concern for contemplation did not encourage conflict and Buddhism fragmented and declined. Weber identifies two important Hindu beliefs. The first is a belief in the transmigration of the soul: the belief that the soul moves into another world on death, and sacrifice and prayer in this world ensure it a peaceful life until eventually it undergoes another death and rebirth into another existence in this world. The second is a belief in *karma*: that retribution for misdeeds in this life involves being born into a lower caste, and proper ritual observances in this life lead to being born into a higher caste. There can be no concept of the 'accident of birth' which lies behind western ideas such as equality of opportunity despite the social class into which people are born. We deserve what we get and, if we conscientiously observe the prescribed rituals, we can do better next time. These are not beliefs likely to fuel criticism, protest, or rebellion.

To buttress their position at the top of the caste system the Brahmins developed an ascetic ideal—an ideal of self denial, in dietary and sexual and other matters—which distinguished them as truly holy men. Here Weber seems to be close to a crude Marxism, an argument that these ideas developed to justify and protect a particular class position. A form of apathetic austerity became the highest ideal of Hindu life. On the birth of the first grandson, the Brahmin should withdraw from everyday life, and seek internal emancipation, a 'blissful state'. When the Brahmins seek emancipation, it is not just from the concerns of this world but from the everlasting cycle of death and rebirth. Yoga is one intellectual method of achieving this special state. Originally, Weber suggests, such ascetics became teachers (gurus) and formed the nucleus of monasteries.

On occasion it seemed that the ideal of the holy man took him well away from the world of religious observance as well, beyond the claims of rituals and of ethical systems—he should aim at a state of indifference as to whether his actions were good or evil, and this brought into question the possibility of salvation for the ordinary person. It also meant that the holy man could be engaged in action and at the same time indifferent to it. Bendix sums up the dominant theme of Brahmin wisdom which:

achieves an image of the world in which not only each man's daily duties but also each man's goal of salvation has become relative to his position in the caste order. Whatever they might be, each man's actions and devotions are valuable *in their own terms*; in a world that has been devalued few men can have more than relative merit.   (Bendix 1966: 182)

The Brahmins managed to hold on to their position despite various challenges and, like the Chinese literati, they tolerated magic and popular religion for the lower orders, which allowed a number of sectarian doctrines to develop. However, the guru was given a new and powerful position with absolute power in the matter of salvation. Under Islamic and later British rule, the Brahmins became ever more important figures.

The overall effect of this on economic activity should be fairly evident. Wealth and professional and economic success could never be seen as a sign of salvation. At the same time, Hindu adherents amongst the masses were involved in every-day economic activities and enthusiastically accumulated wealth, but this was not carried out in the rational, calculative way in which it was pursued in the West. It was, rather, intimately bound up with magic and magical practices. Weber refers to it as a 'magical garden' from which rationality could not develop. The acquisitive drive has to be incorporated into the inner worldly life ethic before it can contribute towards the development of capitalism, and the force of tradition in the caste system as well as the beliefs of Hinduism did not allow this.

Palestine: ancient Judaism

In his study of Judaism, Weber focuses on what differentiates western from eastern religion. The crucial factor is the notion of positive ethical action—of changing the world for the better under God's guidance. But in the end it is the *unintentional effects* of religious belief that are most important.

There are important suggestions in both Judaism and Christianity that people should make themselves the tools of God, the means by which God pursues his ends in this world. The world is a constant temptation, threatening to take people away from God's purposes; and a particular danger lies in sitting back and simply fulfilling ritual expectations. This latter course was represented by medieval mystical Christianity. This is important for Weber, because for him the uniqueness of the West lay in the Judaic tradition of prophecy. The Jewish experience of religion was radically different from the Indian. It was a matter not of ritual observance but of seeking a radical change. The tribes of Israel were the chosen people, the children of God who had lost their privileges, and that privileged position had to be restored. In a very real sense the world had to be turned upside-down—it was not a matter of eternal cycles of the same thing but of a long, changing process. Judaism was soaked in what we would now call history:

The whole attitude toward life of ancient Jewry was determined by this conception of a future God-guided political and social revolution. This revolution was to take a special direction. Ritual correctitude and the segregation from the social environment imposed by it was but one aspect of the commands upon Jewry. There existed in addition a highly rational religious ethic of social conduct; it was free of magic and all forms of irrational quest for salvation. To a large extent this ethic still underlies contemporary Mid-Eastern and European ethics. World-historical interest in Jewry rests upon this fact.   (Weber 1921/1952: 5)

The development of ancient Palestine was rarely a peaceful one—the history of conquest and war runs through the Old Testament. Weber argues that this was in part the result of contrasting ways of life in the region. Settlement and cultivation were possible in the north, whereas, to the south and the east, some settlement was possible but it usually involved seasonal migration, or there was the possibility of a permanent nomadic existence. There was regular conflict between nomads, herdsmen, peasants, and city-dwellers. Under the reign of Solomon, Israel was a major power, developing from the confederacy of tribes that followed the Exodus from Egypt. This period was in turn followed by decline and Babylonian captivity. The basic tenets of Judaism were developed through the period leading up to the monarchy, and, after its fall, they became the basis for the prophetic movement to which we owe the development of the modern world.

The time of 'confederacy' saw no permanent institutions; social cohesion was provided by common religious beliefs which united disparate extended families. The tribes came together as a political unity mainly in times of war. There were a number of specific features of Judaism and its belief in Jahwe (or Jehovah), who was to become the Christian God. 'Everywhere', Weber argues, 'deities are the guardian of the social order. They sanction its violation, reward conformity to it' (ibid. 120). But Israel had a special agreement with God set out in Moses' tablets of stone. God would be Israel's God and no other nation's. And, in return, the Israelites promised obedience to Jahwe and no other God. Originally Jahwe was a God of war and natural catastrophes such as plagues of locusts and snakes and famines and floods; there is perhaps an ironic memory of this in the way the term 'Act of God' is used by modern insurance companies. On occasion he could be angry at being slighted and bring about dramatic punishment to remind people of his power. He was a fierce God, fiercer than the Christian God, but we still have a sense that there might be this fierce absolute power some-where. Jehovah did not sanction a permanent order. He had an agreement with His people which could change if He so desired. He could direct events according to His will, to reward or punish His people. The notion of a special covenant with God was unique in the Middle East. There were long battles with different beliefs within and outside Judaism; the important internal divisions were between priests (the Levites) and various mystic or orgiastic tendencies.

Whereas the Gods of other tribes would respond to sacrifices, Jehovah expected obedience, and this was the only way to seek his favour. This under-mined the power of both magicians and priests; when things went wrong, it generated relatively rational argument about which commandment had been broken and how and why.

It was this tradition which developed when Israel went into Babylonian captivity. Israel was not one of the three great Middle Eastern centres of civilization—rather it was at the crossroads between such societies, and this enabled creative interaction of intellectuals and socially declassed citizens to produce new religious ideas. Weber points out that it is on the margin of great empires or centres of civilization that new religious ideas emerge. He might have added that it was not only religious ideas that emerged in such situations. Marx had also pointed out that new ideas in general come from the edges of the great centres of social change rather than from within them. For Weber, life at the centre of the great civilization is caught up unreflectively in the existence and beliefs of that society, whereas on the edges, where the effects of that life are felt, albeit at a distance, people begin to ask their own questions and learn to develop their own way of dealing with life. There is space and a necessity to reflect on these issues. We find the same happening in modern Europe: it was the German philosopher Hegel who was the first to try to systematize an understanding of the French Revolution—something that could be done only from a distance but not too far a distance. And it is was the thinkers of the Scottish Enlightenment—the philosopher David Hume, the economist Adam Smith—who began thinking through the implications of the industrial revolution in England. As Bendix (1966: 233) puts it: 'The possibility of questioning the meaning of the world presupposes the capacity to be astonished about the course of events, and surprise is not always possible when one is in the midst of events.'

Returning to ancient Palestine, the monarchy developed into an autocratic state of the Egyptian model. This provoked a rebellion and a split into two, Israel and Judah, which survived because of a lull in the expansionary ambitions of the surrounding empires of Egypt and Mesopotamia. Once these started their wars of conquest, the region witnessed scenes that Weber says reached a frightfulness and magnitude never seen before:

Blood fairly drips from the cuneiform[1] inscriptions. The king, in the tone of dry protocol, reports that he covered the walls of conquered cities with human skins. The Israelite literature preserved from the period, above all the oracles of classical prophecy, express the mad terror caused by these merciless conquerors. As impending gloom beclouded the political horizon, classical prophecy acquired its characteristic form. (Weber 1921/1952: 267)

The form taken by that prophecy is perhaps not surprising and Weber argues that it could develop only under external threat and against the king and his prophets, who were seen as of declining importance:

usually the prophet spoke on his own, i.e. under the influence of spontaneous inspiration, to the public in the market place or to the elders at the city gate. The prophet also

---

[1] The name given to the characters of Assyrian script.

interpreted the fates of individuals, though as a rule only those of politically important persons. The predominant concern of the prophet was the destiny of the state and the people. This concern always assumed the form of emotional invectives against the over-lords. It is here that 'the demagogue' appeared for the first time in the records of history. (ibid. 269)

Old Testament prophecy was authoritarian in character and gained power from the fact that it was uttered by a private citizen; the rulers reacted with fear, wrath, or indifference as the occasion demanded. During this period we find the first examples of political pamphleteering. But it would be wrong to draw too close a parallel with modern politics and political situations. These prophets were asserting absolute ethical positions and had little contact with the political real-ities of their situations. In fact, their prestige depended in part on their separa-tion from the nation's politics. We can get a hint of what this might have been like when political outsiders take up moral positions in contemporary political debates—Ross Perot in the 1994 American presidential election comes to mind. But their prestige also depended on their high social status. However, they cursed both the great and the uneducated masses, and—perhaps not surpris-ingly—they gained little public support.

Their most distinctive feature as a status group, Weber argued, was the gratu-itous nature of their prophecies: they were free and spontaneous, very different from the official prophets and the 'industry of prophecy'. As Weber puts it: 'One does not pay for evil omens.' What he calls their inner independence was, he argues, not a result of their activities but a cause of it. This is an interesting way of seeing it and it takes us back to my earlier comments about charisma. I sug-gested that Weber did not see charisma as a social product, but as a sort of independent psychological variable. Here he is talking not about charisma but about an inner independence, which he seems to see too as an independent psychological variable. But I think we are entitled to ask whether this inner inde-pendence would have arisen without the security of a high-status background—only Amos of the prophets came from a shepherd background.

This type of prophecy was a sign of the weakness of the priesthood—and here Weber acknowledges that their family background was important and kept the enmity of the priests at bay. The prophets saw themselves as tools of God, but not as specially privileged humans in the sense that they did not claim to be free from sin. The prophet delivered his own personal message from God, but did not offer any magical solution or sign to prove his communication with Jehovah. The populace at large seemed to assume that the prophetic message was validated by the fact that nobody in his right senses would risk incurring the wrath of the powers that be without some special reason, and hearing the voice of God would be such a reason. The insistence of the moral law against all earthly powers that tried to persecute them was the achievement of these prophets—it made the *morally correct actions of everyday life into the special duty of a people chosen by the mightiest God*' (Bendix 1966: 247; emphasis in original). And the will of this God was open to understanding—not a matter of obtaining a mystical state and not requiring metaphysical speculation. If misfortune befell the people, then it was because of God's will, and if God willed them misfortune, then it was because of disobedience. Weber makes much of the fact that they could have constructed alternative explanations, but that would have moved towards irrationality. Disobedience lay in oppressing the poor, idol worship, neglect of rituals, and—surprise, surprise—suppression of prophecy. But redemption was always possible and the pious would be rewarded. This explanation enabled the transformation of Jehovah into a Universal God, not one among many in competition with the others. He alone was responsible for the fortune and misfortune of his special people. The worse things became, the more the prophecies were fulfilled, the greater the Israelites' devotion to God. And these beliefs prepared the way for the emergence, many centuries later, of the Saviour.

The Protestant ethic and the spirit of capitalism

Introduction

So we come at last to Weber's much heralded classic work on the Protestant ethic. As you might expect if you have read the previous sections, the rise of Puritanism crowns and hastens the process of rationalization that originated with the pact between Jehovah and Israel and was developed by the Old Testament prophets and the arrival of Christianity. This, in turn, led to the development of western capitalism.

The three books that have just been discussed are what we might call sociological histories of religion, looking at the relationship between religious beliefs, economic situations, and social structures and the way in which they interlock in social development. They are *stories*, tales of development. There is a similar element to the Protestant ethic, but that is perhaps less important than the *analytic* aspect. Weber is not simply telling a story but he is suggesting a causal connection between what he calls the spirit of capitalism and the Protestant ethic. The connection is an 'elective affinity'—it is as if one way of thinking about the world seeks out and encourages another. But this affinity is not necessarily a conscious one, working itself out directly through people's thinking and action. It is more indirect. The Puritans do not decide singly or collectively to set out to develop an economic system called capitalism; rather they faithfully follow their beliefs and the growth of capitalism is what some contemporary sociologists would call an 'unintended consequence'.

Bendix (1966) talks about Weber's own work ethic, the punishing demands he made upon himself at the outset of his career which eventually led to his breakdown, and suggests that he took on this attitude to his work from his entrepreneur uncle, who worked hard and lived frugally, in a way Weber thought typical of the great entrepreneurs of early capitalism. Modern psycho-analysis would see this tendency in terms of a strict, if not punitive superego, a strict, internalized authority figure which constantly demands more and more in the way of effort and will allow little relaxation and enjoyment. A very differ-ent thinker, the twentieth-century Marxist philosopher Herbert Marcuse (1969), has employed psychoanalytic ideas to argue that capitalism establishes itself on the basis of an immense internal repression that pushed people into the sacrifice of pleasure. We have seen that Freud's argument was that some repres-sion was necessary to make civilization possible at all; Marcuse's point was that capitalism made very special demands in this respect—rather than consuming wealth for enjoyment, it must be reinvested for the accumulation of capital.

I hope this is not so much of a diversion as it might appear; Weber's thesis in *The Protestant Ethic* is very similar but does not draw on notions of the uncon-scious. It is concerned with conscious beliefs and ideas, which he sees as moti-vating action in a comparatively unproblematic way, and he goes on to the way in which these actions have, for the actors, unintended consequences. I will look first at what Weber has to say about capitalism, and then at his discussion of Protestantism, following the order of his argument.

The spirit of capitalism

Capitalism, 'the most fateful force in our modern life', is defined as entailing a particular sort of action which:

rests on the expectation of profit by the utilization of opportunities for exchange, that is on . . . peaceful chances for profit. . . . Where capitalist acquisition is rationally pursued, the corresponding action is adjusted to calculations in terms of capital. This means that the action is adapted to a systematic utilization of goods or personal services as a means of acquisition in such a way that at the end of a business period, the balance of the enter-prise in money assets . . . exceeds the capital, i.e. the estimated value of material means of production used for acquisition in exchange.   (1904/5/1930: 17–18)

More simply, capitalist economic action aims to make a calculable profit. Such capitalism has existed at all times in most places, but in the West it has taken on a new form, involving the capitalist organization of free labour, the separation of business from home, and the development of rational bookkeeping. He notes the importance of technology and the systematic and rational application of technology to capitalist production, which owed much to the pre-existing 'rational structures of law and of administration' (ibid. 25). At this point Weber seems to be compiling a list of contributing factors rather than ordering them into some tentative causal explanation, although he does emphasize the import-ance of free labour. However, the crucial factor is the peculiar rationalism general to western culture and a general willingness to accept rational techniques. In other cultures religious beliefs and practices have inhibited such activities.

Weber points out that Protestant areas seem to favour the growth of capitalism. This revolt against traditional religion was not against religion as such but the replacement of a very relaxed religious control by a very strict and all pervasive religious control. At Weber's time it was possible to argue that Protestants were much more acquisitive than Roman Catholics, but in the past the opposite had been the case; the original Protestants were Puritans, not concerned with the 'joy of living', with personal pleasure, or consumption.

To build up his conception of the spirit of capitalism, Weber draws on the writings of Benjamin Franklin, an eighteenth-century American who might now be called a 'management' or 'business' consultant and who wrote popular books on how to get rich. The two from which Weber takes his model go under the titles of *Necessary Hints to Those that Would Be Rich* and *Advice to a Young Tradesman*, written in 1736 and 1748 respectively. Franklin sets out what Weber regards as the spirit of capitalism in its pure type. Here I will simply summarize his points with the odd quotation. Many of them take the form of sayings which have entered into common usage:

1. Time is money.
2. Credit is money.
3. 'Remember that money is of the prolific, generating nature. Money can beget money, and its offspring can beget more, and so on. . . . He that kills a breeding-sow destroys all her offspring to the thousandth generation. He that murders a crown, destroys all that it might have produced, even scores of pounds.'
4. 'The good paymaster is lord of another man's purse'—i.e. if I pay my debts when they are due I will always be able to borrow as much as I can. 'The most trifling actions that affect a man's credit are to be regarded. The sound of your hammer at five in the morning, or eight at night, heard by a creditor, makes him easy six months longer.'
5. Keep careful accounts of income and expenditure—basically look after the pennies and the pounds will look after themselves.
6. Always be known for prudence and industry, don't spend time idly; all money that is spent idling loses not only its own value, but the money that it might have been turned in to.

Weber points out that the implication of this is that increasing capital is a duty, not simply a matter of 'business astuteness'. However, the virtues that Franklin proposes are strictly utilitarian; they serve an end and need be espoused only at the level of appearance. It is important that I appear to be honest and hard-working, so that people will trust me and bring me business. Weber argues that it is not quite so simple as this. For Franklin there is something more profound—a real religious conviction and search for salvation:

the *summum bonum* [greatest good] of this ethic, the earning of more and more money, combined with the strict avoidance of all spontaneous enjoyment of life, is above all completely devoid of any . . . hedonistic admixture. It is thought of so purely as an end in itself, that from the point of view of the happiness of, or utility to, the single individual, it appears entirely transcendental and absolutely irrational. Man is dominated by the making of money, by acquisition as the ultimate purpose of his life. Economic acquisition is no longer subordinated to man as the means for the satisfaction of his material needs. This reversal of what we should call the natural relationship, so irrational from a naive point of view is evidently as definitely a leading principle of capitalism as it is foreign to all peoples not under capitalist influence.   (Weber 1904/5/1930: 53)

This is the same phenomenon that Marx understood in terms of the subordination of use value to exchange value and the accumulation of capital. But, whereas for Marx it was the result of a change in the relations of production, for Weber it is the result of a change in ethical orientation towards the world. For both, however, once capitalism is established, it has an almost unstoppable expansionary dynamic.

Returning to Franklin and the spirit of capitalism, Weber argues that the making of money as an end in itself is not quite that but a sign of something else—of 'virtue and proficiency in a calling'. When Weber was writing, the notion of a 'calling' was more familiar that I suspect it is today. It involves the idea that we might be 'called upon' to do something in our lives, called upon by God and perhaps society as well, to pursue a particular employment, a particular line of business, and this must be done to the best of one's ability.

Weber himself makes the sensible reservation that an established capitalism does not depend on such a notion of a calling—it has become an 'immense cosmos' which presents itself to the individual as an unalterable situation to which he or she must adjust; in a statement which would not shame a Marxist, Weber writes:

It forces the individual, in so far as he is involved in the system of market relationships, to conform to capitalistic rules of action. The manufacturer who in the long run acts counter to these norms, will just as inevitably be eliminated from the economic scene as the worker who cannot or will not adapt himself to them will be thrown into the streets without a job. Thus the capitalism of today, which has come to dominate economic life, educates and selects the economic subjects which it needs through a process of economic survival of the fittest.   (ibid. 54–5)

But the system had to originate somewhere in the activities of a group of people who acted in the same way. At many other periods of history the sentiments expressed by Franklin would not have met universal acclaim; and the areas where unscrupulous money-making was acceptable were not the areas in which capitalism developed. Capitalism is characterized by a moralized money-making and its main enemy is characterized by Weber as 'traditionalism'.

Where the worker is concerned, the traditionalist attitude is one that I find I have myself possessed for a large part of my working life: what is important is the preservation of a way of life, and I have been content with earning enough to enable me to live in the way that I desire. If I were imbued with the capitalist spirit, I would be seeking to maximize my earnings even if it meant living in a different way that I did not find attractive. The example that Weber uses is of agricultural workers paid piece-rates (i.e. according to the amount of work they do) at harvest time. He claims that, in situations where the piece-rate has been raised, the workers have produced less—they do not aim to maximize their income, simply to maintain it, and if they can do so by doing less work, all well and good. The obvious solution (to the employer) of increasing work by paying less has its limits—low wages do not keep workers in good health, or attract workers with the necessary skills.

Capitalism cannot, or at least at its beginning could not, rely on workers to adopt the attitude that labour was an end in itself, not simply a means to enjoyment, a comfortable life, and so on. Workers who did adopt such an attitude—such as Methodist workers in Britain—often incurred the hostility of their workmates, who would go as far as destroying their tools. If one or two workers in the group work harder than their colleagues, then everybody will be expected to work harder.

Just as workers can maintain traditionalist attitudes to work, so can employers. Many large enterprises can be content to make 'enough' profit without setting about it in a systematically rational way. Weber's example is of the 'putter-out' in the textile industry in the nineteenth century. Peasants would bring their product to the putter-out, who would buy it and then sell to customers who came to him. He rarely sought customers personally, relying on letters and samples; working hours were moderate, enough to maintain a respectable life. He would have a good relationship with competitors and devote part of the day to socializing. The ease of such a life was changed when some ambitious youngster would start organizing himself more efficiently, personally soliciting customers, supervising his workers more closely, thereby changing them from peasants to labourers, and reinvesting profits in the business. Weber argues that it was not the sudden investment of new money which brought about this transformation but a change in attitude, the appearance of a new spirit.

It is worth going off on a detour here, because this argument seems on the face of it to be very close to contemporary right-wing rhetoric about the way in which the poor should be treated. It is argued that, if social security payments are too high, then the recipients develop a dependent culture, and lose the desire to work—in Weber's terms, they develop a traditionalist attitude, which, so the argument goes, must be changed. However, Weber's point is that such an attitude cannot be changed by varying financial rewards, or the absence of financial rewards, or financial punishments. It is a value choice motivated by something unconnected with finance of any sort, and part of a changing collective consciousness—or even *conscience collective*—which is not brought about by an act of will.

One might think that the moral qualities of sober hard work involve a rational, enlightened attitude that modern sensibilities might regard as the opposite of religious belief. If entrepreneurs were asked why their lives were dedicated to work rather than the other way round, why they were so constantly restless, seeking new achievements, they would produce all sorts of subjective reasons, such as providing for their children, which would have operated equally strongly in traditional societies. Power might be a motive, but the true capitalist seems little interested in its trappings:

> The ideal type of the capitalist entrepreneur . . . avoids ostentation and unnecessary expenditure, as well as conscious enjoyment of his power, and is embarrassed by the outward signs of the social recognition which he receives. His manner of life is distinguished by a certain ascetic tendency . . . a sort of modesty which is essentially more modest than the reserve which Franklin so shrewdly recommends. He gets nothing out of his wealth for himself, except the irrational sense of having done his job well.   (ibid. 71)

This attitude would be incomprehensible to the traditionalist, as would the obligation felt by many entrepreneurs to provide for their fellow human beings. Weber here cites Benjamin Franklin's attempts to bring about civic improvements in Philadelphia.

The Protestant ethic

The emergence of capitalism cannot be seen as part of a slow and universal process of rationalization which was uneven, and Enlightenment rationality did not find its adherents primarily in the countries where capitalism was most advanced. Legal rationalization did not proceed hand in hand with the development of capitalism either—in Britain, for example, the legal system went into reverse, and law was always at its most rational in Roman Catholic countries. So where did the peculiar rationality of European capitalism come from? It originates in Protestantism, more specifically in the writings of Martin Luther after he became a reformer. Most importantly, we find there the notion of a 'calling': 'the valuation of the fulfilment of duty in worldly affairs as the highest form which the moral activity of the individual could assume' (Weber 1904–5/1930: 80). All callings had the same value in the eyes of God. At the beginning, the search for material rewards beyond one's personal needs was seen as a sign of a lack of grace, especially since it could be achieved only at the expense of others. Moreover, as Luther developed and emphasized the notion, he came to place a faith in Providence. It is, for example, God's will that I should clean streets; it is 'meant' and my duty is to do it as well as I can. In this sense, Luther's conception of a calling is traditionalist—I have to adapt to God's will. There is no direct relationship with the idea of the calling as we find it in the spirit of capitalism. To get a clearer idea of the connection, Weber turns to the doctrines of the Scottish Protestant John Calvin, which, he suggests, have always been seen as the real enemy by the Roman Catholic Church and even drew the disapproval of the Lutherans. In moving over to the study of Calvinism, Weber presents a statement of his method and of what he is trying to do which clearly represents the complexity of his analysis and its movement to and from causal explanations:

we are merely attempting to clarify the part which religious forces have played in forming the developing web of our specifically worldly modern culture, in the complex action of innumerable different historical factors. We are thus enquiring only to what extent certain characteristic features of this culture can be imputed to the influence of the Reformation. At the same time we must free ourselves from the idea that it is possible to deduce the Reformation, as a historically necessary result, from certain economic changes. Countless historical circumstances, which cannot be reduced to any economic law . . . especially purely political processes, had to concur in order that the newly created Churches should survive at all.

On the other hand, however, we have no intention of maintaining such a foolish and doctrinaire thesis as that the spirit of capitalism . . . could only have arisen as a result of certain effects of the Reformation, or even that capitalism as an economic system is a creation of the Reformation . . . we only wish to ascertain whether and to what extent religious forces have taken part in the quantitative formation and quantitative expansion of that spirit over the world.   (ibid. 91)

Weber suggests that there are four main forms of ascetic (i.e. self-denying) Protestantism: Calvinism, Pietism, Methodism, and the Baptist sects. These groups engaged in all sorts of struggles with each other and with established churches over doctrine, but Weber is less interested in the details of dogma than in what he calls the 'psychological sanctions' which direct peoples' actions. The essential element of Calvinist belief was predestination: the idea that we are already chosen for eternal life or eternal damnation, and we cannot do anything about it. Salvation is a gift of God, not my own achievement. We can find the same idea in Luther, but it is not central. For Calvin, we could not know God's choice. We might get glimpses of it, but basically it was just like that—not a matter of justice or personal worth: 'for the damned to complain of their lot would be much the same as for animals to bemoan the fact that they were not born as men' (ibid. 103). The psychological effect of this must have been to produce an 'unprecedented inner loneliness'—I am damned or I am saved, I cannot know which and I cannot change matters through my own actions, nor can I find anybody—a priest, for example—who might offer forgiveness and consolation. This is the state of existential loneliness *par excellence*. At the same time, worldly goods and pleasures are denied me—they are signs of corruption and would confirm that I am one of the damned. All this comes across in John Bunyan's *Pilgrim's Progress* (1928), the classical Puritan story. Even religious ceremony is rejected.

For the Puritan, there was no problem about the meaning of life; God had ordered the cosmos to serve the utility of the human race and humans were meant to work out God's purpose on earth; the Puritans were lonely but in a situation where they did not have to search for meaning. Yet there was a search for some confirmation that the individual was one of the saved. Calvin personally had no problem with this: the lucky man was sure that he was one of the elect. However, this would not work for the mass of his followers. The advice given to the faithful was to reach a psychological certainty of their own election, of their own salvation, through the daily struggle of work. Instead of a collection of humble and repenting sinners, Puritans offered an army of self-confident saints. Perhaps the public figure who comes nearest to this model in contemporary British public life is the Reverend Ian Paisley, the Northern Irish Protestant leader. Such people are, of course, completely unbearable if one is not a believer.

Anyway, the Calvinists recommended hard work as a way of achieving the certainty of one's own salvation and dispelling doubts. This is a long way from the mystical communication with God which the Lutherans aimed to achieve. The Calvinist becomes convinced of his salvation (there seems to be little reference to women in all this) through systematic self-control and good works; it is this systematicity, a sense of a planned life, that was missing for the Roman Catholic lay person. Weber points to the relevance of the name 'Methodist' given to those who participated in the eighteenth-century Protestant revival. The aim was to control and suppress spontaneity and impulse enjoyment and bring order into every aspect of life.

Calvinism for Weber was the pure type of Protestant asceticism and the other Puritan sects moved away from it in one way or another. Pietism placed too much emphasis on emotional experiences which undermined the rational orientation of everyday life. Even so there were two important elements of Pietism which he thinks outweighed its emotionalist tendency—the beliefs.

(1) that the methodical development of one's own state of grace to a higher and higher degree of certainty and perfection in terms of the law was a sign of grace; and (2) that 'God's Providence works through those in such a state of perfection', i.e., in that He gives them His signs if they wait patiently and deliberate methodically.   (ibid. 133)

Despite this the Pietists encouraged humility rather than self-confidence and there was a distinct Lutheran tendency.

Methodism was also an ascetic form of Protestantism, but had a strong emotional base and rejected many of the beliefs of Calvinism. It held that the emotional certainty of forgiveness was the only sure sign of salvation, but added nothing new to the notion of a calling. The Baptists also placed an emphasis on emotionality, but here Weber suggested another way in which Protestantism influenced everyday life: 'But in so far as Baptism affected the normal workaday world, the idea that God only speaks when the flesh is silent evidently means an incentive to the deliberate weighing of courses of action and their careful justification in terms of the individual conscience' (ibid. 149). The decisive point for all these forms of Protestantism, however, is the belief in a state of grace which marks its possessor off from worldly degradation, and it is this which leads us to the link between protestantism and capitalism. It should be evident to you, if you think back to Benjamin Franklin's maxims, that the systematic and rational pursuit of profit is clearly similar to the systematic and rational pursuit of one's everyday duties. In the modern development of the Protestant ethic, wealth is disapproved of in so far as it is an incentive to idleness and enjoyment—'But as a performance of duty in a calling it is not only morally permissible, but actually enjoined' (ibid. 163). One's calling is a moral duty for the benefit of the community, but it is more than that. If God shows the chance of a profit, He has His reasons and the chance must be taken to enable His purpose on earth to proceed. And so business success became a sign to reassure the uncertain and lonely believer that he was in fact one of the chosen; it offered psychological comfort; in economic terms, the impetus to make money without spending it on personal consumption and enjoyment led to the accumulation of capital.

It is not a matter of Protestants deciding that they wanted to be capitalists, but of their following the teaching of their prophets, which led them into systematic rationally organized day-to-day life, carrying out God's purpose on earth. Their belief in predestination meant that they experienced an inner loneliness, for nothing they or anyone else could do could effect their salvation. Success in day-to-day business activities came to be taken as a sign of salvation. Since the beliefs forbade their personal pleasure and aggrandisement, profits were reinvested into the business, and business success bred business success.

Conclusion

I have set out Weber's arguments at some length, first because it is an example of historical and comparative sociology which people are still producing today. In fact there has been a rebirth of this type of work (see Giddens 1981, 1985; Runciman 1983, 1989; M. Mann 1986; Anderson 1990), and I think Weber offers a particularly clear example of the genre. More importantly, however, Weber offers a fundamentally important analysis of the growth of capitalism and of modernity that provides dimensions not touched upon by any of the other thinkers discussed in this book. Weber is the theorist of instrumental rationality. The moral philosopher Charles Taylor calls the problem presented by instrumental rationality a 'massively important phenomenon of the modern age':

No doubt sweeping away the old orders has immensely widened the scope of instrumental reason. Once society no longer has a sacred structure, once social arrangements and modes of action are no longer grounded in the order of things or the will of God, they are in a sense up for grabs. They can be redesigned with their consequences for the happiness and well-being of individuals as our goal. The yardstick that henceforth applies is that of instrumental reasons. Similarly, once the creatures that surround us lose the significance that accrued to their place in the chain of being, they are open to being treated as raw materials or instruments for our projects.

   In one way this change has been liberating. But there is also a widespread unease that instrumental reason has not only enlarged its scope but also threatens to take over our lives. The fear is that things that ought to be determined by other criteria will be decided in terms of efficiency or 'cost benefit' analysis, that the independent ends that ought to be guiding out lives will be eclipsed be demands to maximise output.   (Taylor 1991: 5)

The other thinkers added to our comprehension of it, Marx through examining its economic roots and its philosophical and psychological results in the theory of alienation, Durkheim by offering us an analysis of the same situation through the way in which the division of labour replaces and revises the *conscience collective*, and Simmel by examining the more intricate psychological effects of the money economy. Despite his explicit statements, we can find in Weber the conception of *society* as something existing over and above the individuals who make it up. He is not happy about the disenchantment that comes with modern rationality, nor is he happy with the iron cage it produces. This is his tragedy.

   In terms of the secondary dualism which is central to this part of the book, Weber is the theorist of modernity as opposed to Marx as the theorist of capitalism. Weber had a lot to say about capitalism, but he did not see any desirable alternative. Socialism would simply be more bureaucratic than capitalism, and perhaps continue the process of disenchantment further than it would go even under capitalism. By emphasizing his view of the free market, John Horton and Bryan Turner try to reject the notion of Weber as a tragic liberal, but it is difficult to see how this position can be maintained in the face of the arguments in *The Protestant Ethic and the Spirit of Capitalism*. The iron cage is a liberal nightmare, not a liberal vision.

   Weber's historical work shows how he moved towards a clearer conception of social cohesion: the power conflicts which both push a society forward and threaten its stability take place within and between wider frameworks of belief, and those beliefs which push towards practical action to reorganize the world (and therefore eventually to practices governed by rational calculability) have the advantage. And, once established, such practices seem unchangeable. It is as if we have developed an instrumentally rational *conscience collective* which holds us together with our compliance or perhaps against our will. We have been separated from our traditional communities and can find alliances only through common instrumental interest. Although the capitalist spirit provided a motivation and a way of looking at the world which might become generally shared, it also encourages both an individuation—a separation from traditional bonds—and an individualism—a concern with personal ends and ambitions which loses overarching commitments to God or community. When this state of affairs is reached, there is only a social system and a fragmentation of social life. With this last point, I don't think we can do better than quote Derek Sayer's comparison of Marx and Weber on modernity. Sayer takes up the way in which instrumental reason manifests itself through science, rather than through the capitalist spirit:

An elective affinity, then, for the modern age: between those qualities we most prize in scientific discourse—objectivity, universality, logic, consistency, simplicity, systematicity, quantifiability, precision unambiguity and a certain aesthetic elegance—and the principles upon which Weber's machines of modernity operate. In neither is there room for the concrete, the particular and the personal. They are banished to the 'irrational' realm of private life. The modern era, as Marx said, is ruled by abstractions. It may be that capitalism is the foundation upon which this rule is first erected; Marx and Weber provide compelling reason for thinking it is. But it may also be that today, this abstraction has gone very far beyond capitalism itself and we will not be rid of it just by changing the title deeds on property (or still less by 'capturing' 'state power'). This is the enduring importance of Weber's analysis of rationalization and bureaucratization, which is its ubiquitous concomitant. Disembodied, the very form of our sociality turns against us, and within them there is no place for humane values. The soulful corporation or the compassionate state are, by virtue of the very constitution of these soulful forms, contradictions in terms. . . . Insubstantial as modern bourgeois liberties may be—and Weber had few illusions on the matter—they are preferable to none at all.   (Sayer 1991: 153–4)

Weber emerges from all this as the ambivalent theorist—ambivalent in his attitude to modernity and the process of disenchantment that it involved, ambivalent in his attitude towards Marx, ambivalent in his personal life as well. We can find the same ambivalence in his political alignments. Apparently he thought often of joining the German socialist party, but we also find some particularly right-wing positions. To begin with he adopted what one might call a 'hard-realist' position, arguing that there can be no 'ethical' politics and the economic struggle for existence never abates—we do not do future generations any good by suggesting that this should be changed. A strong Germany should be ready to exercise its power in international affairs, but Weber did not think that the ruling class that had united Germany—the old aristocracy—were strong enough to do this, but neither were the new bourgeoisie or the proletariat. Giddens suggests that from this point Weber's main concern was to encourage the development of a liberal political culture in Germany. However, social inequalities and domination will not be removed by democracy and there was a continual conflict between democracy and bureaucracy. Whilst the growth of democracy actually entails an expansion of bureaucracy, the expansion of bureaucracy does not entail the extension of democracy. This is why an elected leadership is important—the worst possible outcome would be unlimited domination by bureaucracy. In his own alignments Weber had to juggle his support for German nationalism with his aim of representative democracy to balance the growth of bureaucracy, but, as Sayer suggests, he was well aware of its limitations.

Perhaps the firmest thing that could be said about Weber is that he was true to his depressive tendency: a carefully protected liberal democracy based on the market is the best we could hope for; socialism would take us in the direction which threatened us most—the triumph of bureaucracy. The trouble is that capitalism

---

Box 13.1. An elaboration of Weber on social integration and system integration

SOCIAL INTEGRATION

Durkheim: in all societies social integration is achieved through the *conscience collective*—shared ways of thinking (logic, conceptions of space and time, shared beliefs, norms, and values. In societies governed by mechanical solidarity, religion is central. In more complex modern societies, the *conscience collective* covers less of our lives but focuses on the ethics of individual freedom—it becomes a religion of humanity.

Marx: a 'false' and rather tenuous integration is achieved through ideologies, and the development of the market constantly threatens whatever integration is achieved. The major contending classes strive towards achieving their own integration in opposition to the others—the proletariat being the class most likely to achieve this.

Weber: at this point there is no real conception of social integration in Weber's work. In his work on religion however, it is arguable that he sees social cohesion as developing through the dominance of rational calculation.

Simmel: social integration is achieved through objective culture—the development of universal symbols and meanings that begins with economic exchange. The growth of such a culture extends human freedom but constricts the integrity and depth of the individual life.

SYSTEM INTEGRATION

Durkheim: where mechanical solidarity predominates, system integration *is* social integration guaranteed by the *conscience collective*. Where organic solidarity predominates, system integration is achieved through the division of labour.

Marx: system integration in capitalism is constantly threatened by class conflict and is supported by the state and by ruling ideologies.

Weber: it is a gross exaggeration to use the word 'system' in connection with the writings we have looked at in Chapter 9. Social structures are held together by different forms of domination and by stability provided by the market. In his work on the world religions, however, there are indications that the growing dominance of instrumental rationality creates a system which can work by itself.

Simmel: no real concept of system integration, except perhaps through economic exchange.

would take us there as well. This second Weber allows us to elaborate on his conception of social integration as well as his views on the secondary dualism.

Box 13.2. Weber on modernity and capitalism/socialism

MODERNITY

Durkheim: a movement towards a balanced society of occupational groups held together by the state and a new humanist 'religion' which emphasized the value of the individual.

Marx: the modern world was moving towards the realization of the values of the French Revolution—liberty, equality, and fraternity. This was not an inevitable or smooth process and entails conflict and revolution.

Weber: modernity is the process of the increasing dominance of rational calculability and the greatest threat is domination by large bureaucratic organizations. A free market economy in the liberal democratic state is the best protection against this.

CAPITALISM/SOCIALISM

Durkheim: Durkheim's concept of socialism was based on his conception of the development of modernity; although problems arise in the abnormal forms of the division of labour, these would be ironed out in continued historical development. He does not seem to see capitalism as a specific form of modern society responsible for either its problems or its benefits.

Marx: capitalism represented immense progress over previous types of society in terms of the ability to produce wealth, although it is driven by contradictions which do not allow it to realize this ability. The competitive market system produces rapid change and fragmentation—seen by many as defining features of modernity; a socialist revolution would create a collectively organized democratic and more stable society which would realize the ideals of the French Revolution.

Weber: socialism and communism would lead to the more rapid development of bureaucratic domination.

Further reading

Everybody should read Weber's *Protestant Ethic and the Spirit of Capitalism* (1904–5/1930). Bendix, *Max Weber: An Intellectual Portrait* (1966) offers good, clear accounts of his religious studies. Weber's *Sociology of Religion* (1922/1965) is also worth reading. For an example of modern sociological history, see W. G. Runciman's two-volume *A Treatise on Sociological Theory* (1983, 1989). On Weber's politics, see Giddens, *Politics and Sociology in the Work of Max Weber* (1972).

For contemporary work on Protestantism and Capitalism, see Gordon Marshall, *Presbyteries and Profits: Calvinism and the Development of Capitalism in Scotland, 1560–1707* (1980) and *In Search of the Spirit of Capitalism* (1982). For an excellent and sympathetic collection on Weber and modernity, see Bryan Turner, *For Weber* (1996).

14 | Simmel: countering an overdose of history?

The decreasing importance of history in Simmel's work; his inversion of Marx; Simmel and Nietzsche; his critique of historicism; history as a genre; Simmel's place in differing existential traditions: his aesthetic perspective.

We do not find in Simmel anything like the careful sociological analysis of other societies that we can find in Durkheim's work on religion, Weber's analysis of the world religions, or even Marx's comparatively sketchy works on pre-capitalist societies. He does not write the history of societies, and in some fundamental sense I would suggest that he actually stands *against* history in so far as it is a manifestation of objective culture which threatens to engulf subjective culture.

Simmel's *Philosophy of Money* contains as much as he offers of a theory of history and here he charts the rise and effects of what he calls objective culture. The individual emerges from the primitive group and develops an individuality through exchange relationships. These relationships create an objective culture against which the individual has to struggle to maintain his or her integrity. We are caught in a trap of our own making. When I discussed this in Part 2, I suggested that this part of his work was closest to that of Georg Lukacs and the early Marx—that he can be seen as giving a more elaborated and intricate exploration of some of the subjective consequences of alienation. However, as time went on this historical dimension was left behind, and he seemed to think of the opposition of these two culture types as a sort of metaphysical state to which all societies, all cultures, are subject. It is part of the existential condition of humankind. In 'The Concept and Tragedy of Culture' he wrote:

The 'fetishism' which Marx assigned to economic commodities represents only a special case of this general fate of contents of culture. With the increase in culture these centres more and more stand under a paradox. They were originally created by subjects for subjects, but in their immediate forms of objectivity . . . they follow an immanent logic of development. . . . They are impelled not by physical necessities but by truly cultural ones.   (quoted in Frisby 1981)

If this is the case, it is just part of the nature of the social world and nothing to do with capitalism. At this point it is worth looking at the relationship between

Simmel and Nietzsche, who is generally regarded as being at the root of post-modern theory. The argument is put well, if not always clearly, by Weinstein and Weinstein (1993). In *The Use and Abuse of History* (1957) Nietzsche argued for what amounts to a rejection of history, of the idea that we are somehow or other determined by our past. We suffer from an 'excess of history', which weakens the inner life. The grand historical theories of the nineteenth century—those of Marx and Hegel most obviously but one might add Comte and many others—invade our inner selves and make it difficult for us to find an authentic voice. We are not puppets of history but come to believe that we are; we can see no point in seeking an authentic voice, since we will be swallowed up by history. In Simmel's terms, objective culture eliminates subjective culture; the personality becomes completely socialized and we descend into cynicism; nothing we can do has any real importance for us.

Weinstein and Weinstein argue that by the first years of the century Simmel, 'whether or not he was aware of doing so', had adopted Nietzsche's way of look-ing at history, talking about it as an 'idol'. It becomes a 'central idea' in terms of which we make moral and cognitive judgements, just as the Marxist militant might have put him- or herself at the service of the movement of history as rep-resented by the communist party, surrendering any independent moral or polit-ical judgement. The party central committee makes 'scientific' judgements about the course of history and the 'correct' policy to be followed.

Weinstein and Weinstein argue, rightly I think, that Simmel's target is rather different from that of Nietzsche—not so much history as *historicism*—the explanation of everything in terms of history. They go on to argue—and I am not so sure about this—that Simmel's solution is one of play: the historian's job is to tell stories on the basis of historical facts, which we cannot do anything to change. This view, as stated by the Weinsteins, is certainly a form of contempo-rary postmodern 'theory':

The freedom of the historian is to construct narratives, that is, to link events or forms of culture into dated temporal sequences according to standards of significance under the control of fact. In this view of history, which is at the antipodes of a 'scientific' history in quest of causes, there are as many histories as there are interests of historians and relev-ant facts for them to weave into narratives . . . there is no 'history' to engulf us and pro-duce us here—history is a *genre*.   (Weinstein and Weinstein 1993: 181–2)

We have detective stories, westerns, romantic novels, and histories. It seems to me that this rather misses the point as far as Simmel is concerned. He was not concerned with arguing for a banal relativism, which it seems to me to be what Weinstein and Weinstein turn it into, but with asserting one value over another—the value of subjective authenticity over objective culture as mani-fested in grand theories of history; this is not a matter of equal values but of one being preferable to, better than, another. It is this stance which puts Simmel in the existentialist tradition from Kierkegaard through Nietzsche to Heidegger and Sartre and Maurice Merleau-Ponty. There is a religious/psychological wing to this movement which begins with Kierkegaard and is alive today in the form of existentialist psychotherapy. There is also a philosophical wing which splits into a leftist and a rightist version. The latter includes Nietzsche, who is often linked indirectly with Nazi philosophy, and Heidegger, who continued to teach throughout the period of Nazi rule. For both, history and society were consigned to the realm of the inauthentic. In this respect the later Simmel belongs to this tradition.

The left-wing tradition through to Sartre and Merleau-Ponty was more concerned, after the end of the Second World War, with the opposition of the individual and society and the relationship between existentialist and Marxist philosophy. The Simmel of *The Philosophy of Money* is closer to this tradition. In his personal politics he remained a liberal reformer throughout his life, taking as his focus not the struggle for power (as did Nietzsche and Weber), but the aesthetics of social life, a much more gentle concern. At times he writes as if any freezing of the life process into concepts is impermissable. It should not or cannot be analysed; we can, however, transform our understanding into an aesthetic appreciation: 'Simmel clearly conceives of the relationship of the sociologist and society as if it were that of the art critic observing a work of art' (Frisby 1981: 153). It is the money economy which first produces this distance between observer and observed, but the aesthetic perspective is privileged because it rescues us from some of the worst excesses of the money economy and modernity. Even here, as Frisby points out, he tends towards a relativism, I suspect because even an aesthetic perspective freezes the life process (just as impressionism became a new form rather than the end of forms) and in the end 'the inward retreat becomes his final political perspective' (ibid. 156).

This is perhaps the final word on Simmel. Returning to the dualisms, Simmel sees society, system cohesion, and social cohesion as objective culture, a process which increases the choices open to the individual whilst at the same time freezing and colonizing the internal life process. We cannot analyse the life process without turning it into its opposite, and in the end there is only the integrity of the individual perspective. This represents a retreat from politics which we can find in much postmodernist thought. The crucial link between Simmel and postmodernism is, I think, via Foucault, who is above all the philosopher who shows how the individual is colonized—but without the sense of the vitality of the life process that Simmel offers us.

Simmel presents an essentially pessimistic view of the secondary dualism (see Box 14.1), and it is appropriate perhaps that this chapter should end suddenly.

Box 14.1. **Simmel on modernity and capitalism/socialism**

MODERNITY	CAPITALISM/SOCIALISM
Durkheim: a movement towards a balanced society of occupational groups held together by the state and a new humanist 'religion' which emphasized the value of the individual.	**Durkheim:** Durkheim's concept of socialism was based on his conception of the development of modernity; although problems arise in the abnormal forms of the division of labour, these would be ironed out in continued historical development. He does not seem to see capitalism as a specific form of modern society responsible for either its problems or its benefits.
Marx: the modern world was moving towards the realization of the values of the French Revolution—liberty, equality, and fraternity. This was not an inevitable or smooth process and entails conflict and revolution.	**Marx:** capitalism represented immense progress over previous types of society in terms of the ability to produce wealth, although it is driven by contradictions which do not allow it to realize this ability. The competitive market system produces rapid change and fragmentation—seen by many as defining features of modernity; a socialist revolution would create a collectively organized democratic and more stable society which would realize the ideals of the French Revolution.
Weber: modernity is the process of the increasing dominance of rational calculability and the greatest threat is domination by large bureaucratic organizations. A free market economy in the liberal democratic state is the best protection against this.	**Weber:** socialism and communism would lead to the more rapid development of bureaucratic domination.
Simmel: modernity is the steady growth of objective culture, dominating the individual life process.	**Simmel:** there is no historical or sociological alternative to modernity; there is an individual alternative in that it is possible to transform both disciplines into art forms.

Further reading

Weinstein and Weinstein's *Postmodern(ized) Simmel* (1993) provides the best account of these issues, but see also Frisby's *Sociological Impressionism* (1981).

15 | Conclusion: the framework of social theory

A discussion of the dualisms of social theory and what happens when they are ignored or when theorists attempt to transcend them; the necessary problems of social theory.

The dualisms that I have referred to in the course of this book set problems for theory but they are not *theoretical* problems, they cannot be worked through and solved by theory or theorists. The same dualisms exist in the real world and they set problems not just for sociologists but for everybody, and not only problems in understanding what is going on in the world, but practical problems in our everyday lives. There are real individuals, real societies, real social structures, real actions, real relationships between real social institutions, and real relationships between real individuals. If am made redundant, then I am one of a number of individuals who lose their jobs through the workings of the society, or a failure in system integration, or contradiction in the social structure. If I join a trade union or a political party or a new political movement, then I am engaging in social action aimed at changing social structure. If my neighbours are constantly hostile, if I feel unsafe walking the streets at night, if people seem to subscribe to alien moral codes or to act without moral judgement, I am dealing with a problem of social integration.

The classical theorists did not formulate these dualisms, but that is basically what they were working with. I have tried to show how they have framed the way in which we think about contemporary society, not only in social theory, but also in terms of contemporary political debates. We *have* to see the world in these terms. If we do not, then we create blind spots of various kinds.

If we take the individual/society dualism as a first example in relation to crime, we open up a prominent contemporary debate in the Western world. If we start from the side of society, we have to say that there is something about a society that produces crime—high levels of unemployment, for example, or lack of moral regulation—and the solution would lie in bringing about some sort of social change. If, on the other hand, we start from the side of the individual, the issue is seen from the point of view of individual morality and the focus moves from social change to issues of punishment or the possibility of reforming criminals.

We might expect a sociologist to start from the side of society and it is from this side that he or she might have most to offer the public debate, since the common-sense perception of crime tends to blame the individual criminal rather than look for underlying causes. However, this sort of sociological understanding does not produce a full understanding of crime or the criminal. Not every unemployed person turns to crime, and not everybody living in a society where morality is subject to argument commits a crime. Sociology can tell us what social conditions make crime more or less likely but not who will commit a crime or what to do about criminals as individuals.

An alternative sociological approach might look at the interaction between individuals and the conditions and mechanisms of the growth of criminal subcultures. This would help us understand a further element in the production of crime, but, in the first place, like the approach from the point of view of society as a whole, it would not tell us why particular individuals are recruited to criminal subcultures. Not everyone who comes into contact with such a subculture becomes a member. It might be that to understand such issues we have to step outside sociology altogether. But we cannot ignore the individual, especially if we adopt an interactionist approach. In the second place such an approach will not lead us on automatically to looking at the wider social dynamics we find if we start at the society end of the dualism.

In fact, neither side leads automatically to the other; one side is blind to the mechanisms of interaction and the other to structural mechanisms—at some point we have to jump. I think that most sociologists would recognize that we have to look at both sides but would tend to gloss the jump—the move to a different *type* of object—when they cross from one to the other.

The same sort of argument can be made in relation to the social action/social structure dualism. Individuals and societies are different forms of being and one does not produce the other, although each depends upon the existence of the other. Similarly, social structures and social action are different forms of being; one does not determine or explain the other, although each depends upon the other. There has to be a jump between two different levels of analysis, and if we start one and do not move beyond it we end up either by ignoring important parts of social reality or by offering an inadequate understanding of them. Elsewhere (Craib 1992b) I have argued that the different twentieth-century schools of social theory all have trouble with this divide. If they start with an understanding of social structure (structuralism, structural Marxism), then, when they move on to understanding social action, the theory begins to have conceptual problems and fragments as people try to produce different solutions. On the other hand, those theories which start with social action either turn into theories of social structure (Parsons's structural functionalism) or have great difficulty (or even find it impossible) in understanding the structural features of social life (symbolic interactionism, ethnomethodology, phenomenological sociology).

We have seen the difficulty of moving from structure to action with Marxism; the move from the analysis of the relations of production to class structure to class actions doesn't work—the wrong people turn up in the wrong places doing the wrong things. We need to look at least at processes of class formation around political and ideological issues at levels closer to the surface, and this involves in turn looking at social action—a switch in object—an understanding of individual and collective interpretations of the world. Structural factors do not account for this interpretive process.

On the other hand, if we try to move from action to structure—the Weberian rather than the Marxist direction—we lose sight of underlying causes and mechanisms and have to resort to 'unintended consequences' to explain the occurrences that are not directly intended by somebody's actions. The surface effects of social structure tend to be systematic and patterned—for Durkheim, this was a central way in which we could identify the effects of 'society'. During an economic depression industries do not decline at random: certain types of industry decline, certain others remain steady, and some even grow, and I do not think it is adequate to see these effects as somehow accidental—which is what explanation by unintended consequences amounts to. People's individual and collective actions are transformed by the underlying structures of relationships in systematic ways—paradoxically it was such a process that produced Weber's iron cage.

If we turn to the distinction between social integration and system integration we find a similar situation: the two do not determine each other. I have suggested that our contemporary situation is one in which there is a high level of system integration, which could be understood in part as produced by the process of globalization, but this has been accompanied by a fragmenting of social integration: it is as if the universalization of norms and values does not pull everybody along behind it and people seek an identity through returning to more local and traditional values or by surrendering attempts to construct values altogether or inventing their own value collages. Similarly, it is possible to envisage a high degree of social integration with a low level of system integration. There are two levels at work, two distinct objects, which require two different forms of understanding.

Perhaps the best illustration of the dangers of running the two together can be found in Parsons's structural functionalism, developed through the middle of this century (Parsons 1951). What I am going to say now is an oversimplification, but I think the point should be clear. As his theory developed, he became more and more interested in systems theory—an approach which its more enthusiastic proponents thought could be applied at almost any level of analysis to almost any object. Parsons developed elaborate models of the social system, the personality system, the economic system, and the cultural system. For systems theorists, the elements which controlled a complex system were high on information and low on energy—just as a washing machine is controlled by the programme rather than the electric motor which drives the drum. In Parsons's theory, this was the cultural system, the universal values of modern society; this was the programmer and the systems and subsystems all fitted together comparatively neatly. It was, in fact, this theoretical system which led to the development of Lockwood's distinction between social and system integration (Lockwood 1964)—societies do not develop in quite as coherent a way as Parsons suggests. Since the Second World War there have been a number of economic crises in the western world, all of which could be seen as crises in system integration but none of which seems to have produced major crises in social integration in the sense of a breakdown of social order and demands for a transformation of the system. Further, I have argued in the course of this book, particularly when discussing Durkheim, that, if there is a contemporary crisis in social cohesion, in the sense of a fragmentation of morality and beliefs, it is due to an increasing level of system cohesion.

Parsons's framework is also a good illustration of the problems that occur when there are attempts to synthesize the dualisms—to find theoretical solutions to real problems: in simple terms, his system began to fall apart. Lockwood's arguments represent one aspect of this; another aspect is represented by Dennis Wrong's paper 'The Oversocialised Conception of Man in Modern Sociology' (1967), which I mentioned earlier. It was Parsons's emphasis on society as opposed to the individual which encouraged, in the 1960s, the popularity of symbolic interactionism and other forms of sociology that seemed to give space not just to individuals but also to the experience of everyday life.

Perhaps the most interesting point about Parsons's synthesis, however, is that in the course of its development he crosses from one side of the action/structure dualism to the other. He begins with an elaborate theory of social action, beginning, as did Simmel, with the dyad, but ends with a highly developed analysis of the structure or system which seemed to obliterate or determine action. In fact, any attempt to bring about a synthesis of different approaches or transcend the dualisms tends to end by giving dominance to one side or another and often implicitly if not explicitly reintroduce the dualisms.

Continuing my policy of oversimplifying, the most recent attempt at synthesis/transcendence is Anthony Giddens's structuration theory (see especially Giddens 1984). Giddens ends up giving action the dominant place. He achieves this by first of all subjecting various structural theories to a criticism which strips them of any determining features and redefines structure in terms of the rules that govern action. Structure, therefore, becomes a property of action. Giddens takes up what he calls the 'linguistic turn' in twentieth-century philosophy and theory, which in sociology has manifested itself in the tendency towards seeing language as actually constituting social reality, and effectively Giddens is saying that action is structured in the same way that language is structured. But structure is dissolved into action; there is no possibility of talking about underlying structures or even surface structures which are not produced by or part of action. He sets up a picture of the social as consisting in and produced and reproduced by rule-governed action, and this 'proper object' of sociology he calls 'social practices'. He then says that these practices can be analysed from two points of view: from the point of view of strategic action and from the point of view of institutional analysis. This seems to me close to reintroducing the action/structure dualism under another name.

So this takes me back to where I began this chapter, and perhaps I can make the same point in yet another way. There is no *one* object of sociology. The three basic dualisms around which I have tried to organize the ideas in this book identify six different objects of sociology and to concentrate on any one takes us away from all the others, yet for any social phenomenon to be understood properly we have to take account at least of the opposing object in a particular dualism, if not all the others. Social theory, then, is engaged in a number of different investigations into different realms of social reality, and, although there must be dialogues between the different approaches, there can be no unified social theory, because the social world itself is not unified.

I have not yet said anything by way of conclusion about the secondary dualism—modernity as opposed to capitalism/socialism; I described this as a secondary dualism because it is not built into social theory as such, as the others are, but represents a focus on one particular historical period and it has to do with the possibilities for change in the modern world. It should be apparent by now that, whichever theorist we choose, we find a more or less ambivalent attitude to the modern world; it represents progress but it also represents a danger. For Durkheim, it establishes the possibility of individual freedom within a comparatively harmonious society, but also runs the risk of increasing anomie and egoism. For Marx, capitalism frees immense productive forces, but it is a system based on exploitation and oppression which offers a future which he posed in the dramatic terms of a choice between socialism and barbarism. For Weber, modernity provides comparative stability at the risk of bureaucratization, the domination of instrumental rationality, and disenchantment; for Simmel, the modern world frees the individual from domination by the primitive group but then subjects him or her to domination by the objective culture against which the individual has to struggle to preserve his or her integrity.

These are issues at the centre of contemporary political debate. There are issues of equality, of the range of differences in wealth that we think is permissible in our society and whether these differences should be linked to differences in power: should the very rich be allowed to build up huge media empires, for example? Should we be concerned with restricting the market economy and to what extent should the state intervene in social and economic affairs? To what extent should we value our individual freedom over and above the demands of society and the local community? To what extent is bureaucracy desirable or undesirable? To what extent do we tolerate those who are different from us or do we try to change them? And, although the classic theorists have comparatively little to say about racism and sexism and the environment, these issues can be understood in terms of the wider debates with which the classical theorists are concerned.

Each of these theorists' conceptions of the modern world is profoundly historical; this is true even of Simmel, who has the thinnest historical analysis of the four—objective culture does not simply arrive but develops over a long time. Their theories of history may vary from the solid evolutionism of Durkheim through to the tentative and reversible process described by Weber, but they all involve some sense of progress towards the contemporary world and the assumption that this contemporary world cannot be understood unless we understand how it has developed. It seems to me that we should always be wary of claims that the world has changed dramatically. I would suggest that there are no radical breaks from what has gone before; we do not wake up suddenly to find ourselves in a different world; perhaps what changes is the range of available ways of living with our problems.

It follows from this that the political choices that were relevant to the classical theorists have been modified but not profoundly changed. The final dualism is essentially about the possibilities of change open to contemporary society. If we stick to the side of modernity, the implications are that the most significant changes that we experience are part of the modern world, whether we like it or not—we might be able to modify their effects but we cannot envisage any more profound change. If we concern ourselves with the capitalism/socialism side of the dualism, then it opens up the possibility that there are other ways of organizing society which perhaps will change our lives in a way we find desirable.

At the time of writing the former point of view seems to have become the dominant view of western social theorists; whereas in the 1970s the terms 'capitalism', 'late capitalism', 'monopoly capitalism', and 'state capitalism' could be found in most sociology books, by the late 1990s 'modernity', 'late modernity', and 'postmodernity' seem to be everywhere. It is paradoxical that, at the very moment when capitalism has reasserted itself on the world stage with many of the ill effects that it has always had, producing regular crises and high levels of unemployment, widening gaps between rich and poor both within and between nation states, and constantly transforming our living and working conditions— melting, as Marx put it, everything that is solid into air—sociologists should give up the sustained critique of modern capitalism that was produced in the 1960s and 1970s.

It might be that sociologists follow the crowd like everybody else and, when radical left-wing politics come to the fore, they produce works of Marxist theory and analysis, and when the right is in dominance, they turn in other directions. However, I think there might be a sociological explanation of this change: that, as technological change has speeded up, particularly with the revolutions in information technology, and as finance capital has used these revolutions to become more and more powerful, it has become easier to be caught up in the surface appearances of the system, and to believe that the surface appearances are all that exist. I think that this is particularly true in the case of Anthony Giddens's work.

What I want to do here by way of a final conclusion is to make a plea for rec-ognizing the importance of the last dualism. One of the implications of talking about necessary dualisms is that sociology is an open-ended pluralist discipline, generating a range of different theories and methods and a range of debates. Attempts to produce syntheses of the different theories are attempts to close down these debates. If sociology reflects the structure of the real social world and the plurality of different 'objects' that make it up, then the 'real-world' equivalent of trying to find a theoretical synthesis is to try to impose a totalitar-ian social order and I do not think that either of these attempts are desirable.

If the family of concepts around the idea of modernity dominate, then I think this has the same effect—it reduces the range of possibilities open to us; the arguments about socialism and capitalism open them up. It seems to me that the most important contribution of the founders of sociology was to produce a notion of 'society' as a significant force in our lives—Marx and Durkheim do so explicitly and happily, Weber almost despite himself, and Simmel with great reluctance—and, even if society turns out to be complex and multidimensional, we still need to hold on to the idea.

Once we have the idea of 'society', there is the possibility of asking what sorts of changes are possible, or desirable, and questioning the range of control that we have over the world we live in. The arguments about socialism and capital-ism that we find in the classic thinkers raise these questions and it is no accident that the two theorists who have the clearest conceptions of society as a whole raise them most explicitly in ways that are still relevant. Even if it is difficult to imagine the socialist revolution in the way that Marx and Lenin imagined it, we should not lose the sight of the possibility that there are other ways of living and other ways of organizing ourselves.

Dramatis personae

In addition to the four major figures—Marx, Durkheim, Weber, and Simmel—I have mentioned a number of other thinkers of whom students might not be aware. What follows are brief details of philosophers, social theorists, and other major thinkers who were: (*a*) predecessors who had a major influence on one or other of the four, (*b*) approximate contemporaries who have made a lasting contribution to the field, and (*c*) significant mid-twentieth-century figures, now dead, who have contributed to the development of modern social theory. I have suggested further reading only in the case of the main social theorists.

Adorno, T. W. (1903–69) A major figure in twentieth-century Marxism, an original member of the Frankfurt School of Social Research, developing the critical Hegelian tradition of Marxism into a powerful critique of modern culture, demonstrating the way in which independent thinking is stifled and people are drawn into the system. See Adorno and Horkheimer (1972).

Althusser, Louis (1918–90) A French Marxist philosopher of science, and a central figure in the development of social thought in the second half of the twentieth century, developing a realist, structural conception of social science through a reinterpretation of Marx's work. His career came to a tragic end—he had always suffered from depression, and during a particularly bad bout in 1980 he killed his wife. He spent the rest of his life in a Paris mental hospital.

Bergson, Henri (1859–1941) A French philosopher whose name is often associated with Simmel. He thought the intellect was incapable of grasping experience and he posited a vital life-force which he thought was responsible for evolution.

Comte, Auguste (1798–1857) A French philosopher, regarded as the founder of positivism, and the first to coin the term 'sociology'. He saw society as moving through three stages—from understanding the world in supernatural terms, to understanding it in metaphysical philosophical terms, to understanding it through the systematic collection of facts and their correlation. He thought that the laws of society that could be derived from this would put an end to political arguments caused by the French Revolution.

Darwin, Charles (1809–82) Darwin's theory of evolution revolutionized thought in the mid-nineteenth century, first by removing humanity from the centre of creation and seeing it as just another species, and secondly by explaining the biological development of human beings as a process of natural selection depending upon adjustment to the environment. It became very difficult to avoid evolutionary thought—it is central to Marx and Durkheim and haunts Weber and Simmel. See Darwin (1859/1970).

Engels, Friedrich (1820–95) A friend and collaborator of Karl Marx, with whom he founded the Communist Party and contributed to the development and popularization of Marxist thought. He ran his father's business in Manchester and saved Marx from dire poverty—an irony that is often pointed out. He was one of the first male writers to make a significant contribution to understanding the position of women in society. See Engels (1884/1968).

Feuerbach, Ludwig (1804–72) A philosopher who critically developed Hegel's thought, particularly in relation to Christianity; his view that religion involved a projection of human powers onto an abstract idea was important in the development of Marx's theory of alienation.

Foucault, Michel (1926–84) French philosopher usually labelled 'poststructuralist' and the author of a very difficult body of work concerned with tracing shifts in the development of western thought and, in the later part of his career, with the development of the human sciences and social control; the development of medicine and the sciences concerned with sexuality and psychology can be seen as means by which, in modern societies, our subjectivity is constituted and controlled. See Foucault (1973, 1977).

Freud, Sigmund (1856–1939) Born about the same time as Durkheim, Simmel but outliving them by over two decades, Freud is the founder of psychoanalysis and throughout the history of sociology there have been regular attempts to integrate psychoanalysis and social theory. Freud's conception of the individual/society relationship is not dissimilar to that of Durkheim (or later, Parsons): the individual must be regulated and directed by the wider social group. For Freud this involves the repression of sexual drives and the development of ego and superego as internal social controls. Civilization goes hand in hand with misery—the more developed society becomes, the more pleasure we have to sacrifice. See Freud (1985*a*).

Hegel, Georg Wilhelm Friedrich (1770–1831) A major European philosopher, perhaps the last of the great system builders. He saw history as a long process via a series of contradictions through which Reason works itself out. Reason, rational thought, is what motivates historical development and it works towards Truth—the most general level of knowledge. Truth can exist only in the context of a totality of knowledge, not as isolated propositions. Marx was seeped in Hegelian thought which he famously 'stood on its head'—seeing the development of thought, and of societies, as a result of human productive activity.

Kant, Immanuel (1724–1804) A a major European philosopher who, like many since, attempted to reconcile empiricist (starting from external reality) and idealist (starting from thought) traditions. He saw the world as divided into things in themselves—objects out there in the world which could not be known in any essential sense—and consciousness, which possessed certain a priori properties, which can best be seen as, for example, a sense of time and space, the basic categories by which we organize the world. Durkheim claimed to find the basis for these categories of thought in social organization, and they can be seen as the intellectual basis for Simmel's 'forms'. Kant's influence can be traced through most types of sociology that begin with the individual or with consciousness.

Kierkegaard, Soren (1815–55) A religious philosopher who emphasized the importance of the experience of the existing individual over and against philosophical systems, particularly that of Hegel. The first of the existentialists.

Lenin, Vladimir Ilyich (1870–1924) Leader of the Russian Revolution and a brilliant political organizer and strategist. He produced a number of political, historical, and philosophical contributions to Marxism, the most important political contribution being the development of a theory of a political party which would lead the working class to victory (as opposed to other Marxists, who thought the working class would sponta-neously rise up and win power). The most relevant sociological contribution was *The State and Revolution*, which discussed the withering-away of the state after the socialist revolution.

Lukacs, Georg (1885–1971) Hungarian philosopher whose personal intellectual history follows the intellectual history of Europe. It has been argued that he wrote the existen-tial work of the century (Lukacs 1971*b*) on the way from passing from Kant to Marx to Hegel, but his main fame is for developing the Hegelian strand of Marxism. He argued that Marx's dialectical method, in which each single proposition only made sense in the context of the whole, and was open to constant revision, guaranteed its adequacy; he argued that Marx had finally resolved the subject/object dualism in western thought, and the experience of the proletariat in the production process enabled this resolution and gave the class a privileged position in understanding the workings of capitalist society. See Lukacs (1971*a*).

Mannheim, Karl (1893–1947) Perhaps best seen as a non-Marxist version of Lukacs, he was one of a circle including Lukacs and Weber who at one period used to meet regu-larly. He is best known for his development of the sociology of knowledge—the theory that all knowledge depends upon the social and existential position of the thinker. This leads to relativism; different points of view are simply different, not better than one another. Mannheim tried to escape this by suggesting that the more inclusive view was best and that free-floating intellectuals were in the best position to produce such a view because they had no special interest or axe to grind. See Mannheim (1938).

Marcuse, Herbert (1898–1979) A German, founder member of the Frankfurt School, who fled to America when Hitler came to power and did not return. As well as develop-ing the critical Hegelian side of Marxism, he wrote a number of works critical of the 'one-dimensional' culture of late capitalism, and a particularly important attempt to combine Marxist and Freudian thought. See Marcuse (1969).

Mead, George Herbert (1863–1931) An American philosopher and one of the founders of the social of sociology known as symbolic interactionism, which concentrates on face-to-face interaction and the social development of the self. Often considered one of the indirect heirs of Simmel's thought. See Mead (1938).

Merleau-Ponty, Maurice (1905–61) A French phenomenological philosopher associ-ated with Sartre and existentialism; he was concerned with exploring the relationship between the body, consciousness, and the outside world.

Michels, Robert (1876–1936) A German sociologist who argued that there is an 'iron law of oligarchy' by which democratic radical political parties develop large bureaucra-cies and come to be dominated by officials who are more concerned with the organiza-tion than with its aims. These ideas fit neatly with Weber's ideas on rationalization. See Michels (1911/1962).

Mill, John Stuart (1806–61) A utilitarian philosopher who introduced Comte's work into Britain and is best known for his work on scientific method. Durkheim was espe-cially critical of the individualism of his social theory.

Nietzsche, Friedrich (1844–1900) A German philosopher, one of the most important of the modern period; he offered a radical critique of Enlightenment rationality and inverted the relationship that the Enlightenment philosophers assumed to exist between knowledge and power—knowledge is seen as a form of domination rather than liberation. He was an important influence on Weber and on the development of postmodernism, particularly Foucault's work.

Parsons, Talcott (1902–79) The most important American sociologist of the second half of the twentieth century, he attempted a massive and systematic synthesis of the classical sociologists—excluding Marx and including Mead rather than Simmel. See Parsons (1951).

Ricardo, David (1772–1823) An economist inspired by Adam Smith who attempted to develop a labour theory of value; Marx developed his theory through a critique of Smith and Ricardo.

Rickert, Heinrich (1863–1936) A German neo-Kantian philosopher, a contemporary of and major influence on Max Weber. His criticism of positivism was important for Weber's methodological writings.

Saint-Simon, Claude-Henri de Rouvroy, Comte de (1760–1825) Ironically, an aristocrat was the founder of French socialism and French sociology. He was imprisoned during the French Revolution but his liberal sympathies saved his life. Many of his ideas were developed by Comte and later by Durkheim—the notion that society moves through three stages, that we can find general laws of society, which should be run by scientists, and that humanity needed to develop a new religion based on positivism.

Sartre, Jean-Paul (1905–80) French existentialist philosopher, novelist, playwright, and political activist and later a Marxist who made a sophisticated attempt to combine the two philosophies. See Sartre (1963).

Smith, Adam (1723–90) Scottish philosopher, economist, and social theorist, a major figure for modern right-wing politicians, who believed in the power of the free market, although Smith himself was able to envisage the state playing a wide social role. He talked about the 'hidden hand' of the market bringing order and stability in a way that Weber assumed, and he developed the labour theory of value that Marx criticized and developed.

Spencer, Herbert (1820–1903) A railway engineer turned journalist turned major English nineteenth-century sociologist. He swallowed evolutionary theory whole, seeing history as an evolutionary process of improvement, pushed forward by the struggle for scarce resources and involving the survival of the fittest. See Spencer (1971).

Tonnies, Ferdinand (1855–1936) A German sociologist who made an important distinction between, 'community' and 'association'. This is echoed in different ways by Durkheim, Simmel, and Weber. The difference is between the deeper and more stable relationships which are reputed to occur in traditional societies and the more fragmented, interest-based relationships more common in modern societies.

Trotsky, Leon (1879–1949) A leader, with Lenin, of the Russian Revolution. He disagreed with and went into exile under Stalin and was eventually murdered by one of Stalin's agents. Wrote widely on politics and the arts as well as developing his own analysis of Russian 'state capitalism'. See Trotsky (1967).

Wittfogel, Karl (1896–?) A founder member, with Adorno, Marcuse, and others, of the Frankfurt School of Social Research. Unlike the others, he was less concerned with the higher reaches of western philosophy, and his major work (Wittfogel 1963) was a development of Marx's comments about eastern empires being seen as a specific mode of production—oriental despotism.

Glossary

action/structure dualism this refers to a major division and necessary division within sociology between approaches which focus primarily on social structure (e.g. Marx, the early Durkheim) and those that focus primarily on individual and social action (e.g. Weber, Simmel)

alienation (Marx) a process in which people become separated from their fellows, the products of their work, and their own life processes

anomie (Durkheim) a state in which there are no clear shared rules or norms of behaviour

ancient mode of production (Marx) a society (such as ancient Rome) in which the city dominates the countryside, and which changes as it reproduces itself

associative relationships (Weber) relationships which depend upon a common, usually material, interest

asiatic mode of production (Marx) a society (e.g. China) in which local communities are dependent upon a strong state, for e.g. constructing irrigation systems

bourgeoisie (Marx) the capitalist ruling class, owners of the means of production

bureaucracy (Weber) the rational form of organization which dominates the modern world

causal adequacy (Weber) an explanation is adequate on the level of cause if, given the same conditions, the same result would follow

charisma, charismatic domination (Weber) special qualities of the personality which enable the person possessing them to exercise power over others (e.g. Christ, Hitler)

citizenship (T. H. Marshall) the status enjoyed by the full members of a community; citizenship rights might undermine class formation especially among the proletariat

class-in-itself (Marx) a group of people defined by a common relationship to the means of production

class-for-itself (Marx) a group of people sharing the same relationship to the means of production, who see themselves as sharing a common interest and act together to achieve it

class, social class (Weber) a group of people who share the same market position

collective representations (Durkheim) shared symbolic systems (such as religious beliefs) through which members of a society represent their organization.

commodity fetishism (Marx) the way in which capitalism transforms, via the market, social relationships into relationships between things

communal relationships (Weber) relationships between people based on common identification (e.g. the family)

conscience collective (Durkheim) refers to the norms and values shared by members of a society and/or the underlying logic and forms of thought shared by a society

determinism, economic determinism (Marx, or attributed to Marx) an explanation in which the result is seen as the inevitable and necessary outcome of a causal process; thus political events and ideas are determined by the relations and forces of production

dialectics, dialectical materialism (Marx) as an argument, dialectics is a debate between opposing positions; as an explanation, dialectical materialism sees society developing through structural contradictions

division of labour (everybody, but especially Durkheim) the way in which different tasks are allocated to different people; Durkheim saw this as a major source of social cohesion

dyad (Simmel) two people, the smallest social group and a starting point for analysis.

egoism (Durkheim) a form of social integration which rests on individual responsibility; not to be confused with selfishness

elective affinity (Weber) refers to the resonance between the Protestant ethic and the spirit of capitalism; not *quite* a causal relationship

emergent properties new elements which emerge from the combination of other elements—e.g. the group can have different properties from the individuals who comprise it

Enlightenment the period beginning in France in the eighteenth century which saw the foundation of modern science and philosophy

epistemology the theory of knowledge and how we come by it

evolution In the social sciences, a notion of steady social development through determinate stages

exchange value (Marx) the value at which a commodity sells on the market; *see also* **use value**

existentialism a philosophical approach which gives priority to our immediate individual experience of the world

false consciousness (various Marxists) a wrong or mistaken view of the world, held by virtue of one's class position

feudalism, feudal mode of production for Weber, feudalism was a form of patrimony—a form of authority resting on personal and bureaucratic power appearing through the routinization of charisma in a traditional setting; for Marx, it was a social order in which the lord 'owned' the means of production, but the peasant controlled; the surplus thus had to be extracted through various forms of rent

forces of production (Marx) the raw materials, tools, and human capacities that are required to produce goods

formal sociology, social forms (Simmel) the organization of social life at various levels in ways that remain the same, whatever the setting; e.g. conflict can be seen as a form of relationship whether it is a matter of two children rowing or a world war

functionalism (attributed to Durkheim) the explanation of the continued existence of a phenomenon in relation to the function it fulfils in the larger whole

Gemeinschaft (Tonnies) close, face-to-face relationships in a stable community, as opposed to *Gesellschaft*

Gesellschaft (Tonnies) relationships based on rational calculation and self-interest in a rapidly changing community

ideal type (Weber) a purely rational construct of a social phenomenon or process, which can then be compared with the real world; a rational 'puppet theatre' (Schutz)

ideology (Marx) a view of the world which is distorted through the self-interest of a social class, or a non-scientific view of the world

individual/society dualism a necessary opposition in social theory which must say something about individuals *and* society, but cannot explain one in terms of the other

instrumental rationality a term used critically by twentieth-century Marxists to refer to a rational organization of activity directed towards practical ends and involving domination over and manipulation of objects and people; Weber develops this conception of rationality but with little critical comment

labour theory of value a theory developed by the classical economists, including Marx, which tries to show that the value of a commodity depends upon the amount of labour expended upon its production

labour power (Marx) this is what the employer buys from the worker; the difference between its use value to the employer and its exchange value (the wage) explains exploitation

legal-rational domination (Weber) the form of authority most appropriate to modern societies, involving bureaucratic organization under the rule of law

lumpenproletariat (Marx) the riff-raff—criminals, the unemployable, etc.—who can be organized by authoritarian leaders

meaning adequacy (Weber) an explanation is adequate on the level of meaning if it tells a coherent, rational story

means of production (Marx) the raw materials and machines used in the production process

mechanical solidarity (Marx) a form of social organization in which there is a minimal division of labour, and the group is united by the *conscience collective*, usually in religious form; evolves into organic solidarity

mode of production (Marx) the basic economic structure of a society, comprising the forces and relations of production

meta-narratives a term used by postmodernists to describe general social theories such as those discussed in this text

objective culture (Simmel) ideas, beliefs, practices which have grown up between people and taken on an objective quality and which then threaten to stifle the life process and the individuality of subjective culture

organic analogy looking at society as if it were a living organism; used by Durkheim

organic solidarity (Durkheim) a differentiated form of society held together by the division of labour and a 'religion of individualism'

overdetermination a concept developed by Lenin and Trotsky to describe the multiple contradictions that create a revolutionary situation

patriarchal authority (Weber) the form of authority in traditional society, based on male heads of households; not to be confused with modern usage, where it means male domination in general

patrimonialism (Weber) authority resting on personal authority and bureaucratic position; develops from the routinization of charisma in traditional settings

peasantry (nearly everybody, but especially Marx) the class of small farmers, according to Marx isolated from each other only to be united by a strong leader

petty bourgeoisie (Marx) the middle class—for Marx, small entrepreneurs and professionals; modern Marxists have included many other groups in the category—including managers and state employees

play forms (Simmel) the point where social interaction becomes an art form; examples of play forms are flirting and sociability

positivism (Comte) a view of social science as empirical investigation aiming to establish general laws of society (*beware*: it has accumulated other meanings during the twentieth century)

pre-notions (Durkheim) common-sense ideas which must be ignored if we are to achieve scientific knowledge

primitive communism (Engels/Marx) a supposed early period of egalitarianism and collective ownership at the beginning of human history

proletariat (Marx) the working class; those who sell their labour power

realism, critical realism a modern philosophy developed by Bhaskar (1978, 1979) which posits a difference between structure and agency and between different (surface and underlying) levels of reality

relations of production (Marx) the crucial relationships between humans and the means of production, which define social classes and modes of production; the two relationships are of ownership and control

social action, meaningful social action (Weber) social action is action directed towards others; meaningful social action is social action to which we attach a meaning. Don't worry about the difference. For Weber, meaningful social action is the proper object of sociology

social currents (Durkheim) sentiments which run through social groups without taking on the solidity of social facts

social facts (Durkheim) social facts have an existence over and above individuals and force themselves upon people—language is a good example

social and system integration social integration refers to principles governing the relationships between individuals, system integration to those governing relationships between parts of a society or social system; such relationships may be complementary or conflictual

species being (Marx) humanity and its defining features

status groups (Weber) a group which shares a particular social esteem, usually involving a similar lifestyle and training; the priesthood is a good example

traditional authority (Weber) *see* **patriarchal authority**

postmodernism the term refers to either or both of (*a*) a new type of society in which traditional boundaries have broken down and which has emerged towards the end of this century or (*b*) various new relativist theories and philosophies which deny the possibility of knowledge

rationality, rational action (Weber) rationality is another feature of the meaningful social action that is the proper object of sociology; it makes social science possible

rationalization (Weber) the process which has dominated the development of the modern world, replacing traditional societies; *see also* **instrumental rationality**

repressive law (Durkheim) law of which the prime purpose is to punish; its dominance is an indication of mechanical solidarity

restitutive law (Durkheim) law of which the prime purpose is to restore the situation as before; its dominance is an indication of organic solidarity

use value (Marx) the (un-measurable) value of a good to the person who possesses it; to be distinguished from **exchange value**

values, value-freedom (Weber) for Weber, our rational lives are bounded by existential (i.e. a-rational) value choices; science is such a value choice, but, once it is chosen, rational value-free investigation is possible within the scientific community

Verstehen (Weber) the rational understanding of people's actions

References

Adorno, T. W., and Horkheimer, M. (1972), *Dialectic of Enlightenment* (New York: Herder & Herder).

Anderson, P. (1976), *Considerations on Western Marxism* (London: New Left Books).

—— (1990), 'A Culture in Counterflow—1', *New Left Review*, 180: 41–78.

Albrow, M. (1990), *Max Weber's Construction of Social Theory* (Basingstoke: Macmillan).

Alexander, J. C. (1982–4) (ed.), *Theoretical Logic in Sociology* (London: Routledge & Kegan Paul).

—— (1988) *Durkheimian Sociology: Cultural Studies* (Cambridge: Cambridge University Press).

Althusser, L. (1969), *For Marx* (London: Allen Lane, The Penguin Press).

—— (1971), *Lenin and Philosophy* (London: New Left Books).

Althusser, L., and Balibar, É. (1970), *Reading Capital* (London: New Left Books).

Anon. (1961), *The Cloud of Unknowing and Other Works*, ed. P. Hodgson (Harmondsworth: Penguin Books).

Axelrod, C. D. (1991), 'Toward an Appreciation of Simmel's Fragmentary Style', in L. Ray (ed.), *Formal Sociology* (Aldershot, Hants: Edward Elgar), 156–67.

Bailey, A. M. (1981), 'The Renewed Discussions on the Concept of the Asiatic Mode of Production', in J. S. Kahn and J. L. Llobera (eds.), *The Anthropology of Pre-Capitalist Societies* (London: Routledge), 89–107.

Barrett, M. (1980), *Women's Oppression Today: Problems in Marxist Feminist Analysis* (London: Verso).

Barrett, M., and McIntosh, M. (1982) (eds.), *The Anti-Social Family* (London: Verso).

Bendix, R. (1966), *Max Weber: An Intellectual Portrait* (London: Methuen).

Benton, E. (1977), *Philosophical Foundations of the Three Sociologies* (London: Routledge & Kegan Paul).

—— (1984), *The Rise and Fall of Structural Marxism* (London: Macmillan).

—— (1993), *Natural Relations, Ecology, Animal Rights and Social Justice* (London: Verso).

Berger, P., and Luckman, T. (1967), *The Social Construction of Reality* (London: Allen Lane, Penguin).

Bhaskar, R. (1978), *A Realist Theory of Science* (Sussex: Harvester Press).

—— (1979), *The Possibility of Naturalism* (Sussex: Harvester Press).

Bion, W. (1976), *Learning from Experience* (London: Heinemann).

Blauner, R. (1964), *Alienation and Freedom: The Factory Worker and his Industry* (Chicago: Chicago University Press).

Blumer, H. (1969), *Symbolic Interactionism* (Engelwood Cliffs, NJ: Prentice-Hall).

Bottomore, T. (1990), 'Giddens's View of Historical Materialism', in J. Clark *et al.*, *Anthony Giddens: Consensus and Controversy* (London: Falmer Press).

Bowlby, J. (1988), *A Secure Base* (London: Routledge).

Buck, N., *et al.* (1994), *Changing Households: British Household Panel Survey 1990–92* (Colchester: ESRC Research Centre on Micro-Social Change).

Bunyan, J. (1928), *A Pilgrim's Progress from this world to that to come* (Oxford: Oxford University Press).

Burger, T. (1976), *Max Weber's Theory of Concept Formation* (Durham, NC: Duke University Press).

Bryant, C. A. (1985), *Positivism in Social Theory and Research* (Basingstoke: Macmillan).

Carver, T. (1975), *Karl Marx: Texts on Method* (Oxford: Blackwell).

Chodorow, N. (1978), *The Reproduction of Mothering* (Berkeley and Los Angeles: University of California Press).

Clarke, S. (1994), *Marx's Theory of Crisis* (London: Macmillan).

Comte, A. (1976), *The Foundations of Sociology*, ed. K. Thompson (London: Nelson).

Coser, L. A. (1956), *The Functions of Social Conflict* (Glencoe, Ill.: Free Press).

—— (1991*a*), 'Georg Simmel's Style of Work: A Contribution to the Sociology of the Sociologist', in L. Ray (ed.), *Formal Sociology* (Aldershot, Hants: Edward Elgar), 139–45.

—— (1991*b*), 'The Sociology of Poverty', in L. Ray (ed.), *Formal Sociology* (Aldershot, Hants: Edward Elgar), 231–42.

Craib, I. (1989), *Psychoanalysis and Social Theory: The Limits of Sociology* (Brighton: Harvester Wheatsheaf).

—— (1992*a*), *Anthony Giddens* (London: Routledge).

—— (1992*b*), *Modern Social Theory: From Parsons to Habermas* (Brighton: Harvester Wheatsheaf).

—— (1994), *The Importance of Disappointment* (London: Routledge).

—— (1995), 'Some Comments on the Sociology of the Emotions', *Sociology*, 29: 151–8.

Crook, S., Pakulski, J., and Waters, M. (1992), *Postmodernization: Change in Advanced Society* (London: Sage).

Darwin, C. (1970; first pub. 1859), *The Origin of the Species* (Harmondsworth: Penguin).

Derrida, J. (1995), *Specters of Marx* (New York: Routledge).

Douglas, J. (1967), *The Social Meanings of Suicide* (Princeton: Princeton University Press).

Durkheim, É. (1915; first. pub. 1912), *The Elementary Forms of the Religious Life* (London: Allen & Unwin).

—— (1952; first pub. 1896), *Suicide* (London: Routledge & Kegan Paul).

—— (1953; first pub. 1897), *Sociology and Philosophy* (Glencoe Ill.: Glencoe Free Press).

—— (1957), *Professional Ethics and Civil Morals* (London: Routledge).

—— (1958), *Socialism and Saint-Simon* (London: Routledge & Kegan Paul).

—— (1962), *Moral Education* (New York: The Free Press).

—— (1964; first pub. 1895), *The Rules of Sociological Method* (New York: Free Press).

—— (1969), 'Two Laws of Penal Education', *University of Cincinnati Law Review*, 38: 32–60).

—— (1977; first pub. 1938), *The Evolution of Educational Thought* (London: Routledge).

—— (1979), *Durkheim: Essays on Morals and Education*, ed. W. F. Pickering (London: Routledge).

—— (1984; first pub. 1893), *The Division of Labour in Society* (Basingstoke: Macmillan).

—— (1990), 'Individualism and the Intellectuals' (1898), in Peter Hamilton (ed.), *Emile Durkheim: Critical Assessments* (London: Routledge), iv. 62–73.

—— and Mauss, M. (1963; first pub. 1903), *Primitive Classification* (London: Cohen & West).

Engels, F. (1940), *Dialectics of Nature* (London: Lawrence & Wishart).

—— (1967), 'Socialism, Utopian and Scientific', in *Selected Works*, ed. W. O. Henderson (Harmondsworth: Penguin).

—— 1968; first pub. 1884), *The Origin of the Family, Private Property and the State*, in K. Marx and F. Engels, *Selected Works* (London: Lawrence & Wishart).

Etzioni, A. (1995), *The Spirit of Community* (London: Fontana).

—— (1996), 'The Responsive Community: A Communitarian Perspective', *American Journal of Sociology*, 61: 1–11.

Faught, J. (1991), 'Neglected Affinities, Max Weber and Georg Simmel', in L. Ray (ed.), *Formal Sociology* (Aldershot, Hants: Edward Elgar), 86–105.

Foucault, M. (1973), *The Birth of The Clinic* (London: Tavistock).

—— (1977), *Discipline and Punish* (London: Allen Lane).

—— (1979), *The History of Sexuality* (London: Allen Lane).

Freud, S. (1985*a*), 'Civilisation and its Discontents', in *Civilisation, Society and Religion* (Pelican Freud Library 12; Harmondsworth: Pelican Books).

—— (1985*b*), 'Totem and Taboo', in *The Origins of Religion* (Pelican Freud Library 13; Harmondsworth: Pelican Books).

Friedmann, G. (1961), *The Anatomy of Work* (London: Heinemann).

Frisby, D. (1981), *Sociological Impressionism* (London: Heinemann).

—— (1984), *Georg Simmel* (Chichester: Ellis Horwood).

—— (1992), *Simmel and Since: Essays on Georg Simmel's Social, Theory* (London: Routledge).

Fukuyama, F. (1992), *The End of History and the Last Man* (Harmondsworth: Penguin).

Gane, M. (1988), *On Durkheim's Rules of Sociological Method* (London: Routledge).

Garfinkel, H. (1967), *Studies in Ethnomethodogy* (Englewood Cliffs, NJ: Prentice Hall).

Gergen, K. (1991), *The Saturated Self* (New York: Basic Books).

Giddens, A. (1971), *Capitalism and Modern Social Theory: Analysis of the Writings of Marx, Durkheim and Weber* (Cambridge: Cambridge University Press).

—— (1972), *Politics and Sociology in the Work of Max Weber* (London: Macmillan).

—— (1973), *The Class Structure of Advanced Societies* (London: Hutchinson).

—— (1976), *New Rules of Sociological Method* (London: Hutchinson).

—— (1978), *Durkheim* (London: Fontana).

—— (1981), *A Contemporary Critique of Historical Materialism, I. Power, Property and the State* (London: Macmilllan).

—— (1984), *The Constitution of Society* (Oxford: Polity Press).

—— (1985), *A Contemporary Critique of Historical Materialism, II. The Nation-State and Violence* (Oxford: Polity Press).

—— (1990*a*), 'Durkheim's Political Sociology', in P. Hamilton (ed.), *Emile Durkheim, Critical Assessments, IV* (London: Routledge), 184–219.

—— (1990*b*), *The Consequences of Modernity* (Oxford: Polity Press).

—— (1991), *Modernity and Self-Identity* (Oxford: Polity Press).

Gilligan, C. (1982), *In a Different Voice: Essays on Psychological Theory and Women's Development* (Cambridge, Mass.: Harvard University Press).

Ginsberg, M. (1956), *On The Diversity of Morals* (London: William Heinemann Ltd.).

Gladis, M. S. (1992), *A Comunitarian Defence of Liberalism* (Stanford, Calif.: Stanford University Press).

Goff, T. (1980), *Mead and Marx* (London: Routledge & Kegan Paul).

Goldmann, L. (1969), *The Human Sciences and Philosophy* (London: Jonathan Cape).

—— (1977), *Lukacs and Heidegger* (London: Routledge & Kegan Paul).

Gouldner, A. (1958), Introduction to E. Durkheim, *Socialism and Saint-Simon* (London: Routledge & Kegan Paul), pp. v–xxvii.

Habermas, J. (1972), *Knowledge and Human Interests* (London: Heinemann).

—— (1974), *Theory and Practice* (London: Heinemann).

—— (1976), *Legitimation Crisis* (London: Heinemann).

—— (1979), *Communication and the Evolution of Society* (London: Heinemann).

—— (1984), *The Theory of Communicative Action, Reason and the Rationalisation of Society* (Oxford: Polity Press).

—— (1987), *The Theory of Communicative Action, II. A Critique of Functionalist Reason* (Oxford: Polity Press).

—— (1990), *The Philosophical Discourse of Modernity: Twelve Lectures* (Oxford: Polity Press).

Hamilton, P. (1990) (ed.), *Emile Durkheim: Critical Assessments* (London: Routledge).

—— (1991) (ed.), *Max Weber: Critical Perspectives* (London: Routledge).

Hall, D., and Gay, P. (1996) (eds), *Questions of Cultural Identity* (London: Sage).

Harding, S. (1986), *The Science Question in Feminism* (Buckingham: Open University Press).

—— (1991), *Whose Science? Whose Knowledge* (Buckingham: Open University Press).

Hartman, H. (1986), *The Unhappy Marriage of Marxism and Feminism*, ed. L. Sargent (London: Pluto Press).

Harvey, D. (1989), *The Condition of Postmodernity* (Oxford: Basil Blackwell).

Hayward, J. E. S. (1990), 'Solidarist Syndicalism, Durkheim and Duguit', in P. Hamilton (ed.), *Emile Durkheim: Critical Assessments* (London: Routledge), iv. 128–44.

Hegel, G. W. F. (1977), *The Phenomenology of Spirit* (Oxford: Oxford University Press).

Held, D. (1980), *Introduction to Critical Theory* (London: Hutchinson).

Hempel, C. (1969), 'Logical Positivism and the Social Sciences', in P. Achinstein and S. F. Barker (eds.), *The Legacy of Logical Positivism* (Baltimore: John Hopkins University Press).

Hindess, B. (1973), *The Uses of Offical Statistics* (London: Macmillan).

—— and Hirst, P. Q (1975), *Pre-Capitalist Modes of Production* (London: Routledge and Kegan Paul).

Hobsbawm, E. (1964), Introduction to K. Marx, *Pre-Capitalist Economic Formations* (London: Lawrence & Wishart), 9–65.

Hochschild, A. (1994), 'The Commercial Spirit of Intimate Life and the Abduction of Feminism: Signs from Women's Advice Books', *Theory, Culture and Society*, 1–24).

Holton, R. J. and Turner, B. S. (1989), *Max Weber on Economy and Society* (London: Routledge).

Horton, J. (1990), 'The Dehumanisation of Anomie and Alienation: A Problem in the Ideology of Sociology', (1964), in P. Hamilton (ed.), *Emile Durkheim: Critical Assessments* (London: Routledge), iv. 145–62.

Jameson, F. (1991), *Postmodernism or the Cultural Logic of Late Capitalism* (London: Verso).

Jones, R. A. (1986), *Emile Durkheim* (London: Sage).

Klein, M. (1957), *Envy and Gratitude* (London: Tavistock).

Lacan, J. (1977), *Écrits* (London: Tavistock).

Lane, C. (1981), *Rites of Rulers* (Cambridge: Cambridge University Press).

Lasch, C. (1980), *The Culture of Narcissism* (London: Sphere Books).

—— (1995), *The Revolt of the Élites and the Betrayal of Democracy* (New York: W. W. Norton).

Leat, D. (1972), Misunderstanding *Verstehen, Sociological Review*, 20: 29–38.

Lee, D., and Newby, H. (1983), *The Problem of Sociology* (London: Hutchinson).

—— and Turner, B. (1996) (eds.), *Conflicts about Class: Debating Inequality in Late Industrialism* (London: Longman).

Lefebvre, H. (1968), *Dialectical Materialism* (London: Jonathan Cape).

Lenin, V. I. (1972), *The State and Revolution* (Moscow: Progress Publishers).

Levi-Strauss, C. (1966), *The Savage Mind* (London: Weidenfeld & Nicolson).

—— (1969), *Totemism* (Harmondsworth: Pelican Books).

Levine, D. N. (1971), Introduction to *Georg Simmel on Individuality and Social Forms*, (Chicago: Chicago University Press).

—— (1991), 'Simmel at a distance: On the History and Systematics of the Sociology of the Stranger', in L. Ray (ed.), *Formal Sociology* (Aldershot, Hants: Edward Elgar), 272–88.

Lobkowicz, N. (1978), 'Historical Laws' in D. McQuarie (ed.), *Sociology, Social Change, Capitalism* (London: Quartet), 120–33.

Lockwood, D. (1958), *The Blackcoated Worker* (London: Allen & Unwin).

—— (1964), 'Social Integration and System Integration', in G. K. Zollschan and W. Hirsch (eds.), *Explanations in Social Change* (London: Routledge & Kegan Paul), 244–57.

Lukacs, G. (1971*a*; first pub. 1923), *History and Class Consciousness* (Cambridge, Mass.: MIT Press).

—— (1971*b*; first pub. 1910), *Soul and Form* (London: Merlin).

—— (1972), *Studies in European Realism* (London: Merlin).

Lukes, S. (1973), *Emile Durkheim* (Harmondsworth: Penguin).

Lyotard, J.-F. (1984), *The Post-Modern Condition: A Report on Knowledge* (Minneapolis: University of Minnesota Press).

McBride, W. L. (1977), *The Philosophy of Marx* (London: Hutchinson).

McLellan, D. (1971), *The Thought of Karl Marx* (London: Macmillan).

—— (1977) (ed.), *Karl Marx, Selected Writings* (Oxford: Oxford University Press).

McLemore, S. D. (1991), 'Simmel's "Stranger": A Critique of the Concept', in L. Ray (ed.), *Formal Sociology* (Aldershot, Hants: Edward Elgar), 263–71.

Mandel, E. (1962), *Marxist Economic Theory* (London: Merlin Books).

—— (1970), *An Introduction to Marxist Economic Theory* (New York: Pathfinder Press).

Mann, M. (1986), *The Sources of Social Power, A History of Power from the Beginning to A.D. 1760* (Cambridge: Cambridge University Press).

—— (1995), 'Sources of Variation in Working Class movements in 20th Century Europe', *New Left Review*, 212: 14–55).

Mann, T. (1961), *The Magic Mountain* (London: Secker & Warburg).

Mannheim, K. (1938), *Ideology and Utopia* (London: Routledge & Kegan Paul).

Marcuse, H. (1969), *Eros and Civilisation* (London: Sphere Books).

Marshall, G. (1980), *Presbyteries and Profits: Calvinism and the Development of Capitalism in Scotland, 1560–1707* (Oxford: Oxford University Press).

—— (1982), *In Search of the Spirit of Capitalism* (London: Hutchinson).

Marshall, T. H. (1973; first pub. 1950), *Class, Citizenship and Social Development* (Westport, Greenwood).

Marx, K. (1964), *Pre-Capitalist Economic Formations* (London: Lawrence & Wishart).

—— (1968a; first pub. 1848), *The Communist Manifesto* in *Marx and Engels: Selected Works* (London: Lawrence & Wishart).

—— (1968b; first pub. 1859), Preface to *A Contribution to the Critique of Political Economy*, in *Marx and Engels: Selected Works* (London: Lawrence & Wishart).

—— (1968c; first pub. 1852), *The Eighteenth Brumaire of Louis Bonaparte*, in *Marx and Engels: Selected Works* (London: Lawrence & Wishart).

—— (1968d; first pub. 1845), *Theses on Feuerbach*, in *Marx and Engels: Selected Works* (London: Lawrence & Wishart).

—— (1969; first pub. 1862), *Theories of Surplus Value, II* (Moscow: Progress Publishers).

—— (1970; first pub. 1867), *Capital, I* (London: Lawrence & Wishart).

—— (1971), *Karl Marx: The Early Texts*, ed. D. McLellan (Oxford: Oxford University Press).

—— (1972; first pub. 1865, *Capital, III* (London: Lawrence & Wishart).

Marx., K. (1973b; first pub. 1859), Introduction to *The Grundrisse: Foundations of the Critique of Political Economy* (London: Allen Lane and Penguin Books).

—— (1974), *Economic and Philosophical Manuscripts of 1844* (London: Lawrence & Wishart).

—— (1976; first pub. 1847), *The Poverty of Philosophy*, in K. Marx and F. Engels, *Collected Works*, vi. *1844–1848* (London: Lawrence & Wishart), 105–212.

—— (1977a; first pub. 1846), *The German Ideology*, in *Karl Marx, Selected Writings*, ed. D. McLellan (Oxford: Oxford University Press).

—— (1977b; first pub. 1875), 'Critique of the Gotha Programme', in *Karl Marx, Selected Writings*, ed. D. McLellan (Oxford: Oxford University Press).

Mead, G. H. (1938), *Mind, Self and Society* (Chicago: Chicago University Press).

Meillasoux, C. (1972), 'From Reproduction to Production', *Economy and Society*, 1: 93–105.

Michels, R. (1911/1962), *Political Parties* (New York: Collier).

Miller, R. W. (1991), 'Social and Political Theory: Class, State, Revolution', in T. Carver (ed.), *The Cambridge Companion to Marx* (Cambridge: Cambridge University Press).

Mitzman, A. (1971), *The Iron Cage: An Historical Interpretation of Max Weber* (New York: Alfred Knopf).

Moore, B. (1966), *The Social Origins of Dictatorship and Democracy* (Harmondsworth: Penguin).

Mouzelis, N. P. (1990), *Post-Marxist Alternatives: The Construction of Social Orders* (London: Macmillan).

Nietzsche, F. (1957), *The Use and Abuse of History* (Indianapolis, Ind.: Bobbs-Merrill).

Nisbet, R. (1967), *The Sociologicak Tradition* (London: Heinneman).

Oakes, G. (1984), Introduction to *Georg Simmel: On Women, Sexuality and Love* (New Haven: Yale University Press).

Ollman, B. (1971), *Alienation* (Cambridge: Cambridge University Press).

Owen, D. (1994), *Maturity and Modernity: Nietzsche, Weber, Foucault and the Ambivalence of Reason* (London: Routledge).

Parkin, F. (1982), *Max Weber* (Chichester: Ellis Horwood).

Parsons, T. (1947) Introduction to M. Weber, *The Theory of Economic and Social Organization* (New York: Oxford University Press).

—— (1951), *The Social System* (New York: Free Press).

—— (1965), Introduction to M. Weber, *The Sociology of Religion* (London: Methuen), pp. ix–lxvii.

—— (1966), *Societies, Evolutionary and Comparative Prespectives* (Englewood Cliffs, NJ: Prentice Hall).

—— (1973), 'The Superego and the Theory of the Social System', in P. Roazen (ed.), *Sigmund Freud* (Englewood Cliffs, NJ: Prentice Hall).

Pearce, F. (1989), *The Radical Durkheim* (London: Unwin Hyman).

Pickering, W. F., and Martins, H. (1994), *Debating Durkheim* (London: Routledge).

Popper, K. (1957), *The Poverty of Historicism* (London: Routledge & Kegan Paul).

—— (1959), *The Logic of Scientific Discovery* (London: Hutchinson).

Poulantzas, N. (1976), *Classes in Contemporary Capitalism* (London: New Left Books).

Powers, C. H. (1991), 'In Search of Simmelian Principles: An Alternative Interpretation of Simmel's Work', in L. Ray (ed.), *Formal Sociology* (Aldershot, Hants: Edward Elgar), 353–5.

Ray, L. (1991) (ed.), *Formal Sociology* (Aldershot, Hants.: Edward Elgar).

Rex, J., and Moore, R. (1967), *Race, Community and Conflict* (Oxford: Institute of Race Relations & Oxford University Press).

Rickert, H. (1962), *Science and History* (Princeton: Van Nostrand).

Rose, N. (1996), 'Identity, Genealogy, History', in S. Hall and P. du Gay, *Questions of Cultural Identity* (London: Sage), 128–50.

Rubin, G. (1984), 'The Traffic in Women: Notes on the "Political Economy" of Sex', in R. Reiter (ed.), *Toward an Anthropology of Women* (New York: Monthly Review Press), 157–210.

Runciman, W. G. (1966), *Relative Deprivation and Social Change* (London: Routledge & Kegan Paul).

—— (1972), *A Critique of Max Weber's Philosophy of Social Science* (Cambridge: Cambridge University Press).

—— (1983), *A Treatise on Social Theory, I. The Methodology of Social Theory* (Cambridge: Cambridge University Press).

—— (1989), *A Treatise on Social Theory, II. Substantive Social Theory* (Cambridge: Cambridge University Press).

—— (1995), 'The 'Triumph' of Capitalism as a Topic in the Theory of Social Selection', *New Left Review*, 210: 33–47.

Rustin, M. (1991), *The Good Society and the Inner World* (London: Verso).

Sacks, K. (1984), 'Engels Revisited, Women, the Organisation of Production and Private Property', in R. Reiter (ed.), *Toward an Anthropology of Women* (New York: Monthly Review Press), 211–34.

Sartre, J.-P. (1957), *Being and Nothingness* (London: Methuen).

—— (1963), *The Problem of Method* (London: Methuen).

—— (1976), *Critique of Dialectical Reason* (London: New Left Books).

Sayer, D. (1991), *Capitalism and Modernity: An Excursus on Marx and Weber* (London: Routledge).

Scaff, L. A. (1991), 'Weber, Simmel and the Sociology of Culture', in L. Ray (ed.), *Formal Sociology* (Aldershot, Hants: Edward Elgar), 106–35.

Schutz, A. (1972), *The Phenomenology of the Social World* (London: Heinemann).

Shils, E., and Young, M. (1953), 'The Meaning of the Coronation', *Sociological Review*, 1: 63–81.

Simmel, G. (1950), *The Sociology of Georg Simmel*, ed. by Kurt H. Wolff (New York: Free Press).

—— (1955), *Conflict and the Web of Group Affiliations* (Glencoe, Ill.: Free Press).

—— (1968), *The Conflict in Modern Culture and Other Essays* (New York: Teachers College Press).

—— (1971), *Georg Simmel on Individuality and Social Forms*, ed. D. Levine (Chicago: Chicago University Press).

—— (1984), *Georg Simmel: On Women, Sexuality and Love*, ed. G. Oakes (New Haven: Yale University Press).

—— (1990; first pub. 1900), *The Philosophy of Money* (London: Routledge).

Solzhenitsyn, A. (1968), *Cancer Ward* (London: Bodley Head).

Spencer, H. (1971), *Structure, Function and Evolution*, ed. S. Andreski (London: Nelson).

Swingewood, A. (1991), *A Short History of Sociological Theory* (Basingstoke: Macmillan).

Taylor, C. (1977), *Hegel* (Oxford: Oxford University Press).

—— (1989), *Sources of the Self* (Cambridge, Mass.: Harvard University Press).

—— (1991), *The Ethics of Authenticity* (Cambridge, Mass.: Harvard University Press).

Thompson, E. P. (1965), *The Making of the English Working Class* (London: Gollancz).

Thompson, K. (1982), *Emile Durkheim* (Chichester: Ellis Horwood).

Tonnies, F. (1957), *Community and Association* (London: Routledge & Kegan Paul).

Trotsky, L. (1967), *History of the Russian Revolution, I* (London: Sphere Books).

Turner, B. S. (1992), *Max Weber: From History to Modernity* (London: Routledge).

—— (1996), *For Weber* (London: Sage).

Turner, J. H. (1991), 'Marx and Simmel Revisited: Reassessing the Foundations of Conflict Theory', in L. Ray (ed.), *Formal Sociology* (Aldershot, Hants: Edward Elgar), 47–58.

Walby, S. (1990), *Theorizing Patriarchy* (Oxford: Blackwell).

Wallerstein, I. (1974), *The Modern World System* (New York: Academic Press).

Wallwork, E. (1972), *Durkheim: Morality and Milieu* (Cambridge, Mass: Harvard University Press).

Weber, M. (1930; first pub. 1904–5), *The Protestant Ethic and the Spirit of Capitalism* (London: Allen & Unwin).

—— (1947; first pub. 1922), *The Theory of Social and Economic Organisation* (New York: Oxford University Press).

—— (1949), *The Methodology of the Social Sciences* (Glencoe: Free Press).

—— (1951; first pub. 1915), *The Religion of China* (Glencoe: Free Press).

—— (1952; first pub. 1921), *Ancient Judaism* (Glencoe: Free Press).

—— (1958; first pub. 1921), *The Religion of India* (Glencoe: Free Press).

—— (1965; first pub. 1922), *The Sociology of Religion* (London: Methuen).

—— (1978; first pub. 1925), *Economy and Society: An Outline of Interpretive Sociology* (New York: Bedminster).

Weinstein, D., and Weinstein, M. A. (1993), *Postmodern(ized) Simmel* (London: Routledge).

Winch, P. (1958), *The Idea of a Social Science* (London: Routledge & Kegan Paul).

Wittfogel, K. A. (1963), *Oriental Despotism* (New Haven: Yale University Press).

Woolf, V. (1929), *A Room of One's Own* (London: Hogarth).

Wright, E. O. (1978), *Class, Crisis and the State* (London: New Left Books).

—— (1989), 'Models of Historical Trajectory: An Assessment of Giddens's Critique of Marxism', in D. Held and J. B. Thompson (eds.), *Social Theory and Modern Society: Anthony Giddens and his Critics* (Cambridge: Cambridge University Press), 77–102.

Wrong, D. (1957), 'The Oversocialised Conception of Man in Modern Sociology', in L. Coser and B. Rosenberg (eds.), *Sociological Theory* (New York: Collier Macmillan).

Zaretsky, E. (1973), *Capitalism, The Family, and Personal Life* (New York: Harper & Row).

Zeitlin, I. M. (1968), *Ideology and the Development of Sociological Theory* (Englewood Cliffs, NJ: Prentice Hall).

Index

International Kierkegaard Commentary

Volume 5
Eighteen Upbuilding Discourses

International Kierkegaard Commentary

Volume 5

Eighteen Upbuilding Discourses

edited by
Robert L. Perkins

MERCER UNIVERSITY PRESS

ISBN 0-86554-879-X   MUP/H654

International Kierkegaard Commentary
Eighteen Upbuilding Discourses
Copyright ©2003
Mercer University Press, Macon, Georgia 31210-3960 USA
All rights reserved
Printed in the United States of America

The paper used in this publication meets the minimum requirements
of American National Standard for Information Sciences—
Permanence of Paper for Printed Library Materials, ANSI Z39.48-1984.

Library of Congress Cataloging-in-Publication Data

Kierkegaard, Søren, 1813–1855.
[Atten opbyggelige taler. English]
Eighteen upbuilding discourses / edited by Robert L. Perkins.
pp. cm. — (International Kierkegaard commentary ; 5)
Includes bibliographical references and index.
ISBN 0-86554-879-X (alk. paper).
1. Spiritual life—Christianity.
I. Perkins, Robert L., 1930–   . II. Title. III. Series.
BV4505.K3713 2003
248.4—dc21

2003005535
CIP

Contents

Acknowledgments

All the contributors to the volume would desire to make acknowledgments, but it is a privilege reserved for the editor. Those whom the contributors would have named will be content to have served their friends and colleagues.

I have the privilege of thanking a number of persons at Stetson University who have supported my work in general and the *International Kierkegaard Commentary* in particular: H. Douglas Lee, president of Stetson University, Grady Ballenger, dean of the College of Arts and Sciences, Rob Brady, chair of the Department of Philosophy.

The advisory board, C. Stephen Evans and Sylvia Walsh, and the volume consultant, George Pattison, read all the contributions, offered valuable insights into the articles, and also made numerous recommendations. Dr. Julia Watkin of the University of Tasmania continues to be particularly helpful in suggesting possible authors and tracking down obscure allusions in Kierkegaard's texts. The interest of Mercer University Press and especially the efforts of Senior Editor Edmon L. Rowell, Jr. are deeply appreciated. Princeton University Press gave permission to quote from *Eighteen Upbuilding Discourses* and other translations to which they hold copyright.

Permission to reprint "When That Single Individual Is a Woman," by Sylvia Walsh and published in *Kierkegaard Studies Yearbook 2000*, was graciously given by the publisher, Walter de Gruyter of Berlin and New York and is hereby gratefully acknowledged.

The several contributors and I also thank our families for the lost evenings and other scattered hours while we pursued these tasks. Finally, I wish to thank my wife, Sylvia Walsh, for assistance at every stage of this project and for making our life together an unutterable joy.

Robert L. Perkins

Sigla

AN   "Armed Neutrality." See *Point of View* (PV).

BA   *The Book on Adler*, trans. Howard V. Hong and Edna H. Hong. Princeton NJ: Princeton University Press, 1995.

C   *The Crisis and a Crisis in the Life of an Actress*. See CD.

CA   *The Concept of Anxiety*, trans. Reidar Thomte in collaboration with Albert B. Anderson. Princeton: Princeton University Press, 1980.

CD   *Christian Discourses* and *The Crisis and a Crisis in the Life of an Actress*,
C   trans. Howard V. Hong and Edna H. Hong. Princeton: Princeton University Press, 1997.

CI   *The Concept of Irony together with "Notes on Schelling's Berlin Lectures,"*
NSBL   trans. Howard V. Hong and Edna H. Hong. Princeton: Princeton University Press, 1989.

COR   *The Corsair Affair*, trans. Howard V. Hong and Edna H. Hong. Princeton: Princeton University Press, 1982.

CUP   *Concluding Unscientific Postscript to "Philosophical Fragments,"* two vols., trans. Howard V. Hong and Edna H. Hong. Princeton: Princeton University Press, 1992.

EO, 1   *Either/Or*, two vols., trans. Howard V. Hong and Edna H. Hong.
EO, 2   Princeton: Princeton University Press, 1987.

EPW   *Early Polemical Writings*, trans. Julia Watkin. Princeton: Princeton
FPOSL   University Press, 1990.

EUD   *Eighteen Upbuilding Discourses*, trans. Howard H. Hong and Edna H. Hong. Princeton: Princeton University Press, 1990.

FPOSL   *From the Papers of One Still Living* See *Early Polemical Writings* (EPW).

FSE   *For Self-Examination* and *Judge for Yourself!*, trans. Howard V. Hong and
JFY   Edna H. Hong. Princeton: Princeton University Press, 1990.

FT   *Fear and Trembling* and *Repetition*, trans. Howard V. Hong and Edna H.
R   Hong. Princeton: Princeton University Press, 1983.

JC   *Johannes Climacus* or *De omnibus dubitandum est*. See *Philosophical Fragments* (PF).

JFY   *Judge for Yourself!* See *For Self-Examination* (FSE).

JP   *Søren Kierkegaard's Journals and Papers*, ed. and trans. Howard V. Hong and Edna H. Hong, assisted by Gregor Malantschuk. Bloomington and London: Indiana University Press, (1) 1967; (2) 1970; (3–4) 1975; (5–7) 1978.

LD   *Letters and Documents*, trans. Hendrik Rosenmeier. Princeton: Princeton University Press, 1978.

NA   Newspaper articles, 1854–1855. See *The Moment and Late Writings*.

NSBL   "Notes on Schelling's Berlin Lectures." See *The Concept of Irony*.

OMWA "On My Work as an Author." See *Point of View* (PV).

P   *Prefaces* and "Writing Sampler," trans. Todd W. Nichol. Princeton:
WS   Princeton University Press, 1998.

PC   *Practice in Christianity*, trans. Howard V. Hong and Edna H. Hong.
        Princeton: Princeton University Press, 1991.

PF   *Philosophical Fragments* and "Johannes Climacus," trans. Howard V. Hong
JC   and Edna H. Hong. Princeton: Princeton University Press, 1985.

PV   "On My Work as an Author," "The Point of View for My Work as an
OMWA Author," and "Armed Neutrality," trans. Howard V. Hong and Edna H.
AN   Hong. Princeton: Princeton University Press, 1998.

R   *Repetition*. See *Fear and Trembling* (FT).

SLW   *Stages on Life's Way*, trans. Howard V. Hong and Edna H. Hong.
        Princeton: Princeton University Press, 1988.

SUD   *The Sickness unto Death*, trans. Howard V. Hong and Edna Hong.
        Princeton: Princeton University Press, 1980.

TA   *Two Ages: the Age of Revolution and the Present Age. A Literary Review*,
        trans. Howard V. Hong and Edna H. Hong. Princeton: Princeton
        University Press, 1978.

TDIO   *Three Discourses on Imagined Occasions*, trans. Howard V. Hong and Edna
        H. Hong. Princeton: Princeton University Press, 1993.

TM   *"The Moment" and Late Writings*, trans. Howard V. Hong and Edna H.
NA   Hong. Princeton: Princeton University Press, 1998.

UDVS   *Upbuilding Discourses in Various Spirits*, trans. Howard V. Hong and Edna
        H. Hong. Princeton: Princeton University Press, 1993.

WA   *Without Authority*, trans. Howard V. Hong and Edna H. Hong. Princeton:
        Princeton University Press, 1997.

WL   *Works of Love*, trans. Howard V. Hong and Edna H. Hong. Princeton:
        Princeton University Press, 1995.

WS   "Writing Sampler." See *Prefaces* (P).

SKS   *Søren Kierkegaards Skrifter*, ed. Niels Jørgen Cappelørn, Joakim Garff, Jette
        Knudsen, Johnny Kondrup, and Alastair McKinnon. Published by Søren
        Kierkegaard Forskningscenteret. Copenhagen: Gads Forlag, 1997ff.

SKS, K *Kommentar til Søren Kierkegaards Skrifter*. Published by Søren Kierkegaard
        Forskningscenteret. Copenhagen: Gads Forlag, 1997ff.

Introduction

Upbuilding, or edification, is the central theme of Kierkegaard's authorship: "only the truth that builds up is truth for you" (EO, 2:354). He stressed life development and the necessity of a lifeview for an author in his first work, the little book on Andersen, *From the Papers of one Still Living*. *Either/Or*, Part One, sketches numerous lives, victims, and victimizers, who are in desperate need of upbuilding or, more pathetically, rebuilding, or is the proper term, rebirth? The letters of Judge William in *Either/Or*, Part Two, lay out the basic psychological presuppositions for upbuilding a life, presuppositions that Kierkegaard never repudiated, although he did deepen and enlarge them even as he rejected the comfortable complacency of the Judge. The crucial sermon that closes the volume shows the necessity of transcendence to break the domination of social conformity and worldliness that can appear as moral smugness. These early works should have made clear to each and all Kierkegaard's basic intention to become an upbuilding religious author, one critical of much in the common life.

Somewhere along the way, probably soon after the publication of *Either/Or*, Kierkegaard developed a plan to publish a number of upbuilding discourses to "accompany" the pseudonymous works, even those he had not yet written. These discourses, collectively called *Eighteen Upbuilding Discourses* are the focus of the commentaries in this volume. We have to infer Kierkegaard's reasons for writing them, but the popularity of the worst modes of life presented in *Either/Or*, Part One, no doubt contributed mightily to his decision (PV, 20).

How the discourses "accompany" the pseudonymous works is far from clear and the putative relation has led to difficulties for those who look for some explicit references back and forth between the two series. Overt connections are visible but also few and far between. The discourses take a tack that is, for the most part, loosely parallel to the pseudonymous literature, but the approach to the issues raised is often oblique. Some key concepts are treated in both series, but the mode of presentation insures the independence of both expositions, though reading them together does enrich our understanding and increases our capacity to appropriate them in our thinking and into our life's practices. Thus Kierkegaard's treatment of the most important issues of human existence is approached from several perspectives. The sheer inventiveness of the two approaches, the pseudonymous writings and the upbuilding discourses, is remarkable.

Kierkegaard also published a large number of other upbuilding, Christian, and confessional discourses, but they are not related to other signed or pseudonymous books the way Kierkegaard claims those collected in *Eighteen Upbuilding Discourses* to be. The discourses have been the most neglected of all his works, though that unfortunate situation is changing. There is a real sense in which the discourses are the keystone of the authorship, a literary production directed to the upbuilding of all, even and especially the inhabitants of Christendom.[1]

There is an odd and nonchalant continuity between the six books that make up *Eighteen Upbuilding Discourses*. The discourses appear to be just thrown together, suggesting an ad hoc, "as we roll along" kind of disorder and casualness. For instance, the subject of patience appears in the title of the last discourse in one book and in both of the titles in the next. Any careful literary critic would wonder why he did not put these three together in one volume. This arrangement, if indeed the contents of the volumes were planned, suggests an overburdened effort to make the discourses appear assembled more or less by accident.

By contrast, if the reader thinks this arrangement is just accidental, that the discourses have no plan, then he or she should

---

[1]I had written this paragraph before reading Pia Søltoft's excellent essay, "Recent Danish Literature on Upbuilding Discourses [of] 1843 and 1844 and *Three Discourses on Imagined Occasions,*" in *Kierkegaard Studies Yearbook 2000*, ed. Niels Jørgen Cappelørn, Hermann Deuser, and Jon Stewart together with Christian Fink Tolstrup (Berlin FRG and New York: Walter de Gruyter, 2000) 251-60. Søltoft's agreement strengthens my confidence in these views. See also Mark L. Taylor, "Recent English Language Scholarship on Kierkegaard's Upbuilding Discouses," 273-99, and Eberhard Harbsmeier," Die erbaulichen Reden Kierkegaards von 1843 bis 45 in der deutschen Rezeption," 261-72, in the same volume.

really think about Kierkegaard as a literary strategist.[2] It just may be that in spite of the financial losses he incurred when the discourses were remaindered, he smiled internally, realizing that his plan for a collection had succeeded by means of a failure. Is it possible that these discourses are as indirect a communication as "The Seducer's Diary" and that Kierkegaard used his own name as a pseudonym? He does make every effort to make them appear to be "without authority."

I would suggest, contrary to both of the views mentioned above, that the collected volume as we have it has a beginning, a middle, and an end; that there is development, even a tightly knit one, and that upbuilding is the unifying theme. I would not go so far as to suggest that once the idea of the "accompaniment" was conceived, the sequence of the subjects of the discourses was determined. The placement of the discourses on patience in two volumes, mentioned above, suggests a growth of conception of the plan to accompany. He just kept thinking about patience. The collection of all the discourses in *Eighteen Upbuilding Discourses* results in a sustained religious and philosophic exposition of a profound moral psychology, perhaps the most original since Augustine[3] in its capacity to unite the religious and the common world of human competence, confusions, and the incoherent but powerful passions into a single compelling vision. Certainly *Eighteen Upbuilding Discourses* is the most conceptually innovative work

---

[2]How to read Kierkegaard has been a much-discussed question since at least the publication of Louis Mackey's *Kierkegaard: a Kind of Poet* (Philadelphia: University of Pennsylvania Press, 1971). Other prominent studies include H. Holmes Hartshorne, *Godly Deceiver: The Nature and Meaning of his Pseudonymous Writings* (New York: Columbia University Press, 1990); Roger Poole, *Kierkegaard the Indirect Communication* (Charlottesville and London: University of Virginia Press, 1993); Sylvia Walsh, *Living Poetically: Kierkegaard's Existential Aesthetics* (University Park PA: Pennsylvania State University Press, 1994); and Michael Strawser, *Both/And: Reading Kierkegaard from Irony to Edification* (New York: Fordham University Press, 1997).

[3]The efforts of Thomas Aquinas and Dante in moral psychology, though both magnificent achievements, appear to be thorough Aristotelian reworkings of the Augustinian synthesis of Christian theology and the Neoplatonism they knew. Their achievements are two of the more important footnotes referred to by Whitehead.

in ethics and moral psychology in continental philosophy between Kant and Nietzsche.[4]

Eighteen Upbuilding Discourses is, as a result, a remarkable book. And full of surprises too. And frustrating cul-de-sacs. One example of each must suffice.

The surprise is that there are eighteen discourses. They were published in just over fifteen months, between 16 May 1843 and 31 August 1844, in six small books. The story of how they were all gathered together has been frequently told, most recently in the historical introduction to the volume in the Princeton series (EUD, xxi-xxii). For most people the eighteen discourses, 401 pages in the current English translation, would be a considerable literary production for so short a time. However, during that time Kierkegaard also wrote and published *Fear and Trembling, Repetition, Philosophical Fragments, The Concept of Anxiety,* and *Prefaces.*[5] This production in itself is virtually unbelievable as a human achievement, but the combination of all this and the discourses provokes wonder and awe.

The cul-de-sac is that Kierkegaard specified that these were to be called "discourses" and not "sermons." He had reasons for this distinction, and several discussions appear in the literature and in this volume.[6] These discussions have some interest, but there seems to be no necessary reason to challenge his designation. Still, some of these discourses appear to be more like sermons than others. By contrast, some passages have the odor of a college lecture hall. However, the capacity of some of the discourses to communicate orally is in doubt. They are addressed to the cultured

---

[4]This comment is extremely limited in scope by the reference to philosophy. Thus the works associated with the pseudonym, Judge William, *Upbuilding Discourses in Various Spirits,* and *Works of Love* are deliberately excluded.

[5]*Either/Or* had already been published on 20 February 1843. *Three Discourses on Imagined Occasions,* the first-named volume of upbuilding discourses, appeared 29 April 1845, followed by *Stages on Life's Way* the next day, 30 April 1845. *Concluding Unscientific Postscript to "Philosophical Fragments"* appeared on 27 February 1846.

[6]See EUD, xiv, for a brief discussion of the principal concerns. European scholarship has been more interested in this issue than American. See the recent work by George Pattison in this volume and in the essays mentioned in n. 1 above.

elite, but many of the elite and most of the ordinary folks would have had a difficult time listening to them had they been offered in the pulpits of Copenhagen.[7] Although the external literary form is that of a discourse, the actual literary genre is not so easy to identify.

How are we to read the discourses? There are as many ways to approach them as there are readers. That is not quite the proper question.

How do the discourses read us? This question is a better approach, for though we are apparently the readers, it is actually the discourses that compel us to reflect and to examine ourselves. The discourses are by no means Socratic interrogations, that is, Platonic dialogues. There is a profound moral psychology in Plato based in reason, irony, and the aporetic. Kierkegaard's is far more complex, for its Platonic presuppositions are nourished by the history of the struggle of Christianity against its environment. It is not that Kierkegaard has done research and knows the history and concepts of Christian moral psychology so much as he reflects on his own experience and culture and re-creates it in current idiom. Thus there is both continuity and difference in his treatment of the age old issues of worldliness, to name just one instance that is common to the whole tradition. The latter's "bondage of the will"[8] is recreated in the aesthete's sense of impotence.[9]

One last remark. The form of a religious discourse is quite off-putting to many of our contemporaries. As a literary form it is moribund, but, no critical reader of philosophy should be put off by the literary expression. Heidegger, for one, was not, though his approval of the upbuilding discourses was, naturally, qualified by

---

[7]Some Kierkegaard lover may object to this remark, but I offer the last five lines on p. 187 and the first two on p. 188 (Hongs' translation) in my defense. Few passages in Kierkegaard so clearly need rewriting. There are other examples.

[8]Augustine, *Confessions*, bk. 8, esp. chap. 5. Of course, the same book records the powerful reintegration and empowerment of his person, an event we should still call by its religious name, conversion.

[9]"I am as timorous as a *sheva* . . . " (EO, 1:22). "I have, I believe, the courage to doubt everything . . . but I do not have the courage to acknowledge anything . . . " (EO, 1:23). A careful reading can multiply these two references many times over.

his own views.[10] Having said that, it is time to turn to the authors so they may share the fruits of their efforts.

Introducing the Authors

When a new reader begins to learn something of the discourses two issues focus his or her attention: the first is the relation of Regine Olsen, Kierkegaard's onetime fiancée , to the discourses, and the second most likely issue is the description of the discourses by Johannes Climacus, the pseudonymous author of *Concluding Unscientific Postscript to "Philosophical Fragments."* Thus, we will begin with that most personal of issues, the colorful closeness of the discourses to the greatest emotional crisis in Kierkegaard's life before proceeding to the more exegetical question of Johannes Climacus's appraisal of the discourses.

Andrew J. Burgess's essay, "Kierkegaard's Discourses on 'Every . . . Perfect Gift' as Love Letters to Regine," reveals the details of the discourses that pertain to the pain both Kierkegaard and she felt over the breaking of the engagement. However, Burgess moves beyond his discovery and interpretation of all the pertinent texts relating to their relation to the recent discussions/debates between Jean-Luc Marion and Jacques Derrida over the nature of gift, giving, and receiving. Burgess explores the closer connection between Kierkegaard and Marion than that between Kierkegaard and Derrida. But the most interesting turn in his argument is that

---

[10]Hubert L. Dreyfus authoritatively discusses the relation of Heidegger and Kierkegaard in his *Being-in-the-World: A Commentary on Heidegger's 'Being and Time', Division I* (Cambridge MA and London: MIT Press, 1991) 283-340. Other pertinent studies of the Kierkegaard-Heidegger relation include John M. Hoberman, "Kierkegaard's 'Two Ages' and Heidegger's Critique of Modernity" in *International Kierkegaard Commentary: "Two Ages,"* ed. Robert L. Perkins (Macon GA: Mercer University Press, 1984) 223-58; Dan Magurshak, "Despair and Everydayness: Kierkegaard's Corrective Contribution to Heidegger's Notion of Fallen Everydayness," in *International Kierkegaard Commentary: "The Sickness unto Death,"*, ed. Robert L. Perkins (Macon GA: Mercer University Press, 1987) 209-37, and Patricia J. Huntington, "Heidegger's Reading of Kierkegaard Revisited: From Ontological Abstraction to Ethical Concretion," in *Kierkegaard in Postmoderninsm,* ed. Martin J. Matuštík and Merold Westphal (Bloomington and Indianapolis: Indiana University Press, 1995) 43-65.

Burgess shows the limits of the biographical approach to Kierkegaard's authorship.

Sylvia Walsh continues the examination of the import of the first two discourses focusing a subtext on gender relations. Walsh finds that though Kierkegaard does not endorse political and social movements on behalf of woman's liberation, there is much in the discourses to support equality between the sexes in social, economic, and political contexts. Basing her argument squarely on the analysis of the single individual, a concept that unites the individual and the universal (EUD, 10), Walsh shows that Kierkegaard spoke broadly against the denial of universality and for spiritual equality (EUD, 13). The most profound and far-reaching notion is that the spiritual equality so strongly stressed in numerous discourses can supply the basis for the universal claim for woman's social liberation. When this universal concept is internalized it becomes the criterion by which to judge or interpret the social world and that in turn creates first the possibility and then the necessity for external or social equality. In the meantime the spiritual ideal becomes the basis of a consolation and hope for those caught in situations of inequality, oppression, and violence. This consolation is not just for heaven but is expressed as hope in this world. This is the substance of the general message of hope addressed to the single individual, be that person Regine or anyone else.

In his article, "Is the Religion of *Eighteen Upbuilding Discourses* Religiousness A?" Thomas C. Anderson examines Climacus's treatment of the upbuilding discourses in *Concluding Unscientific Postscript to "Philosophical Fragments."* Anderson examines three central notions: the nature of God, eternal salvation, and the human being's relation to God and to eternal salvation. His first finding, one which others have also detected, is that Climacus's treatment of Religiousness A in *Concluding Unscientific Postscript* is not altogether clear. This discovery is not very encouraging, but Anderson pursues his question, and his general conclusion is that much of the language in *Eighteen Upbuilding Discourses* draws upon Christianity for its concept of God and as a result goes beyond immanent religion. Much of the confusion concerning Religiousness A is caused by Climacus's mixing of two senses of it, a Socratic and a Platonic version. At the same time, the Socratic is used to criticize the Platonic understanding of the religious. Another complication is that Climacus to some extent agrees with Religiousness A that religious deepening can lead persons to recognize that, in relation to God, they can do nothing. Obviously this conclusion enforces the difference between God and persons, so Religiousness A can never lead one to lose his or her existence in some abstraction or lead to pantheism as Climacus claims about the Platonic form. Also when he suggests that the reality of God can be asserted only on faith, Climacus agrees with the Socratic understanding of Religiousness A. By contrast, regarding immortality, there are indications that Climacus believes in the natural immortality of the soul in agreement with the Platonic version of Religiousness A and in contrast to the Socratic understanding where such a belief is simply a matter of faith. Finally, some of the discourses do refer directly to Christian theological notions. Given all these complications, Anderson concludes that, "at the very least" it is incorrect, without serious and detailed qualification, to classify the discourses within Religiousness A, as Climacus thinks.

The next several articles, those of Pattison, Shakespeare, Mooney, and Lotti, examine Kierkegaard's rhetoric and language as performative acts.

George Pattison in his essay, "The Art of Upbuilding", examines the understanding of the notion of upbuilding in the age of Kierkegaard. Although (probably unfortunately) the notion is moribund today in the "age of entertainment," it had a currency in the Golden Age of Denmark, and, Pattison claims, familiarity with it will help us understand what Kierkegaard meant to accomplish in the religious discourses. The way in is through an early work of J.P. Mynster, "Remarks Concerning the Art of Preaching" (1810). There is no evidence that Kierkegaard knew Mynster's work, but Kierkegaard was familiar with his "live" sermons and read the printed versions when they appeared. The aim of Pattison's essay is to offer a short exposition of Mynster's understanding of preaching, emphasizing those ideas that Kierkegaard would react to, whether positively or negatively. Mynster, for his part, says in a review that one of the discourses was a "sermon," a remark that no doubt caught Kierkegaard's attention. However, perhaps the crux of the issue between them is Mynster's remark that "the Church is not a mission station." Kierkegaard, more aware of the crisis of Christianity in the modern age, could not accept the comforting understanding of upbuilding Mynster deduced from this view of the church and the limits it put on other goals of preaching. A perceptive reading of *Eighteen Upbuilding Discourses* in the light of Mynster's view of the church prophesizes the final attack Kierkegaard made on the institutional church in Denmark.

Steven Shakespeare in his article, "A Word of Explanation: Transfiguring Language in Kierkegaard's *Eighteen Upbuilding Discourses*," attempts to resolve, in a rather deconstructive way, some of the difficulties many experience when they first read the discourses. The discourses seem primarily to be polished literary works and the collection more so, written by an author who is very much in charge of the scene. However, appearances can be deceiving. The difficulty is further complicated because the discourses do not conform to the ordinary expectations of upbuilding writing. Shakespeare points out that the Prefaces to each collection of discourses deny authorial authority as clearly as any pseudonym, forcing the reader to come to terms with the discourses themselves rather than with the author. What is true for the discourses is also true for the language of the discourses. It attempts to unlayer the accretions of public custom, private practice, and social cliché in order that the demand, the requirement, the criterion can speak with authority again for itself.

Edward F. Mooney in his essay, "Words that Silence as They Build: Against a Boundlessly Loquacious Mind," asks: How do the discourses instill silence? Using language borrowed from William James, Mooney suggests that though the analytic ability of the modern intellect is indeed useful, some moderns forget the interests and passions that pointed us down discursive paths in the first place. Reality is now measured by the analytic tools of a specific area, that is, chemistry or sociology, tools that cannot grasp the existential, religious, and spiritual dimensions of our lives. The result is an overintellectualization of the common life that neglects or despises primitivity, simplicity, and silence. Mooney attempts to clarify the experiences, intuitions, and felt convictions to which Kierkegaard appeals by looking at his stylistic modes. Kierkegaard uses words to limit, to abridge the power of words by using language discursively and nondiscursively at one and the same time. There are, however, times when the discursive and nondiscursive uses of language must be kept separate, an example for Kierkegaard being the use of language in liturgical or worship contexts as distinct from academic activities such as research and writing. Kierkegaard's capacity to handle language and issues in this multilayered way is one source of his fascination for many.

Michael Lotti goes to the heart of the many fundamental educational issues in his essay, "An Education in Possibility." Lotti's question is: What is the fundamental end of education? Is it the accumulation of a lot of data between the student's ears or is it dedicated to the eliciting and provoking of the students' growth toward maturity and authenticity? Both of these are legitimate goals in the education of youth, but the achieving of maturity and authenticity is the more difficult of the two. To focus the existential growth of persons, Lotti recovers the term, "education in possibility" from *The Concept of Anxiety* and then interprets it in the light of the discourses to show how they offer a genuine education in possibility. He discusses a number of Kierkegaard's literary techniques and shows how they lead the person to a deeper self-understanding.

Piety struggles with the eternal mystery of the reality of evil and the forgiveness of sins; how one "discovers" sin but does not "see" it.

In her essay, "Good Faith," M. G. Piety forces an issue concerning the two discourses entitled, "Love will hide a multitude of sins" (EUD, 55-78). These discourses discuss an almost intractable problem: the Christian faith is either foolish or unrealistic to deny the reality of evil, specifically the evil of human sin, or it is contradictory because the reality of evil is very much a teaching of orthodox Christianity. Trying to maintain both positions suggests that the faith is an expression of what Jean-Paul Sartre called "bad faith," and hence the title of her article. As one would expect of Piety, she undertakes to discuss the tough cases of gratuitous evil. She argues steadfastly for the neither/nor, that Christianity is neither hypocritical nor foolish, but rather that it exercises good faith.

The next two articles, those by Roberts and Colton, probe Kierkegaard's significance for virtue theory.

In his essay, "The Virtue of Hope in *Eighteen Upbuilding Discourses*," Robert C. Roberts argues that Kierkegaard is a member of the group of ethical thinkers he calls "virtuists." He uses this expression rather than "virtue ethics" or "virtue ethicists" in order to emphasize that the tradition of virtue ethics includes ethical virtues such as a sense of duty or justice, prudential virtues such as industry and cleanliness, and also theological or spiritual virtues such as faith or hope. "Virtuist" is an inclusive term denoting all these varieties, though one may study, write, or speak of only a small range of them. To be a virtuist is to believe that persons are capable of forming identifiable characters, for instance, as when we say, "You can depend on Mary." However, nothing is guaranteed in human life, for some persons go astray and fail to develop themselves as stable characters. The reason we can make this distinction is that there is some minimal human possibility that can be developed or lost. The way we exist, the full range of our actions, indicate our virtues or lack thereof. Turning to the virtue of hope, Roberts exploits Kierkegaard's brief explicit discussions of the concept, but then he pays much more attention to the way hope underlies other virtues and appears in unexpected contexts. It may just be that this virtue has found its spokesman in "The Virtue of Hope in *Eighteen Upbuilding Discourses*."

Ronald G. Colton continues Roberts's focus on virtue ethics in a detailed close reading of *Four Upbuilding Discourses* (1843) in the context of virtue theory by recalling, as an hermeneutical tool, Kierkegaard's concept of repetition in his article, "Perception, Emotion, and Development in the *Four Upbuilding Discourses* of 1843: Narratives of Repetition and Kierkegaard's Moral Pedagogy." Colton takes seriously the claim made by Kierkegaard that the discourses "accompany" the pseudonymous works. The third discourse in this series receives special attention, for it focuses the strategies of repetition, which in turn thematically shape the narrative account of moral perception, emotion, and moral development implicit in *Eighteen Upbuilding Discourses*.

The remaining articles focus on upbuilding virtues and debilitating vice. Those of Possen, Ferguson, and Perkins focus on the virtue of patience, while that of Andic takes a hard look at cowardliness.

David D. Possen begins and ends his article with reference to Meno's unanswered question, "Can virtue be taught?" In Plato's dialogue, *Meno*, the question is unanswered because it is unanswerable within Meno's suppositions, based as they are on the Sophistic teachings about "virtue." The Sophists can offer a primer for their version of virtue or teach the whole course for x-number of drachmas; Socrates cannot. However, if one changes the presuppositions, then it may be possible for virtue to be taught, though not by the issuance of a manual but by the tasks and events of life itself. Possen's article is about necessary presuppositions for gaining and losing one's soul. And, this is the important point, we gain and/or lose our souls in and through the suffering and trials we endure in life. In Kierkegaard's moral psychology, impatience is not just an annoyance to ourselves and others. Rather it is testimony to the lack of a person's centered focus on the essentials of his or her own moral choice of the self. At the end of the article, we have learned that patience cannot be taught in Meno's sense of the word because, according to Possen, patience is taught not just by life and its trials, but also by the thought of death.

Harvie Ferguson in his essay, "Patience: the Critique of Pure Naïveté," approaches the concept through earlier dogmatic formulations and through Kierkegaard's own approach that challenges the tradition, after first briefly discussing his unique literary approach. On this last matter Ferguson leaves us with the paradox that only the patient who does not need the discourses can read them and the impatient who needs them cannot—because they are impatient. (That may well express what many have felt when they read the discourses for the first time.) Commenting briefly on Tertullian, Augustine, and Petrarch, Ferguson urges that Kierkegaard is not attempting to revive these points of view in spite of their insights. Rather, a new understanding of patience is necessary based on the psychological and sociological assumptions of modernity. In this age patience is devalued as complacency, indifference, or in popular parlance, "hanging in there." The last bastion of patience is the endurance of an illness—hence our use of the word, patient. The modern world has committed itself to the concept of autonomy, but that is a very narrow concept that undercuts family, community and even the political order. Some of the unexpected outcomes of this concept are pointed out in *Two*

Ages: leveling, envy, indifference, boredom, to name a few. Kierkegaard (a.k.a. Anti-Climacus) set out the etiology of these manifestations in *The Sickness unto Death* under the rubric of despair. The foundation of Kierkegaard's critique of modernity found in *Two Ages* and in *The Sickness unto Death* originates in the analysis of patience and impatience found in *Eighteen Upbuilding Discourses*. Kierkegaard restructures the concept of patience as an expression of the authentic choice of oneself consonant with modernity; patience is autonomy in its fullest sense, a sense that does not lead to despair but rather to responsibility and care.

Martin Andic examines the penultimate discourse, "Against Cowardliness," in an essay of the same name. The Biblical text that Kierkegaard quotes (II Timothy 1:7) mentions neither courage nor cowardliness, but rather, "a spirit of power and of love and of self-control." These three are, of course, spiritual virtues based in faith, and they scarcely sound like cowardliness. Rather the opposite, courage. Following his understanding of a Christian moral psychology, Kierkegaard does not try to relate faith to courage in any "how to" fashion, but to define spiritual courage as a gift of God, courage becoming almost a stand-in for faith. Spiritual courage is qualitatively different from the natural virtue but does not supercede it; rather it transforms it by presupposing it. Once we recognize that in relation to God we are always in the wrong and/or that our need of God is our highest perfection, God then is able to complete our natural courage as a divine grace affirming God's confidence in us. Now God goes with us to face every trial, even that last enemy, death. Spiritual pride is self-defeating and a form of cowardliness, the denial of our finitude, our sin, and our mortality. Humility, knowing who we are, is then the key to spiritual courage.

The last things anyone thinks about when reading *Eighteen Upbuilding Discourses* are politics and the common life. Thus Robert L. Perkins's essay, "Upbuilding as a Propaedeutic for Justice", comes last in the collection. *Eighteen Upbuilding Discourses* accentuates the individual, personal piety, the religious, the spiritual virtues, etc. Yet Perkins argues that the text is and should be an important one in the education of political leadership. The origin of this strange idea is found in the Preface to "The Single Individual," sometimes also called "Two Notes" (PV, 103-104), where Kierkegaard in passing urges patience on "the impatient politician." Moreover, Kierkegaard claims that "the religious is the transformed rendition of what the politician . . . has thought in his most blissful moment" (PV, 103). As a thought experiment Perkins invents a figure, the patient politician, and interprets the essay that urges young people to remember their Creator while they are young (EUD, 233-52) as the fundamental conceptual and intellectual preparation for political leadership, for the patient politician. Perkins then offers a political reading of the three discourses in which patience is named in the title, concluding with another argument against that Hydra of Kierkegaard criticism, otherworldliness: If even *Eighteen Upbuilding Discourses* has clear political import, then the charge of Kierkegaard's otherworldliness is just wrongheaded.

Thus far the authors can lead us. We invite the readers of *International Kierkegaard Commentary* to learn what they can here and then by their development of better analytical and synthetic skills to become our teachers.

Robert L. Perkins

1

Kierkegaard's Discourses on "Every . . . Perfect Gift" as Love Letters to Regine

Andrew J. Burgess

Although Søren Kierkegaard speaks to a wide audience, his works sometimes carry a message addressed to one particular reader, his former fiancée, Regine (Olsen) Schlegel. Looking back later, near the end of the nineteenth century, Regine herself reports she used to recognize "bits of her past, memories of the engagement period, studies of him and of her" in the writings he sent to her.[1] This is especially true of the three 1843 discourses on their favorite Bible passage, the text James 1:17: "Every good and every perfect gift is from above and comes down from the Father of lights, with whom there is no change or shadow of variation" (JP, 6:6800; cf. 6:6965). Regine claims that when she looked into the volume that contained the first of these three discourses, and saw its dedication to "An Unnamed Person," she believed it was dedicated to her.[2] For his part, Søren admits in 1849 that he had not only intended the volume for Regine but that, in the same first discourse on the James text, he had even included a private message to her (JP, 6:6472, 18).

This discourse, and the passage within it with the hint to Regine, thus offers a special challenge for interpretation, and the two later discourses on this text only increase the difficulty. Although Kierkegaard commentators often have to remind students of the dangers of becoming distracted by the details of his

---

[1]Bruce H. Kirmmse, *Encounters with Kierkegaard: A Life as Seen by His Contemporaries* (Princeton NJ: Princeton University Press, 1996) 42.

[2]Kirmmse, *Encounters*, 51.

romance with Regine, here is a piece of text that seems to cry out for just this sort of analysis. If not the three discourses as a whole, at least the private hint to Regine asks, indeed begs, to be footnoted to events in his life. How else shall the reader make sense of it? The investigation thus proceeds in several stages. First, it has to do some biographical work on the setting for the particular part of the 1843 discourse that was meant for his former fiancée, and also on a possible message she may have sent him. Then, it will tackle the perplexing question of what it could possibly mean for anything to be a "good and perfect gift" from God in the sense the discourses describe. Finally, having looked separately at the life setting and conceptual content of the discourses, the essay will turn around and reflect on a problem that can arise when the two are inappropriately put together.

A Secret Message to Regine

Before the exercise can get underway, some methodological remarks are in order. The reasons Kierkegaard's works invite attention to his life lie deeply rooted in his philosophy. The story of his broken engagement, for example, plays a key role in all three of the pseudonymous works he published in 1843—*Either/Or, Repetition*, and *Fear and Trembling*—and it returns again at even greater length in *Stages on Life's Way*, published in 1845. Both *Either/Or* and *Stages on Life's Way* include long diaries containing circumstances that partially correlate with known events in Kierkegaard's life. *Stages on Life's Way* even includes verbatim the note with which he sent back Regine's ring when he broke the engagement (JP, 6:6472, 8).

Recently scholarship on Kierkegaard has been enriched by the publication of two major studies of the relation between his life and works, Joakim Garff's *SAK: Søren Aabye Kierkegaard—En Biographi*[3] and Alastair Hannay's *Kierkegaard: A Biography*,[4] as well as by the translation of such works as Jørgen Bukdahl's *Søren Kierkegaard and the Common Man*.[5] The need for such an approach is

---

[3](Copenhagen: Gads Forlag, 2000).
[4](Cambridge: Cambridge University Press, 2001).
[5](Grand Rapids MI: Eerdmans, 2001).

indisputable. As Hannay writes, "It is impossible to read Kierke-gaard properly without knowing where he stood in relation to his time, its culture, even life in general, and as I anticipate the reader will come to agree, it would be ridiculous to suppose that the life can tell us nothing about how the texts are to be understood."[6]

The achievement of these works is all the greater in that a biographical approach to Kierkegaard faces dangers that earlier scholars were not always able to avoid. Writing about Kierke-gaard's discourses, including one on the text "Every good and every perfect gift," George Pattison warns his readers about "the murky waters of the Brandes-Heiberg-Lowrie school of explaining the authorship by means of the life."[7] Pattison's statement will be welcome words to any professor who has ever struggled to dissuade a student from writing a term paper along those lines.

Although any author can be misused in this way, Kierkegaard is particularly susceptible, because of his notion of "subjective truth." According to the work *Concluding Unscientific Postscript*, written by Kierkegaard's pseudonym Johannes Climacus, there are at least two ways in which something can be said to be true (CUP, 1:199-204). In the usual sense of truth, which Climacus calls "objective truth," something is true when the object of truth is as reported. But there is also a second sense of truth, in which truth consists not in correspondence to reality, nor in coherence of ideas, but rather in putting into practice the truths one professes. This second sense of truth Climacus calls "ethical truth" or, because it is truth in relation to an ethical agent or subject, "subjective truth." A reader attracted to Kierkegaard's notion of subjective truth may thus be inclined to depend upon Kierkegaard's biography to evaluate the truth of his works. After all, such a reader may think, what better way is there to find out whether Kierkegaard's works are "subjectively true" than to check whether someone has put them into practice?

The hint to Regine Schlegel that Søren Kierkegaard wrote into the first 1843 discourse on "Every Good and Every Perfect Gift" is

---

[6]Hannay, *Kierkegaard*, xi-xii.

[7]George Pattison, "A Dialogical Approach to Kierkegaard's *Upbuilding Discourses*," *Zeitschrift für neuere Theologiegeschichte* 3 (1996): 188.

a good example of a passage with respect to which this danger can arise. Here is a piece of text that cannot be fully interpreted without drawing on external information from Søren and Regine's lives, tempting a reader to judge the truth of the discourses on the basis of whether Søren and Regine put into practice the ideas of the rest of the discourse.

Just getting started on the historical investigation, however, is not easy. The set of discourses bristles with unanswered questions. What is the passage referred to? Can Søren expect Regine to identify it with the discourse? How would she appreciate its significance?

In 1849, six years after publishing this discourse, Søren writes in his journal a tantalizing note about its personal relevance for his relationship to Regine: "The preface to the two upbuilding discourses is intended for her, as are many other things: the date of the book, the dedication to father. And in the book itself there is a slight hint about giving up, that one loses the beloved only if one gets him to act against his conviction. She has read it—that I know from Sibbern" (JP, 6:6472, 18). The mention of Sibbern here refers to his teacher F. C. Sibbern, who deliberately kept in contact with both Regine and Søren and thus kept them in communication. But what is the passage referred to? Plainly, only one passage fits his description, and it is located at a point Regine could not have missed. The discourse starts out speaking of the people who tried to accept the words of the biblical text but could not penetrate them. Then the viewpoint shifts abruptly from the third person to the second: "and you, my listener, said it was bound to happen" (EUD, 35). From that point a section several pages long begins, addressed to the "troubled one" and "the grieving," telling how "you" (his "listener") had begged heaven with a wish, how you had struggled ever harder, even tempting God.

The steps of this struggle between the listener and God recall the five stages Elizabeth Kübler-Ross defines in her classic study of the stages of grief in circumstances of death and dying[8]—denial and isolation, then anger, bargaining, depression, and finally acceptance. The discourse follows twice through this grief cycle,

---

[8]Elizabeth Kübler-Ross, *On Death and Dying* (New York: Macmillan, 1969).

the first time playing down and the second time emphasizing the stage of anger. At first the grieving ones were in denial, "continually disappointed" as they tried to lift themselves up (EUD, 34-35), but since they were "slow to anger" they did not become upset and defiant even when they were "tossed about by the passion of the wish" (EUD, 35). The listener then began to bargain, trying to get eternity to give the wish because of a willingness to "wait in quiet longing" (EUD, 36). Then, "when your fruitless wishes had exhausted your soul" in depression (EUD, 36), your mind "developed in itself the meekness that is receptive to the word that was implanted within you" (EUD, 36). Alternatively, the discourse goes on, a page later, you (the listener of the discourse) may have been too "old," too "mature" for such "childish ideas about God" (EUD, 37). Instead, your denial took the form of "defiance" and you were "swift to anger" and "your heart grew hard" (EUD, 37). In this case the bargaining with God would become bitter, a penetrating scream, because you believed that your voice was "so powerful that it was bound to resound through the heavens and call God out of his hidden depths," but just as before "the chill of despair froze your spirit" (EUD, 38). Still, "when you then humbled yourself under God's mighty hand and, crushed in spirit, sighed: My God, my God, great is my sin, too great to be forgiven—then heaven opened again" (EUD, 38). Although the grief cycle in the discourse explicitly describes the anguished petitioner before God, it is hard not to imagine Regine applying the ideas also to her own personal struggle over the engagement with Søren, as she read this passage aloud to herself.

Suddenly, right between the twin cycles of grief stages described in the discourse, comes a paragraph that slightly interrupts the context and seems to be the very message Søren wanted to convey to Regine:

> Let us for a moment speak foolishly and in a human way. Suppose there was someone whom you really trusted because you believed he had your welfare at heart; but you had one idea of what was beneficial for you, and he had another. Then would you not try to persuade him? You would perhaps plead with him and implore him to grant your wish. But when he persisted in his refusal, you would stop imploring him and you would say: If by my pleas I moved him to do what he did not consider to be right, then something even more terrible would happen. I would

> have been weak enough to make him just as weak; then I would
> have lost him and my trust in him, although in the moment of
> intoxication I would have called his weakness love. (EUD, 37)

Here is exactly the hint Søren said he wanted to make to Regine,
about "giving up, that one loses the beloved only if one gets him
to act against his conviction." The message is set so neatly into the
context that it works for the general reader as well, but the fit is
loose enough that the passage might easily be an insertion into the
discourse.

Could Søren be confident that Regine would discover such a
message? That would be the easiest part of his task. Reading
sermons aloud is just what Søren used to do with Regine; we learn
from his journals that the two were accustomed to read Mynster's
sermons together once a week (JP, 5:5689). In fact, with these
particular discourses, he knew from Professor Sibbern that she was
reading them. Regine corroborates Sibbern's report herself. In her
memoirs a half century later she says the "religious discourses"
were for her the favorite part of Kierkegaard's writings, and she
even describes how she and her husband Fritz Schlegel used to sit
together and read the writings aloud to each other and discuss
them.[9]

Søren could be sure she would understand the message
because of the hours he had spent with her. The text "Every Good
and Every Perfect Gift" was part of a special bond between them.
Years later, in 1852, he tells how in the previous year he was in
church and Regine was sitting nearby when they heard the pastor
Paulli begin to preach on this text from James 1:17:

> Upon hearing these words she turns her head, hidden by the
> one sitting next to her, and looks toward me very fervently. I
> looked vaguely straight ahead.
> The first religious impression she had of me is connected
> with this text, and it is one I have strongly emphasized. I actually
> did not believe that she would remember it, although I do know
> (from Sibbern) that she has read the *Two Discourses* of 1843,
> where this text is used.

---

[9]Kirmmse, *Encounters*, 37.

... Paulli finished reading the text aloud. She sank down rather than sat down, and I actually was somewhat worried as I was once previously, for her movement is so vehement.

Now to go on. Paulli begins to preach. I believe I know Paulli fairly well; it is inexplicable how he came to think of such an introduction. It may have been intended for her. He begins: These words, all good gifts, etc., "are implanted in our hearts." Yes, my listeners, if these words should be torn from your hearts, life would lose all its value for you etc. I seemed to be standing on thorns.

For her it must have been overwhelming. I had never exchanged a word with her, had walked my way, not hers—but here it seemed as if a higher power were saying to her what I had been unable to say. (JP, 6:6800, p. 443)

If this text could affect her so strongly nearly ten years after the engagement was broken, no doubt it would have had even more meaning for her back in 1843, when *Two Discourses* were written. Nor should it be surprising, then, that three of the nine discourses he wrote during that first year were based on that text, at a time when he was acutely aware she was reading the discourses. He did not publish another discourse on the text until two months before he died.

Thus, in a discourse about good and perfect gifts, Søren gives Regine a private gift of consolation. Or was it the "higher power" that gave the gift, as he speculated after Paulli's sermon? He does not know. Whether it was for her a perfect gift, whether indeed she even received it as a gift, is uncertain. In a letter the year after Søren died, Regine writes that she had not been aware of the full depth of their relationship until she saw the posthumous papers, since, she says, "my modesty frequently forbade me to see things in that light—a light to which, however, my unshakable faith in him repeatedly led me back."[10]

A Secret Message to Søren

If the messages Søren sent as gifts to Regine were sometimes enigmatic, her gifts to him were no less so. Of course, some of her gifts and messages were simply the conventional exchanges

---

[10]Kirmmse, *Encounters*, 50.

between lovers. After his death, for example, Regine wrote his nephew Henrik Lund for certain rings and broaches and for all the letters, some of which "were supposed to be burned,"[11] and it may be surmised that some of these things, perhaps all, came from her during the engagement period. The breakup of the engagement in 1841, however, changed everything, including the kind of messages they sent to each other.

In 1852, three years before he died, Søren received a little gift on Christmas eve. What the gift was he does not tell the reader, only that it was sent with *Flyveposten*, a popular magazine, and that, he says, it "pertains to the preface to *Upbuilding Discourses in Various Spirits*, but also, if I am not altogether wrong, to the two upbuilding discourses of 1843." Then he adds: "I do not know why, but it occurred to me—could it be possible that she could have done this." Later he sees her on the way to church, and her behavior leads him to think that she is waiting for him there and wants to speak with him, but before she can do that he has entered the church. He is altogether uncertain and writes: "Maybe she was waiting for someone else out there in the passage, maybe she was waiting for me, maybe that little gift was from her, maybe she wanted to speak with me, maybe, maybe." (JP, 6:6835).

"Maybe . . . maybe, maybe." His conclusion leaves the reader as puzzled as he was, with one other puzzle besides: what was the gift that he received that pertained to the preface to *Upbuilding Discourses in Various Spirits*?

A glance at that preface shows why it would recall Regine and the earlier discourses, since that preface, like all the other prefaces to the books of discourses that preceded it, starts out with a set formula, which in a paragraph addresses itself to "that single individual," he calls it, who was initially Regine, but becomes in later discourses, more generally, the ideal reader. The distinctive part of the preface to *Upbuilding Discourses in Various Spirits* comes in the other paragraph, which develops a new theme. It runs:

> When a woman works on a cloth for sacred use, she makes every flower as beautiful, if possible, as the lovely flowers of the field, every star as sparkling, if possible, as the twinkling stars of

---

[11]Kirmmse, *Encounters*, 49.

the night; she spares nothing but uses the most precious things in her possession; then she disposes of every other claim on her life in order to purchase the uninterrupted and opportune time of day and night for her sole, her beloved, work. But when the cloth is finished and placed in accordance with its sacred purpose—then she is deeply distressed if anyone were to make the mistake of seeing her artistry instead of the meaning of the cloth or were to make the mistake of seeing a defect instead of seeing the meaning of the cloth. She could not work the sacred meaning into the cloth; she could not embroider it on the cloth as an additional ornament. The meaning is in the beholder and in the beholder's understanding when, faced with himself and his own self, he has in the infinite remoteness of separation infinitely forgotten the needlewoman and her part. (UDVS, 5-6)

In a sense the gift comes from the woman, true, but properly speaking it comes only from God. The woman's gift has to remain anonymous so that the ultimate donor may be recognized.

What kind of gift could it have been that would have reminded Søren both of *Flyveposten* and of such a preface? Perhaps there was something in a special issue of the magazine that recalled this preface, but in that case it is hard to see why Søren would have thought of Regine. Or the apparent reference to a magazine may simply say that the gift arrived "by express mail." Or it may have been that the gift Søren received was an embroidery Regine had made, suitable for an altar cloth, showing a bird that has come and picked a little flower and is about to fly away (EUD, 5). It could be placed within an issue of the magazine and left at his apartment with no other clue, except for a private understanding they shared about this image. Such a hypothesis would help account both for Søren's suspicion and his puzzlement.

A distinctive mark of this particular gift is its elusiveness. Thus if a new historical datum were to be discovered next week in some attic—an issue of the journal bearing Regine's name, for example, a plain reference to her in a poem in an issue of *Flyveposten*, or some marginal marks in her handwriting—then that could not have been the gift Søren received, because then he would not have been so uncertain. This gift he could not identify with any confidence as coming from Regine, only "maybe . . . maybe, maybe."

This inquiry about gift giving stretches the outer limit of strictly historical research, where it might easily become mere speculation, but it still cannot provide a result satisfying to the student fascinated by testing Kierkegaard against the standard of "subjectivity is truth." Were Søren and Regine giving gifts in these instances? Maybe, maybe; and it does not matter much either way. Were they appropriating the message of the scripture text and giving good and perfect gifts? That is a different question, which could only be answered, if at all, after a scrutiny of the discourses.

Good and Perfect Gifts

What is a perfect gift? The discourses and other writings of 1843 contain a remarkably well-developed presentation of what it means to be a gift from God, but each of the three gift discourses repeats the theme in a different way.

After the preface, which contains the message to Regine, the first gift discourse focuses on receiving God's gifts. Each time he repeats the text he returns to this theme. Echoing Paul in I Timothy 4:4, he insists that "Everything created by God is good if it is received with thankfulness" (EUD, 42), even punishment, which should be received as a gift from God, in repentance (EUD, 45-48). Every gift is a gift from God if it is received in thanks to God, even punishment accepted with thanksgiving. Some of the ideas may reflect his personal torment at the time, but none of this comes out in the discourse, since that matter is between him and God. Reflecting much later, in 1849, on the course of his relationship to Regine, he writes that

> I once prayed to God for her as for a gift, the most cherished gift;
> at the time I glimpsed the possibility of carrying out a marriage.
> I also thanked God for her as for a gift; later I had to regard her
> as God's punishment on me—but always I have committed her
> to God and have honestly persisted in doing this. (JP, 6: 6473, 5)

Even one's reception of the gift is a gift of God, so that it is like the gift of a child that is actually purchased by the parents. For example, he says: "In repentance, you receive everything from God, even the thanksgiving that you bring to him, so that even this is what the child's gift is to the eyes of the parents, a jest, a receiving of something that one has oneself given" (EUD, 46).

The second discourse on the gift brings together all three elements of the gift giving: the giver, the gift, and the condition for receiving the gift:

> What earthly life does not have, what no man has, God alone has, and it is not a perfection on God's part that he alone has it, but a perfection on the part of the good that a human being, insofar as he participates in the good, does so through God. . . . What is the good? It is God. Who is the one who gives it? It is God. . . . because God is the only one who gives in such a way that he gives the condition along with the gift, the only one who in giving already has given. (EUD, 134)

As the good, God is both the giver and the gift, and God also gives the condition for receiving the gift. The passage has a heavy Platonist and exemplarist coloring. The good is God; and human beings, insofar as they participate in the good, do so through God. More specifically, David Kangas points out, the passage, together with the whole second discourse on the gift, owes a debt to a Platonist strain in late medieval Christian mysticism.[12] Kangas identifies a distinctive theme, from Meister Eckhart, also in an earlier discourse, where Kierkegaard writes that "God gives not only the gifts but himself with them" (EUD, 99). Kangas concludes, "What links Kierkegaard's concept of God to Eckhart's, and what constitutes the ultimate basis of his critique of Hegelian theology, is the (paradoxical) idea that God is the Good that gives itself, the Good that exceeds itself through itself."[13]

With this terminology of giving of self and of excess, Kangas brings Kierkegaard close to the position of Jean-Luc Marion, in Marion's extended debate with Jacques Derrida over the question of the gift of God.[14] In his lecture "In the Name" Marion derives

---

[12]David Kangas, "The Logic of Gift in Kierkegaard's *Four Upbuilding Discourses*," *Kierkegaard Studies Yearbook 2000*, ed. Niels Jørgen Cappelørn, Hermann Deuser, and Jon Stewart (Berlin: Walter de Gruyter, 2000) 113-18.

[13]Kangas, "Logic of Gift," 115.

[14]Jean-Luc Marion, *Reduction and Givenness: Investigations of Husserl, Heidegger, and Phenomenology* (Evanston IL: Northwestern University Press, 1998; orig., 1989); Jacques Derrida, *Given Time I: Counterfeit Money* (Chicago: University of Chicago Press, 1992; orig. 1991) and *The Gift of Death* (Chicago: University of Chicago Press, 1995; orig. 1992); Jean-Luc Marion, *Being Given* (Stanford CA: Stanford University Press, 2002; orig. 1997); *God, the Gift, and Postmodernism*, ed. John D.

a position similar to Kierkegaard's from the work of the early Christian mystic Dionysius the Areopagite, identifying a "third way," besides positive or negative theology, which goes beyond naming or conceiving God. According to Marion, in this third way "the excess of intuition [a Husserlian term] overcomes, submerges, exceeds, in short saturates, the measure of each and every concept."[15] In the ensuing discussion between Marion and Derrida, Marion then applies this way of speaking about God to the notion of God as giver of self and as gift. To Derrida's objection that as soon as something is identified as a gift, either by the giver or receiver, it is canceled as a gift and becomes merely a matter of barter,[16] Marion asserts that "you can perfectly well describe a fully achieved or given gift" in cases where one of the three factors in gift giving (giver, gift, or receiver) is missing.[17] For example, the giver or receiver may be anonymous, or the receiver may be someone from whom no gratitude or repayment can be expected.

Inserting Kierkegaard into this Marion-Derrida dialogue stretches the imagination, but it is not impossible. Kierkegaard might perhaps not share Marion's desire to be considered a true follower of the ruling philosophy (in this case, Husserl's phenomenology), but he would be on Marion's side regarding the question of the whether it is possible for human beings to give genuine gifts. His justification for that view, however, would differ from Marion's. Whereas Marion chooses extraordinary circumstances (such as money found whose owner is unknown, for an example of a gift without a giver), Kierkegaard picks his examples from among everyday cases where selfishness or ingratitude might be expected but where a person might possibly be so transformed in attitude as to overcome the obstacles to a true gift giving spirit. The only perfect gift one human being can give another, he says,

---

Caputo and Michael J. Scanlon (Bloomington: Indiana University Press, 1999); Robyn Horner, *Rethinking God as Gift: Marion, Derrida, and the Limits of Phenomenology* (New York: Fordham University Press, 2001).

[15]In *God, the Gift, and Postmodernism*, 40.

[16]Derrida, "On the Gift," *God, the Gift*, 59; also in *Counterfeit Money*, 10-14, 24, 30, 156; and, with respect to the treatment of Abraham's sacrifice of Isaac in Kierkegaard's *Fear and Trembling*, in *The Gift of Death*, 95-96.

[17]"On the Gift," *God, the Gift*, 62-63.

is love (EUD, 157), but love is "from above," that is, from God, so that love is not only the giver and the gift but also the condition love gives in order that human beings can receive love. All of this sounds abstract and unrealistic, and one can imagine how exasperated Derrida might get at such talk, but Kierkegaard thinks concretely, especially in the third discourse on good and perfect gifts. To Kierkegaard the decisive point in each case he brings up is that, since every perfect gift is from God, no human "giver" has any business feeling proud, and no human "receiver" needs to feel indebted. Anyone who does so has simply misconstrued the situation.

Still, might not a human being end up feeling deeply indebted to God and thereby, in Derrida's terms, cancel the gift? That is a question John Caputo poses also to Marion at the end of the dialogue with Derrida, but with the time for discussion over he answers it himself:

> I worry whether we do not end up in debt in Marion. But is not for-giving the highest moment of the gift? Should anyone end up in debt from a gift? Should we be in debt to God for the gift of creation? If creation is a gift, then it is not a debt but something we affirm and celebrate.[18]

Love Letters from God

One principle Kierkegaard shares with both Derrida and Marion is the anonymity of the gift. If Kierkegaard does not insist, with Derrida, on the absolute unknowableness of the pure gift, he agrees with both of the others that this should be gift giving's ideal. This principle also underlies Kierkegaard's hermeneutic for scriptures, making them what he calls "love letters from God."

Kierkegaard's clearest statement of the principle comes in the third discourse on the gift, where the thrust is on the equality of all people and of all good gifts. For, he says,

> when you consider that every good gift is from above, then the right hand you stretched out to give will quickly hide itself, and the left hand will never find out anything; then you will rejoice

---

[18]Caputo, in "On the Gift," *God, the Gift*, 77.

> in secret, as a benefactor may, rejoice in the same way as he who
> received the gift, and both of you rejoice over the same thing,
> that the gift came from above, since there really was an invisible
> hand that gave it—it was your hand; and you are convinced that
> there is an invisible hand that will truly make it a good gift—it
> is God's hand. (EUD 148)

That is, since all good gifts are from above, from God, the
human giver can only rejoice in secret. Both the giver and recipient
are happy that the gift comes from the "invisible hand" of God. Or
rather, the "invisible hand" is both the secret hand of the anonymous donor and also, as giver of a good and perfect gift, the hand
of God. The secrecy of the donation therefore does not eliminate
thankfulness but only adds to it. Since all good gifts are from God,
both giver and receiver will unite in thanking not only each other
but also God (EUD, 152).

This passage sheds a peculiar light on the 1852 incident in
which Søren came to think that Regine might have left him a gift
without letting him know it was from her. For if that gift was
indeed from Regine, and if, following his own advice, Søren
thanked God for it, then, according to the Bible passage on "Every
good and every perfect gift is from above" both of them shared,
that gift was a good and perfect gift, a gift from God. And in that
case, Regine possibly did understand Søren's message and replied
in the only appropriate way, with silence.

The passage also illuminates part of what the preface to each
of the books of discourses means when it dedicates the books to
"that individual," thereby designating both Regine and the reader
who may approach the discourses in the same spirit as she did. To
the extent that the discourses Søren wrote as a gift to Regine were
good and perfect gifts they have to be considered pseudonymous
writings, for the actual author is God. Moreover, the reader who
receives those discourses properly, whether that person is Regine
or someone else, might be understood as pseudonymous too.

If all that holds true, then the same principles Søren put
forward for understanding scripture also apply to his own
upbuilding discourses—*if*, of course, they are given and received
in the proper spirit, as gifts of God. According to a famous passage
in *For Self-Examination*, scripture is to be read as if it were love
letters from God (FSE, 26-30). The lover, he says, knows that before

he can start to read the letter there are some preliminaries that have to be gotten out of the way, such as translating the letter if it is in a foreign language, but he willingly does this in order to start reading. And when he starts reading, he wants to be "alone with the letter," for otherwise, he says, I am "not reading the letter from my beloved" (FSE 30). Similarly, if someone is reading the scriptures properly, then the consulting of the scholarly apparatus, the translating and the commentaries and the puzzling over obscure passages, is only preliminary to the main event, which is to be alone with the text and hearing it as love letters from God. Now, although Kierkegaard's discourses are certainly not scriptures, to himself or to anyone else, the same principles apply to his writings, if they are read as messages from God. First the discourses have to be translated, their sources uncovered, commentaries compared, and every scrap of available biographical information brought to bear. All the scholarly methodology has to be applied. Nonetheless, even after all this has been done, "that individual" for whom the discourses are written has not yet gotten alone with the letter and begun to read it.

"Alone with the letter"—what a curious phrase. For Kierkegaard it does not mean that the individual is physically isolated but rather that someone is conscious that the text applies directly to oneself and not to anyone else. That is why the notion that one can think that one can check on the truth of Kierkegaard's writings by looking to see whether he applied them to himself is so misleading. It turns the category of subjective truth completely upside down. In fact, Søren Kierkegaard did try to apply his ideas in his own life with great care, but the discourses insist this is not the way in which you, the reader, can find their subjective truth. As *Either/Or* says at the end, "only the truth that builds up is truth for you" (EO, 2:354). The real question is not "Has my neighbor Christophersen done it; has he actually done it?" but "Am I able to do it?" (SLW, 440; CUP, 1:322). Whether Søren or Regine actually did it is irrelevant for you as "that individual," that is, as "subjective thinker." The important question is whether you did it yourself. From your standpoint the discourse, understood as a love letter, is directed to you, not to Regine. Reading the discourses in any other way is just as misguided as sneaking a look at someone else's mail. It follows that the biographical origin of a discourse may be not more but less relevant to an understanding of Kierke-gaard's writing than it would be of some other author, at least if someone is trying to understand him on his own terms. "Subjec-tive" understanding means applying the principles to oneself, not checking on whether someone else has done so.

That is why the negative result of the search for Regine's gift is so appropriate, and why it illustrates how a biographical approach is only the start, not the end, for true reading of such a text. If Regine offered an almost perfect gift in 1852, then the reader could still not be anywhere near as certain of this as Søren was, because to the extent of its perfection the gift would be from God to him. By the same token, if Søren's two 1843 discourses were almost perfect gifts to Regine, she would still not find them to be messages from Søren as much as messages from God to her. Most important of all, insofar as the discourses were Søren's almost perfect gifts, his readers would not be inclined to find him in them, much less his relation to Regine, because insofar as the discourses were perfect gifts they would be first and foremost from God.

After all, what, humanly speaking, would a perfect gift be, in Kierkegaardian terms? I imagine finding tucked away in some Copenhagen parsonage a yellowed altar cloth, once used in the nineteenth century but now preserved only out of respect for its age and because of a reluctance to destroy anything hallowed through use at the altar. Embroidered on the cloth are some unfamiliar symbols, centrally among them a bird that has come and picked a little flower and is about to fly away. No one remembers any more who wrote the preface to the upbuilding discourse on which the imagery is based, and no one has found out whose patient fingers embroidered the pattern. I am, of course, not saying there ever was such a cloth. I am only saying that, if there was, it was a good and perfect gift.

2

When "That Single Individual" Is a Woman

Sylvia Walsh

Kierkegaard's *Eighteen Upbuilding Discourses* is a collection of his religious discourses from 1843 and 1844. Nine discourses were published each of these two years, grouped into three series of two, three, and four discourses respectively and issued separately at various times during the year. Each series is accompanied by a preface that is repeated, with minor variations, throughout the collection. The preface always begins with a statement attesting that the speaker is neither a preacher nor a teacher but rather an author without authority who sends these upbuilding discourses— in themselves only a "trifle" or "superfluity"—on a journey in search of "that single individual" (*hiin Enkelte*) who will be "favorably disposed" to receive them and become his reader (EUD, 5, 53, 107, 179, 231, 295).

This designation for the intended reader of these discourses poses an interesting puzzle as to the identity of this figure, but it also prompts a reconsideration of the relation between the particular and the universal, difference and sameness, with respect to the audience and meaning of the discourses. In his journals Kierkegaard remarks that "the point of departure of the pseudonymous writers is continually in the differences—the point of departure in the upbuilding discourses is in the universally human" (EUD Supplement, 476; Pap. VIII2 B 192). The upbuilding discourses thus may be understood as being addressed to every individual and are upbuilding for precisely that reason; that is, they apply equally to all individuals regardless of differences in sex, class, age, education, and religious sophistication (EUD, 240).[1]

---

[1]For example, concerning the difference between the simple or uneducated person and the cultured or educated person, Kierkegaard says: "In my opinion,

This emphasis on sameness, or our common humanity, rather than on differences or particularity as the point of departure for the upbuilding discourses is immediately apparent in the opening discourse from 1843, where Kierkegaard states that faith

> is not only the highest good, but it is a good in which all are able to share, and the person who rejoices in the possession of it also rejoices in the countless human race, "because what I possess," he says, "every human being has or can possess." The person who wishes it for another person wishes it for himself; the person who wishes it for himself wishes it for every human being, because that by which another person has faith is not that by which he is different from him but is that by which he is like him; that by which he possesses it is not that by which he is different from others but that by which he is altogether like all. (EUD, 10)

Consequently, Kierkegaard goes on to affirm in this same discourse that, with respect to sexual differences, "whether he is the mighty male who defies the storm or the defenseless female who only seeks shelter from the gale—this has nothing to do with the matter, my listener, absolutely nothing" (EUD, 13).

---

culture by no means makes upbuilding superfluous: it just makes it more and more necessary . . . because the *cultured person*, if he understands himself . . . will become aware that what we call culture leaves a whole side of the soul unsatisfied, without nourishment and care . . . and he will make it his concern to see to it that this need for upbuilding will increase equally with his increasing culture. . . . With regard to upbuilding, the explicit task is precisely *to develop* deeper and deeper the need that everyone *ought to have.*—For the *simpler people,* however, who also have the advantage neither of the time nor of the circumstances for the cultivation of the spirit, the upbuilding becomes that which cultivates, that which genuinely and nobly cultivates one who nevertheless remains uninitiated into that which cultivates intellectually and esthetically.—Genuine education never makes one grow away from the upbuilding as something one needs less and less, but makes one grow up to the upbuilding as something one needs more and more. . . . The upbuilding does not want to consolidate differences between people any more than the ocean wants to separate. Just like love, the upbuilding wants to unite, if possible, the most different in essential truth" (EUD Supplement, 474; Pap. VIII2 B 188). See also EUD Supplement, 470 (Pap. VII1 B 220), where Kierkegaard writes: "Something that is supposed to serve for upbuilding must never contain a split, as if there were one kind of upbuilding for the simple and another for the wise."

Although differences are downplayed in favor of unity and sameness in the universal human reference of the upbuilding, they nevertheless play an essential role in the identity and experience of that single individual who is the intended recipient of the discourses. In Kierkegaard's journals the category of the single individual is defined dialectically and ironically on the one hand as "the most unique of all," and on the other as "what every human being is" (EUD Supplement, 475; Pap. VIII2 B 192; see also JP 5, no. 5975; Pap. VIII1 A 15). This double meaning of the category, Kierkegaard claims, is operative in the distinction between the pseudonymous works, which employ the first meaning, and the upbuilding discourses, which understand it in the second sense. But this duplexity of meaning, I shall contend, is also operative within the upbuilding discourses themselves.

To see how this is so, let us return to the opening discourse of 1843 on faith, where Kierkegaard uses the example of a "perplexed man" who wishes, in a paternalistic fashion, to do everything for someone he loves in order to procure faith for that individual (EUD, 10-16). What the perplexed man comes to realize is that this is the wrong way to love and that no human being can give faith to another. Thus he is constrained to let go of the other, leaving that person alone to will or grasp faith for himself or herself (EUD, 10-14). This release or withdrawal on the part of the perplexed man precipitates a change in both parties and in their relation to one another: They become like strangers to one another in the installation of the perplexed man "in his limits" and the other "in his rights" (EUD, 14). But the perplexed man also comes to perceive that this separation constitutes "the true meaning" of their relationship, for if he were able to bestow the highest good upon the other, this would mean that he would also have the power to deprive the other of it (EUD, 15). Thus, he thanks God that the other owes him nothing in this regard.

This example is used by Kierkegaard to emphasize not only the singularity of each individual with respect to acquiring faith, which is at the same time a possibility for everyone, but also the need for a proper separation between individuals in personal relations which protects them from abuse of power by one over the other. Given the fact that the first party in the example is referred to as a perplexed man (*Mand*) rather than a perplexed person

(*Menneske*), one is tempted to interpret the text as alluding specifically to heterosexual relations (although it need not be limited to them) and thus to the need for establishing and maintaining nonpaternalistic (if not nonpatriarchal) and nonabusive treatment of women by men in religious matters.[2] If that is its meaning, then the discourse contains a promising message of edification for women in particular—a possibility we shall return to consider more closely later in the paper.

Kierkegaard goes on in this same discourse to further underscore the importance of particularity and difference in individuals by noting that "[w]hen two people learn different things from life, it can be because they themselves are different" (EUD, 22). He illustrates the point this time with an example of two children who are brought up together and always share the same things but "still learn altogether different things" (EUD, 22). Several discourses from 1844 make the same or a similar point. In discussing the necessity for patience in expectancy, Kierkegaard points out the diversity of expectancy in human life, suggesting that persons expect "very different things according to different times and occasions and in different frames of mind" (EUD, 206). In another discourse he notes that what separates individuals from God is "very different for different people" (EUD, 246). And in distinguishing between indifferent and concerned truths—an important epistemological observation that anticipates the distinction between objective and subjective truth in *Concluding Unscientific Postscript*—Kierkegaard characterizes concerned or subjective truths as "not applying universally to all occasions but only specifically to particular occasions" (EUD, 233).[3] In contrast to indifferent or

---

[2]One is reminded here of the notorious passage in *The Sickness unto Death* in which Anti-Climacus states that "in most cases the woman actually relates to God only through the man" (SUD, 50n).

[3]On the contextual nature of feminist epistemology and its compatibility with Kierkegaard's epistemology in *Concluding Unscientific Postscript*, see my article, "Subjectivity versus Objectivity: Kierkegaard's *Postscript* and Feminist Epistemology," in *International Kierkegaard Commentary: Concluding Unscientific Postscript to "Philosophical Fragments,"* ed. by Robert L. Perkins, (Macon GA: Mercer University Press 1997) 11-31. This article is reprinted in slightly revised form in *Feminist Interpretations of Søren Kierkegaard*, ed. Céline Léon and Sylvia Walsh (University Park, Pennsylvania State University Press, 1997) 267-85.

objective truth, which is "equally valid [*lige gyldig*] whether anyone accepts it or not" and "indifferent to the individual's particular condition," concerned truths "are not indifferent to the single individual's particular condition," nor are they "indifferent to how the individual receives" the truth, that is, "whether he wholeheartedly appropriates it or it becomes mere words to him" (EUD, 233). In making a similar distinction between self-knowledge and general truths, Kierkegaard points out in another discourse that

> General discussion of general truths can certainly give a person much to remember and can develop his understanding, but it is of only very little benefit to him. . . . Above all, generality is not for upbuilding, because one is never built up [*opbygges*] in general, any more than a house is erected [*opføres*] in general. *Only when the words are said by the right person in the right situation in the right way, only then has the saying done everything it can to guide the single individual to do honestly what one otherwise is quick enough to do—to refer everything to oneself.* (EUD, 276, emphasis added)

These passages amply demonstrate the particular, contextual nature of the upbuilding discourses within a universal frame of reference. They indicate that context matters; indeed, it is what gives content to, or puts flesh on, the bare bones of the universal, without which the discourses would become general or abstract and consequently not upbuilding for anyone.

Another way Kierkegaard tries to emphasize the importance of context in these discourses is by making a "pilgrimage . . . with the text into differences," that is, multiplying the number of possible situations addressed in the text, as in the discourse on "Every Good Gift and Every Perfect Gift Is From Above" from 1843 (EUD, 145). Almost half the paragraphs in this discourse begin with an "Or" that introduces another variation on the conditions under which a person might be willing to give to others (EUD, 147-56).

Of course, it is impossible to mention every possible situation in a text, and Kierkegaard addresses just this impossibility and its possible consequences in a discourse from 1844. Here he has the single individual protest that "my experience was very different from what you are talking about," implying that the discourse does not apply to him or her (EUD, 193). To this Kierkegaard replies that when "this emphasis on the different" becomes "a staring at heterogeneity" it is not conducive to preserving one's soul and that "if unity does not lie at the base of diversity, similarity at the base of dissimilarity, then everything has disintegrated" (EUD, 193). Even if one's particular situation is not specifically mentioned in a text, then, there is still a common core of human experience to identify with in it.

A second qualification with respect to specificity is set forth in a discourse from 1844. Reflecting on the passage in Ecclesiastes 12:1 which admonishes the reader to "think about your creator in the days of your youth," Kierkegaard suggests that even though the admonition "can be repeated again and again and applies to countless numbers of people, it speaks every time to the single individual . . . as if it spoke to him alone, as if it came into existence solely for his sake, as if it were unconcerned about all the rest of the world" (EUD, 238). Yet, while "it is indeed the case that the admonition's concerned truth addresses itself specifically to the single individual in a particular circumstance of life . . . the discourse about it nevertheless must take good care lest it make the upbuilding conditional upon the accidental," thus becoming untrue (EUD, 239). This would be the result "if one wanted to be built up by the thought of old age, but in a special way so that youth could not be built up by the same thought," or vice versa (EUD, 139-40). Even though a discourse may specifically address itself to a particular condition or time of life, then, it must be applicable to other circumstances or ages as well.

Taking these two qualifications into account, we may nevertheless conclude that both the discourses and "that single individual" who is their intended recipient must be understood specifically as well as universally, in terms of the particular situation and differences that characterize each reader, yet without excluding anyone on the basis of those factors. Since the particular situation and distinguishing characteristics of individuals vary from reader to reader, we may also conclude that the understanding of the discourses will vary according to the particular circumstances of each reader. While each discourse has a general message that applies universally to everyone, it will not be interpreted and appropriated by all readers in the same way, as if their circumstances in life were all the same. Rather, the message is interpreted within the context of the particular circumstances of each person's own life, so that, on the basis of these differences, what each person gleans from them is context-specific, understood and appropriated in terms of the particular conditions of that person's life rather than as a generality.

On the basis of these conclusions, let us now pose a test case of the specificity or contextuality of reference and meaning in this particular collection of discourses. Let us suppose that, on occasion, "that single individual," or the "favorably disposed" intended reader of these discourses, is a woman. As a matter of fact, there is textual evidence that Kierkegaard had one particular woman in mind—Regine Olsen—as the designated reader of these discourses, especially the first series of discourses from 1843, for he indicates as much in his journals (JP 5, no. 6388, 6472; Pap. X1 A 266, X5 A 149). Moreover, Regine confirms in her memoirs (as told to Hanne Mourier and Raphael Meyer) that the religious discourses were dedicated to her, that a copy of the first ones was sent to her by Kierkegaard through F. C. Sibbern, and that she read them with her fiance and later husband, Fritz Schlegel.[4]

If a third party thus reads the first two discourses with Regine Olsen specifically in mind as their intended recipient, it is obvious that Kierkegaard is quite explicitly addressing her recent experience of loss, sorrow, disappointment, and unhappiness over the breakup of their engagement to one another. In the first discourse he encourages her to face the future in the victorious expectancy of faith, which is based on the eternal and thus is never disappointed, rather than approach it with "multifarious expectancy" or "expectancy of something particular," which may or may not be substantiated in time or eternity (EUD, 27-28, 36). Kierkegaard entertains the possibility that her continued faith in him "when the inexplicable happened" may have been wrong (even though commendable in comparison with others who turned away from him) because it is inappropriate to have faith in a human being "in this way," possibly leading one to forget that there is a higher faith in God. However, he rejects this scenario and credits her instead

---

[4]*Encounters with Kierkegaard: A Life as Seen by His Contemporaries*, collected, edited, and annotated by Bruce H. Kirmmse and translated by Bruce H. Kirmmse and Virginia R. Laursen (Princeton NJ: Princeton University Press, 1996) 36-37, 40.

with having, or at least successfully regaining, the expectancy of faith that will see her through this crisis and others (EUD, 24-26). Read in this context, it becomes apparent too that "the perplexed man" mentioned earlier in the discourse is Kierkegaard himself, who records here his own realization that faith, like love, must be presupposed in others and in any case is not something that can be wished into existence for Regine by him or anyone else (EUD, 13, 15; WL, 216-24). In view of the nonpaternalistic, nonabusive character of the relationship that evolves between the perplexed man and his beloved in the discourse, it reveals considerable maturity in Kierkegaard's understanding of the proper attitude and behavior he should maintain toward Regine Olsen in religious matters. Not only does she not owe him anything, he credits her with perseverance in faith at a time when it might have been lacking, precipitating her downfall in doubt and despair.[5]

The second discourse encourages Regine to thank God for the many good and perfect gifts bestowed upon her rather than tempting God to make the divine idea of what is best for her coincide with her own wishes or trying to persuade and implore her beloved (Kierkegaard) to do something he did not consider to be right (EUD, 19-21, 35, 37). In a journal entry from 1849 Kierkegaard alludes to the latter possibility, suggesting that "in the book itself there is a slight hint about giving up, that one loses the beloved only if one gets him to act against his conviction" (JP 6, no. 6472; Pap. X5 A 149:18). Entertaining the possibility that, for a time at least, she may have succombed to anger, hardness of heart,

---

[5]In response to a diary entry in which Kierkegaard presumably states that "she [Regine] was not religiously inclined," Regine suggests in her memoirs that this statement "must have been based on a passing impression" since "the fact that he dedicated the whole of his religious works to [me] . . . indicates that he must have regarded [me] as religious" (Kirmmse, *Encounters with Kierkegaard*, 35-36; see also 40). As Kirmmse points out, the statement attributed to Kierkegaard cannot be found in the journals, but he does say in one entry that "she has no intimation of the specifically religious" (JP 6, no. 6304; Pap. X1 A 15) and in another that she "has had no religious upbringing" (JP 5, no. 5689; Pap. IV A 142). Against the latter charge Regine counters in her memoirs that she "had had a profoundly religious upbringing" (Kirmmse, p. 40). Of course, what Kierkegaard meant by "religious upbringing" may have been very different from what Regine understood it to mean.

despair, and complaints against God because of her suffering and grief, Kierkegaard goes on to remind Regine that when she finally humbled herself before God, "your countenance was renewed, and God's compassionate grace had loved forth [*fremelsket*] in your barren mind the meekness that is receptive to the words" of scripture referred to in the text (EUD, 37-38). In using the phrase "loved forth"—a beautiful expression that is employed again in *Works of Love* in variant forms (*opelsker* and *at elske frem*) to convey the need "to love forth love" in others—Kierkegaard alludes to an earlier communication to Regine (JP 5, no. 5526; Pap. III A 171; WL, 217; see also EUD, 508, note 100). In it he credits her with having loved forth a flowering plant by her "ardent gaze" and the "warmth of her love," reminding her that "there were also times when you despaired of my love or had fearful intimations that our happiness would not last, and a gentle dew of tears refreshed it, and look, it doubled its growth, became twice as beautiful; in this way, too, it was loved forth." Thus, like the first discourse from 1843, the second one in the series is filled with very specific personal allusions and meaning for Regine Olsen in particular, and both are meant to be upbuilding for her specifically in her time of trouble.

But surely these discourses and others in the collection were not written for her alone. We have seen that as upbuilding discourses they have a universal significance which makes them personally applicable to other "favorably disposed" readers as well, including other women. Indeed, we know from the recent research of Bruce Kirmmse and Habib Malik that Kierkegaard had a sizable coterie of female readers in his own time—not altogether to his liking.[6] The celebrated Finnish-Swedish writer, Fredrika (or "Frederikke") Bremer (1801-65), reports in her book, *Life in the North (Liv i Norden)*, published in 1849, that Kierkegaard "has gained a not inconsiderable audience in happy, pleasant Copenhagen, particularly among ladies," who were attracted to his "philosophy of the heart."[7] As the following passage from Kierke-

---

[6]See Kirmmse, *Encounters with Kierkegaard*, 94, 95, 101-103, 297, 106, 110, 124; and Habib Malik, *Receiving Søren Kierkegaard: The Early Impact and Transmission of His Thought* (Washington DC: Catholic University of America Press 1997) 54-77.

[7]Kirmmse, *Encounters with Kierkegaard*, 94. See also Malik, *Receiving Søren Kierkegaard*, 57.

gaard's journals of that year indicates, he thought her statement absurd: "Frederikke has made me into nothing but a psychologist and has supplied me with a considerable audience of women [*Dame-Publikum*]. That is really ridiculous, how in all the world I can be seen as a ladies' author [*Dame-Forfatter*]" (Pap. X1 A 658).

Nevertheless, it is true that women as well as men at that time in Denmark and abroad were attracted to Kierkegaard's writings, especially his religious discourses. Regine reports in her memoirs that she loved the religious discourses "more than all the rest," and Petronella Ross, a friend of F. C. Sibbern, comments in a letter to him that Kierkegaard's "writings are my favorite reading—among the religious sort," although she admits that she has read only "a little of him."[8] Moreover, H. C. Rosted, an assistant school inspector and local historian of the town of Hørsholm, reports in his memoir that Kierkegaard regularly sent copies of his writings to Regine ("Tagine") Reinhard, proprietress of the inn at Hørsholm where he frequently stayed, and that he often had long talks with her about religious questions.[9]

These citations, of course, provide only anecdotal evidence of interest in Kierkegaard's authorship among women of his time, but they do establish that his contemporary audience included female as well as male readers. Of particular interest to us here, however, is whether this group of female readers may have included any *feminists* among them, and if so, whether it is possible for "that single individual" to be a female feminist (assuming that men can be feminists too) who may find something upbuilding in these discourses for her specifically as a feminist. With regard to the first question, recent scholarship indicates that at least two of Kierkegaard's early female admirers were leading feminists of the time.

---

[8]Kirmmse, *Encounters with Kierkegaard*, 40, 101. Kirmmse notes that in an earlier letter to Ross, Sibbern especially recommended to her the discourse on Job's words in the series of four upbuilding discourses from 1843, and on one occasion Ross wrote to Kierkegaard requesting a copy of his *Christian Discourses*, which he apparently sent to her.

[9]Kirmmse, *Encounters with Kierkegaard*, 110. See also Malik, *Receiving Søren Kierkegaard* (72-75), who reports that the diary of Linda Keyser Preus (1829–1880), wife of a Norwegian immigrant pastor in Wisconsin, indicates that she also read several of Kierkegaard's religious works.

One was Fredrika Bremer, who in addition to writing travel books started the Swedish suffragette movement and wrote a novel, *Hertha* (1856), on the condition of women in Sweden; the other was Camilla Collett (1813–1895), a Norwegian novelist and advocate of women's rights who published an anonymous novel, *The Governor's Daughters* (*Amtmandens Døtre*), in 1855 on the condition of women in Norwegian society.[10] In spite of the fact that Kierkegaard personally offended both women by refusing to meet with them when they came to Copenhagen, Bremer contemplated, but finally decided against, including long excerpts from *The Moment* in the English translation of her novel because she thought Kierkegaard would be "almost incomprehensible to foreigners," and Collett may have crafted the heroine of her novel with several female characters from *Either/Or* in mind.[11] Although Malik credits Kierkegaard with being a "negative stimulus" for these women inasmuch

---

[10]Kirmmse, *Encounters with Kierkegaard*, 95; Malik, *Receiving Søren Kierkegaard*, 62-68, on Bremer, including references to secondary works on her, and 68-71 on Collett, with corresponding references to secondary literature on her. See also Julia Watkin, "Serious Jest? Kierkegaard as Young Polemicist in Defense of Women," in *International Kierkegaard Commentary: Early Polemical Writings*, ed. Robert L. Perkins (Macon GA: Mercer University Press, 1999) 7-25. Watkin also refers to Mathilde Fibiger (1830–1872), a teacher and social theorist who wrote a sensational book, *Clara Raphael, Twelve Letters* (1850), challenging the social and ecclesiastical narrow-mindedness of the time, but it is not known whether she was acquainted with Kierkegaard's writings. However, her sister, Ilia Marie Fibiger, was Kierkegaard's nurse at Frederiks Hospital when he was dying, and Kierkegaard's close friend, Emil Boesen, reports that she sent him flowers, which made him happy (Watkin, "Serious Jest," 14 and n.29; Kirmmse, *Encounters with Kierkegaard*, 124, 126).

[11]Malik, *Receiving Søren Kierkegaard*, 64-65 and 69-70. See also Fredrika Bremer, *Hertha*, trans. Mary Howitt (New York: G. P. Putnam & Co., 1856). The English translation does retain some specific references to Kierkegaard, including a brief quotation from a short tract from 1855, "This Must Be Said: So Let It Now Be Said," which the heroine initially responds to quite favorably, according to the narrator, who reports that "she felt that a combating and suffering heart throbbed here in unison with her own, embittered, bleeding, loving, and still, though as in the midst of the flames, seeking to lay hold upon God; and she felt less solitary in the world" (242-43). Later, however, her despair at presumably having been deceived by her lover became so great that "[t]he words of Kirkegaard no longer consoled her," and she threw the tract into the waters of the falls where she had stopped on her journey to confront him (245).

as their novels represent a protest of conventional views of woman reflected in his authorship, neither of them seems to have been positively affected by Kierkegaard on the subject of woman, especially on the burning issue of female emancipation, which he consistently opposed in both his pseudonymous and nonpseudon-ymous writings.[12] It would appear, therefore, that Kierkegaard had little or nothing upbuilding to say to them or other feminists on this score.

If that were the case, however, it would serve to undermine the universal reference and character of the upbuilding disourses, making the female feminist an exception to the universal and presenting a situation to which the discourses do not apply. To consider this possibility, let us return, "once more with feeling," to the upbuilding discourses of 1843 and 1844 and read them empathetically through the eyes of a modern feminist who, if she has any prior acquaintance with Kierkegaard's writings, may not be as kindly disposed toward them as Regine and other conven-tional female readers of his time were inclined to be.[13]

Beginning with the first discourse from 1843 and interpreting it in terms of her own expectancy about the future, our feminist reader may at first be encouraged by the gender inclusiveness or universality of the possibility of faith affirmed in it, and by the nonpaternalistic, nonabusive character of male-female relationships advocated by the author with respect to the acquisition of faith. But her expectancy or wish, like that of Regine, is for something particular in the world. For her, however, it is not marriage to the beloved for which she yearns, as in the case of Regine, but rather for social equality. As she reads on in the text, however, she learns, as did Regine, that her wish may not be granted. Indeed, in a sub-

---

[12]Malik, *Receiving Søren Kierkegaard*, 67, 71.

[13]The quoted phrase is from Louis Mackey, "Once More With Feeling: Kierke-gaard's *Repetition*," in *Points of View: Readings of Kierkegaard* (Tallahassee: Florida State University Press 1986) 68-101. For a range of feminist critiques of Kierke-gaard's views on women, see the essays in *Feminist Interpretations of Søren Kierke-gaard*. See also my article, "Issues That Divide: Interpreting Kierkegaard on Woman and Gender," in *Kierkegaard Revisited*, Kierkegaard Studies Monograph Series 1, ed. Niels Jørgen Cappelørn and Jon Stewart (Berlin: Walter de Gruyter 1997) 191-205.

sequent discourse from 1843, Kierkegaard suggests that while equality before God obtains for both man and woman and is the basis of every upbuilding view of life, it constitutes the divine law and has validity "only when the single individual fights for himself with himself within himself and does not unseasonably presume to help the whole world to obtain external equality, which is of very little benefit, all the less so because it never existed" (EUD, 143). Thus our feminist reader is seemingly being advised not only to give up her wish for social equality but also her fight for it in the world, since such external activity "produces nothing but confusion and self-contradiction, as if true equality could be expressed in any externality as such, although it can be victorious and be preserved in any externality whatever" (EUD, 143).

Here we encounter very early in Kierkegaard's writings a point of view that remains constant throughout his authorship and which presents a problem not only for feminist readers but for other modern social theorists as well. For while a spiritual equality between man and woman, rich and poor, high and low before God is unqualifiedly endorsed in his writings, he does not envision a corresponding social equality that would give concrete expression to this spiritual ideal in external forms. Anticipating the claim in *Works of Love* that Christian equality is not the same as worldly similarity, in these discourses Kierkegaard clearly is not willing to equate genuine equality with a particular external condition or state of affairs in the world (WL, 72).[14] But in the final clause of the statement quoted above, he does leave the door open for the victory and preservation of true equality within any and every external order. However, this concession is also problematic inasmuch as it would seem to be exceedingly difficult if not impossible to establish and preserve true equality for women under certain social conditions—as in the current situation of

---

[14]On the social ethic of *Works of Love*, see my article, "Forming the Heart: The Role of Love in Kierkegaard's Thought" in *The Grammar of the Heart: New Essays in Moral Philosophy & Theology*, ed. Richard H. Bell (San Francisco: Harper & Row, 1988) 234-56. See also Jamie Ferreira, "Other-Worldliness in Kierkegaard's *Works of Love*," in *Philosophical Investigations* 22/1 (1999): 65-79, and my response to her article on subsequent pages in the same issue, "Other-Worldliness in Kierkegaard's *Works of Love*—A Response," 80-85.

Afghanistan women under Taliban rule, or the wholesale marketing of girls and women for sex slavery in Asia and Africa, or the objectification and denigration of women both locally and globally in pornography over the internet and in literature and films readily available at media outlets everywhere—to mention only a few of the ways in which women continue to be subjugated, abused, and exploited in patriarchal cultures of the present age. Surely some social climates are more conducive than others to securing a measure if not the full realization of social equality for women as well as other disenfranchised groups in the temporal realm. But that insight, true as it undoubtedly is, is somewhat beside the point being made here by Kierkegaard, since for him the issue is not quantitative, that is, a matter of particular societies being more or less receptive to the rights of women, but qualitative, inasmuch as in his view true equality is not equivalent to social equality, however much the latter may be realized in any particular society.

Given the inherent imperfection of the temporal realm, which in Kierkegaard's view is wedded to the preservation of differences rather than sameness or equality of persons in likeness to God, how then can true equality be victorious and preserved in the world? The answer put forth in these discourses is that it is only in and through "the hallowed place," that outer and/or inner sanctuary where "every externality is discarded as imperfect, and equality is true for all" and where the single individual is "educated to preserve increasingly this equality in the clamor of the world and with it to penetrate the confusion" (EUD, 141-42, 267). It is clear from the last passage quoted that our feminist reader is not being admonished to give up her fight for equality in the world. On the contrary, she is encouraged

> to fight the good fight with flesh and blood, with principalities and powers, and in the fight to free [her]self for equality before God, whether this battle is more a war of aggression against the differences that want to encumber [her] with worldly favoritism or a defensive war against the differences that want to make [her] anxious in worldly perdition. (EUD, 143)[15]

---

[15]In order to indicate the context-specific character of the text in relation to the female feminist reader, I have substituted and placed in brackets female pronouns for the male ones used by Kierkegaard in the passage quoted here and in

She must continue to contend with the differences, then, but not for the sake of establishing social equality for herself and others in the world. Rather, she must contend with them in order to free herself inwardly for an inner appropriation of the spiritual equality before God which she already has. The goal of this spiritual struggle, as Kierkegaard sees it, is not to do away with the differences as such but rather to blind one's eye to them, allowing the divine equality to burn, like a fire, "ever more intensely in the difference without . . . consuming it" (EUD, 143).

According to Kierkegaard, what is needed to sustain our feminist reader in this fight with differences is, first of all, an eternal goal (*Maal*) and criterion (*Maalestok*) that will always be valid and which can serve as a measure for understanding herself in temporality in such a way that neither good fortune and prosperity nor sorrow and affliction can rob her of hope (EUD, 260-61). In Kierkegaard's estimation the goal and criterion of experience in temporal life are too low and too limited since "events can still come along that are beyond the scope of experience," making one prey to despair (EUD, 260). "[E]ven if [she] manages to slip through life without having any such misfortunes challenge [her] calculations, then, if [she] has learned nothing higher in life, [she] is still a child of temporality for whom the eternal does not exist" (EUD, 260).

For Kierkegaard the goal and criterion of the eternal, as opposed to those of temporality, are to be found in the expectation of eternal salvation, which in his view has a meaning and consequences for the present life as well as in heaven in that it provides "comfort beyond all measure" and "is a refuge in distress, a fortress that life cannot take by storm, an assignment that distress and sufferings cannot cancel" (EUD, 263). Kierkegaard goes on to aver that "life together with this conception is more nourishing for a person than mother's milk to the nursing child, and [she] returns from this conception strengthened, strengthened most of all precisely when [her] striving is not to wean [her]self from this nourishing but to make it [her] wont" (EUD, 263, 264).

---

passages quoted below.

It is perhaps here that one finds the greatest relevancy of the upbuilding discourses to the lives of women, especially those who continue to suffer greatly from maltreatment in patriarchal societies around the world. For even if it is impossible, humanly speaking, to free themselves from such temporal conditions, the expectation of eternal salvation provides a consolation and hope that can help them to endure their awful situations and be saved from despair (EUD, 267).[16] But even the modern feminist who has gained a measure of freedom and social equality in the temporal realm and looks forward to a full realization of these in the future may benefit from an expectancy of eternal salvation, as it will provide an eternal goal and criterion against which the relative gains and losses of temporal equality may be measured. In that way, she too may be saved from despair when her fondest earthly wish does not fully materialize or is lost after having once been gained.

Another internal requirement for fighting the good fight for female equality in the temporal realm is patience. Kierkegaard devotes no less than three discourses in this collection to the need for patience in the battles of life, although he concedes that "it cannot be endorsed with full certainty as the one thing needful in the external: perhaps at times impatience would be more profitable and would hasten the gain of what is coveted" (EUD, 169). Even in the spiritual realm he credits "apostolic speech," which in his view is essentially different from all human speech, with being "as impatient as that of a woman in labor" (EUD, 69). Extending the analogy to feminist speech, one may liken the impatience of apostolic speech to it as well, inasmuch as apostolic speech, like much feminist discourse, is

---

[16]Anticipating *The Sickness unto Death,* Kierkegaard speaks here of the expectancy of eternal salvation as "the eternal remedy that heals all sickness, even the sickness unto death," and the two forms of despair—despair in weakness and despair in defiance—are prefigured as well in the distinction between "the soft person" and "the defiant person" in an earlier discourse (EUD, 111). For an analysis of the two forms of despair in terms of their association with gender categories, see my article, "On 'Feminine' and 'Masculine' Forms of Despair," in *International Kierkegaard Commentary: The Sickness unto Death,* ed. Robert L. Perkins (Macon GA: Mercer University Press 1987) 121-34, reprinted in slightly revised form in *Feminist Interpretations of Søren Kierkegaard,* 203-15.

concerned, ardent, burning, inflamed, everywhere and always stirred by the forces of the new life, calling, shouting, beckoning, explosive in its outbursts, brief, disjointed, harrowing, itself violently shaken as much by fear and trembling as by longing and blessed expectancy, everywhere witnessing to the powerful unrest of the spirit and the profound impatience of the heart. (EUD, 69)

Kierkegaard distinguishes this "very different apostolic impatience," which maintains calm and order in anticipation of the end of all things, from "the rashness of an excited person" who acts impatiently in such a way as to throw everything into disorder in times of crisis (EUD, 71). Although he would undoubtedly label feminist impatience as an example of such rashness, I would argue that it bears a closer resemblance to apostolic impatience in its ardor for human equality and that, given the unequal social status of most women in the world today, feminist impatience is not only needed and but also justified in the fight for social equality.

But patience is also needed, especially since "the most crucial issues are decided slowly, little by little, not in haste and all at once" (EUD, 199). While almost every endeavor in life requires a measure of patience, Kierkegaard points out that it is even more imperative in the spiritual realm, where patience is needed to gain and preserve that inner being or soul by which one relates oneself to God or the eternal and possesses oneself in one's eternal validity independently of the external realm. Contrary to what one might expect, the model for patience set forth in these discourses is not Job, although he does serve as a prototype for humanity in other respects elsewhere in the collection (see EUD, 109-24). Rather, it is the New Testament prophetess Anna, who is lauded not only for her decision to remain faithful to the memory of her deceased husband and to herself in freely continuing to bind herself to him in love, but also for setting her expectancy in the future on the coming of the eternal in time (EUD, 209). Unlike the foolish and impatient virgins in the gospel story from Matthew 25:1-13 with whom she is contrasted in the discourse, Anna patiently sustained an expectancy for the eternal regardless of its fulfillment or nonfulfillment in time and thus was never disappointed (EUD, 213-23).

Finally, Kierkegaard suggests that "the armor of love" and forgiveness will also be needed for a victorious fight for true equality in the world, especially on the battleground of one's inner being where that single individual who is a woman must fight "for [her]self with [her]self within [her]self" (EUD, 77, 143, 378).[17] Reminding us "that every human being, if he [or she] is honest, only all too often catches himself [or herself] in being able, protractedly, penetratingly, and expertly, to interpret the sad truth that revenge is sweet" in such a way as to justify it, Kierkegaard indirectly entreats his feminist reader to forego revenge against those who have wronged her, forgiving them in such a way as to abolish the partition wall of differences between them (WL, 57-58). Concerned not to admonish or judge others on this score, however, he emphasizes instead the power of Christian love "to love forth . . . the good in the impure" by hiding a multitude of sins in oneself and others (EUD, 57, 61). Once again, the human paradigm used to exemplify the point being made here is a woman—the woman in Luke 7:36-50 who is forgiven much and who forgives much because she loved much (EUD, 75-78).[18] In the discourse that focuses most explicitly on equality, however, Kierkegaard suggests that it is in the giving of love and receiving it in turn as a gift that true equality between human beings is effected and preserved in the temporal realm (EUD, 157-58). Since the gift of love is "from above" and thus more significant than either the giver or the receiver, it establishes an equality in love between them which is the only thing that is temporally lasting (EUD, 158).

---

[17]On the need for forgiveness in contemporary feminist liberation movements, see Wanda Warren Berry, "Finally Forgiveness: Kierkegaard as a 'Springboard' for a Feminist Theology of Reform" in *Foundations of Kierkegaard's Vision of Community: Religion, Ethics, and Politics in Kierkegaard*, ed. George B. Connell and C. Stephen Evans (Atlantic Highlands NJ: Humanities Press, 1992) 196-217.

[18]Kierkegaard returns to this biblical figure numerous times in his later religious writings, where she is extolled as a prototype of piety. See especially "An Upbuilding Discourse," in *Without Authority*, ed. and trans. Howard V. Hong and Edna H. Hong (Princeton NJ: Princeton University Press, 1997) 149-60. For a list of scripture references to her, see the appendix in L. Joseph Rosas III, *Scripture in the Thought of Søren Kierkegaard* (Nashville: Broadman & Holman Publishers, 1994).

In conclusion, our empathetic reading of the early upbuilding discourses from the standpoint of that single individual who is a woman and modern feminist suggests that while they do not endorse female liberation movements designed to secure social equality for women in the temporal realm, a feminist reader may still find much in them that is upbuilding and supportive of her fight for true equality in the world. First and foremost, her fundamental and complete spiritual equality as a human being before God is affirmed and recognized as the qualitative criterion against which any and every expression of social equality or inequality in the temporal realm must be measured. Second, while no particular form of temporal equality is endorsed, the victory and preservation of true equality in the world remains a possibility for every woman, especially in the inner battleground of the soul where she must fight for self-preservation and freedom against temporal influences and gain the inner strength and resources to persevere in life no matter what her external circumstances, gains and losses, victories and failures. Third, spiritual consolation for herself and her sisters is offered in temporal situations of subjugation and abuse that seemingly are intractable and show little or no possibility of change. Fourth, the discourses are supportive of gender inclusiveness and nonpaternalistic, nonabusive treatment of women by men in religious matters and, by extension, in other areas of sociality as well through the establishment of temporal equality in love. Fifth, guidance for women in particular is provided through the use of female models who exemplify essential qualities needed in the fight for true equality.

Far from finding the eighteen upbuilding discourses irrelevant to her particular situation, therefore, that single individual who is a woman and a feminist may turn to them for the inner support, perspective, and guidance needed to be victorious in her fight for true equality in the world. What a pity, though, that Kierkegaard could not, or did not, embrace and support that cause in external forms which seek to establish female social equality as well—or at least to make a substantial difference in woman's earthly lot and situation. For that his favorably disposed feminist readers may forgive him, but only those who love much in spite of what must be regarded as a major shortcoming in these otherwise truly upbuilding discourses for "that single individual" who is a woman.

3

Is the Religion of
Eighteen Upbuilding Discourses
Religiousness A?

Thomas C. Anderson

Introduction

In *Concluding Unscientific Postscript to 'Philosophical Fragments'* (hereafter, *Postscript*) in an appendix entitled, "A Glance at a Contemporary Effort in Danish Literature," the pseudonymous author, Johannes Climacus, offers some brief comments about the discourses now collected in *Eighteen Upbuilding Discourses*.[1] He states that they were "purely philosophical" in character for they "did not use Christian categories at all" (CUP, 1:256-57n.). As philosophical, their categories or concepts were only those of "immanence" (CUP, 1:256, 272). This means, Climacus explains later in *Postscript*, that their categories have "only universal human nature as [their] presupposition" (CUP, 1:559); that is, they can be generated and understood by the *natural* powers that all human beings possess.[2] As he often puts it paraphrasing Scripture,[3] they are concepts that have "arisen in man's, that is, humanity's heart" (CUP, 1:580). Specifically Christian categories (he mentions Christ, the God-man, sin and forgiveness of sin, and the atonement) can not be attained by our natural powers of thought. They require every human being to "relinquish his understanding and his thinking" (CUP, 1:557), Climacus claims, for Christian concepts are not just beyond human understanding, they are "against [and] . . .

---

[1]CUP, 1:256-57, 272-73.
[2]CUP, 1:557-59, 584.
[3]See 1 Corinthians 2:9.

contrary to all thinking" (CUP, 1:570). If they had not been revealed by God, human beings would never have been aware of them and even after they are divinely revealed we still cannot understand them.[4] Thus he characterizes the difference between the two categories as the difference between "what comes from God and what comes from man" (CUP, 1:580).

Climacus also designates the categories used in the upbuilding discourses as "ethical" (CUP, 1:256) rather than Christian in nature. I believe he uses the term ethical here not to refer to the ethical stage specifically, but broadly (as he does throughout the *Postscript*), to refer to the general task or obligation each human being has to become a subject. I say this because Climacus's statement that the upbuilding discourses are ethical comes three hundred pages before he has discussed non-Christian religion, the religion of immanence called Religiousness A, and distinguished it from the ethical and from Christian religion. Once he has made those distinctions, it becomes clear that the upbuilding discourses are more accurately classified as religious in nature.[5] To my knowledge, all commentators who address the issue so classify them; some, in fact, accept Climacus's designation and locate the discourses in Religiousness A.[6] However, in spite of what Climacus says, it seems questionable, at least on the face of it, to simply place *Eighteen Upbuilding Discourses* within the religion of immanence.

For one thing, fourteen of the discourses consist of commentaries by Kierkegaard on passages from the New Testament. Even

---

[4]CUP, 1:557-61, 579-85.

[5]See CUP, 1:572. The concept of God in religion (whether A or B) is more personal than in the ethical stage where God is equivalent to moral obligation or law (FT, 68). Also, the ethical stage's concept of guilt is not as total as is the religious concept (CUP, 1:537). On the other hand, there is a sense in which the ethical, meaning the obligation to become a subject, is contained in the religious, as we shall see.

[6]David Gouwens, *Kierkegaard as Religious Thinker* (Cambridge: Cambridge University Press, 1996) 117; Reidar Thomte, *Kierkegaard's Philosophy of Religion* (New York: Greenwood Press, 1969) 123-24, 146; Louis Mackey, *Kierkegaard: A Kind of Poet* (Philadelphia: University of Pennsylvania Press, 1971) chaps. 3 and 4; C. Stephen Evans, *Kierkegaard's "Fragments" and "Postscript"* (Atlantic Highlands NJ: Humanities Press, 1983) 158.

more significant is the fact that citations from the New Testament and commentaries on those citations are pervasive in all of the eighteen discourses.[7] Furthermore, many do mention religious categories that Climacus (and Kierkegaard) clearly consider to be specifically Christian, such as sin (even original sin) and forgiveness of sin, the resurrection of the dead and Christian love which is discussed in detail in the third and fourth discourses. They also contain references to Christ, to Christianity and to the Holy Spirit and speak of God as love and as our father. Of course, the fact that *Eighteen Upbuilding Discourses* contains many Christian references and notions does not necessarily make it primarily Christian in nature. That depends on the overall way the discourses present some fundamental religious notions—such as the nature of God, of eternal salvation or happiness (*salighed*), and of human beings' relation to God and to eternal salvation. And that brings me to the topic of this paper.

I will attempt to answer the following question. Does the religion set forth in the eighteen discourses generally correspond to Religiousness A as that is described in the *Concluding Unscientific Postscript* and differentiated from Christianity? I confine myself to the *Postscript*'s presentation of Religiousness A because it is the single most extensive discussion (over 200 pages) of that religion in all of Kierkegaard's works.[8] I will concentrate on the way the eighteen discourses and the *Postscript*'s Religiousness A treat the major religious notions mentioned above: the nature of God, of

---

[7]The Hongs' index to these discourses list hundreds of citations to the New Testament. Of course, all of SK's works cite the New Testament but *Eighteen Upbuilding Discourses* contains an usually large number, even more than *Christian Discourses* and *Practice in Christianity*!

[8]I recognize that Climacus classifies *any* religion that is not Christianity in the strict sense as Religiousness A, even the Christianity in Christendom (CUP, 1:557) and, therefore, that features of Religiousness A can be found in many of Kierkegaard's works. Needless to say, it is impossible in one essay to deal with all of those works. The most thorough treatment of Religiousness A that I am aware of in the secondary literature is Arnold Come's *Kierkegaard as Humanist* (Buffalo NY: McGill-Queen's University Press, 1995). In addition to *Concluding Unscientific Postscript*, Come makes extensive use of *Sickness unto Death, Works of Love*, and *Soren Kierkegaard's Journals and Papers* to understand Religiousness A.

eternal salvation, and of the human being's relation to God and to eternal salvation. I begin with Religiousness A.

Religiousness A and Its Differences from Christianity

As others have noted, Johannes Climacus's presentation of Religiousness A in his *Postscript* is not altogether clear.[9] There are a couple reasons for this. For one thing, Religiousness A is an extremely broad category which includes any religion that is not Christianity in the strictest sense. For another, at least two different kinds of Religiousness A are discussed in the *Postscript*.[10] One is exemplified by Socrates who emphasizes the concrete temporal existence of the individual and his or her need here and now to venture and *believe* in immortality and in God's reality. The other, initiated by Plato and present also in contemporary speculative thought according to Climacus, claims that persons can come to *know* their essential immortality and find the reality of God within themselves. Accordingly, it de-emphasizes the importance of existence in time and the need for faith.[11] Before pursuing this point any further, however, let me set forth the general characteristics of God that are present in both versions of A.

The nature of God

The author of the *Postscript* describes Religiousness A's God as an eternal, all knowing, infinite, omnipresent, creator and governor of all things who is absolutely different from his finite, temporal,

---

[9]Come, *Kierkegaard as Humanist*, 283; Mark Taylor, *Kierkegaard's Pseudonymous Authorship* (Princeton NJ: Princeton University Press, 1975) 241.

[10]I want to thank Robert Perkins for the helpful suggestion that I distinguish these forms of Religiousness A. Lee Barrett uses an analysis of Climacus's apparently contradictory statements, "Subjectivity is Truth" and "Subjectivity is Untruth" to point out differences between these two forms of Religiousness A. See Barrett's "Subjectivity As (Un)Truth: Climacus's Dialectically Sharpened Pathos" in *International Kierkegaard Commentary: Concluding Unscientific Postscript to "Philosophical Fragments,"* ed. Robert Perkins (Macon GA: Mercer University Press, 1997) chap. 15.

[11]CUP, 1:205-207, 226-27, 270-73.

totally dependent creatures.[12] Although this God is radically different from creatures in his ontological characteristics, he is not placed in a totally transcendent realm by Climacus but is said to be within all creatures. This God is also described in very personal terms as sympathetically concerned about each individual human being's needs and weaknesses, as giving comfort and assistance to everyone, as patient and understanding even with sinners, and as pleased when an individual "desires the highest goods, peace of soul, his soul's salvation" (CUP, 1:507).[13] God cares so much for each individual that he insures that everything he gives each person (including pain and suffering) is for his or her good. And if any individual sincerely seeks to do God's will, God "will help him find what is the right thing" (CUP, 1:496). (However, as we will see later, it does not seem that humans really need God's assistance to achieve their eternal salvation.) In one place, Climacus indicates that he believes that the relation between individuals and God is so intimate that the religious individual can say "*Du*" to God (CUP, 1:90), that is, can address him like a family member, relative, and close friend.[14]

Needless to say, many of these features of Religiousness A's God are also found in Christianity's conception of God. Of course, the most significant difference between the two religions is that Christianity proclaims that the God who is the eternal, infinite, omniscient, omnipresent Creator is incarnated in the finite, historical individual Jesus of Nazareth. Such a God is totally unknowable by, and incomprehensible to, the natural powers of human understanding and, as a result, human reason considers the Incarnation foolish, offensive and absurd according to Climacus.[15]

---

[12]All of these feature and those which follow are found in Climacus's lengthy discussion of Religiousness A in CUP, 1:387-586. It is worth noting that explicit discussion of the distinction between Religiousness A and B takes place in very few of these pages, namely, 555-61, 571-73, 581-86. (I will use masculine pronouns when referring to God simply because Kierkegaard always does.)

[13]CUP, 1:406, 415, 489-95.

[14]*Du* is the familiar form of the Danish second person singular pronoun. (See the translators' n. 52 in CUP, 2:202.) I must point out, however, that this statement occurs very early in the *Postscript*, long before Climacus distinguishes between Religiousness A and B.

[15]CUP, 1:209-14, 556-61, 574-85.

The relation between humans and God
(and eternal salvation) in Religiousness A

I noted earlier that Climacus states that in Religiousness A God is viewed as present *within* all creatures, which is perhaps another reason why he calls it a religion of immanence. Accordingly, he also maintains that self-conscious creatures, human beings, can come to know God's presence by an "inward deepening" of their self-knowledge, that is, by internally reflecting upon themselves to such a depth that they find or discover that they are grounded in God.

As many have noted, Climacus often calls this process of deepening self-awareness "recollection," a term he acknowledges borrowing from Plato.[16] Recollection for Plato was the process of self-awareness by which individuals recall (remember) the knowledge they, or more precisely their souls, learned before their birth. It implies that the soul is immortal, at least that it existed prior to one's birth. And Climacus does say that through self-knowledge or recollection an individual will "discover that he must presuppose himself to be ["essentially"] eternal" (CUP, 1:573). Plato in the *Phaedo* (78A-81A) also couples the soul's immortality with its presence in the realm of the divine, a realm where it not only knows the forms but "forever dwells . . . in company with the gods". Similarly, as we noted, Climacus states

---

[16]CUP, 1:205, 208, 226, 270; PF, chap. 1. Each of the following discuss what Kierkegaard means by recollection: Pojman, *The Logic of Subjectivity* (Tuscaloosa: University of Alabama Press, 1984) chap. 3; Evans, *Kierkegaard's "Fragments" and "Postscript"*, chap. 8, and Taylor, *Kierkegaard's Pseudonymous Authorship*, chap. 6, sect. B. Robert Wood makes an interesting comparison between Kierkegaard's and Plato's views of recollection in "Recollection and Two Banquets: Plato's and Kierkegaard's," in *International Kierkegaard Commentary: Stages on Life's Way*, ed. Robert Perkins (Macon GA: Mercer University Press, 2000) 49-68. George Pattison in his interesting comparison of Climacus's and Augustine's notions of recollection, "Johannes Climacus and Aurelius Augustine on Recollecting Truth" in *International Kierkegaard Commentary: Philosophical Fragments and Johannes Climacus*, ed. Robert Perkins (Macon GA: Mercer University Press, 1994) argues that the form of recollection that Kierkegaard encountered in his day was that of Hegel not Plato, 245-46, 255-57.

that by recollection a person in Religiousness A can come to the awareness of God, a God who is within.[17]

One type of self-knowledge or recollection that leads to an awareness of God is called ethical by Climacus. In this kind of self-awareness God is present as the ultimate foundation of the absolute character of one's moral obligation to become a self (subject) and attain eternal salvation. In fact, the entire second part of the *Postscript* (which is all but 58 pages of the work) is devoted to the ethical for it describes "the highest task assigned to a human being" (CUP, 1:129), the task to become a subject. Throughout his discussion Climacus joins this ethical task, which, he says, each individual can discover within himself or herself, with the inner presence of God. Note the following passages: "the individual actually and essentially comprehends the ethical only in himself because it is his co-knowledge with God" (CUP, 1, 155) and "the ethical is discovered by the individual's becoming immersed in his self and in his relation to God" (CUP, 1:144). The following is especially clear: "when a person rubs [the lamp of freedom] with ethical passion, God comes into existence for him, . . . the Lord" (CUP, 1:138-39).[18]

This kind of ethical becomes part of Religiousness A because it, like all religions according to Climacus, "has passed through the ethical and *has it within itself*" (CUP, 1:388, my emphasis). Accordingly, he states that the religious individual's ethical-religious "task" (CUP, 1:461, 525-27) or "absolute requirement" (CUP, 1:466, 503), which "is in one's innermost being" (CUP, 1:548), is to transform his or her individual temporal existence by absolutely willing his/her absolute end, his/her soul's eternal salvation and happiness, and God. (Climacus, without offering any argument, identifies one's absolute end, eternal salvation, with God.[19] This is

---

[17]CUP, 1:556-61, 571.

[18]Similar passages are CUP, 1:137, 140, 156, 183, 244.

[19]CUP, 1:410-15; 560-61. For example, he writes: "The absolutely differentiating one [who differentiates between absolute and relative ends] relates himself to his absolute *telos*, but *eo ipso* to God" (CUP, 1:413). John Glenn, " 'A Highest Good . . . An Eternal Happiness': The Human Telos in Kierkegaard's *Concluding Unscientific Postscript*," in *IKC: Concluding Unscientific Postscript to "Philosophical Fragments*," chap. 13, has an interesting comparison of Climacus's notion of

not surprising since he is writing to professed Christians who no doubt believe that their eternal salvation involves possession of, or, better, being with, God.) Climacus uses the terms resignation or renunciation to designate the religious individual's ethical-religious task. Resignation involves the self-awareness that one is capable of nothing, absolutely nothing, in relation to an infinite God, and the corresponding decision to give up, renounce, die to, any and all finite things, including oneself in his or her finitude, in order to commit oneself totally to attaining his or her absolute end and to living this commitment every moment of his or her life.[20] Individuals who renounce all the finite, including themselves, and commit themselves totally to their eternal salvation with God will, Climacus asserts, suffer greatly but also find their relationship to God within themselves. "Self-annihilation" he says, " finds the relationship to God within itself . . . finds its ground in it , because God is the ground only when everything that is in the way is cleared out [i.e. renounced], and first and foremost the individual himself in his finitude" (CUP 1:560-61).

Climacus seems to be referring here to another way that self-awareness or recollection becomes conscious of God within oneself. For, along with the awareness that one can do absolutely nothing, comes the awareness that "the person . . . through God is capable of everything" (CUP, 1:430, 471, 486). Climacus's suggestion, and it is only that, is that if we recognize that we are totally powerless, that we are able to do nothing and that in ourselves we are nothing, and yet we know that we are and do all kinds of things, we come to see that this is only possible because a Creator who is capable of everything is within us supporting and assisting us.[21] In other words, when we realize that by our own powers we can neither cause ourselves to exist nor to continue in existence, nor can any finite thing, we understand that we must be grounded in an all powerful being who is present within us and causing and sustaining us in being.[22] (To look ahead, we will see that this argu-

---

eternal happiness with Aristotle's and Kant's. However, he does not discuss Climacus's identification of eternal happiness and God.

[20]CUP, 1:404-407, 430, 472.

[21]CUP, 1:430, 471, 484-86.

[22]This is the way Mackey expresses Climacus's argument, *Kierkegaard: A Kind*

ment, only suggested in *Postscript*, will be clearly set forth in *Eighteen Upbuilding Discourses*.)

Now although Religiousness A can through recollection come to know the eternal dimension of the existing individual and the presence of God within, the *Postscript* describes two quite different reactions to this knowledge, the Socratic and the Platonic. The Socratic, which Climacus obviously favors since 90% of the Religiousness A he discusses is of this type,[23] places so much emphasis on the individual's concrete existence that it does not pursue the path of recollection. Socrates, according to Climacus, ignores the fact that he is by nature eternal and has God within himself and focuses instead on the fundamental difference between the eternal and the temporal, the absolute, divine realm and the finite, relative realm of creatures.[24] His ethical goal is, through renunciation of the finite and the suffering of self-annihilation, to express in his existence his absolute relation to the absolute and eventually attain eternal salvation. Thus this form of Religiousness A, Climacus writes, "accentuates existing as actuality, and eternity, which in the underlying immanence still sustains the whole, vanishes." The eternal still underlies and sustains everything but, since the entire stress is on one's existence, it is hidden: "in [this form of] Religiousness A, the eternal is *ubique* and *nusquam* but hidden by the actuality of existence" (CUP, 1:571).

The Platonic form of Religiousness A, on the other hand, "pursue[s] recollection and immanence" and "loses [it]self in speculative thought," Climacus says (CUP, 1:205-206). That is, since

---

of Poet, 120-21. Come, *Kierkegaard as Humanist*, chap. 6, also finds this argument in Religion A but primarily uses *Sickness Unto Death* to flesh it out.

[23]Of the more than 200 pages devoted to Religiousness A, only about thirty actually discuss the Platonic version: (CUP, 1:204-10, 226-27, 270-73, 555-61, 571-73, 581-86). Indeed, since Climacus puts much of this discussion in footnotes, in an appendix and in "The Intermediate Clause," it has the appearance of being rather peripheral—even though the positions set forth are very important. This incongruity is, I believe, an instance of Johannes Climacus, the humorist, at work (CUP, 1:270-73). For a most interesting discussion of these and other "paratextual" literary structures in the *Postscript*, consult Hugh Pyper, "Beyond a Joke: Kierkegaard's *Concluding Unscientific Postscript* as a Comic Book," in *IKC: Concluding Unscientific Postscript to "Philosophical Fragments*," chap. 8.

[24]CUP, 1:206.

the Platonic form of Religiousness A emphasizes recollection and its knowledge that "every individual is essentially structured equally eternally and essentially related to the eternal [God]", it considers my temporal existence, as just "an element within my eternal consciousness . . . [and] consequently a lesser thing" (CUP, 1:573). As Climacus puts it, "the moment in time is therefore *eo ipso* swallowed by the eternal." The individual's "existence in temporality has no decisive signification because there is continually the possibility of taking oneself back into eternity by recollecting" (CUP, 1:206).[25] Because this form of Religiousness A, by stressing recollection, minimizes existence in time or absorbs it into the eternal, Climacus calls it pantheism. "The only consistent position outside of Christianity is pantheism," he writes, namely, "the taking oneself back into the eternal through recollection" (CUP, 1:226).[26] To repeat, since Platonic Religiousness A tends through recollection to "swallow" (Climacus's term) the individual existent into the eternal being so that "the moment of existence in time . . . is something vanishing" (CUP, 1:226), it is pantheistic. Thus Climacus asserts that in this form of Religiousness A, God is not only "within the individual" but is in fact *everything*: "in immanence God is neither a [particular] something, but everything, and is infinitely everything" (CUP, 1:561).[27]

Of course the Socratic version of Religiousness A, the one to which Climacus devotes most of the *Postscript*, considers it ludicrous to suggest that an individual can attain *his* or *her* eternal salvation by ignoring a person's individual existence or by

---

[25]See also, CUP, 1:572, 582.

[26]Most commentators simply ignore Climacus's linking of recollection and pantheism. One of the few who is aware of it is Alastair Hannay, *Kierkegaard* (Boston: Routledge & Kegan Paul, 1982) 45. Niels Thulstrup, *Commentary on Kierkegaard's "Concluding Unscientific Postscript"* (Princeton: Princeton University Press, 1984), has a good discussion of the kinds of pantheism Kierkegaard was exposed to. He especially concentrates on the Hegelian kind, chaps. 5–7.

[27]Climacus also often labels speculative thought and the Hegelian system pantheistic for the same reason; they either ignore existence or attempt to absorb it into thought or the system. See, e.g., CUP, 1:121-23, 209, 217, 305-306, 355, 456. SK himself defines pantheism in much the same way as "abolishing . . . the qualitative difference between God and man" SUD, 117. See also, JP, 4:3887, p. 36.

absorbing it into the eternal.[28] Nevertheless, the fact remains, and Climacus himself points it out, that an individual living in Religiousness A can at any time "take oneself back into eternity by recollecting" (CUP, 1:206) and thus "has a possibility of escape [from existence] . . . of a withdrawal into the eternal behind it" (CUP, 1:572). This means, he adds, that "it is as if everything were not actually at stake." And, indeed, since the individual is by nature eternal and has God within, everything is not at stake in Religiousness A. For when it comes to one's eternal salvation, Climacus admits, "every human being, viewed essentially, participates in this eternal happiness and finally becomes eternally happy" (CUP, 1:581). This is so because eternal happiness/salvation is the attaining of one's absolute goal, abiding with God for eternity, and according to Religiousness A every individual is already by nature eternal (immortal) and possesses God within him/her self. And so Climacus does not hesitate to draw the humorous[29] conclusion that in Religiousness A "it makes no difference one way or another to the existing person" how he or she lives his or her temporal life. Although some individuals strive day after day to attain their eternal salvation and others pay no attention to it "they both, viewed eternally, go equally far" (CUP, 1:582).

Needless to say, this is very different from Christianity. Before addressing that difference, however, I want to note one final contrast between the Socratic and the Platonic version of Religiousness A. Because the Socratic type of Religiousness A disregards the knowledge obtainable by recollection, Climacus exhorts it to take the risk to *believe* in immortality and in God and eternal salvation.[30] But the Platonic, by pursuing recollection, is able, he says, to *find,*

---

[28]For example, Climacus insists that the existing person cannot "transform himself from an existing into an eternal person" (CUP, 1:452, 456).

[29]Incongruity is the basis of humor for Climacus. Thus it is humorous that no matter how much or how little effort individuals expend on attaining their eternal salvation, recollection reveals that all in fact attain it. Note the following passage where Climacus links humor and recollection: "Humor is always a revocation of existence into the eternal by recollection backwards" (CUP, 1:602). See also CUP, 1:270-72 and 582.

[30]CUP, 1:201-207, 422-29.

discover or *become aware* of one's immortality and God's reality within the individual.[31]

Much of this is in sharp contrast to Christianity as Climacus points out. Although Christianity also insists on the need for an individual to renounce the finite and establish an absolute relation to the absolute ("You must love the Lord your God with all your heart, with all your soul, with all your mind and with all your strength" [Mark 12:30]), and does believe that God is in some sense within each human being as both creator and law giver, its "doctrine is not to merge [the individual] in God through a pantheistic fading away or . . . blotting out of all individual characteristics" (JP, 4:3887, p. 36). Nor, according to Climacus, does it believe that humans are essentially eternal nor, a fortiori, that they naturally participate in eternal salvation. Climacus understands Christianity to teach that human beings become eternal and eternally saved only by believing that "the eternal [God] is present at a specific point in time" (CUP, 1:57) in the God-man Jesus. This means, like the Socratic version of Religiousness A maintained, that every person's temporal existence has "decisive significance" (CUP, 1:206), for each individual must at some moment in their lives commit themselves in faith to Christ in order to become eternal and attain eternal happiness/salvation with God. In other words, Climacus notes, Christianity proclaims that "the individual who was not eternal now [through faith in Christ] becomes eternal," which is another belief that "is inaccessible to all thinking" (CUP, 1:573).

One way Climacus highlights this difference between Religiousness A and Christianity is to say that the latter, unlike the former, believes there is no "immanental underlying kinship between the temporal and the eternal" (CUP, 1:573). The primary reason that Christianity denies an underlying kinship between God and human beings is its belief in human sin. This brings us to the

---

[31]CUP, 1:205-206, 424, 560-61, 573, 582. It is interesting to note that because he did not distinguish between Socrates and Plato in his *Philosophical Fragments*, Climacus spoke there of Socrates as knowing, not believing, his immortality and God by recollecting the truth which was within him (PF, 9-13). Thus, he writes, "Socrates did not have faith that the god existed. What he knew about the god he attained by recollection" (PF, 87).

final difference in the way each religion conceives the human relationship to God.

According to Climacus, Religiousness A recognizes that in this life human beings never completely die to self, renounce all finite things, and establish an absolute relation to God—and it considers them guilty for not doing so. However, this guilt remains within immanence, he says, for it does not sever the underlying relationship between God and human beings, nor does it negate the fact that all humans are by nature eternal (immortal) and essentially partake of eternal salvation. Christianity reveals what human understanding could never arrive at, that human beings are sinners and that their sin causes a fundamental rupture or "break" (CUP, 1:532, 583) between them and God. Because of sin, Climacus explains, "all connection [between humans and God] is cut away"[32] (CUP, 1:572) and "every communication of immanence by way of recollection through regression into the eternal is broken" (CUP, 1:583). Christianity also teaches that every individual is "born in sin" and so from the beginning of his life "he is prevented from taking himself back into eternity through recollection" (CUP, 1:208). Furthermore, sin *essentially* changes every human being, according to Christianity. By sin one has "lost continuity with himself [and has] become someone else" (CUP, 1,576), "another person" (CUP, 1:583). Christianity maintains, Climacus says, that the only way the break can be overcome and connection with God reestablished is by God taking the initiative and revealing that through Christ and his Atonement humans are offered forgiveness of sins.[33] If we, with God's help, choose to believe this revelation, even though it is against human understanding, if we believe in Christ as our Redeemer, Christianity promises that we will be essentially changed, reborn, "a new creation" (CUP, 1:573, 576). We will become eternal (immortal) and intimately related to God both now and forever and thus attain eternal salvation.

---

[32]Of course this cannot literally be true, for God is still present to every creature as their creator and sustainer. However, according to Climacus, sin makes it impossible for a human being to come to know that by recollection or to rely on it as a guarantee of eternal salvation.

[33]CUP, 1:207-10, 570, 573, 576, 582-85.

Summary of Religiousness A

As we have repeatedly pointed out, because it concentrates on existence, the Socratic version of Religiousness A disregards recollection and the knowledge of God and of one's eternity that can be obtained through it. Nevertheless, even though the Socratic ignores many of the following characteristics, all of them are ascribed by Climacus to Religiousness A.[34]

1. In immanent religion, Climacus describes God as the eternal, infinite, omniscient, all powerful creator, sustainer and governor who is within all things and is everything. God is also described as lovingly concerned with creatures and as assisting them in reaching their ultimate end.

2. By their natural powers, human beings are able to find God within themselves, Climacus states. This can happen if they reflect deeply within themselves (recollect) and come to recognize their absolute moral obligation to be a self and that they are themselves capable of absolutely nothing. However, because the Socratic from of Religiousness A leaves recollection aside, it must venture to believe in God's reality. (Neither it nor the Platonic is aware that God became a particular existing historical individual human person, Jesus of Nazareth.)

3. Not only can human beings by their own powers discover God within themselves, they are also able to see that they are by nature eternal. Since they are naturally eternal and essentially possess God, they essentially possess their eternal salvation. Also, Climacus explicitly links Platonic recollection with pantheism since it (recollection) involves "the taking oneself out of existence back into the eternal" God (CUP, 1:226). (In Christianity, existing human

---

[34]Climacus does say the Religiousness A, or more precisely its Socratic emphasis on the existential pathos (manifest in resignation, suffering and guilt) of the existing subject, is a prerequisite for Christianity (CUP, 1,556-60). However, he never says that everything found in Religiousness A is in Religiousness B, as one of my readers seemed to suggest. Quite the contrary. As the preceding discussion, summed up in the following list, shows, there are many significant differences. (Just as, similarly, the religious stage contains the ethical but not every single item of the ethical, not, for instance, its belief in human self-sufficiency nor in the primacy of the moral order.)

beings are not by nature eternal nor in possession of their eternal salvation nor essentially with or within God.)

4. Humans are guilty for not totally committing themselves to God but such guilt, Climacus maintains, does not destroy their basic kinship with God nor their eternal nature nor their possession of eternal salvation. (Religiousness A is not aware of sin and the breach it causes between God and human beings, nor, therefore, of our need for forgiveness and rebirth, nor of Christ and his Atonement.)

Is the Religion of Eighteen Upbuilding Discourses *Religiousness A?*

This section will compare the religion of Kierkegaard's eighteen discourses with the *Postscript*'s two versions of Religiousness A. We shall see that in some cases the discourses express views similar to the Platonic version, sometimes to the Socratic version, sometimes to neither. Yet, overall, one could say that they are Socratic in nature for their emphasis is on personal existence. The purpose of all eighteen discourses is to "build up" the individual readers to whom they are addressed. They are not intended just to directly inform their readers about religion, but to "win them over" and "move them" to live, to exist, in a genuinely religious manner.[35] They never suggest that the individual can or should attempt to ignore or escape from existence by withdrawing or vanishing into the eternal; they evidence no tendency toward pantheism.

The Nature of God in *Eighteen Upbuilding Discourses*

In many respects Kierkegaard's description of God in these discourses matches that given by Climacus in Religiousness A. Thus, Kierkegaard says that God is the eternal, omniscient, omnipresent, almighty, providential Creator of everything.[36] God is the supremely good author of all good things and, in fact, everything he creates, even pain and suffering, is a gift to humans

---

[35]See the Hongs' introduction to the discourses, EUD, xvi.

[36]One or more of these characteristics can be found in EUD, 7, 19, 28-29, 36, 87, 133-34, 145, 199, 243, 303, 310, 393.

through which he leads them to eternal salvation.[37] Like Climacus, Kierkegaard describes God in personal terms as loving, merciful, compassionate and faithful toward his creatures.[38] In a couple of places he even states that "God is love" (EUD, 325, 388).[39] More frequently, he says that God's love for us is a father's love and very often he calls God our Father.[40] Indeed, Kierkegaard insists that the term Father is not just a metaphor but is "the most beautiful, the most uplifting, but also the truest and most expressive of names" for God. To say "that God is a Father in heaven," he goes on, "is not metaphorical, imperfect, but the truest and most literal expression" (EUD, 99). For Kierkegaard to apply this name to God throughout these eighteen discourses suggests to me that in them he conceives God to be in a most intimate relationship with his human creatures, a relationship that is more than is present in a creature's relation to its Creator or even to a lover or dear friend.

To my knowledge, Climacus in the *Postscript's* Religiousness A *never* refers to God as our Father. As I mentioned above, the only time he alludes to an intimate loving relation between God and creatures is early in CUP (long before he introduces the distinction between Religiousness A and B), where he says the religious person can say *Du* to God. My strong suspicion is that Climacus, who surely knows that Christians frequently call God their Father, avoids that name when discussing God in Religiousness A because to use it would be to go beyond what can be known about God by natural human powers alone. Accordingly, I suggest that insofar as *Eighteen Upbuilding Discourses* names God as Father, and it does

---

[37]EUD, 14, 19, 28-29, 40-42, 87, 99-100, 111, 132-33, 148, 156, 167, 325, 369.

[38]EUD, 39, 46, 87, 100, 129, 136-37, 214, 325, 340, 388.

[39]In *Soren Kierkegaard's Journals and Papers*, Kierkegaard does indicate that he considers the identification of God with love to be proper to Christianity: JP 2:1446, p. 146, and 3:2448, p. 55.

[40]These are just some of the places where he does so: EUD, 28, 36-40, 98-100, 125, 133, 138-39, 271, 388, 400.

so frequently, its religion is not totally within the limits of immanence.[41]

Like Religiousness A, a couple of the eighteen discourses speak of God as within the individual or, more specifically within one's "inner being." The whole of the fifth discourse is a discussion of a person saving his soul by being "strengthened by God's spirit in his inner being" (EUD, 83).[42] Kierkegaard refers there to the witness of God in one's inner being from which one learns "in the full assurance of faith" (EUD, 98) that everything, including spiritual trial and suffering, is a good gift from a faithful, loving, comforting and approving God. The witness, he says, is itself "a gift from God," therefore, "from the Father in heaven" by which one "understands and is convinced that God is a Father in heaven" (EUD, 98-99). Here, too, in referring to the God within as a Father, Kierkegaard apparently goes beyond what can be known of him by natural human powers.

The Relation between Human Beings and God (and Eternal Salvation) in *Eighteen Upbuilding Discourses*

Inasmuch as God's spirit is a witness within one's inner being, it is not surprising that, like the *Postscript*, Kierkegaard states in the discourses that we come to know God through "deeper and more inward self-knowledge" (EUD, 276). In the fifth discourse, for example, he writes that a person who "allows his soul to sink deeper and deeper into [his] concern" about God and himself and the relation between them will eventually discover the witness of God within his inner being (EUD, 95). Yet the self-knowledge required is very difficult, he says, and needs God's assistance because ultimately one must come to realize that a person's "task,"as Climacus said, is to admit that he or she is capable of nothing[43] "The highest is this," Kierkegaard states, "that a person

---

[41]In JP 2:1432, pp. 137-38, Kierkegaard states that God only becomes our Father through the mediatorship of his son, Jesus.

[42]In the sixteenth discourse Kierkegaard also speaks of God's witness testifying within an individual's heart, EUD, 333-34.

[43]EUD, 167, 226, 273-76, 306-09, 317-18, 345, 368-69. Of course, if I can do nothing at all, this means that by my own power I cannot even become aware that I can do nothing at all! And that is precisely what Kierkegaard says, "at most [a person] is capable of being willing to understand" that he or she is capable of

is fully convinced that he himself is capable of nothing, nothing at all" (EUD, 307). He also agrees with Climacus that such self-knowledge should lead an individual to "renounce the world" (EUD, 216, 374) or, more strongly, to "die to the world" (EUD, 325) and undergo the "death of self-denial" (EUD, 288) and the "annihilation" of the self (EUD, 309). Those who die to all earthly things, including their earthly selves, who humbly admit they can do nothing—and, in particular, that they cannot attain their eternal salvation themselves—will come to recognize their absolute need for God, Kierkegaard says, "the God who is capable of all things" (EUD, 310). And in his fifteenth discourse he claims that the person who goes this far in self-knowledge "comes *to know God*," (EUD, 321). In fact, he asserts that such a person is able to "experience" God in "every moment." "Someone who is conscious that he is capable of nothing at all has every day and every moment the desired and irrefragable opportunity to experience that God lives" (EUD, 322). Why? because "the person who is himself capable of nothing at all cannot undertake the least action without God's help, consequently without becoming conscious that there is a God" (EUD, 322).

Kierkegaard's reasoning here seems to be what Climacus hinted at in his *Postscript*. Those who attain the self-awareness that they literally can do nothing to cause themselves to be, act, or to continue to be, and yet who obviously do exist and act, must become conscious of a Creative Power through whom they exist and act. When a person "understands that he himself is capable of nothing at all," Kierkegaard states, "in and with this understanding God is also present immediately" (EUD, 323). Needless to say, this is very close to Climacus's conception of recollection in Religiousness A, especially its Platonic version.

Yet there are other discourses where Kierkegaard's position seems much closer to the Socratic version of Religiousness A which, as we saw, disregards recollection. In his first and second discourses, rather than speaking of one "becoming conscious that there is a God" of our having the "irrefragable opportunity to experience that God is" through self-knowledge and renunciation,

---

nothing (EUD, 309).

Kierkegaard states that God's reality can be professed only by faith, faith that is a gift of God.[44] Yet in the same breadth he asserts that *"every* human being has it [faith] if he wants to have it" and that "if you do not have it, then it is your fault and a sin" (EUD, 11), which makes it sound as if he considers this faith to be something human beings can achieve through their own powers.

But this cannot be correct for, if we can do nothing without God's assistance, that must mean we cannot believe in God without his assistance. Of course, such faith need not be specifically Christian faith for it is obvious that many non-Christians believe in God. I suggest that Kierkegaard is talking here about a faith or belief that he thinks *all* human beings will be offered by God, if they sincerely want to have it. Since an individual remains free to accept that gift or not, it is a person's fault if he or she does not. Kierkegaard apparently believes that a loving God who is our Father will respond to anyone who sincerely seeks him: "One who seeks God always finds [him]" (EUD, 97), he states. He seems convinced that, if a human being humbly recognizes that he or she needs the assistance of Divine Power to be or do anything, including to believe in God, and sincerely asks for faith, God will grant it because "God is faithful and does not leave himself without a witness" (EUD, 88).[45] Such faith is what some have called natural human belief in God, meaning that it is not beyond or against human understanding as is Christian faith.[46] It is the general kind of faith that has entered into the human heart and that Climacus attributed to Socrates and his version of Religiousness A.

I turn next to the issues of immortality and eternal salvation. There can be no doubt that Kierkegaard in these discourses considers the individual human being, or, more precisely, the individual human soul, to be eternal in the sense of immortal. Almost every one of the eighteen discourses explicitly refers to man's or the soul's immortality and some, like the thirteenth, "The Expec-

---

[44]EUD, 24-26, 35-36.

[45]See also EUD, 137-39, 250. Kierkegaard also states this view in other works: CD, 244-45; FSE, 13-14, 69; UDVS, 77, 173, 227; PC, 67.

[46]Come, *Kierkegaard as Humanist*, 304-10, 321-22; Pojman, *The Logic of Subjectivity*, 101; Evans, *Kierkegaard's "Fragments" and "Postscript"*, 147-53.

tancy of Eternal Salvation," make it one of their major themes.[47] What is unclear is why Kierkegaard considers the soul to be immortal; is it immortal by nature or only by a special grace of God?

Unfortunately, he never specifically addresses that issue. Nowhere in any of the eighteen discourses does he speak, for example, of a person coming through self-knowledge to recognize that he/she is essentially eternal—as Climacus did in the Platonic Religiousness A. Yet he also never says that the soul's immortality is a divine gift that can only be known by faith—as in the Socratic Religiousness A. The best I can do is offer the following things that Kierkegaard does say about the soul that suggest to me that he considered it to be immortal by nature.[48]

1. Kierkegaard describes the soul as our "inner being" and our "deeper self." That self, he says, is the part of us that is concerned about God and our eternal salvation and he sharply contrasts it from our sensuous self which is selfishly concerned only with temporal worldly things.

2. Sometimes Kierkegaard refers to our soul or our inner being as spirit and contrasts it to the flesh.[49] He states that the "home of the spirit is in the eternal and infinite" (EUD, 337). The word home suggests that the spirit (soul) naturally belongs with the eternal and with God who is spirit and that implies that it is not temporal in nature like the flesh is.

3. As we will see later, Kierkegaard believes that the souls of those who do not attain eternal happiness are still immortal. Unlike Climacus, he does not say that because every human is immortal (eternal), every human will attain eternal happiness. Now since he makes it perfectly clear in many places that he believes that the soul's eternal *happiness or salvation* is a gift of God,

---

[47]Accordingly, I am perplexed why Come, *Kierkegaard as Humanist*, 24, 114, 269, states that Kierkegaard denies there is anything eternal in man.

[48]Kierkegaard talks about the soul often in the discourses. It is a central topic of three of his discourses: the fifth, "Strengthened in the Inner Being" (for the inner being is the soul), the ninth, "To Gain One's Soul in Patience," and the tenth, "To Preserve One's Soul in Patience." Mackey, *Kierkegaard, A kind of Poet*, 102-106, has a helpful discussion of some of Kierkegaard's most difficult remarks on the nature of the soul.

[49]EUD, 334-38.

if Kierkegaard also thought that the soul's very immortality was also a divine gift why wouldn't he clearly say so in at least one of the many places where he refers to it?

Let me repeat, I offer these reasons not as conclusive proof but as indications that Kierkegaard considered the human soul to be immortal by nature.[50] However, note that unlike Religiousness A none of the reasons appeal to recollection.

In any case, as I've said, Kierkegaard is crystal clear that eternal salvation, or "saving one's own soul" (EUD, 82), is entirely God's gift. Although he does say that God is within each individual as his/her creator, sustainer and witness, he insists that there is nothing one can do, no condition one can fulfill, to deserve or merit the gift of eternal salvation.[51] "Every person has heaven's salvation only by the grace and mercy of God," he writes (EUD, 271). To claim that one's eternal salvation comes inevitably, Kierkegaard complains, makes God "resemble a weak human being who does not have the heart to deny eternal salvation to anyone, whether one desires it or not" (EUD, 251). This statement should remind us of Climacus's view of eternal salvation/happiness in Religiousness A for in that religion human beings do indeed attain that goal inevitably whether an individual desires it or not and no matter how he or she lives in this life. Because Religiousness A considers everyone essentially to be eternal and to possess God, it follows that everyone inevitably attains eternal salvation or happiness which is the eternal possession of God. This is another point, then, on which the religion of *Eighteen Upbuilding Discourses* differs significantly from Religiousness A. (I must add, however, that the Socratic version of A, in which the individual disregards his/her natural immortality and possession of God, and passionately ventures to believe in immortality, God and eternal salvation is similar to the religion of these discourses on this point.)

The difference in their conception of eternal salvation inevitably leads to a difference of opinion about the importance of temporali-

---

[50]Taylor, *Kierkegaard's Pseudonymous Authorship*, 255-57, claims that Kierkegaard does not consider the soul immortal by nature. However, he supports this conclusion only by citing *Climacus's* version of Christianity in the *Postscript*, not Kierkegaard's own words in works written under his name.

[51]EUD, 28, 167, 174-75, 198, 220-23, 258, 264-73, 316-18.

ty or, more precisely, of the moment in time. Since Religiousness A considers human persons to be essentially eternal and eternally saved, none of the choices people make during their temporal existence really have any bearing on their eternal happiness. In the discourses, however, the choices people make in this life are crucial for their eternal life according to Kierkegaard.[52] An individual must earnestly desire to save his or her soul and at some moment ("this very day" [EUD, 200, 356]) renounce the world and acknowledge that he or she can do nothing to attain salvation. Only those who acknowledge their absolute need for God and choose to commit themselves totally to God will be willing to accept faith and believe in a God who offers eternal salvation. Of course, one can refuse to believe. Those who reject God's gift of faith still possess an immortal soul but instead of eternal salvation or happiness they will gain eternal "perdition," Kierkegaard says. In traditional terms, they will "lose" their soul "for all time and for eternity" (EUD, 186). On this point, then, the discourses appear to be much closer to Christianity, which also makes one's eternal salvation depend on one's choices in time, than to Religiousness A.[53] (Yet, again, I must acknowledge that the Socratic version of A also emphasizes the need for individual decision and choice in time in order for one to exist in the proper relation to their absolute end, eternal salvation, God.[54])

The final topic to be addressed is the concept of guilt or sin. Recall that in the *Postscript* Climacus said that the guilt of Religiousness A did not destroy the essential relationship between human beings and their eternal salvation and God. On the other hand, he described Christianity as teaching that human sin does cause a fundamental break or rupture between human beings and their eternal salvation with God. This breach is so severe, he said, that in order to reestablish the relationship to God and gain eternal salvation, we need to be recreated or reborn and this will take

---

[52]EUD, 200, 222, 356.

[53]Not only does SK speak of the soul's immortality in the discourses, he also refers to the Christian belief in "the resurrection of the dead; of both the righteous and the unrighteous" (EUD, 216).

[54]CUP, 1:463, 481, 497, 506.

place only if we accept in faith God's forgiveness through Christ's Atonement.

The first thing to be said about *Eighteen Upbuilding Discourses* is that it does not often deal with such matters. When it does, Kierkegaard's language again seems closer to Christianity than to Religiousness A. For example, he uses the term sin more often than the term guilt and he talks about forgiveness of sin, and Climacus himself said both notions were specifically Christian. Kierkegaard even spends a couple of pages discussing original sin[55] and states that human beings are "born in sin" (EUD, 349) and that sin separates us from God.[56] Since all people are sinners, he states, they need forgiveness and so must turn to God and totally rely on his mercy. If we do repent and confess our sins and our unworthiness, God will respond with his "compassionate grace" (EUD, 38).[57] Finally, in at least one passage, Kierkegaard even uses the language of re-creation, although he does not directly connect it with forgiveness of sins. He states that if a person admits that he or she can do nothing and comes to know that God is love, then God will sanctify him or her for God "is always creating . . . and he wants to create in him [or her] a new human being" (EUD, 325). Still, in none of these places does Kierkegaard speak of Christ or his Atonement for sin or of our need to believe in him in order to be forgiven and recreated. Nor does he engage in any discussion of the extent of our separation from God caused by sin. He never says whether sin involves a total rupture in our relationship or something less severe as in Religiousness A.

Conclusion

If, to be labeled Christian, a discourse must explicitly discuss faith in Jesus of Nazareth as the God-man who by his death redeemed us from sin and offers himself as the way to our eternal salvation, then the eighteen discourses are not Christian, just as Climacus claimed in his *Postscript*. However, as I have tried to show, if we investigate *Eighteen Upbuilding Discourses*' conception

---

[55]EUD, 125-26. See also 130.
[56]EUD, 248.
[57]See also EUD, 249-50, 353, 359, 367-69, 375.

of the nature of God and its understanding of human beings'
relation to God and to their eternal salvation, then the issue is not
so clear cut. In some places the discourses present a religion that
is clearly different from Climacus's description of Religiousness A
in his *Postscript*; sometimes, in fact, it seems close to Christianity.
Yet in other places the religion of the discourses is quite similar to
at least one of the versions of Religiousness A that *Postscript*
discusses. To be specific:

1. There is a great deal of agreement between the eighteen
discourses and Religiousness A about the nature of God as a
caring all powerful creator. There are also places where God is said
to be within human beings. However, throughout the discourses
Kierkegaard repeatedly refers to God as our Father, something that
Religiousness A never does. This suggests that in attributing that
name to God, *Eighteen Upbuilding Discourses'* religion is drawing
upon Christian revelation and thus going beyond immanental
religion.

2. In some discourses Kierkegaard agrees with Religiousness A
that knowledge, even experience, of a God who is capable of all
things can be attained by human beings internally deepening their
self-knowledge to the point where they recognize they can do
absolutely nothing. However, such self-knowledge is never
advanced as a way a person could withdraw or escape from his or
her existence, nor is it, therefore, a path to pantheism, as the
Platonic from of Religiousness A is said to be. Moreover, in other
discourses Kierkegaard speaks as if God's reality can only be
asserted by faith, a position that is similar to the Socratic version
of A.

3. Nowhere in the discourses does Kierkegaard suggest that a
person can discover that he/she is eternal or immortal by deepening his/her self-knowledge, as Religiousness A does with its
notion of recollection. Yet there are some indications in them that
Kierkegaard believes the human soul is naturally immortal. If this
is correct, that would be similar to the Platonic Religiousness A
and contrary to the Socratic where immortality was only a matter
of faith, (as well as to the view of Christianity that Climacus
presented).

4. Even if persons are immortal by nature, this does not make
their temporal existence irrelevant for their eternal salvation

because whether they are eternally saved or eternally damned depends upon the choices they make in time. The discourses unambiguously state that eternal salvation is entirely a gift of a loving and merciful God. Unlike Religiousness A, which in the final analysis considers the temporal existence and choices of humans unimportant for their eternal salvation, Kierkegaard's discourses exhort human beings to seize the moment and here and now choose to believe in a loving God if they wish to receive the gift of eternal salvation from him.[58]

5. Even though it contains no lengthy treatments of such notions, some discourses do refer to specifically Christian categories such as sin (more often than guilt), original sin, forgiveness of sin, and, at least once, to God's creation of a new human being in an already existing individual. (I should add that Kierkegaard also devotes two discourses to discussions of Christian love.)[59]

Thus, the very least that one can conclude is that it is incorrect simply to classify the discourses within Religiousness A—no matter what Johannes Climacus says. Even though some of them do express positions which agree with those found in one or another version of A, they also present views of God and of the human being's relation to God that are clearly contrary to that religiousness. In addition, they also put forth some specifically Christian beliefs.

---

[58]The Socratic form of Religiousness A also stressed the import of existence in time and the need to choose absolutely one's absolute end, eternal salvation, but since recollection discloses that every individual is naturally immortal and inevitably attains eternal salvation, Climacus ultimately speaks of the "illusory" character of temporal decisions (CUP, 1:271n.) and considers the whole situation humorous. See the texts cited in note 29.

[59]I have not discussed *Eighteen Upbuilding Discourses*'s treatment of Christian love in this paper because the *Postscript*'s account of Religiousness A contains almost no mention of human relationships. Still, I might note that Kierkegaard's discussion of Christian love in the third and fourth discourses include many notions that he will later treat in detail in *Works of Love*.

4

The Art of Upbuilding

George Pattison

Like other parts of his authorship, Kierkegaard's upbuilding writings were, from the beginning, carefully considered elements in a larger communicative strategy (even if that strategy was not quite as calculated as Kierkegaard himself sometimes suggested). Also like other parts of the authorship, the upbuilding works did not emerge from a vacuum, but from a specific cultural context, and the assumption guiding this essay is that a better acquaintance with this context will help us to a better understanding of what Kierkegaard's upbuilding discourses were about. The main features of the cultural background of the pseudonymous works are well known and much discussed: the literary world of Romanticism, the philosophical universe of Hegelianism, and the political and intellectual radicalism and nihilism of the 1840s. All of these remain relevant to the discourses as well, but here more particular sources and debating partners come into view. Kierkegaard himself often paid tribute to the importance that Bishop J. P. Mynster's sermons had had for him, counting them amongst his most regular devotional reading.[1]

Famously, Kierkegaard disallowed calling the discourses "sermons," although several of his contemporaries insisted on seeing them as such—including Mynster himself, a man who, we might presume, knew a sermon when he saw one![2] Even if we take Kierkegaard's part in this terminological debate, however, the very

---

[1]Perhaps the most accessible account of Mynster in English is in chap. 10, 'Piety and Good Taste: J. P. Mynster's Religion and Politics,' in Bruce Kirmmse, *Kierkegaard in Golden Age Denmark* (Bloomington: Indiana University Press, 1990).

[2]See Kts (pseudonym of J. P. Mynster), "Kirkelig Polemik" in *Intelligensblade* 41-42 (1844): 111.

fact of his disclaimer suggests that he was aware of the possibility that the discourses might be read as if they were sermons and, indeed, several of them maintain the conceit that they are transcripts of spoken words, addressing the reader as "My hearer!" and, at least in the case of the first, speaking of the hearers being gathered in church. It therefore seems likely that we will gain at least some insight into the background of the discourses by turning to the one Kierkegaard regarded as the master of preaching: Mynster himself.

Turning to Mynster, then, we are immediately struck by a further intriguing fact: that Mynster was not merely a master preacher, he was also the author of a treatise entitled "Remarks concerning the Art of Preaching" (1810). Although this was written at an early period in Mynster's career (published in the same year as the first of many volumes of his collected sermons), and before the appointment as Chaplain to Vor Frue Kirke in Copenhagen (where he was to be parish priest to the Kierkegaard family), it is profoundly consonant with his whole practice as a preacher during the next forty-four years. It was originally delivered as a lecture to a clergy meeting, where it was so well received that Mynster himself subsequently said of it that it was this lecture that first made him widely known in clerical circles.[3]

My aim here is therefore to offer a brief exposition of this somewhat forgotten text, drawing attention to those points that are most relevant to Kierkegaard's discourses. To find such an exercise attractive does not require us to make the strong claim that Kierkegaard himself would have been familiar with these "Remarks". He could have been, but I know of no evidence that he was. He was, however, familiar with Mynster's sermons and other religious writings, not to mention his personal presence in the pulpit and in society, and insofar as the "Remarks" distil key elements in Mynster's own practice as a preacher as well as clarifying the theoretical assumptions underlying that practice they help us to focus the issues around his significance for Kierkegaard.

---

[3]See J. P. Mynster, *Meddelelser om mit Levnet* (Copenhagen: Gyldendal, 1854) 177.

Mynster's early association with many of the leading spirits of Danish Romanticism is evident from the opening lines of the treatise on preaching, where, rejecting the view that the human being is a *tabula rasa* who can be taught to do anything simply by being provided with the relevant rules and methods, he speaks about how the beautiful image that the artist brings forth must have been long prepared inwardly and in secret, secret even from the artist himself. So it is with the art of preaching: preaching and its effects must be a reality before we can begin to reflect on it theoretically, and, indeed, there has only recently been much in the way of theorizing about preaching. Yet it is astonishing, given both this lack and the singular demands of preaching that we hear so many good sermons. The preacher must, after all, fit his words to the solemnity of the place, to the variety of his audience (which might at any one time include both princes and beggars), while abstaining from academic demonstrations and sensuous seductiveness, and do so week by week, year after year.

This situation is ameliorated by the fact that it is not the preacher's task to establish Christianity or found a congregation. He does not have to proclaim some new teaching, and his congregation should not expect it. Of course, he must have an inward, heartfelt relation to what he sets forth, and the congregation must be willing also to listen rightly and not want merely to be passively stirred and swayed. The action of divine worship must be the fruit of a common devotion in which all hearts are united. It is not a matter of learning some new information, though that is not necessarily ruled out, but of being confirmed in what is already known, something that simple but honest words can achieve as well as any. But if the sermon should not be a matter of artifice, this does not mean that it will not benefit from the application of some art, and it is to the furtherance of such art that Mynster hopes his treatise will contribute.

The first point he considers is that a sermon will rarely achieve a conversion or revolution in the life of the auditor: "the church is not a mission station", he writes.[4] Nor does preaching offer a

---

[4] J. P. Mynster, "Bemærkninger om den konst at prædike," in *Blandede Skrivter af Dr. J. P. Mynster* (Copenhagen: Gyldendal, 1852) 87. Further references are to

"course" in religion and morality, for the church is not an educational institution either. Those who gather for divine worship must be presumed to agree in the main points of faith: the point of such worship, therefore, and of the preacher's contribution to it must be "upbuilding". In accordance with this, the best word for preaching itself is "Talks" (*Taler*), a name that reflects the good-natured tone and the personal warmth that are integral to the communicative act of preaching in an established congregation.

Mynster, as we have seen, did not see preaching as an academic exercise. Nevertheless, the preacher must address the understanding as well as the heart. For Mynster, a man of the Romantic era, heart and head are indeed not essentially divided. The understanding may be spoken of as cold and indifferent to what should chiefly concern our deepest longings, and it is easy to see examples of how the understanding can overreach its limits. This is indeed particularly so (he says) in the case of many English sermons which are so metaphysical that they are more likely to awaken doubt than to edify (although, in case we might suspect any anti-English sentiment in the aftermath of 1807, Mynster gives the counter position in words from *Tristram Shandy*: "'Tis not preaching the gospel, but ourselves. For my own part, I had rather direct five words point blank to the heart" [BKP, 105])[5]. The point is that both understanding and the heart must be given their due: we should not forget that "thought is a light that illuminates all that is in a person" (BKP, 90). At the same time, "if one is to address the understanding concerning religious and ethical matters, then the feeling for religion and the ethical must first live in the heart" (BKP, 90).

This, of course, is precisely where philosophers, from Aristotle to Kant, will feel uncomfortable, suspecting some ruse to bypass rationality. Mynster recognizes the possibility of abuse but does not believe that this should lead us to condemn all rhetoric.

---

this edition and are given in the text as BKP.

[5]It is striking that Mynster quotes English sources at several points, and in English. For Kierkegaard's generation, however, English had fallen far behind German and even French as a familiar foreign language. Kierkegaard's own access to English authors such as Shakespeare or Swift is chiefly through German translations.

Nevertheless, the question goes to the heart of the matter. Take the example of a court of law. When the defense goes beyond the bare facts of the case itself and draws the judge's attention to mitigating circumstances or to the accused's previous service to the people or to the dishonor to his name resulting from the case, is he wrong to do so? Surely these are matters that the judge *should* consider. The fault is only when such considerations are allowed to override respect for the law itself. It would be only "half-humans" who could neither laugh nor cry, and we should not imagine that law is only undermined by these: the pretence that we are dealing with bare facts to which human feelings are irrelevant can itself be used to subvert justice. Sophisms, after all, can insinuate themselves into even the most abstract discourse.

This last comment leads Mynster to reflect on the relation between preaching and philosophy, and to address the objection that the preacher merely offers a superficial version of what metaphysics achieves in greater depth and with greater rigor. But here too it would be a mistake to deny the relevance of feeling. Rationality alone can never establish "primordial truth, the highest principle, from which all truth proceeds" (BKP, 95) which can only be "immediately cognized (*erkiendes*)". This is a matter of the heart and of conscience, and the task of scientific knowledge can only be the exposition thereof. Even the most rigorous philosophers accompany their lectures with illustrations that attempt to make their subject more plastic, more accessible to their hearers. Firmness in possession of the truth "demands the unscientific as well as the scientific" (BKP, 96). Mynster cites Cicero, Bayle and Jacobi as exemplifying the need to acknowledge a higher kind of truth than that which reason alone can make available. In Jacobi's words, quoted by Mynster, "Transcendental philosophy will not tear this heart from my breast—should I let myself be set free from dependence on love in order to become blessed through pride" (BKP, 97)? In a similar vein he deprecates modelling the form of a sermon on a philosophical discourse—not that a sermon should not have a certain form, but this need not be forced or apparent (BKP, 105). In these comments we might hear a considerable if unexpressed anxiety that philosophy (N.B.: not Hegelian philosophy, for this is a whole generation before the influence of Hegel is felt in Denmark) is threatening to usurp the traditional territory of the preacher, namely, to offer guidance in the ultimate issues of belief and morals.

We certainly do not need to attribute any direct influence on Kierkegaard to such passages, but they do make clear that something of the critique of philosophy that Kierkegaard was to develop in specific relation to Hegel was already latent in Mynster's thought, as in that of other leading figures of Danish Romantic philosophy such as F. C. Sibbern and P. M. Møller. Mynster, however, is by no means prepared to drive this point in the direction of a radical separation of religion and philosophy. On the contrary, in pursuing his own proper task, the preacher is helping to lay the foundation for what true science requires. The essential task of the preacher is "to set forth the highest objects before the eyes of men, to open their eyes to see what is in front of them, when he places the most holy knowledge in that place where the artifice of sophistry can do nothing, where man has his true treasure, freed from the transient folly and wisdom of time" (BKP, 98).

Typical of Mynster is his emphasis on the visual aspect of what the preacher is to accomplish. So, he continues, the preacher "must know how to make his object visible, to invite each person to come and see it as it is" (BKP, 99). To reject the false, we must show it in its true form. The same applies to the good, the true and the beautiful.

> A portrayal of what dwells in a pious soul, its faith, its hope, its love, its contentment, its humility, its strength, its care, its comfort, its joy and peace, how it regards the world, itself, its relation to God—who would dare to say that such a portrayal is ineffective, without the power to convince, even if it is far indeed from anything we might call a demonstration. (BKP, 99)

The most powerful inducement to religion is that we, mortals as we are, *see* its beauties.

It is then to this goal of enabling the listeners to visualize the object of the discourse that the preacher's modes of expression are adapted—"His similes and figurative words, his personifications, his manner of address, now to the whole company, now to each individual in particular, his frequent questions . . . " (BKP, 100). If he can do this then he will unite the clarity of thought with feeling, and this unity is itself the ground and proof of conviction.

The emphasis on visuality is highly relevant to Kierkegaard, and in several seemingly contradictory respects. On the one hand it is precisely this that is the object of attack in such later works as *Practice in Christianity*, where the preacher's call to his congregation to "observe" is linked to the kind of false admiration that inhibits the believer from active discipleship. Mere seeing, mere contemplation, in other words, induces mental and moral habits of passivity and detachment. Yet Kierkegaard's own discourses are replete with intensely visual figurative expressions. Again and again we are called to "behold" this or that: "Look at him, that lucky one whom good fortune delighted to indulge in everything [EUD, 89]. . . . Just look at the favored one [EUD, 90]. . . . Just look at him! [the person who is intimate with adversity, EUD, 92]. . . . Look at him, the *concerned one*! [EUD, 94]." I have explored this contradiction elsewhere, and would only reiterate here that, as I understand it, it is one of the keys to Kierkegaard's communicative strategy that he lures us into the contemplative space of free-playing possibilities conjured up by figuration and visualization in order to recall us the more sharply to the unrepresentable freedom within which the religious relation to God must be worked out.[6] Whereas Mynster, then, sees the visual nature of the subject matter of the sermon as leading to a direct intuition of the ultimate objects of religion, Kierkegaard practices what could be called an implicit negative theology in which the visual metaphor is subjected to an internal critical deepening. This can go so far that the image itself is rendered paradoxical—a sign of contradiction.

Mynster is insistent on preaching being what we might call a "live" art. It is part of the assimilation of preaching to a more academic kind of discourse that the preacher organizes his material to focus on a series of "points" and likewise with a growing custom for people to leave the service after the sermon. The outcome of this is the fashion for printed sermons in order for readers to "study" them at leisure. But, Mynster says, the written

---

[6]See, e.g., George Pattison *Kierkegaard: The Aesthetic and the Religious* (London: SCM, 1997) esp. chap 6; idem., "The Theory and Practice of Language and Communication in Kierkegaard's *Upbuilding Discourses*," in *Kierkegaardiana 19* (1998): 81-94; idem., *Kierkegaard's Upbuilding Discourses. Philosophy, Literature, Theology* (London: Routledge, 2002) esp. chap 6.

text of a sermon is "only preparatory, not the work itself" (BKP, 113) and he quotes Fox's saying "Speeches are made to be spoken, and not to be read."[7] This fact shows itself in a certain formal aspect in that a spoken address can be more repetitious and discursive than a written one and take grammatical liberties that would be unacceptable in writing. Also, the "live" speaker will adapt his words and ideas to his particular audience, and not simply give free rein to what he wants to say and how he wants to say it. All of which leads Mynster to disagree with what is apparently a growing disapprobation of improvised preaching. Some liberty must be allowed in this regard, he insists.

Printing has widened the sphere of the arts, but, as Plato had already warned, writing can weaken our power of "inward recollection" (BKP, 117). This must be especially true of an art such as preaching whose content is ultimately more than verbal, and where merely formal understanding must not be confused with the matter at issue. The preacher is and must be personally engaged in his speaking. Through varied words and on many occasions he communicates essentially the same message, and whatever variety of expression he uses "his heart is permeated by the same feeling and his conscience acknowledges the same truth"—and this is what the listener will take away, rather than the memory of this particular phrase or that particular idea (BKP, 119). The Christian God does not dwell in a purely transcendent light, He has instead involved himself in time and history with the whole drama of human life, its fall, its corruption, its redemption, in short "the whole person" (BKP, 122). Preaching must reflect this, as must the preacher himself in his manner of engagement with his task.

Today, of course (he continues), there is no article of faith that has not been exposed to doubt, no symbol or expression that has not been exposed to ridicule or whose ancient meaning has not been questioned. Everywhere there is a longing for novelty and a critical spirit prevails. If this might seem to go against the grain of the earlier comment that the church is not a mission station, it is characteristic for Mynster that, despite acknowledging the presence of critical voices in society, he is instinctively defensive of the idea

---

[7]Presumably the reference is to Charles James Fox—Mynster does not specify.

of a "Christian society" or, more specifically, of the idea that the Danish Church is still in a real sense the heart of Danish society. Although many are now rootless, they are not unwilling to hear. They have needs and aspirations that the preacher must address if he is to win them. Complaints that the time of preaching is past are not new. Even today "we will still be able to make our preaching fruitful for everyone who cares to gather their fruits" (BKP, 128). Moreover, given that the subject of preaching is religion, preachers themselves should apply the consolations of religion to their own endeavors, and pursue their task with faithfulness, humility and confidence. Therefore in the face of today's challenges we should not despair, and we may yet carry forward the same work as that of the apostles.

There are several points here we might relate to Kierkegaard and, in particular, to the discourses.

To begin with, it is striking how Mynster specifies the designation "Upbuilding Discourses" (*Opbyggelige Taler*) as most suited to describing the nature of the contemporary sermon. When, then, Mynster praises the first volume of Kierkegaard's discourses and says that despite Kierkegaard's refusal to call them sermons they are "really" sermons, he is, in his own terms, being entirely consistent. Yet precisely because this expression relies upon the assumption that, in some sense, Denmark "is" a Christian country and that the church is not required to be a mission station we can see already something of the reasons why it was precisely Mynster's version of Christianity that became the object of Kierkegaard's iconoclastic "Attack on Christendom" twelve years later, at the other end of his authorship. For Kierkegaard, it would seem, the real proclamation of Christianity that was needed would have to be more than an "upbuilding discourse." It is notable in this connection that Mynster's comment about Kierkegaard's discourses was made in the context of an article responding to the charge made in a review of *Either/Or* that the cultured classes of Copenhagen had abandoned the church. This article was, in turn, part of a cycle of articles and counterarticles provoked by *Either/Or* that I have elsewhere described as having "an eerie prophetic significance, anticipating the final polemics of Kierkegaard's own 'Attack

upon Christendom.' "[8] Mynster, of course, knew as well as Kierkegaard himself knew, that Kierkegaard was not ordained and
therefore not technically licensed to preach, and his remark is very
much apropos the content rather than the pragmatic context of the
Discourses. At the same time, given his own emphasis on the
essentially "live" nature of the art of preaching, he might have
been observant of the fact that, although several of Kierkegaard's
later addresses for Friday communion were delivered in church,
the early *Upbuilding Discourses* are entirely and very self-consciously literary works, written texts, that could not possibly have been
preached in a "live" situation (apart from matters of style, just
compare the length with that of Mynster's own printed sermons!).

This may seem like a small point, but again it points to the
deep gulf between the basic conceptions underlying Mynster's
church practice and Kierkegaard's idea of Christian communication.

Kierkegaard shares with Mynster a desire to resist the assimilation of the religious address to a merely academic discourse on
the subject of religion, but how can he give effect to this resistance? We have already noted his own use of visual effects, and,
we might add that, like Mynster's preacher, he is constantly
engaged in questioning the listener/reader to make them aware of
their involvement. But he also asks the reader to read aloud, a
practice that is designed expressly to make the act of reading more
personal and more engaged, in opposition to the disinterested
critical distance that might be relevant if we were reading academic texts. But is there more to the question of writing than this?

Mynster's treatise makes clear that already in the early 1800s,
under the social pressures resulting from the Napoleonic Wars and
the ideological influences of the Enlightenment and of Romanticism, public religion was in a state of crisis in Denmark. What he
complains of in his contemporaries—the restless pursuit of novelty,
the prevalence of a critical spirit—are points that will be central to
Kierkegaard's critique of the age. Of course, they were and are also
shared by many others who, following Schiller, saw modernity as
suffering a series of radical dualisms: heart and head, individual

---

[8]*International Kierkegaard Commentary: Either/Or II*, 304-305.

and society, etc. What specifically unites Mynster and Kierkegaard is the question as to what this situation means for the communication of religion. Kierkegaard's way will ultimately prove more negative, at least as far as the role of the church is concerned. His early decision not to move on from his theological qualification to ordination but to devote himself to writing is, we sense, already a pointer in that direction.

Is it going too far to say that the very fact that he chooses to write his religious addresses, to pursue the goal of upbuilding as an author, reflects his acceptance of the irresistibility of the modern age and its culture of writing that is the fate of our times. In *The Point of View for my Work as an Author*, Kierkegaard will, famously, characterize the present age as essentially esthetic and argue that this is why he himself had to begin by writing esthetic books— only so could he meet his readers where they were and win their attention. In other places, however, he draws attention to different aspects of the age. In *Two Ages* it is to its being mired in reflection. Elsewhere it is precisely the massive output of printed writing that comes to the fore. Kierkegaard's complaints against science and scholarship are well known, but these would not have the grip they do if it were not for their transmission in printed texts. In his unpublished *Lectures on Communication* Kierkegaard wrote:

> The powers of the human world have been fantastically extracted and a book world has been produced (one now becomes an author simply and solely by becoming a reader—instead of by primitivity, just as one becomes a man now becomes a man simply and solely by aping "the others," instead of by primitivity), a public of fantastic abstractions. As soon as one writes he is no longer a single individual human being himself, nor is the reader that to him, either. (JP, 1:650:4)

The social constitution of knowledge is inseparable from "the whole mob of publishers, booksellers, journalists, authors" (JP, 1:649:5), from "scholarly periodicals" (JP, 1:655) and mass readership (JP, 1:655). This is, of course, not a different complaint from that which finds the age too esthetic or too reflective, it is simply another dimension of the same essential problem. Writing—the book-world and periodical-world—is the cultural embodiment and instrument of reflection, a continual abrogation of the immediacy of speech and a constant invitation to lose oneself in an esthetic relation to reality, rather than to exist in one's primitivity. In this situation the relation of pastor to congregation and society is also changed and, Kierkegaard says, becomes "a poet-relationship" (JP, 1:653:18), something that, we infer, again points to the secondhand, literary nature of the pastor's way of communicating, where "live" sermons are "written" with a view to publication.

In accordance with the pedagogical logic of *The Point of View*, however, we can only work against such a situation by accepting its conditions. Accepting them—but not on their own terms, for it is precisely Kierkegaard's strategy to turn these conditions against themselves—in this case, by attempting a kind of writing that is constructed so as to enact a countermovement against mere bookishness and to resist being appropriated in the manner of abstract or objective knowledge, a kind of writing that repeatedly attempts to turn readers back to themselves and to their individual situation vis-à-vis God. So, where Mynster sets out to work for the improvement of the age by preaching and by the subsequent printing and circulation of his sermons in published collections, Kierkegaard chooses the printed word from the very beginning— and does so precisely as a means of curing bookishness. Through inviting readers to a different kind of reading from that with which they are familiar he seeks to awaken them to a different kind of relation to their own reality from that which occurs in the mediation of the book. The preacher is not ashamed either of his authority or of his "I" and Mynster's sermons duly make plentiful use of the "I" of one who, as an ordained pastor, is entitled to speak authoritatively in his own voice to his flock. Yet such authority and such personal asseverations on the part of the preacher are not going to make any impact on a society that is questioning its very relation to the church. Kierkegaard, then, produces in his discourses sermon-like works that are distinguished from sermons precisely by their lack of authority and by the absence of the authorial "I." The work of reading the discourses is not that of deriving views and opinions secondhand from the authoritative author telling you what to think. The author, as Kierkegaard puts it in one of the prefaces to the discourses, "continually desires to be as one absent on a journey" (EUD, 179). The aim is not to draw the reader into the fellowship of the church or to confirm the reader in that fellowship (and the social dimension of religion is never far from Mynster's mind) but to leave the reader alone with God. For all the analogies between them, Mynster's sermons and Kierkegaard's discourses, and Mynster's understanding of the art of preaching and Kierkegaard's understanding of the art of upbuilding are marked by a fundamental divergence, that suggests the inevitability of Kierkegaard's final rejection of Mynster's policy of accommodation and amelioration in relation to the crisis in the relationship between church and society.

5

A Word of Explanation:
Transfiguring Language in Kierkegaard's
Eighteen Upbuilding Discourses

Steven Shakespeare

The more one thinks about it, the stranger earthly life and human language become. (EUD, 301)

The *Eighteen Upbuilding Discourses* seek to make life and language strange to us again. My intention in this essay is to show how an appreciation of this sharpens our reading of them, and sheds light on the grammar of Kierkegaard's religious communication.

The question of language, its nature, use and abuse, is now acknowledged as a key theme in Kierkegaard's writings.[1] It is a question that cuts across traditional divisions between the pseudonymous works and those which appeared under the author's own name. It helps to highlight the complexity of those texts in which Kierkegaard appears to speak in his own name.[2]

---

[1]See, e.g., Mark C. Taylor, "Language, Truth and Indirect Communication," *Tijdscrift voor Filosofie* 37 (1975): 74-88; R. Hall, "Language and Freedom: Kierkegaard's Analysis of the Demonic in *The Concept of Anxiety*," in *International Kierkegaard Commentary: The Concept of Anxiety*, ed. Robert Perkins (Macon GA: Mercer University Press, 1985) 153-66; R. Hall, *Word and Spirit. A Kierkegaardian Critique of the Modern Age* (Bloomington and Indianapolis: Indiana University Press, 1993); Peter Fenves, *"Chatter": Language and History in Kierkegaard* (Stanford CA: Stanford University Press, 1993); Steven Shakespeare, *Kierkegaard, Language and the Reality of God* (Aldershot: Ashgate, 2001).

[2]For a striking deconstruction of the author's voice, even in a work as seemingly authoritative as *The Point of View for My Work as an Author*, see Joachim Garff, "The Eyes of Argus," *Kierkegaardiana* 15 (1991): 29-54.

Commentators are increasingly compelled to point out how even Kierkegaard's most apparently direct authorial interventions are haunted by the specter of what must remain unsaid, what renders discourse about life and faith, ethics and religion, intrinsically wayward and broken. The discourses are no exception. They are not the pristine creations of a sovereign writer, transparently declaring the truth of things. They inhabit, or better, they evoke and create their own fictional world, their own rhetorical situation. In form and content, they invite us to engage with the communication of the incommunicable.[3]

Kierkegaard's understanding of language and signs is inseparable from this paradox. For language itself is the medium and the expression of those contradictions which structure and disturb our sense of human selfhood, existence, value, and faith.

There is one particular play on words that exemplifies this, and which will bring our deliberations into focus. The movement from explanation (*Forklaring*) to transfiguration (*Forklarelse*) is woven throughout these texts, to emerge in its most provocative form in the final discourse, "One Who Prays Aright Struggles in Prayer and is Victorious—in that God is Victorious" (EUD, 377-401). The presupposition that our words can give us a clear, distinct and rational access to what is real founders before the ambiguities of existence. However, the point is not to leave language behind, but to transform it from within. For language is where real and ideal meet, the sign of both our temporality and our relationship to eternity. Given this, communication about existence and its ultimate meaning can never be straightforward. Kierkegaard's discourses awaken us to the mystery that inhabits our words, threatening us, provoking us, and luring us out of our mute complacency.

The Errant Discourse

If nothing else, the prefaces to the discourses should make us pause before assigning these texts to the category of direct communication. They renounce their own authority, exposing

---

[3]See George Pattison, " 'Who' Is the Discourse? A Study in Kierkegaard's Religious Literature," *Kierkegaardiana* 16 (1993): 28-45.

themselves to the risk of interpretation as they journey through the world beyond the author's perception and control (EUD, 5). They seek a reader whose "voice breaks the spell on the letters" who "with his voice summons forth what the mute letters have on their lips, as it were, but are unable to express without great effort, stammering and stuttering" (EUD, 53). It is this reader who "sanctifies the gift, gives it meaning, and transforms it into much" (EUD, 107), whilst the author "desires only to be as one absent on a journey" (EUD, 179).

The discourse is changed. Leaving its home "inclosed in itself" it relies on that reader whose interest "brings the cold thoughts into flame again, transforms the discourse into a conversation," who "accomplishes the great work of letting the perishability of the discourse arise in imperishability" (EUD, 231). In the final preface, Kierkegaard bids a last adieu to his work, and describes his own joy as being one "who continually comes to his reader only to bid him farewell" (EUD, 295).

Even this brief travelogue through the discourses alerts us to their complexity. Consider the characters involved. There is the author, who has the godlike power to create and initiate, and yet whose very act of creation renders him hidden and powerless to control what results. There is the discourse, personified as a solitary wanderer with nowhere to lay its head and whose Christ-likeness is underlined by references to its transformation, resurrection and exaltation.[4] And finally, we meet the reader, who seems to take over the divine power to create, transform, and raise from death.

Woven through this trinity are the tangled threads of language and communication. It is language that breaks free of its author's control. And yet language in the abstract, as a set of rules and signs, is dead unless it becomes conversation, the dialogue in

---

[4] This is not to suggest that the discourses are taking any particular position as regards Christological doctrines. However, as will be argued, they have to be regarded as *performative works*, rather than depositiories of objective doctrinal information. In this sense, it is intriguing that they echo the pattern of Christ's own lived mode of communication. Perhaps the boundaries between the discourses and more decisively Christian Kierkegaardian works need to be questioned.

which neither authorial intention, the meaning of the text, nor the one who interprets it are left unchanged.

A Difference of Language

It should not surprise us, therefore, that the very first discourse announces the need for "a different kind of talk (*en anden Tale*)" about faith (EUD, 9). Faith is incomparable to any worldly good or possession. It does not stand at the top of a hierarchy of goods, but is "qualitatively different" (EUD, 10). And this introduces a kind of tension in the way we must speak of faith. On the one hand, the mark of faith's difference is that it is accessible to anyone. It is not a commodity which can be bought, sold, measured out, or hoarded. It eludes the codes of bourgeois property, exchange and competition. To wish it for oneself is to wish it for all people.

At the same time as faith is presented as the most accessible reality of all, it is nevertheless inexpressible in any direct way. It is "more blessed than language can describe" (EUD, 25), and the God to whom faith relates does not meet us in visible signs, but in secret (EUD, 26).

Any discourse on faith must bear this tension within itself. It must not distort faith by turning it into a possession for those who have the correct moral or religious capital. Faith is utterly open and egalitarian. And yet at the same time, all talk of faith must hold a secret at its heart. This is not a hidden piece of knowledge, but the fact that faith can never be directly expressed or communicated, that no words or signs can grasp it.[5]

To put it strongly, communication about faith is both necessary and impossible. This comes out more clearly as we look at some of the ways language is treated in the discourses, at once illuminating and hiding the eternal.

Kierkegaard acknowledges that some complain that existence is a "dark saying" (EUD, 88). In the same discourse, he later describes the one who becomes afflicted and seduced by external concerns, and loses all hope in life: "He saw what others saw, but

---

[5]See Jacques Derrida, "Passions," in *On the Name* (Stanford CA: Stanford University Press, 1995) 3-31.

his eyes continually read an invisible handwriting in everything, that it was emptiness and illusion" (EUD, 94).

Language here appears as a metaphor for what obscures and leads astray. But despite some of Kierkegaard's repeated concerns about the confusion and dissipation which careless words foster, his attitude to language is never one-sided. For example, the passage which begins "Every Good and Every Perfect Gift is From Above," quoted from James 1:17-22, refers to receiving the word that is implanted in us. Commenting on this, Kierkegaard writes that the apostle's words are neither casual nor idle, but urgent and powerful, admonishing us against our delusions. Moreover, these words "are not spoken without any bearing on other words" (EUD, 32).

The gift of God is thus likened to a word which is already within us, and which nevertheless needs to be received by us. The strange logic is similar to that which Kierkegaard uses when dealing with the soul. The soul is ours, it is in a sense the most essential part of us. And yet it must be received as a gift. The words "to gain one's soul in patience" are utterly alarming to conventional wisdom, disrupting as they do all sense of our self-possession and complacent self-assurance (EUD, 159-60). If life's task is to gain the very thing that life seems to presuppose, meaning and words seem thrown into confusion. And yet this is unavoidable, because the soul is "the contradiction of the temporal and the eternal" (EUD, 163).[6] Our life is utterly contingent and time bound, and yet precisely as such, it offers us the possibility to be dispossessed of our illusory self-sufficiency and awaken the trace of eternity within us. At the same time, eternity is never something pure, silent and static. It is the gift of life at every moment, a word implanted in us.

The communication of the eternal, must, like the words about gaining one's soul, contain a "redoubling repetition" (EUD, 169). "Repetition" is one of Kierkegaard's limit concepts, appearing in various texts to break open closed systems of thinking.[7] Without

---

[6]Compare SUD, 13-14, for Anti-Climacus on the paradoxes of selfhood.

[7]See Stanley Cavell, *Must We Mean What We Say?* (Cambridge: Cambridge University Press, 1969).

repetition, there is no creation (R, 133). Repetition is transcendence (R, 186; CA, 21), setting decision and passion in motion (CUP, 1:312-13). And, in one of Kierkegaard's most insightful texts on language, repetition is bound up with the very nature of signs. It occurs when time and eternity, the real and the ideal touch: "Here is a redoubling, here it is a matter of repetition" (JC, 171). This collision, this contradiction, gives human consciousness its distinctive interest in existing, and all of this is possible only because of language. Language, the word, brings the real and the ideal together, brings existence to expression (JC, 168). And even as it does so, it makes us aware of all that can never be fully or directly expressed.

In their own errant way, the discourses are a practical exercise in exposing language and communication to what exceeds them. whilst always maintaining that it is only within human, linguistic, temporal existence that we encounter these paradoxes.

The recurring theme of the implanted, fruitful word underlines this. God, we are told, "brought us forth by the word of truth" (EUD, 137), and we are called to be slow to speak that we may better listen to the divine Word "which sounds now, as formerly, when one is silent" (EUD, 138). And yet the word which sounds on the interior of the soul cannot be divorced from public expression. Even the Bible, whose "language has shaped the discourse of the God-fearing about the divine" (EUD, 327), whose words resonate in holy places, is vulnerable. Its words are carried off into strange secular contexts, so that "we sometimes hear a scriptural expression that has wandered from the sacred out into the world" (EUD, 327). However, far from this being simply a story of loss and decay, it repeats the necessary journey of the discourses themselves, the risk of communication which takes them beyond settled contexts and the security of an enclosed sacred realm.

The language of eternity can never lose its bearing on other languages, its complicity with the errancy of words or else it becomes like cowardliness, "the speech that is never heard, that in its superiority disdained every word and phrase the language offered" (EUD, 361). Words about the sacred may become platitudes, and Kierkegaard may stress the silence and secrecy of goodness, for "it is God's nature to live in secret" (EUD, 370). But this secrecy is, as we have seen, the excess, the hidden and broken heart which accompanies all communication, not an invitation to self-inclosing reserve. The good which remains silent is easily misjudged. Indeed, silence becomes a temptation rather than a virtue when it lets "rouged untruth" go unchallenged (EUD, 371).

Language must be seen differently, expose us to what is other. Kierkegaard praises Anna who recognizes the infant Jesus in the temple, as an example of expectancy, who "said with a mind dedicated to God, solemn as eternity's language is, confident as eternity's expectancy is: It must happen" (EUD, 217). Another play on words between "maaskee" (meaning "perhaps") and "maa skee" (meaning "must happen") highlights the closeness and the difference between eternity's language and the language we use every day. The point, then, is not to abolish language and time, but to free them from the narrow, utilitarian instrumentalism which thinks it knows what happiness is and how it is achieved. Whilst prayer is considered "idle talk on earth" (EUD, 223) where impatience rules, it is still language that clears a space for the eternal to appear, as it does in Anna: "Although ordinary human speech becomes silent at the sight of her, the most profound expression in language must call her in the strictest and noblest sense: the expectant one" (EUD, 225).

Language's inescapable potential for duplicity means that the most urgent of all concerns, eternal salvation, can become a mere "play on words . . . a loose and idle phrase, at times virtually forgotten, or arbitrarily left out of the language" (EUD, 255). Salvation does not lie in abandoning language, therefore. The life without any expectancy of an eternal salvation is like "writing in the sand that the sea erases" (EUD, 263). Language and communication are utterly vulnerable, and Kierkegaard constantly warns us against superficial and light-minded interpretations of the scriptures he chooses for the discourses. And yet the expectancy he recommends is even more intimate a communication than receiving one's mother's milk (EUD, 263).

Understanding this means reading life's text in such a way as to include oneself in the reading:

> And even though in every other sense it is just a figurative expression to say that we see the finger of God in life, a person who is concerned about himself understands it quite literally, because all deeper and more inward self-knowledge is under

> divine guidance and continually sees the finger of God that points to him. To miss one letter confuses the whole word, and yet this confusion is nothing compared with the confusion that occurs when a person, in understanding life in its totality and the history of the human race, skips over one human being—himself—since the individual human being is, after all, not like a single letter, in itself a meaningless part of the word, but is the whole word. (EUD, 276)

A person cannot be built up in general, but only in the context where one's own existence and meaning is at stake (EUD, 276).

Life is uncertain, and the discourses seek to make us tremble before this. "To Preserve One's Soul in Patience" ironically poses itself against the "written word" which "stands fast" as a futile attempt to preserve meaning and value intact against the vagaries of time and existence (EUD, 184). The discourses nurture an anxiety that what matters most cannot be preserved in this way. Indeed, the horror of losing one's soul is such that "Language is unable to articulate it clearly" (EUD, 185). No instant solution is possible. We cannot leap over our temporality and language, for time "talks in between" the moments of our life (EUD 188). Impatience wants to evade all this through fantastic wishes that take leave of existence. Patience dares to interrupt these illusions (EUD, 189), until by the end of the long winding path of the discourse, it is shown to accentuate the passion of existing: "This, you see, is why we chose to let patience itself speak! It does not seek confirmation in someone's experience but, as it says, will gloriously strengthen every experience" (EUD 203).

What happens in the course these texts is not that any new information is given or any intellectual puzzles solved. Rather, we are invited into a process of reading that changes us as it changes our language, gives it another grammar.

This is indicated by the way in which Kierkegaard deals with the language used by apostles in scripture. Kierkegaard held the apostle up as an ideal source of authoritative communication. At the same time, however, what the apostles had to say was inevitably paradoxical and indirect. The second "Love Will Hide a Multitude of Sins" discourse opens by stating that "Just as apostolic speech is essentially different in content from all human speech, so it is also in many ways different in form" (EUD, 69). This is explained by saying that apostolic speech is "ardent, burning, inflamed, everywhere and always stirred by the forces of the new life" (EUD, 69). It is as "impatient as . . . a woman in labour" (EUD, 69). This speech of fire proclaims judgement and gives birth.

However, the essential difference between apostolic and other speech is not easy to isolate. The characteristics mentioned could be applied to other instances of fiery rhetoric. The issue only unfolds as we follow the discourse, and find that the apostle speaks from a different presupposition, that of the eternal love which can never be deceived or refuted by what happens in the world.

This is what I meant by saying that the discourses invite us to use a different "grammar" of communication, to change our fundamental attitude to time and language. Kierkegaard underlines this shift by making the surprising claim that apostolic words about love hiding sins are "a faithful thought, a valid witness, which in order to be understood must be taken literally (*maa tages efter Ordet*)" (EUD, 59). This is not to suggest that the words are simply copying an independent reality on the far side of our language, since "all observation is not just a receiving, a discovering, but also a bringing forth" (EUD, 59). It is rather that the apostolic words have the capacity to bring into being the reality they describe, to give birth to love in actual existence, not merely as a romantic ideal.

This strange literalism recurs when Kierkegaard considers calling God "Father." He writes that only for the one who judges by externals is this a figurative expression. For the one who looks beyond these, "this expression is not metaphorical (*billedligt*), imperfect, but the truest and most literal expression" (EUD, 99). The word translated metaphorical here is better rendered as "figurative." Kierkegaard is saying that Fatherhood is not an image drawn from human life and secondarily applied to God. The reason for this is that Kierkegaard identifies the essence of fatherhood with the giving of gifts. But God does not merely give gifts that are separate from God's own being, for "God gives not only the gifts but himself with them in a way beyond the capability of any human being" (EUD, 99).

God is the giver. Before birth, language, teaching, ideas, love, God is the first, the origin of all. Faith sees all things as given, as gratuitous. It reads the world as gift, and therefore "the human distinction between what might be called gift and what the language is not inclined to designate as gift vanishes in the essential, in the giver" (EUD, 99). Even as the discourses affirm our creativity in bringing to birth a new reality, so they dispossess us of our illusions of mastery. At the height of our creative interpretation, we are exposed, receptive to an infinite gift. Language, which can become mired in dualism and externalities, is also the medium through which the paradox of faith is made possible.

When Kierkegaard admonishes the reader to leave figure behind for actuality (EUD, 133-34), it is not because there is a direct language available which copies divine reality. He is describing a process in which the words are transformed, in which they become part of a way of living which refers all things to God: "Let us, then, try to make a pilgrimage, as it were, with the text into differences as we continually let the words remind us *that every good gift and every perfect gift is from above*" (EUD, 145). If this happens, the apostolic words are heard as a "divine refrain" (EUD, 145).

This "hearing as" involves something like learning a new language. For instance, in "To Need God is a Human Being's Highest Perfection," the word that we should be "contented with the grace of God" confuses ordinary language (EUD, 300). It is a word that wounds to death in order to save life, "a little magic formula that transformed everything" (EUD, 300). It is hard to understand this because it is "a new language . . . one that is so very different" (EUD, 300). There is a "language difference" between God's eternal faithfulness and an immature faith which thinks that grace only occurs when things work out well in life (EUD, 302).

Word Play

This transformation of everything, this shift in language, is indicated throughout the discourses in various ways. One persistent motif is that of playing on the different senses of the Danish words for clarification, explanation and transfiguration.

Kierkegaard uses a variety of words in the discourses to indicate radical change and transition: *forandre* (to alter or change), *forvandle* (to transform) and *forklare* (to transfigure). The latter verb can also be translated "to explain" or "to clarify" and gives rise to the related nouns *Forklaring* (explanation) and *Forklarelse* (transfiguration).

A key example of this is found in the continuation of the discourse "To Need God." Having alerted us to the need for a new language, Kierkegaard goes on to indicate how, when one longs for grace "everything has been changed (*forandret*)" (EUD, 303). Words of grace call a person aside "where he no longer hears the secular mentality's earthly mother tongue, the speech of human beings, the noise of the shopkeepers, but where the words explain themselves to him (*Ordet forklarer sig for ham*)" (EUD, 303). Later in the discourse, we read that when the first, shallow understanding of the self struggles with the deeper self that halts it, "in that minute everything can be changed" whilst the deeper self sits with "transfigured (*forklarede*) gentleness" for the sickness to give way to new life (EUD, 314-15). Others may try to help the first self out with "the explanation (*Forklaringen*)" (EUD, 315), but this only obstructs the deeper change to which the self is called. God is compared to the friend to whom one goes for some explanation of life's trials (EUD, 324). However, God does not offer reasons, but sanctification: "Wherever God is in truth, there he is always creating" making a person into "a new human being" (EUD, 325).

God is known by the effect of transformation, of new creation, through which a person is able to be dispossessed, vulnerable and yet steadfast. And this is a spiritual journey from the demand for explanations and clear reasons for things, to a faith that is a gratuitous response to grace.

The first discourses examine our desire for explanation (EUD, 15, 35) our search for coherence and order in all things which approaches the world "with a question, extorts an explanation from it, demands a testimony" (EUD, 84). The language here is all about power, demand, control, but the truth is that a person "is not the lord in such a way that he is not also a servant" (EUD, 85). We flee from this "more profound explanation (*Forklaring*)" (EUD, 85) which is not a matter of gathering more knowledge, but of allowing knowledge to be "transformed into an action the moment it is possessed" (EUD, 86), a knowing that is poured out in witness and passion. The craving we have for explanation is contrasted with the way in which God "explained himself" to us by making us coworkers in creation (EUD, 87).

The quest for objective certainty is changed into a resolution to create meaning, and God too is changed from the ultimate guarantor of the world's coherence and legibility, to the one who awakens desire and empowers creativity. The "dark saying" of existence (EUD, 88) is not clarified by additional knowledge but transformed by faithful appropriation (see EUD, 158).

This is worked out more fully in a number of discourses. In "The Lord Gave and the Lord Took Away; Blessed be the Name of the Lord" we follow the story of Job, whose story defies rational comprehension. Job walks alongside us when every explanation falls silent (EUD, 111). What has been explained and understood can always be changed (the verb *forklare* is used) into fodder for new illusion and self-deception (EUD, 118). The point is to wait for "the Lord's explanation" (EUD, 118), in which all is traced back to God.

In "Think about Your Creator in the Days of Your Youth," we see how the immediacy of the young person's thought of God as creator becomes fissured by reflection. Language is complicit in this separation. Indeed "language itself is so selfish that it talks only of their own affairs and very little of God's, whose concern this separation is" (EUD, 246). And yet however much youth is idealized here, this interruption marks a stage in life's growth towards something deeper. Near the end, Kierkegaard writes of one who is helped by their recollection of youth's immediacy, which transforms or transfigures (*forvandle* and *forklare* are used in parallel sentences) life's beautiful earnestness "into an even more beautiful jest" (EUD, 249).

This recollection is not merely a return to Socratic inwardness, since it is itself transfigured by the interruptions of time and language. It has to be lived and received, not as absolute knowledge but as jest, not as certainty but as witness.

The most striking example of the wordplay Kierkegaard uses comes in the final discourse, "The One Who Prays Aright." He begins by contrasting the random word about easy victories, which quickly gathers a crowd, and the "more profound explanation" which drives them away (EUD, 378). The discourse is a precarious and daring venture, which seeks to communicate something about which no direct communication is possible, since no one can give the eternal to another (EUD, 381-82).

The discourse describes those who encounter loss and grief, and seek some explanation for them. The child is able to attribute good things to God and bad things to other forces, but this childlike view cannot persist into adulthood. If it remains "unclarified" it is judged immature (EUD, 386). The word used here (*uforklaret*) could also mean "untransfigured".

The one who has gone beyond childishness turns to God in prayer looking for another explanation. And this initiates a struggle, in which the one who prays contends with God. Some contend for good things and honors, some against past horrors or for the fulfillment of a wish, but Kierkegaard maintains that in each case "it is a matter of making oneself clear to God, of truly explaining (*forklare*) to him what is beneficial for the one who is praying" (EUD, 388).

The struggle persists because "To look forward to an explanation is still always a comfort" (EUD, 389). But the struggle becomes a transformation, a deepening of inwardness that becomes an end in itself rather than a means to achieve something else (EUD, 392). As the one who prays changes, so God is changed too, in a paradoxical way: "Has God become changed? An answer in the affirmative seems to be a dark saying, and yet it is so, he has become changed, for now it has indeed become manifest that God is unchanging" (EUD, 393). Far from being chill indifference, this is the changelessness of an eternal presence and concern. The changelessness of God can only become apparent in time as change, as the struggle that releases the chance of new creation.

At this stage, the prayer becomes a demand for God to explain himself. It remains a long way from "*the explanation*" (EUD, 394), the decisive point at which the passion of understanding brings about its own downfall. To human ways of speaking, faith is utterly foolish, and yet God remains "the first inventor of language" (EUD, 395), whose self-gift sets creation, time and language in motion. For faith, however, it is the understanding that is a dark saying which is powerless to explain (EUD, 395), and therefore powerless truly to change a person.

Faith's explanation can only come through dispossession, as the Comforter, the Spirit, came only when Christ was removed from the possession of the disciples (EUD, 396). In absence, in the loss of all reference points, in the void, "the Comforter comes with the explanation; then he makes all things new" (EUD, 396).

The explanation comes, but it is not what was imagined or expected at the beginning, for "prayer is the means by which the explanation will correspond to the way he prays about it" (EUD, 397). The pray-er creates his or her own reality even as it is received from elsewhere. And this is the victory, "that instead of receiving an explanation [*Forklaring*] from God he was transfigured [*forklaret*] in God, and his transfiguration [*Forklarelse*] is this: to reflect the image of God" (EUD, 400).

Too much emphasis should not be placed on these words. Elsewhere, the discourses speak disparagingly about transfiguration, when it is imagined as a passport to instant glory (EUD, 338, 348). And yet Kierkegaard's play on words attempts to sketch a spirituality which transfigures thinking, language and time. It is a spirituality which holds to the eternal as the secret that impels and surrounds our words and our living, and does not sacrifice temporality and communication to silent eternal absolutes. The new language of the eternal makes all the difference in the world, but it is still a language, and one inextricable from our contradictory existence.

Erasure

For the discourses, words remain vulnerable but irreplaceable traces of the eternal other within time. The appearance of the eternal as discourse, textual and temporal, means that it is forever opaque to systematic rational comprehension. And there will always be an ambiguity about its status. Do we struggle with God in prayer, or with ourselves? After all, "A person is not in an exclusively receptive relation; he is himself communicating" (EUD, 45), changing the world by the way we relate to it.

Language is structured and fractured by this repetition, the repetition that makes creation and transcendence possible, whilst tying us yet more intimately to time and communication. In "To Gain One's Soul in Patience," Kierkegaard describes the way in which the admonition to patience is "transfigured in heavenly glory" as the world falls apart around us (EUD, 170). And yet the believer's response is to remain utterly still, because gaining one's soul is not like any other form of gain. The phrase about gaining one's soul in patience exposes something at the heart of language:

> [T]he words in their entirety are a kind of picture of the whole process of gaining, that it takes place much as the words proceed with their communication—that is, it is all a repetition. It is not a question of making a conquest, of hunting and seizing something, but of becoming more and more quiet, because that which is to be gained is there within a person, and the trouble is that one is outside oneself. (EUD, 170-71)

That which is most essentially within us is that which dispossesses us of mastery. Our ownmost selves, and the language in which consciousness comes to birth, reveal a transcendence whose limits we cannot draw.

There is another kind of drawing in the discourses:

> Is he not one who draws, he who struggles in prayer with God for an explanation? Will not the explanation draw a boundary line between him and God so that face-to-face with God he begins to resemble himself? Ah, but now comes the difference, because the child has to be helped by the addition of something, but more and more is taken away from the struggler. (EUD, 399)

What is taken away is any sense that we can explain away transcendence or create God in our likeness. Ironically, it is when our images of God as an external addition are removed that God is most radically other, and we are set free to resemble ourselves.[8]

The drawing, the writing, the making of signs that constitutes the discourses is predicated on an understanding of language as an invention of the divine, as gift, and yet one that must be given back, given away if it is to transform us. When Jesus draws in the ground in the story of the woman taken in adultery, he is "writing in order to erase and forget" (EUD, 67). It is easy to create new

---

[8]Cf. UDVS, 192-93, where Kierkegaard stresses the inverse relationship between a human being and God, expressed in worship. Worship, far from alienating us from ourselves, is what allows us to be content to be human and reveals the glory of humanity, free of illusions of mastery: "To worship is not to rule, and yet worship is what makes the human being resemble God, and to be able truly to worship is the excellence of the invisible glory above all creation" (UDVS, 193).

burdens of accusation and guilt, new idols of power. The language of eternity, even as it is spoken, has to be erased.

6

Words that Silence as they Build:
Against a Boundlessly Loquacious Mind

Edward F. Mooney

Poets, theologians, philosophers, preachers, the imprisoned—the assortment of persons drawn to Kierkegaard's discourses is no doubt endless.[1] These brief writings, digestible at a sitting, are meant to cultivate or form or rebuild a soul, without regard to their reader's status, learning, occupation, or wit. Each discourse is intimately addressed by Kierkegaard to one he calls "my reader," the "special individual" he hopes will listen, read, in special confidence. A line in the preface to each small collection of discourses has Kierkegaard seeking a special intimate who will accept his heartfelt address. It is like the refrain in a song of unrequited love. But who is that "special individual" he calls "my reader"? Perhaps several will understand him. Each is addressed, nevertheless, uniquely, pleadingly, as *"my* reader." The tone confides loss and hope for reconciling communion. Can I escape the passing thought that these words are addressed quietly, revealingly—to *me*? And if I am indeed now privately addressed, how am I to respond? With formalities? Do I answer appeals to the heart with scholarly disquisition?

Different works from my Kierkegaard shelf address me differently. The massive *Concluding Unscientific Postscript* swaggers, struts, and stings with mock-scholarly rigor. *Fear and Trembling*, in its early lyric sections, sings with romantic ardor of the hero and his publicist.[2] Both can seem theatrical—the *Postscript*, for example,

---

[1] I have in mind figures as diverse as W. H. Auden, Martin Heidegger, and Dietrich Bonhoeffer.

[2] See my *Knights of Faith and Resignation: Reading Kierkegaard's Fear and Trembling* (Albany: State University of New York Press, 1991).

in its satire and parody of academic nonsense. Of course, *Postscript* is not only that. Most books from Kierkegaard-and-company have serious points to make in addition to whatever role lyric, irony, or parody might play in their delivery.[3] Yet the early discourses seem to be the exception here. They have no glittering, witty, ironic surface to dig beneath. They seem, shall we say, sincere—in the best sense, "simple," but nonetheless profound and endlessly repaying thoughtful attention. They elaborate themes and motifs with clear counterparts in the more dialectical, literary, and lyrical pseudonymous works. "Repetition" and the long-suffering Job appear both in the book *Repetition* and in the early discourse "The Lord Gave, and the Lord Took Away." Kierkegaard meant the sermonic discourses to be read alongside the literary pseudonymous works. He took pains to have "The Job Discourse" and *Repetition* published simultaneously in 1843.[4]

Whatever the overlap of theme and motif among the early discourses and the rest of the authorship, the former stand out in their relative simplicity of address, lacking artifice, and also in their demanding something "plain and simple." The discourses leave us profoundly quieted, "simplified"—even as a correlative "plain and simple" response might start to brew. As a consequence, I can feel that their intent and spirit are violated if I treat them only academically, because to do so would violate a religious silence that they instill. The academic heart and mind is put at odds with the religious mind and heart. Why should this be? William James might give us a clue.

---

[3]For the theatrics of *Fear and Trembling*, see my "Moriah in Tivoli: Introducing the Spectacular *Fear and Trembling*," *Kierkegaard Studies Yearbook 2002*, ed. Niels Jorgen Cappelørn et al. (Berlin: de Gruyter, 2002), as well as *Knights of Faith and Resignation*.

[4]I discuss "The Job Discourse" from *Eighteen Upbuilding Discourses* and its connection to Kierkegaard's master idea of "repetition" in chap. 3 of *Selves in Discord and Resolve: Kierkegaard's Moral Religious Psychology* (New York: Routledge, 1996). I discuss the slim book *Repetition* in "Repetition: Getting the World Back," in *The Cambridge Companion to Kierkegaard*, ed. Alastair Hannay and Gordon Marino (Cambridge: Cambridge University Press, 1997). I place "repetition" as a barrier against nihilism in "Kierkegaard's Category of Repetition," *Kierkegaard Newsletter* (Fall 2000).

James refers to the boundless "loquaciousness" of the "rational-ist" mind in its encounter with religious experience.[5] And he reminds us that such boundless loquaciousness all too easily overrides our "gut feelings" and instincts. These are an essential source of our being, and part and parcel of any deep immersion in the flow of religious experience. James claims that an exclusively rationalist or discursive loquaciousness will darken the center of religious experience.[6] The rich phenomena that initially trigger our reflective interest can quickly disappear under the pressure to provide a discursive account *of* that phenomena. Something gets lost in translation as one moves from the immediacy of religious reception and response to the "loquaciousness" that is adopted as essential to transform an impact, impulse or response into a well-formed proposition for examination and debate.

From a purely academic point of view, it's a bad thing to forget the interests and phenomena that set us down a discursive, conversational, or dialectical path. But from a more deeply spiritual, existential, or religious point of view, it's a bad thing also. We are full time human beings even as we're professional academics.[7] A concern for the fullness of our lives means that we have an urgent, "existential" stake in those "felt-convictions" that form the fabric of our lives. A flurry of discussion or debate can easily suppress the reflective immediacy of religious feeling and conviction. Kierkegaard would resist an impertinent "loquacious-ness" that drowns out a religious mood or ambiance, the space that deep-felt spiritual convictions inhabit.

---

[5]See the use of these passages from *The Varieties of Religious Experience* in Charles Taylor, *Varieties of Religion Today: William James Revisited* (Cambridge MA: Harvard University Press, 2002) 52.

[6]See "The Sentiment of Rationality" and "The Will to Believe," collected in *William James: The Essential Writings*, ed. Bruce Wilshire (Albany: State University of New York Press, 1986), as well as *The Varieties of Religious Experience* (many editions).

[7]TV news anchor Dan Rather "unprofessionally" broke into tears on camera recalling the events of September 11. David Letterman comforted him with the words: "You're a professional—and for God's sake, you're a human being!" As Kierkegaard might plead, "You're an academic—and for God's sake, you're a human being!" But first, he'd have to open our eyes, as "9/11" opened Rather's eyes.

If I'm on track here, there are several questions to ask: What is it about the discourses that brings about a "silencing effect"? How is this silence at odds with the requirements of an academic project? Could conflating the religious and the academic violate a latent taboo? What sorts of "experience," "intuitions," or "felt-convictions" are at stake for Kierkegaard in his drive to establish quietude? Finally: In what light can these "felt-convictions" be seen as matters of ultimate concern, well worth preserving? Starting, then, with the first query: How can discourses instill silence?

1. Instilling Silence

As I read parts of the *Eighteen Upbuilding Discourses* before me, I do not find *Postscript* puzzles or dialectics to which I can respond by removing or intensifying or explaining their sting. Nor do I find the lyric sections one can frame as parables, or fairy tales, or imaginative inventions of that "freelance" poet and dialectician Johannes de silentio penning *Fear and Trembling*. The discourses do not seem geared to provoke what James called a "loquacious" philosophical, literary, theological, or psychological response. Instead, they invoke a state of being or composure rather different from a readiness to engage in a discursive response. They do not immediately put at stake my powers of wit or intellectual insight or interpretative finesse. Instead, they seem to put at stake the very core of my religious, spiritual being. They don't ask me to consider the *importance* of quietude. They seem bound to *enact* or *instill* that state of quietude. If I resist, I resist not a claim or viewpoint but the attempt of words to place me somewhere I refuse to go. Thus these early discourses especially seem fairly to cry out *not* to be written about—surely not in standard *academese*. We may refuse them, it seems, but not argue with them—perhaps not even discuss them. This is the radical, and for the most part unarticulated, possibility I want to explore and elaborate here.

We have before us writings to be read as sermons, however "unauthorized" or "unofficial" they may be from the standpoint of the institutional Christianity in place in Kierkegaard's Copenhagen. As Kierkegaard is quick to remind us in the opening prefaces to each of the discourse sets, their author has not been invested with ecclesiastical authority to preach *bone fide* sermons. Nevertheless, the fact that he feels compelled to insert such a prefatory note emphasizes the point that the writing is immediately recognizable as "sermonic," with a declared scriptural "lesson," and an intimate maternal (or paternal) preacherly address. Two of the earliest of these early eighteen discourses begin forthrightly with a prayer. These are neither speeches before a debating society nor diversions printed up for an evening's read or cafe-society discussion. They are not treatises to be debated by academic and cultural elites, nor meant to win votes in the next election. As sermonic, they only accidentally end up on library shelves as part of an archival record.

This characterization of the discourses as presupposing a frankly sermonic setting involves papering over some subtle complications. I spell out these qualifications at length in section 5, below. But for the moment, it's safe to say that the immediate impact of the discourses is to evoke the setting of sermons heard "live" by a worshipping congregation. They are part of a ceremonial address within the architectural confines of a church or cathedral, and part of the longer address, including music and liturgy, that makes up a practice of religious worship within a recognizable tradition.

The silence or quiet that they effect is an outcome of their design as vehicles of worship, constituent and prominent parts of the practices of worship. These practices require, among other things, a reverence for something other than ourselves. It may be expressed in sounds of joy or song, but even these sounds are responsive to something "other" and "prior." They are responsive to the wondrous, sacred, or holy, a power that initially quiets and defeats our typically inflated sense of self-centeredness, self-importance, and readiness to hold forth—readiness to speak out on *our* terms. Worship quiets the clamorous soul.

Understanding this power of words to stop wordiness, or even to stop an inept type of thinking in words, relies on a rough contrast between discursive and nondiscursive use of language. I might vocalize loudly a sound others would identify easily as "teach!" I might shout it with the single aim of testing the resonance of a concert hall. This would be as close to a purely nondiscursive utterance of language as I can imagine. In fact, the utterance may have left the domain of language entirely, and be considered best as merely sound. For in the context of testing acoustics, almost any vocalization would have served as well. In contrast, imagine a purely discursive uptake of "teach," as when I have a friend read the entry for "teach" from my etymological dictionary. I could find myself utterly concentrated on the information conveyed, oblivious to any affect in, or wider surrounding for, my friend's reading. I sift single-mindedly for the discursive sense alone. In practice, discursive and nondiscursively linguistic reception-and-response will often occur simultaneously. A love song will effect me discursively through its words, and also nondiscursively through its melody. I might attend, or take up, the verse discursively, for content, and then attentively take up the melodic line. In time I might find the words and lyric intonation merge imperceptibly as one.

Think of T. S. Eliot's lovely verse, "Teach me to care and not to care; Teach me to sit still." I could listen for a discursive "message" to ponder intellectually and to interpret, perhaps against the background of various religious and cultural traditions. Alternatively, I might become immersed in the nondiscursive rhythm, repetition, and alliteration, of words—hearing the music of the verse, as it were. Or letting a quite different dimension settle in, I might hear the verse neither as message alone (a claim, for example, that it's good to sit still, a claim to ponder or assess), nor as "music" alone (words to be enjoyed as I might enjoy poetry read aloud in a language I do not understand). Instead, through this third attunement, I might let myself relax into the verse's prayer-like plea. I might hear its cry for help: "Lord, *help* me to care!"

Kierkegaard's early discourses offer words that can be taken up discursively or nondiscursively or both simultaneously—not unlike the variety of ways we can take up with Eliot's "teach me to care and not to care." To catch the flow and focus of these early discourses relies on our familiarity with scriptural themes and passages. It relies on a discursive attunement. Yet there is also obvious poetic music in their unfolding, and catching this flow and focus relies on a nondiscursive attunement. And perhaps the dominate attunement these discourses offer or effect is a sort of quietude. To be caught up in this quietude relies on a nondiscursive attunement. It's as if their culminating impact were to let the discursive Wittgensteinian ladder fall away as we attain—or are taken over by, or taken to—a spirit of quiet worship or prayer. If they in fact effect a religious stillness, a clamorous aspect of the self is quieted while a comforted, quiet aspect of the self is energized. Words build even as they silence.[8]

Words in discursive space invite discursive response, and when we respond to sentences discursively we have already, by our response, assumed a discursive background to the words we address. Consider an architectural analogy. If I enter a cathedral carrying scaffolding to repair chipped plaster, to that extent I enter a space demanding a carpenter's and plasterer's response. If I enter a cathedral with a video camera to catch the play of light on mullioned glass, to that extent I enter a space inviting a tourist's or art historian's response. If I enter a cathedral in which a funeral is being conducted, I may have a journalistic aim: to list the dignitaries present and mark what they say for the morning edition. On the other hand, I may set camera and notepad aside, enter a space of mourning and eulogy, and join in worshipful communion.

Kierkegaard invites us to a place of liturgy, worship, and prayer. In the cathedral of these discourses one *can* take notes on the prayer, identify the historical context of scriptural allusions, or become fascinated with alliteration or metaphor. Or one might become fascinated with this congregation's fashionable Sunday attire. How do we attend to *Eighteen Upbuilding Discourses?* Our attention will vary as we locate ourselves as academics, worshipers, or bibliophiles. Our stance will unveil or alter or selectively distort the space they occupy.

A Kierkegaardian discourse can serve as a crib for next Sunday's sermon, as a challenge to one's translation abilities, or as the bookend to a crowded shelf. More aptly, I might sift the discourses for accounts of humility, patience, or love, to be instructed, or to line them up with corresponding *Postscript*

---

[8]Robert Perkins has suggested in correspondence that to instill quiet might be an instance of indirect communication. A state of being is communicated rather than a straightforward claim to be assessed. I discuss instilling states of being and empowerment in "Exemplars, Inwardness, and Belief: Kierkegaard on Indirect Communication," *International Kierkegaard Commentary: Concluding Unscientific Postscript,* ed. Robert L. Perkins (Macon GA: Mercer University Press, 1997).

passages for mutual illumination. [9] I could take up early discourse expositions of steadfastness or *The Book of Job* and compare these with familiar religious, secular, or literary accounts of their themes. But I might also hear these discourses religiously and noncomparatively, letting them quiet the soul. If they are like a heaven-reaching gothic arch that humbles and readies us for prayer, and if we respond in keeping, then they will suppress an exclusively academic, loquacious mind. An academic response is permitted, even to some extent encouraged by the discourses—just as a great cathedral can permit, even encourage a glazier's, photographer's, or art historian's response. But we'd sense that for worshipers, the cathedral must at some basic level repel attempts to capture its resonances exclusively through the eye of the glazier, photographer, or historian. The early discourses, for a reader in the least attuned to the background of Christian worship and its traditions, evoke a context of worship and prayer: and they evoke, instill, a strain of nondiscursive quiet thoughtfulness.

2. Academic Opposition

The context of worship, prayer, and reverence that these discourses sustain accounts for their palpable "silencing," quieting effect. Turning to our next large question, we can ask how a context sustaining reverence can become opposed to a context sustaining academic pursuits.

It is not an accident, as Kierkegaard surely knows, that what James called the "loquaciousness" of the "rational mind" can both sweep away the phenomena of quiet worship or prayer and also cripple our understanding of the latter's importance. These discourses instill an attitude of *communion with*—not abstract *thoughts about*—the words through which we are addressed. But the discursive mind is geared precisely to focus with some detachment *on and about* its issues. This is a gearing that goes counter to demands for communion *in and with* the words or issues of a discourse. Even the most sympathetic reader of the discourses

---

[9] See George Pattison, *Kierkegaard's Upbuilding Discourses* (New York and London: Routledge, 2002) and Michael Strawser, *Both/And: Reading Kierkegaard from Irony to Edification* (New York: Fordham University Press, 1997).

risks overlooking or violating their letter and their spirit, which can never be academic only, but always prominently religious.

Blurring this distinction between a religious and an academic uptake and response can be seen, first, as an intellectual *confusion of categories*, a violation of the conceptual distinction between scholarly academic response and religiously modulated response. Seen from this angle, the remedy would be to square up our dialectical response-frames in order to more precisely mark the divide between "the religious" and "the scholarly." Perhaps that's a Kierkegaardian *Postscript* aim.

Alternatively, blurring this distinction can be seen as missing the *practical impasse* presented by conflicting demands that cannot be simultaneously fulfilled. We have incompatible demands of equal weight bearing on our will with no "grand principle" to break the deadlock. Seen from this angle, the remedy is not to correct an intellectual error but to acknowledge a humbling *limit of the will*, a limit on the powers of practical reason.[10] A religious perspective demands something like the quietude of worship; and an academic perspective demands something like an exercise of the discursive, loquacious mind. But the latter inherently violates the ambiance of worshipful quiet. The practical agent gets caught in a volitional knot that reason can't untie.

Finally, the blurring of this distinction can be seen as an embarrassing, even shameful or offensive, *violation of a taboo*. Worship institutes a taboo against the abstract chatter, disruptive uproar, or mechanical droning of academic discussion. Academic discourse, in turn, institutes a taboo against worshipful attitudes because they short-circuit or damp down readiness to assertively make a case, to be clear, explicit, and "objective" before an audience of rational responders. One's job is not to pray quietly but to lay out one's cards for all to assess and debate.

Taboo is noticed less in its observance than in its violation. Kierkegaard charges his contemporaries with violating a taboo, and with covering up their violations. *Postscript*, for example, tries

---

[10]On Kierkegaard's setting limits to the will through discursive devices in *Either/Or*, see my "The Perils of Polarity: Kierkegaard and MacIntyre in Search of Moral Truth," *Kierkegaard after MacIntyre: Essays on Freedom, Narrative, and Virtue*, ed. John Davenport and Anthony Rudd (Peru IL: Open Court, 2001).

to awaken its readers to the violation both of piety and of scholarship when religious institutions adopt the lingo and presumptions of an intellectualist philosophy. The latter may subscribe to the maxim that scholarly truth lies in objective methods of historical inquiry. Religious institutions and persons must subscribe to the countermaxim that truth lies in cultivating a deep subjective responsibility toward self and the divine.

If worship, or meditation, or respect for the felt-convictions or promptings of a reverent faith should be kept separate from the exercise of a discursive or disquisitional mind, then not to honor this distinctness becomes like the violation of a taboo. Both academics and ecclesiastics can mistake advances in the powers of the discursive intellect with advances in piety, religiosity, or prayerfulness. This trespass of boundaries can become commonplace. Kierkegaard's dialectical authorship aims to bring its readers back to a perspective where the religious and the academic can be seen as distinct, and the violation of their respective regions can be seen both as a comic blunder and as dangerously breaking a taboo.

3. Taboo

Let me recount a simple anecdote that brings home the problematic wedding of academic and religious aims in the early discourses, and that highlights the presence of prohibition or taboo wherever the academic and the religious are too closely joined. Imagine reading an undergraduate Princeton honors thesis in philosophy signed off with a simple "Amen." This might be little more than an undergraduate *faux pas*. One mentally erases the offending word to cover up a minor shame. Now imagine that this "Amen" closed out a thesis written by someone who was to become a prominent philosopher. One's impulse to erase might be slowed as one searched for clues that might make the closing appropriate in a way not immediately apparent. The thesis is titled *In Demonstration of the Spirit*. It was written in the 1930s by a philosopher who went on to serve for a time in the 1950s as an assistant professor at Harvard. Even as an undergraduate, Henry

Bugbee knew the academic drill, its customs and taboos.[11] His rationale, weak academically, but strong "existentially" or "religiously," is to underline the theme, announced in the preface, that his writing all along has been not only a scholarly exercise but a spiritual one as well, a kind of sustained prayer or meditation.

The author undertakes his writing as a blessing, a gift, a time of affirmation, wonder, hope and attentiveness. But to honor this religious strand in his work through an explicit "Amen" violates or tests a taboo. Philosophical *"demonstrations* of the spirit" must not be mixed with prayer-like *"acclamations* of the spirit." Blurring boundaries in this way creates impurities. Apparently one must choose: *either* the academic *or* the religious. An honors dissertation is clearly an academic undertaking.[12]

Our human practices, moral and religious, political and academic, run smoothly by the incorporation of key distinctions constitutive of these practices. In a worshipful setting, if we are participants, we do not snap pictures of the priest performing mass nor, in a classroom setting, do we kneel before professors. An academic thesis ending with "Amen" seems to violate a taboo, for it slows down or inhibits elaboration or critique of the thesis advanced. In this context, it's just out of place, "impure," to engage in "overt" reverential silence and thanksgiving.

Yet life does not always fall simply within prescribed, "self-evident" purity-maintaining boundaries. Any reader of Kierkegaard knows that his writing can embrace a strange mixture of scholarly strands and more affective tremors of personal expectancy, fear and trembling, hope, despair, and thankfulness—attunements to the world that are less characteristic of disciplined academic endeavor than of religious or worshipful undergoings.

---

[11]See Henry Greenwood Bugbee, Jr., *The Inward Morning: A Philosophical Exploration in Journal Form*, original introduction by Gabriel Marcel, with a new introduction by Edward F. Mooney (reissue: Athens GA: University of Georgia Press, 1999; orig.: State College PA: Bald Eagle Press, 1958). Bugbee's *Journal* can be seen as an extended attempt to write reflectively in a vein both religious and philosophical, both meditative, prayerful, and "not unacademic."

[12]The taboo isn't a matter of failing to honor the familiar "liberal" separation of private from public spheres. Much academic work is done in relative privacy, and prayers can be public crowd-gathering ceremonies.

Part of our fascination with Kierkegaard is his daring both to insist on and simultaneously to challenge or blur distinctions between the religious and the academic, the religious and the ethical, the religious and the aesthetic. His writing inhabits the region of taboo.

If I were an academic advisor at Princeton, I would no doubt have erased "Amen" from the closing lines of this thesis. But if I were a pastor, I might consider leaving it intact. And if I am a pastor and an academic, I could fall into a practical impasse that highlights limits of the rational will. Henry Bugbee's chapters on art and religion are thorough and persuasive. They unfold for academic analysis through their discursive acuity, if not through Jamesean "loquaciousness." Yet this discursiveness forces another aspect of the writing beneath the horizon of our attention. It forces out of view the aspect tagged by the closing "Amen." By excising the quiet, prayerful dimension, we concentrate on the academically discussible topics. We defuse the worry that a taboo has been broken by "forgetting" the closing "Amen."

As I work through the early Kierkegaardian discourses in an academic frame of mind, I no doubt temporarily erase the prayerful, religious quiet they beg to have observed. To honor their religious call would block the effectiveness of my discursive mind. It seems I can't have it both ways. Facing what James would call a "forced option," I must either will to embrace the domain of academic loquaciousness, discussion, and debate, or else will to remain immersed in the mood of worship and prayer that are so central to the discourses. As full-fledged philosophers, religionists, or academics how do we manage both to remember and to forget the quiet of a Kierkegaardian prayer? There must be a third shadowed alternative. And there is. We can enter the dangerous region of taboo, and wrestle with its demons.

Without appearing to violate a taboo, there are wonderful discursive studies that trace thematic resonances among the pseudonymous works and the simultaneously appearing discourses. Other studies trace the specific way Kierkegaard interprets, "reads," the specific biblical passages that give each discourse its pedagogical launch[13]—though to be sure, Kierkegaard tells us he

---

[13]See, e.g., Timothy Polk, *The Biblical Kierkegaard: Reading According to the Rule*

is no teacher, implying, perhaps, that the words sound out their *own* teaching, for him and for us, wielding power of their own. There have been essays probing the extent to which the early discourses may be more a piece of "indirect communication" than had been supposed, and others that place their meaning biographically in Kierkegaard's struggle to clarify a vocation, somewhere in the mix of allure and aversion among parsonages, siblings, parents, townsfolk, professors, friends, and fellow poets.[14] And there are the later discourses (more properly, deliberations), the series of writings called *Works of Love*, that repay endless scholarly philosophical and theological study, and that bring into play the same dialectical imagination so necessary in responding to *Postscript*, say, or *The Sickness Unto Death*.[15]

But do these successful responses violate what I've called the demand of the discourses for quiet? Struggling for a discursive response to them can feel somewhat maladroit—as one might feel exiting a cathedral overcome with grief, only to be asked by a TV news reporter to comment on the service within.

4. Modes of Silence

I've argued that the discourses can be responded to discursively, but are designed to play a nondiscursive role as well, the role of quieting academic discursiveness. This role has been underappreciated (naturally) by academics. It deserves increased appreciation. We can learn the physics of gothic architectural wonders, and still confess the relevance of the service held within, and perhaps the personal need to let ourselves be absorbed in its ambiance. This would be to let the cathedral trigger, invite, and enhance all manner of worshipful, prayerful response—quite apart

---

of *Faith* (Macon GA: Mercer University Press, 1997).

[14]For "indirection" in even the signed works, see Strawser, *Both/And*. For a brilliant intellectual biography, see Alastair Hannay, *Kierkegaard: A Biography* (Cambridge: Cambridge University Press, 2001).

[15]For a study of the deliberative *Works of Love* (which inherits the style of the early discourses) see M. Jamie Ferreira, *Love's Grateful Striving* (Oxford: Oxford University Press, 2001); and Pattison's *Kierkegaard's Upbuilding Discourses*. Both works weave together the discourses with the "dialectical" writings of Johannes Climacus and Anti-Climacus.

from the physics of the place. The early discourses can both excite and damp down the loquacious academic mind. Approached as sermon-like deliverances, they can't help but still the inquisitive or disputatious mind.

A related point is this. The sort of quiet that the discourses instill is an experiential mood of reverence or humility rather that a discursive *category of,* or *claim about,* quiet or humility. Silence is an important "dialectical category" in Kierkegaard's authorship, but it would be a mistake to link the experiential silence instilled by the early discourses with "silence" as a topic or category of investigation in other parts of the authorship.

Even if one were to think of "silence" as a pervasive Kierkegaardian theme, one would have to distinguish an array of differences that are most likely too varied to yield to a single, all-purpose account. The "quieting" of the early discourses is not Kierkegaard (or his pseudonyms) wrestling with the silence-producing "offense" of the crucifixion, nor is it Abraham's silence toward Sarah and Isaac, nor, the breathless silence of exasperation and puzzlement at the three page testament at the end of *Postscript* averring that the book's arguments are not the writer's own. Nor should discourse-instilled silence be assimilated to the silence of Mary in the presence of Jesus and Martha, or the silence of the "sinful" woman attending Jesus, each discussed by Kierkegaard. Nor is it the silence Kierkegaard may seem to want of women *generally*—as if voiceless women were preferred to disquisitional ones, Christianly speaking.[16]

My main point, however, is not that Kierkegaard has many sorts of silence at work in the authorship, each dependent on local context for its specific meaning. All this is true, yet the larger point is quite different. Despite this fact of differences in the sorts of silence Kierkegaard takes up topically, or aims to effect rhetorically in his readers, another major fault line remains to be mapped. This is the fault line between the quiet that the early discourses aim to

---

[16]See Wanda Warren Berry's discussion of modes of speech and silence in "The Silent Woman in Kierkegaard's Later Religious Writing," *Feminist Interpretations of Søren Kierkegaard*, ed. Celine Leon and Sylvia Walsh (University Park PA: Penn State University Press, 1997), and my account of Abraham's silence in *Knights of Faith and Resignation*.

instill, and the many sorts of silence discursively elaborated (and nondiscursively effected) elsewhere in Kierkegaard's authorship.

There is, to my ear, a culminating quiet in these early discourses that is unique in the authorship. It seems to be a *dominating* effect. There is a special extradiscursive and powerful *imposition* of a silence specific to these discourses. The outcome is to humble or override an impulse to discuss or interrogate. Kierkegaard directs us to read these discourses aloud. Silence, it seems, is enacted and undergone *through* the enunciation and absorption of spoken or written words. To be caught up by the worshipful or prayerful imposition of such silence is not to discuss, or to be readied to discuss, anything at all—least of all, the silence so enacted. Words that still the soul make no claim *about* silence. And with no discursive claim on the table, there is nothing to discuss, nothing to be answered, countered, or clarified.

This silence seems to differ in quality and degree from other moments of Kierkegaardian silence. The categories and even enactments of silence in the *Postscript*, or in *Either/Or*, or in *Fear and Trembling* cry out almost immediately for philosophical and exegetical exploration. There are local passages in the discourses, to be sure, that invite discursive exploration. But if their dominate effect is the installation of the quiet of prayer, then we've entered different territory. We're led to undergo the experience of silence, the very silence of "silence," in a dramatically sustained and thoroughgoing way. It becomes something raw and primitive in its inescapable imposition—like rolling Midwest thunder claps. Discussion, if it enters the picture at all, comes sometime and place down the line. Worship, like thunder, stills the clamorous soul.

5. Full-fledged Sermons?

Here we can enter some serious qualifications to a full assimilation of the discourses to a sermonic setting, a context of worship. First, Kierkegaard delivers up these "sermons" to a publisher to be transformed into jacketed books to be read out of church by the Danish book-reading public and cultural elites. Second, he admits no authority to preach them, and third, although he urges us to read these discourses aloud, he fails to specify the audience to be addressed. Can we coherently preach to ourselves? Or are we surreptitiously allowing Kierkegaard to violate his own reticence by having *him* preach to us—indirectly, surreptitiously—as we read? Furthermore, he wants to be remembered as a writer, not as a preacher. This is true generally of Kierkegaard, and the point carries over explicitly to the discourses. They have prefaces and dedications whose tone and content place them as pieces of literature—modeled on sermons, but framed nonsermonically. And they are surely to be read as part of a much larger literary-spiritual production, most of which makes no pretense at being worshipful. Last, it is not beyond his cunning for Kierkegaard to "try on" the speech and ambiance of Christian worship, in particular, its sermonic segments, with less than full commitment to their force as vehicles of worship.

Kierkegaard might use his rhetorical skills just to display his "postmodern" talent for decentering the writing self. More likely, he blocks direct access to his authorial intent because his commitment lies less in producing exemplary sermons than in underlining the fundamental gap between honest, authentic worship and its shallow simulacra. He is dedicated to establishing a contrast between the authentic and the counterfeit throughout the authorship. And he adopts the strategy of complicating access to his intent to achieve his end. He adopts the strategy of "trying on" a mode of audience address with less than full commitment to it. He "tries on" the ambiance of a dialectical mock-Hegelian disquisition in *Postscript*, or "tries on" the ambiance of a traditional academic dissertation in *Concept of Irony*, or "tries on" the ambiance of a seductive literary tale of adventure and betrayal in *Either/Or I*. For that matter, he famously "tries on" a spectacular, dramatic reenactment of the trial of Abraham.[17] In the following section, I'll say more about his interest in this task of bringing out the sham he finds about him. For the moment, it's enough to say that "trying on" the ambiance of worship, if that's what we have before us in these early discourses, entails a "hedged" commitment on Kierkegaard's part. The upshot is that his commitment to the discourses as vehicles of worship is less that simple or straightfor-

---

[17]"The spectacular" in *Fear and Trembling* is contrasted with "the religious" in my "Moriah in Tivoli."

ward, even though he surely means them to be imitations, or models of such vehicles.

Kierkegaard no doubt relishes the scholarly inquisitiveness these discourses will provoke. We are forced to objectively, discursively, plot the location of these "quasi-sermons" within a nonsermonic authorship, and simultaneously to acknowledge their silence-instilling, subjectivity-enhancing force. The trick is to embrace this tension—to let ourselves be captives of a Kierke-gaard-induced "double vision," something like an irony that we are meant neither to evade nor to damp down.[18] This means *angst* in knowing that we violate a taboo, which ever way we turn.

6. Felt Conviction and Content

What sort of experience or felt-conviction is brought to light through the quiet-instilling force of these discourses? What experiential "contents" are allowed to well up or to be wrought in this ambiance? The ambiance is already one of reverence, prayer, and worship, as we've seen, and has for its more specific content the meanings, experiences, and felt-convictions native to a Christian's faith, a kind of Lutheran faith, as Kierkegaard and his readership would understand it. More generally, the "content" of this engendered space of worship will include suffering anxiety and freedom, as one absorbs, as best one can, the full dimensions of this space. And as we've seen, it will include a sense of inhabiting a region of taboo as one oscillates between academic and religious uptake and response; between being tempted to engage the discursive mind and letting nondiscursive quiet prevail; between falling victim to the aesthetic spectacle all about (social, architectural, musical, discursive, and otherwise) and dropping more appropriately into honest prayer.

Assuming one finds oneself for the moment in a space of relatively unmixed piety, the discourses open a space of possibility for any number of Christian virtues to resonate, speak, as we are

---

[18]See Thomas Nagel, *The View from Nowhere* (Oxford: Oxford University Press, 1986). Nagel argues that we must live with "double vision" in philosophy, a condition created by the irresolvable conflict between "subjective" and "objective" standpoints.

readied to hear. It will be a space given over to meditations and resolves on trust, hope, charity, generosity of spirit, mercy, as these await infusion and nourishment in a faith-life. For academics and other part-time warriors, this space of quietude harbors humility as the candid recognition of our limits in projects of mastery of the world, others, or the self. Patience and renewal have space to thrive. This is the quiet space of "upbuilding" or "edification" that the discourses work to clear. It is a space not just for faith's platitudes, but a place where virtue can take hold and enter the fabric of a life. Content as well as quietude is instilled.

William James pleads for the importance of "felt convictions" and "intuition" for a person's religious identity. Such convictions or "gut feelings" remain at risk in a culture dedicated to the projects of self-assertion and control through the tools of rationalized technology, bureaucracy, and "free market" competition and its supportive, well-fueled ideology of consumerism. "Felt conviction" is discredited when it slides unchecked toward zealotry, or where it erupts in violence. It is equally discredited when it slides toward "mere preference" or "subjective choice" and thus falls outside the pale of worthy discussion. Thus we are left in a region of "taboo" between loquaciousness and "dumb intuition." To live as religiously thoughtful academics we must cultivate languages and ways of speaking and attunement that can retrieve the importance of what all too easily gets assimilated into the disrepute of mere "felt-conviction" or "dumb intuition" or the disrepute of empty loquacity.

Kierkegaard harnessed his own abundant discursive gifts in the interest of "felt-conviction" and the subtle, even silent, appeals of reverence, worship, and prayer. He indulged his great talent for words as an inoculation against using words in an exclusively "loquacious" way. As William James put it, in struggling to defend "dumb intuition" against excessive academic intellectualism, "if you have intuitions at all, they come from a deeper level of your nature than the loquacious level which rationalism inhabits."[19] As he sees it, the detached academic impulse has "more prestige" than felt-conviction because "it has the loquacity" which (he says

---

[19]See Taylor, *Varieties of Religion Today*, 52.

bluntly) "can challenge you for proofs, and chop logic, and put you down with words."[20]

In Kierkegaardian perspective, the region of faith is the nonloquacious region of "felt conviction," and the latter must defend itself "without words."[21] In *Either/Or*, he gives us a taste of the excesses of aestheticism. He hoped, thereby, to undercut its allure. In *Postscript*, he gives us a taste of dialectical acrobatics, thereby undermining its allure. In the present case, he gives us a taste of worship, prayer, and reverence to undermine their shallow counterfeits. The premise is that the Copenhagen churchgoing fashion of "see and be seen," of sociable loquacity, is a counterfeit of piety. Churchly aestheticism is reinforced through rituals of mutual congratulation among a self-important congregation Add a refined hauteur among its priests, and you have, not *gravitas*, but refined illusion.

In calling attention to the upbuilding, forming capacity of Kierkegaard's sermonic discourses, we do not escape the risk of believing we are submitting to their prayerful, quieting effect just in the course of writing *about* this quiet. But of course we then remain academics. We talk *about* the discourses and their intended effects even as we insist that they are meant to still the academic mind. We remain fascinated onlookers, not worshipers, as we write of Kierkegaard's desire that we drop the scholar's stance. The point remains worth making. While we are trained as academics in philosophy or theology to seek and respond to a text's dominant discursive drive, the early discourses, in the interest of an authentic piety, seem bound to subvert this drive.

The point can be elaborated further by considering the way immersion in prayer, music, or scripture evades the bustle of a discursive mind.

7. Prayer, Music, Scripture

Imagine a prayer delivered by a pastor to a congregation. It's meant to build up a spiritual mood or passion or feeling that might alter or infuse the heart. Those joining in the prayer may

---

[20]Taylor, *Varieties of Religion Today*, 52.
[21]Of course, ironically, words remain Kierkegaard's métier throughout.

"follow along" with the words, letting themselves be swept up in its arc of significance. Being so swept up might be an essential phase in upbuilding of spirit. Of course, as we've noted, discourse prayers are not exactly prayers. They're framed by literary introductions that locate a reader *outside* the space of worship. Be that as it may, the prayer and subsequent body of the discourse are surely meant to model, if not fully replicate, prayerful worshipful attention. A prayer is not the first ploy in a conversational exchange, and however dialectically provocative a sermon can be, its ambiance is worship, not an academic debate. We save our objections and commentary for outside the chapel door.

If prayer is addressed to "Our Father," we are expected to present a petition or a word of thanks or acclamation in a manner that is not declamatory, insistent or peevish—however urgent the plea or heartfelt the gratitude. When another speaks a prayer, we submit or surrender to the tenor of these words' appeal, diminishing as best we can our critical distance from them, and maximizing as best we can our immersion in them. At best they are words that flow from our passional (as opposed to our loquacious) self—a self whose most prominent desire is to join the concerted appeal of speaker, listeners, and words, and then to await whatever response might be divinely granted. Reverence and respect quiet the will. They give us a stance opposite to a readiness for riposte, objection, or hermeneutical paraphrase.[22] Insofar as our writing or thinking is immersed in the world of prayer or worship, our distinctively academic capacities for discursive response are shut down or challenged. Our ability to take hold of an object or topic to "make sense of it" are set aside (if only temporarily). Prayer invites us to *release* our control on words or topics, allowing words to take the course initiated by another, or even allowing words to sound "on their own."

Like prayer, music too invites us to deactivate or quiet an academic, disquisitional response. It typically suspends or stalls our impulse to "get a word in edgewise" or otherwise raise objections or arguments in response to what we have heard. Of

---

[22]See Berry's "The Silent Woman." On quieting the will as an aim of *Either/Or*, see my "Perils of Polarity."

course, texts or verse can be set to music in hymns, chants, or arias. Nevertheless, an oration delivered musically—an oratorio—is not just another speech. The "book" of an opera, and its theatrical realization become full opera only with the successful incorporation of music. The recently commissioned opera "Dead Man Walking" grips us through its discursive elements: in this case, the death penalty is under scrutiny. However, a difference remains between the opera, on the one hand, and the movie or the book, on the other. The opera's script is supplemented by a musical score, by the nondiscursive demands of orchestration, vocal delivery, pitch, timbre, rhythm, and other purely musical factors. One might find the music of the opera unsurpassed while finding the opera's discursive "script" and stage realization quite shallow or objectionable.

Music scored apart from associated verse or text can seem discursive. The "statements" or "subjects" of a Bach fugue interweave in conversation. "Descriptive" or "programmatic" music can seem to "paint a picture" that activates discursive minds. But a response to music requires more. It must open the soul to tones to which we can give ourselves nondiscursively. When music becomes the focus of discursive debate, its special wordless power to gather listeners and singers is for the moment set aside. When debate *about* music gets too heated, we know that music's capacity to instill a reverent or joyful or grief-filled mood is forgotten. It becomes relegated to an onlooker's object of contention.

From the standpoint of academic philosophical or theological endeavor, we *want* animated constructive or deflationary discussion. Yet it would be a scandal to have such animated discussion run headlong after the cadence of a prayer or benediction or hymn. The painter Barnett Newman is said to have quipped, at the expense of art critics, that criticism or aesthetics is to painting as ornithology is to birds.[23] We can imagine the Kierkegaardian transposition. Discourse *about* worship is to worship as ornithology is to birds. And what Kierkegaard wants to deliver, if not worship

---

[23]Newman's quip as it bears on the contrast between moral responsiveness and moral theory *about* responsiveness is discused by Michael Stocker in his *Valuing Emotions* (Cambridge: Cambridge University Press, 1996).

itself, is awareness of the difference between its authentic shape and loquacious conversations *about* it. Quite ironically (or comically), in the present age it takes all too many words to make the point.

The first of Kierkegaard's eighteen collected discourses, "Expectancy," welcomes in the new year with a passage from scripture. It builds up our hope as music or prayer might, not by announcing a simple proposition to debate, but by calling on words whose power resides deep in a traditions of hope and expectancy, and have spoken to Christians continually through the ages. In a sense, scripture attains a life of its own, in which each generation is invited to participate. Attunement to scripture is as far from attunement to an newsprint op-ed piece as attunement to a Handel oratorio is from attunement to a Presidential oration.

Why should a mood of prayerful, quiet attention in the ambiance of music and scripture be any part of spiritual upbuilding? Formation of spirit might require preliminary downsizing of presumptions of grandeur, self-importance or self-sufficiency. To kneel or sit quietly in worship is to forego an attitude of dominance over others and one's situation. Even petitionary prayer is supplication, neither demanding nor commanding. A Kierkegaardian discourse does not position readers to enter a sphere of active give and take, but rather, positions them to enter a space of *patience*—of expectancy, listening, waiting. Such stillness, such abrogation of dominance or mastery in a moment of reverence, is an essential phase of spiritual growth. Giving up *our* turn to speak creates the space where another can speak to and through us, in prayer, or in scripture, or sermons, or in hymns.

A discourse opening with a prayer privileges receptivity over self-assertion, and its following scriptural quotation privileges authoritative words of another place and time over words of our own "invention." This reminds us that we do not just wield language as we will, but inherit its authority and power, which arrives mysteriously from time immemorial. Scripture is not sound we use to make our way, but words that carry us through worlds. It empowers us, as great music lets us sing. It does not lie at hand for any neophyte to use at will. Words that still, words of worship or prayer or meditation—sermonic discourse passages—make space for us to live in words not first our own but may become our own.

We've considered the sermonic setting and the mood of worship as constitutive of the space the discourses occupy, and opened lines of sight on that space, a space for prayer, for Christian virtues (such as patience and humility), for the music of verse and hymn, and for a scriptural basis of a discourse elaborated as "the lesson of the day." Lastly, we can open what I'll call a pervasive line of mystery.

8. Preserving Mystery

The early Kierkegaardian discourses typically quiet us by recalling us to what I rather awkwardly call the alluring and repelling *mystery* of existence, which first and foremost defies our self-importance, cognitively and volitionally. It comes to us not just through the music of worship, the majesty of vaulted ceilings, or the wonder of sacraments enacted at communion rails. Mystery comes not just in the sight of scudding clouds or geese in silhouette against a city sky. It arrives most distinctively through verbal juxtapositions and repetitions of meanings—repetitions that help embed them, and are played out in rhythmic phrases of arresting power.

Here we encounter the paradoxical juxtapositions of a strength that is weakness, a hope that is madness, a pain buoyed by delight, a Lord concerned with the least sparrow's fall (as Kierkegaard notes in the opening discourse), a flower amidst offal, the Lord's giving and taking quite beyond any measure of justice, a child always already loved. These juxtapositions are registered not just as intellectual scandals or dialectical enigmas (though they may be taken up as such, say, in *The Concept of Anxiety* or *Postscript*). What are taunting conundra for the dialectical mind become in a religious setting sustaining wonders for the religious soul.

In the discourses, these tensed and otherwise troubling juxtapositions of the Kierkegaardian authorship slip by in melancholy, wistful, or contemplative ways as reminders of the inexhaustible depths of significance we precariously and faithfully inhabit. It is an ambiance untamable yet not thereby an insult or offense to spirit. Encased lyrically, as it were, these striking formulations lay the background for a heartening reminder. Such inexhaustible mystery vouchsafes the inexhaustible horizons of our hope and delight—whatever the descending dark. We live in possibility, hopeful possibility, which must indeed seem something of a mystery from the standpoint of anyone set to take stock of our situation from a stance of utter mastery or control.

In ways akin to prayer or scripture, the mystery of things opens up to the grounding power on which we can be silently, safely built.

7

An Education in Possibility

Michael Lotti

Like most writers, Søren Kierkegaard wanted to educate his readers through his writing. What sets Kierkegaard apart from most writers is not only the depth of his thought but also the unique way he goes about educating. Much has been written about the multifaceted educational strategies in Kierkegaard's pseudonymous works, but less has been written about the education offered in *Eighteen Upbuilding Discourses* which accompanied his first pseudonymous production. In this essay, I want to show why these discourses are best described as an "education in possibility." To do this, I will first point out a few things about education in general. Then I will examine part of *The Concept of Anxiety*, for it is in that often impenetrable work that Vigilius Haufniensis introduces the term in a surprisingly clear way. Then I will turn to these discourses themselves, demonstrating how they offer a reader a genuine education in possibility.

Education in the Facts

When we think of education, we are prone to think of a general pattern like this: the teacher knows X, the student does not know X, and the teacher tries to instruct the student so that he or she learns or knows X. Nearly all of what we call "education" is like this, from the ABC's of preschoolers to the physics, accounting, and, yes, even philosophy and theology classes of college students.

We could refer to such education as an "education in facts," for by it the student comes to know the facts about something or about how something is done. No infant knows that there are nine planets in the solar system, but many adults do; somewhere along the line, the adult had to be educated in the facts about the solar system. Likewise, every auto mechanic had to be educated in the facts of engine design. And every historian of the early church had to learn about the Scriptures, the early councils, and the Latin and Greek languages used by the church fathers. These examples also indicate that an "education in the facts" is often not simply about "knowing X," but also about "knowing how to do X." The auto mechanic does not simply learn about engines, but also about how to diagnose and repair engine problems. In learning Greek and Latin, the historian of the early church learns the skill of translating along with learning grammar and vocabulary. Even someone who learned something basic like the nine planets of the solar system had to learn how to read, listen in class, take notes, and perhaps even use a telescope.

Most assuredly, the possibility of living a Christian life or a moral life depends upon some amount of an "education in the facts." An ethical person needs to learn about what is right and what is wrong and how to make ethical judgments in various circumstances. A Christian, of course, needs to learn the stories of the Scriptures, the creeds, and how to engage in various church practices like praying, singing, or memorizing psalms.

Yet however important such education in the facts is for the Christian and the ethical person, most of us would follow Kierkegaard (and, for that matter, Judge William, Frater Taciturnus, Vigilius Haufniensis, and Johannes Climacus) in thinking that such an education is not enough. A moral person is not someone who only knows about rules of conduct or moral theories. To count as moral, a person must actually perform moral actions and perform them for the right reason. This person must have an inner sense, one might say, of what it means to be ethical. The same is true of a Christian. One can know an enormous amount about the Bible, church history, and theology and still not be much of a Christian. To count as a Christian, one must *exist* in a particular way, and again we could say that a Christian must have a particular inner sense; in particular, an inner sense of the living Christ.

Anyone who has taught subjects such as these knows that it is simply impossible to bestow such an "inner sense" on students. One can lecture back and forth and up and down about the Gospel of Matthew, for example, and some students will come to feel that God, through the text, is making a demand on them, while other students will simply learn that some people think that God, through the text, is making a demand on them. Importantly, this happens even though the material is the same for both sets of students. To use a less loaded example, an enthusiastic physics teacher can generally get all of his or her students to know the basics of physics, but only some students (or none at all) will pick up on the beautiful intricacy of atoms and molecules and come to share the teacher's enthusiasm for physics. The teacher cannot bestow, at will, such enthusiasm.

But to say that it is not possible to bestow a particular inner sense upon a learner is not to say that one does not ever learn to have or develop such a sense from someone else. Nor does it mean that a teacher ought not to try to awaken it. What this means is that another type of teaching and learning is necessary, one that does not follow the standard format of an "education in the facts." This brings us to Vigilius Haufniensis, who labels such an education an "education in possibility."

An Education in Possibility in The Concept of Anxiety

To understand what an "education in possibility" is, we must begin with the fourth chapter of *The Concept of Anxiety*, where Vigilius Haufniensis, Kierkegaard's pseudonym in this volume, broadly describes two types of people: those who are "in dread of evil" and those who are "in dread of the good."[1]

For Haufniensis, being in dread of evil—and it is only one's own evil one can dread—presupposes "inwardness," which is a concern for oneself in light of those things which are "eternal;" i.e. ethical and religious demands. Being in dread of evil is, then, both a bad and a good state to be in. It is bad because it is painful; no one likes to face his or her own sinfulness or his or her propensities toward evil. Being in dread of evil is good, however, because it is honest. One at least acknowledges that "good" and "evil" are categories that apply to oneself. One recognizes, in other words, that one is under judgment, and this means, echoing language

---

[1] In my opinion, "anxiety" does not adequately capture the weightiness of the Danish word *angst*, at least as it is used by Haufniensis. I use the term "dread" in this essay except when I refer to the title of Haufniensis's work.

from *Either/Or II, Stages on Life's Way,* and *Concluding Unscientific Postscript,* that one possesses an inner "seriousness" or "earnestness" about one's life.[2]

It is precisely this seriousness or earnestness that is avoided by one who is "in dread of the good," and Haufniensis goes so far as to compare such a person to the demons in the Gospels. The person who is in dread of the good is not so much an evildoer as a person who simply evades disclosure and transparency about themselves (CA, 127). As Haufniensis expresses it, they will to exist in untruth (CA, 128). Like the demons who wanted nothing to do with Jesus, those who are in dread of the good fear what is good because in acknowledging goodness at all, they would be acknowledging a standard of behavior. And to acknowledge a standard of behavior is to acknowledge that one is answerable to that standard and thus under judgment, and judgment is just what the demonic person wants to avoid.

Haufniensis articulates the "dread of evil" and the "dread of the good" in another way. Playing upon the multiple senses of the word "freedom," he describes those who are in dread of evil and those who are in dread of the good as both free and unfree. Those who are in dread of evil are unfree because they are, to use the classical Christian terminology that Haufniensis appropriates, in bondage to evil. Like the Apostle Paul, they do not do the good that they want to do, but the evil they do not want to do (Romans 7:19). But they are free because they are firmly planted in "the freedom of the eternal." They understand the claim that goodness makes on them, and this frees them from the slavery of their own corrupt reasoning and, potentially, from corrupt living itself. Such "freedom of the eternal" is just what the demonic person fears, for it means bondage (or "unfreedom") to him or her (CA, 120). This

---

[2]George Connell has discussed the positive and negative aspects of "seriousness" in Kierkegaard's writings, especially with regard to Judge William, in "The Importance of Being Earnest: Coming to Terms with Judge William's Seriousness," in *International Kierkegaard Commentary: Stages on Life's Way,* ed. Robert L. Perkins (Macon GA: Mercer University Press, 2000) 113-48. I use the term—and I think Haufniensis uses the term—in the positive sense described by Connell, that is, as describing an honest concern about one's own significance over and against a frivolous (or possibly demonic) indifference to one's own existence.

person's idea of freedom amounts to the ability to follow his or her inclinations, not the demands of goodness. Thus, the greatest freedom possible for one in dread of the good would be life without "goodness" altogether, and the greatest bondage possible for such a person would be a life within "the freedom of the eternal." As Haufniensis summarizes, one who is in dread of evil simply dreads evil in the freedom of the eternal; one who dreads the good dreads such freedom itself.[3]

No one is born earnest, according to Haufniensis (CA, 150), and of course there are literally hundreds of ways to be like the demons and avoid being transparent to oneself. One of these ways should be familiar to any reader of *Either/Or I*, in which the aesthetic author revels in "possibilities" but for no apparent purpose other than articulating them. He lacks the earnestness to make his possibilities truly educative. In *The Concept of Anxiety*, Haufniensis emphasizes that another evasion—and again, we can discern the voices of Judge William, Frater Taciturnus, and Johannes Climacus here—is to become educated in the facts, especially in the facts pertaining to "the eternal." Educated responses to "the eternal" are "evasions" according to Haufniensis, for they all treat "the eternal" as something, at most, to be thought about but not produced in action (CA, 138). To put it in terms we have been using, such an evader may understand a lot of facts about "the eternal," but never thinks of the eternal as informing his or her own possibilities as an existing human being. In other words, such a person can possess great understanding about morality and theology, but will avoid understanding himself or herself in religious or ethical terms.

One who is in "dread of evil," on the other hand, fears the possibility of actually being evil, so his or her education in "the eternal" is naturally directed toward understanding (and perhaps changing) his or her own life. According to Haufniensis, this is analogous to the situation of a lover. One who loves, he points out,

---

[3]A more extended (and slightly different) development of the relationship between sin, the demonic, freedom, and unfreedom can be found in Ronald L. Hall's "Language and Freedom: Kierkegaard's Analysis of the Demonic in *The Concept of Anxiety*," in *International Kierkegaard Commentary: The Concept of Anxiety*, ed. Robert L. Perkins (Macon GA: Mercer University Press, 1985) 153-66.

will hardly have an interest in tracking down a precise definition of love (CA, 147). He does not want *to know about* love, but to *be in love* and to *grow in love*. If he wants to *know about* anything at all, it will be the things that need to be known and continually accomplished which help his love abide and expand. Haufniensis puts this another way: to understand what you say is quite different from understanding yourself in what you say (CA, 142). The former is the goal of an education in the facts; the latter is the goal of an education in possibility.

But what is this "education in possibility" which the demons avoid and which those who are "earnest" embrace? Woven into Haufniensis's elliptical prose in chapter 4 are four key distinguishing marks; I will present them in the order that they appear in this essay. First, an education in possibility takes place in a literal or figurative place like the Jutland heath, where "the greatest event is a grouse flying up noisily" (CA, 159). Second, the goal of an education in possibility is not to change reality, but to understand oneself in light of that which is unchanging—i.e. "the eternal." This means that an education in possibility is not an education in the possibility of good fortune, which trades on the wish for actuality to change, either by chance or by one's own work (CA, 156-57). Third, the student of possibility, unlike the demonic person who is fearfully closed in upon himself, can experience an inward expansiveness of that which is good or God (CA, 134)—or again, as Frater Taciturnus and Johannes Climacus might say, an inward ethical or religious expansiveness. Fourth, the student of possibility, being far removed from the frothing waves of world history, can gain a sense of his or her infinite guilt in light of "the eternal" (CA, 161). Haufniensis is audacious enough to say that enough practice in such an education can actually result in what must be its goal: the learner becomes an ethical autodidact or, in the case of understanding oneself religiously, a theodidact, one taught by God himself (CA, 162).

Anyone familiar with the practice of self-examination and confession should be able to recognize in Haufniensis's "education in possibility" a descriptive framework of the dynamics of coming to grips with oneself ethically or religiously (or both).[4] What is missing in *The Concept of Anxiety* is probably just as obvious, however: the actual substance of an "education in possibility." One can write at length—as Haufniensis does—about "dread," "the eternal," "inwardness," "sin," and even "God," but such writing remains firmly in the mode of trying to describe the facts about such matters. It is one of the many ironies of *The Concept of Anxiety* that while its author praises honest self-reflection and warns against evasive learnedness, he neatly avoids ever stepping out of his role as a "psychologist" who only talks about the earnest topics mentioned above (and, of course, "earnestness" itself). He offers a blueprint for an "education in possibility," but assiduously avoids going into the actual house. To be fair, one can note that in a few instances, some of Haufniensis's descriptions of human possibility—especially in his brief discussions of Jesus confronting various demons—may help a reader to be more self-reflective in a specifically religious way. But if this is so, it is accidental so far as Haufniensis is concerned. His goal, stated clearly in the introduction to *The Concept of Anxiety*, is to articulate a view of the human psyche that is at odds with the one proffered in the speculative philosophy of his day. If a reader wants the "education in possibility" that Haufniensis describes, then he or she must turn elsewhere. It is my claim that the most obvious "elsewhere" is *Eighteen Upbuilding Discourses*, and it is to this work that we now turn.

Inviting the Learner to the Jutland Heath

Having a place of solitude like the Jutland heath is important for an education in possibility. As Vigilius Haufniensis notes, a solitary place gets one away from the "frothing waves of world history" and the thought that such world history constitutes (or

---

[4]It is worth noting that in *Concluding Unscientific Postscript*, Johannes Climacus practically reverses Haufniensis's terminology while making the same point. For Climacus, the only important "fact" is one's own "actuality" as an ethically existing subject, while the realm of "possibility" is the realm of disinterested, abstract thought (CUP, 314-20). Climacus sounds more like Haufniensis when he states that an earnest individual is educated by possibility insofar as he or she wants to transform a possibility into a way of actually existing (CUP, 320-24).

should constitute) one's own self-understanding (CA, 159). A Jutland heath is even more important in that the dread of evil is a problem for a single individual. That is, many people may experience the dread of evil, but they cannot resolve the problem of *my* dread. Having a dread of evil, in other words, presupposes (or is the manifestation of) an individual conscience before God.[5] As such, it can only be meaningfully addressed within that same framework, which means that one must be, figuratively at least, *alone.*

The first invitations to the Jutland heath in *Eighteen Upbuilding Discourses* occur, quite naturally, in the prefaces that accompany the six smaller collections of discourses that make up the larger volume. As discussed in the previous section, the starting point for a valuable "education in possibility" is seriousness or earnestness, and this necessarily involves an inward orientation. Given that most education is directed outwardly to a subject independent of the teacher and learner, Kierkegaard obviously thought that it would be wise, in the prefaces, to remind or even encourage the learner to reorient himself or herself.

One primary obstacle to a properly earnest orientation is authority. If there is an authority beyond "the eternal" or God for the learner, then he or she is no longer alone on the Jutland heath. In most teacher-learner situations, there is a proper authoritative relationship. The teacher knows, the student does not know, and the student ought to submit to the teacher's authority. The same holds true in many understandings of the pastor-parishoner relationship, especially when the pastor performs the duties unique to him or her by virtue of ordination; i.e. preaching or administering the sacraments. Thus, Kierkegaard is at pains, in the prefaces, to disassociate himself from all authority to teach and to preach. He,

---

[5]From this point on, I will only say "God" and not "the good or God," "goodness and God," or other such awkward references to the centerpoints of ethical and religious truth. I do not, of course, deny the distinction between an ethical and a religious point of view. What I acknowledge is what Johannes Climacus notes (CUP, 1:138): to understand oneself as answerable to an absolute demand is, by definition, to have a god. I would also say that it is fairly obvious that the *Eighteen Upbuilding Discourses* were written with such a presumption in mind.

in fact, insists that he departs from the scene altogether. If the reader follows Kierkegaard's cues, including his repeated plea that a *single individual* read his words, he or she will be left alone with the discourse.[6]

Earnestness involves more than being alone, however, so Kierkegaard also emphasizes in the prefaces that the reader he wishes for is "favorably disposed" (EUD, 53), possessing "good will and wisdom" (EUD, 179) and "honest confidentiality" (EUD, 231). This does not mean, he notes, that the reader must be either solemn or cheerful (EUD, 5), but simply willing to make the thoughts in the discourse his or her own thoughts, and thus to have a conversation with the discourse.[7]

However obvious it may be, it should be noted that the prefaces do not *make* the reader honest or good or "favorably disposed," nor do they seem designed to do so. And this is, in fact, the first instance of Kierkegaard educating the reader in possibility. By use of his revocation of authority and his reminders about the importance of the "favorably disposed" single individual, Kierkegaard shows the reader that a different type of learning is possible. And the presentation of this possibility is at the same time an invitation—but no more than that. The reader can take up Kierkegaard's invitation and all of the dread that, if Haufniensis is right, will necessarily accompany a choice to stand alone before "the eternal" and be educated. But the reader can also decline the invitation and either put down the work altogether or, as some of the

---

[6]I am aware that Kierkegaard often had Regine Olsen in mind when he used this phrase, and sometimes exclusively so. As the Hongs note in the historical introduction to their translation, however, Kierkegaard also thought that his personal concerns, when not described as personal concerns, gave expression to the universally human (cf. EUD, xvii-xxi). Every reader becomes, potentially, "that single individual." It is in this spirit that I analyze these discourses. For a more substantial argument for this position on the "single individual," see Sylvia Walsh's "When 'That Single Individual' is a Woman," in *Kierkegaard Studies Yearbook 2000*, ed. Niels Jørgen Cappelørn et al. (New York: Walter de Gruyter, 2000) 1-18. (Walsh's article is reprinted in the present volume.)

[7]For more on the nature of such a dialogue and the difficulties with instigating it and carrying it out responsibly, see Pia Søltoft's "To Let Oneself be Upbuilt," in *Kierkegaard Studies Yearbook 2000*, ed. Niels Jørgen Cappelørn et al. (New York: Walter de Gruyter, 2000) 19-39.

secondary literature on *Eighteen Upbuilding Discourses* demonstrates, take up an impersonal, analytic posture. Importantly, Kierkegaard's prefaces do not condemn the possibility of taking up such an analytic posture. They only depict one possibility, and the depiction is the invitation. The response to that invitation is in the learner's hands.

After the prefaces, Kierkegaard makes a conscious effort to sustain this possibility or invitation in the texts of the *Eighteen Upbuilding Discourses*. The reasoning behind this should be obvious enough: it would not do much good, after the gentle yet pointed prefaces, to simply quote verses from Scripture and admonish the reader to believe them. It would even be dangerous for Kierkegaard to slip in a few references to himself, for any use of "I," even in the form of a personal anecdote, subtly asserts a kind of authority of the author over the reader. Kierkegaard avoids the latter fate by continually referring not to himself or his thoughts, but to "the discourse." Sometimes, it is a concept like "patience" or "love" which speaks. In such cases, the reader is reminded that they are not discussing Scripture with Kierkegaard, but thinking along with the thoughts of the discourse. By continually making himself absent in this way, Kierkegaard also indirectly reminds the reader that he or she is on the Jutland heath, where one is alone before God.[8]

Kierkegaard also avoids all forms of judgment as a way of maintaining the Jutland heath for the reader. The emphasis of each discourse is not, indeed, on the reader, but on the theme: love, faith, patience, suffering, cowardice, prayer, etc. When the reader is directly addressed, it is usually a rhetorical device that points toward a better understanding of the theme; it is up to the reader to discern the possibility of judgment from that understanding. Even when the development of a theme seems to inevitably lead to a harsh judgment of the reader, the discourse leaves the reader alone. In the first discourse entitled "Love Will Hide a Multitude of Sins," for example, the discourse notes how easy it would be to

---

[8]George Pattison discusses this and other features of the prefaces in " 'Who' Is the Discourse? A Study in Søren Kierkegaard's Religious Literature," *Kierkegaardiana* 16 (1993): 28-45.

harshly judge a reader in light of the magnificence of love, but chooses the easier task of dwelling on love, with no attention to the perfections or imperfections of the reader (EUD, 58-59). Another example occurs at the end of the discourse on Job, where it is stated that there is no honest escape from the terrifying reality that Job represents; the discourse, however, does nothing to console the reader (EUD, 124). Job and his possibility simply stand there, and whatever judgment follows from that comes either from the reader or from God, not the discourse.

Eighteen Upbuilding Discourses also calls the reader to the Jutland heath by never demanding anything from the reader but attentiveness. The discourses generally let the Scriptures speak, introduce a context in which those Scriptures make sense, and then elaborate on the Scriptural theme. No call to action or demand for repentance is ever issued. As we will see, *Eighteen Upbuilding Discourses* rather presents possibilities for a way of thinking and living and then leaves the reader with these possibilities. This is consistent with the prefaces, of course. Any interference or even prompting on Kierkegaard's part would be nothing less than an assertion of authority, however subtle. Some might find this odd in that Kierkegaard is often labeled an existentialist, and existentialists always seem to want some kind of commitment or choice from their readers. Kierkegaard's absence, however, signifies his commitment to the idea that any decision made has to be made for the right reasons, which means that it must be made for the reader's own reasons. In other words, the decision and even the desire to decide must come from the reader (or perhaps from God), and thus they would be the reader's own. Any interference or even prompting on Kierkegaard's part would make a commitment from the reader suspect.

Before moving on, a possible misinterpretation must be addressed. It could be thought that in emphasizing this "Jutland heath" in *Eighteen Upbuilding Discourses*, Kierkegaard is advocating a type of enlightened self-absorption. This is not the case, however. For one, the reader is invited to take on *Kierkegaard's own thoughts* (EUD, 53). The reader, in other words, is invited to have a conversation with another, even if that other is a discourse written "without authority." When a person reads a book in isolation, he or she is in dialogue with the thoughts of the author, and reading

Eighteen Upbuilding Discourses is no exception. Secondly, personalities like Paul and themes like love in the discourses demonstrate that the goal of an education in possibility is not continual self-examination, but a life that bears fruit in one's relationship with God and one's neighbor. The Jutland heath of *Eighteen Upbuilding Discourses* is a place to make an ethical or spiritual beginning, not the place where ethics and religion end.

Deepening the Reader's Self-Awareness

The point of an education in possiblility is not, of course, simply to stand alone before God on the Jutland heath, but to *learn* before God on the Jutland heath. In particular, the point is to learn about oneself before God.

To be educated about oneself before God, however, one must first know oneself. And while knowing oneself may be a natural capacity of human beings, it is certainly not an oft-realized capacity. Being conscious of oneself is a learned skill, and one of the discourses, at least, acknowledges that it is difficult to attain (EUD, 275). It is vital, then, that an education in possibility help develop the reader's self-awareness.

As self-awareness cannot be commanded or taught like mathematics or chemistry, Kierkegaard had to develop other methods in *Eighteen Upbuilding Discourses* to elicit it. Three methods in particular are used: questioning, utilizing recognizable vocabulary, and withholding concrete details.

Questioning

By "questioning," I do not refer to the effortless and extraordinarily effective use of rhetorical questions that fill the *Eighteen Upbuilding Discourses* and which generally serve to elucidate a point. I am referring to the practice, seen in only some of these discourses, of directly asking questions that should enable the reader to understand himself or herself better. This technique was used effectively by Socrates, and Kierkegaard takes it in only a slightly different direction by removing himself from the scene and letting the discourse, as it were, do the asking—and, we might add, letting the reader decide whether to do the answering.

The best and most extended example of this is in the first discourse on "Every Good and Every Perfect Gift." The discourse notes that it can seem easy to accept the idea that "all things serve those who love God," but then presents this series of questions:

> Are, then, the apostolic words that every good and every perfect gift is from above and comes down from the Father of lights a dark and difficult saying? And if you think that you cannot understand it, do you dare maintain that you have wanted to understand it? When you had doubts about what came from God or about what was a good and perfect gift, did you risk the venture? And when the light sparkle of joy beckoned you, did you thank God for it? And when your allotted portion was little, did you thank God? And when your allotted portion was suffering, did you thank God? And when your wish was denied, did you thank God? And when you yourself had to deny your wish, did you thank God? And when people wronged you and insulted you, did you thank God? (EUD, 43)

This is just a sample: the questions continue for another page. The point is easy to see: if a reader asked these questions of himself or herself, the result would, indeed, be a movement from a lesser to a greater self-awareness. And as Haufniensis would say, it would be a movement from understanding a truth ("every good and every perfect gift is from above and comes down from the father of lights") to understanding oneself in that truth.

Similar but much less extended examples of such questioning occur throughout *Eighteen Upbuilding Discourses*. I will briefly mention three. From the second discourse on "Every Good and Every Perfect Gift," there is a telling question: why would you not want to abide in God? (EUD, 134) At the end of the discourse on Job, there are a series of questions that lead the reader to compare himself or herself to Job (EUD, 123-24). In "The Expectancy of Eternal Salvation," there is another telling question: if the gift of salvation were from a God who is like a weak old man, would you want to receive it (EUD, 257)?

Utilizing Understandable Vocabulary

Another way of deepening the reader's self-awareness is less direct than questioning. With one exception, Kierkegaard only uses ordinary vocabulary in *Eighteen Upbuilding Discourses*.[9] By only using ordinary words that any reader can relate to, the discourses avoid trying to initiate the reader into something unfamiliar, but rather bring deeper reflection to bear on that which is already known.

A few examples will bring out this point more clearly. The first discourse on "Love Will Hide a Multitude of Sins" presumes that reflecting on normal concepts like love, fear, stinginess, envy and impurity (and a few others) will help a reader understand the verses of 1 Peter 4:7-12. Likewise, the second discourse on "Every Good Gift and Every Perfect Gift" elicits reflection on James 1:17-22 by discussing common terms like grief, judgment, choice, death, humility, and gifts. The next discourse on "Every Good and Every Perfect Gift" works in large part by asking the reader to reflect on the many ways that one can do something quite normal like giving or receiving a gift.

To drive this point home about the use of ordinary language, one could perform the interesting exercise of comparing the index of *Eighteen Upbuilding Discourses* with the index of *The Concept of Anxiety* or that of *Philosophical Fragments*.[10] Attending only to the references to Kierkegaard's text (i.e. not to the *Journals and Papers* or other supplementary material), one can easily note that there is virtually nothing unrecognizable in *Eighteen Upbuilding Discourses*: "faith," "love," "fear," "doubt," "suffering," and so on. Such words, as Paul Holmer used to say, make up the diction of the human race. *Philosophical Fragments*, on the other hand, has at least a dozen terms with which it is difficult to have any immediate resonance: "actuality," "first cause," "necessity and coming into existence," "the dialectic of contemporaneity," "the paradox of thought," and so on. *The Concept of Anxiety* is the same: "metaphysical determinant," "immediacy," "the negative," "nothingness," and then the redoubtably opaque twins of "activity-passivity" and "passivity-activity." Much can be said about the different vocabularies of Kierkegaard and the pseudonyms Johannes

---

[9]The exception is in the discourse "To Gain One's Soul in Patience," where the discourse introduces and discusses the technical terms "redoubling" and "repetition."

[10]I am referring to the indexes in the Hong editions.

Climacus and Vigilius Haufniensis. The point here is that *Philosoph-ical Fragments* and *The Concept of Anxiety* were written by pseud-onyms who, according to Kierkegaard, have a point of view and a sphere of interests that are not the same as their creator's. Their thoughts are directed outward, toward knowing about something, and the terms used are, appropriately enough, like some kind of abstraction from existence instead of about any one person's existence. *Eighteen Upbuilding Discourses* is directed toward the reader understanding verses from Scripture or a religious theme in light of his or her own life, and again, appropriately enough, the terms are quite obviously related to one's own existence.[11] This is not to say that the pseudonymous works cannot be upbuilding. They can, but in a much different way than *Eighteen Upbuilding Discourses* is upbuilding. More will be said about this later.

It is important to note that Kierkegaard never directly deni-grates the abstruse vocabulary of *Philosophical Fragments, The Con-cept of Anxiety*, and other works, nor does he directly criticize the theoretical interest that gives rise to it. The extent to which he in-directly denigrates it is an ongoing interpretational issue, of course, but his indirect point in *Eighteen Upbuilding Discourses*—if it can be called a "point"—is clear enough. The intellectual orientation taken by a theoretician is qualitatively different from the intellectual orientation of one who is examining himself or herself, and each way of learning calls for a different kind of education. As it is put at the beginning of "Think About Your Creator in the Days of Your Youth," there is a difference between *indifferent truths* and *concerned truths* (EUD, 233-34); it is the latter which is explicated or presumed throughout the discourses, and the language used is appropriate enough for any concerned person.

---

[11]My point here is a general one. For the most part, the way Kierkegaard uses specific images in *Eighteen Upbuilding Discourses* remains to be explicated. Two such analyses are Arne Grøn's "Temporality in Kierkegaard's Edifying Discours-es," which examines Kierkegaard's emphasis on temporality and images of time throughout *Eighteen Upbuilding Discourses*; and Helle Møller Jensen's "Freeze! Hold It Right There," which examines Kierkegaard's use of images of stillness and movement in the discourse "To Preserve One's Soul in Patience" (*Kierkegaard Studies Yearbook 2000*, ed. Niels Jørgen Cappelørn et al. [New York: Walter de Gruyter, 2000] 191-204 and 223-39).

Withholding Concrete Details

Although the vocabulary used in *Eighteen Upbuilding Discourses* is clear and concrete, it is often not situationally specific, and this vagueness is another technique that fosters self-awareness.

The best way to be clear about this is to note what Kierkegaard does *not* do in *Eighteen Upbuilding Discourses*. If a reader personally invests himself or herself in the discourse—as Kierkegaard hoped—then that reader is compelled to use his or her own examples to fill out these broad concepts. For while everyone is, of course, conversant in "the diction of the human race," everyone's reference points with regard to such terms are somewhat different. My experience of hopefulness is different from my neighbor's experience of the same, and his is different from his neighbor's, and so on. When "Love Will Hide a Multitude of Sins" is expounded in relation to fear, stinginess, envy, and impurity, for example, there are no specific examples of fear, stinginess, envy, and impurity to help the reader along the way. Another example: in the third discourse on "Every Good Gift and Every Perfect Gift," several kinds of giving are described in a general way: giving with the expectation of reciprocation, giving with the humble knowledge that one is also in need of gifts, giving with the hope of admiration, giving sympathy without violating the recipient, and others. The reader can only actively think about gift giving along these lines by reflecting upon the actual instances of gift giving (or gift receiving) that he or she has experience of. This avoidance of attaching specific situations to specific moral and religious vocabulary allows and even encourages the reader to provide his or her own examples and personal meaning to the content of the discourses, and this is obviously a means of fostering self-awareness.

Expanding the Reader's Moral and Religious Consciousness

Thus far, we have seen how Kierkegaard invites the reader to the Jutland heath and stirs the personally engaged reader to self-reflection. As such, we have also seen how *Eighteen Upbuilding Discourses* fits part of Vigilius Haufniensis's description of an education in possibility. But we have not seen, to any great extent, why *Eighteen Upbuilding Discourses* can be called an education in possibility; we have only seen how Kierkegaard's techniques can be possibly educative. The justification for labeling the *Eighteen Upbuilding Discourses* as an "education in possibility" becomes most clear when it is seen that these discourses do not simply help a reader become aware of who he or she is, but actually expand the ethical and religious possibilities for the reader.

To understand what Kierkegaard is doing in this regard, something has to be made clear which is not readily obvious, but which seems to have been obvious to Kierkegaard. It is this: becoming morally or spiritually educated is not a straightforward matter. It can certainly seem like a relatively straightforward matter; to become formed as a Christian, one might say, a person should simply learn Christian tenets and try to live by them. The most obvious places to start would be the classic lists from the Scriptures and the Christian tradition: the Ten Commandments, the Beatitudes, the gifts of the Holy Spirit (Galatians 5:22-23), the seven deadly sins, and the seven cardinal virtues. The next thing to do, especially to avoid the accusation of seeking only an education in the facts about such matters, is to examine oneself in light of these lists. Do I covet? Am I generous? Am I a peacemaker? Do I harbor wrath or pride? Do I practice charity? And so on.

If someone were to do as much, he or she would certainly count as "earnest" and undoubtedly win praise from Vigilius Haufniensis and Kierkegaard. Haufniensis might even say that such an endeavor in self-examination is a kind of education in possibility. The learner, in constantly subjecting himself or herself to possibilities of living that have not been realized, will actually become more self-aware and perhaps even more knowledgeable about the possibilities of evil and goodness.

It is not too much to say, however, that any one person's understanding of these possibilities is limited, no matter how ardently he or she engages in self-examination. I may have a good sense for the intricacies of hope, for example, but be somewhat less clear about the workings of greed—and my neighbor may be just the opposite. The point is simply that when it comes to understanding the possibilities of human existence, especially the moral and religious dimensions of human existence, every person needs some (and probably a lot of) education. This point reinforces my earlier claim about the solitude of an "education in possibility" like

Eighteen Upbuilding Discourses. Such solitude is not complete isolation, for the education that happens from these discourses depends on having someone like Kierkegaard to open doors to self-examination that would otherwise remain closed.

It is also important that one's understanding of the possibilities and difficulties of living in light of the Ten Commandments, the Beatitudes, and the other lists grow and deepen as one's life progresses. An adolescent conception of love, for instance, is not enough to sustain a marriage, no matter how pure and sincere it is. Nor can a young person's struggle with covetousness, even if undertaken with great earnestness, adequately teach him or her about all the forms of covetousness in the world and in the heart that will be encountered as he or she gets older. Gaining a more mature understanding of these things is necessary, for if one's understanding does not keep pace with one's life, doubt and despair about the possibility of goodness can easily set in—and just such a situation is constantly alluded to in some of the earlier discourses.[12]

To secure a deep and mature understanding of "the diction of the human race," one needs an education where the possibilities of faith, love, generosity, and other traits are explicated in light of the complexities of human life and the human heart. Kierkegaard presents these possibilities by carefully eliciting and guiding his reader's imagination, helping him or her to conceive of a possi-

---

[12]The passages in the following discourses discuss the long-term battle with mature and sophisticated doubt: "The Expectancy of Faith" (EUD, 23-28); "Every Good and Every Perfect Gift Is from Above" (EUD, 41); "Love Will Hide a Multitude of Sins" (EUD, 65); "Every Good Gift and Every Perfect Gift Is from Above" (EUD, 127-28, 130-32).

bility that could not have been conceived previously.[13] Let us see how he accomplishes this.

Articulating Connections in the Human Heart

In *Eighteen Upbuilding Discourses*, Kierkegaard attempts to educate by repeatedly showing how the human heart can be swayed and where it can be swayed to. In doing this, he articulates connections and possibilities in the human heart that are not obvious and thereby educates the earnest reader.

Who, for example, is naturally inclined to think of doubt as something "crafty"? For that matter, who is naturally inclined to analyze doubt as a condition that affects the heart and not merely the mind? Yet that is precisely what is suggested in the first discourse, "The Expectancy of Faith." This discourse goes on to describe possible nonintellectual origins of doubt regarding God that are not obvious: disappointment in life, disgust at the unreliability of human beings, preoccupation with visible signs, and expecting certain circumstances to materialize (EUD, 23-26). At the same time, of course, the possibility of a faith that overcomes such doubts is also articulated. Another example: who would think that prosperity and good fortune can strengthen one's inner being, along with misfortune and adversity? The discourse "Strengthening the Inner Being" describes how this is possible, but even then it goes on to describe how being strengthened by adversity,

---

[13]The imagination, I would say, is a much-neglected component of moral and spiritual reasoning, and it is because Kierkegaard counts on an active imagination from his reader that the discourses can be difficult for the modern reader, who more often than not preconceives the study of morality and spirituality as the study of rules, creeds, and theories about rules and creeds. One can reasonably say that Kierkegaard's ability to awaken and guide the reader's imagination in order to expand his or her moral and religious consciousness is the most consistently impressive feature of *Eighteen Upbuilding Discourses*. More detailed studies of Kierkegaard's understanding of the role of imagination in ethical and spiritual development are David Gouwens's *Kierkegaard's Dialectic of the Imagination* (New York: Peter Lang, 1989) and *Kierkegaard as a Religious Thinker* (New York: Cambridge University Press, 1996) and M. Jamie Ferreira's *Transforming Vision: Imagination and Will in Kierkegaardian Faith* (Oxford: Clarendon Press, 1991). As with many studies of Kierkegaard's thought, however, the latter two books virtually ignore *Eighteen Upbuilding Discourses*.

misfortune, and wrongdoing can save one from despair, bitterness, disappointment, and anxiety, and even lead to a greater love of people. And if that is not enough, the discourse then articulates the additional not-so-obvious possibility of being strengthened by a spiritual trial, where one feels only the wrath of God's judgment. And even then it goes on describe the possibility of such a trial leading to false boastfulness and thus making it harmful to the bearer (EUD, 87-98).

Let us consider two more examples of such education in possibility. The first is from "To Gain One's Soul in Patience," which is based on Christ's words of Luke 2:19. This discourse begins by describing several kinds of recognizable patience: the patience of a hiker who rests during a journey; the patience of a farmer who waits for the harvest; the patience of a mother during sleepless nights; and the patience of one who writes and speaks even though no one in particular is reading or listening. But even though most readers would not have been aware of all these types of patience as genuine possibilities, the discourse presses on to articulate a patience that has no goal in this world. The possibility of this latter patience, says the discourse, is the possibility of fulfilling Christ's words and gaining one's soul. The second example is from "Think About Your Creator in the Days of Your Youth," which considers how people get separated from the thought of their Creator. The possibilities of inconsolable guilt, pleasures, and worry separating one from God are discussed, but they are fairly obvious candidates. What is striking (and educative) are the descriptions of the way that aging, gaining knowledge, and harboring seriousness can also separate one from God. And then, of course, the possibility of consolation in the thought of the Creator is drawn out with new clarity.

Examples like these could be listed for pages, but I will leave it to the reader to explore *Eighteen Upbuilding Discourses* at a different time. We shall now turn to another way that Kierkegaard educates his reader in possibility.

Considering Biblical Figures

In many ways, the consideration of Biblical figures in the *Eighteen Upbuilding Discourses*—Job, Anna, Paul, and John the Baptist get extended treatment—is much like what was described above. A discourse takes a familiar moral or spiritual concept and deepens it by articulating a possibility that was probably not clear or even present to the reader beforehand. Here, though, the concept has the shape of a concrete human life and can thus be an even more concrete possibility for the reader. Let us briefly examine two of these figures, Paul and John the Baptist.

The opening of "Strengthening the Inner Being," via notable (and unreproducible) artistry, gives the reader a sense of just how different Paul was. Paul was in prison willingly, writing about the "inner being"—an unusual possibility, to say the least. Even more unusual was Paul's being in Rome, supremely unnoticed by that great city's standards, yet believing that the whole world needed his words and that his message would conquer the whole world (EUD, 80-84). Such an introduction to Paul's words ought to awaken in any reader a sense of the extraordinary man who wrote them, and such a sense can be the beginning of hearing Paul's words about "the inner being" as words about a possibility in human life rather than as a foundation for the defense or criticism of doctrine. Paul's extraordinary character—and the possibility of life that he represents—is given more extended treatment in "The Thorn in the Flesh." Several exceptional and educative insights can be found in this discourse, but two in particular stand out. First, Paul's sinfulness was like that of few others, for he not only had to repent of the sins that he had always known about, but also of persecuting Christians, which he at one time thought was a good thing to do. As the discourse puts it, Paul had the anguish of repenting of his very best (EUD, 341). But such anguish and sinfulness, constantly being pressed upon Paul via the thorn in the flesh, was side-by-side with intense joy. Such a man exhibits not only the possibility of experiencing intense suffering and intense beatitude, but also of holding them together at the same time out of a love for God.

John the Baptist was quite different from Paul, but he still embodied a possibility of living that most would need to be educated into. Who can easily imagine living one's whole life to be superceded and to say, with utter finality, "He must increase, I must decrease"? Moreover, who would consider that such an utterance would not be made with bitterness, spite, revenge, enviousness, or even simple resignation, but with genuine joy? For that matter, who would be able to think of all these alternatives to joy?

Deepening the Reader's Sense of "Infinite Guilt" (and Something More)

We have considered how *Eighteen Upbuilding Discourses* invites the reader to the "Jutland heath," deepens a reader's self-awareness, and expands a reader's moral and religious sensibilities. As such, we have also seen how *Eighteen Upbuilding Discourses* fits three of Vigilius Haufniensis's criteria for an "education in possibility." Let us now examine these discourses in light of Haufniensis's fourth criterion, which is that an education in possibilty must awaken a reader's sense of "infinite guilt."

The term "infinite guilt" can sound decidedly negative, and in one sense, at least, it is. As mentioned before, facing one's own sin is always difficult, and choosing to be (and not just feel) guilty before "the eternal" is not exactly a natural inclination. But it is also true, as was also said before, that willfully existing in "infinite guilt" is the precondition for ethical and spiritual growth. To have a sense of "infinite guilt," a reader has to be earnest, and as we have seen, Kierkegaard certainly presumes such earnestness in the reader of *Eighteen Upbuilding Discourses*. He does more than presume it, however. He attempts to accentuate it. He accentuates something more, however, and this something more is just as important as "infinite guilt," yet it receives no mention in *The Concept of Anxiety*. More about this in a moment.

Let us first look at how *Eighteen Upbuilding Discourses* conform to Haufniensis's description of the awakening and strengthening of "infinite guilt" in an education in possibility. As we have seen, Kierkegaard expands the reader's sense of ethical and religious possibilities. What this amounts to for an earnest reader, however, is an expanded sense of judgment. An expanded sense of ethical and religious possibilities, in other words, is at the same time an expanded sense of what one should be but is not, or of what one should not be but is. A reader may even experience, like Paul did, the crushing realization that one not only falls short by one's own standards, but that one's standards themselves fall short. The result of an earnest reader working through the *Eighteen Upbuilding*

Discourses, then, should be a greater and greater sense of "infinite guilt" or even, as Vigilius Haufniensis would also put it, a greater and greater sense of one's original sin.

The reader is reminded of this throughout *Eighteen Upbuilding Discourses*. The very first discourse, "The Expectancy of Faith," says that doubt invades thought through the normal exigencies of life; therefore the battle of faith is fought every day, from young age to old. As mentioned before, the first discourse on "Love Will Hide a Multitude of Sins" extols love, but then frankly acknowledges the judgment one feels when confronted with the gloriousness of love. The second discourse on "Love Will Hide a Multitude of Sins" opens by recalling the Apostle Peter's sense that because time is short, love demands ardent attention. It goes on to catalog the ways that love, as it reveals a person's sinfulness, is always unsettling and difficult. Also as mentioned earlier, the reality of Job is presented as terrifying because of the possibility of suffering he presents to every person. The discourse "Patience in Expectancy" flatly states that Anna, the woman who waited ceaselessly in the Temple for the coming of the Messiah, can not only teach us how to live, but can also make us weep over ourselves (EUD, 209). "The Expectancy of an Eternal Salvation" ends with a prayer that emphasizes the humanly unbridgeable gulf between oneself and God (EUD, 272-73). Each of the last four discourses in the collection, which were originally published together, also accentuate "infinite guilt." The discourse "To Need God is a Human Being's Highest Perfection" emphasizes that one is never done needing God, and in fact ought to need God more and more as life progresses. "The Thorn in the Flesh" says that Paul's suffering is a sign that we should face the terror of knowing ourselves, even under the most extreme judgment (EUD, 344-45). The discourse "Against Cowardliness" says that avoiding self-examination is pride and cowardice, and that "this very day" is always the time to begin becoming humble and brave (EUD, 359-60). The last discourse says that no other desire in human life is more important than the desire to yield to God and become more transparent to him (and oneself) in prayer.

As much as *Eighteen Upbuilding Discourses* can accentuate "infinite guilt," however, they also emphasize joy and beatitude as the result of undergoing an education in possibility, and this is the "something more" that *The Concept of Anxiety* lacks. It is stated repeatedly throughout *Eighteen Upbuilding Discourses*, for example, that the Scriptural passages and themes demand much of the earnest reader, but they also possess a healing grace in that they provide much and are pressed upon the reader only by a loving and merciful God. A few specific examples substantiate this claim. In the first "Every Good and Every Perfect Gift," it is quite explicitly stated that our sense of imperfection, brought on by earnestness, leads to repentance, but that such repentance gives birth to love, which is healing and, in fact, the movement of God himself in us (EUD, 45-46). Seemingly following up on this idea, the very next discourse ("Love Will Hide a Multitude of Sins") claims that the power of love to forgive and heal the wounds of sin is real, and that by becoming loving people we actually become God's coworkers in love (EUD, 62). In "To Need God is a Human Being's Highest Perfection," infinite guilt is described as "becoming nothing before God," but such nothingness is also said to be followed by being made into something new by God and thus being filled with God (EUD, 325). The difficulty of expectancy, articulated in several of the discourses, is followed by one of two things: the joyous fulfillment of the expectancy (as in the cases of John the Baptist and Anna) or the joy of serving God for that which is to come (as in the cases of Peter (EUD, 69-70) and Paul). The last discourse boldly restates this recurring theme: the victory in losing the world via struggle and prayer is that we actually become like God (EUD, 399).

Given Vigilius Haufniensis's self-described indifferent standpoint (or, as Johannes Climacus would put it, "objective interest"), it should not be surprising that he fails to see and describe the joy that often accompanies "infinite guilt," even though it is a possible result of an education in possibility. The other pseudonyms that parallel *Eighteen Upbuilding Discourses* are similar. "A" of *Either/Or I* is certainly "indifferent" to any ethical or religious demands. Constantine Constantius, Frater Taciturnus, and Johannes Climacus are all acute observers, but they never allow themselves to be more than observers. To his credit, Johannes Climacus actually contemplates the possibility of a loving union between God and a human being, but it only seems to move him insofar as it is a fascinating possibility to think about. Judge William is the only pseudonym in this group who counts as an earnest personality. His writing, however, is still didactic and admonishing; far different, in other words, from the intense, yet gentle and almost apersonal tone of *Eighteen Upbuilding Discourses*. It is no wonder, then, that at the first (supposed) end of his authorship, Kierkegaard so willingly attached his name to *Eighteen Upbuilding Discourses* (CUP, 1:627) while practically begging for the pseudonyms to be read as independent authors with their own points of view (CUP, 1:626, 629). He knew and wrote about joy; his pseudonyms, with the half-exception of Judge William, did neither.

Again, this does not mean that the pseudonymous works cannot be upbuilding; it only means that the pseudonymous authors do not aim at upbuilding. The author of the pseudonymous authors clearly thought that in composing the pseudonymous works he was aiming at the same goal when writing the discourses: namely, to reintroduce Christianity to a Christendom that had essentially forgotten it (POV 7-8, 41-56).[14] The strategy of the pseudonymous works is, of course, quite different, aimed more at engaging a reader's reflectivity and not, as with *Eighteen Upbuilding Discourses*, a reader's self-reflectivity. But for either strategy to work toward upbuilding, the reader must be earnest, which means that whether a work is upbuilding or not depends on the reader. This leads to the last section of this essay.

The Limit of an Education in Possibility

At the end of "To Gain One's Soul in Patience," a warning of sorts is issued: knowledge of patience alone does not help gain a soul. Like one who hears the Word but does not do it, the one who simply knows about patience is supremely deficient with regard to patience (EUD, 172-74). And then comes the final point, directed not at the reader but at the discourse itself. As the discourse is a description of patience and not the gaining of it, it is imperfect; and as the description is something which "the world and time"

---

[14]At least two other commentators in the English-speaking world have agreed with this self-assessment of Kierkegaard: David Gouwens in *Kierkegaard as a Religious Thinker* and Harvie Ferguson in part III of *Melancholy and the Critique of Modernity* (New York: Routledge, 1995).

can take away, it is not even a necessary condition for gaining patience (EUD, 175).

This is, of course, similar to the point that Haufniensis makes about the evasions of the learned. When thinking about "the eternal," they fill their heads with several notions about "the eternal," but never confront the "the eternal" as it relates to their own lives. In other words, they become educated in the facts, but not in possibility. What is different is that this point is made in a discourse which, from its preface to its closing words, does just about everything possible to bring the reader to a place of earnestness and educate him or her in that earnestness. One might think that the discourse is saying that it might not be an education in possibility, and one would be right.

The point, again, is this: whether *Eighteen Upbuilding Discourses* is an education in possibility depends entirely on the reader. One can read them as an example of religious thought in 19th century Denmark, or one can read them with fear and trembling as one allows oneself to be ever more exposed to God. One can read them to find thematic parallels with Kierkegaard's other works, or one can read them to prepare for confession. One can, in other words, read them to be educated in the facts, or one can read them to be educated in possibility.

The same is true for any other works as well. For the reader who chooses only to know, the most exquisitely crafted attempt at an education in possibility will fail to make that reader earnest. The earnest reader, on the other hand, is like Paul, for whom everything was a means for edification (EUD, 345). Thus, an education in possibility—or, one should say, the *attempt* at an education in possibility—quickly reaches its limit when it encounters a reader. And it is always up to the reader to move beyond that limit or not.[15]

---

[15]This essay is a development of ideas presented in my first publication, "Going Back to the Religious Beginning," *Wittgenstein Studies* (Feb. 1997). I am indebted to Stacey Ake and George Connell for the comments and suggestions they made on earlier drafts of this essay.

8

Good Faith

M. G. Piety

Kierkegaard is fascinated by the claim at I Peter 4:8 that "love hides a multitude of sins." He treats this issue repeatedly throughout his authorship but focuses on it particularly in two edifying discourses for which it is the title (EUD, 55-78). These are two of the loveliest and most moving of Kierkegaard's discourses, yet they appear to present an intractable philosophical problem. Kierkegaard claims that a loving vision "sees not the impure but the pure" (EUD, 61) and yet that "the love that hides a multitude of sins is never deceived" (EUD, 61). To assert that one can see no sin while never being deceived is to suggest that sin is not real. The reality of sin is, however, one of the basic tenets of Christianity, and it is a presupposition of the dialogue, which exhorts the reader to turn away from the "'evil eye [that] comes from within'"(EUD, 60) and "discovers much that love does not see" (EUD, 60). But if the Christian refuses to see in the world what he or she nevertheless posits must be there, Christian conviction looks either foolish or very much like the hypocritical self-deception Sartre identifies in *Being and Nothingness* as "bad faith."[1] That is, it would appear that in order to rescue faith from the charge that it is either foolish or hypocritical, one must choose between the veracity of a loving vision or the reality of sin.

Kierkegaard clearly wants to claim, however, both that sin is real and that a loving vision of the world is veridical. I will argue that it is, in fact, possible for Kierkegaard to reconcile these two apparently irreconcilable claims: that sin is real and that a vision

---

[1]Jean-Paul Sartre, "Bad Faith," *Being and Nothingness*, trans. Hazel E. Barnes, new introduction by Mary Warnock (London: Routledge, 1991; orig. complete English translation: New York: Philosophical Library, 1956) 47-70.

that refuses to see it is not self deluded. I will argue that such a reconciliation is possible as a result of the combination of Kierkegaard's epistemology, his ontology and an ambiguity in the terminology of the original Greek text of I Peter. That is, I will argue that Kierkegaard's interpretation of what it means for a loving vision to "hide" sin makes the Christian neither a hypocrite nor a fool.

Introduction

There are two issues inextricably intertwined here: the epistemological and the ontological. So we need to look both at the interpretation of reality, or the "knowledge" of reality, to which a loving vision gives rise, and at the actual nature of the reality. Getting at the reality behind appearances has always presented difficulties to philosophers, and the present discussion is not immune to those difficulties. We are fortunate, however, in that we can make certain ontological assumptions. They may be mistaken, but to the extent that the discourses in question themselves make those assumptions, this possibility should not concern us. The particular assumption I have in mind is that sin is real, so our task is to examine first how a loving vision that does not see sin actually works as a vehicle for presenting reality and then whether this can be reconciled with the view that people are, in fact, sinful.

"Love is blind," observes Kierkegaard:

> When love lives in the heart, the eye is shut and does not discover the open act of sin, to say nothing of the concealed act . . . When love lives in the heart, the ear is shut and does not hear what the world says . . . When love lives in the heart, a person understands slowly and does not hear at all words said in haste and does not understand them when repeated because he assigns them a good position and a good meaning. (EUD, 60-61)

How such a loving vision might work can be seen in the example of the relation between a hypothetical mother-in-law and daughter-in-law that Iris Murdoch describes in *The Sovereignty of Good*.[2] The

---

[2]Iris Murdoch, *The Sovereignty of Good* (London: Ark Paperbacks, 1985) 17. See also David J. Gouwens's treatment of this example in *Kierkegaard as Religious Thinker* (Cambridge: Cambridge University Press, 1996) 203-204.

mother-in-law feels some hostility toward her daughter-in-law. She feels the girl is "lacking in dignity and refinement," that she is "brusque, sometimes positively rude, [and] always tiresomely juvenile."[3]

Murdoch explains, however, that the mother-in-law is "well intentioned," and that she thus endeavors to see her daughter-in-law in a more favorable light. She tells herself that she is "old fashioned and conventional," perhaps even "prejudiced and narrow minded." She endeavors to see her daughter-in-law in a more favorable light and "discover[s]" that she is "not vulgar but refreshingly simple, not undignified but spontaneous, not noisy but gay, not tiresomely juvenile but delightfully youthful, and so on."[4]

Murdoch does not say that it is love that alters the mother-in-law's vision of her daughter-in-law. In fact, she asserts that the mother-in-law's more positive interpretation of her daughter-in-law is the result of "careful and just *attention*."[5] Such an assertion would appear to preclude that the unfavorable assessment could have been correct. Yet it could have been correct. Christianity assumes that people are far from perfect. From the perspective of Christianity, it must thus be possible that the daughter-in-law really was brusque, rude and "tiresomely juvenile." So "is the woman indeed seeing the girl truly, or is she self-deceptively sacrificing her critical discernment in this new judgment of her daughter-in-law?"[6]

Murdoch's example is fairly innocuous. The mother-in-law's judgments of her daughter-in-law are primarily concerned with points of etiquette, not ethics. What some people find brusque or rude others would find appealingly straightforward. It seems reasonable to suppose that a person can be *willfully* indifferent to how her behavior is received by others and that such willful indifference could be considered unethical. Most of the time, however, what passes for rudeness is actually an unintentional failure to appreciate the nuances of various social situations. Different social or cultural situations, or different personalities or

---

[3]Murdoch, *Sovereignty of Good*, 17.
[4]Murdoch, *Sovereignty of Good*, 17-18.
[5]Murdoch, *Sovereignty of Good*, 17.
[6]Gouwens, *Kierkegaard as Religious Thinker*, 204.

levels of sensitivity in individuals can mean that what is inoffensive behavior in more familiar contexts can become offensive behavior in less familiar ones.

Kierkegaard's concern is not etiquette, but ethics. Still, Murdoch's example is useful in that it provides us with a template for a more substantive example. Let's assume that the daughter-in-law actively dislikes her mother-in-law and makes no attempt to conceal this. On the contrary, she takes every opportunity to insult her mother-in-law and to flaunt in her face that she has supplanted her in her son's affections.[7] What if the mother-in-law is a Christian and thus endeavors to see her daughter-in-law lovingly? Can she really give her daughter-in-law's behavior a "good meaning"? She accepts, after all, that people are sinful. She may endeavor to see her daughter-in-law's slights as unintentional, but won't she be aware, on some level, that she is deceiving herself about her daughter-in-law's true character or about the significance of her behavior? So why does Kierkegaard assert that "the love that hides a multitude of sins is never deceived"?

It is possible to argue that what Kierkegaard means when he says that "the love that hides a multitude of sins is not deceived" is that in the *infinite conception of love . . . to be deceived simply and solely means to refrain from loving, to let oneself be so carried away as to give up love in itself and to lose its intrinsic blessedness in that way*" (WL, 236; italics in original). There is no question that Kierkegaard is primarily concerned with "deception" in this sense, that is, in what one could call the ontological rather than epistemological sense. The difficulty is that however compelling this view is, it leaves the question of epistemological deception essentially unanswered. But if the Christian is deceived in the ordinary sense, it appears that she will be subject to the dialectic of what Sartre famously identifies in *Being and Nothingness* as "bad faith," and if that turns out to be true, then it would appear that the Christian would be deceived in the more profound sense as well. That is, bad faith is self-deception. The Christian, if subject to this dialectic, would appear to be hypocritically claiming to himself or herself to

---

[7]Compare Gouwens, *Kierkegaard as Religious Thinker*, 204.

view others lovingly while, in fact, continuing on some level to condemn them.

Bad Faith

Sartre did not discover the phenomenon of self-deception, but his is one of the clearest articulations of it; hence it provides a nice framework for laying out what would appear to be difficulties inherent in Kierkegaard's concept of Christian faith. "Bad faith," asserts Sartre in *Being and Nothingness,* is faith that decides first the nature of truth.[8] That is, it decides what truth is before observing reality rather than discovering what it is as the result of such observation. This would appear to be precisely what Christianity does, according to Kierkegaard. Christianity decides that we should view others as inherently lovable, yet it also posits sin, which would appear to make people unlovable. That is, it appears to command us to see what may not always be there (i.e., a lovable nature) as well as not to see what is there (i.e., sin).

"Love is blind," observes Kierkegaard, and a person becomes increasingly blind the more he or she loves. Yet Kierkegaard insists that such blindness is not an imperfection.

> Or did love become more imperfect when, having first deceived itself by refusing to see what it nevertheless saw, it finally did not even see it anymore? Or who concealed better—he who knew that he had hidden something or he who had forgotten even that? To the pure, all things are pure, declares an old saying, and does not thereby suggest an imperfection in the one who is pure. . . . Or was it an imperfection in the one who is pure that he, having first kept himself unspotted by the impurity by refusing to know [*vide*] what he nevertheless knew (*vidste*), finally did not even know anything more about it? (EUD, 59)

But can one become truly ignorant of the fact that one is "deceiving"[9] oneself in this way? Sartre argues that this is not

---

[8] Sartre, *Being and Nothingness,* 68.

[9] I have used quotation marks here because it is not yet clear whether one is, in fact, deceiving oneself.

possible.[10] Self deception is a lie told to oneself. The difficulty, however, as Sartre puts it, is that

> [T]he one to whom the lie is told and the one who lies are one and the same person, which means I must know in my capacity as deceiver the truth which is hidden from me in my capacity as the one deceived. Better yet I must know it very exactly *in order* to conceal it more carefully—and this not at two different moments, which at a pinch would allow us to reestablish a semblance of duality—but in the unitary structure of a single project.[11]

It is for this reason that "bad faith," according to Sartre, cannot actually "succeed in believing what it wishes to believe."[12] On some level, the person in bad faith knows that he is trying to hide something from himself. He accepts, on some level, what he is trying to reject, and he *knows* that he is doing this. That is why Sartre calls this type of activity "bad faith." He argues that some consciousness of what one is hiding from oneself must always be present or the deception will not be effective. One has to know where to erect the screen, so to speak. One has to remember why the screen is there (i.e., what is behind the screen), otherwise one might inadvertently move it and expose the "truth."

The problem for the Christian is that it would appear that hiding the multitude of others' sins would require that he in fact be aware of those sins in order more effectively to obscure them. That is, it looks like the Christian will have to be aware of others' sins in order to know precisely where to erect the screen that would hide them. But if the Christian is aware, on some level, of others' sins, even while resolving not to see them, then it would appear that he or she is in bad faith. It is difficult, at first glance, to imagine how Kierkegaard is going to avoid this problem.

Untangling the Knot

I believe Kierkegaard does avoid the problem of bad faith. There are three strands, or cords, to Kierkegaard's defense against

---

[10]See n. 8 above.
[11]Sartre, *Being and Nothingness*, 49.
[12]Sartre, *Being and Nothingness*, 70.

the charge that a loving vision is in bad faith. The first is his epistemology, the second is his ontology and the third is what one could call the indeterminacy of translation.

The Epistemological Cord

What would it mean to be aware of another's sin? "Love," says Kierkegaard, "is to be known by its fruits" (WL, 15). This suggests that there should be some sort of unequivocal external expression of sin. We assume there is such an expression to the extent that we make moral judgments primarily based on people's actions, on what we can observe of their behavior, or on what we know about them. Yet according to Kierkegaard, this is precisely what we should *not* do. "Only half-experienced and very confused people," he argues, "think of judging another person on the basis of knowledge [*Viden*]" (WL, 231). "Is it not so," asks Kierkegaard, "that one person never completely understands the other? But if he does not understand him completely, then of course, it is always possible that the most indubitable [*Utvivlsomme*] thing could still have a completely different explanation that would, note well, be the true explanation" (WL, 229).[13]

It is not *what* one does, according to Kierkegaard, that determines whether one behaved well or ill, but *how* one has done it. It is how a thing is done that is "essential" (WL, 13) on his view. "One can do works of love," he asserts, "in an unloving, yes, even in a self-loving way, and if this is so, the work is no work of love at all" (WL, 13). "There is no work," he asserts, "not one single one, not even the best, about which we unconditionally dare to say: The one who does this unconditionally demonstrates love by it. It depends on *how* the work is done" (WL, 13).

This may seem, at first, like an extreme claim, but it is actually relatively uncontroversial. Cynics have long been fond of pointing out that even the most apparently altruistic behavior could simply be a concealed expression of self interest. A mother-in-law, for

---

[13]The Hongs actually have "indisputable" where I have "indubitable." The former is the more idiomatic expression but the latter is a more literal translation of *Utvivlsomme* (see *A Danish-English Dictionary*, ed. J. S. Ferrall and Thorl. Gudm. Repp [Copenhagen, 1845] 356) and conveys more effectively the subjective nature of the original.

example, may endeavor to appear loving in her relations with her daughter-in-law out of fear that if she did not, she would alienate her son, or out of a desire to appear to others to be a good person. Even if one accepts, however, that there is no unequivocal expression of goodness, it would appear that there are at least unequivocal expressions of evil. Mother Theresa may not actually have been a saint,[14] but Hitler, one may object, was certainly evil.

Kierkegaard is emphatic, however, that the uncertainty that characterizes positive judgments characterizes negative judgments as well and that "even something that appears to be the vilest behavior could be pure love" (WL, 228). "It has been said," he observes,

> that some day in eternity we . . . shall with amazement miss this one and that one whom we had definitely expected to find there; but will we not with amazement also see this one and that one whom we would have summarily excluded and see that he was far better than we ourselves, not as if he had become that later, *but precisely in that which made the judges decide to exclude him.*
> (WL, 234; emphasis added)

"[Y]ou can credit even the worst person," asserts Kierkegaard, "with the good, because it is still possible that his badness is an appearance.[15] There is no way to know, from a person's behavior alone, whether that behavior emanates from love or from sin. "[O]ne honest, upright, respectable, God-fearing" person, asserts Kierkegaard, "can under the same circumstances do *the very opposite* of what another human being does who is also honest, upright, respectable [and] God fearing" (WL, 230, emphasis added).

---

[14]See Christopher Hitchens, *The Missionary Position: Mother Theresa in Theory and Practice* (London: Verso, 1995) and Matt Cherry, "Christopher Hitchens on Mother Theresa (Interview)," *Free Inquiry* 16 (1996) accessed at <http://www.secularhumanism.org/library/fi/hitchens_16_4.html>.

[15]WL, 228. I have winessed putative Christians object that this sounds nice, but that it cannot be applied universally. Terrorists, they argue, for example, are clearly evil. Christ, they explain, did not understand this because he did not have to deal with terrorism. Such a view seems, however, in the words of Kierkegaard, something "both to be laughed at and to be wept over" (WL, 242).

This does not mean, of course, that the Christian should give characters like Hitler, or suicide bombers, a free rein. To love does not mean to do whatever the beloved wants. "If your beloved or friend," asserts Kierkegaard, "asks something of you that you, precisely because you honestly loved, had in concern considered would be harmful to him, then you must bear the responsibility if you love by obeying instead of loving by refusing a fulfillment of the desire" (WL, 19-20).

We have a responsibility to stop Hitler, or the suicide bomber, just as we would have a responsibility to stop Abraham from what would appear to any observer to be the imminent murder of his son, not because we know these people to be sinful, but because their actions would appear to be harmful. It is possible, after all, to harm others even while one intends to help them.[16] The difficulty is that the intentions of others cannot be objects of direct observation.[17] We must act to stop what would appear to us to be harm, or what we define socially and politically as a "crime," but must refrain from judging the criminal in a moral sense.[18]

---

[16]Many people who appear to be genuinely moral will, for example, defend war as an attempt to help the enemy by liberating them from an oppressive dictator. That is, they will defend killing people as a means of helping them. More charitably, one could say that they will defend, in a utilitarian manner, killing some innocent people to help what they hope will be more innocent people. Other people, however, who also appear to be genuinely moral, often find such a position morally repugnant.

[17]I disagree here with Jamie Ferreira's suggestion in *Love's Grateful Striving: A Commentary on Kierkegaard's "Works of Love"* (Oxford: Oxford University Press, 2001) that our inability "to infallibly determine motivation" is not inconsistent with the claim that there is a point at which "mitigating explanations" can be "falsified" (175). There is no such point for Kierkegaard. Certainly some mitigating explanations can be falsified but others would still be possible. Mitigating explanations are *always* possible. To explain an action is not the same thing, however, as to justify it. It is, after all, possible to actually harm someone one is trying to help. The intention to help can explain how the harm came to be done. It does not, however, justify the harm. The difficulty, I would argue, with Ferreira's position is that she conflates "excuse" with "explanation" (175), which is to say that she confuses explanation with justification.

[18]It is, of course, possible to argue that characters like Hitler and suicide bombers are simply insane and that moral categories thus do not apply to them. The prevailing opinion of the psychiatric community is unsurprisingly that Hitler was seriously disturbed. See, e.g., "A Psychiatrist Looks at Hitler," *Lancet* 238

Epistemologically, Kierkegaard's position is that we never really know the motivation behind other people's actions. A person's actions, viewed independently of their motivation, will yield nothing conclusive as to their deeper significance.[19] We may know *what* people do, but we can't ever be certain *why* they do it. "[K]nowledge of this kind," asserts Kierkegaard, "is equivocal, explains now this and now that, and can mean the opposite" (EUD, 86).[20] This is, in fact, precisely what we saw in Murdoch's example of the relationship between the mother-in-law and her daughter-in-law. One and the same set of actions will support two radically different interpretations. The interpreter will likely be more strongly inclined in one of these directions, but this, asserts Kierkegaard, says more about him or her than it does about the person whose behavior is being interpreted.[21] The mother-in-law's revised judgment of her daughter-in-law is not the result of any change in the daughter-in-law's behavior, but of a change in the mother-in-law's attitude. The same behavior simply receives a different interpretation.

(1940): 44-77; P. Hopkins, "Observations on Some Criminal and Pathological Traits in Dictators," *Journal of Criminal Psychopathology* 4 (1942): 243-51; Bolterauer Lambert, "War Adolf Hitler eine originaere Fanatikerpersoenlichkeit?" *Sigmund Freud House Bulletin* 13 (1989): 12-20; Edleff H. Schwaab, *Hitler's Mind: A Plunge into Madness* (Westport CT: Praeger, 1992); and Desmond Henry, Dick Geary, and Peter Tyrer, "Adolf Hitler: A Reassesment of His Personality Status," *Irish Journal of Psychological Medicine* 10 (1993): 148-51. Such a characterization of mass, or serial, killers is controversial, I would argue, only if one confuses explanation with justification. It should make no difference, however, to the Christian whether the "criminal" is insane, wicked, or merely confused. The Christian has a responsibility to act to prevent what would appear to him or her to be harmful behavior as well as to refrain from condemning, or unnecessarily harming, the agent of such behavior.

[19]Compare Anthony Rudd, "Believing All Things: Kierkegaard on Knowledge, Doubt, and Love," *International Kierkegaard Commentary: Works of Love*, ed. Robert L. Perkins (Macon GA: Mercer University Press, 1999) 121-36, and Marilyn Piety, "Kierkegaard on Knowledge" (Ph.D. diss., McGill University, 1995; UMI Dissertation Services, ISBN 0-612-05775-5) 269.

[20]Compare WL, 230-31.

[21]Compare "[W]hen knowledge in a person has placed the opposite possibilities in equilibrium and he is obliged, or wills to judge, then who he is, whether he is mistrustful or loving becomes apparent in what he believes about it" (WL, 231).

One could thus argue that, from an epistemological point of view, a loving vision does not literally refuse to see what it nevertheless saw. That is, to the extent that sin is not *what* one does but *why* one does it, sin cannot ever have been an object of observation. One "saw" another's sin only in the sense that one imputed it to the other on the basis of his or her behavior. One "sees" sin because one decides to see it. The loving vision simply makes a different decision from the unloving one. The mother-in-law of our example does not thus have to hide her knowledge of her daughter-in-law's sinfulness from herself. Even if the daughter-in-law were actually trying deliberately to hurt her, this was not something the mother-in-law could have known. What she knows is simply that it was possible to judge her daughter-in-law in an unloving way and that that is what she had initially done.

Kierkegaard asserts, however, that it is indeed possible truly to discover sin. He illustrates this with the hypothetical example of a man who is genuinely loving in the Christian sense but whose wife is not. The wife loves her husband, however, in what Kierkegaard calls the "preferential" sense[22] and "just because she loved him she would discover how he had been sinned against in a multitude of ways. Injured and with bitterness in her soul, she would discover every mocking glance; with a broken heart she would hear the derision—while he, the one who loves, discovered nothing" (WL, 288). What the wife discovered, according to Kierkeggard, she discovered "with truth" (WL, 288). She was able to discover how her husband had been sinned against in the sense that her assumptions in this regard correspond with the facts, not in the sense that she knows, or can directly observe, the sins of those who wrong her husband. She can "see" how her husband is sinned against in the sense that through her bitterness, she imputes nefarious motivations to the actions of others and happens to be correct. "An understanding of [*Forstand paa*] evil," asserts Kierkegaard, "involves an *understanding* with [*er . . . i Forstaaelse med*]

---

[22]The difference between preferential love and genuine Christian love is a frequent theme of Kierkegaard's. See, e.g., EUD, 320, and the entry under "preferential love" in the index to *Works of Love*.

evil" (WL, 286).[23] She has truly discovered evil in the fortuitous
sense that a clock that has stopped truly states the correct time
twice a day. That is, sin is out there, according to Christianity,
hence if one is to go about imputing it to others one will invariably
occasionally be correct.[24]

Kierkegaard also asserts, however, that "in a certain sense [*i en
vis Forstand*], the one who loves can know [*Vide*] whether someone
deceives him, but by refusing to believe it, or by believing all
things, he keeps himself in love and in this way is not deceived"
(WL, 239).[25] This would certainly appear to suggest that a loving
vision is disingenuous, or that the Christian is really a hypocrite.
The key to unraveling this apparent contradiction with what Kierkegaard says throughout his authorship about the ethical-religious
indifference of knowledge concerns the qualification "in a certain
sense [*i en vis forstand*]." That is, one "knows" one is deceived in
what I have elsewhere identified as the loose sense in which Kierkegaard uses the expression "know."[26]

But if it is not possible to know, in the strict sense, whether a
particular action is loving or sinful, why does Kierkegaard insist
that "love is to be known [*skal være kjendelig*] by its fruits"? (WL,
15). Does that not suggest a yardstick by which we could measure
the goodness of others? The answer is no and no. First because it
does not follow, according to Kierkegaard, from the fact that love

---

[23]The Hongs actually have "knowledge" both places where I have substituted
"understanding." The Danish expression *Forstand paa* is more accurately
translated, however, as "an understanding of." The Hongs do actually translate
Forstand in the sentence immediately preceding the one in question as "understanding." The Danish expressions normally translated into English as "knowledge" are *Viden* and *Erkjendelsen*. See *A Danish-English Dictionary*, ed. J. S. Ferrall
and Thorl. Gudm. Repp (Copenhagen, 1845) 364 and 71, respectively; also see
Piety, "Kierkegaard on Knowledge."

[24]Compare this with Kierkegaard's claim that someone who has an understanding with evil can "discover" evil even where it does not exist (WL, 287).

[25]I have altered the Hongs' translation here to make it more accurate. The
Hongs omitted the qualification "certain" (*vis*) and apparently mistook the article
en ("a" or "an") for the adjective *een* ("one") (see Ferrall-Repp, *Dictionary*, 69 and
65, respectively). They have also confusingly translated *Viden* as "be aware of"
(see n. 23 above).

[26]See Piety, "Kierkegaard on Knowledge," 34-40, 139-98.

is known by its fruits "that you are to take it upon yourself to be the . . . knower" (WL, 15)[27] or from the fact that a tree is known by its fruits "that there is one tree that is to take it upon itself to judge the others—on the contrary" (WL, 15). God would appear to be the one who is the knower and the judge. Second, because the expression here that is translated as "known" is *kjendes*," which refers to acquaintance knowledge rather than propositional knowledge.[28] "[T]o judge someone else," asserts Kierkegaard, "is to judge yourself, or to be disclosed yourself" (WL, 233). To say that God "knows" the Christian by his or her fruits is thus not to say that God knows *that* someone is Christian by these fruits, but to say that one comes before God through this process of self-disclosure, that God becomes acquainted with the Christian through this process.

"Like," asserts Kierkegaard, "is known [*kjendes*] by like; only someone who abides in love can know [*kjende*] love, and in the same way his love is to be known [*er til at kjende*]" (WL, 16). Since God is love, to abide in love is to encounter divine love. But an encounter of this sort is fundamentally an ontological rather than an epistemological phenomenon.

The Ontological Cord

Even if we assume that it is possible to decide either to "see" sin or not to "see" it, how is it possible for a person who decides his or her initial unloving vision was mistaken to secure this new conviction? That is, how is it possible for the mother-in-law of our example to be confident in the veracity of her new judgment rather than merely in the exemplary nature of her decision? Recognition that a person's actions will support either a positive or negative interpretation will not, in itself, support that the positive interpretation is more likely the correct one. That people often behave badly is a fundamental part of Christian doctrine. If the daughter-in-law *seemed* hostile, she may have *been* hostile. It would appear that the possibility that the initial judgment was correct will

---

[27]The Hongs' translation reads "expert knower." "Expert" does not appear, however, in the original text.

[28]See Piety, "Kierkegaard on Knowledge," 201, 298-99.

always be lurking in the background of the consciousness of the mother-in-law, undermining her confidence in her judgment. This possibility may even incline the mother-in-law, once she has reformed her vision of her daughter-in-law, in the direction of arrogant self-congratulation, which is to say, in the direction of self-love in what Kierkegaard would call the negative sense.[29] If this is the case, then Christian conviction would still be equivalent to "bad faith."

The problem of bad faith is that the "deceived" and the "deceiver" are the same person. It is not difficult to deceive someone else, but it would appear impossible, for the reasons stated above, to deceive oneself. One has to know what one is hiding from oneself in order to be able to hide it effectively. The mother-in-law of our example is not literally hiding her daughter-in-law's sins, because it is clear, according to Kierkegaard, that these sins cannot ever have been an object of observation. What the mother-in-law is "hiding" from herself is that her daughter-in-law's behavior could just as well support a negative interpretation as the positive interpretation she is now giving it. That is, she is "hiding" from herself the objective uncertainty in her subjective conviction that one of the possible interpretations of her daughter-in-law's behavior is correct and the other is not.[30] It would appear, however, that she cannot entirely obscure to herself the possibility that the *other* interpretation is correct and that no matter how exemplary her loving vision is, it is not accurate.

The ontological cord of Kierkegaard's defense against the bad faith charge is that the person who "saw the sin" and the person who no longer "sees" it are, in an important sense, different people. One becomes a "new person" when one becomes a Christian.[31] Christianity thus reestablishes the duality of the

---

[29]The distinction between positive and negative self-love is a frequent theme of Kierkegaard's. See, e.g., WL, 17-24.

[30]This is, in fact, what I believe Kierkegaard means when he says in the *Postscript* that "[a]n objective uncertainty held fast through appropriation with the most passionate inwardness is the truth" (CUP, 1:203). That is, for love to hold fast to the uncertainty is for love to obscure it in its positive embrace (κάλυξ from καλύπτω; see the section entitled "The Indeterminacy of Translation" below.

[31]Compare *Philosophical Fragments*, 30-31.

"deceiver" and the "deceived" that Sartre argues is essential for successful "deception." The person who "saw" others' sins is not the same person as the person who does not see them.

The difficulty with this attempt to rescue the loving vision of the Christian from the charge that it is in bad faith is that even the transformed individual accepts the reality of sin. This would appear to imply that however genuine a particular loving judgment might be, the Christian would be driven to mistrust these judgments in a general sense. But if one mistrusts a loving vision in general, how can one rely on it in a particular instance? If sin is out there in the world, then it could be *anywhere*, even right here in the most apparently innocent act.

Kierkegaard's response to this objection would be that to mistrust love is itself a sin and that the true Christian is so preoccupied with rooting sin out of himself or herself that there is simply no time to find it in others. The claim of Christianity that everyone is in fact sinful has no more than abstract significance for the true Christian. He keeps "the straying thoughts in the bonds of love by the power of conviction" (EUD, 82). The person who is entirely preoccupied with rooting out his or her own sin does not refuse to see what he or she nevertheless sees. The true Christian cannot "see" sin in others because no time is left to direct his or her gaze outward in that sense.[32]

> How would the eye [Øie] that loves find time for a backward look, since the moment [Øieblik, glance of a eye] it did so it would have to let its object go! How would the ear that loves find time to listen to the accusation, since the moment it did so it would have to stop listening to the voice of love! (EUD, 74)

And when this is true of a person, that person is indeed no longer the same person who actively hid the sins of others from himself or herself. Such a person does not have to hide others' sins. The true Christian has become "blind."

It is natural at this point to object that what I have described is the ideal of Christian existence, an ideal which Kierkegaard himself emphasizes is never perfectly instantiated in the life of any human being, no matter how passionate his or her commitment to the truth of Christianity. The Christian is not without sin, and to the extent that the Christian continues to be sinful, it would appear that he or she is capable of seeing sin in the world. The Christian is, in a sense, able to see sin in the world. What the Christian sees "in the world" is not other people's sin, however, but his or her own. That is, Kierkegaard's epistemology precludes that one could ever *literally* have seen other people's sin. One simply *supposed* one saw it when one was confronted with behavior that mirrored behavior one knew in oneself to be an expression of sin.[33]

The "open act of sin" was never there to be discovered in others, not because it was not there, but because our relation to others is such that their sin is epistemologically inaccessible to us. We *think* we see it, but what we see, according to Kierkegaard, is, in fact, our own sin, the sin of choosing to see others unlovingly.[34] "It does not depend then," explains Kierkegaard, "merely on *what* one sees, but what one sees depends on *how* one sees" (EUD, 59, emphasis added).

Love does not "hide" sins, according to Kierkegaard, in the sense that their multiplicity is "just as great whether the understanding discover[s] it or not. . . . [T]hen it would be equally true that the understanding discovered the multiplicity of sin and that love hid it, but one would not be more true than the other" (EUD, 62). But one *is* more true than the other according to Kierkegaard. The perspective from which sin is seen as repugnant, or as an expression of something inherently unlovable in the sinner, and the perspective from which it is not seen as repugnant or inherently unlovable are not equally valid perspectives. Love's version is veridical. "What is it," asks Kierkegaard, "that is older than

---

[33]One cannot, according to Kierkegaard, hide one's own sins from oneself (see, e.g., WA, 182).

[34]Not everyone would call what they would take to be expressions of the inherently unlovable nature of others as expressions of "sin." Kierkegaard could use this term with impunity because the overwhelming majority of his readers were either Christian (at least in the nominal sense) or Jewish. It is of no consequence, however, what one calls expressions of what Kierkegaard would call "sin." It is all ontologically the same thing, regardless of the name one gives it. It is thus sin one "sees" whether one calls it that or not.

everything . . . that outlives everything . . . that is never changed even though everything is changed? It is love" (EUD, 55).

When someone who is not Christian (or who is only nominally Christian) revises his or her vision of another to see that person more positively, he or she is indeed in bad faith, because the revision is arbitrary. Viewed objectively, people are neither inherently lovable nor inherently unlovable. They just *are*. A loving judgment has no more validity than an unloving one. Whether people appear lovable or contemptible would depend on one's mood, whether one was having a good day or a bad day. One could endeavor to see people consistently one way or the other, but one would always be aware that one's vision of them was merely a production of one's own design.

On the other hand, the Christian is distinguished from someone who is not Christian in that the judgments of the Christian have a foundation which those of the latter lack. The Christian is committed to the view that others are lovable. That commitment is not arbitrary, but the natural consequence of the conviction that God is love, that *everyone* is loved by God and that everyone is thus *lovable*. The Christian loves others out of gratitude for the fact (or what is taken to be the fact) that *he* or *she* is loved.[35] The Christian endeavors to see others as lovingly as God sees them out of a conviction that this is the way they are *supposed* to be seen, not simply because it is good to be loving but because the view that others are lovable *must be correct*.[36]

---

[35]Compare Gouwens's claim in *Kierkegaard as Religious Thinker* that "The Christian life is joyful gratitude in performing the works of love" (196).

[36]My position here is similar to Gouwens's view when he claims that "[w]ithout ignoring evil, love 'hides' the multiplicity of sins *in light of a larger imaginative vision of the other person*, one that 'hopes in love' for them 'that the possibility of the good means more and more glorious advancement in the good from perfection to perfection or *resurrection from downfall or salvation from lostness* and thus beyond' " (Gouwens, *Kierkegaard as Religious Thinker*, 206, and WL, 237; italics added). But there is an important difference, I would argue, between my interpretation and Gouwens's. The "larger imaginative vision" of which Gouwens speaks is certainly part of a loving perspective. Gouwens's account makes it appear, however, that a loving vision loves a person *despite* his sin for what he *could be*, whereas I am claiming that a loving vision loves others *as they are*, sin and all.

The Christian may succumb occasionally to feelings of his or her own unworthiness, or unlovableness. When one does not oneself feel loved, one has de facto loosened one's grip on the conviction that God is love. Thus when the Christian lapses into feelings of unworthiness or harsh self-recrimination, those feelings may express themselves in harsh judgments of others. The Christian has something, however, that the person who is not Christian does not have. The Christian has the memory of his or her encounter with divine love. That is, the Christian has the memory of feeling loved by God, of the belief that God *is* love and that God thus loves everyone equally. This memory serves for the Christian as an impetus to renew his or her faith. But the renewed faith that rejects negative judgments of others does not literally *hide* facts from the believer. The facts in question are something the Christian freely admits: I failed to see others as lovable because I doubted that I was loved. This is the sense in which the Christian is a new person. Not that the believer has suddenly become perfect, or incapable of sin, but in the sense that he or she has had an experience the person who is not Christian has not had—the experience of feeling loved—and this has yielded a new understanding of his or her experience, an understanding that does not hide any part of that experience. The Christian freely admits even his or her own sins.

To say that "love hides a multitude of sins," to the extent that it is interpreted epistemologically, is thus to speak figuratively. The sins of others cannot, strictly speaking, be seen, and one's own sins are something the Christian strives actively to confront. No sin escapes God's detection, so love does not literally hide sins even from God. "God in heaven," asserts Kierkegaard, "is not halted by any deception . . . his thought is vivid and present . . . it penetrates everything and judges the counsels of the heart" (EUD, 66).[37] It does hide them figuratively, however. It "hides" the purported sins of others that, to an unloving vision, seem all pervasive. In an analogous fashion it "hides" one's own sins from oneself in that it deprives them of their sting. This is presumably what Kierkegaard means when he says that "the comfort is precisely this—that love

---

[37]Compare EUD, 78.

is able to live in the same heart in which there is a multitude of sins and that this love has the power to hide the multitude" (EUD, 72). Conviction that one is loved makes the sins recede in importance in the face of the love that surpasses all understanding. "But when love takes it from him, then love indeed hides it" (EUD, 74). But if they are no longer important, then they are no longer sins in the traditional sense. Now you "see" the sin, and now you don't. That is how love "hides" sins.

The Indeterminacy of Translation

We have so far looked to Kierkegaard's ontology primarily as a means of supporting the view that the Christian faith is not "bad faith." That is, we needed to reestablish the duality of the knower and the known, or of the Christian and the knowledge that the phenomena of the behavior of others could just as well support negative as positive interpretations, in order to rescue the Christian from the charge that he or she is a hypocrite. We are not yet in a position, however, to rescue Christian faith from the charge that it is foolish. The Christian may sincerely "see" other people as loveable, but it is hard to imagine that they, to the extent that they are sinful, could actually *be* lovable.

I mentioned in the introduction to this essay that I believed Kierkegaard exploits an ambiguity in the original Greek text of I Peter to help the reader to a more profound understanding of Christian truth. This ambiguity provides a key, I believe, to rescuing the Christian from the charge that he or she is a fool. We must thus turn, at this point, to a consideration of the Greek text.

"[T]he apostolic word,"[38] asserts Kierkegaard, is not "deceitful" or "poetic," "but a faithful thought, a valid witness, which in order to be understood must be taken at its word [*maa tages efter Ordet*]" (EUD 59).[39] It is not "just a rhetorical expression," asserts Kierke-

---

[38]I have corrected the Hongs' translations here. The Danish is *det apostoliske Ord* (SKS, 5:69). *Det* is the singular article, not the plural. The plural would have been *de apostoliske Ord*. This is important because "the apostolic word" (as opposed to "words") has the connotation of a promise or an oath.

[39]This is a difficult expression to translate. The Hongs have "literally" where I have "at its word." *[E]fter Bogstaven*, or "according to the letter(s)," is the locution that was commonly translated into English as "literally" (see Ferrall-

gaard, "to say that love hides a multitude of sins, but it is truly so" (EUD, 62). It is not immediately apparent, however, what it means to say that it is really true rather than just a figure of speech, that love hides a multitude of sins. "Apostolic speech [*Tale*]," Kierkegaard observes, is different in both form an content from "all human speech" (EUD 69).

The reference to love's hiding a multitude of sins comes at I Peter 4:8. The Greek term that is rendered as "hide"(*skiuler*) in the authorized Danish translation of this passage is καλύπτει, the third person present indicative conjugation of the Greek καλύπτω. "Hide" was an acceptable translation of this expression during the period of Kierkegaard's writings,[40] and it was indeed translated this way in the authorized Danish version of the New Testament. Notably, however, "wrap" ("*tilhyller*"),[41] "*encompass*" or "surround" ("*omgiver*"),[42] "embrace" and even "comprehend" ("*omfatter*")[43] were also acceptable translations.[44] The average Dane would not have been aware of this, of course. The average Danish theology student would have, however, which means that Kierkegaard would have.

Repp, *Dictionary*, 40), but the Danish text actually reads *maa tages efter Ordet*. I could not find this locution in any of my three nineteenth-century Danish-to-English dictionaries. Neither is it to be found directly in Christian Molbech's *Dansk Orbog* ("Danish Dictionary") (Copenhgaen, 1859). *At tage en paa Ordet* means "to take one at his word" (Ferrall-Repp, 231) as does *at tage en ved hans ord* (see Christian Molbech's *Dansk Orsprog* ["Danish Proverbs"] [Copenhagen, 1850] 168). Kierkegaard has *efter* where one would expect to find either *paa* or *ved*. *Efter* was often used interchangeably, however, with both *paa* (see Molbech, *Dictionary* 1:404) and *ved* (see Molbech, *Dictionary* 2:383). The most reasonable translation would thus appear to be the one I have substituted for the Hongs's. It is possible Kierkegaard chose *efter* instead of either of the more common prepositions because of its connotations of imitation (*Efterfølgelse*). That is, it is possible he means to suggest that in order to understand "the apostolic word," we must take it as a promise that brings with it the obligation to live according to it, or to "hide," through our own love, the sins of others.

[40]See *Græsk Dansk Ordbog* ("Greek-Danish Dictionary") ed. Paul Arnesen (Copenhagen, 1830) 704.

[41]See Ferrall-Repp, *Dictionary*, 328.

[42]See Ferrall-Repp, *Dictionary*, 222.

[43]See Ferrall-Repp, *Dictionary*, 221.

[44]See Arnesen, *Ordbog*, 704.

What does it mean to "comprehend" sin? The Christian, according to Kierkegaard, assigns a "good meaning" to the behavior of others. It seems worse than foolish, however, to call sin "good." It would seem downright dangerous and certainly not how God would want us to view sin. "Good" can have a variety of meanings however. The mother-in-law of our example need not be blithely ignorant of the fact that her daughter-in-law is actively trying to hurt or humiliate her. Comprehending such behavior may see it as stemming from her daughter-in-law's own pain and confusion. She may see her daughter-in-law as simply "lashing out blindly at what seem[s] to [her] a cruel world."[45] A "good" interpretation may mean forgiving her because she knows not, in the deepest sense, what she does. Is that not, after all, the very plea the crucified Christ made to God on behalf of all human beings, including his executioners? Christianly understood, sin does not make one unlovable. That God loves us, sin and all, is the message of Christianity. Even willfully hurtful people are thus lovable. To see them as otherwise is indeed to see sin, but not *their* sin—rather one's own.

"When love lies in the heart," asserts Kierkegaard, "a person . . . does not hear words said in haste and does not understand them when repeated because he assigns them a good position and a good meaning" (EUD, 60-61). Not to understand "words said in haste" because one "assigns them a good position and a good meaning" (EUD, 60-61) means not to understand those words the way *the world* understands them, as an expression of an inherently unlovable nature, but to see them as expressions of pain and confusion. The understanding sees sin as repugnant, as condemnable; love does not.

Love does not, of course, see sin as something positive. God loves people, one could argue, in a manner analogous to the manner in which animal lovers love animals. Animal lovers love all animals, regardless of how attractive or well behaved they are. The animal lover does not despise the vicious animal. Some animals, he or she acknowledges, are a threat to others and must either be isolated or "put down." These animals are the objects, however, of

---

[45]Rudd, "Believing All Things," 135.

special sympathy and sorrow, not contempt or condemnation. From this perspective, even characters such as Hitler, or suicide bombers, are thus properly objects of Christian love.

This does not mean that sin is not real. Sin may be defined as the failure to love, and the one who fails to love fails to receive love—not because love is not given, but because the one who refuses to love refuses to accept it.[46] To fail to see others as lovable is *ipso facto* to fail to believe that they are loved by God which, in turn, is to fail to believe that God *is* love and this, finally, is to fail to believe oneself loved by God. That is sin, to refuse to accept that God is love. Damnation, whatever else it might also be, is the failure, as the result of this refusal, to *receive* the love God offers[47] and continues to offer even in the face of one's refusal to receive it.[48]

Conclusion

Kierkegaard's concern in the two discourses entitled "Love Will Hide a Multitude of Sins" was clearly more ontological than epistemological. His concern, I would argue, is not primarily with knowledge, in the propositional sense, of sin but with knowledge in the acquaintance sense, or with what love *does*, substantively, or

---

[46]Compare this to Kierkegaard's claim at the beginning of the *Fragments* that the truth (i.e., love) is not withheld from one but that one *excludes oneself* from it (PF, 15).

[47]This is what I take Kierkegaard to mean when he says that "God is actually himself this pure like for like, the pure rendition of how you yourself are. If there is anger in you, then God is anger in you; if there is leniency and mercifulness in you, then God is mercifulness in you" (WL, 384). That is, God does not himself condemn you because, as Martin Andic points out, "to characterize God as relentless to the relentless seems to contradict the notion that God is Love that is perfect and equal and loves everyone, just and unjust, saint and sinner alike" (Martin Andic, "Love's Redoubling and the Eternal Like for Like," *International Kierkegaard Commentary: Works of Love*, 11). God does not condemn a person for failing to love; that person condemns himself. The unloving person condemns himself or herself to a loveless world and all God's efforts to rescue such a person will be to no avail if he or she refuses to be rescued.

[48]Compare this to Kierkegaard's claim that the person who has lost the condition for understanding the truth "himself has forfeited and *is forfeiting* the condition" (PF, 15; empahsis added).

ontologically, with the sins with which it is presented.[49] Love comprehends sin not in the sense that it knows *that* some particular individual has sinned. It comprehends sin in the sense that it encounters the sin, or grasps it, in the embrace of the sinner. Love embraces a person with his or her sin.

I believe Kierkegaard wanted to emphasize the apparent contradiction in an epistemological reading of I Peter 4:8 and in this way to point the reader in the direction of an ontological rather than an epistemological reading. His project was edification rather than elucidation.[50] Contradictions can often be edifying. That is part of the thinking behind the Buddhist *koan*.[51] That is, confronting the apparent contradiction in the claims that "love hides a multitude of sins" and that yet it is "never deceived" could impel the reader to a new understanding of the text, a new perspective, a perspective from which the apparent contradictions in the earlier perspective are resolved. This new perspective would involve what we could call an ontological, or spiritual reading. Such a reading would be an expression of Christian faith, an expression of God's love. Had Kierkegaard intimated, however, that the claim "Love hides a multitude of sins" was not essentially an epistemological claim, but an ontological or spiritual one, he would have risked his reader's interpreting this to mean that it was true only in a sense, or to a certain degree; and this was emphatically *not* what he meant! Love, according to Kierkegaard, does not "kind of hide," or "sort of hide" sins. It "hides" them absolutely in its all encompassing embrace. And yet it is never deceived, because enveloped in the embrace of love is precisely where sins belong.

---

[49]I have treated the theme of the difference, for the Christian, between propositional knowledge and substantive knowledge more fully in both my dissertation (see n. 19 above) and in "Kierkegaard on Religious Knowledge," *History of European Ideas* 22/2 (1996): 105-12.

[50]Compare this with Rudd's claim that "Kierkegaard wishes to separate clarification clearly from edification" (Rudd, *Believing all things*, 132).

[51]A *koan* is a question that has no rational answer. A classical example is "What is the sound of one hand clapping?"

9

The Virtue of Hope in
Eighteen Upbuilding Discourses

Robert C. Roberts

Meursault

The strange hero of Albert Camus's *The Stranger* is to many of us only barely recognizable as a human being. As Camus wrote in 1955, "readers have been tempted to regard [Meursault] as a human wreck."[1] Camus defends Meursault, however, as an understated hero of self-expressive honesty who is strange to his society because he refuses to "play the game" of pretending to be nicer than he is: "he is animated by a passion that is deep because it is tacit, a passion for the absolute and for truth." This description is itself strange, because the strangeness of Meursault is his utter lack of sustained passion. In nothing that he does has he any larger plan in view; rather, he just "goes with the flow" of the events of his life, the elemental stimuli of his environment.[2] He does not seem to mind that his mother has died, except for the annoyance of having to go to the funeral. When his girlfriend asks him whether he loves her he says that it doesn't matter, but he doesn't; but he is willing to marry her. When she says that marriage is a serious matter, he says it isn't. He is indifferent about advancement in his work. He falls in with Raymond, a pimp, and becomes a willing accomplice of the man's petty but violent

---

[1] *Avant-Propos* written for a student edition of Albert Camus's *L'Étranger* edited by Germaine Brée and Carlos Lynes (New York: Appleton-Century-Crofts, 1955) vii.

[2] If ever a character fit the behaviorist S-R model of human action, it is Meursault.

revenge against his mistress, and testifies before the police that the mistress was cheating on Raymond—something Meursault does not know, nor does Raymond have any but circumstantial evidence. He goes to the beach with Raymond and there meets his undoing: aimlessly floating in response to physical comforts and discomforts and trivial emotions he kills an Arab who is the brother of Raymond's abused mistress. He does not plan this act or have any but the most momentary intention of doing it. Later when asked why he did it he says it was because of the intense sunlight; and asked whether he regrets having done it he says that he feels more annoyance than regret. Repeatedly he comments that this or that is of "no importance" or "doesn't mean anything" or "does not matter." He does, however, care about physical comforts and pleasures: he is pleased by the warm sun on his body, sex with Marie, cigarettes, a cup of coffee, a dry towel in the restroom at work. He is also mildly bothered when people disapprove of him. The novel contains no detectable evidence for Camus's claim that Meursault has a passion for truth. It is true that he is disarmingly frank (though not with complete consistency), but one has the impression that he is so by default rather than by concern for truth. Meursault is a very different character from Joseph Conrad's Charlie Marlow, who comments,

> I would not have gone so far as to fight for Kurtz, but I went for him near enough to a lie. You know I hate, detest, and can't bear a lie, not because I am straighter than the rest of us, but simply because it appalls me. There is a taint of death, a flavor of mortality in lies—which is exactly what I hate and detest in the world—what I want to forget. It makes me miserable and sick, like biting something rotten would do. Temperament, I suppose.[3]

That describes a person with a passion for truth.

How can Camus regard this human wreck as a hero? The answer is that Meursault exemplifies an eccentric theory of human nature to which Camus was committed. As he writes in the foreword from which I quoted, "I tried to sketch in my character

---

[3]*Heart of Darkness*, chap. 1 (towards the end), in Joseph Conrad, *Heart of Darkness & The Secret Sharer* (New York: New American Library, 1960) 84.

the only Christ that we deserve."[4] Meursault is a pioneer of a new humanity. Jean-Paul Sartre makes this clear in a review of Camus's novel. I quote Sartre at length.

> Camus also comments . . . about love in *The Myth of Sisyphus*: "What we call love," he writes, "is nothing but a socially constructed way of seeing, for which books and legends are responsible, that links certain beings." Similarly we read in *The Stranger*, "She wanted to know whether I loved her. I answered . . . that that meant nothing, but that no doubt I didn't love her." . . . above all the word "love" is without meaning. No doubt Meursault put his mother in the home for the aged, "because he was short of money and they didn't have anything to say to one another." Also no doubt, he didn't go to see her very often, "because that took his Sunday—not counting the effort it took to go by bus, to get the tickets and spend two hours on the road." But what does that mean? Isn't he completely in the present, completely devoted to his present feelings? What one calls a dispositional attitude [*sentiment*] is nothing but an abstract unity and the meaning of discontinuous impressions. I am not always thinking about those I love, but I claim that I love them even when I don't think about them—and I could compromise my tranquillity in the name of an abstract attitude, if I didn't feel any real, episodic emotion. Meursault thinks and acts differently: He does not acknowledge great attitudes that are continuous and all alike; for him, love does not exist, nor do loves. Only the present counts, the concrete. He'll go see his mother when he gets the urge, and that's that. If the desire is there, it will be strong enough to make him take the bus because another such concrete desire will be strong enough to make this sluggard run all out and jump into a moving truck. But he always refers to his mother with the tender and childish "mama" and does not miss an opportunity to understand her and to identify with her. "I acknowledge nothing of love but this mixture of desire, of tenderness, and of understanding that binds me to another." So we see that we must not neglect the *theoretical* side of the character of Meursault.[5]

In Camus's metaphysics of persons we are nothing but the episodes of our lives. Only the present counts because only it is

---

[4]Camus, *L'Étranger*, viii.

[5]Jean-Paul Sartre, "Explication de *L'Étranger*," in *Situations* I (Paris: Gallimard, 1947) 99-121; quotation from 107-109.

real; traits are social fictions having no reality. This is a radical empiricism, a positivism of the episodic, with obvious ethical implications. Honesty about oneself, to oneself and to others, is a sheer spontaneous expressivism of the moment: you say how you feel now and only that, without reference to your dispositional personality, since this is only a fabrication, nor to your history, since it contains only episodes to summarize, no indicators of any stable characteristics. Love as a trait of persons, or as an ongoing dispositional relationship, does not exist. When Meursault tells Marie that he doesn't love her, he is not searching his heart and the history of their interactions for patterns that indicate how he "really feels" about her. Instead, he is giving voice to the metaphysical premise that what people think they are talking about when they so search their hearts and histories is an empty social construct, a concept without reference. And the same must be true of justice and courage and the sense of duty. This metaphysic of the momentary and the discrete lies behind the personal emptiness that is Meursault. Or rather, Meursault is the fictional projection, the biographical thought experiment and Christ myth, that corresponds to this "theory" of human nature and its redemption.

Kierkegaard and Virtuism

If Sartre's interpretation is right, Camus's novel is a philosophical objection, in the form of a story, to an ancient and historically abiding supposition on the part of thinkers about human nature, ethics, and related matters. I will call this supposition "virtuism,"[6] numbering among its adherents Plato, Aristotle, Seneca, the church fathers, Augustine, Thomas Aquinas, Adam Smith, Immanuel Kant, Friedrich Nietzsche, and John Rawls, as well as countless less distinguished thinkers. Characterized most generally, virtuism is the view that people have traits or personal qualities that partially explain their actions, perceptions, judgments, desires, and emo-

---

[6]I use this broad term rather than "virtue ethics" because the kind of traits with which the tradition is concerned are not limited to ethical ones, at least not in the usually narrow sense of "ethical." The traits in question may also be "spiritual," such as hope and faith, or mostly prudential, such as industry and cleanliness, as well as ethical, such as justice and the sense of duty.

tions. If the traits are genuinely explanatory, as the tradition supposes, they are not merely socially constructed fictions, but real traits. These can be good (virtues) or bad (vices), good traits making persons good, functional and well, and bad ones making them bad, dysfunctional, and unwell. So virtuists tend to think it quite important, ethically and otherwise, for people to develop virtues and overcome or avoid vices. It is not just momentary acts, impulses, and feelings that are important, but what kind of stable dispositional attitudes characterize a person—what kind of person one is. Virtuists differ widely among themselves on many questions, including the question which traits exactly are virtues and which ones are vices. For example, Nietzsche's and Aristotle's lists of virtues diverge strikingly from those of the Christians I mentioned above, as well as from each other's.

I want to argue that Kierkegaard belongs to this group of thinkers and therefore decidedly not to the much smaller and less distinguished dissenting group represented by Camus and Sartre around the time of World War II—despite the fact that the standard textbook interpretation of Kierkegaard in the 20th century associated him precisely with this group (Kierkegaard "the father of existentialism").[7] But we can distinguish, among virtuist orientations, a mainline whose high point is arguably Aristotle (or Aristotle and Aquinas) from the less fertile variants represented by Stoicism, Kant, and others. And I want to claim that Kierkegaard belongs in this mainline. Indeed, it seems to me that his writings are not only an extremely rich instance of this stream of the virtuist way of thinking about persons, but significantly extend it. In what follows, my references to virtuism will be to this mainline part of the tradition.

---

[7] During the past twenty years this association has been especially associated with Alasdair MacIntyre, who perpetuated the freshman doctrine of Kierkegaard-the-existentialist in his *After Virtue* (Notre Dame IN: University of Notre Dame Press, 1981). See the very able critiques of MacIntyre's perpetuation in the articles by Charles K. Bellinger, Norman Lillegard, and Edward F. Mooney, in *International Kierkegaard Commentary: Either/Or Part II*, ed. Robert L. Perkins (Macon GA: Mercer University Press, 1995). See also *Kierkegaard after MacIntyrre: Freedom, Narrataive, and Virtue*, ed. John J. Davenport and Anthony Rudd (Chicago and La Salle IL: Open Court, 2001).

In two other essays[8] I have proposed that most of Kierkegaard's writings can be profitably read as explorations of various traits of character—of Christian and quasi-Christian virtues, as well as formations or deformations of character that are alternatives to those virtues, such as the formations of the various aesthetes of *Either/Or* volume one. In one of those papers I suggest that Kierkegaard's exploration of the virtues is a kind of conceptual analysis that can be called "grammatical" (following Ludwig Wittgenstein). In the other I stress that Kierkegaard's preoccupation with emotions and passions and his construals of the virtues as configurations of these constitutes a striking continuity with the kind of "ethics" that stems from the ancient philosophers, especially Aristotle.

Eighteen Upbuilding Discourses lends itself admirably to this kind of reading. The chief virtues explored in these discourses are hope ("The Expectancy of Faith," "Patience in Expectancy," and "The Expectancy of an Eternal Salvation"), gratitude (all three of the discourses entitled "Every Good and Every Perfect Gift Is from Above," "The Lord Gave, and the Lord Took Away; Blessed Be the Name of the Lord," and "One Who Prays Aright Struggles in Prayer and Is Victorious—in That God Is Victorious"), love (both discourses entitled "Love Will Hide a Multitude of Sins"), patience ("To Gain One's Soul in Patience," "Preserve One's Soul in Patience," and "Patience in Expectancy"), humility ("He Must Increase; I Must Decrease," "To Need God is a Human Being's Highest Perfection" [which is also about joyful trust of God]), spiritual integrity ("Strengthening in the Inner Being"), and courage ("To Preserve One's Soul in Patience" and "Against Cowardliness"). "Think about Your Creator In the Days of Your

---

[8]"Kierkegaard, Wittgenstein, and a Method of 'Virtue Ethics,' " in *Kierkegaard in Post/Modernity*, ed. Merold Westphal and Martin Matustik (Bloomington: Indiana University Press, 1995) 142-66; and "Existence, Emotion, and Character: Classical Themes in Kierkegaard," in *Cambridge Companion to Kierkegaard*, ed. Alastair Hannay and Gordon Marino (Cambridge: Cambridge University Press, 1997) 177-206. "Dialectical Emotions and the Virtue of Faith," in *International Kierkegaard Commentary: Concluding Unscientific Postscript to "Philosophical Fragments,"* ed. Robert L. Perkins (Macon GA: Mercer University Press, 1997) 73-93, is a companion to "Existence, Emotion, and Character."

Youth" is perhaps not about any single virtue (unless it be something rather summary like piety), but it is certainly about virtue in the sense of good disposition; for it is about establishing in one's mind the thought of God, and returning to it again and again. I have listed, for the most part, only the virtue that is the primary focus of each of these discourses. The discussion of any virtue typically involves reference to other virtues and vices, as well as to matters closely allied with the virtues and vices, such as emotions, concerns, choice, rationality and deliberation, imagination, action, finitude, death; such reference is a necessary part of the conceptual or "grammatical" elaboration of the virtues.

In the present essay I shall look at the three discourses in which Kierkegaard focuses on hope, in an effort to make out that his approach to the upbuilding belongs in the virtuist tradition. What are some of the features of mainline virtuism that we should look for in these discourses? I will just mention them without trying to prove that they are characteristic of this tradition. First, persons are thought of as capable of having a stable character, that is, enduring traits or qualities not merely of our bodies (say, height, complexion) but of us as persons (say, gentleness, patience). Second, virtuists think of human beings as having a given human nature independently of our trait development, and of the traits as either satisfying or failing to satisfy or frustrating the developmental demands of that basic nature. So some people develop into personal successes, while others become wrecks, and still others fall somewhere between these extremes. Third, these traits are neither a kind of passivity (receptive event) nor a kind of activity (initiatory event), but a determinate way of being human; they are neither something one undergoes, nor something one does, but something one is. (This three-way distinction perhaps throws light on Kierkegaard's rather peculiar use of the word "existence," as well as his preoccupation with passion and action.) In the virtuist tradition, because we "exist" in a certain way, we are subject to certain kinds of episodes of passivity (passions) and disposed to perform certain kinds of actions. But our traits dispose and do not simply determine our actions. We act out of them, and our actions may in turn form them. So, fourth, the traits are dispositions to passive or quasi-passive episodic states of the subject such as emotions, perceptions, and thoughts. Such episodes, like actions, are thus indicators of the presence of the traits from which they arise. What we feel, perceive, and think is a consequence of who we are (our traits, our mode of "existence"). Actions are indicative of virtues only as arising out of such motivations, perceptions, and thoughts; mere "behavior" tells little about character. Fifth, traits are associated with patterns of thought, deliberation, "practical reason." In the paradigm cases, actions arising out of the virtues are chosen in accordance with the canons of the virtue, and in this way the virtue can be indirectly chosen. A full-blown, paradigmatic virtue is one that its possessor endorses and confirms and consolidates by his own deliberate choices in accordance with the canons of the virtue. Sixth, traits are interconnected, supporting one another or destroying one another (the "unity of the virtues"). Seventh, virtues and vices make or fail to make for the well-being, happiness, eudaimonia, or flourishing of those who possess them and those who associate with those who possess them. Some such traits also make for their possessors' moral worth and other kinds of admirability (or the opposites). Thus, eighth, virtuists are typically preoccupied with moral and spiritual education, upbringing, upbuilding, formation, deep psychological development. Such development is a formation of proper concerns, patterns of reasoning, and dispositions to emotions, perceptions, and actions.

Kierkegaard on Hope

The reader may be struck that while I claim that three of the discourses are about the virtue of hope, Kierkegaard only rarely uses the word "hope" (*Haab*) in them, speaking instead of expectancy (*Forventning*). However, he is talking about hope in these discourses. He begins the main body of "The Expectancy of Faith" by commenting that "those who are expecting something are indeed the happy and fortunate ones" (EUD, 16). But somebody who was expecting failure, tragedy, disaster, degradation and annihilation would not be described as happy and fortunate. Clearly, Kierkegaard can call the expectant happy only if he is discussing the kind of expectancy that is hope—expectancy of something good (see WL, 249). In "The Expectancy of Faith" the object of the expectancy he has in mind is "victory" (EUD, 19); in "Patience in Expectancy" his model is Anna the prophet, who is expecting Israel's Messiah;

and in "The Expectancy of Eternal Salvation" his model is the Apostle Paul, who is expecting glorious eternal life. Someone might object, too, that "The Expectancy of Faith" is not about hope, but about faith. It is of course about the virtue of faith, but its focus is the *expectancy* of faith, which is hope.[9]

That, in conformity with the virtuist tradition, Kierkegaard thinks of this expectancy as a formed disposition of the person of faith rather than as just a series of discrete acts of faith, is suggested by the way he speaks of it and expounds it. He says that the person who expects an eternal salvation "accustoms himself to" (*vænne sig til*) it as a kind of nourishment for his soul (EUD, 263).[10] He says that "the object of expectancy, the more glorious and precious it is, form[s] (*danne*) the expectant person in its own likeness, because a person resembles what he loves with his whole soul" (EUD, 219). Speaking of someone who expects something important and genuinely proper to himself, but in a thoughtless and rote way with a "deadened will" and as a matter of course, he says, "One who expects in this way is not educated (*dannes*) by his expectancy, either—on the contrary, his nature degenerates" (EUD, 218). That Kierkegaard is talking about traits is also suggested by an expository device that he uses fairly frequently in *Eighteen Upbuilding Discourses*, namely portrayal of "characters."[11] For example, in "The Expectancy of Faith" (EUD, 19-23), Kierkegaard makes vivid the character of the person with genuine hope by juxtaposing him with four other characters that we might call the Youthful Optimist, the Defeatist, the Person of Experience, and the Discouraging Doubter. This small-scale device bears a certain resemblance to his grand-scale pseudonymous personæ, which seem to me to be "characters" one and all, and the "stages" they represent, which are prescriptions for types of character.

---

[9]Hope puts in a brief appearance in "Strengthening in the Inner Being" (EUD, 93-95), and there Kierkegaard's word is *Haab*.

[10]The Hongs translate "to make it his wont."

[11]This device is reminiscent of William Law's *A Serious Call to a Devout and Holy Life*, which Samuel Johnson so much appreciated and imitated in his *Rambler* essays and elsewhere.

In contradiction of Jean-Paul Sartre's dictum that, where human beings are concerned, "existence precedes essence,"[12] Kierkegaard's accounts of the properly formed human being start from a conception of a nonnegotiable given human nature which lays down the parameters of development, dictating that some formations are proper and healthy and others are not. The part of human nature that is particularly pertinent to the virtue of hope is, most basically, the human sense of the future, which Kierkegaard calls "the greatness of human beings, the demonstration of their divine origin" (EUD, 17). The ability, indeed the necessity, to be occupied with the future is intimately connected with human beings' occupation with the past, and our power to be outside the current moment and for our present to be qualified by our construal of the future distinguishes us from the animals, who are "in bondage . . . to the service of the moment" (EUD, 17). But not just any orientation to the future is satisfactory or fulfiling for human beings. Only hope—the expectancy of what one construes to be *good*—is fulfilling. People can bring themselves to think that they have found fulfillment without hope, but this is possible only through self-deception: "Even though in the world we hear at times of someone who expects nothing at all, even though such a person is sometimes thought to have attained the proper assurance, because he craftily made it impossible for himself to discern the loss, yet it is also admitted that this wisdom is of later origin and no one has it in early youth" (EUD, 220). "Originally," everybody lives on hope of one sort or another, and this feature of youth is an indication of something deep in human nature; so the the price of trying to contravene our need to hope is (*pace* Freud) always the degeneration of the person. The key to fulfillment is not to learn not to hope, but to learn a mature hope, to place one's hope in what is worthy of a being with "spirit." So human nature demands that one be occupied with the future, and that one find the future to be good. But that is not all. Kierkegaard also thinks that the human spirit demands an assurance with respect to its future good, an absolute reliability across time, or transcending time.

---

[12]See Jean-Paul Sartre, *L'Etre et le Néant* (Paris: Gallimard, 1943) 515.

The future good that is adequate to human spirit is one that will not let us down, one that is not temporary (temporal) but eternal.

> When the sailor is out on the ocean, when everything is changing all around him, when the waves are born and die, he does not stare down into the waves, because they are changing. He looks up at the stars. Why? Because they are faithful; they have the same location now that they had for our ancestors and will have for generations to come. By what means does he conquer the changeable? By the eternal. (EUD, 19)

In this aspect, the fulfilling hope is the opposite of anxiety, which is a sense of insecurity with respect to one's future good. Anxiety is thus one of the indicators of the three aspects of nonnegotiable human nature relevant to the virtue of hope that we have identified in Kierkegaard's thought: orientation to the future, "demand" that the future be good, and the need for security with respect to the future.

Neither anxiety nor hope, insofar as they are episodes (rather than dispositions), are something the subject does, but something he undergoes. They are what Aristotle calls πάθη (passions) and which he thinks to be one of the two kinds of things whose falling in a mean between extremes makes for the virtues.[13] (The other kind of thing is actions.) In his stress on passions in moral psychology[14] Kierkegaard agrees with almost everybody in the virtuist tradition, both the Aristotelian mainline and the other strands, including even Kant[15] (though Kant is ambivalent about emotions in moral psychology). The idea in virtuism, at least in the mainline, is that the passivity or receptivity of the virtuous person is a *formed* receptivity. So, for example, in situations where hope of victory (see EUD, 19) is an "issue"—say, one is facing the failure of one's life's project or the death of a loved one—the feeling of hope is a more or less spontaneous reaction. I say "more or less

---

[13]See Aristotle, *Nicomachean Ethics*, book 2, chaps. 5 and 6.

[14]See my "Existence, Emotion, and Character: Classical Themes in Kierkegaard."

[15]See the passages on feeling (*Gefühl*) in *The Metaphysical Principles of Virtue*, in *Ethical Philosophy: Grounding for the Metaphysics of Morals & Metaphysical Principles of Virtue*, trans. James W. Ellington (Indianapolis: Hackett Publishing Company, 1995).

spontaneous" because we will count a person as having the virtue of hope even if he needs to remind himself of his eternal hope, after initially feeling a wave of despair. Even to be able to feel such hope after a reminder requires an impressive formation in this virtuous kind of receptivity.

This quasi-spontaneity characterizes not only emotions, but judgments. In a passage reminiscent of Aristotle's discussion of φρόνησις[16] (practical wisdom), Kierkegaard asks what kind of person is most likely to make a good deliberator about "what [attitudinal] consequences the expectancy of an eternal salvation has for this earthly, troubled life" (EUD, 254). And the answer is that the best deliberator about this matter is a person who is himself deeply concerned about his eternal salvation. Just as, for sound judgment in civic matters, one does not consult "aliens and foreigners" or "loafers and irresponsible tramps" or "robbers and agitators" (see EUD, 255), but instead well-formed citizens who have a stake in the well-being of the country whose policy is being deliberated, so in questions about an eternal hope's impact on everyday life, one consults the person who has the virtue of hope. Such practical wisdom is intimately entangled with the concern for an eternal salvation that is at the heart of such a virtue. Kierkegaard himself exemplifies, in his person and in the discourses we are considering, this interlocking passion and practical wisdom. I say that his hope is, with respect to the judgments he registers here, a "quasi-spontaneity" because he no doubt must make some effort to formulate the insights of the last two-thirds of "The Expectancy of an Eternal Salvation". And yet these insights have the stamp of originality, not in the sense that they have never been formulated before, but in the sense that they spring from the mind of one who has firsthand experience.

Let us note in a little more detail some of the emotional consequences that Kierkegaard identifies as marks of the virtue of hope. Ordinary hopes, for power, pleasure, wealth, etc.—the hopes in which the "person of experience" trades—can be disappointed by unfulfillment, by late fulfillment, and by not turning out to be what they were cracked up to be. Kierkegaard stresses that

---

[16]See Aristotle, *Nicomachean Ethics*, book 6.

genuine hope, by contrast, cannot be disappointed. The good—the resurrection of the dead, reunion with dead loved ones, a state of blessed understanding with God and with oneself—"never mocks a person" (EUD, 216). This expectation cannot disappoint for several reasons. First, unlike finite hopes, it is bounded by no time limit, and so one is never justified in supposing that since it has not yet been fulfilled, it will not be fulfilled. For a similar reason there is no such thing as late fulfillment: No time limit can be set beyond which it could be legitimately thought that the Kingdom of God had come too late. This grammatical fact constitutes a criterion. If someone thinks he has the virtue of hope, but then succumbs to disappointment, he must conclude that his hope was not genuine.

Kierkegaard further explores the character of Christian hope by posing and answering an objection, in an empiricist style, that we might call the "circle" objection. "'An expectancy without a specified time and place is nothing but a deception; in that way one may always go on waiting; such an expectancy is a circle into which the soul is bewitched and from which it cannot escape'" (EUD, 23). In other words, an expectancy that cannot be disappointed is not really an expectancy, in much the way that a proposition that cannot be falsified was once thought to be no real proposition, but just a string of words that do no work. Kierkegaard answers by admitting that the expectancy of faith "remains in itself," not subjecting itself to empirical tests, but he denies that it follows from this feature that it is not real expectation. Its indefeasibility in the face of empirical changes is in fact part of the glory of such expectation. That we are capable of it is an expression of the "infinite" and the "eternal" in us, our potential for transcending the vicissitudes of the changing, undependable temporal world and living in fellowship with God. Indeed, the fact that this expectancy is predicated on belief in the God of Abraham and Jesus is crucial to its indefeasibility:

> But if you had faith in God, how then would your faith ever be changed into a beautiful fantasy you had better give up? Would he then be able to be changed, he in whom there is no change or shadow of variation? Would he not be faithful, he through whom every human being who is faithful is faithful; would he not be without guile, he through whom you yourself had faith? Would

> there ever be an explanation that could explain otherwise than
> that he is truthful and keeps his promises? And yet we see that
> people forget this. (EUD, 25)

Those who insist that an undisappointable expectancy makes no
sense are simply noting that Christian hope is a different *kind* of
expectancy from the everyday variety that calculates probabilities
and stands or falls by the vicissitudes of temporality, and are refusing (in severe detriment to their nature, according to Kierkegaard)
to practice a kind of expectancy that entrusts everything to God.

So one emotional mark of a person with Christian hope is that
he does not experience disappointment of that hope. But this is not
to say that the person cannot be disappointed, as well as suffer
other emotional afflictions. In "The Expectancy of an Eternal
Salvation" Kierkegaard identifies two other kinds of emotional
consequence of hope, and one of these is that it makes affliction
light. The biblical text for this discourse is 2 Corinthians 4:17-18,
where the Apostle says, "For this slight momentary affliction is
preparing for us an eternal weight of glory beyond all comparison,
because we look not to the things that are seen but to the things
that are unseen; for the things that are seen are transient, but the
things that are unseen are eternal." Kierkegaard points out that the
Apostle's afflictions are anything but light when measured by the
ordinary standards of human "experience":

> [T]hat this man was halted on the road of offense and conse-
> quently was indeed tried in the mortal dangers of the soul, that
> he was caught up into the third heaven and consequently was
> indeed tempted to have a distaste for earthly life, that he
> witnessed with an enthusiasm that made him seem a raving man
> to his hearers, that for forty years he was knocked about in the
> world, without a fixed residence, outlawed and abandoned, to
> the Jews an offense, to the Greeks foolishness, rejected by the
> world, in mortal danger, in hunger, in nakedness, in prison, and
> that he finally was executed as a criminal. . . . (EUD, 262)

Add to this that Paul was sometimes sorely disappointed "when
the congregations went astray, when false teaching and human
fickleness jumbled meanings together so that the way of truth
became impassable" (ibid.), and the description of all this as a
"slight momentary affliction" is seen to express an extraordinary,
even paradoxical, formation of character. Paul can experience such

afflictions as slight and momentary (though they stretch out over forty years) because he measures them against (experiences them in light of) that "eternal weight of glory beyond all comparison" that he expects.

The other emotional consequence of hope that Kierkegaard identifies in "The Expectancy of an Eternal Salvation" is that it makes one nonjudgmental towards one's neighbor. In fact, a person's attitude towards his neighbor's salvation is a criterion of whether that person's hope is the virtue or a misleading *simulacrum*. Frequently, in the history of the church, people have sought observable signs of their own and others' salvation, "let these conditions be acts, specific conceptions, moods" (EUD , 269), by which they could assess themselves and others in this respect. Kierkegaard believes that there are no such signs, since a person's salvation belongs to the infinite (it is God's business) and the signs are always finite (psychological facts of one sort or another). "[S]omeone who is truly concerned [about his eternal salvation] surely grasps that there must be a condition, but he will never be able to fathom it finitely, since the concern will prevent a finite fathoming" (EUD, 268). The concern prevents a finite fathoming because of the object of the concern (which thus defines it as the concern that it is). The object of this concern is an eternal salvation conceived as it is in Christian theology: the believer "expects eternal salvation *by the grace of God*" (EUD, 268). Thus the grace of God is the condition, and this condition cannot be fathomed by observing psychological states. The believer thus remains in a state of "uncertainty" with respect to both his own and anybody else's salvation. The uncertainty that Kierkegaard speaks of here is compatible with being "altogether certain through grace— something we indeed wish for the single individual" (EUD, 269). This "uncertainty" is not the same as doubt of one's salvation; instead, it seems to be a kind of epistemic humility which refrains from drawing conclusions about people's salvation from psychological premises. And this humility is not only epistemic, but also social: in refraining from "judging" another's salvation, one is also refraining from putting oneself in the down-looking position characteristic of judges' benches. Such humility is prescribed by the grammar of salvation as it is conceived in the Christian tradition. This is why the quality of the hope (the virtue) of those who occupy themselves with figuring out who is and who isn't saved is called into question by this activity: it misconceives the object of that hope.

Kierkegaard commends this epistemic humility in another way. After denying that one can fathom the condition for salvation, he says "[b]ut suppose also that there were particular conditions that could be expressed accurately in words and by means of which observant thought could test the state of the single individual . . . " (EUD, 268-69). Even if such psychological marks of salvation existed, he says, the individual who was properly concerned for his eternal salvation could never be satisfied with whatever degree of evidence such marks afforded; and if he could not even make a confident judgment about his own salvation on the basis of psychological marks, he certainly would refrain from making such judgments about his fellow human beings. Thus again, the person who has genuine hope of eternal salvation does not judge his neighbors in this respect.

It may seem that Kierkegaard contradicts himself in laying down a psychological condition for the genuineness of hope—namely, that the subject be not disposed to lay down psychological conditions for anybody's salvation. However, this would be a contradiction only if Christian hope were tantamount to salvation. But to make any of the virtues tantamount to salvation is a kind of salvation by works that Kierkegaard eschews in the final prayer of "The Expectancy of an Eternal Salvation": "Father in heaven, when I think about the matter of my salvation, I do not take out the accounting, . . . And I will not build my salvation on any work . . . " (EUD, 272). Later in life, Kierkegaard becomes yet more decisive and clear about the primacy of the work of Christ in our salvation. Although in the following journal passage from 1852 he makes the point with respect to the work of imitating Christ, he could just as well have made it with respect to virtues like hope, patience, gratitude, humility, and love.

> No, the Atonement and grace are and remain definitive. All striving toward imitation, when the moment of death brings it to an end and one stands before God, will be sheer paltriness—therefore atonement and grace are needed. Furthermore, as long as there is striving, the Atonement will constantly be needed to prevent this striving from being transformed into agonizing anxiety

in which a man is burned up, so to speak, and less than ever begins to strive. Finally, while there is striving, every other second
a mistake is made, something is neglected, there is sin—therefore
the Atonement is unconditionally needed. (JP, 2:1909, p. 353)

The person who passionately expects an eternal happiness for
which he can take no credit himself, but for which all the credit
goes to God, will be reconciled "with his neighbor, with his friend,
and with his enemy in an understanding of the essential" (EUD,
265). In him, alienating emotions will be replaced with their
reconciling opposites: judgmental anger with compassion and a
contrite sense of solidarity with fellow sinners, contempt with a
generous sense of the difficulty of achieving excellence and the
paltriness of whatever excellence one may have achieved oneself.

I said earlier that in the virtuist tradition traits are associated
with patterns of thought and that actions arising out of virtues are
chosen in accordance with these patterns so that the action
expresses the virtue and the virtue can be indirectly chosen by
performing such actions. Kierkegaard's reading of the expectancy
of Anna the prophet illustrates this feature of the tradition. The
Gospel tells us that Anna was widowed early and never remarried
(Luke 2:36-37); by the time we meet her, her practice is not to leave
the temple, but to worship there "with fasting and prayer night
and day" (v.37). Kierkegaard reads her long widowhood as a
choice not to remarry and thus not to seek consolation for her grief
in a replacement man. Given her intense practice of worship, Kierkegaard sees this choice as a renunciation of temporal consolation
and a decision to find her consolation only in the eternal. She
"then found the grace to see eternity as an expectancy in time"
(EUD, 218). That is, she chooses eternity but she does not choose
to see eternity as something to be realized in time; this she finds
by "grace" in her Judaism. The thought that is crucial to Anna's
expectancy, and in terms of which she makes the choice that Kierkegaard attributes to her, is the distinction between the finite and
the infinite, the temporal and the eternal. This thought is essential
to the virtue of hope and by deliberately choosing the eternal Anna
makes her hope *hers* and a *virtue* in a way that she would not have
done had the virtue lacked this painful history of renunciatory
action. Kierkegaard sometimes formulates in a way that might
seem to suggest existentialist punctiliarism. For example, he says

that faith "can be had only by constantly being acquired and can be acquired only by continually being generated" (EUD, 14). Is he saying that faith is an "act" and not a disposition, in conformity with the Sartrean doctrine that what we are in the moment exhausts our being, any reference to a personality that transcends or lies behind the action being nothing but socially constructed illusion? Not at all. The quotation is more plausibly read as expressing the classical view that virtues like faith are, among other things, dispositions to choose, which are acquired and retained by periodic deliberate action as ordered and formed by the virtue's "logos" (reason, grammar).

"Patience in Expectancy" provides also an excellent illustration of the thesis of the interdependence of the virtues ("the unity of the virtues") that is so characteristic of the virtuist tradition in its mainline.

> [P]atience and expectancy correspond to each other, and not until these two have found each other, find and understand each other in a person, not until then is there like for like in the friendship that is to be continued; expectancy in patience is like a good word in the right place, like a golden apple in a silver bowl. (EUD, 220)

Kierkegaard offers a little developmental story of how these two virtues come to "find each other."[17] In an ordinary healthy childhood and youth, the individual is full of hope, and the hope is essential to his or her happiness. This hope is an enthusiastic expectancy of good fortune, of finite enjoyments and triumphs. This nearly unalloyed optimism about temporal prospects is naïve and unrealistic about the nature of temporality—its admixture of misfortune, its unreliability, the ultimate defeat of all finite wishes by the march of time. And yet there is something right about it. It is an immature and unstable version of how people ought to turn out—confidently hopeful and happy in their hope. In response to the essential hopelessness of temporality, people can develop in a variety of ways. We can become decisively cynical and gloomy

---

[17]In a parallel passage, Kierkegaard traces how hope matures through "strengthening in the inner being," expounding something like the developmental sequence described in Romans 5:1-5. See EUD, 93-95.

about life, we can ignore the hopelessness as much as possible and make do with the crumbs of small hopes that finitude can supply, we can rebel in passionate protesting despair against whatever it was that put this highly unsatisfactory universe together, or perhaps we can do as Meursault does in his cell in the early hours of the day of his execution as he imagines the scene of the guillotine, and construe the meaninglessness of the universe as something fitting and "tender" and highly congruent with our own aimless life. But none of these courses of development preserves the enthusiastic happiness of youthful hope. This freshness is preserved only when hope is infused with patience. But what is patience?

In general, patience is the ability to sustain, over time, some activity or attitude, against certain emotions that tend to undermine the activity or attitude. Emotions of this sort are discouragement and impatience. It may seem trivial and unhelpful to define patience as the ability to resist impatience, but not if we see that impatience is a fairly discrete type of emotion. Impatience is a concern based construal,[18] based on a concern that something happen or a concern to get something done. Based on such a concern, impatience is the construal of the event or accomplishment as *not coming soon enough*. Thus impatience is a kind of frustration. As such, the emotion is a motivation to hurry the activity (often to its detriment) or quit the activity or give up on something's happening. The impatience that would be relevant to Anna would be the construal of the Messiah's coming as being too long delayed, and it might be manifested in anger at God, or in an impulse to throw in the towel and see if she can't find a new husband, or an impulse to lament, or perhaps just in pacing around the temple and compulsively consulting the wise rabbis. But Anna is patient in her expectancy. She has no such impulses, but is and has been, for these last many years, confidently and joyously preoccupied with Messiah's coming.

---

[18]I have developed this account of emotion in "What an Emotion Is: A Sketch," *The Philosophical Review* 97 (1988): 183-209, and further in chap. 2 of *Emotions: An Essay in Aid of Moral Psychology* (Cambridge: Cambridge University Press, 2003).

However, Anna's is a special kind of patience. Kierkegaard distinguishes two kinds (see EUD, 213). One is what people ordinarily have in mind when they speak of patience. This is a virtue of which almost everybody has a modicum; if one had no tolerance at all for waiting for things to happen or for getting something accomplished, one would be a dysfunctional human wreck. Everybody has a certain "natural power of endurance" (EUD, 213) corresponding to his various expectancies. I suppose that this is relative to such factors as age, knowledge, and the character of one's expectancy. Thus if one is old enough to understand that bush beans require several weeks between planting and harvest, and if one has only a normally intense passion for these delectable pods, one simply watches them grow, weeds and waters, with expectancy and without impatience. But if one has a young married daughter and no grandchildren as yet and an intense passion to get some, as the years pass and no pregnancy occurs, one's natural power of endurance may be surpassed, and any patience that one enjoys must be a product of will and work. Though Kierkegaard pictures Anna's patience as a matter of choice, the patience of the potential grandmother is not yet the second kind of patience, not yet Anna's patience. The would-be grandmother may be nearly heroic in her patience without her patience being Anna's, for as Kierkegaard remarks, "temporal patience has provisions on hand for a long time, doggedly perseveres, seldom rests . . . " (EUD, 223).

Anna's patience is special to the object of her hope. It makes sense to calculate probabilities and compute times if one is exemplifying temporal patience. In the gardener's almanac I look up the appointed time for the appearance of bean blossoms and if mine are overdue by a few days I tell myself, "Be patient; maybe the weather's been a little cold and the rain a little scarce." Thus I tap some of my provisions for patience. But at a certain point, if the blossoms don't appear, the calculations make it reasonable for me to run out of patience and give up my hope of a crop this year. Because Anna's hope is in God, whose time is his own, so to speak, and is on no human or finite schedule, and is absolutely trustworthy, such calculations of probabilities and times are not appropriate. Her patience is "infinite," which is to say that there are no conditions under which, if she is true to the logic of the situation, she will become impatient for the Messiah to come, or suppose that the Messiah has delayed too long, or that it is too late for him to come, or that he will, after all, not come. Of course the historical Anna, though she is a great spiritual model, is not a perfect human being, and it is likely that she did feel impulses of impatience from time to time during those many years of eager expectancy. She needed to tap decisively the resources of infinite patience. What are these? If infinite patience is not, for imperfect human beings, an "original natural power of endurance" (EUD, 213), how does one practice it?

Any wavering of the true expectancy results from inappropriately assimilating it to ordinary expectancies with their probabilities and dependencies on the vagaries of human will (what Wittgenstein might call falling prey to "misleading analogies"). Infinite patience is a preservative[19] of eternal hope and consists largely, if not wholly, in the concerted use of the practices associated with eternal hope. As Kierkegaard says, "the true expectancy, which requires patience, also teaches patience" (EUD, 221). If discouragement of eternal hope always involves something like "forgetting" that probability thinking and finite conditions do not apply to it, then the practice of patience will consist largely in calling oneself back to hope by "reminding" oneself of the ways of God. Reminders of the logic of eternal hope are just what Kierkegaard provides, in a literary and conceptual way, in his upbuilding discourses on hope. But to think that an assimilation and repetition to oneself of Kierkegaard's reminders would amount to the practice of infinite patience would be a comical intellectualist misunderstanding. Kierkegaard stresses that Anna is said to have spent her time "worshiping with fasting and prayer night and day" (Luke 2.37). She does not just remind herself, intellectually, of the grammar of Jewish hope, but in the temple lays her body on the line day after day, night after night, in the practices of that hope. Kierkegaard repeatedly says that Anna's kind of expectancy is "always equally close to fulfillment" (EUD, 222) and that it "cannot be disappointed" (EUD 26; see 23-28), and surely that

---

[19]Compare Plato's discussion of courage and its relation to wisdom in *Republic*, book 4, at 429a-430c.

imperviously unvarying closeness to fulfillment is largely due to the expectant person's intimate fellowship in prayer with the God in whom she hopes.

In the mainline virtuist tradition virtues are thought of, not just in a narrowly deontological way, as dispositions to do what is right, nor in a narrowly consequentialist way, as dispositions to precipitate good states of affairs, (or both), but also and primarily as aspects of personal and social well-being, health, strength, proper functioning, fulfillment, and happiness. This is also true of Kierkegaard's account of the Christian virtue of hope. We have seen that on his account, one of human nature's requirements is a kind of security or assurance about the goodness of the future. As long as one relies on the temporal future, only an unstable and deceitful semblance of such assurance is possible; "experience" can calculate the probabilities, but such calculations easily go wrong, and are always only probabilistic anyway. Thus he says that a person who expects only in temporal and probabilistic terms "wastes the power of his soul and the content of his life in calculations and the virulent unwholesomeness of probabilities"[20] (EUD, 219). Unwholesomeness is relative to the organism; one animal species' poison is another's food. For Kierkegaard, the human being is an organism that cannot, without being poisoned, or at any rate fatally undernourished, feed its need for future good on a sole diet of probabilities. In addition to this drive for security, the human self also has a basic need to have a life that makes some kind of ultimate sense. To make sense, a life needs "a goal and a criterion," but if we find our goals and criteria only in the finite, then this need is again fulfilled only deceitfully. (Imagine someone who finds the goal of his life in being a prominent Kierkegaard scholar; and uses his standing in the community of Kierkegaard scholars as the criterion of his success in achieving the goal. Kierkegaard thinks that anyone who is clear about the needs of his heart, on the one hand, and the nature of this goal and criterion, on the other, will immediately see that the latter is

---

[20]The Hongs translate the phrase "the irascible [*hidsige*] unwholesomeness of probabilities," but "irascible" fits the context so poorly that I have ventured a different translation.

fundamentally inadequate to the former.) The life of a person who tries to live in this way is really "without a goal and criterion" and is "inconsolable and disordered," and Kierkegaard describes it in metaphors of futility. Such a life "is only aimless running that becomes lost on the wrong path, is shadowboxing in the air that the wind blows away, writing in the sand that the sea erases." The human self is so constituted as to need an eternal goal as its goal and criterion, and the object of genuine hope is such a goal. Kierkegaard says that one who really experiences the futility of temporal goals "will no doubt seek a goal that is always valid, a criterion that is always valid." The language in which he describes a human spirit's assimilation of such a goal and criterion is rich in metaphors of well-being. The expectancy of an eternal salvation is "a refuge in distress, a fortress that life cannot take by storm, an assignment that distress and sufferings cannot cancel; and life together with this conception is more nourishing for a person than mother's milk to the nursing child, and he returns from this conception strengthened" (EUD, 263).

Finally, I said that a mark of the virtuist tradition is to be concerned with moral and spiritual development and education. Though this point hardly needs to be reiterated since notions of personal development have pervaded our discussion, let me close by simply recalling that Kierkegaard calls the discourses we have been discussing "edifying" or "upbuilding." It is clear that what he intends to build up in people is such personally essential attributes as gratitude, humility, patience, courage, and hope—that is, he intends the discourses to contribute, in some small way, to the building up of people as people. Such a project is radically at odds with the picture of human nature represented by Camus's novel and Sartre's philosophical commentary on it.

10

Perception, Emotion, and Development in Kierkegaard's Moral Pedagogy

Randall G. Colton

Introduction

In December 1843, Kierkegaard published a volume of four upbuilding discourses. The first discourse proposes Job's life as a paradigm because he had the faith, patience, and gratitude to receive again as a gift what had been taken from him in his sufferings.[1] The next three show how those virtues can make possible a similar recovery of what has been lost for the discourses' reader, employing a narrative pattern identified in some of Kierkegaard's works as a "repetition." But they aim at more than description. They intend to "win" or "move" their reader to a genuinely religious existence (see JP, 1:641)[2] and especially to the virtues most central to Job's exemplarity. Throughout the four discourses, repetition as a narrative pattern, paradigmatically present in Job's life story, structures both content and pedagogy. In the third discourse, for example, repetition appears as a pedagogical strategy in thirteen short narratives, and the attention paid to the virtues of giving and receiving reinforce the nature of repetition itself as a gift. My present essay focuses on that discourse's pedagogical strategies to show that repetition as a

---

[1] See George Pattison, " 'Who' Is the Discourse? A Study in Kierkegaard's Religious Literature," *Kierkegaardiana* 16 (1993): 28-45, for a discussion of the personification of the discourse in Kierkegaard's upbuilding discourses.

[2] For a similar claim, see Andrew J. Burgess, "Patience and Expectancy in Kierkegaard's Upbuilding Discourses," in *Kierkegaard Studies Yearbook 2000*, ed. Niels Jørgen Cappelørn, Hermann Dueser, and Jon Stewart (Berlin/New York: Walter de Gruyter, 2000) 217.

narrative pattern shapes the accounts of moral perception, emotion, and moral development implicit in the discourses.

Each of the upbuilding discourses aims to cultivate properly religious concerns in the reader and to clarify the concepts with which the reader grasps the objects of those concerns. This task is a central one for a religious discourse because one can reliably and accurately see the significance of oneself and one's world only when one sees them in the light of the proper objects of concern, religiously understood. When one grasps those objects of concern under faulty concepts, one is liable to lose them and, with them, one's sense of the meaning of one's world. Getting that meaning back by acquiring a more adequate conceptual grasp of one's objects of concern—i.e., coming to see oneself and one's world accurately by seeing their significance in relation to proper objects of concern understood in the most adequate way—is a crucial part of becoming religiously virtuous. Since to construe one's world on the basis of one's concerns is, arguably, to experience an emotion, becoming virtuous also entails a transition to more appropriate emotional responses. Because they are finally received as gifts, such transitions form a trajectory best described in narrative or conversational form; they come contingently, sometimes surprisingly, rather than necessarily. These three claims—that reliable and accurate moral perception depends on a repetition, that moral perception is or can be an emotional response, and that the development of proper emotions takes the form of a narrative or conversation—provide the focal points for my reading of the third discourse.

The first section sets the context for reading the third discourse by describing the relation between the Job discourse and the other three. The second section details the third discourse's use of narratives of repetition as a pedagogical strategy. The third section elucidates the kind of moral perception those strategies aim to cultivate by contrasting it with prominent contemporary accounts of moral perception, while the fourth section clarifies its connections with the emotions. The final section argues that a narrative, conversational model of moral development best fits the process of becoming religiously virtuous.

The Four Upbuilding Discourses of 1843

Kierkegaard takes as his title for the first discourse the latter part of the verse that he also takes as his text: "The Lord gave, and the Lord took away; blessed be the name of the Lord." This sentence of Job's, Kierkegaard's discourse notes, has become a proverb everyone knows and repeats, passing it down through the generations. But it alone does not make Job "the teacher of humankind" everyone knows he is (EUD, 109), nor will that kind of repetition encourage anyone in the right way. One may properly call Job a teacher of humankind, not because he has left behind a proverb but because he has "left . . . only himself as a prototype, his life as a guide for everyone" (EUD, 109; cf. 112). Job's exemplarity lies in his struggle to recover what he had lost, overcoming doubt with faith, ingratitude with thankfulness, and impatience with long-suffering. Job's task, and the concepts that shape his responses to testing, form the context for the three accompanying discourses and for the pedagogical strategies Kierkegaard pursues in them.

Job's struggle, as recounted in the first discourse, began when he was informed by several messengers that he had lost everything he valued most, including even his children, the source of his greatest joy (EUD, 114). With these losses, Job was in danger of losing himself, a possibility the discourse describes in arresting images: Job might have been "starved out in the insatiable craving of the lack" (EUD, 117); consumed by the "worm of craving that would not die in his soul" (EUD, 117); wasted "in a demented possession of what had been lost" (EUD, 118); or he might have "[thrown] himself away" or become a "wanton" (EUD, 118).

Just a few weeks before publishing these upbuilding discourses, Kierkegaard had published pseudonymously another short work, *Repetition: A Venture in Experimenting Psychology*, which explores some of the same disturbing possibilities as the Job discourse.[3] Letters from a young man to an older adviser, in which

---

[3]See Edward Mooney, "*Repetition*: Getting the World Back," in *The Cambridge Companion to Kierkegaard*, ed. Alastair Hannay and Gordon D. Marino (Cambridge: Cambridge University Press, 1997) 282-307, and "Getting the World Back: Kierkegaard on the *Book of Job*," in *Selves in Discord and Resolve: Kierkegaard's Moral-*

he expresses his despair at losing his beloved, comprise portions of the book. Noting the same text that the discourse expounds, the young man calls on Job as a fellow sufferer, imagining Job as an advocate for him in his own suffering (R, 197-98). Though surely the reader should not take at face value the young man's equation of his own suffering with Job's, the young man's description of his loss of self captures vividly the possibilities that the discourse notes only in the third person. The young man laments, "I am nauseated by life; it is insipid—without salt and meaning. . . . One sticks a finger into the ground to smell what country one is in; I stick my finger into the world—it has no smell. Where am I? What does it mean to say: the world? What is the meaning of that word? Who am I" (R, 200)? The young man has lost his beloved and, worse still, finds himself ineluctably cast as the guilty party even though he remains utterly convinced of his own innocence. In such an experience, the concerns by which he had previously oriented himself in the world fail to provide significance and direction to his choices and responses, rendering him immobilized (R, 214).[4] At the end of the letter containing this lament, he cites a catechism's definition of "world": "As a rule, the word 'world' includes both heaven and earth and everything found therein" (R, 203). Unfortunately, the young man cannot find himself in the world, since the cares and concerns that previously attached him to the world in particular ways have dissolved. He has lost sight of the value and significance of the other elements of his world because he has lost his primary object of concern, his beloved. He longs for a repetition; that is, he longs to see again the significance in himself and

---

Religious Psychology from Either/Or to Sickness unto Death (New York/London: Routledge, 1996) 27-40, for lucid discussions of the themes in the Job discourse and *Repetition*.

[4]Stephen Crites argues that in the passage referred to here, "I am inside" should be translated "Here I sit." The latter better pictures the young man's claim at the end of the paragraph that he has remained "for a whole month now, without moving a foot or making one single movement" (R, 214) and more vividly captures the loss of his world that threatens the young man. See Stephen Crites, " 'The Blissful Security of the Moment': Recollection, Repetition, and Eternal Recurrence," in *International Kierkegaard Commentary: Fear and Trembling and Repetition*, ed. Robert L. Perkins (Macon GA: Mercer University Press, 1993) 233n.3, 244.

the world that he saw before losing his beloved (R, 214-15), to "have a double sense of [their] meaning" (R, 221).[5] Against all reasonable expectation, he predicts that such a repetition will occur after he has prepared himself to be a dutiful husband and so to marry his beloved. Surely then, he fondly imagines, she will return to him.

Eventually, the young man sends a letter asserting that he has finally experienced his repetition of meaning, though he has not experienced an external repetition as he had anticipated.[6] Of course, he is of dubious reliability as a narrator, and the reader may suspect that the young man has not completely grasped the concept of a repetition nor completely escaped self-deception.[7] Nevertheless, his story suggests the possibility of a genuine repetition, and, in the discourse's telling, Job seems to have experienced one. After all, his brief words end not in lament but in praise: "Blessed be the name of the Lord!" Surely only someone who had seen again the significance his world had lost could respond as Job does. Furthermore, since anyone may face a test like Job's, his example opens the possibility of repetition for all (EUD, 123-24). As a prototype, Job's life should encourage everyone to respond as he does. But such a task is no easy one, requiring nothing less than a transformation. Each one must acquire the virtues attributed to Job in the discourse, especially the virtues of gratitude, patience, and faith.

---

[5]Alastair Hannay explains, "Repetition is 'repeating' or 'resuming' one's earlier experience from a higher vantage point, giving it a new, and deeper, unity." See *Kierkegaard: The Arguments of the Philosophers* (London: Routledge, 1991) 69.

[6]The gap between the young man's anticipated repetition and the repetition he claims actually to have experienced indicates that there are different kinds of repetition. In a passage in his papers, Kierkegaard distinguishes three kinds of repetition roughly corresponding to the aesthetic, ethical, and religious lifeviews. See Mooney, "*Repetition*," 303n.11.

[7]Such suspicions increase when the reader learns that Kierkegaard altered the story from its original form to include the young man's self-proclaimed repetition, a repetition that occurs when he discovers his beloved is marrying another man, only after Kierkegaard himself discovered that Regine was marrying. See Hannay, *Kierkegaard*, 346n.52.

Only a spirit of thankfulness enabled Job to exclaim, in the midst of his losses, "The Lord gave and the Lord took away" (EUD, 115-16). His thankfulness in this instance, no doubt, had a different character than the gratitude he expressed before his losses but was nevertheless equally honest. Because of his thankfulness, Job could recall the genuine beauty—neither lessened by regret nor increased by nostalgia—of what he had lost, the beauty that reflected the goodness of God, who gave the gifts to begin with (EUD, 116). Without this ability to remember the significance of what he had lost, Job could not have experienced a repetition, "a double sense of meaning." Similarly, his gratitude enabled him to relinquish his attachment to his losses, "as if it were not the Lord who took it away but Job who gave it back to him" (EUD, 116-17), since he saw them as gifts and not as achievements or entitlements. This relinquishment freed Job to see again the value of what he had lost, liberating him from a "nagging" fixation on his original sense of its meaning (EUD, 118).

But Job's gratitude did not imply a mere resignation to the vagaries of fate or a stoic refusal to credit the value of contingent goods. In the midst of his thankfulness, the discourse says, "he did not evade the thought that [everything] was lost" (EUD, 118). But that thought failed to vitiate his thankfulness because "his soul remained quiet until the Lord's explanation again came to him and found his mind, like good earth, well cultivated in patience" (EUD, 118-19). Patience is a "soul-strength" (EUD, 160) that, paradoxically, makes one weak with respect to the things of the external world (EUD, 172). Patience holds the soul still and quiet, as it seeks to gain itself in relation to God through suffering in the external world (EUD, 171-72; cf. EUD, 116-19). Had Job not been patient, his suffering would soon have overwhelmed his thankfulness, and he would have lost his soul rather than gained it.

Job's patience and thankfulness both depended on his faith. By faith, Job saw God at work in his own suffering (EUD, 121). Rather than blaming his enemies or nature or even himself, Job simply confessed, "the Lord took away" (EUD, 119-20). "Job traced everything back to God; he did not detain his soul and quench his spirit with deliberation or explanations that only feed and foster doubt, even though the person suspended in them does not even notice that" (EUD, 121). But seeing God at work in one's suffering does not necessarily result in gratitude and patience; it may even work against such virtues. C. S. Lewis, for example, reflecting on the death of his wife, writes, "Not that I am (I think) in much danger of ceasing to believe in God. The real danger is of coming to believe such dreadful things about him. The conclusion I dread is not, 'So there's no God after all,' but, 'So this is what God's really like. Deceive yourself no longer.' "[8] So Job's faith did not just see God but saw him as unconditionally good and as the source of every good. As a discourse published earlier in 1843 puts it, "he, the Father of lights, ever constant, at every moment makes everything good, makes everything a good and perfect gift for everyone who has enough heart to be humble, enough heart to be trustful. . . . Every gift is a good and a perfect gift when it is received with thankfulness" (EUD, 40-42). Or as the second of 1843's four discourses has it, "What, then, is the good? It is that which is from above" (EUD, 134). In faith, Job saw what he had lost, and his losing it, in relation to the God who gives all and only good things.

Job's faith made his gratitude possible. Only one who sees God as the source of good and of nothing but good can give thanks to God when he loses his world. Job's patience sustained his faith by keeping his soul still and quiet, so that he did not lose his perception of God as the source of goodness. But at the same time, the reader might think that Job's patience depended on his faith, too, since in it he had a perception of God that made waiting for a repetition seem worthwhile.

Faith, gratitude, and patience make a repetition possible for the one who has suffered loss. Consequently, these four upbuilding discourses aim to encourage their reader to grow in those virtues. The second of the four, titled "Every Good and Every Perfect Gift Comes From Above," concerns the virtue of faith and the struggle with doubt. Gratitude and its complement, generosity, form the subject matter for the third, which repeats the previous title. The fourth ruminates on "gaining one's soul in patience." Though Job does not appear on stage in any of these last three discourses, his

---

[8] *A Grief Observed* (London: Faber and Faber Press, 1963; repr.: New York: Bantam, 1976) 5.

prompting sounds clearly in the background. For example, his conviction that God is the source of all and only good provides the object for faith and doubt in the second discourse and the shape of gratitude and generosity in the third. And his repetition provides the model for growth in virtue presupposed by the other discourses. The rest of this paper will explore the narrative pattern of repetition present in the third discourse's pedagogical strategies and their implications for concepts of moral perception, emotions, and moral transitions.

Before moving to that exploration, note one last contextual feature. Besides Job's experience of repetition, his thankfulness, and his faith that God is the source of all and only good, yet another element structures the third discourse's meditations. As a corollary to the last conviction, the third discourse also insists on the equality of every person. Referring to the concept of divine goodness as captured in the title passage, the discourse asserts, "If that stands firm, then the difference is indeed canceled, because a difference in imperfection, which is indigenous in people's gifts, can only be transient, then at last the words of the apostle are continually heard as a divine refrain that is able to perfect every difference in equality before God" (EUD, 145). Concepts of divine goodness and its corollary equality provide the context for the gratitude and generosity prized by the discourse. So the responsive reader moves, not from ingratitude to gratitude, but from one sense of giving's significance to another, more adequate one, shaped by genuinely religious concerns and concepts; and so as well for generosity. The responsive reader must, then, lose the first sense of giving and receiving significance and meaning, so that he can see them again with eyes sharpened by the discourse's thoughts. The next section finds that pattern at work in the discourse's pedagogical strategies.

Kierkegaard's Pedagogical Pattern in the Third Discourse

Arne Grøn argues that the characters described in the upbuilding discourses play "a methodological role" in Kierkegaard's attempt to depict virtues such as patience and courage as modes of resistance to the acids of temporality that threaten the human self.[9] Grøn rightly underscores the significance of Kierkegaard's use of characters and the importance of the passing of time for them. But Kierkegaard aims not merely to depict the virtues but to move his reader to acquire them. To that end, Kierkegaard configures the passing of time for his characters into a structured and repetitive set of narrative patterns. This section of my paper describes the patterns of repetition that plot the discourse's narratives.

The bulk of the discourse comprises thirteen brief narratives each of which describes someone who moves from lacking generosity or gratitude to exemplifying one of those virtues. Written in the second person, these stories intend to bring "you the reader," as you see yourself in the characters, to lose your naïve grasp on the significance and value of giving and of giving thanks, and then to find a new perspective in which you see again their significance and value. This new sense, of course, is distinctively religious, shaped by genuinely religious concerns and concepts.

The discourse does not address the moral skeptic who needs to be convinced of the virtues' value. It assumes that, as someone "favorably disposed" to the discourse, you are already professedly committed to becoming religious (EUD, 107), but that you are also liable, in certain circumstances, to see giving and receiving in the light of concepts other than James's essential truths. Even worse, you tend to conceal from yourself the tenuousness of your virtues, preferring to think of yourself as morally mature. Consequently, the discourse sets you in circumstances that disclose the limits of your ability to see giving generously and receiving gratefully as of central significance for you. Those disorienting circumstances reveal that you actually see the significance of giving and receiving only in relation to concepts and concerns that fail to exhibit religious earnestness. But they also provide an opportunity for the discourse to reshape your perception in distinctively religious ways. After you better grasp the religious concepts that the discourse uncovers, and connect them to your concern for becoming religious, you may learn to see giving and receiving

---

[9] "Temporality in Kierkegaard's Edifying Discourses," in *Kierkegaard Studies Yearbook 2000*, ed. Niels Jørgen Cappelørn, Hermann Deuser, and Jon Stewart (New York: Walter de Gruyter, 2000) 200-201; see also 195.

anew. You may finally come to see them in a religiously authentic way. Three examples of this strategy follow.

Imagine yourself first as a *joyless giver* (EUD, 145-46). As this character, you see the significance of giving in terms of its effectiveness at meeting the manifest needs of another, especially for that which will ensure the equality of all. Giving's value follows from its place in a kind of hypothetical imperative: if this need is to be met, you must make the gift that will meet it. Since, as the "favorably disposed" person you are (EUD, 107), you are committed to the value of meeting others' needs, you can easily see that you should make this gift. So you are willing to give, but you find no joy in the giving, any more than you would find joy in the calorie counting necessary for your desired weight loss. But you can, of course, easily imagine circumstances in which giving would lose even the significance your present perspective assigns it and in which, consequently, you would find yourself immobilized, not readily able to act decisively in a giving manner. For instance, if you could imagine that anyone else might make the gift that meets the need, you would find it difficult to decide to give yourself. Circumstances like those, then, loosen your grasp on the significance of giving. But the discourse loosens your grasp in another way as well. Since all good things are from God and human equality before God depends on that truth, the discourse points out, your gift is always unnecessary and never sufficient for achieving the equality at which it aims. With those truths fixed in your mind, you may find it difficult to recognize the same sort of significance that you saw before in any kind of giving. Your grasp on giving, then, is deficient in two ways: it cannot be counted on in a wide variety of circumstances and, even when you do give, it lacks the affect of joy that should accompany it.

But the discourse's story raises new hopes. If you can lose that sense of giving's significance, perhaps you can recover another. Since giving depends on the divine goodness, perhaps you can begin to see giving's significance now in the way that it puts you and the receiver together, equally, before God. In a later passage, the discourse describes how giving admonition to another (as the discourse does to the reader), enacting a kind of repetition, can make the admonition "as fresh and vivid in your soul as it was in the moment of acquisition" (EUD, 149). Perhaps in this story, in the character of the joyless giver, you hope that the significance of giving can again become fresh and vivid, even if different from your naïve perspective. But the discourse disappoints this hope. Almost accusingly, the discourse declares, "But you learned another kind of wisdom, that there is no good gift either up there or down here, and you could just as well keep everything or give everything away" (EUD, 146). Seeing yourself in the story's mirror, you can imagine how such circumstances might take away your perception of giving's significance, since it would no longer demonstrate your ability to bring about equality for others (itself a perception that subtly undermines genuine equality). You continue to read, hoping to find in the story a new way of seeing giving in such circumstances. But no repetition is forthcoming; turning dizzily in the darkness from heaven to earth, you fail to see again the significance of giving. You have learned the aesthete's version of wisdom, a wisdom that makes true choice impossible: whether you give or do not give, you will regret it either way (EO, 1:38-39).

Nevertheless, as the reader you are not bound by the perceptions of the characters in the discourse's story. The significance of the story, according to the preface of *Four Upbuilding Discourses*, finally lies not in its own narrative world but in its repetition in the reader's life. Your appropriate reception of the story "sanctifies the gift, gives it meaning, and transforms it into much" (EUD, 107). Just as you could not predict the conclusion of the story as the discourse tells it, neither can you predict with certainty the prospects for the story's repetition in your own. But by turning your reflection against you through the story, the discourse has at least made possible the loss that must precede the repetition.

Imagine yourself next as a bitter, *reluctant giver* (EUD, 149-50). As this character, you see someone facing a problem or circumstance relevantly similar to one you yourself have faced at some earlier time. You recall that, after much bitter struggle, you overcame the adversity, and you recognize that you are now in a place to help others by passing along what wisdom you have gained. So you see a significance to giving in these circumstances— your gift will produce equality between you and another by transferring your hard won advantage to that other. At the same time, your grip on that significance is quickly failing, and your circumstances have all but robbed you of it. You, after all, won this wisdom the hard way, and you set a high value on it accordingly. You consider, then, that it might be better to make this one who needs such wisdom also pay for it in the bitterness of struggle, before receiving your advice. Perhaps that person will then value it as highly as you do.

So this scenario takes you, as the "favorably disposed" reader, from a willingness to give to circumstances in which, in the story's mirror, you lose completely your grasp of the positive significance of giving. But your loss proves that your perception was, in the first instance, naïve at best. If the bitterness of your struggle compared with the potential ease of the receiver could cloud your vision, then you must have seen the source of the gift's goodness in your effort in the struggle. And though you were willing to give so as to effect equality between you and the receiver, you had in mind only a certain kind of equality. You wished for an equality in achievement, and the gratuitousness of your gift threatens that possibility. So that perception of giving's significance cannot provide for reliability in giving or enable a giving free from bitterness and reluctance. The reluctant giver is also joyless.

James's guiding words—every good and every perfect gift comes from above—shape a different perception. Seen in their light, the gift of admonition has its value not in view of its relation to the bitter experience that produced its wisdom but in light of God's goodness and ability to make it fruitful in the life of another. Since you cannot know what God and the other will make of it, the discourse insists that you see yourself as more insignificant than your gift. The goodness of the gift comes from God, not from the giver's effort. And consequently, the gift makes possible an equality before God, relegating differences in achievement to the inessential.

The discourse opens the possibility, then, of gaining back your sense of giving's significance, this time in a form more impervious to the threats of changing circumstances. But once again, the discourse does not neatly answer expectation. Rather than provide the ending to the story, the discourse provides words of advice: "If, then, you do have an admonition to give, do not lift your head high in censure, do not open your eyes to probe, but bow your head and your eyes under the admonition so that it may sound from above just as meaningfully for you as for the other" (EUD, 150). As you follow that advice in imagination, the story suggests the possibility of a repetition. But the discourse refuses to provide a definitive resolution, just as it refuses to predict your reception of its gift of itself. Whether, you, as the reader, will experience your own repetition is something neither story nor discourse nor, perhaps, even you can declare with certainty.

Imagine yourself, finally, as a *dominated receiver*, obliged to accept a gift from a rich and powerful person (EUD, 153-55). This powerful person disregards you, "since the whole affair was trifling and meaningless to him" (EUD, 154). The giver sees himself as so superior to you that he sees value in neither the gift nor the thanks. He is like Aristotle's magnanimous man, who, "if he is honored by just anyone, or for something small, . . . will entirely disdain it."[10] You, however, are to see yourself not as the magnanimous man, but as the lowly one who seeks to thank him for some boon, vital to you but inconsequential to him. If the magnanimous man perceives the situation correctly, then you harm yourself by expressing thanks, since that act confirms your inequality (EUD, 153-54). Perhaps you can already feel your sense of the significance of giving thanks slipping away, and resentment boiling to the surface. In such circumstances, you may easily lose your grip on the significance of thanking your benefactor, since such acts seem to make you complicit in your own domination by another.

The discourse ruthlessly takes from you your sense of thanksgiving's significance—but only because your naivety makes you unreliable and bitter. Your naïve perspective sees the magnanimous man as he himself does, as the source of the goodness of the gift. Consequently, giving thanks has meaning only in relation to him. Furthermore, you desire equality with him, but only the kind of equality he can recognize and respect. His calloused disregard of you and your thanks makes achieving that impossible. But when James's words shape your perception, you see the same story in a different way, so that you can see again the significance

---

[10]Aristotle, *Nichomachean Ethics* (1124a10-11), trans. Terence Irwin (Indianapolis: Hackett Publishing Company, 1985) 99-100.

of giving thanks in relation to God's goodness and the corollary human equality.[11]

According to the discourse, "The lowly man is served by the powerful, and in your thanksgiving you lifted your heart up to God for having used that powerful man as an instrument to help you" (EUD, 154). Now you see that the gift reveals not an inequality between you and the magnanimous man but a common dependence on God. He, even if unknowingly, expresses his dependence on God through giving, and you through thanking, and together you are united in a common confession that each is *"more insignificant than the gift"* (EUD, 156-57).

Like the other two, this little story exemplifies the kind of repetition suggested in the narratives of Job and *Repetition's* young man. In each case, the reader can discern at least four possible moments. First, the stories present the central characters as attached to some finite object of concern, which provides them with a first, naïve sense of the value and significance of their world. Next, some external event or circumstance causes them to lose their grasp on the object of concern. After that, they become unable to maintain their naïve vision of the significance of themselves, their activities, their surroundings, and so on. That inability renders them immobile and despairing. Finally, in the moment most properly termed a repetition, they may gain a new vision of their world, seeing it anew in the light of a more adequate object of concern and finding a more reliable and appropriate sense of its significance.

These moments vary in their intensity, length, and depth. The young man's experience of the third moment—the loss of his beloved and the consequent loss of significance in his world—is of much greater duration and force than the corresponding experi-

---

[11]When you give thanks to the magnanimous man in light of your new concept of gratitude, he may not recognize your words or actions as gratitude, since they will not credit him as the final source of the goodness of his gift. In his papers, Kierkegaard asserts that if you love your neighbors in the Christian sense, "you must be able to bear that your love for them is regarded as hate" (WL, 441). Similarly, gratitude repeated might not look like gratitude at all to those who, like the magnanimous man, have never suffered the loss of their naïve perception. I owe the formulation of this point to a conversation with my father, Robert E. Colton.

ence for Job. In fact, Job moves so quickly from loss to repetition, that the blindness to significance the young man suffers seems almost a mere possibility in his story. The young man's repetition, on the other hand, seems shallower than Job's; one wonders if the young man's experience should even count as a repetition rather than an instance of self-deception.

In another contrast, some of the characters in "Every Good and Every Perfect Gift" find their way to a repetition and some do not. The joyless giver, for example, does not, while the reluctant giver's fate is left ambiguous. Only the dominated receiver experiences a true repetition. But despite the diversity of these stories' endings, they are similar in other resects. Some of these similarities will illuminate the following sections of my paper.

Because the discourse addresses itself primarily to the "favorably disposed" reader, one might expect that it would deploy characters with fundamentally religious concerns. But if one pays careful attention, one can see that these characters are not concerned most of all with their relation to God, though they seem to have convinced themselves that they are. Since these stories are mirrors for the reader, as you read them they aim to uncover your hidden concerns as well. You may take Kierkegaard's reference to the "favorably disposed" reader as a congratulating pat on the back, as acknowledging your own maturity. But as you see yourself in the stories of the discourse, that pat becomes a different kind of blow all together, knocking from you your moral self-complacency. As the joyless giver, for example, you are most concerned not with your relation to God but with your unique ability to bring about equality for others through your own efforts and, perhaps, with others' recognition of that ability. Consequently, circumstances that reveal you as unnecessary for the equality of others take from you that object of concern and cause you to lose sight of the significance of giving generously. Similarly, as the reluctant giver, your concern is for your status as a self-made individual. Circumstances that suggest the triviality of that status threaten your sense of giving's significance. As the dominated receiver, your concern is for others' recognition of your equal status and worth. The callous attitudes of the dominating giver cause you to lose your perception of the significance of giving thanks.

In all these stories, adverse circumstances reveal your concerns as not genuinely religious and as fixed instead on finite, external objects. Those inadequate concerns distort your perceptions of giving generously and receiving gratefully, rendering you incapable of acting virtuously. But in the last example, that of the dominated receiver, the discourse shows the difference made by cultivating a concern for one's relation to God and understanding that concern under properly formed concepts. Taking your relation to God as your central concern and understanding God as the source of goodness and the guarantor of human equality, reshapes your perception of the significance of giving thanks even in the most difficult of circumstances. The next section of my paper describes the kind of moral perception these stories aim to form.

Moral Perception

Through its pedagogical patterns, the discourse emphasizes metaphors of vision and perception for understanding the difference between genuinely virtuous persons and actions and those that are vicious or merely immature. It assumes that reshaping moral perception can aid one in the process of becoming virtuous. The following two sections attempt to elucidate this connection, first by contrasting the discourse's approach to moral perception with that of some contemporary ethicists, and then by exploring the perceptual features of the emotions at the heart of character.

Contemporary ethical discussion has made much of vision metaphors for central aspects of the moral life and a whole literature has grown up around the effort to describe the nature and significance of moral perception. One might think, then, that this discourse presents a natural point of contact between Kierkegaard's reflections and contemporary ethics. And in a sense, it does. Nevertheless, the kind of perception the discourse strives to form in its reader does not neatly correspond with the accounts typically offered in the contemporary debate.

Lawrence Blum's essay "Moral Perception and Particularity" offers a helpful framework for comparing the discourse with the contemporary discussion, since he comments on much of the literature available and arrives at fairly moderate conclusions. Blum argues that "principle-based" moral theories have overlooked the important role of moral perception, the capacity for assessing the moral significance of particular situations. Specifically, he contends that such theories have not done, and, within the limits of their conceptual resources cannot do, justice to moral agents' capacity for three "operations" he identifies as the most significant elements of moral perception.[12] Blum's account focuses on the separable features of some set of circumstances, describing a capacity for distinguishing those that are "morally relevant" from those that are not. He describes this distinction in the following way: "If I am presented with a specific situation I must know for example that the fact that it involves promise keeping and harm to an individual means that it involves two morally relevant features, whereas its involving taking a walk or eating cereal is morally irrelevant."[13] Those with acute moral perception will note easily and accurately the presence and "weight" of the morally relevant features, while those with less acute moral perception may find their view somewhat blocked, so that they do not register them.

But this characterization of moral perception does not fit very closely the narratives of Kierkegaard's discourse. In particular, it seems ill suited for the narrative pattern of loss and recovery. The characters in the discourse do not move from vice or immaturity to virtue by improving their grasp on the separable features of the situation. What changes, as you identify with these characters, is your sense of the significance, not so much of the features of the situation, as of the value of giving generously or receiving gratefully. Moral perception requires a grasp of both the concrete particulars of a situation and of their import for the perceiver. For example, imagine yourself again as one receiving a much-needed gift from a powerful person, who is completely indifferent to your thanks. In such circumstances, you lose, most of all, your perception of the value of receiving with gratitude. Your circumstances and the giver's indifference to the significance of the gift compel you to see as the giver does: "that your expression of thanks had

---

[12]Lawrence Blum, "Moral Perception and Particularity," in *Moral Perception and Particularity* (Cambridge: Cambridge University Press, 1994) 44-45.

[13]Blum, "Moral Perception," 41.

no value" (EUD, 154). But when your vision is shaped by genuinely religious concerns and concepts, you can regain that sense of significance. Giving thanks again becomes, for you, an important act. At the same time, giving thanks enables you to penetrate to the deeper truths of your circumstances, past the appearance of inequality due to accidental differences and to the essential equality of giver and receiver before God. As one commentator puts it, in the moment of repetition, *"nothing new is added to the old, but the old has become new."*[14]

If one tries to explain the discourse's strategy in Blum's terms, one might suggest the following. The discourse picks out certain morally relevant features of the situation it describes so that you, in the place of the character, can see that choosing to give thanks, or choosing to give, is the morally praiseworthy action in the situation. In this case, the morally relevant features are the divine source of the goodness of the gift, and of all goodness, and one's equality with the other.

But this interpretation seems forced in at least two ways. First, the stories enact a pattern of loss and recovery, but separable features of situations are not lost and recovered in that way. One sees them or one does not. The distinguishing feature of the repetition, that the significance or value of the thing lost is restored in a higher key, makes little sense with respect to separable features. Second, these features seem to differ markedly from the kinds of features Blum otherwise appeals to, such as "suffering, racism, dishonesty, violations of someone's rights, [and] temptations to compromise one's moral integrity."[15] Blum's examples (all negative in some fashion, one might note) are events, attitudes, choices, feelings, and so on. But the morally relevant features this interpretation picks out of the discourse's narratives do not fit comfortably in any of those categories. More importantly, these features do not seem much like particulars at all, and Blum insists that perception is of particulars. The discourse insists not just that God is the source of the goodness of this particular gift but that he

---

[14]Niels Nyman Eriksen, *Kierkegaard's Category of Repetition: A Reconstruction*, Kierkegaard Studies Monograph Series 5, ed. Niels Jørgen Cappelørn and Jon Stewart (New York: Walter de Gruyter, 2000) 9.

[15]Blum, "Moral Perception," 46.

is the source of all goodness. With the apostle James, the discourse aims to bring an idea alive in the single individual; and ideas have some degree of generality.

Nor is it clear that the characters are supposed to look *at* the divine source of goodness or the equality of giver and receiver and then decide how to give or receive. Instead, they look at their giving and receiving *through* those concepts; their perception of giving and receiving is *shaped* by the ideas James and the discourse aim to "bring to life in the single individual" (EUD, 141). When they see in this way, generosity and gratitude come to seem natural, compelling, and significant. The discourse is concerned not so much with the perception of particular separable features of a situation as with the perception of the *import* of particular acts, for the single individual, given the situation as a whole.

Blum's framework for the debate about moral perception leaves little room for the kind of perception the discourse has in mind. Lest one think that the problem is only terminological, that Blum must simply use another name for what the discourse is after, one should consider the "Postscript" to Blum's article, provided for its inclusion in a collection of his essays. There Blum describes "*seven* steps that take the person from a given situation to action based on moral principle."[16] Moral perception, understood in Blum's specific sense, occupies only two or three of those steps. Yet none of the others involves the kind of perception the discourse describes, though steps 3 and 4 come the closest.

Those steps, called "agency engagement" by Blum, require one to ask whether one should take action in a given situation and then to answer that question with a judgment. When circumstances cause one to lose one's grasp on the value of thanksgiving for oneself, the question of whether one ought to give thanks in those circumstances does arise. And when one regains a sense of gratitude's significance, one may perhaps form a judgment that one ought to give thanks. But Blum seems to have no sense of the perceptual character of either of these steps and he consequently reduces their richness and texture by overintellectualizing them. One who faces the kind of loss the discourse's stories describe does

---

[16]Blum, "Moral Perception," 57.

not merely raise a question, but instead faces an immobilizing dizziness. Receiving gratefully seems valuable to the individual before the loss of some important object of concern, but after that loss the individual suffers a disorientation that makes action not just a matter for judgment but a frightening or angering or otherwise emotionally weighted possibility. Such anger or fear or despair is, of course, readily apparent in Job's story or in that of the young man in *Repetition*. But even in the miniature stories employed in the third discourse, emotions like those are frequently palpable; and were they not, one might question the reality of the character's concerns in the first place. Blum's sequence of steps fails to take such essential phenomena into account.

Perhaps Blum's omission results from the "analytical separateness" of his steps.[17] The first two represent moral perception; the second two, agency engagement; and the next two, selection and specification or application of rules and principles. Though he admits that sometimes several of these operations occur simultaneously, he nonetheless assumes that they can be defined separately. Thus, one may identify the morally relevant features of a situation without recourse to the commitments implied by agency engagement and rule-application. This seems to me less than plausible, for reasons one may learn from Kierkegaard. In a discourse titled "Strengthening in the Inner Being," published on the same day as *Repetition* and *Fear and Trembling,* one finds a distinction between "indifferent" knowledge and "concerned" knowledge. An indifferent knowledge of the world does not relate the world to anything outside it, and so tells me nothing about how to act with respect to it. A concerned knowledge of the world relates the world to the objects of my concern, to my possibilities and ideals, and so gives me orientation to navigate my way through it. Without concerned knowledge, the world confronting me underdetermines any particular interpretations. I can always see it in another way. Consequently, moral perception requires concerned knowledge. But concerned knowledge synthesizes the steps Blum wants to keep analytically separate. It introduces a

---

[17]Blum, "Moral Perception," 57.

third element between agent and situation and complicates the picture of moral perception.

Of course, Plato has already described that complication in the *Republic* (507d-508b), in the image of the sun. Sensible perception requires a perceiver, an object, and a source of illumination—the sun. Moral perception has the same structure. And just as an eclipse disorients one's physical senses, the discourse suggests, so the loss of a central object of concern disorients one's moral capacities. When circumstances rob one of the status or recognition for which one had an abiding concern, one no longer sees clearly particular acts of, for example, giving and receiving. Without that clear perception, one can only act unsurely, as if in the dark. Or one might use a more contemporary image. After my wife has gone to sleep, I often sit up, reading by the glow of the book light she gave me. At such times, my vision is shaped by the boundary between the bright ellipse the light projects and the darkness of the rest of the room. When the batteries die and the light fades, I lose my sense of the meaning of the page before me. If I turn on the brighter bedside lamp, I can see again, but now in a whole new way, my vision no longer elliptical but circular and much more comprehensive. The source of light determines the shape of my effective vision, just as my objects of concern determine the shape of my moral perception and the range of my action. "Every Good and Every Perfect Gift" describes such perception, its loss, and the possibility of repetition. Consequently, it uncovers aspects of moral perception that Blum's essay leaves unremarked.

More briefly, I should also distinguish the discourse's presentation from another current model of moral perception to which it might be assimilated. Blum discusses and rejects Kantian views of moral perception, including Barbara Herman's version, articulated in her essay "The Practice of Moral Judgment." Herman describes "rules of moral salience," inculcated in agents from childhood, that enable them to "identify morally significant elements in the situations" they face.[18] Rules of moral salience are "an interpretation, in rule form, of the respect for persons (as ends in themselves) which

---

[18]Barbara Herman, "The Practice of Moral Judgment," in *The Practice of Moral Judgment* (Cambridge MA: Harvard University Press, 1993) 82.

is the object of the Moral Law."[19] Thus, like Blum, Herman attempts to describe and explain a capacity for perceiving the significance of separable features of situations. Like the discourse, she also includes in her description a third element, besides the perceiver and the situation, so one might think that she and the discourse offer roughly the same alternative to Blum's view.

But the discourse does not suggest the possibility of repetition through learning or applying new rules. Nor do the discourse's central ideas pick out otherwise unnoticed features of problematic situations. Those ideas are not rules but truths about God and his relation to humans. The truths the discourse attempts to bring alive in the heart of the individual reshape moral vision—and so make possible a repetition—because, through its imaginative exercises, the reader cultivates more genuinely religious concerns and comes to understand their objects under more adequate concepts. Furthermore, rules can play the role of the discourse's truths only insofar as they reveal some truth about objects of concern. But at that point, their significance lies not in their rule-like form but in their indicating a possibility or possibilities with respect to which one can experience fear or longing, despair or hope, and so on. And when they do that, they've become something other than Herman's rules of moral salience.

But thinking through this difference with Herman has brought the discussion to a consideration of affective states like those just named, and the discourse's pedagogical strategies rest on certain assumptions about them. As an orientation to these issues, I will close this section with a brief comment on "Strengthening in the Inner Being," alluded to above. This discourse describes the deep connections between moral perception and character by focusing on the individual's concern for meaning. It develops three themes: 1) a concern for meaning in one's circumstances, which may become a concern about God or a concern about some finite or temporal object; 2) the inner being, or character of the individual, revealed in and shaped by the concern; and 3) the emotions and virtues that indicate the status of the individual's inner being and provide a kind of perceptual access to the meaning he seeks. One's

---

[19]Herman, "Practice of Moral Judgment," 86.

"inner being" becomes manifest in one's deepest concern, a concern for "the meaning the world has for him and he for the world" (EUD, 86). A person without this concern, on the other hand, has no inner being, no character. He is "light-minded" (EUD, 89), venturing into the world with a childish, naïve hope intact (EUD, 94). But once this concern has been awakened in his life, the meaning of his circumstances becomes lost, and the shape of his character depends on how he recovers some kind of meaning.

For instance, the discourse imagines an individual who faced adversity and attempted to find its meaning through a continual close attention to "the anarchy into which everything seemed to have disintegrated" (EUD, 94). He "saw what others saw, but his eyes continually read an invisible handwriting in everything, that it was emptiness and illusion" (EUD, 94). The description of this person's experience suggests that his understanding of his circumstances presents itself in emotional responses such as despair and anxiety. But the discourse imagines another person who, faced with similar adversity, transformed his concern for meaning into a concern about God, and discovered, not emptiness and illusion, but strengthening in the inner being. This individual displayed "joyful thankfulness" in relation to his circumstances, rather than anxiety or despair, as did the first. This parable suggests that an emotional response, dependent on the concerns at the core of one's character, constitutes one's moral perception, at least in many instances.

The pedagogical strategy of the discourse on which this essay focuses relies on this kind of claim. Reshaping moral perception can help to reshape moral character because the concerns in the light of which one perceives meaning in one's actions and circumstances are the concerns on which one's emotions depend, unless some pathology intervenes.[20] In the next section, I explore this connection between emotions and perception more closely.

Emotions and Moral Perception

Imagine yourself again as the joyless giver. In this story, your naïve sense of giving's significance makes it a mere means to an end separate from itself. Considered apart from its utility in bringing about the equality you desire, it has no particular positive significance for you, constituting instead a mere drain on your resources. Even considered as a means to your desired end, giving is necessary but not particularly desirable. To the extent that you experience joy, you experience it merely in the outcome, not in the act of giving itself. But if you developed a concern for God as the source of goodness and saw the significance of giving in light of your relation to him, the act of giving itself would have a deep and positive meaning and would be a source of joy for you. Your joylessness, then, suggests that your perceptions are faulty and that you have failed to internalize the truths of the text the discourse expounds. You have not grasped the true import of these acts of generosity or gratitude. Imagine yourself as the reluctant giver or as the dominated receiver and you can trace the same pattern. Your emotions change with your perceptions and indicate the extent to which you have internalized the truths about God's goodness and human equality at the center of the discourse. Explaining the discourse's pedagogy, then, depends on an account of the emotions that weaves tightly together their perceptual quality and their intimate relations to concepts and concerns.

In "Existence, Emotion, and Virtue: Classical Themes in Kierkegaard" Robert C. Roberts clarifies Kierkegaard's understanding of the emotions. His remarks can explain the assumptions about the

---

[20]Part of the pedagogical task is to identify and address the particular pathologies that divide particular individuals' moral perceptions from the concerns at the center of their emotions. For example, the first volume of *Either/Or* catalogs a variety of aesthetic lifeviews that feature various kinds of dissociation. Kierkegaard's insistence that, to help another, one must begin where the other is (PV, 45) and his wide variation in style and approach reflect his concern with that aspect of the pedagogical task. But his rich insights into that challenge require another essay.

emotions on which the discourse's pedagogy depends. Emotions are based on concerns, shaped by thoughts, and experienced as perceptions. A concern is an interest, passion, or attachment of a person that provides the ground for a range of emotions. Roberts uses the example of someone who owns a small business that is the object of her chief concerns. She is likely to feel joy when business is going well, pride when her products and services are excellent, and so on. Her emotional responses depend on her interest in her business. Thoughts play their role too, however. Though Kierkegaard does not simply identify emotions with thoughts, he does insist that the ways in which one conceptualizes the objects of one's emotions shape them into the kinds of emotions they are. Roberts writes, "In his upbuilding discourses Kierkegaard repeatedly instructs us on how to *think* so as to have, or not to have, a given emotion."[21] Certainly in this discourse Kierkegaard spends much of his energy on the concepts that underlie correct or incorrect moral perceptions. But his repeated use of perceptual metaphors in this discourse suggests another point. Roberts writes, "While emotions are shaped by thoughts, the fact that they focus specific kinds of features of the situations they are about, and do so in terms of the concerns on which they are based, makes them as much like perceptions as like *mere* thoughts."[22] Emotional responses, then, are "a kind of immediate impression of the way things are (the way God is, the way oneself is, the way the world is), the most natural metaphor for which is sense perception."[23] Anger, for instance, may be a perception of someone's action toward oneself as an undeserved slight to one's dignity. In that case, it is also a perception of the importance of one's dignity for oneself. Thus, it depends on one's concern for

---

[21]Robert C. Roberts, "Existence, Emotion, and Virtue: Classical Themes in Kierkegaard," in *The Cambridge Companion to Kierkegaard*, ed. Alastair Hannay and Gordon D. Marino (Cambridge: Cambridge University Press, 1998) 190. For a fuller description of the emotions and their moral significance, see Roberts's *Emotions: An Essay in Aid of Moral Psychology* (New York: Cambridge University Press, forthcoming).

[22]Roberts, "Existence, Emotion, and Virtue," 195-96.

[23]Roberts, "Existence, Emotion, and Virtue," 197.

one's own dignity and a concept of that dignity that specifies what counts as a slight to it.

This account of the emotions comports well with the discourse's pedagogical strategy. As already noted, the preface to *Four Upbuilding Discourses* declares that the reader who can receive the discourses meaningfully is one who is "favorably disposed" (EUD, 107). The discourse's strategy assumes the reader's professed concern for becoming religious, though it also reveals opposing concerns hidden in the reader's own inner being. Consequently, the discourse assumes that it has no need to convince the reader that he or she ought to love his or her neighbor or to give generously or to receive with thankfulness or even to value human equality. If you can imagine yourself in the discourse's stories as being without these concerns and their attendant construals, then you will surely miss their drama.

So the discourse focuses on the concepts of God's goodness and its corollary human equality. It shows that a naïve perception of the significance of giving or receiving often results from false or inadequate conceptualizations of central objects of concern. The discourse uncovers them by putting the reader into circumstances in which certain conceptualizations of God's relation to humans cannot sustain a perception of the value of giving generously or receiving gratefully for the reader. In this way, it opens the possibility of a repetition that enables the reader to see their significance again, but this time in a more adequate and stable way.

If emotions are modes of perception, then this repetition may appear as a shift in emotional responses. The characters' new vision is not a mere matter of reflective cognition, but more a matter of an immediate perception-like grasp, as they begin, in the best scenarios, to give gladly rather than grudgingly or to receive joyfully rather than reluctantly. For the reader, reflecting in a concerned way on the discourse's imagined narratives promotes this kind of moral seeing.

If emotions are based on concerns and shaped by thought, then a change in one's concerns and thoughts may alter one's emotional responses. This discourse's pedagogy is directed towards the latter, changing the thoughts that shape its reader's emotional responses. But one cannot change one's emotions just by deciding to change one's thoughts. Emotions have a perceptual aspect, and perceptual transitions cannot, at least normally, be directly willed. After all, the discourse does not always present stories that end as the reader hopes, nor does it even claim knowledge of the resolution for every story. Moral transitions, such as the ones the discourse describes, are not the inevitable result of effort, but gifts for which one waits in patience and faith and gratitude. Like gifts, they are not necessary, but neither are they arbitrary. The next section describes in more detail this feature of moral transitions.

Developmental Models

One of the most interesting features of the biblical book of Job is its dialogical format. Conversations structure its narrative, as God, Satan, Job's wife, Job's friends, and Job himself offer rival interpretations of Job's life and the meaning of his suffering. Something of this conversational motif survives in *Repetition's* exchange of letters between the young man and Constantin, but the Job discourse, at first glance, seems to suppress it. The most dramatic and central conversations in the biblical book of Job, those between Job and his friends and between Job and God, receive no attention at all. Instead, the discourse focuses on a saying handed down as a proverb. But contrary to first appearances, the Job discourse does indeed make conversation a central motif. In so doing, it suggests a model for understanding moral transitions that fits the pedagogy of the third discourse better than some other plausible alternatives. So the present section of my paper has both critical and constructive aims. I argue against the adequacy of syllogistic or organic models for capturing the transitions involved in developing the virtues the third discourse depicts, and I argue for an autobiographical, conversational model suggested by the Job discourse.

The discourse deploys its pedagogical narratives with the aim of sparking a perceptual transition, necessarily involving the emotions, as a moment in the task of becoming virtuous, religiously understood. Nothing about Kierkegaard's pedagogical strategy compels his reader from one kind of perception to another. There is no causal force, no psychological conditioning with a necessary, Skinnerian result. Nor is there a deductive move from one perception to another, no syllogism, the necessary conclusion of which is the new perception. As examples of repetition, the recovery of what was lost, the transitions to more complete virtue depicted in the discourse cannot be forced. *Repetition's* young man and the discourses' Job must simply wait for a storm that gives their worlds and themselves back to them. As John McDowell writes in a similar context, "The transition to being so motivated is a transition *to* deliberating correctly, not one effected *by* deliberating correctly; effecting the transition may need some nonrational alteration such as conversion."[24] So the transition is contingent. What kind of model captures the notion of moral development the discourses imply, if one discards the analogy of a deductive syllogism or forcible conditioning?

Organic growth provides an intuitively appealing image. A plant's growth to maturity—a seed, fallen from the plant and buried in the ground, develops its potential through stages of growth, and finally brings forth new life and new seeds—suggests several of the aspects of moral development already discussed. The plant's life moves from less adequate to more adequate stages of functioning as it responds to its environment, just as a person moves from less to more adequate moral stages in response to its environment. Even its burial in the ground could represent the loss of meaning that precedes a repetition. Its environment introduces an element of contingency, so that no one can predict with certainty whether this seedling will move successfully through its stages of maturity or not. Thus organic growth depicts a movement through stages that a deductive syllogism obscures, but at the same time suggests also a principle of reasonable explanation for growth or its absence. In talk about moral growth or cultivating souls, or even the concept of development itself, some such set of analogies must be in play.

But the organic model proves inadequate in at least two ways. First, it fails to capture the right kind of contingency. A normal seed might or might not grow to maturity because its environmental conditions might or might not prove conducive. And with the

---

[24]John McDowell, "Might There Be External Reasons?" in *Mind, Value, and Reality* (Cambridge MA: Harvard University Press, 1998) 107.

right knowledge and the right tools, with the ability to manipulate a seed's external conditions as necessary, one could be pretty confidant that one could cause the seed to grow as one wished. But the contingency built into moral transitions is not this way. There is no knowledge, no tools, and no skill that can make moral transitions as predictable as hydroponic gardening. Their contingency extends even beyond the unpredictability of a particular human's choosing, for they do not follow necessarily even when willed. Like a perceptual gestalt shift, they sometimes take place suddenly after much desire and a long wait.

This contingency raises the specter of arbitrariness. If the transition does not have to go the way it does, then why is one kind of transition better than another or better than none at all? After all, a syllogistic or organically causal connection gives one assurance that the next move is the right one. But without any such connection, how can one be sure which next move is the right one?

One may take a cue here from Aristotle's discussion of tragic narrative in the *Poetics*. Aristotle argues that a tragic narrative represents one complete action and that the incidents that make it up "have the greatest effect on the mind when they occur unexpectedly and at the same time in consequence of one another."[25] On this account, successful narratives have an aspect of contingency in that one cannot predict their transitions, but they are nevertheless nonarbitrary, since the incidents occur "in consequence of one another." He attributes these features to tragic narrative specifically, but a little reflection on one's own experience with stories reveals that the surprising but fitting connection between events is a characteristic of stories in any genre. What stories require for unity and nonarbitrariness, then, is not a necessary, predictable connection between incidents. Instead, their unity lies in connections discernible in retrospect as fitting. The moments of the narrative follow one another in an appropriate way, even if one could not have predicted their sequence before the narrative unfolded.

---

[25]Aristotle, *Poetics* (1452a1-4), trans. Ingram Bywater, in *The Basic Works of Aristotle*, ed. Richard McKeon (New York: Random House, 1941) 1465.

But if this is true of stories, then Kierkegaard's narrative pedagogy assumes that it is also true of moral transitions, since it presents them in narrative form. If "rational" means "effected by syllogistic deliberation" or "explainable by cause and effect relations," as in a plant's growth, then, as McDowell points out, such transitions will be nonrational. But being nonrational in that sense does not entail any sort of vicious arbitrariness or irrationality. Instead, the moral transition the discourse works to bring about will be entirely reasonable if it can be seen to fit with what came before from a retrospective point of view. The discourse supplies the means to see that fittingness when it offers the conceptual clarification that allows the characters to see again the significance of activities whose value had been obscured by the loss of central objects of concern. That clarification follows on a kind of unmasking, in which the discourse reveals the ways in which you as the reader, seeing yourself in the mirror of a character's story, have worked to keep authentically religious concepts and concerns from shaping your vision. As the reluctant giver, for instance, your attachment to your own sufferings as proof of your wisdom and courage makes you seem peculiarly significant, in a way that has its appeal to your pride, even if it makes it impossible to sustain generosity in the circumstances the discourse's story depicts. Furthermore, you can explain why you were formerly satisfied with your naïve perception, by referring to the concerns and concepts Kierkegaard's pedagogy uncovers. Finally, you can explain the fittingness of the denouement as a recovery, in a fuller and more adequate form, of what you lost through the accidents of changing circumstances. Your account of your moral transition, then, will be autobiographical and not strictly syllogistic or available from a third-person perspective as in a description of organic growth.[26] And, thus, it will be no more arbitrary than any other autobiography.[27]

---

[26]See Charles Taylor, *Sources of the Self: The Making of the Modern Identity* (Cambridge MA: Harvard University Press, 1989) esp. 62-75, for further argument along these lines.

[27]Of course, some autobiographies are quite arbitrary, and perhaps all are to some degree. The discourse's pedagogical strategy offers some defenses against such arbitrariness in its unmasking of base motives, in its dialogical method

An organic model also fails because it explains moral growth chiefly by reference to the capacities latent in the seed. Everything required for the maturity of the plant, apart from external environmental factors, is present in the seed. Given the right environment and coaxing, those latent capacities naturally unfold into a mature plant, as it fulfills its essential possibilities. But consider, for example, the peculiar character of faith, gratitude, and patience, the virtues that prepare Job for his repetition. They are less fulfilling than emptying of the person they characterize, as the following claims from the *Four Upbuilding Discourses* demonstrate. The call to *patience* will "always come inopportunely, capable of simultaneously killing every bold expectancy that longs for renowned deeds, for inspired achievements" (EUD, 159), insisting that "a person can truly possess the imperfect only by surrendering it" (EUD, 165). The person who receives *gratefully* "confesses that *he is more insignificant than the gift*" (EUD, 156-57), voiding his or her own claims to independent meaning and abandoning himself or herself to another. *Faith* requires renouncing demonstration and dying to the doubt that makes one strive for it (EUD, 135). A discourse published in 1844, titled "To Need God is a Human Being's Highest Perfection," even goes so far as to claim that "the highest [power of a human being] is this: that a person is fully convinced that he himself is capable of nothing, nothing at all" (EUD, 307). One struggles for one's own "annihilation," since "the annihilation is his truth" (EUD, 309).

These sentences are hard sayings, undoubtedly meant to provoke, and resolutely turning from concepts like health and flourishing that are at home in an organic context. Becoming religious, they insist, means not to achieve but to receive. They present gratitude as central because the condition for a repetition lies not in the individual but in God. The recovery of meaning and the acquisition of virtues are finally gifts from another. A model of moral development that overlooks this fact overlooks the exem-

---

(which requires you, the reader, to take account of another's interpretation of your own life), and in its bringing you, the reader, to awareness of your God-relation (which provides the final, inescapable context for the truth and intelligibility of judgments on life-stories, since God is the source of all and only good).

plarity of Job, and will make it very difficult to bring alive in the individual essentially religious ideas like those of James.

In this respect, even a narrative model of development has its dangers. If one thinks of the retrospective fittingness of events in a narrative as analogous to the way in which God's gifts meet needs one never fully understands one has until one receives the gift, then one may remain close to the spirit of the religious discourses. But if one thinks, as seems reasonable, that the retrospective fittingness of events in a well-constructed narrative is obvious because those events fulfill some tension, some fore-shadowing, initially overlooked in the preceding events of the story, then the essentially religious point becomes lost. Instead of directing attention to one's God-relation, such a narrative model focuses one's sight on one's own capacities. So, as an analogue for moral development, that feature of narrative intelligibility may suggest what the organic model suggests: that becoming virtuous fulfills some positive capacity latent in the individual. Timothy Jackson identifies this kind of doctrine as "Pelagianism": "the doctrine that we can have faith and earn salvation by means of our own intrinsic resources; human nature is perfectible, and no special grace is required."[28] Jackson argues convincingly that Kierkegaard rejects any version of Pelagianism throughout his religious writings. What model, then, can capture the sense of nonarbitrary contingency found in narratives but without losing the religious spirit?

The Job discourse suggests an answer. As noted above, the biblical book of Job moves its narrative by recounting the rival interpretations of Job's life and sufferings offered in a number of conversations, through which Job grows deeper in faith, patience, and gratitude. Despite neglecting the most central and dramatic of those conversations, the Job discourse nonetheless repeats that motif. On the most general level, as George Pattison notes in another context, "the religious works are pervaded by the conceit that the reader is a 'listener' listening to the words of a 'speak-

---

[28]Timothy P. Jackson, "Arminian Edification: Kierkegaard on Grace and Free Will," in *The Cambridge Companion to Kierkegaard*, ed. Alastair Hannay and Gordon D. Marino (Cambridge: Cambridge University Press, 1998) 236.

er.' "[29] Within that conceit, the Job discourse presents or refers to no fewer than eight conversational pairs.[30] These conversations are about the meaning and significance of a life: the life of Job as presented in the biblical text and that of the reader as reflected in the discourse itself. The interlocutors exchange interpretations of Job's life as a narrative whole, and the reader is challenged in turn to make a good confession concerning his or her own, just as Job does in the titular benediction (EUD, 124).[31]

If confessing is, though only in part, telling one's story to another, then perhaps one can turn to conversation for a profitable model of moral development.[32] The way in which one develops the virtues may be like the way in which one gains understanding in one's conversations. If one imagines oneself in conversation with another—whether God, the discourse, or simply other humans— one can see that conversation captures features of both narratives and gifts. First, its parts have that retrospective fittingness characteristic of narratives.[33] Second, one's potential for gaining understanding in the conversation is a potential for responding to the gift of the other. Without the other's gift—whether promise or command or threat or so on—one's capacity is only a need for the other. The gift of the other transforms what appears as mere need into a capacity for response, and so for movement. Similarly,

---

[29]" 'Who' Is the Discourse?" 36.

[30]For those keeping score: Job's wife speaks to Job (111); the messengers speak to Job (114 and 119); Job speaks to God (his benediction on 114 and 118 and throughout in praise and thanksgiving); the storm speaks to the sufferer and the sufferer to the storm (121); the voice of comfort speaks to the troubled one (122); the discourse speaks to the listener (throughout) and the listener to the discourse (123); the listener speaks to himself or herself (123); and the listener speaks to God (123).

[31]Though much has been made of Kierkegaard's relation to Socrates, and rightly so, these particular themes find an even better exemplar in Augustine's *Confessions*.

[32]See Edward Mooney's *Selves in Discord and Resolve*, 6-8, for a description of practical reasoning in Kierkegaard's works as dialogical in form.

[33]See *After Virtue: A Study in Moral Theory*, 2nd ed. (Notre Dame IN: University of Notre Dame Press, 1984) 211, where Alasdair MacIntyre describes conversations as "enacted narratives."

developing the virtues depends not on a self-sufficient unfolding of latent potential, but instead on the reception of a gift.

Of course, every analogy limps, and this one is no exception. Part of its deficiency is evident in the last paragraph's ambiguity between need and capacity. In conversation, the need for the gift of the other is a hidden capacity for response; but in the individual's relation to God, God gives both the gift and the condition for receiving the gift (see PF, 14). Nevertheless, in one's attempts to aid another in the task of becoming religious, this model may stand one in good stead. These discourses, after all, initiate a kind of conversation, in which the initiating speaker's artful absence may turn one to a conversation with oneself and with God.

Conclusion

The *Four Upbuilding Discourses* of 1843 present a connected series of meditations meant to aid the reader in acquiring the faith, gratitude, and patience exemplified by Job. His benediction, the keynote for his paradigmatic life, expresses a repetition. After the loss of his most central objects of concern, Job's faith, patience, and gratitude enable him to see again the meaning and significance of his world. Each of the other discourses attempts to cultivate in the reader one of those virtues, so that the reader's own story can also have the character of a repetition. Cultivating those virtues requires a transformation of moral perception, consisting in a renewed pattern of emotional responses, and received as a gift in the context of a confessional narrative.[34]

[34]I am grateful to Gregory Beabout and Robert Roberts, as well as to Robert Perkins and the anonymous readers for the *International Kierkegaard Commentary*, for helpful comments and criticisms.

11

Can Patience Be Taught?

David D. Possen

Meno asks Socrates, "Can virtue be taught?" (*Meno*, 70a). They haggle; Socrates, who insists that neither he nor his fellow citizens even know what virtue is (*Meno*, 71b), repeatedly invites Meno to examine the *nature* of virtue instead (*Meno*, 71d, 75b, 77b, 79e, 86c). But Meno will not be deterred from his original question (*Meno*, 86c). After surveying various self-proclaimed teachers of virtue, they arrive at an answer: *No*, at least not straightforwardly (*Meno*, 87d). The virtuous acquire their virtue only as a gift from the gods (*Meno*, 100b).

I ask: Does Kierkegaard believe that patience can be taught? Whereas Meno is motivated by the sight of Sophists plying a brisk trade in the teaching of virtue, I am driven by Kierkegaard's tantalizing title "Upbuilding." Can Kierkegaard "build" me "up," I wonder, without *teaching* me? I am further enticed by the individual titles of the *Eighteen Upbuilding Discourses*, which read like a list of exemplary human qualities: confidence, gratitude, love, inner strength, perseverance, patience, maturity, humility, courage. I can hardly open an "upbuilding discourse" entitled, for example, "To Gain One's Soul in Patience," without imagining that, in the pages I am about to read, Kierkegaard will *summon* me to patience, thereby *assisting* me to gain my soul.

Now, Kierkegaard explicitly addresses a listener with just such a reaction: "To gain one's soul in patience—are not these words . . . to the adult what a father's voice is to the child when he calls him from his noisy play, in which he was king and emperor, to the quiet task of patience?" (EUD, 159).

I believe the aim underlying this rhetorical question is, in fact, to prompt us to reflect critically on the reaction in question. In his closing paragraph, Kierkegaard admits that the discourse will inevitably fail to satisfy, will tempt his listener "to impatience in demanding a new discourse" (EUD, 175). On my reading, what the discourse fails to satisfy is precisely the listener's expectation of a primer in patience useful for gaining a soul. In fact, as it will become clear, such expectations would leave the reader with little patience for the discourse itself.

Before going further, let me specify exactly what I am asking. Does Kierkegaard believe patience—as he himself defines that term—can be taught? By "taught" I simply mean teaching as we usually encounter it, a process of motivating the student to learn, describing the relevant subject matter, and *aiding* the student to master the subject, whether by breaking the subject down into manageable steps (providing instructions), or by furnishing a compelling model of mastery (teaching by example). As I will explain, Kierkegaard's discourses on patience *do* provide not only ample description, but motivation as well: he praises patience, and, with cutting rhetorical questions, goads his listeners to search for it. However, *instructions* for patience are noticeably missing.

Instead, Kierkegaard directs us to an *exemplar*, the widow Anna. But Anna, as I will argue, in fact aids us much less as an example than as a riddle, as an arrow pointing to the secret of her own patience: a life illuminated by love for the dead. To explain this, I pursue my question with a stubbornness modeled on Meno's tenacity, and arrive at an answer not far from that of the *Meno*: No, not straightforwardly, not by the three discourses on patience, nor by anything *in* those discourses, either. Yet these three discourses turn out not to tell the whole story. My paper ends by following the riddle of Anna to two later texts on the educative power of death. I conclude by suggesting how Death, on Kierkegaard's account, *can* teach us earnestness, and can thereby assist us to discover, gain, and preserve our souls in patience.

Kierkegaard's Sense of Patience

Much as Meno and Socrates cannot address Meno's question without at least attempting to clarify the definition of virtue, some preliminary remarks on Kierkegaard's understanding of patience are warranted at this point. In his three discourses on patience, Kierkegaard employs that word (*Taalmodighed*; less frequently,

Taalmod) in a severely restricted sense of the word. Patience commonly refers to a variety of habits and behaviors we praise, inculcate, and hope to encounter. Thus, in childhood, patience is the capacity to wait; in social life, it is the habit of suspending judgment; in deliberation, it is the ability never to lose sight of what endures, to keep our eyes on the prize. Here, instead, we read: "Let us at least have the patience to believe the words, the patience not to postpone the deliberation until a more opportune time and, lacking this quality ourselves, the patience not to beg the words to have patience, the patience to separate what is inseparably joined in order to put it together again" (EUD, 160). The patience described here involves *suspending* intellectual caution and *refusing* to delay decision. It means refusing to depend on the patience of our beholder, personified here by the Gospel's own call to patience. Finally, *Taalmodighed* requires that we set aside an underlying truth—that we are all, at all times, already faced with a soul to lose or acquire—in order to learn to live according to that truth.

Our words *patience* and *passion* both derive from the Latin *pati*, which, like the Danish *taale*, root of *Taalmodighed*,[1] means to "suffer" in both that word's senses: suffering and sufferance. We commonly appreciate patience—the knack of suffering or sufferance—as a means to praiseworthy ends, from survival to serenity. In ordinary talk, writes Kierkegaard, "the condition for attaining what is desired is patience—therefore [one] is not really gaining patience but gaining what is coveted" (EUD, 161). Now, Kierkegaard does hold that *Taalmodighed* is the *condition* for acquiring a soul; in this case, however, "the condition stands in a special relation to the conditioned" (EUD, 167)—namely, "the condition and the conditioned are . . . inseparable" (EUD, 169). As we learn at the end of the discourse, the *means*—the gaining of

---

[1]In the text commonly known as *Purity of Heart*, Kierkegaard makes much of this etymology: "But what, then, is patience [*Taalmod*]? Is not patience the courage [*Mod*] that freely takes upon itself the suffering that cannot be avoided?" (UDVS, 118). Accordingly, Flemming Harrits analyzes Kierkegaardian *Taalmod* as "suffering's courage, a disposition suited to endure" (my translation). See Harrits, "Wortwörtlichkeit des Geistes," *Kierkegaard Studies Yearbook 2000*, ed. Niels Jørgen Cappelørn, Hermann Deuser, and Jon Stewart (Berlin: de Gruyter, 2000) 127.

patience—turns out to be coextensive with the *end*—the very gaining of the soul itself: "The person who wants to gain his soul in patience . . . never abandons patience, not when he has gained it, since it was indeed patience that he gained, and as soon as he gives up patience, he gives up the acquisition again" (EUD, 174). In other words, summoning me to patience cannot *assist* me to gain my soul, but *is* nothing other than to summon me to gain my soul. We must therefore avoid the trap set for us in the title, that is, refuse to inhabit the fantasy that patience can be acquired in some useful, separate step, as an undertaking more manageable than the larger task of gaining a soul.[2]

When I ask, then, whether or not Kierkegaard believes patience can be taught, I am asking nothing less than the question, "Does Kierkegaard believe the gaining and preserving of souls can be taught?" This, in turn, is an instance, restricted to the trilogy of discourses on patience, of three general questions on the intent and effect of the book as a whole, of "upbuilding" communication itself: How does Kierkegaard believe he can *help* us? What do "upbuilding discourses" *teach* us? Last, how do they actually *change* us?

Does Kierkegaard, then, believe patience be taught? The texts present conflicting answers. The first two discourses on patience are threaded with self-referential passages, which depict communication about patience as an enterprise fraught with confusion and subject to stark limitations. The third discourse, on the other hand, offers Anna, a human exemplar of patience. Let us examine these texts, then, one by one.

To Gain One's Soul in Patience: Standards for Speaker and Listener

The literary engines of an upbuilding discourse are its incisive rhetorical questions. By their sheer frequency, they evoke the press

---

[2]Here I follow George Pattison, who writes: "Patience is not simply a *means* to the end of acquiring a self, not just one condition of selfhood among others, but . . . it is precisely in and by becoming patient that we also 'acquire' a self." See Pattison, *Kierkegaard: The Aesthetic and the Religious* (New York: St. Martin's Press, 1992) 160-61. Beyond this point, however, my reading diverges from Pattison's, as I indicate in nn. 6 and 7 below.

and intensity of dialogue: the reader, addressed directly, is held in place, bound to agree or disagree on each point before proceeding. This can be tiring for the interpreter, who faces the constant temptation to reduce each question to the proposition it rhetorical-ly espouses. For us, however, it will often prove fruitful to resist this urge, and to hunt instead for answers in the questions' wording, sequence, and trajectory.

The opening of "To Gain One's Soul In Patience" paints patience not as trait or knack but as something that *comes*: it is unassuming, yet blessed with quiet grandeur. Patience comes as a poor, unadorned bird; as a soft breeze; then, as "the incorruptible essence of a quiet spirit" (EUD, 159). The last phrase is Scriptural, contrasting gaudy female sensuality with the human being's hidden, imperishable (*aphthartos*) core, deeply cherished by God (1 Peter 3:3-4).[3] Next, the relation between patience and life is specified by the Hippocratic formula *ars longa, vita brevis*:

> Patience is a poor art, and yet it is very long. Who learned it properly from life—who had the patience for that? Who taught it to another person in the right way—ah, perhaps there was someone who taught another patience very well by being very impatient himself! Who spoke fittingly about it, so that he did not rush into impatience of expression and hastiness of phrase? Who listened to the discourse about it in the right way, so that he did not understand it and then impatiently demanded a new discourse and thus certainly comprehended patience and the discourse about it but did not comprehend that it was not to be understood in that way! (EUD, 159)

Patience, here, is not an art characterized by its uses for life; rather, life itself is too short to encompass the art of patience. This prompts a series of questions. Can patience nonetheless be *learned* from life? This question is quickly answered by the wording of the next, "Who had the patience for that?" In other words, to learn

---

[3]The same phrase is employed in part one of *Either/Or*: it is the standard by which A diagnoses the ceaseless yearning behind Marie Beaumarchais's veil of sorrow as fruitless vacillation, rather than patient expectancy. Marie's heart is not the "incorruptible essence of a quiet spirit," but the "barren busyness of a restless spirit" (EO, 1:184). For a brief discussion of this diagnosis, see Harvie Ferguson's *Melancholy and the Critique of Modernity: Søren Kierkegaard's Religious Psychology* (London: Routledge, 1995) 91-92.

patience from life, one must already possess patience. This line of inquiry, it seems, will not teach us how patience can be learned in the first place.

If I cannot learn patience from my own life, can I at least learn it from another's? Can patience be taught me? The succeeding question casts doubt even on this hope: perhaps the *impatience* of another is as good a teacher as any. The question that follows next, however, calls our attention to another way of speaking about patience—soon identified as "the discourse"—which is "fitting" insofar as it avoids hypocrisy, that is, as it avoids impatience in *words*.

We seem, then, to be rushing toward an answer. Evidently, if *any* text can teach us patience—not by plunging us into an encounter with another's impatience, but by teaching us as we are usually taught, with descriptions, recommendations, and instructions—then "the discourse" can, whether the one we are holding, or another, superior to it.[4] If so, then we are left with only a single worry: *How* do we learn patience from such a discourse?

The wording of Kierkegaard's final question, however, suggests a difficulty: the right way to listen to the discourse is not the right way to understand patience. I have listened properly to the discourse only when I have *failed* to understand it and have demanded a new one. In so doing I have "comprehended patience and the discourse about it," in other words, beheld the two side by side, and recoiled from the difference between them. But I have still not understood patience. In its proper listeners, therefore, the discourse in fact prompts *impatience*: an insightful, revolutionary impatience perhaps, but impatience nonetheless.

We have so far analyzed the *wording* of the last question, but not the question itself. What it asks is, "Who?" Who listened properly to the discourse? Did you? Since this is the first page of his first published discourse on patience, Kierkegaard is obviously not expecting an immediate answer. Rather, this question, like its

---

[4]Kierkegaard's questions regarding "the discourse," as I mention and cite below, are repeated on the final page of this discourse (EUD, 175), where their self-reference is no longer ambiguous. I infer that *these* instances of the phrase "the discourse" are self-referential as well, and, accordingly, drop the quotation marks in what follows.

predecessor, is intended to dog us while we read and confront us when we are finished. The two questions thus constitute a working contract of sorts, with goals for both author and reader. We ought not finish Kierkegaard's discourse without asking: Has he spoken fittingly about patience? Have we listened well?

In fact, we *cannot* avoid these questions at the end of the discourse, since Kierkegaard abruptly repeats them in his concluding paragraph:

> Should we now ask, "Who described this conflict properly?" As if the proclamation were not always imperfect, and as if the proclamation were not always something other than the gain? As if the description would not tempt the speaker to impatience in the expression of passion and the listener to impatience in listening and to impatience in demanding a new discourse, whether he found the one heard to be too elaborate (and then the speaker should praise him if it did not mean that his soul was utterly thoughtless) or too simple, which certainly should not be praised (for the person who thinks that multiplicity and multitudinousness assist him in the gain is like the person who believes that simplicity stops him), since only the simple is an assistance. Or was not the description itself something that the world and time were capable of taking away without taking away the patience and the gain that is in patience, which even in the moment of death gains a person his soul for the eternal if he dies in patience? (EUD, 175)

These convoluted sentences deserve extra attention, not only as the end of this discourse, but as the last paragraph of the volume (the *Four Upbuilding Discourses* of 1843). How are we to read these words, particularly as *parting* words?

In the first line, one question lies nested in another. What would it mean to ask here, "Who has properly described the conflict between patience and impatience?" Presumably, since Kierkegaard's discourse nowhere compares itself to discourses by others, to ask the question rhetorically is to prompt one of two replies. Either Kierkegaard himself has written a proper discourse, or no one has, because no one can.

Yet in the first line's frame, as in the remainder of the paragraph, Kierkegaard directs us *away* from that question. This serves, I submit, similarly to direct us away from either of the above "answers," and thus to allow Kierkegaard to defend the discourse, in what follows, as something entirely other than a success or a failure.

Two rhetorical questions follow, both of the form "As if it were not the case that. . . . " Such phrasing signals the dismantling of fantasies. First, there is the mirage mentioned in this essay's introduction: the expectation of a perfect discourse that can assist me toward the "gain." Second, there is the illusion that such a discourse can steer clear of the Scylla and Charybdis of Kierkegaard's opening paragraph: the speaker's temptation to impatience of speech, coupled with the listener's to "impatience in listening" and "impatience in demanding a new discourse." Here, however, these pitfalls seem unavoidable in any "description."

Kierkegaard began, we saw, with three suggestions: that the right way to teach patience may well be *impatiently*; that only a discourse that avoids impatient language is "fitting"; and that the right way to listen to the discourse may well be to cry foul and demand a new one. This passage explicitly endorses the last suggestion (provided that what is demanded is a *simpler* discourse). And what of the first two? In my view, since the passage calls into question whether anyone can write without impatience, it is more compatible with the first than with the second.

Taken together, on my reading, these passages discourage the assumption that, to find a discourse effective in teaching patience, we ought to measure the degrees of patience within a discourse, in its speaker's style, or in its listeners' docility. Instead, it seems, patience is best provoked by the shock of *example*—specifically, by examples of impatience. A teacher's impatient lapse can sharpen our senses, and lead us, through self-criticism, to avoid his missteps. Our own impatient rejection of a discourse can similarly hone our sight; without self-criticism, however, we cannot employ this sight to find patience in ourselves. As it turns out, then, a discourse on patience is effective insofar as it provokes me to confront impatience *in existence*. So the question "Can this discourse, or any, teach me patience?" is best addressed not to the discourse, nor to Kierkegaard, but is a question for each of us, to be asked anew at each reading.[5]

---

[5]On this point I agree emphatically with Flemming Harrits, who asserts, at the

We are left with Kierkegaard's parting question. Is not the discourse perishable, he asks, hence incidental to patience and its imperishable power, "which even in the moment of death gains a person his soul for the eternal if he dies in patience?" (EUD, 175). Although the first half suggests that no discourse can, in itself, convey patience (let alone teach it), the final clauses strain against these limits by urging us: at least *die* in patience! How are we to read this?

In my view, the question's two parts are linked by the theme of *mortality*. Discourses are perishable, like human lives; patience cannot be gleaned from a book, just as it cannot be learned afresh from life-experience (EUD, 159). Rather, patience can be developed in the self-scrutiny that is prompted by encounters with *impatience*, encounters that may certainly be occasioned in lives and discourses.[6] The end of the discourse and the volume, like the death of another, is an occasion particularly evocative of impatient reactions, and simultaneously a time especially ripe for the self-scrutiny patience demands.

---

climax of his essay "Wortwörtlichkeit des Geistes," that the discourses generally

> are thought of, spoken, and written as a musical score, intended for those who care to read it aloud and thereby to endow it with its own voice, so that the reader can speak, hear, and—perhaps—understand herself or himself in the libretto. . . . Haunted by the possibility that it may, as a source of authority, miss its notes, the discourse *refuses* to be didactic, much less admonitory; it would rather act with no authority other than what the addressee confers upon it. The discourses, therefore, are not designed "for upbuilding another," as if they came from an outsider; on the contrary, they are self-referential, and "upbuilding" *inter pares*. (Harrits, "Wortwörtlichkeit," 133; my translation.)

[6]Commentators on the *Discourses* rarely mention Kierkegaard's view that an appropriate dose of impatience is indispensable for edification. Harvie Ferguson in fact denies this: "Impatience of any sort is inimical to spiritual growth" (*Melancholy*, 196). George Pattison, meanwhile, identifies the forms of impatience with the forms of despair; this simplistic equation, in my view, mars his otherwise promising account of patience (*Kierkegaard*, 162, 198-99n.). An exception is Sylvia Walsh, who draws on Kierkegaard's distinction between apostolic impatience and "the rashness of an excited person" (EUD, 70). In "When 'That Single Individual' is a Woman," Walsh sketches a Kierkegaardian ideal that incorporates both apostolic impatience and patient expectancy (*Kierkegaard Studies Yearbook 2000*, 15).

We have not yet, however, satisfactorily accounted for the form of Kierkegaard's last words: why end with a question? Part of the reason, as I have mentioned, is the rhetorical question's curious ability to *goad* a reader who would remain detached—something which Kierkegaard's declarative sentences and mine cannot do. Yet surely there is more to this choice. Isn't it possible that Kierkegaard wishes to leave the final question's door ajar by a crack? Isn't it possible that he wants to preserve the tantalizing possibility that the imperishable can take on substance in a book—indeed, may already have, in what we might call a Book—which, though ostensibly perishable, can nonetheless teach? Or, repeating the analogy of books and lives, what if Kierkegaard similarly means to preserve the possibility of patience embodied in a human exemplar? We have spoken of examples of impatience as instructive; what, then, of an example of patience, and of a discourse that celebrates such an example?

To Preserve One's Soul in Patience: Letting Patience Speak

When we move from the first discourse on patience to the second, we are passing from winter to spring, from December 1843 to March 1844, to a thin new book (*Two Upbuilding Discourses*) dedicated entirely to patience. Once again, a title tempts, this one with the thought that we are making progress, since to preserve we must have already gained. The sense that we have moved on to new material is reinforced by Kierkegaard's long, enthralling introduction. He engages the standard heroic equation between superhuman endurance and earthly life-threatening dangers, only to overturn that equation by insisting that spiritual danger is the deeper threat (EUD, 181-85). "To lose one's soul," Kierkegaard argues, *that* "is the danger; that is the terrible thing, and what one does not preserve one can indeed lose. Thought itself scarcely comprehends this horror. Language is unable to articulate it clearly. Only the soul's anxiety has a presentiment of what the obscure talk is about" (EUD, 185). But if words themselves cannot fully describe the danger, how can the words of the discourse teach us to avoid it? The end of the introduction provides the answer:

> Just as there is only one means for preserving [the soul], so is this means necessary even in order to understand that it must be preserved, and if this were not the case, the means would not be the only means. This means is patience. A person does not first gain his soul and then have the need for patience to preserve it, but he gains it in no other way than by preserving it. . . . *To preserve one's soul in patience* [is] through patience to ascertain what it is that one has to preserve. If a person does not use the help of patience, he may, with all his efforts and diligence, come to preserve something else and thereby to have lost his soul. (EUD, 187)

Thought and language, we saw above, cannot give the mind a firm hold on the horror of losing the soul; but patience alone, this passage indicates, allows us to draw from this horror its only lesson—that we must not lose our souls—and patience alone allows us to respond appropriately.

The sentences just quoted further clarify the relation between the two discourses. I do not first gain my soul, then preserve it; rather, I gain my soul *by* preserving it.[7] How do I preserve my soul? In patience. What does this mean? By detecting, or discovering, my soul, that is, by distinguishing the imperishable in me from the perishable. As the end of the passage makes clear, any attempt to preserve the self without patience is an objectless conservatism, a foolish consistency not merely little-minded, but void of soul.

Banish, then, another fantasy. Though we have opened a new book, we have *not* moved on to a new topic, or stage, in upbuilding; only our angle of approach, perhaps, has changed. Acquiring the soul, we saw, is coextensive with acquiring patience; preserving the soul, we now learn, is similarly coextensive with patience; and to acquire the soul *is* to preserve it. What is at stake in all three—patience, gaining one's soul, preserving one's soul—is the discovery, in self-scrutiny, of the imperishable. But this is precisely

---

[7]This marks my second point of disagreement with George Pattison. According to Pattison, "once we have 'in patience' acquired a 'soul,' we cannot just leave patience behind but must 'in patience' 'preserve' the 'soul' we have in this way 'acquired' " (*Kierkegaard*, 161). Such a sequential view, however, ignores Kierkegaard's claim that one "gains [his soul] in no other way than by preserving it" (EUD, 187).

what cannot be *taught*: there are no instructions to fill a manual. Perhaps we can, as I have been suggesting, be shocked into self-scrutiny by encounters with impatience. Perhaps we can, as I will next discuss, derive inspiration from exemplars of patience. But these possibilities are beyond the scope of a *discourse*. A discourse succeeds in affecting the individual precisely insofar as the individual discovers self-scrutiny for himself. As Flemming Harrits writes of the discourse in general, "Its [specifically] written character fades; it becomes what in a double sense it [already] was and is: a speech of turning toward the self."[8]

In arguing that the underlying topic has not changed, I do not mean to neglect the value of "To Preserve One's Soul In Patience" as a separate piece. To the contrary, that discourse sets forth, in my view, two arguments crucial to Kierkegaard's account of his communicative technique. In the first such argument, Kierkegaard answers an objection to his use of three archetypal fables to address the reader personally. Each tale depicts a "young person" setting out upon the path of life. In the first, the youth masterfully completes his journey, fortified by patience; in the latter two, the youth is overwhelmed by fortune and misfortune, respectively, and soon becomes mired in impatience (EUD, 192-95). To listeners who refuse to see themselves in these parabolic sketches, Kierkegaard replies as follows:

> So, then, the young person went out into the world. My listener, whether this discourse seems like an old story that wants to anticipate what you are just about to do, or whether it comes afterward like an old story about what you left behind long ago, this is how it is, this is how the young person goes out into the world. But the next part, yes, it is very different, and the single individual—well, if the discourse were to address all individuals, then each one might shake his head and say, "No, it did not happen that way with me; my experience was very different from what you are talking about." Perhaps so; the discourse certainly desires no praise. But would not this emphasis on the different, if it becomes a staring at heterogeneity, have a certain similarity to the wish, and [would not] impatience, which once was the ingratiating friend, become the ingenious confidant? Try to break with it sometime, and then you will see how this thought

---

[8]Harrits, "Wortwörtlichkeit," 133; my translation.

becomes violent and vehemently complains about patience, as if it wants to make life sheer boredom, wants to make everyone a poor repetition of the same. And yet if unity does not lie at the base of diversity, similarity at the base of dissimilarity, then everything has disintegrated. If, then, no one else dares to say a well-intentioned word against the diversity that will enrich life to the point of disorder, patience does. . . . Patience wants to preserve only the soul; it has the courage to give up everything else. (EUD, 192-93)

In my view, this is an ingenious—and telling—argument. We surely agree, Kierkegaard asserts confidently, that the sketches' uniform beginning, "The young person went out into the world," is relevant to one and all. The disagreements only start later—in the details of the journey. The parables describe only three fates: mastery of life in patience; surrender to impatience amid good fortune; and surrender to impatience amid misfortune. You may certainly object that your particular journey fits none of these types. But does not your objection then betray your own resistance to patience? Just try relinquishing your objection, and you will *feel* this resistance.

The argument works so well on us because Kierkegaard, at this point, so smoothly substitutes "patience" for "the discourse." Describing his thought experiment's certain results, Kierkegaard predicts that the mind will blame *patience*—not the discourse, nor the fables' author—for wanting "to make life sheer boredom" (EUD, 193). The switch is natural, since patience is the fabular sketches' chief criterion, and is in that sense their instigator. Yet, however natural, the switch has another effect, suspiciously convenient for Kierkegaard's defense of the discourse: the point of view of the discourse, which classifies all adult lives according to the three fables, turns out to be identical to that of patience itself. This emerges bluntly in the passage's final sentences. It is *patience* that dares to deny diversity by promulgating the parables, whose leveling of human lives is, in fact, *constitutive* of patience's concern for the soul.

In this discourse, then, Kierkegaard offers us a metaphor for upbuilding: patience is a summoning standard, personifiable by the discourse and by two Scriptural phrases,[9] that will, if only we let it, identify and preserve our souls. For example: "The words came to your mind, and your soul became sober again, and patience began its good work again" (EUD, 202). By investing the Gospel words, and the discourse itself, with the authority of patience, the metaphor encourages us to think that the words themselves can teach us patience.

Kierkegaard ultimately retracts the metaphor, but it is a defensive and strangely situated retraction. First, the discourse announces its abrupt end: "Praised be the God of patience. This is the end of the discourse" (EUD, 202). Then, immediately *after* the declared "end," come two more paragraphs, followed by a repeated announcement of the "end."

> We have spoken about the power of patience to preserve the soul. We have spoken as if patience were outside a person; we are well aware that this is not so. And nevertheless I ask you . . . since you have known it better, more inwardly, and for a longer time—was it nevertheless not so at times, when concern and your laboring thoughts piled up deliberations that were of no benefit except to give birth to new deliberations, that then the plain, simple, but nevertheless forgotten words of patience prodded you from another direction, was it not as if patience stood on the outside? We have made it appear is if patience were outside, and we have let it speak, as it were, for itself. Who speaks properly about it? The older person[,] venerable in patience? . . . But sometimes it is not easy for the older person to speak simply, solely, and purely out of patience and to witness only to that. He saw much, he experienced much, he learned many priceless words, which still are not those of patience but of life experience, with which he can benefit himself, also others, but not always another.
>
> The younger person knows so little; the moment may come when it is manifest that he exerted his thought and eloquence for nothing, that his words were a fraud, not to deceive others, far from it, but a fraud in which he himself was deceived. Then he will even have done damage, done damage with the view that perhaps could not be carried through, done damage by making people busy themselves with ridiculing the physician who cannot help himself, ridiculing the one who was strong in patience at a

---

[9]"This very day," Luke 23:43, and "God will make the temptation and its outcome such that we can bear it," 1 Corinthians 10:13 (EUD, 200-201).

distance and thereby forgetting to pay heed to themselves and to consider the business that every human being has with himself. This, you see, is why we chose to let patience itself speak! It does not seek confirmation in someone's experience, but, as it says, will gloriously strengthen every experience. . . . Praised be the God of patience. This is the end of this discourse. (EUD, 202-203)

Let us first address the doubled assertion, "This is the end of this discourse." I prefer to avoid reducing the matter to a logic puzzle, where precisely one of the two sentences must be adjudged true, the other false, depending on where the discourse *really* ends. I will instead say simply that Kierkegaard casts doubt on these paragraphs' status: are they included, or not, in the discourse?

Assume they are not. Then these paragraphs constitute an apologetic appendix or postscript, designed to defend the discourse's practice of letting patience "speak for itself" as an outside force, that is, by speaking in the name of patience. Although he admits the metaphor misleads, Kierkegaard offers three justifications for it: (1) the metaphor matches how we hallucinate the voice of patience during bouts of *impatience*; (2) older people, though "venerable in patience," cannot isolate their accomplishments in patience from the broader tapestry of their life-experience, and digest them into communicable form; (3) younger people lack the life-experience to avoid self-deception, and thus risk inviting the ridicule of listeners whom they mean to be urging to self-scrutiny. The metaphor thus allows the discourse to sidestep challenges to its relevance, and speak with the authority of the listener's existing impatient fantasies.

Now assume these paragraphs *do* have the last word. Then Kierkegaard's retraction of the central metaphor is integral, not auxiliary, to the discourse. Reinterpreting the rest of the passage in this light, we now see three further complications. (1') Since the discourse both depicts and assumes the role of patience as it appears to an impatient person, it follows that, insofar as the metaphor helps change us, it does so precisely by leading us to encounter *impatience*. This can lead to patience, as I have argued, but it is not the same as to teach it. (2') In fact, no one, however aged or venerable, can *teach* patience. (3') The young speaker—indeed, Kierkegaard himself—must continually struggle to keep the listeners' attention directed inward.

On both readings, the central rhetorical question, "Who speaks properly about it?", suggests that neither an old nor a young speaker can do so. The discourse's employment of the voice of patience is, then, a semi-pseudonymous attempt to jump the fences restraining direct communication. Does the attempt succeed? The discourse's enigmatic ending suggests an equivocal answer. In vividly simulating, and informing, the experience of impatience—perhaps. In simulating and informing the experience of patience—perhaps not. We turn, therefore, to the one possibility left unexplored: communication through a human exemplar of patience.

Patience in Expectancy: The Case of Anna

Kierkegaard's final discourse on patience differs in several obvious ways from the previous two. "The soul" has vanished from the title; the term "expectancy" takes center stage; most important, Kierkegaard introduces us to Anna, exemplar of patience in expectancy. How, exactly, is "patience in expectancy" related to the task of patience set forth in the first two discourses? Andrew Burgess explains the relations among patience, expectancy, and "patience in expectancy" as follows: expectancy is the hallmark of true patience, while one's degree of patience serves as a barometer of the merits of one's expectancy; "patience in expectancy" refers precisely to this complementary function, in which each serves as the criterion for the other's appropriateness.[10] But patience and expectancy are also, it turns out, mutual prerequisites: "Only the true expectancy, which requires patience, also teaches patience" (EUD, 221). To learn patience, then, means to acquire it in expectancy; but this does not simplify our problem, unless Kierkegaard can actually *teach* us patience in expectancy through Anna's example.

To do this, he must first persuade us to take Anna as an exemplar valid and compelling for *us*. Remarkably, with the exception of a single passage arguing that "the most profound expression in language must call" Anna "the expectant one" (EUD,

---

[10]Andrew Burgess, "Patience and Expectancy in Kierkegaard's Upbuilding Discourses," in *Kierkegaard Studies Yearbook 2000*, 209.

224), Kierkegaard influences us to accept Anna as exemplar not by assertion, but by prodding us, once again, with rhetorical questions. *"Is Anna, then, not expectant?"* (EUD, 210). *"Is Anna not patient in expectancy?"* (EUD, 213). *"Is Anna not patient in her expectancy?"* (EUD, 219). Kierkegaard defends this strategy as a way of holding his readers' impatience at bay: "If I were to add, 'This is what expectancy looks like,' and go on to say, 'Oh, that it might always look like this!'—there might be someone who impatiently would turn away from this same picture" (EUD, 212). Rather, the rhetorical questions force us to give Anna a chance to serve us as an instructive example. Unfortunately, we next learn, we will not be in a position to *understand* Anna until we have become like her: "Not until a person tries his hand at it in such a way that he . . . chooses expectancy, not until then can Anna truly become the object of contemplation" (EUD, 212).

This daunting caveat notwithstanding, we will need to start somewhere in interpreting Anna and the discourse; its Scriptural roots are as good a place as any. Two witnesses observe the presentation of the Christ child at the Temple in Jerusalem: a man named Simeon, and a prophetess named Anna (Luke 2:25, 36). In his retelling, Kierkegaard works to draw us to Anna: "The Gospel just read mentions Simeon only briefly but dwells all the more solicitously on Anna, as if it first and foremost wanted to make her the object of our attention" (EUD, 208). This is, I daresay, misleading. Anna rates two descriptive verses to Simeon's one, true, but Simeon is the sole actor in ten of the eleven verses describing the encounter, while Anna's only role is to thank God and spread the word to "all those patiently awaiting (*tois prosdechomenois*)" (Luke 2:38). Most intriguingly, while the description of Anna gives parentage and a brief personal history, it is the description of Simeon that confirms we have found the exemplar we seek: Simeon is "just and pious, patiently anticipating (*prosdechomenos*) Israel's aid" (Luke 2:25).

Instead, Kierkegaard chooses Anna. He assumes, evidently, that the Gospel's juxtaposing her to Simeon and to the other expectant ones indicates that she, too, is *prosdechomene*, and that her brief biography serves as a study in patient anticipation. This is a reasonable and useful assumption, since the figure of Simeon, defined as patiently expectant and little else, cannot teach us how to imitate his example. Yet it is noteworthy that Kierkegaard does not make clearer what he is doing: investing an unobtrusive New Testament woman with apostolic authority.

A superb essay by Mark Lloyd Taylor surveys Kierkegaard's entire upbuilding literature and argues that "Kierkegaard's portrayal of several apostolic women provides him with the opportunity to practice the apostolic authority he otherwise eschews."[11] Taylor enumerates six such women, then elaborates: "Kierkegaard in telling their stories lets the apostolic authority of the New Testament authors speak without needing to claim the title of apostle for himself."[12] Unlike Anna, all the women Taylor's essay describes encounter the adult Jesus; all are nameless, or named Mary. Insofar as these women "see Jesus Christ in his abasement and love him nonetheless," these women "present a picture and a prototype or pattern for all subsequent Christians. They show with singular clarity how one should seek and receive forgiveness. The fact that they are *women* emerges as crucial to Kierkegaard's depiction," since woman's "inner life is simpler, more unified; she finds it easier to come to a decision without the endless, stalling deliberations typical of a man."[13]

It is noteworthy that Anna does not make Taylor's list, considering that Kierkegaard similarly portrays her as an example: "The most profound expression in language must call her in the strictest and noblest sense: the expectant one" (EUD, 224). I do not know Taylor's reasons, but I agree with his decision. Not only is Anna's role too minute, her encounter with Jesus too formal and too early, but in her role as exemplar of patience in expectancy, she does *not*, I contend, "show with singular clarity how one should" anticipate in patience.

What is exemplary about Anna? She is eighty-four years old, widowed after only seven years of marriage, and committed to a life of fasting and prayer in the Temple (Luke 2:37-38). It is precisely in what she does *not* do—remarry, bear children, or

---

[11]Mark Lloyd Taylor, "Practice in Authority: The Apostolic Women of Søren Kierkegaard's Writings," in *Anthropology and Authority: Essays on Søren Kierkegaard*, ed. P. Houe, G. Marino, and S. H. Rossel (Amsterdam: Rodopi, 2000) 86.

[12]Taylor, "Practice," 87.

[13]Taylor, "Practice," 87-88.

generally develop loving family ties—rather than in what she does do, that Anna distinguishes herself. The *fact* of her long, static widowhood demonstrates, to Kierkegaard, that Anna "chose to remain faithful to her late husband, as he had been faithful to her, or to say it in another and more truthful way, even though it might not seem as beautiful to her, she chose to remain true to herself; after all, every external bond was dissolved, and only that love bound her in which she had her freedom and without which she would not have known herself again" (EUD, 209). The phrases "only that love" and "without which" bear considerable load here: Anna's spiritual achievements would have been impossible, claims Kierkegaard, without her love for her late husband. Thus we seem to be on the verge, at last, of a set of *instructions*: like Anna, love only the dead, and you will have the freedom to discover yourself. Does this also apply, in particular, to patience in expectancy?

Just before the end of the discourse, Kierkegaard performs a thought experiment whose results furnish this final link:

> What if Anna had been a mother, what if the one dead had remained with her . . . what if the child now being presented had been [her great-grandson], what if three generations had never forgotten her?—And now! Anna had experienced the pain of life and had sown with tears, had lost her husband early, since then had remained childless and forsaken; then in her eighty-fourth year she came forth in the temple, concealed the expectancy of all ages in her devout figure, and so she stands, always remembered as the witness of expectancy.—Blessed is the one who became poor and forsaken, blessed is the barren one, blessed is the one who lost the world in such a way that expectancy's desire for it never awakened in his soul, blessed is the one whose expectancy walked through the gate of death into the eternal in order to apprehend his expectation until he saw it with earthly eyes and did not desire to see it anymore in time. (EUD, 225)

If we are to take Anna seriously as an exemplar of patience in expectancy, it seems, we must concede that the fact of her widowhood is indispensable to her achievement, much as, conversely, married life would have been exclusive of it. The blessings that follow, meanwhile, encourage us to emulate, or at least appreciate, a life without family ties, and end by directing our attention, as at the close of "To Gain One's Soul in Patience," to the decisive test of death.

But this return to the moment of death—the universal doom as well as, Christianly, the universal opportunity for salvation—is, I believe, an important hint. Does Kierkegaard *really* intend, by furnishing us with Anna as an exemplar, to convince us that patience demands a childless, unmarried life? On my reading, Kierkegaard tempts us to think so—then backtracks hastily in the discourse's final paragraph:

> If, however, a person knew how to make himself truly what he truly is—nothing—knew how to set the seal of patience on what he had understood—ah, then his life, whether he is the greatest or the lowliest, would even today be a joyful surprise and be filled with blessed wonder and would be that throughout all his days, because there is truly only one eternal object of wonder—that is God—and only one possible hindrance to wonder—and that is a person when he himself wants to be something. (EUD, 226)

How can we reconcile this with what has come before? How can Anna's patience be entirely dependent on the mere fact of her widowhood, as the two previous passages suggest, when patience in general, as these words imply, is available to the "greatest" and the "lowliest" alike?

The answer can only be, I contend, that the thrust of the earlier passages is not to limit patience to the barren and forsaken, but rather to insist that only a single set of life experiences can teach us patience, namely, experiences of loving the dead. I base my claim on the following passage, which I consider to be Kierkegaard's clearest explication, and most convincing recommendation, of the figure of Anna:

> [Anna] remained faithful to the departed one, and she considered herself well taken care of, as she was indeed, since there is nothing that so forms, ennobles, and sanctifies a person as the memory of one who is dead hidden in a sincere heart; there is nothing that next to God himself so uncompromisingly tests and searches a person's innermost being as does a commemoration of one who is dead preserved in an always present memory; there is nothing that maintains a person's soul in this kind of persevering and faithful endurance as does the thought of one who is dead, which never slumbers. . . . The person who loves one who is dead serves his entire life for his love. (EUD, 210)

Here is the true *sine qua non* of Anna's exemplary patience: her love for her departed husband. And precisely this love for the dead, on my reading, is the teacher we have been seeking. For nothing, "next to God himself," can prompt fruitful self-scrutiny as this love can; similarly, nothing can preserve—hence gain—one's soul as this love can. What is essential in such love is not that it replaces or excludes marriage, but rather that it regrounds life itself and all of its commitments, from the greatest to the lowliest.

All this sounds promising, and spurs a final question: *How*, exactly, does the relation to the dead accomplish this? But our brief passage, published in 1844, does not say. Now, I believe an answer does emerge in later writings on the same theme, particularly in the 1845 discourse "At a Graveside" (TDIO, 69-102), and in "The Work of Love in Recollecting One Who Is Dead," published in 1847 as chapter 9 of *Works of Love*. I will turn to this answer in my concluding remarks. Here, however, I want to stick to the three discourses on patience, and repeat my original question: Does Kierkegaard believe patience can be taught?

I say that the question cannot be answered from within our chosen discourses. Consider: we have chased the question from discourse to discourse, from concept to concept, and have wound up with a *hint*. To acquire patience, we saw, is no lesser a task than to gain one's soul; this, in turn, is no lesser a task than to preserve one's soul; and nothing can accomplish this last—we have just learned—as love of the dead can. Meanwhile, we learned what *isn't* a teacher of patience: Kierkegaard's discourse cannot teach it directly. No living speaker, however old or venerable, can teach it directly. "Only the true expectancy," we then learned, "teaches patience"; but expectancy also "requires patience" (EUD, 221). So we are really seeking a teacher of patience *in* expectancy. Can Anna, the exemplar, teach us this? If so, then only to one who has already *chosen* expectancy (EUD, 212). In a sense, this is a welcome result, for it confirms that the figure of Anna, like the personification of patience in the second discourse, does not do anything that Kierkegaard has claimed, in the self-referential passages we have cited, is beyond the scope of a discourse. On the other hand, this result leaves us no better off than Socrates and Meno, denied the pleasure of a clear answer.

We find ourselves in a maze, with at most one way out: to follow Anna back to her own teacher,[14] to the source of her own patience in expectancy—that being not the mere fact of her widowhood, but its secret, "the memory of one who is dead hidden in a sincere heart" (EUD, 210). But this topic is taken up in full only elsewhere. Thus it is that, in chasing patience's teacher, we have been tracking a series of conceptual "arrows," statements that define patience in terms of further, prerequisite concepts to be elaborated. But each arrow has pointed only to another, and the chase has led us across all three discourses, with few results. Ironically, our most hopeful sign comes here, as we contemplate an arrow that points out of the book itself, to the realm of Death, where "all paths meet" (WL, 345), and where, presumably, all arrows end.

Afterword

I have hinted that "At a Graveside" and "The Work of Love in Recollecting One who is Dead" together provide an account of how a relation to death can teach us many things, patience among them. I will conclude with a brief sketch of this account, together with its implications for the question with which I began.

"Patience in Expectancy," we saw, ends with the recommendation that a person "make himself truly what he truly is—nothing," since a person's "desire to be something" is what hinders him (EUD, 226). *Works of Love* offers a helpful rejoinder: "No one can make himself *no one* as well as one who is dead, because he is no one" (WL, 347). The dead one can, as an example of being

---

[14]It is precisely here, for the first time, that the parallel with the *Meno* breaks down completely. Both Socrates and Anna exemplify patience, meditate on death, and, instead of lecturing or providing a doctrine, exhibit their excellence in their existence (I owe this thought to Robert Perkins, in correspondence). However, whereas Plato offers little in the way of instructions for emulating Socrates (notoriously, many interlocutors exit their encounters with Socrates unaltered or even worsened), Kierkegaard does provide general accounts of what can be instructive—to us as to Anna—in three types of encounter with death: love of the dead, shame before the dead, and the earnest thought of death itself.

"nothing" and as a reminder of our own inability to do so, make us aware of our own presumption in a way no living speaker can. This is because "one who is dead is no actual object; he is only the occasion that continually discloses what resides in the one living who relates himself to him" (WL, 347). Encountering the dead, then, provokes the constant self-scrutiny we saw is constitutive for patience. "In the relationship to one who is dead, you have the criterion by which you can test yourself" (WL, 358).[15] Accordingly, Kierkegaard simply urges us to "Go out and practice it; recollect the one who is dead and just in this way learn to love the living unselfishly, freely, faithfully" (WL, 358). The lesson seems simple: merely recall a dead one lovingly—a typical (if occasional) human activity, and therefore one that need not be taught separately—but do so earnestly and continuously, and you will learn to live and love others as you should.[16]

"At a Graveside" offers similar recommendations, but emphasizes less one's love for the dead than the thought of one's own

---

[15]In the text commonly known as *Purity of Heart*, Kierkegaard offers parallel observations under the rubric of "a beneficial sense of shame" (UDVS, 52-55). Even where there are others who properly inspire such shame, insists Kierkegaard, if that "is to become truly beneficial to the modest person, it is still an unavoidable condition that he be most ashamed before himself. Therefore it is legitimate to say that it is truly most beneficial for a person to have a sense of shame before one who is dead, and if he has it before a living person, then to have it before him as before one who is dead" (UDVS, 54). In other words, admonished regard for the dead teaches admonished self-regard, which is the prerequisite for properly admonished regard for others. Recollecting the dead in shame thus serves as an educative withdrawal from the society of the living, a withdrawal made necessary because "the living . . . can still make mistakes, can still be changed, can still be carried away in a moment and by a moment" (UDVS, 54).

[16]This interpretation is deeply indebted to M. J. Ferreira, who provides a thorough defense of this account of love for the dead against Adorno's suspicion that Kierkegaard wishes us to "behave toward all men as if they were dead." Rather, argues Ferreira, love for the dead "serves the purposes of testing one's love" because it is "the relation in which faithfulness or unfaithfulness can best be isolated and tested because of the radical unresponsiveness of the beloved." It is thus a " 'criterion' or 'test,' " and "not necessarily put forward as the model of relation we should strive to bring about." See M. J. Ferreira, "Mutual Responsiveness in Relation: The Challenge of the Ninth Deliberation," in *International Kierkegaard Commentary: Works of Love* (Macon GA: Mercer University Press, 1999) 195, 197-98.

death. For example, "Death can expressly teach that earnestness lies in the inner being" (TDIO, 73). The discourse itself then explicitly instructs the listener in how to learn properly from this thought: "If you, my listener, will fix your attention on [the thought of death] and concern yourself in no other way with the consideration than to think about yourself, then this unauthorized discourse will become an earnest matter also with you. To think of oneself as dead is earnestness" (TDIO, 75). In other words, this discourse can help me precisely when I am reading it as relevant to myself—to my own death.

But if the discourse can help me, can it not then *teach* me? No, replies Kierkegaard; the discourse can help only insofar as the listener is already being taught—by death. Death is the teacher, not the discourse, for no discourse can convey the urgency that is death's alone. "The unauthorized discourse cannot carry this out in earnest as here described; there is no death waiting for it so that all can be over. But despite this, you, my listener, can pay heed to the discourse" (TDIO, 73). The discourse on death thus serves as our final arrow, directing us to Death itself, teacher of the earnest self-scrutiny that is prerequisite for patience. But even in so pointing, does not this discourse accomplish far more than Kierkegaard allows, when in "To Gain One's Soul in Patience" he describes all discourses as imperfect and of no help to their subject matter, tempting to speaker and listener alike? Once again, we find Kierkegaard's clarification in his discourse's final words:

> The person who has spoken here is, of course, not your teacher, my listener; he is merely letting you witness, just as he himself is doing, how a person seeks to learn something from the thought of death, that teacher of earnestness who at birth is appointed to everyone for a whole lifetime . . . the teacher who will at some time come to give a test and examine the pupil: whether he has wanted to use his instruction or not. And this . . . final examination of life, is equally difficult for all . . . because it is the test of earnestness. (TDIO, 102)

Here Kierkegaard presents himself as an exemplar, a witness to death's educative power. Yet here too, as in the case of Anna, the exemplar is not the teacher, but *points to* it. The teacher, meanwhile, need not be hired, just noticed—the lecture is already underway; the teaching, for its part, need not be solicited, just listened to—it is already proceeding. Although Kierkegaard can name the teacher, and even describe what is communicated, he cannot replace either.

This is the great paradox of the "upbuilding discourses": they are shot through with the language of teaching and learning, urgings, assertions, and rhetorical questions, yet if they do succeed in altering their listener, it is precisely *not* by teaching, but when "that single individual" is reminded to attend to the teacher within. To try, despite Kierkegaard's repeated warnings and revocations, to assess the discourses' own educative value, is to risk what James Conant identifies as the temptation to say things such as, "These sentences will only show something to someone who is already on the verge of grasping what it is they want to know."[17] For to speak this way cannot teach; to speak this way about the discourses is not to disclose hidden content, but merely to continue in their tone.

In this essay, Kierkegaard's self-referential passages have served both as a persistent obstacle and a prolific resource, deflecting and directing our search across five discourses. We asked: does Kierkegaard believe patience can be taught? Now we can answer: He believes no discourse can teach patience, nor can any living person, nor can even the example of Anna. Yet the answer to the question is *yes*. Patience *can* be taught—by the earnest thought of death.[18]

---

[17]James Conant, "Must We Show What We Cannot Say?" in *The Senses of Stanley Cavell*, ed. R. Fleming and M. Payne (Lewisburg PA: Bucknell University Press, 1989) 250.

[18]I would like to express deep thanks to Gordon Marino, for his guidance throughout the reading and writing process; to Cynthia W. Lund and others at the Hong Kierkegaard Library, for their hospitality, support, and friendship; and, finally, to Niels Jørgen Cappelørn, for first directing me, in conversation, to the ambiguous case of Anna.

12

Patience: The Critique of Pure Naïveté

Harvie Ferguson

The will that waits and endures is not the same will that makes it possible for people to get out of bed in the morning or to choose between this necktie, this silk scarf, or that. (William Maxwell, *Time Will Darken It*)

The purpose of this essay is to demonstrate the centrality of patience to the reflection that Kierkegaard calls "upbuilding" and to explore its peculiarity. Fully to grasp the radical character of the discourses on patience requires some preliminary consideration of their unconventional literary form. The specific meaning of patience within the discourses can then be approached by way of contrast with older dogmatic positions and, more particularly, through Kierkegaard's own views of the transformation of modern society that challenges such traditional teaching. In this context patience emerges as an essential but hidden aspect of a culture that values impatience above all else.

Modernity consists in the long process of working through the implications of human autonomy. Since the Renaissance this has been considered primarily in terms of a continuously developing and strictly human capacity to act rationally in relation to self-determined goals. All such action requires effort, determination, and persistence which, from the viewpoint of the discourses, are just the characteristics of impatience. Genuine patience, however, which might be described as naïveté, remains a requirement of life in modern society. It is only in patience that we are reconciled with the radical project of modernity and the frustrating contradictions, failures, and disappointments that inevitably issue from it. The enigma of modern humanity is just that it generates in equal measure from within itself *both* patience and impatience.

The Superfluous Text

Reading *Eighteen Upbuilding Discourses* (hereafter, the *Discourses*) demands patience; only the patient reader can become intimate with the significant truth they contain. This requirement is due neither to exceptional length nor inherent difficulty; individually the *Discourses* are much shorter than the pseudonymous works they accompanied and, certainly, they are less dialectically complex, technical, or allusive than the more explicitly philosophical works within the authorship. They invite patience in the particular sense in which the *Discourses* themselves talk of patience. The text is not to be appropriated by force. Nor does it invite surrender, as does a favourite novel, by virtue of an imaginative content that takes on a life of its own. The *Discourses* are free of both philosophical conceit and literary deception; they are addressed neither to reason nor imagination but rest serenely in themselves. The enigmatic text is to be read naïvely for what it is.

The *Discourses*, therefore, assume everything that we might think they are obliged to demonstrate. Above all they require of their reader the very quality into which they seemingly promise initiation. Only the patient can read the *Discourses* appropriately, but do not need to do so; and those who do stand in need of their spiritual offering cannot read them properly. They are superfluous.

Yet patience is a pivotal concern of the authorship as a whole and, in a literal sense, is central to the series of eighteen discourses finally collected and published in a single volume. Of these the eighth, ninth, and tenth are devoted to patience, so that just as much comes before patience as follows after patience. "To Gain One's Soul in Patience" is the fourth of *Four Upbuilding Discourses* (1843), while "To Preserve One's Soul in Patience" and "Patience in Expectancy" form the *Two Upbuilding Discourses* (1844) that immediately follow it. At first sight, indeed, one might think a more sensible plan for publication would have been to place them together in a single volume. But it would be quite against the spirit of the enterprise as a whole thus artificially to isolate one of the interrelated and overlapping terms through which it is conducted. Patience makes its presence felt throughout the discourses; seeping out, as it were, from this central location to illuminate what comes before as effectively as what is to follow. All the discourses, in fact, enfold the reader in the aura of patience which is their specific virtue. Patience, that is to say, is their inherent quality rather than, or as well as, their communicable meaning. More than this, patience, gradually and without any intellectual fuss, subsumes the entire authorship within its expanding horizon. In patience these seemingly brief essays come to occupy the reader in a peculiar way, gradually enlarging and, as it were, thickening their substance. Here patience *is* discourse; that is, neither a dialectical exercise nor a dialogical exchange, but a set of *practices* embedded in everyday life. And here patience is also upbuilding in the sense that, *if* the reader can enter the world of the text then, truly, it constitutes the starting point for a process of existential enrichment.

The *Discourses* should not, therefore, be misread as a direct and clear statement of the author's "position" in relation to the literary and philosophical ventures of the pseudonyms and the worlds they reflect. They promise, or seem to promise, a welcome relief from the indirect and allusive aesthetic writings, or the dialectical complexity of the philosophical works. But neither "S. Kierkegaard" who claims authorial responsibility on the original title pages or the "S.K." that signs the "Preface" to each collection of the discourses, carries any guarantee of authenticity, especially in the context of the maieutic art that was simultaneously being conducted pseudonymously by an author known to be Søren Kierkegaard. And whatever judgements might be reached as to Kierkegaard's own views they could not provide the reader with a readymade "meaning" for the text. There can be no direct communication of the existential plenitude that the *Discourses* open up and which is their real subject matter. Nor can there be a defensible "position" to be taken in relation to this reality, which is either made actual or held in abeyance by the reader.

And whether or not the discourses were intended to convey a private meaning to Regine Olsen, they were, in being published, gifted to contingency. The text is a gesture cast into the chaos of the world in the knowledge that it will be ignored, rejected, or misunderstood by all but the "single one who is my reader". In that potentially large number of singular readers, however, the discourses on patience will elicit an appropriate existential response. Here the accidental becomes essential in a way pioneered by Novalis in the fragments he had published under the title *Pollen* and which, like minute airborne seeds, served to stimulate in an unknown and unchosen reader, a decisive act of self-reflection.[1]

The discourses, that is to say, break with modern conventions of reading. The "Preface" to each collection of discourses enjoins the reader to speak the text aloud in solitude. This unexpected instruction subverts the established practice of reading as imaginative inwardness, and seems all the stranger given the author's commitment to rescuing "inwardness" from the objectifying illusionism of the present age. It seems that Kierkegaard is invoking an older tradition in which the text bodies forth the immediate authority of the spoken word. If such were the intention, indeed, it would, simultaneously, reverse the ordering of the sensorium that had been a central motif of the development of modernity since the Renaissance.[2] Mechanical printing, mass production, and a culture of individualism combined to make reading, the private and silent appropriation of a text, a popular leisure activity.[3] In a quite literal sense its primary significance in Kierkegaard's own culture was effectively to pass the time. Reading even "kills" time and generally serves as a substitute for the genuine patience that is at the heart of the *Discourses*. The *Discourses* are not themselves to be consumed in this way, aesthetically. Reading aloud provokes a different and more appropriate relation between the reader and the text. Yet Kierkegaard is not seeking to revive a premodern context or form of understanding; the *Discourses* are unconventional but decisively modern. What is externalised and bathed in the aura of speech is nothing other than the reader's own voice; the reader's self. It is the self "objectified" and given a momentarily vivid presence in contrast to the

---

[1]Novalis (Friedrich von Hardenberg), *Pollen and Fragments* trans. Arthur Versluis (Grand Rapids MI, Phanes Press, 1989).

[2]David Michael Levin, ed., *Modernity and the Hegemony of Vision* (Berkeley and Los Angeles: University of California Press, 1993); *Sites of Vision* (Cambridge MA: MIT Press, 1997); Jonathan Crary, *Techniques of the Observer* (Cambridge MA: MIT Press, 1990).

[3]Roger Chartier, *The Order of Books*, trans. Lydia G. Cochrane (Cambridge and Oxford UK: Polity Press, 1994); Lucien Febvre and Henri-Jean Martin, *The Coming of the Book*, trans. David Gerard (London: NLB, 1976); Paul Saenger, *Space between Words: The Origins of Silent Reading* (Stanford CA: Stanford University Press, 1997).

self who is the listening subject. And it is just the actuality of a second, patient self, which it is the task of the *Discourses* to invoke.

The text of the *Discourses* is first of all an occasion and an opportunity for naïveté; coming upon it in the right way is a fortunate encounter rather than the point of departure for a logical train of thought or the work of interpretation. Reading is, in this way, an existential encounter of the self with the self; an encounter in which the text acts ultimately as an invisible mediator.

The role of patience in the *Discourses*, then, has to be understood in relation to the entire authorship. The *topos* of patience had long been unpopular and, in the context of the otherwise radical modernity of the authorship, Kierkegaard's earnest and subtle meditations on the theme are surprising. The decisive sense in which the discourse of patience is also a thoroughly modern practice becomes evident, however, in relation both to an older dogmatic literature and, more significantly, to Kierkegaard's own secular analysis of modern culture as the "Present Age."

The Demands of Fortitude

The early church fathers commended patience as a virtue. In a tradition stretching back to Cyprian and Tertullian patience is viewed in the light of God's perfection. Divine patience is manifest in His condescension; not only in His binding Himself to the natural process of gestation, growth, and maturation of the life of Jesus but also in His self-limitation and self-humiliation in the acceptance of human suffering. In relation to God's monumental patience, "the magnitude of which is the reason why pagan nations reject the faith", human patience is a frail and imperfect imitation.[4] Genuine patience, which is a difficult combination of courage and humility, comes only from God. Patience "illuminates" faith; it is "both subsequent to and antecedent to faith",[5] such that impatience is nothing less than "the original sin in the eyes of the Lord".[6]

---

[4]Tertullian, "Patience," in *Tertullian: Disciplinary, Moral and Ascetical Works* (Washington DC: Catholic University of America Press, 1959) 197.

[5]Tertullian, "Patience," 203.

[6]Tertullian, "Patience," 202.

What more generally is viewed as patience within the human community is, in fact, its very opposite. For a pagan culture, patience is recognised in relation to the pursuit of purely human ends. We are frustrated by every obstacle that stands in the way of our attaining secular goals and, though we might bear this suffering with courage, or Stoic indifference, it is within a Christian perspective properly called impatience because it turns us away from all higher goals. Tertullian enjoins us to a more demanding practice; "Let the whole world fall in ruins provided I gain the patience to endure it!".[7]

For Augustine, also, patience has a central place as a Christian virtue because, living in the midst of sin, we rarely gain what, even legitimately, we hope for or intend. Our reason can never wholly penetrate the tangle of contingency and clarify a possible route to highly valued goals. Thus we experience loss and the sadness of disappointed aspirations, and the deeper perplexity of chance; "Patience, then, allows people to be properly saddened by their own and the world's state yet also remain unimpeded in their pursuit of and adherence to valuable goals".[8]

The *Discourses* should not be read, however, as an attempt to revive these ancient views of patience. A marked affinity, certainly, links the writings of Kierkegaard with those of Tertullian. As significant, however, is their resemblance to Petrarch's secular encomium on patience as the mutual disdain of good, as well as bad, fortune;[9] a viewpoint that seems equally to open the way to a revival of Stoicism and a positive valuation of indifference and nihilism. And, more importantly, such thematic similarities that apparently link the *Discourses* to premodern traditions have to be interpreted in the changed context of cultural and psychological assumptions of modernity.

---

[7]Tertullian, "Patience," 206.

[8]Lee H. Yearley, *Mencius and Aquinas: Theories of Virtue and Conceptions of Courage* (Albany: State University of New York Press, 1990) 137.

[9]Petrarch, Francesco, *Petrarch's Remedies for Fortune Fair and Foul*, trans. with a commentary by Conrad H. Rawski (Bloomington and Indianapolis: Indiana University Press, 1991) vol. 1, *Remedies for Prosperity*; vol. 3, *Remedies for Adversity*.

The Impatience of the Present Age

The discourses on patience are unexpected and challenging just because the Kierkegaard of the pseudonymous works so clearly grasped the extent to which modernity is in a preeminent sense *impatience*. In modern society the principle of human autonomy makes any sense of loss self-undermining; in claiming the world for ourselves we simultaneously become responsible for our own sadness and grief. And in renouncing all premodern forms of dependence we seem to have cut ourselves off from any source of consolation. Modernity is impatient because it cannot readily find an antidote to its self-inflicted wounds. Now there is no transcending and incommensurable source of happiness to weigh against the pervasive and obscure melancholy that colors modern experience. In this context, patience or, rather, what is generally called patience, becomes devalued as complacency and indifference. Patience is viewed negatively as dull conformity; at best laziness and at worst a ready acceptance of injustice. The domain of genuine patience has, as it were, shrunk and now clings to the experience of illness as its final stronghold. Patience rather than being a spiritual disposition has become uniquely predicated on bodily infirmity and a sick person undergoing treatment is still justifiably referred to as a patient.[10]

The authorship as a whole, in its variety and complexity, charts the spiritual implications of the transformation of modernity for the structure and meaning of existence. This is a rich documentation of the actual content of historical newness. The enormous significance of the *Discourses* lies in their grasping that newness religiously. The *Discourses* do not oppose religious existence to modernity, as tradition to newness but, rather, bring into awareness the forms of religious life immanent in modernity itself. Kierkegaard knows only too well that older forms of consciousness and feeling, secular as well as religious, do not simply disappear, and that the most widespread conception of religion in modern society remains steadfastly rooted in the unreality of a distant past; and

---

[10]Stanley Hauerwas, *The Hauerwas Reader* (Durham NC and London UK: Duke University Press, 2001) 348-66.

against all such remoteness the varied aspects of the authorship seeks to grasp the specific character of modern life, including the religious, through forms that themselves emerge only with the development of modern society.[11]

For people born into a modern society reality is, thus, defined in terms of *experience*. Modernity begins with the rejection of tradition as a binding authority on the present or future; this is the cultural assumption given with, and enabling the development of, modern society. The imperative of the past, including the oral and textual meanings through which the world had previously been understood and grasped, as well as the institutions and everyday routines in which people's lives had been ordered, was broken. Experience, direct, living, human experience, was to become the ultimate ground of all authority, the vital source of morality, the privileged route to valid knowledge, and the uniquely credible source of self-understanding. Withdrawn from participatory modes of identification and action, humanity had no option but to create for itself a world of self-sufficient and interrelated representations.

It is important, thus, to recognise that the modern notion of experience, and modern experience itself, was constituted as an act of separation from those larger and more inclusive realities that had shaped the premodern world. There is a sense in which the *postulate* of autonomy already and, as it were, at a stroke, destroyed everything that had gone before.[12]

The world of objects that appear outside of us, the world of the past and of the possible future, and the world imagined, are all characterised by human attributes; all are understood and grasped only because they are thoroughly humanised as images and representations. Modern discourse, therefore, turned inwards and with increasing determination settled on the task of self-exploration.[13] Only human beings have genuine knowledge of the world

---

[11]Harvie Ferguson, *Modernity and Subjectivty, Body, Soul, Spirit* (Charlottesville: University Press of Virginia, 2000).

[12]Hans Blumenberg, *The Legitimacy of the Modern Age*, trans. Robert M. Wallace (Cambridge MA: MIT Press, 1983); Reinhart Koselleck, *Futures Past: On the Semantics of Historical Time*, trans. Keith Tribe (Cambridge MA: MIT Press, 1985).

[13]Dalia Judovitz, *Subjectivity and Representation in Descartes: The Origins of Modernity* (Cambridge: Cambridge University Press, 1988).

because they alone have withdrawn from it; they alone *require* knowledge to deal with a world from which they now stand back and observe as an objective reality.

Of course, the founding principle of autonomy does not mean that we are free to fashion ourselves just as we please. The self, the experiential core of reality, also has a structure and a nonarbitrary tendency to development and growth; a structure in which history, society, and the body take root. Identity, thus, is not wholly a matter of freedom and choice; it is simultaneously a discovery and an unearthing of what is already given. Like art, the self is created but created as something necessary and essential; as that which, once revealed, could not have been otherwise.[14]

In the liberating atmosphere of newly discovered autonomy, however, these limitations and ultimate constraints were easy to ignore. That the new human world was continually in danger of self-parody, of losing itself in a labyrinth of self generated representations, was already a theme explored by the most significant creative writers, including Cervantes, Montaigne, Shakespeare, and Calderon as well as by philosophers in the wake of Descartes's decisive shift towards subjectivity.[15] The ambiguity of waking and sleeping, the enigma of madness, and the challenge of Otherness within the family of humankind made autonomy a double-edged weapon in the struggle against tradition and authority.[16]

The implications of modernity for the conduct of everyday life are brilliantly exposed by Kierkegaard in his review of Gylembourg's novel *Two Ages*. The historic project of claiming autonomy has, in fact, issued in meaningless convention, in the stultifying and spiritless world he calls bourgeois philistinism. For the present age "everything is manifestly nondescript, thus trivial, formless, superficial, obsequious, and openly so. Here there is no great revolution and no deep, dark secret, but all the more superficiali-

---

[14]Roman Ingarden, *The Literary Work of Art*, trans. George G. Grabowicz (Evanston IL: Northwestern University Press, 1973).

[15]Anthony J. Cascardi, *The Subject of Modernity* (Cambridge UK: Cambridge University Press, 1992).

[16]Johannes Fabian, *Time and the Other* (New York: Columbia University Press, 1983).

ty" (TA, 29). Nothing is sufficiently different and distinct to stand out against the general characterlessness of the age. "The present age" he remarks succinctly, "is essentially a *sensible, reflecting age, devoid of passion, flaring up in superficial, short-lived enthusiasm and prudentially relaxing in indolence*" (TA, 68).

This, in part at least, is a generalisation of the description of boredom which, reflected in the singular member of the public, had been presented pseudonymously in the first volume of *Either/Or* "with its flashes of enthusiasm alternating with apathetic indolence" (TA, 74). This is an orientation that "lets everything remain but subtly drains the meaning out of it; rather than culminating in an uprising, it exhausts the inner actuality of relations in a tension of reflection that lets everything remain and yet has transformed the whole of existence" (TA, 77). The draining of tension "from the coiled springs of life relationships" transforms everyone into a spectator, an outsider. The established order persists by virtue of inertia and a soporific indifference rather than commitment, even amongst those privileged by its institutional arrangements (TA, 80).

Echoing Rousseau, Kierkegaard argues that the only unity and in such a society comes from envy:

> Reflection's envy holds the will and energy in a kind of captivity. The individual must first of all break out of the prison in which his own reflection holds him, and if he succeeds, he still does not stand in the open but in the vast penitentiary built by the reflection of his associates, and to this he is again related through the reflection relation in himself. (TA, 63)

Envy is the general form of social relation in such a society. Individuals, though they hardly justify the term, "mutually turn to each other in a frustrating, suspicious, aggressive, leveling reciprocity" (TA, 63).

The annulment of the disjunction between subject and object undermines all the essential distinctions in which selfhood might take root and fabricates in its place a culture typified by abstraction, the public, envy, leveling, and chatter.[17] The present age, thus,

---

[17]Peter Fenves, *"Chatter": Language and History in Kierkegaard* (Stanford CA: Stanford University Press, 1993).

seems to be supremely *impatient* and, as "busyness", regards impatience as something valuable. This is an impatience that is agitated by the passage of time, however short it might be, required for the accomplishment of any task and the achievement of any goal. The overwhelming instrumentality of human activity in modern society seemingly condemns us to a life of impatience.[18] At the same time we live in a society in which a specific form of secular *patience* has become institutionalised as indifference and boredom. Any goal becomes arbitrary, no accomplishment appears worthwhile, and every striving is emptied of inner meaning. It is an age in which "Life's existential tasks have lost the interest of actuality" (TA, 105) and become mere phenomena. For many, "trapped in everydayness and habit (EUD, 347), the present age is altogether too easy and good fortune is accepted as luck or the reward for well-directed effort.

> Free from care, they go their way; a friendly fate makes everything easy for them. Every wish is fulfilled; their every enterprise prospers. Without understanding how, they are in the midst of the movement of life, a link in the chain that binds a past to a later time; unconcerned about how it happens, they are carried along on the wave of the present . . . they go on living amid the changes of life, at no moment desire to tear themselves free from them and honestly give everyone his due . . . For them life has no riddle, and yet their life is a riddle, a dream. (EUD, 33)

Events cease to have any significance beyond their bare occurrence, so that "everyone is experienced in indecisiveness and evasions and waits for someone to come along who wills something—so that they may place bets on him" (TA, 105).

In this sense every person is enfolded in a drifting miasma of complacency. The young man depicted in the first volume of *Either/Or* is at one with the present age and is both impatient and patient; he is *bored*. Patience in any more demanding and decisive sense seems contrary to the fundamental character of modernity as autonomous selfhood. As a term or a concept patience has become

---

[18]*Two Ages* might be read in the light of Max Weber's later and fundamental development of the theme of rationalization in modern society; Max Weber, *Economy and Society*, 2 vols., ed. Guenther Roth and Claus Wittich (Berkeley and Los Angeles: University of California Press, 1978).

redundant; the very stuff of the superfluous text. How can the *Discourses*, then, appear as anything other than a symptom of modern, we might now say postmodern, nihilism; a symptom that lacks even the scintillating glamour of the aesthetic writings that, momentarily, served the purpose of distraction?

Yet it is just the enabling assumption of the *Discourses* that patience is a reality in the fullest possible sense. It is its own reality; the epitome, rather than the denial, of autonomy. The critique of patience begins with acknowledging the actual presence of patience itself however implausible this might seem. The question is not "How is patience possible?" but, rather, *given patience* "What does patience reveal about the character of human possibility?" The discourse on patience must assume its own existence; it cannot begin with a starting point which is not itself patience; as wisdom is said to begin in wonder or knowledge in doubt. Patience is itself a primitive orientation to reality that cannot be analysed into more elementary components or traced to some unsuspected point of departure. The discourse, that is to say, cannot subject patience to the impatience of a rational framing concept or narrative structure.

The literary challenge facing the *Discourses* is to fashion a language that, while remaining comprehensible, opens onto a world that is alien to all the self-conscious forms of reflection upon modern life and experience.

Wishfulness

A vocabulary emerges, fragmentary, suggestive, and undogmatic that, suspicious alike of traditional religious terminology and modern philosophical abstraction, creates for itself a space for "upbuilding" thoughts. The *Discourses* begin with talk of bewilderment, expectancy, concern, and most intriguingly, wishfulness, and the gift. Eschewing a logical and conceptual starting point or a narrative point of departure the *Discourses* wish themselves into existence.[19]

---

[19]The first of *Two Upbuilding Discourses* (1843), "The Expectancy of Faith," opens with a consideration of "well-wishing" and the difficulty of "wishing something definite with respect to what is indefinite and indefinable. But we do

Wishing, unlike intention or desire, is egoless; it does not presume or project selfhood. The wish is free of the implications of ethical self-development or self-expression that inform all the "higher" forms of modern culture and lends to the undemanding and degraded conventions of bourgeois philistinism a flimsy aura of respectability. Equally, the wish rejects from the outset the entire dialectical development that claims to terminate in completed selfhood. Such a process, brilliantly conceived by Hegel and, equally, by the author of the first volume of *Either/Or* in the wonderful essay on "The Immediate Stages of the Erotic", is rooted in the incompleteness of the self, on the absence of trust in itself and in its own world.[20] But the wish does not rouse the will or desire, it does not call for an energetic and determined focus on something outside and beyond immediacy; it is neither consequential nor decisive. The counterpart of the wish, thus, is neither an aim nor a hope, but an expectation.

What later generations of psychologists were to consign to childhood and to the primitive as a "magical" world view is, for the *Discourses*, the bridge between the familiar conventions of modern selfhood and what that selfhood conceals. There is no distance between the wish and expectation, no tension or striving. Wish and expectation are simply different expressions for a foundational trust in reality. The wish, contrary to a common view that Freud was also to challenge, is not self-expressive or self-demanding. In a strange way the wish is quite *disinterested* in what it wishes for; hence its mobility and insincerity, its openness to suggestion, and its friendly and sociable character.[21]

The wish is the relation between the powerless and the powerful; it rests confidently in the protection of a higher power.

---

not let this difficulty block our way, we do not give thought the time to disturb the puzzling and vague impulses of the heart" (EUD, 8).

[20]G. W. F. Hegel, *Hegel's Phenomenology of Spirit*, trans. A. V. Miller (Oxford UK: Clarendon Press, 1977); Alexandre Kojève, *Introduction to the Reading of Hegel*, trans. James H. Nichols, Jr. (New York: Basic Books, 1969); *Hegel's Dialectics of Desire and Recognition*, ed. John O'Neil (Albany: State Univeristy of New York Press, 1996).

[21]Harvie Ferguson, "Sigmund Freud and the Dynamics of Modernity," in Anthony Elliott, *Freud 2000* (Cambridge UK: Polity Press, 1998).

The wish wishes for gifts; it is receptive to gifts; gifts shower upon it; it wishes for just those gifts it is able to receive. The *Discourses* reveal a deep complicity between wish, expectation, and gift; an interrelational complex that at first sight seems to be quite distinct from the anthropological understanding of the gift as an elementary form of exchange.[22] In the perspective that has come to dominate all academic discussions of the phenomenon, the gift is viewed as the form upon which society itself is founded. Social relations of solidarity and trust are frequently conceived as consequential upon the process of gift giving, the fundamental structure of which involves mutual obligations to give, to receive, and to return some valued object, person, or symbol. In what remains the most insightful anthropological analysis Marcel Mauss clearly grasps the essential character of the gift as a bearer of spiritual qualities. It embodies, rather than merely represents, the giver.[23] In time the useful physical properties and form of the gift displaced its "personality" and became the central focus for rational and functional modes of exchanging goods and, finally, of commodities and signs. But, even in modern society, the private gift giving and receiving ceremonies that punctuate personal relationships retain the identifying characteristics Mauss ascribed to the gift in general. It is just the spiritual character of the gift that the *Discourses* take to be essential and provides the reader with a point of transition from logical reflection to edifying meditation. The *Discourses*, that is to say, seize upon a radical notion of the gift as both freely given and freely received; it is without compulsion of any kind. There is no moral obligation to receive the gift "from above", nor does its acceptance entail a reciprocal duty to present a gift in return. But the perfect gift, the gift "from above", cannot

---

[22]See particularly the three discourses that appear under the title "Every Good and Every Perfect Gift Is from Above," the second of *Two Upbuilding Discourses* (1843) and the second and third of *Four Upbuilding Discourses* (1843).

[23]Marcel Mauss, *The Gift: The Form and Reason for Exchange in Archaic Societies*, trans. W. D. Halls (New York and London: W. W. Norton, 1990); Christopher Gregory, *Gifts and Commodities* (London and New York: Academic Press, 1982); Maurice Godelier, *The Enigma of the Gift*, trans. Nora Scott (Cambridge and Oxford UK: Polity Press, 1999); Alan D. Schrift. ed., *The Logic of the Gift* (New York and London: Routledge) 1997.

be returned and does not initiate a process of communication and exchange as between equals. It remains utterly incomprehensible.

Modern secular gift giving, that is to say, establishes a network of ambitions and calculations. The gift ensnares the subordinate in obligations. Typically we give in order that something be given back; respect, subservience, or admiration as well as material goods. The rich want "to make the needy anxious in subservience" (EUD, 146). But the absolutely free relation of giving is, and remains, asymmetric and its real character is summed up in the humanly frightful text from Job "The Lord gave, and the Lord took away; blessed be the name of the Lord". The relation of giving and taking away, as distinct from giving and receiving, establishes a wholly different reality; one that might be thought of as established through the consciousness of absolute dependence that Schleirmacher had understood to be essentially religious.

In the face of the gift freely given and freely withdrawn Job is unable to offer any explanation; "What good would human wisdom do here?", comments the *Discourses*, "Would not human wisdom rather make everything more difficult! Would not eloquence, which despite all its gloriousness never once managed to articulate the variety that simultaneously dwells in a person's heart, rather anesthetize the energy of the act and let it fall asleep in protracted deliberation" (EUD, 113). In this bewildering situation, however, if the gift is properly received in the first instance, then the "quiet sorrow" over its withdrawal does not turn to despair.

The Gift of Patience

Now we may see that patience is a gift; it is a gift "from above"; it is *the* gift from above. It is the gift which, properly received, even though it is withdrawn *as a gift* remains the secure possession of the recipient. Job reveals the unsuspected resilience and richness of this gift. Patience is such that, when every other gift is withdrawn, and even the gift of patience itself is withdrawn, Job is nonetheless consoled by patience over this loss. In every loss is revealed to him the free action of God; this is the insight of patience and cannot be lost. And, in the process of consoling over the loss of a gift, patience is appropriated as a wholly human possibility; as the possibility in which the human comes to be truly human. Patience once seized persists; "He never abandons patience, not when he has gained it, since it was indeed patience that he gained" (EUD, 174).

The condition of receiving the perfect gift is itself perfect; no earthly need can be the condition for receiving the gift from above, it must be rooted in a need for perfection itself, the need for God:

> Before this need awakens in a person, there must first be a great upheaval. All of doubt's busy deliberation was mankind's first attempt to find it . . . There is then a new beginning that is not attained by the continued influx of doubt, for then there would really never be a beginning that would begin with something other than doubt. Therefore, whereas in the old order of things man came last and it was doubt's task, as it were, to fathom everything that had gone before, now man is the first, has no intermediary between God and himself, but has the condition he cannot give himself, inasmuch as it is God's gift. (EUD, 136-37)

This new beginning brings the human into relation with God, not through the intermediary of a world opaque and estranged as *things*, but in terms of the absolute need for the Absolute. Doubt and knowledge, which are the polarities of a distinctively modern perspective, are founded in relative needs and therefore presents an obstacle to our capacity to receive perfection. God is the *only* good and not the summit of a series of humanly calculable utilities. And inasmuch as humanity participates in good it does so only through God; "it is not a perfection on God's part that he alone has it, but a perfection on the part of the good that a human being, in so far as he participates in the good, does so through God" (EUD, 134). The essential task, then, is properly to receive the gift rather than struggle to will to become good, or seek strenuously for knowledge of divine things, or contemplate the beautiful as a sign of some sort.

In purely human terms, as Hegel's dialectic of lordship and bondage had demonstrated, need is the imperfection that brings about a separation and distance between the needy self and the other who is required to complete the self.[24] The difference and separation between self and other allows reason *and* feeling

---

[24]Hegel, *Phenomenology*, 111-19.

mutually to develop. But in religious terms the need for God is the perfection that is itself the condition for receiving the gift that satisfies this need. He receives "that which was there before he received it . . . This he receives, the good and perfect gift by which the need that was itself a perfection is satisfied" (EUD, 139).

The absolute gift is offered freely and inclusively to all, yet, paradoxically, the gift absolutely singles out each recipient. It is characteristic of the *upbuilding* that the particular is contrasted *both* to the universal and to the indifferent mass of the modern public; "In the world, the differences work frantically to embellish and to embitter life, as beckoning goals, as rewards of victory, as oppressive burdens, as attendants of loss; in the world, external life takes arrogant pride in differences" (EUD, 142). But the upbuilding begins in blindness to human difference, for "every upbuilding view of life first finds its resting place or first becomes upbuilding by and in the divine equality that opens the soul to the perfect and blinds the sensate eye to the difference" (EUD, 143). Nor does this singling out, in contrast to the envious impulses of the present age, subsequently divide people from each other, rather, it unites them in thankfulness.

The Soul of Patience

It is in the last of the *Four Discourses* (1843), "To Gain One's Soul in Patience", that patience emerges as the central phenomenon or the religious life. Luke's words "In your patience you will gain your soul" (Luke 21:19), serve as a summons to earnestness, as a father calls to a playing child. And it is in earnestness, which is the "mood of patience", that we "embrace all life" (EUD, 159).

A person does not immediately "possess" his or her soul. It must be gained; "life must be gained and it must be gained in patience" (EUD, 160). People immediately understand the requirement for perseverance in any task oriented towards a goal. But, everything thus accomplished by perseverance remains outside the person and cannot be the gaining of patience in the sense in which the discourse speaks. Perseverance is reinforced by a host of intermediary rewards and by the continual renewal of intention and the rational hope of eventual success. But, conceived externally as a goal of striving and rational action, the soul recedes as we advance towards it and remains forever out of reach. If our relation to patience is modelled on the calculable relation of means to ends then we condemn ourselves impatiently to despair.

In this context the discourse meditates on the notion of possession, as distinct from the modern and much discussed idea of ownership. Attention to the relation between possessing and being possessed by, unlike that between owning and not owning, and in a way that is comparable to the focus on unconditional gift giving rather than gift exchange, turns the discourse towards existential issues. The soul does not belong *to* a person as an alienable property, it is essentially constitutive *of* the person. To gain the soul is to discover and fully acknowledge this obscure relation. To possess the soul is simultaneously to be possessed by the soul, which is no more to be "gained" by effortful action than the perfect gift can be received as a limited good; "But if a person possesses his soul, he certainly does not need to gain it, and if he does not possess it, how then can he gain it, since the soul itself is the ultimate condition that is presupposed in every acquiring, consequently also in gaining the soul. Could there be a possession of that sort, which signifies precisely the condition for being able to gain the same possession" (EUD, 163).

Radically to possess something is also to be possessed by it; to be identified with and, as it were, absorbed in the possession. Internally to possess is to possess only the essential, and to be possessed by the essential in such a way as to be free of self-contradiction; "it was actually temporality that made it impossible to possess and to gain the external simultaneously, because that which is in the moment either is or is not, and if it is, then it is not gained, and if it is gained, then it is not" (EUD, 163). But "in the eternal there is no such self-contradiction. . . . The eternal is not either a something possessed or a something gained but is only a something possessed that cannot be gained any more than it can be lost" (EUD, 163).

Properly speaking "It is a question not of making a conquest, of hunting and seizing something, but of becoming more and more quiet, because that which is to be gained is there within a person, and the trouble is that one is outside oneself" (EUD, 170-71). The soul is gained *in* patience, and "The person who grows in patience does indeed grow and develop. What is it that grows in him? It is patience" (EUD, 169). This development is quite different from impatient striving and the desire for self-expression; it neither presupposes, nor issues in, an objectifying and alienating selfhood. To *gain* the soul cannot be the work of a decisive moment but "turns the mind to quiet but unflagging activity" (EUD, 170). We are admonished to patience; not to patience above all else, but to patience *alone*. Patience is not to be construed, as it is in all romantic psychology, as the interminable task of retrieving a soul that has, somehow, been concealed *beneath* the forms of modern experience. The soul, rather, is in patience in such a way as to be *patience* itself; "so that it is patience itself in which the soul in patience inclosingly spins itself and thereby gains patience and itself" (EUD, 171). To gain the soul, in patience, is simultaneously to lose the world as an external good, that is, as the occasion of impatience.

Patience and Experience

Modernity can be viewed as nothing other than the culture of experience; as the world founded in the claim that experience and reality are identical. But patience is not born of experience and does not accumulate experiences; it is timeless rather than enduring. In the present age, and seemingly to an increasing extent, "experience certainly knows how to comfort in many ways" (EUD, 263), and provides itself with its own forms of consolation. The fragmentary and instrumental character of experience provides us with so many readymade measures of progress and adaptation to a world for which we claim responsibility:

> "[T]emporal life is piecemeal. . . . Experience has the advantage of always having a goal (*Maal*) by which it measures (*maal*), a goal towards which it strives, and as it divides up the range of finitude it always knows how to measure out (*udmaale*) the particular, and as it proceeds from the certain it knows how to calculate the uncertain; it has a criterion (*Maalestok*) for power and endurance, for resistance, for danger and difficulties, and, whether life enters in favorably or disturbingly, it knows how to cope with it accordingly. (EUD, 206)

There is much to be learned in experience, but experiences do not necessarily bring wisdom or fulfilment, far less give rise to patience; "He saw much, he experienced much, he learned many priceless words, which still are not those of patience but of life experience, with which can benefit himself, also others, but not always another" (EUD, 202). Genuine consolation, patience, is an *in*experience that is not founded in experience; it is *naïveté*. Patience "has not been formed by the dubious wisdom of experience" (EUD, 19-20) and "does not seek confirmation in someone's experience but, as it says, will gloriously strengthen every experience" (EUD, 203). Experience, in fact, is the contrary of patience, the "indefatigable enemy, time" (EUD, 193). It is not that time as persistence or duration will finally conquer the most patient self, who can wait no longer, but that the self whose existence is wholly in time and is, therefore, bound by time's accidents and contingencies, has no being other than the succession of experiences. Only in patience, that is otherwise than in the bare succession of experiences, can the self truly constitute itself as a self.

The common reaction to such talk is to reject the very idea of patience; "is patience perhaps a phantom figure that beckons in the clouds, that has itself experienced nothing, attempted nothing in life?" (EUD, 197). The *Discourses* care, however, to distinguish patience from the

> miserable commonsensicality that has not the courage to attempt anything and continually fears for the worst and treads carefully on the cautious middle ground, knowing that desire nevertheless ends sometime and ends in nausea, that hardship sometimes ends in despair, and therefore thinks the sagacious thing to do is to take care to be neither cold nor hot—as if this were not the most despairing condition of all? (EUD, 198)

It is not the task of patience to *avoid* experience and the invigorating plunge into the impatient turmoil of the present age; but it is only in patience that we can endure its lively contradictions without despairing, and struggle against its cruelties without losing hope. Patience does not replace impatience, but impatience continually threatens so to obscure patience as to tempt us to deny its essential presence for us.

The assumption of the *Discourses*, however, is that a religious reality has begun to unfold. This remains incomprehensible from a nonreligious perspective, and unnecessary to explain from a religious perspective. But the change is radical in terms of the entire world of existence. "How changed everything is when the fulfilment has come! . . . how forgotten, then, the past is, like yesterday, short as a sigh, brief as a moment. The person who has experienced this marvels at it and scarcely comprehends it. The person who has not experienced it does not understand what the talk was all about or what it says about the pangs of childbirth" (EUD, 205).

Patience does not come from experience but, once gained, its invisible presence dignifies every possible experience. The fundamental trust in reality that the discourses talk of as patient expectancy is undramatic and quiet; it knows nothing of the dreamy intoxication of the present age. Purely temporal expectation is destructive both of the soul and the modern rational self; "He wastes the power of his soul and the content of his life in calculations and the irascible unwholesomeness of probabilities; his proud achievement disintegrates and he is decomposed into empty noise: his energy is deadened in cowardly superstition" (EUD, 219). In the present age the steadfastness of expectation is easily dissipated into a cloud of possibility, by "impatience's short, hasty, precipitous, frivolous, arrogant, shrewd, comfortless "maybe"" (EUD, 217).

The Charm of Finitude

Modernity founded itself on the premise of autonomy and the separation of humanity from its historic but inessential dependence on nature and God; it began with a proclamation of trust in itself. But this did not imply that human reality became, or would become, transparent to itself. Rather, it meant that everything dark and mysterious in reality became an aspect of humanity itself. The self took into itself everything it had at one time conceived as lying obscurely beyond the limits of its own knowledge and, rather than clarifying reality, this served only to darken the interiority of selfhood. The self became a stranger to itself, uncannily aware of itself both as a familiar presence and as an enigmatic other. Every effort to force this mystery from its hiding place, to unmask, illuminate and reveal the true face of humanity, ended in failure. And this failure, taken into the heart of Enlightenment thinking, provoked increasingly desperate efforts to conquer and subdue an alien self-presence. The uneasy spirit was tranquillised, anaesthetised, and denied; transformed into nothing more than an alternative *representation* of relations and processes that had their origin in the same lucid acts of self-will that gave rise to the immediate forms of everyday experience. Finally, the aggravating intruder was assimilated to a purely theoretical and empty *concept* of the unconscious—and forgotten. As reality became identified with existence, the self-transcending self slid into nothingness. The human became banal. There was no longer any need for patience because the mystery that patience revealed and to which it reconciled us had dissolved into the illusory unreality of the past. In robust perseverance we could now get on with the task of claiming our world as our own.

Yet what endures is not the world of experience that we believe we have fashioned for ourselves but patience itself. Patience is a mystery at the heart of modern culture; the very culture, that is to say, that self-consciously roots itself in the negation of all mystery. Without patience we could not face the contradictory and shocking world that we have in fact created. The discourses reveal a vast, dark presence, albeit one that, just because it is not accommodated by the conventional forms of experience or forced into the reflective categories of reason, has been neglected. Concealed in the midst of the very impatience of the present age, patience rests serenely in itself. The *Discourses* rediscover the language, or, rather, the speech, of patience; the speech in which patience itself resides. Patience, in the end, is not difficult, it is not demanding. Patience has been overlooked rather than abandoned and, rendered invisible, it no longer arouses the momentary attention that would be required for its destruction. Patience dwells in conventional forms of life but remains distinct from them. The self that identifies itself with the creation and transformation of its own experience is reconciled to the world of experience by the patient self that is its unacknowledged companion. Patience, as it were, draws us out of these self-limiting forms and reconciles us to the contingency of time. Equally, it draws us back into time and reclaims the world of experience for us. Patience has a genius for the particular; a talent for finitude. Now the crucial life task confronting the individual is to sink into the particular and become absorbed in it. The self-transcending self is *also* the self of everyday experience; it is not something ethereally "beyond" itself. Patience, thus, saves us from all "higher" values in the same manner that, potentially, it saves us from mundane superficiality and nihilism. Patience is naïveté, rather than innocence, in the face of life's contingency. At the same time, patience is the critique of pure naïveté; it is that which makes naïveté possible. And, more than that, patience is that which renders possibility *and* necessity bearable.

13

Against Cowardliness

Martin Andic

God did not give us a spirit of cowardliness but a spirit of power and of love and of self-control. (2 Timothy 1:7)

Kierkegaard places these words of Paul at the head of his discourse "Against Cowardliness," the third of his *Four Upbuilding Discourses* of 1844, and the seventeenth of the collection we call *Eighteen Upbuilding Discourses*. He writes against cowardliness, by which he means our irresolution and pride that dare not make the venture of faith decisively and scrupulously and openly. But more especially he writes positively for courage, which he understands in terms of faith. To him this is the real courage, and what is usually called by this name in common life is actually cowardliness. His fundamental thesis about courage, here and in the upbuilding discourses generally, is meant to support and illustrate and develop what Paul has written. It is that faith, so far from weakening our courage in life, leads to the best and fullest and most authentic kind there is, that which God confers on those who truly seek it (EUD, 352-53). There are degrees or levels of courage, and the highest in worth and difficulty and passionate intensity is that which is directed by faith to our highest good, and that receives everything as a good and perfect gift from God, even courage itself (EUD, 44). His intent, accordingly, is not to point out a causal connection between faith and courage as we naturally understand it, but to define genuine courage as a *gift* of God that is acquired by faith; or more exactly, that *is* faith and is perfected by God. It is a spirit that God gives us when we desire it and ask for it, having done what we can for God and having admitted that without God we can do no real good at all. Kierkegaard thus treats true courage as a religious excellence that completes the natural excellence that we develop and exercise by our own effort, not superseding that effort and making it unnecessary but *transforming* and perfecting it while constantly presupposing it. Our action is indispensable, but it is not enough; the decisive condition is our submission to and dependence on the divine even for the condition (EUD, 136-37).

Kierkegaard's account of the highest and best courage thus emphasizes resolution and existence before God, as well as existence for other human beings; but he holds all three, and courage itself, to be qualified until we have sought and acquired the grace to work for God as "unworthy servants" who claim no merit of our own for what we do with his help. In an older terminology, courage is a supernatural virtue, come down to us from heaven to fulfil the human and raise it to its highest level; yet it does this precisely by lowering us, or what is merely all-too-human in us, so that we become nothing in ourselves but an instrument that God can use.

Because Kierkegaard underlines our personal resolve and venture and taking courage, he often calls the fullest courage the confiding and witness and assurance of the Spirit, God's confidence with us, the bold confidence acquired by faith;[1] but he would also say that we resolve to take this courage from *God*, who completes what is ours and gives it to us renewed and strengthened and brought to its highest. It is this confidence that we need in facing God's justice in death and already in this life, lest we lose the greatest good, the eternal. In giving us such confidence God goes *with* us to face death and all the challenges of existence.[2]

Moreover, because Kierkegaard makes humility the decisive condition, he speaks freely of pride as cowardliness: for in the end our pride is the obstacle to receiving this condition of true courage and confidence and the fullest resolve.

---

[1]A second reason would be that God has confidence, but not courage, which is correlative to the fears and dangers and opportunities that *we* face in existence and time. Thus, e.g., WL, 147, 244: God has and shows us boundless confidence but gives *us* real courage.

[2]Cf. Genesis 15:1; 26:24; Deuteronomy 31:23; Joshua 1:9; Psalms 23:4; 27:1, 14; Isaiah 43:1-2; 57:15.

In setting this out, I will focus on this discourse, "Against Cowardliness," but I will also draw freely on the other upbuilding discourses, and on Kierkegaard's authorship generally. My discussion is organized as follows.

First, I will begin with the resolution and existence before God that depend on us, showing how Kierkegaard links resolution with earnestness and passion, and existence before God with humility and self-denial. For our failures in courage are failures especially in these. How do they become the courage that is received from God? They acquire it and even "win" it, Kierkegaard says (EUD, 44); and yet he repeats again and again that it cannot be earned by any merit of our own.

Second, to clarify this, I will offer a close reading of the argument of "Against Cowardliness," which sets out obstacles to this transformation: our unwillingness to resolve ourselves, to fulfil our resolve, and to let it be known by others. I will focus on the call to work with God as his "unworthy servants" who do only what we are told to do; and on Kierkegaard's demand for transparency, which seems contrary to his usual praise and practice of indirection, maieutic, and irony. For him, however, these are stages on the way to explicit truth and witness. He refers to Jesus' command to let our light shine before people, and Paul's reminder of openness before God, and I suggest he may also be thinking of Plutarch's similar appeal for openness as a debt of humanity that we owe to one another; Kierkegaard would add that we really owe this debt to God.

Third, I will examine how he applies Paul's words in 2 Timothy 1:7, so that the spirit of power and love and self-control that God gives us takes up and transmutes our courage; I link this with the traditional view of Thomas Aquinas that religious courage is a Gift of the Spirit that disposes us to be moved towards our highest end and allows God to work in us so that we may share in the divine nature.

Fourth, to sharpen this notion of true, religious courage as God-given, higher than the highest human courage in the good that it aims at and the good that it can achieve, I will compare Kierkegaard's discussion with Aristotle's. Both writers redefine fear and confidence and revalue their objects, respectively the danger-ous and safe, because evil and good; but while Aristotle understands these as baseness and honor, Kierkegaard takes them to be falseness and truth to God. For Aristotle, courage is willingness to sacrifice everything else for nobility, even risking death for it; for Kierkegaard it is *dying* to self and to everything that the world (and even the noblest pagan) calls nobility. It is self-annihilation before God, so that we may become an instrument of the divine will: that is the true nobility. It becomes clear at this point that all that we can *do* to accomplish this, and to acquire the highest and fullest courage—we might also say faith, and confidence, and authentic identity—from the divine, is to desire and ask that it be done in us by the divine itself; this is a point brought forward more recently by Simone Weil, and it is what Thomas says as well.

Fifth, and finally, I will address the question, should we read Kierkegaard's call for openness, as many have done, as a personal rebuke to himself for a cowardly failing to confess his own psychological and physical weakness? He has taught us to look to a person's actions and life to see the meaning and truth that one's words have for the one who speaks or writes them, to see whether one's life verifies and illustrates them or refutes them and makes them meaningless. So should we take his words as warning himself to resolve more earnestly and with fuller humility to submit himself to God, with all his weakness openly confessed, and to ask God to give him the courage that he needs? Kierkegaard's words are aimed at every single individual, and they apply to himself as well as to everyone else. But the important ethical question, so I will argue, is not what is their meaning and truth for *him*, but what is their meaning and truth for ourselves, each one of *us* individually. If we understand him, and understand ourselves in what we understand, then we dare not allow our concern with him to displace our proper self-concern. Our interest in his weakness is liable to be a diversion from our task, and thus cowardice. It is our weakness that first requires our attention and a conscientious accounting before divine justice. Kierkegaard intends to show us that it is our courage that is in question, and that we can acquire the assurance that we most need from God alone.

Resolution and Existence before God

The *resolution* involved in courage is decision and choice, venture and risk, and one might also wish to call it faith and confidence. Resolution and courage are qualified when there are limits to what we will risk; but Kierkegaard is speaking of religious and moral resolve and courage to serve the good, which require venturing everything for it as a good that is present to us only in this venture. It is true of all resolution, however, that it is not merely words; it is not just telling ourselves that we are resolved, or that it is good and admirable to be so. Resolution is action or at least readiness for action; it is looking for the situation in which to do what we have resolved so as to be in character with it, and seeing the task in everything. Thus it is beginning at once to do what we can; and in religious and moral courage it is constantly beginning all over again, with the understanding that existing individuals cannot attain the good once and for all, nor even begin where we left off before, with a result achieved by ourselves or another on this way. It is fulfilling our resolution in every detail, however small and troublesome and unwelcome, just because they are details of it, while recognizing what remains undone that should be done. Some resolutions may be hidden, for example, not to betray a secret; but the religious and moral resolution to serve the good of which Kierkegaard is speaking requires being "open before God . . . [and] people," in other words witnessing.[3]

Resolution is wholehearted and all-venturing, thus fervent and impassioned.[4] It is resolving "the most sacred power in a person, the will," into one purpose that fills us with confidence and zeal (EUD, 191). It is above all the expression of our *earnestness* in self-concern, that is to say inwardness. Elsewhere Kierkegaard defines earnestness, like inwardness, as relationship to the eternal, so that the thought of God, and of death and judgment, comes with everything that we do and think and say. Earnestness is the

---

[3]Situation, task: JP, 4:4056, 4491. Beginning, fulfilling, being open: EUD, 357, 363-64, 374-75. Witnessing: JP, 1:656, 2:1901, 1957, 4:4967.
[4]See EUD, 9-10, 219, 233, 359-62, 374.

primitivity that sets first the first thing and risks everything for it; that constantly goes back to the beginning to be inwardly alone with the idea that defines our life; it is the originality of spirit. Earnestness is part of repetition, starting over again and again, suffering for the idea in person and not only in words praising another's suffering. Earnestness is truth that is honesty or openness before God, and fulfilment in actions and life; it is sharing the truth, with irony that helps others to be earnest and related to God.[5]

Kierkegaard's pseudonym Vigilius jokes that there exists so far as he knows no single definition of earnestness; we would welcome and expect that with existential concepts, since we can scarcely grasp by a definition that which has to be understood by realizing it ourselves but which in definition easily becomes something foreign; and as it is with love and (faith in) God, "so also with earnestness, which is so earnest a matter that even a definition of it becomes a frivolity" (CA, 147). He is reversing Polonius's words in *Hamlet* 2.2.93-94 "to define true madness, What is't but to be nothing else but mad?" There is a serious point as well, explained in the *Postscript*: subjective existential concepts and truth cannot be understood merely by objective reflection, but only by subjectivity that exists in these as a single individual.[6] Accordingly, to define true earnestness is *not* to be earnest, sc. unless we mean to be what we say it is.

Kierkegaard for his part generally links it to doing and saying and thinking things with *all* our heart, to trying to get them right,

---

[5]Earnestness as self-concern and inwardness: EUD, 269, 276, 340, 399. Eternal: JP, 1:235, 2:2112, cf. CA, 146, 151; WL, 320, SUD, 68-69; TDIO 75, 88, cf. EUD, 350-51, WL, 190, 227-28, 320. Primitivity: JP, 2:1135, cf. 2035, 1:84-85, 3:3561, 4:4050, 4296, cf. 1:379, 912. Repetition: R, 133, cf. TDIO, 96, PC, 189-90, JP, 3:3795. Truth: EUD, 254, 269 FT, 121, JP, 3:3166; 1:649-23. See further Michael Theunissen, *Der Begriff Ernst bei Soren Kierkegaard* (Freiburg: K. Albers, 1958).

[6]CUP, 1: 52 -53, 130, 199-200, 224, 350-51, 379-80. In questioning the definability of earnestness, however, one may also be pointing to its ambiguity, between worldly definitions of it as busily chasing after money and prestige and power, and religous and ethical definitions as doing right and loving one's neighbor: thus WL, 83, 320, CD, 89-90. Even within religious and ethical definitions of existential concepts there is ambiguity, for "Everything Depends on 'How' " they are applied (JP, 6:6784).

to understanding ourselves and them before God; and generally with reference to *fear* of what is truly evil and fearful, the loss of the eternal; and with enduring and persisting despite fear of what is not truly evil after all, the loss of temporal goods, for it cannot make us worse human beings. Thus he says that a person concerned with eternal salvation has "the earnestness to reject the flirting of light-minded ideas, the fear and trembling to be terrified at the thought of breaking with heaven or of taking it in vain" (EUD, 258); at other times he writes that someone becomes earnest and finds guidance when one will "work out his own soul's salvation in fear and trembling" (TDIO, 61), while his pseudonym Silentio mentions "an honest earnestness that fearlessly and incorruptibly points to the tasks [and] lovingly maintains" them (FT, 121). In the *Journal* Kierkegaard notes that so-called religious inwardness "can also be cowardice, which does not dare to be too earnest" (JP, 4:4372), from which it follows that courage *does* dare, and is real earnestness.[7]

Earnestness is thus the fiery purpose and focus and the fearless or fear-defying assurance in courage and its resolve, the heart and the will in it to press forward and hasten on; we might wish to say that true and full earnestness *is* courage.

But *existence before God*, and more particularly existence before God in *humility*, is also part of courage and even of what it resolves, so Kierkegaard thinks. He explains in the second upbuilding discourse that God "makes everything a good and perfect gift for everyone who has enough heart to be humble, enough heart to be trustful" (EUD, 40-41); he connects the two again when he asks who has courage to admit to oneself "I do understand [James'] words, all right, but I am too cowardly, too proud, [and] too lazy to want to understand them perfectly"? (EUD, 43). The earnest person has the courage to be a master by serving, and the humility to rule only as a servant (EUD, 85).[8] Kierkegaard mentions the cowardice that prevents the humbling understanding with God that one will serve him with all one's

---

[7]See also SUD, 5-6; JP, 1:235; 2:1743; 3:3166; 4:4183.

[8]That is to say, one rules with God, and serves God, by serving people freely as God's coworker. EUD, 86, 282, 333; cf. WL, 160-61, 279, 362. Matthew 20:26-28; 1 Corinthians 3:9; cf. 2 Corinthians 5:20; 6:1.

power and yet deserve nothing for it (EUD, 352-53, 359); a person prays well, he says, who earnestly struggles for this understanding and "only when he himself becomes nothing, only then can God illuminate him so that he resembles God" (EUD, 399, cf. 379).[9] In other places Kierkegaard writes that faith gives "the courage and humility to become an individuality" (JP, 2:2083), that love has "the courage for this God-pleasing venture of humility and pride— *before God* to be oneself" (WL, 271). To him true humility and true pride are united in authentic courage: "true humility and pride are one . . . , [to] fear only God—otherwise nothing" (JP, 2:1388). Courage is shown in venturing all one has for the good, including the human pride of doing this by oneself and meritoriously, so that humility is part of this courageous venture and fulfils it:

> Christian humility . . . presupposes a pride which carries its head higher than proud human humility but which then humbles itself. . . . If a person really gets serious about the humility which abases unconditionally, . . . it will be condemned as the most frightful arrogance [pride] . . . [Christianity] demands . . . the passion to venture everything. "That's all you have to do," says God; "I will do the rest." (JP, 3:2679)

Since seriousness and the passion to venture everything are earnestness, it follows that such humility is part of and perfects the deeper earnestness that could be identified with courage: the fully earnest person humbly does all for God and claims no merit for it. Thus we need "the courage to go forward in humility, certain of being persecuted more. . . . [For] the world ridicules the humble person" (JP, 4:4623, 3:2482).[10]

---

[9]Only then, when one knows oneself in one's nothingness before God, can one *know* God so that God can "create in him a new human being." EUD, 321, 325.

[10]Cf. CUP, 1:49: love's equality shows itself in relation to God in "the humility that entirely acknowledges its human lowliness with humble bold confidence before God as the one who certainly knows this better than the person himself." UDVS, 239-40: "There is courage [*Mod*], which bravely defies dangers; there is high-mindedness [*Hoimod*], which proudly lifts itself above grievances; there is patience [*Taalmod*], which patiently bears sufferings; but the gentle courage [*sagte Mod*] that carries the heavy burden lightly is still the most wonderful": high-mindedness is pride, while gentle courage is "meekness" [*Sagtmod*], namely, a humility that has courage in it.

Moreover, when we dare to venture all for God, giving up even our proud notion of doing it by ourselves and deserving well for it, God purifies and intensifies our courage: God sends the spirit to witness to and confirm it, to confide itself and give us confidence. Because God transforms our venture into faith's bold confidence in this way, Kierkegaard argues that true courage is acquired from God, who turns into this our *earnest* desire to serve and our *humble* understanding that it is God who does everything and that we do nothing by ourselves. If we are honest about this, Kierkegaard says, we may "win the courage" to thank God for everything as a good and perfect gift that is from above, and "the faith to receive this courage, since it, too, is a good and a perfect gift" (EUD, 44).[11]

A difficulty arises just here: if we do *nothing* by ourselves, how do we "win" this courage? And if our very faith and courage are acquired from God who gives them freely without any regard to our merit, then are our earnestness and humility and our venture *God's* actions and not ours, so that it is not *our* fault either if God freely withholds them? We will address this explicitly in what follows.

One more preliminary point. The resolution and humility in courage, as Kierkegaard presents it, cannot entirely be separated: we must resolve to be nothing, and humble ourselves simply to be God's dedicated, wholehearted instruments. Our failures in courage come down to irresolution and pride; but we should consider as forms of cowardliness faults that cannot be classed with just one of these rather than the other. Laziness and thoughtlessness are lack of earnest resolve, while defiance and impatience are self-will. Crafty doubt and dishonesty seem to be both of these

---

[11]Cf. EUD, 122, 129, 151-52, 264, 273, 370; JP, 2:1433: "the understanding with God is that this suffering indicates God's love—this is the confiding of the spirit . . . God's confidence"; 4:4337: "have faith, and you will you see, you will gain the courage to understand [misfortune] differently—that these things happen simply as an assistance in the task, so that it may be served with more purely religious powers"; 4346, 4690, 4694: "say to yourself: The question is not whether I have the courage or not, as if it were left up to me to decide—no, I must; and then the Spirit witnesses with my spirit"; 4939. Romans 8:15-17; John 14:15, 21-23, 26, 15:26-27; 1 John 5:7; Ephesians 2:8.

together, a stubborn evasion, a sly and sagacious misrepresenting the task to make the difficult easy and the easier difficult, in order to avoid both submission and commitment.[12] On the other hand we see both humility and resolution in the religious courage to receive and serve, to believe and understand, to love, to wait and hope, to exert ourselves and to venture, that Kierkegaard speaks of in the discourses; and likewise in the courage that he and his pseudonyms mention elsewhere, the faith-based, God-given courage to know, to believe in people, to be forgiven, to be meek; to take hold of time with faith and speak and act like Abraham, to will repetition, to renounce anxiety without anxiety, to become a single individual and spirit; to exist for everyone in our heterogeneity.[13]

Our particular concern here is with what Kierkegaard says about courage and the failures of courage in "Against Cowardliness," so let us now turn to this discourse to consider it carefully.

Resolution, Fulfilment, Openness

The discourse has a scriptural text and an introduction on the concept of resolution generally, followed by three sections, one on each of three main failures of courage: first, in fully resolving to serve the good so as directly to begin to act wholeheartedly and simply before God, without doublemindedness and presumption of piling up merit; second, in carrying out one's resolve in every particular even if trivial, inconvenient, and awkward; and third, in performing it intelligibly and transparently so that none need mistake it, although people may nevertheless choose to take offense and respond with mockery and hostility.

If time (temporality, dependence on worldly goods that time can bring or take) can make one forget the eternal, resolution can

---

[12]Laziness: EUD, 43, 221, 236, 340, 349. Defiance: 35-39, 118, 195-97, 216, 373, 386. Craft: 23, 41, 135, 348-49, 355-56, 374. Cowardliness is something shameful, contemptible, and intolerable; even the most worldly person turns away from it in others and in oneself (EUD, 353-54), once one is shown that it is there, i.e., that what is there *is* cowardly.

[13]EUD, 43, 85-86, 65, 75, 201, 334, 92, 375. CI, 26*; WL, 244; WA, 154; UDVS, 240; FT, 49, 120; R, 132; CA, 117; FT, 116-17; SUD, 43; JP, 4:4183.

join one back to it, and even "bring the eternal into time for him" (EUD, 347), so as to give time (life, existence) deeper meaning and value again.[14] But the resolution to act, in the sense that one *says* to oneself that one is resolved to act, is not in itself action, and to praise resolution is a temptation to admire and talk and *do* nothing.[15] Talk lets one imagine that one need only deliberate whether to act, as if going to a party, not saving oneself from danger. The truth is, everyone *needs* resolution, for everyone needs the eternal. Everyone is in religious and moral danger: the danger not only of *misfortune* but of *despair* and *sin* in losing the worldly goods that one lives for and with them one's courage and faith, one's sense of purpose and meaning in life, one's moral integrity and hope, if one has based these on worldly goods; worst of all, the danger of *death* at any time, though certainly it will come in time, with the final *judgment* of God hereafter, and here already[16] one is "under indictment," with oneself as informant and witness, even accuser and judge: an earnest person acknowledges this divine justice, "indicting himself so terribly that he cannot acquit oneself but learns to need mercy" (EUD, 350-51, 309, 340), and only so to acquire bold confidence in it (I John 4:17-18). Resolution is not the work of a moment but a continuing active state, constantly renewed; it is not itself the victory on which it sets one's heart, but

---

[14]See EUD, 175, 192, 337, 356 (time); 324-25, 331-32, 356-57, 361, 382 (meaning); 174, 259, 322-24 (eternity in time).

[15]EUD, 363; cf. WL, 91, 94, 359-74. EUD, 350: "it is wretched to have an abundance of intentions and a poverty of action, to be rich in truths and poor in virtues." Cf. La Rochefoucauld, *Maximes*, trans. Leonard Tancock (New York: Penguin, 1959) 187: "The word virtue is as useful to self-interest as the vices"; 432: "To praise noble deeds unreservedly is in a sense to have a share in them." That is to say, reserve no action to practice what you praise, and you share in this nobility; reserve no words only, and you share in words only. Kierkegaard cites *Maximes* 271 in CI, 49: Alcibiades' unfulfilled enthusiasm for Socrates and his ideals is like "the fever of reason."

[16]WL, 227-28: "Alas, many think that judgment is something reserved for the far side of the grave, and so it is also, but they forget that judgment is much closer than that, that it is taking place at all times, because at every moment you live existence is judging you, since to live is to judge oneself, to become disclosed"; CD, 205: "Immortality is judgment. . . . not a continued life . . . in perpetuity, but . . . the eternal separation between the righteous and the unrighteous."

simply and constantly starting over again to do what may lead to this, and working toward it one day at a time; and while it makes one proud to say that one resolves, it is humbling to admit that every day may be difficult and a drawn out struggle with success always deferred (not to mention, what will be developed later, that one can do nothing by oneself); yet there is an eternal power in a resolution toward the eternal, and so Kierkegaard repeats "Do what you can for God, and he will do for you what you cannot do" (EUD, 352).[17] It is said that fear of God, Christianity, and the pious humility in resolution make one cowardly; but the text from Paul assures us that "it is just the reverse."[18] Anyone is deeply cowardly who is *not* knighted by God's strong hand, because one was too proud to accept it at the cost of admitting that one does not deserve it. Knighthood is the great and noble service of God, and more exactly the noble courage given to those who venture themselves to it.[19]

It is cowardliness to delay and avoid this good resolution, and euphemistically to call that pride, as is usually done. Cowardliness is dishonest, deceptive (EUD 43, 348-49, 374), it *hides* itself behind all the other passions and "buries itself deep in the soul" (EUD, 355-56);[20] but it is common, for "everyone is somewhat cowardly"

---

[17]See also EUD, 368-69, 375. Cf. 250: "Spiritually, the fulfilment is always in the wish"; 393: "he who prays aright is always victorious, for it is one and the same . . . while he had sufficient inwardness to pray, he was also assured that the wish would be fulfilfilled if he prayed aright," and now he does pray aright; that he prayed, however imperfectly, "helped him, namely, to concentrate his soul on one wish," namely, for right understanding with God.

[18]To doubters fear of God is cowardice, but to believers the cowardice is doubt itself. See EUD 23, 41.

[19]This knighthood is worn lightly, however, for God does not bestow it as owed to you for any merit of your own. EUD, 46: "God is the one who does everything good in you and then gives you the childlike joy of regarding [even] your thanksgiving as a gift from you," and so with love offer him your deeds to receive like a child's gift, "a jest, a receiving of something that one has oneself given"; cf. JP, 2:1121, 1156, 3:3415, echoing *Two Gentlemen of Verona* 1.2.143-44, 171-74.

[20]This is said of self-love by La Rochefoucauld in *Maximes* 563 and Pascal in *Pensées* 978, and implied by Plato in *Laws* 5.731d-2b; self-love is as close to pride as self-interest and self-seeking are to self-satisfaction, as close as desire to gratification. Kierkegaard says that self-love is consumed *only* by the love of God

(EUD, 355) and knows this, and consequently (and wisely) mistrusts even one's own boldest actions. There is a rare "false pride" (EUD, 354-55, 371) that sleeplessly, wearily, and fearfully means to do right all by oneself, without relying on anyone else for understanding and approval and help, not even on God's coknowledge and confidence: but this is cowardly too, for it is not daring to admit that one does nothing without God.[21]

First of all, it keeps one from *acknowledging* what is good, that it is the truly great and noble that one should resolve wholeheartedly to strive for always. It warns against haste, grandly sets the goal infinitely far off, and abides in "continued striving" (EUD 357, cf. 272), although this must sometimes *begin* in resolution if it is ever to arrive.[22] Cowardice is proud of one's ability and waits until the task seems difficult and dangerous, drawing strength from the fear of danger, whereas the real difficulty is to begin and have to feel one's own inability; or it admits one's inability and waits for it to increase rather than risk it too soon, not daring to think that "it must indeed always be enough, and the less one begins with, the greater one becomes" (EUD, 359). Just as the poorest widow gives the most when she gives everything she has with mercy (EUD, 362, cf. WL, 317-18), so the weakest person is greatest when one ventures everything one has with *all* one's heart and the understanding with God that it is really *God* who does any good one does. One must dare to do *now* what one can, in faith that with heaven's help it will be enough, and not wish and dream that one had more so that one could *then* resolve to give all. As it is foolish cleverness to hold back when one can win nothing except by risking everything (EUD, 359-60, cf. 378-79), so it is cowardliness and pride to wish to be more than one is and to delay resolution with make believe assent to it (EUD, 359-60, 363), thus rewarding oneself twice for deferring it.

---

that it evades in cowardliness: EUD, 309, 330, 374.

[21]He seems to be thinking of Socrates here, perhaps at *Apology* 28b; but see also 23b, *Euthyphro* 13a, *Republic* 2.379bc, 10.612e-13b, *Meno* 99d (with *Sophist* 267c, 268a), cf. *Laws* 1.644d-44b, where dependence on God is emphasized.

[22]Cf. Franz Kafka "There is a goal, but no way; what we call the way is just wavering." *Reflections*, in *Dearest Father*, trans. Ernest Kaiser and Eithne Wilkins (New York: Schocken 1954) 26.

Second, cowardliness keeps one from *doing* the good one resolved to do. If one imagines that a resolution settles everything and the fulfilment is just a detail, then one's resolution is itself just "a glittering delusion . . . a seducer and deceiver instead of a trustworthy guide" (EUD, 363, cf. 348-49). Truly "the splendor of eternity shines upon the resolution" (EUD, 363); but this is only the beginning, and one must find eternity *in* the particulars of fulfilment, so that one "neither disregards them nor is lost in them" (EUD, 364), and life goes on with the coherence and grace that the resolution to serve God can give it.[23] Resolution then requires being careful with money, restraining anger, enduring annoyances with a good grace, persisting although tired or bored, forgetting an insult. Resolution always "knows the one thing needful and that it is the one thing needful" (EUD, 356), namely to do what is good rather than what is merely clever; yet it calls one to do it in minute particulars, *as* particulars and because one did resolve.[24] Cowardliness, however, wants to do important things because it flatters one to do what is important and, if one fails, to have failed in what is important; so it belittles the task that everyone has and then avoids it because it is little. Yet whatever one does accomplish on one's own, God does not *need* it, for "however great one may be, one is still only a servant" (EUD, 367); what matters to God is that one has resolved, "has promised everything to the good, . . . along with one's weakness, and [will] leave it to God" what comes out of it, "satisfied with being willing to be an unworthy servant" (EUD, 367-68). Kierkegaard refers here to Christ's remark in Luke 17:10 that even at our best we are still "unworthy servants" who only do our duty: our best *is* to do only

---

[23]Thus it is said that Zen means doing everything "perfectly," unselfconsciously yet mindfully and freely: with the perfect love of God for everything and everyone. Cf. Matthew 5:48; and George Herbert, *The Elixir*, 5: "A servant with this clause [namely, in all things God to see] Makes drudgerie divine: Who sweeps a room, as for thy laws, Makes that and th' action fine."

[24]William Blake: "He who would do good to another must do it in Minute Particulars . . . & every Minute Particular is Holy." *Jerusalem* 55.60, 69.42, in *Complete Writings*, ed. Geoffrey Keynes (Oxford, 1976) 687, 708. Cf. JP, 1:179, quoting Augustine: "God is so masterful in great matters that he is no less so in little ones," 2:1371, 1426, 3:3062, cf. Plato, *Laws* 10.900c-903b; Matthew 10:29-30; Luke 16:10.

our duty, and to claim no merit for it before God.[25] As Simone Weil says, "For glass, there is nothing better than absolute transparency. For a human being there is nothing more than to be nothingness [before God]. . . . Zero is our maximum."[26] Thus if one imagines that what one cannot make oneself do "is nothing," how much more truly nothing, before God, is what one *can* do by oneself. If one does much for an ideal, one will notice whether one does *all* that one could; and admitting the discrepancy may teach one to know oneself and God and so transform one's activity and renew one's resolution, for as Paul says "God does not give a spirit of cowardliness but a spirit of power, of love, and of self-control" (2 Timothy 1:7). Humbly confess the weakness in which you become aware of God, aware that without God you can do nothing at all; so that you "Do what you can for God, and God will do for you what you cannot do" (EUD, 368-69). The only and greatest thing that anyone can do for God is "to give oneself completely, consequently one's weakness also, for obedience is dearer to God than the fat of rams" (EUD, 369).[27]

Third, cowardliness keeps one from *acknowledging* the good that one does do. Kierkegaard means, the good one *intends*, for only

---

[25]*Douloi achreioi* are literally worthless slaves. Kierkegaard also says that we are to be "coworkers with God": he is following Paul (see n. 8 above), who writes in Romans 6:20-22 that we are slaves of God and no longer of sin, and yet in 8:14-17, 29 that in God we are no longer slaves or servants but adopted children and heirs with Christ. It comes to the same. For seen from below, we are slaves; from above, heirs and fellow workers; yet we should always think of ourselves from below, in humility, for we (in our natural worldly egoism against which we contend so long as we exist) are always below and we do not know what we shall be (1 John 3:2; EUD, 173, 399-400).

[26]Simone Weil, *First and Last Notebooks*, trans. Richard Rees (London: Oxford University Press 1970) 354. Cf. JP, 4:4384: no human being has, though it is the goal, "pure transparency in willing solely what God wills, so that there is no residue of his original subjectivity." For both writers, with transparency to the will of God we acquire a new transformed subjectivity that is faith and single individuality or, as she prefers to say, love and the spirit of truth.

[27]First Samuel 15:22; UDVS, 61, PV, 73. See also JP, 2:1436 "the most insignificant thing of all can be transformed into what is more important than all world history, as soon, that is, as it pleases God to accent it as a task of obedience"; 1476 "the indulgence is the deepest secret of the individual conscience with God, face to face with the requirement," 1492; 4:4922.

God knows what good it accomplishes.[28] True, one should prefer to appear to others worse than one is rather than better, which is dangerous if one causes this oneself: one should not practice one's piety before people, but before God in secret (Matthew 6:1), and when one has done wrong one should not risk discrediting the truth by hypocrisy. But when one does what is right and good one must not be afraid to let people see it, rather than mislead them to their harm by being oneself the cause of this.[29] Good action begins in silence, in secret confidence with God (cf. FSE, 48-51); but it is easily misunderstood, and it is tempting like Lear's daughter Cordelia not to defend oneself but "to break off relations with people and shut oneself in with the good in silence" (EUD, 371); it is tempting even for the humble person condemned by powerful hypocrites to let people think that the hypocrites are right and by silence to seem to confirm the condemnation, and to take one's secret to the grave. When all others promise obedience to God and praise each other for this, one is inclined to be quiet and privately try to perform what others vow publicly; when all grieve loudly, to fast in secret but appear unfeeling; when all are well-known benefactors and crowd around the person made famous by being wronged and visit the prisoner notable for being detained, to go covertly to see to the widow, the orphan, and the prisoner who is despised. One may not dare to serve God for fear of misjudgment; but even if one does dare, and *invites* misjudgment, it is still cowardliness: for then one does not venture to be simply an unworthy servant who deserves nothing for only doing his duty, but slyly wants to be more than one is and to deserve more than one gets: "he wants his deeds to judge others and in a crafty way

---

[28]EUD, 131: "a person may know how to give good gifts, but he cannot know whether he is giving a good gift" in the sense in which knowledge is religious and moral concern; 272: one must say to God "I will not build my salvation on any work, . . . since you alone know whether it was a good work . . . [or] will become a good work."

[29]Cf. WL, 297: The one who denies forgiveness "enlarges the sin, makes it seem greater . . . provides the sin with sustenance . . . that a sin continues is a new sin. And this new sin you could have prevented by forgiving in love and taking away the old sin, just as does the one who loves, who hides a multitude of sins." Cf. Socrates in the *Apology* 33a: "I have never let anyone do wrong," that is to say, when I could stop it.

. . . wants to build up a larger balance with God" (EUD, 372). Thus anyone who occasions misjudgment must test oneself to see "whether it is God's call he is following or a voice of temptation, whether defiance and anger are not mixed embitteringly in his endeavor" (EUD, 373). Is one submitting to God's will by doing right and taking whatever comes as a good and perfect gift from above, or is one *angry* with one's poor reward and *defying* God's will by inciting more wrong against one in order to deserve better compensation? Or accepting that wrong from people as a punishment from God for weakness that one dare not confess and so possibly mitigate the wrong? Even if one does not do it in order to deserve a greater reward (as in "false pride"), might one be taking people's misjudgment as a punishment for this weakness,[30] hiding *guilty* gloom under outward frivolity and indifference, thus punishing oneself by allowing them to be mistaken? This is "a hatred of oneself that wrongs the person himself. . . . But hatred of oneself is still also self-love, and all self-love is cowardliness" (EUD, 374).

Let everyone test oneself, then, to see if one does recognize the good for which one lives and that moves and fills one's heart. If one can do this, retiring and humble, decent and unpretentious as the good is, one will bear with the world's continued misunderstanding and is not to blame for it, for then one is truly "open before God" (EUD, 374; 2 Corinthians 5:11). Otherwise one is proud as well as cowardly: not daring to do what is difficult, one dishonestly calls it easy and what is easy difficult, then becomes full of oneself and imagines oneself to be better than others for doing the good secretly, rather than simply a useless servant like everyone else (which is harder). If one pays oneself a worldly reward to renounce the world, one does not renounce it. Loving the good requires that one acknowledges one's love because "It is the truth, and the acknowledgment is the truth he owes to his neighbor" (EUD, 374), to keep the other from doing wrong that

---

[30]Kierkegaard, here and in what follows, need not be speaking of himself in his own psychological and physical weakness. He may be thinking of anyone's self-indulged failures in resolve, even little ones such as extravagance, irritability, impatience, laziness, resentment: EUD, 364.

one could prevent.[31] If "your life certainly must teach you to believe that a person is better than he seems" (EUD, 375), then you ought to believe it of others, sc. that they will respond rightly and well to your example. "God gives a spirit of power, of love, and of self-control . . . [when you] do what you can for God" (EUD, 375). Venture, then, resolve yourself and have courage, to *do* the good, to see to the *detail* of it, and to *recognize* the good "even if you do not gleam with it" (EUD, 375), sc. as if it were simply and entirely your own. Do it without shame before people, even if "you always feel your own imperfection and lower your eyes [in shame] before God" (EUD, 375). Venture in trust in God, you who dared the judgment of conscience and your punishment, and dare instead to "endure the sympathy of people, [you] who endured the punishment" (EUD, 375) when they misunderstood. Do not be misled by the sophistry that "it is more difficult to serve the good when misjudged" (EUD, 375): for it cannot be better if it is less *true*, and easier for *you*.

Kierkegaard's call to recognize the good, even if you do not "gleam"with it, is an allusion to Christ's words in Matthew 5:16: you shall *shine* with the divine light of love and justice and truth, but so that people may see it and praise, not you for your piety, but *God* from whom it comes down. Christ goes on to say that you show it not by words without deeds, but by *deeds* with or without words, so that by fruits the tree may be known. It is God who accomplishes what is good in your deeds (above your egoistic self-knowledge), so that when you feed the hungry and refresh the thirsty, welcome strangers, clothe the naked and visit the sick or imprisoned, you do not know that it is God.[32] It is your role to

---

[31]Truth does not increase error, any more than love increases hate and sin, or justice injustice by returning harm for harm and making people worse. See *Republic* 1.335; WL, 285-288, 334-38.

[32]Matthew 5:16: "Let your light so shine before men, that they may see your good works and give glory to your Father who is in Heaven." Cf. 4:16, quoting Isaiah 42:7; 6:1; 7:20-21; Luke 6:46; James 1:22-27; 2:8-26; Matthew 13:43; John 1:4, 9; 3:21; 7:16; 14:10: "The Father who dwells in me does his works"; Matthew 25:37: "Then the righteous will answer him, 'Lord, when did we see you hungry and feed you . . . ?' "; cf. 6:3-4: "do not let your left hand know what your right hand is doing, so that your alms may be in secret," namely, hidden from *you* in your worldly self-love; Mark 10:18, 27: "No one is good but God alone . . . [but]

become nothing in yourself, only an instrument that God can use to feed and refresh, welcome and clothe and comfort, and in this service to become understandable to others so that they need not be misled into deeper error and deeper wrong; if they choose not to understand, then you need not answer for that. This truth that you owe to people is part of the openness to God that you owe to God, because the divine has opened you to yourself and itself to you in confidential understanding with you.[33]

This openness and truth, to be ventured earnestly, humbly, and courageously, is clarified by notes in the *Journal*:

> This is the measure of what a man is: for how large a portion of his contemporaries does he dare to exist, allowing his life to judged by them. . . .
> Courage is to dare to will to exist for the whole range of one's contemporaries. (JP, 4:4183, cf. 4163, WL, 74-75)

One must dare to exist for others in a difference from them that they will misunderstand, even as one works to overcome this misunderstanding and difference. For one will not believe and value what others do; and by allowing them to think that one does, at least at first, one works to dissuade them from the egoistic and sensate, aesthetic concepts by which they act and live, and to persuade them into higher and truer, religious and ethical ones.[34] People shall recognize what the truth is, and that one lives by it or means to do so, so that if they take offense then at least they cannot misunderstand, and if the difference persists it is by their own wilfulness and cowardliness. If one hides one's faith or denies that one has it, one puts people to the test of their faith, which only Christ may do, or one risks demoralizing them and giving up oneself. Moreover, there is demonic pride in "avoiding the appearance of being as good as one is," for "A sinner can never delude himself into thinking that he can be so good that it would be dangerous for the world or men to find out how good he is"

---

all [good] things are possible with God"; James 1:17, 2 Corinthians 12:9: "My power is made perfect in [your] weakness"; see also Psalms 5:8; 23:3; 25:9; 143:2; Isaiah 26:12; Jeremiah 9:23-24. (All these quotations are taken from the Revised Standard Version.)

[33]EUD, 374, 388, 394-95, 399-400; cf. WL, 189-90, 160-61.

[34]JP, 6:6577, 6916, cf. 4:5022, 6:6932; PV, 7, 53-55, 77.

(JP, 3:3745). Indirection must aim at *transparency*, and one must become as open as possible.[35]

Thus when Kierkegaard declares that "Socrates took every-thing, everything, with him to the grave, . . . [and] kept it for eternity" (JP, 4:4303), his point is not that *Socrates* did not dare to exist for others (cf. EUD, 371), for he thinks that Socrates made his defense "which embittered the judges and made them condemn him to death . . . [into] the situation which made it clear what there really was to Socrates" (JP, 4:4278); the point is that Socrates took his truth with him, his earnest and humble and courageous service of the good, for he never abandoned it, and everyone must start all over again from the beginning and find one's own. (Cf. PC, 210.) Thus "Socrates belonged together with what he taught, . . . his teaching ended in him, . . . he himself was his teaching" (JP, 6: 6360).[36] Kierkegaard says something similar of himself in the famous passage comparing to a tapeworm the professor who will take over from him the intellectual capital in his authorship but only lecture about it and not live it, and about only lecturing about it, but "in another sense I will take it with me" who have lived it (JP, 6:6817-18).

In emphasizing the transparency in courage, Kierkegaard has in mind Jesus' words about letting one's light shine so that people see it and praise God (Matthew 5:16) and Paul's call for openness before God (2 Corinthians 5:11). But Kierkegaard also read the classical authors with close attention and well-focussed imagina-tion, and he read Plutarch,[37] in whose essay "Is it a wise precept

---

[35]JP, 2:1957-58, 1962, 6.6577; 3:3105, 3228: a Christian must not withhold and hide oneself, but constantly make one's word of truth "a pure and personal transparency, that his life may be his teaching." See also JP, 2:2202, 3:3449, 4:4480.

[36]Kierkegaard constantly returns to Socrates' heroism and courage, as if rebuked and made sleepless by him, like Themistocles by Miltiades: see, e.g., JP, 2514, 2652; 4:4271, 4288, 4480: "Socrates was the man who attained the highest [courage]"; CUP, 1:359-60. For who *else* has ever been willing to die for practicing philosophy? If there are any other examples, then they too attained the highest courage that a person can show, humanly speaking. Kierkegaard will say, however, that the courage that Christian faith needs and takes only from God is higher still.

[37]He cites Plutarch from memory in JP, 6:6180 on the difference between fear and cowardice: a man trembling remarked that his body would tremble even

to live unknown?"[38] he could have found these suggestive words: "The ancients called man 'wight' [*phos*] because from our kinship with one another a strong love is implanted in each of us being known and knowing [wit]." Moreover, some philosophers believe that the soul itself is light [*phos*], because it hates most ignorance and everything unlit and dark, which it fears and mistrusts, whereas light makes everything cheerful and agreeable. "But he who throws himself into the unknown state [sc. hides himself] and wraps himself in darkness and buries his life in an empty tomb would appear to be aggrieved at his very birth and to renounce the effort of being." In a related passage in "Epicurus makes a pleasant life impossible," Plutarch also writes that "To learn the truth itself is a thing as dear to us and desirable as to live and be, because it brings us to knowledge, and the most dismal part of death is oblivion and ignorance and darkness."

He might have said, spelling this out, that openness brings us together in the mutual knowledge and love that is our human life and being, so that in kinship we *owe* it to one another.

Kierkegaard for his part would add that the one to whom we really owe this debt of transparency and availability is *God*, who gives us everything, so that we repay (and renew) the debt and fulfil the gift by giving it to each other, helping one another to give. We receive the knowledge and love of God insofar as we give it to each other as God's, working not on our own but as servants who at our best do "only" as we are told. Our work is an earnest joke, although it takes courage to offer it: the joke is on us,

---

more if it only knew in what danger it was going to be. Kierkegaard says that this is in the *Moralia*; but though it is close to *Contentment* 475d-76a, it is still closer to Seneca's *Letters* 11.1-2, 57.4-5, 67.6, 71.29, 88.29. Such a remark is ascribed to Marshal Turenne in the seventeenth century, and quoted by Nietzsche and by Simone Weil. I will say more about this difference between feeling and behavior below.

[38]*Plutarch's Moralia*, trans. Benedict Einarson and Phillip De Lacy, Loeb Classical Library (Cambridge MA: Harvard University Press, 1967). The words quoted here and in what follows about our love of openness and the effort of being occur at 1130ab and 1093a. Cf. EO, 2:322 openness gives meaning and actuality to life; CUP, 1:91-93, 121-23 the continued striving of existence.

for we have nothing to give to God and for God but what already is and always will be God's.[39]

God-given Courage Is a Spirit of Power, Love, and Self-control

Full courage for Kierkegaard is acquired from God, who "does not give a spirit of cowardice, but a spirit of power [*dunameos*] and of love [*agathes*] and of self-control [*sophronismou*]," in the words of the scriptural text from Paul. The courage that God breathes into us enables us to dare earnestly and humbly to *begin* resolutely to serve the good and to *perform* in details and to let it *show* in our actions and life that we intend this. We might suppose at first that the three elements of courage are meant for the three challenges to courage, respectively; but the truth is, all three elements of courage are needed for each of them. The writing in this passage (EUD, 360) is uncharacteristically gnarled and the reasoning elusive, so let us look at it closely.

We need this spirit, Kierkegaard says, in order (A1) to *know* what is good, truly good and noble, its meaning to us and for us, sc. to know what it requires of us and gives to us at any time; (A2) to *love* it selflessly and desire and rejoice to be its unworthy servant, sc. to serve it freely and not for reward, which would defile it; and (A3) to be *constant* in the self-control that makes fruitful the resolved effort toward it, sc. to restrain the cowardly pride that wants to be more than a servant and to do something worthy by ourselves. "This acknowledgement, this assent of resolution, is the first dedication" (EUD, 360, cf. 361 "resolution . . . is the true acknowledgment"). Love and constancy, that is to say, are parts of the knowledge shown in resolution: knowing the good this way *is* loving it freely and joyfully and serving it unpretentiously and wholeheartedly, even knowing ourselves to be loving and serving it so; and the resolution to dedicate ourselves consists of this knowledge.

Kierkegaard goes on to exclaim how rarely we do, even in resolving to devote ourselves, *renounce* fantasies of importance, and *receive* the power (B1) to see the good, (B2) to love it selflessly, and

---

[39]See WL, 160-61, 189-90, 280-82, 365; JP, 2:1156.

(B3) to come to sound understanding with it,[40] so that we have (C1) the power lucidly to hold ourselves to the good that seems to destroy us (in our natural egoistic sensuality), sc. the power to hold on to the conviction that what is truly best and great and noble is the good, (C2) the love not to shrink from this destruction, sc. the love to deny ourselves for the good, and (C3) the sanity not to betray ourselves, sc. the sanity to be true to our resolve toward the good.

In his first two triads, Kierkegaard mentions three forms of power that Paul says one has in the spirit of God as a whole, and in the third he refers to the three aspects or operations or gifts of that spirit, power being one along with love and self-control.[41]

All three elements of the spirit that comprise courage are present in all three challenges to courage, however, because the challenges arise together just as the elements work together.

This treatment of courage as given by God may be compared with Thomas Aquinas's account of the Gifts of the Spirit. The virtues that make us good, he explains, make our lives good or happy; and there are two levels of happiness, a human happiness that we can attain ourselves, and a superhuman one that we can get only from God so that we take part in the divine nature; we cannot attain this by ourselves, he says, but must have divine help: "It is necessary for man to receive from God some additional principles, by which he may be directed to supernatural happiness, even as he is directed to his connatural end by means of his

---

[40]EUD, 360 "to make the pact of self-control with it"; the Swensons' translation has "to enter into a sober covenant with it." Both versions are valid, since the Greek word *sophronismou* is the genitive of *sophronismos*, controlling oneself, sobering, chastening, linked to *sophrosune*, self-control and sobriety, and to restraint especially in sensual pleasures and so particularly to sexual chastity and purity, but more generally to moderation and prudence and discretion, sanity, and soundness of mind. *Sophronismos* would preserve our earnestness and humility by preventing intoxication, dizziness, swooning, thoughtlessness, lightmindedness.

[41]Paul has written *agathes*, goodness, excellence, where Kierkegaard speaks of love; but for both writers the best person is the loving person, so that goodness is love. Moreover, for both, God who is good is love that is a love of love, so that in God above all, goodness is love: thus, e.g., WL, 3-4, 264-65; Romans 5:1-5; 13:8; 1 Corinthians 13:13; 2 Corinthians 13:14.

natural principles, albeit not without the divine assistance."[42] These additional principles are the faith, hope, and charity infused or poured into us by God, "which God works in us without us, [which is to say] without any action on our part, but not without our consent."[43] Thomas goes on to discuss Gregory the Great's list of seven Gifts of the Spirit—fortitude (sc. courage), piety, fear, counsel, understanding, science, and wisdom—and explains that these are called gifts, "not only because they are infused by God, but also because by them man is disposed to become amenable to the divine inspiration, according to Isaiah 50:5: 'The Lord . . . hath opened my ear, and I do not resist.' "[44] God instigates us, pricks us on, prompts us to obey by giving us, among other things, fortitude which "prevents the soul from being afraid of neglecting the body and rising to heavenly things."[45] This is the religious courage that we need to pursue our highest end, the supernatural happiness of sharing in divinity. God-given fortitude thus perfects those things which are done by us, of which Thomas says that "God causes them in us, yet not without action on our part, for He works in every will and in every nature."[46] The faith and courage to see God's action in everything is itself God's action.

---

[42]*Summa Theologiae* 1.2.62.1, in *Basic Writings of Saint Thomas Aquinas*, 2 vols., ed. Anton C. Pegis (New York: Random House 1945). See also 1.1.62.4 (speaking of beatified angels): "An act cannot be meritorious as coming from free choice, except in so far as it is informed by grace. . . . [One does] not merit beatitude by a natural conversion towards God; but by the conversion of charity, which comes through grace." We have no "merit" but grace; yet even if God prompts our desire for it, we have to consent to this desire and receive, as God's, what God gives. 1.2.114.1 reply 2: "God seeks from our goods not profit, but glory, i.e., the manifestation of His goodness."

[43]ST 1.2.55.4 reply 6. Cf. Ephesians 2:8: "For by grace you have been saved through faith; and this is not your own doing, it is the gift of God."

[44]ST 1.2.68.1. Cf. Psalms 40:6: "Sacrifice and offering thou dost not desire; but thou has given me an open ear"; 119:36-37: "Incline my heart to thy testimonies and not to gain. Turn my eyes from looking at vanities, and give me life in thy ways."

[45]ST 1.2.61.

[46]ST 1.55.4 reply 6. Cf. Philippians 2:12-13: "work out your own salvation in fear and trembling, for God is at work in you, both to will and to work for his good pleasure." Nature must cooperate with grace, assisted and transformed and raised by it. See further JP, 6:6969, and n. 52 below.

The Incompleteness of Human Courage

Thomas's distinction between levels of happiness and levels of excellence, and his claim that the highest form of courage is *given* to us with faith, help us to understand how Kierkegaard would read a philosopher like Aristotle who treats courage as a natural virtue. The comparison will help us to focus more sharply the humility and renunciation, the self-annihilation and passivity in religious courage, as Kierkegaard understands it, in relation to the resolve and integrity, personal venture and activity in it, and both in relation to transformative grace.

For Aristotle, following Plato, a *virtue* is a quality of intellect or character that makes us and our lives good; it improves us and benefits us so that we live well, that is to say rightly and happily. A virtue belongs to our fulfilment, to the best and most complete life that we can live. Aristotle thinks that our full happiness requires exercising all the virtues, both intellectual and moral, but especially intellectual ones, for it includes as much contemplation of truth in science and philosophy as consists with restraint, courage, and the rest of moral and political virtue and nobility. We are social and political animals as well as reasoning ones, and we owe help to one another in friendship and justice. Nevertheless, intellectual virtues are the most important for our happiness; the others are indispensable but secondary.[47]

Aristotle considers that the worldly person can know the virtues only up to a point. One can recognize that courage is a middle between feeling too much and feeling too little fear and confidence, but one will not know how to feel these as one should, at the right time, toward the right objects, for the right reason and in the right way, unless one already understands virtue, or as he says nobility [*to kalon*], to be the best life and aspires to it and discerns it in particulars. This understanding cannot be reduced to a few simple rules that can be taught like grammar and arithmetic,

---

[47]See Aristotle, *Nicomachean Ethics*, esp. 1.7, 10; 2.1, 6.12-13, 10.7-8. Cf. Plato, *Meno* 87c-89a, *Republic* 1.333e, 335, 352e-54a; 7.519b-21b.

for it is a way of action and life. One learns courage by doing as brave people do, and practice brings understanding.[48]

More particularly, courage is shown in defying fear and danger in pursuing the good of nobility, but it is not properly speaking a disregard of any and all evil whatever, such as poverty and disease and friendlessness, envy and insult to one's wife and children, and shame and death generally. It is right and not cowardly to dread these, but it is not courage not to dread them and to resist them; rather, he thinks, it is courage steadfastly to endure what is terrifying in struggle for a noble end, and it is what is most terrifying—death in battle (for one's city)—that most brings out courage, when someone fearlessly faces a noble death.[49] We must distinguish affect and action here. Aristotle does not mean that the courageous person *feels* no fear but that one feels it as one *ought* to, and so *behaves* "fearlessly," not moved by fear basely and cravenly away from what is right and best but moved by one's choice of the good honorably and bravely towards it despite one's fear. As for poverty and disease and evils that do not show one's baseness and are not one's fault, since these do not dishonor they are not truly harmful, and one should not at all costs avoid them but have a due fear of them; to defy these is called courage only by similarity to the defiance of death for a noble cause.[50]

Actually Aristotle says that courage has due confidence as well as due fear; but he resists saying that these consist simply in correctly estimating the *odds* of success and failure, for they also

---

[48]*Nicomachean Ethics* 2.2, 4, 6.

[49]More courage is needed to stand and face sudden dangers, Aristotle says, because there is no time to calculate; but courage in battle is greater than courage at sea and in illness, not only because the end is nobler but also because a soldier overwhelmed could save his own life by running away, but sea voyagers who expect to drown and the fevered who wait for death cannot save themselves so. Greek *phobos* means both fear and flight: hence soldiers can be fearless to a higher degree because they can *resolve* not to flee. See *Nicomachean Ethics* 3.6-9, esp. 1115a25-35, 1117a16-23, and 1115b22-24, 1116a10-12; cf. Plato, *Laches* 191ce, *Protagoras* 358d.

[50]NE 3.6 1115a17-19. Cf. Socrates in the *Gorgias* 509c-12: we should defend ourselves from the worst evil of *doing* wrong, and leave it to heaven to defend us from the lesser one of *suffering* wrong; *Apology* 30cd, 41cd a good person cannot be harmed.

involve setting rightly the *value* of the honor as opposed to the life and prestige and wealth that are at stake. Thus a cowardly person does not endure when one should and a reckless person endures when one should not.[51]

Kierkegaard similarly treats courage as a noble quality that makes us pursue the goal of human life, involving well directed confidence towards this and fear of missing it, and sacrifice of everything else for it. But he understands nobility and the best life as relationship to God (EUD, 352-53). He will say, *Aristotle* knows the virtues only up to a point. There is a higher kind of happiness demanding a higher valor, a religious courage not available to him and to the Greeks.[52] The blessedness Aristotle mentions in passing (NE 1.9) is only a divine acknowledgment of an excellence that we can achieve by ourselves.[53] But that excellence is pride.[54] True

---

[51]In NE 3.8, Aristotle says that we call courageous *only* by analogy (1) citizen soldiers who keep their position and weapons because of the *praise* that they hope to receive if they stand and the *disgrace* that they fear if they run; (2) fighters whose *training* and *experience* makes them hold and endure so long as they know themselves stronger but clear out when they realize that they will die; (3) *fierce* people who are roused by pain and anger and vengeance, by feeling not reason and the choice of honor; (4) confident soldiers whose *success* makes them expect to prevail, but think with their legs when they foresee death in defeat; (5) those *ignorant* of the danger they are in who bolt as soon as they understand it. Cf. *Laches* 192b-193d.

[52]This is not easily said, because Socrates' courage rebukes him and all of us: see n. 36. Nevertheless, Kierkegaard insists, Socrates was a pagan and did not know the deeper religiousness of divine transcendence and human guilt and redemption by Christ. See further JP, 1:115: "*Paganism—Immortality*. One often learns the most from an occasional remark . . . 'there is such a thing as wishing for the impossible, as for example, for immortality' " (NE 3.2 1111b20-22). Kierke-gaard would contrast this with Matthew 19:26 and John 6:51; 12:25.

[53]Aristotle observes in NE 10.9 that we assume the gods are active and that they care for human beings who care for what the gods love and are, namely, in-telligence; but he never says that they are active *in* our justice and courage and generosity, only that they rejoice simply to *see* these: their whole and only action is contemplation. See esp. 1178b8-23, 1179a23-33. Plato is closer to Kierkegaard: see n. 21; cf. n. 46.

[54]Thus WL, 268-69: "Only the spirit's love has the courage to will to have nothing at all . . . therefore it gains God—by losing its soul. Here again we see what the early fathers understood in saying that the virtues of the pagans are glittering vices"; cf. 53, 196, 319. Lactantius, *Institutes of God* 6.9; Augustine, *The*

courage requires our acknowledgment that by ourselves we achieve nothing at all, and that we have no excellence but what we receive from God.

The best virtue requires the humility of *not* knowing that what we do for others is good for them, much less that what we have done is good enough to win salvation.[55] We must acknowledge, or understand with God, that only God makes good for others what we do for them, that we *do* nothing good on our own ever, and *are* nothing before God. This is *nullifying* ourselves, so that we become only God's instrument, or can become one: for we do not know whether we serve God by what we do until after we have ventured it.[56] To understand that we are nothing and can do nothing without God, and so to *need* God, is our highest perfection, our fullest virtue, humanly speaking, and "the first mystery of truth" (EUD, 326, cf. 156, FT 104).

But even that is saying too much. The highest we can do is to *desire* with all our heart to understand it.

> This is the annihilation of a person, and the annihilation is his truth. . . . To comprehend this annihilation is the highest thing of which a human being is capable; to brood over this understanding, because it is a God-given good entrusted to him as the secret of truth, is the highest and the most difficult thing of which a human being is capable—yet what am I saying—he is incapable even of this; at most he is capable of being *willing* to

---

City of God 19.25. Thus EUD, 354-55, 371: false pride.

[55]EUD, 39: "God is not like a person [namely, like one of us] who, if he had a good gift to give, yet gave it away in the dark, with uncertainty . . . because he did not really know whether it would really be of benefit to the other"; EUD, 131: "a person may know how to give good gifts, but he cannot know whether he is giving a good gift"; EUD, 137: James would encourage the single individual "to doubt himself, his own capacity and competence"; cf. Socrates in the *Charmides* 164ac; 165b, 166c, 167ab, 173a; *Gorgias* 511c-12. EUD, 269-70: The earnest and truly concerned person knows that one cannot guarantee by one's actions and life that one has assured one's salvation, and the thought that it is assured "may very well make him lose salvation, just as the consciousness of the good deed causes one to lose the reward."

[56]Mark 10:18, 26-27. EUD, 151, 226: A person must "make himself truly what he truly is—nothing"; 312; cf. JP, 2:1106, 3:3719, 4:4460: "To know that God is using one—this is a dangerous thought for a man to have; this is why he does not get to know it until afterward." It is dangerous because it is presumption, pride.

understand that this smoldering brand only consumes until the fire of God's love ignites the blaze in what the smoldering brand could not consume. (EUD, 309, emphasis added)[57]

Here the difficulty we have noted emerges with full force. If we cannot give ourselves even this understanding that we are totally dependent on God, since we depend on God for this too, and can do nothing to deserve and assure it, then how can we *win* it (see EUD, 44), and how can it be *sin* not thus to have acquired from God what is given to us freely without regard to any desert of ours (Ephesians 2:8-9)?[58]

Kierkegaard's solution is that we acquire this understanding and faith when we *ask* God to take everything that stands in the way, and *let* ourselves in our sensate worldliness be created "a new human being. . . . transfigured in God, . . . to reflect the image of God" (EUD, 325, 399-400). This consent to what God offers to do for everyone is our whole and only freedom, so that

in the moment of dedication [one] *renounces* all dreams and fancies, every mirage that wants to inflate him and cause him to be

---

[57]Cf. EUD, 136-37: "But to need the good and perfect gift from God is a perfection. . . . Before this need awakens in a person, there must first be a great upheaval. . . . the condition he cannot give himself, inasmuch as it is God's gift." The smoldering brand is the self-love (EUD, 330) that Anti-Climacus says cannot die to itself and into God and the faith and authentic selfhood and spirit that alone fulfils it: despair of this is "an impotent self-consuming that cannot do what it wants to do . . . [that] has inflamed something that cannot burn or be burned up . . . whose worm does not die and whose fire is not quenched" (SUD 18-19, quoting Isaiah 66:24). Cf. JP, 4:4376: "Spiritual trial is a terrible thing. Yet . . . an intimation of a higher and more blessed understanding constantly smolders therein," namely, that the divine gives itself only when one gives everything else away.

[58]Kierkegaard is concerned with this too, and concludes: "There are many, many envelopes, but there must still be one point or another where there must be a halt at subjectivity . . . unless we want to have fatalism" (JP, 4:4551). There must be "a moment of freedom, of acceptance" (JP, 3:2672). There must be a movement of *resolution*. In his final journal entry Kierkegaard speaks of a man who is ready to give his soul back to God with thanks for helping him to do "what only freedom can do . . . as if it were God who did it" (JP, 6:6969). One must freely ask for what God in turn freely gives and must give in order to *be* God (so that there is both freedom and necessity on both sides). One thanks God afterwards for everything good, thus including one's asking because that too is good.

amazed at himself, and instead *receives* the power to envision it as it is, the power to embrace it with self-denying love, the power to make the pact of self control with it. (EUD, 360, emphasis added)

In the previous paragraph Kierkegaard remarks that the good we see does not leave us indifferent to it, but draws a "pledge" (EUD, 359) from us that we never forget and that torments and saves us. If we might ever not dare at once to fulfill this pledge with our whole heart and our full renunciation of pride,[59] this must be a pledge that we then only partly give, although it is with the best part of us; and all that we can do is to *ask* God to draw us more and more fully into this pledge. That is all that we can do; it is enough, "God will do the rest" (JP, 3:2679).[60]

This is Thomas's solution too. The act of faith, he says, is "an act of the intellect assenting to the divine truth at the command of the will moved by the grace of God," responding to the divine promises of good.[61] We assent to the good we see and desire and love; God has instigated the assent and given the fortitude to fulfil it despite fears of what it costs. God has caused us to do what we do yet not without consent and action on our part.

Thus it is with courage as Kierkegaard says it is with patience, that it is "just as active as it is passive, and just as passive it is active" (EUD, 187, 197): the activity is *passive*, because we must renounce, give away, open to the spirit God offers; but this

---

[59]EUD, 9: Is there any wish for a good "so certain that one would dare to put his whole soul fervently into it without holding back any part of it"; 223, 254, 258, 393, 399.

[60]Simone Weil argues that this *consent* (to God's "de-creating" us in our wilful separateness and re-creating us as divine means or instruments of selfless justice) is what is meant by the taste of the pomegranate seed that ensnared Persephone. See *Notebooks*, trans. Arthur Wills (London: Routledge 1956) 126, 401, 545; *Intimations of Christianity*, trans. Emma Craufurd (London: Routledge, 1976) 3, cf. 187; and *Waiting for God*, trans. Emma Craufurd (New York: Harper, 1973) 163, cf. 133-34, 209. See further *Intimations*, 186: "to be free, for us, is to desire to obey God"; similarly, *Waiting*, 129, and 211: those who in love of God turn with all their souls from worldly things "do not turn toward God. How could they do so when they are in total darkness? God himself sets their faces in the right direction." This is very much in the spirit of Kierkegaard in EUD, 136-37, 309, 359-60.

[61]Thomas, ST 2.2.9 reply. See also above at nn. 42-44.

passivity is *active*, because we must freely and bravely venture it, "embrace it with self-denying love" (EUD, 360). The renunciation and the venture require all our heart and all our might and our whole soul (EUD, 10), though all we can really do is to *want* and pray and suffer God to help us and work with us.[62] We bring all our courage to be transformed and united to God's own boundless confidence and assurance.

Is Kierkegaard Speaking of Himself?

Kierkegaard says that it is better to appear to people *worse* than one is, rather than better, which is especially dangerous if one is responsible for this: for if one does wrong and hides it under a piety practiced publicly before others to draw their attention and praise, one risks discrediting the truth by one's falsehood and misleading others not only about oneself but also about what piety is, and thus harming them as well as oneself. But when one truly means to do right and piously serve the good, one must dare to let people see it rather than conceal it and mislead them to their ruin (EUD, 369-70). Two paragraphs before this, Kierkegaard says that someone who achieves much good and wins great praise will nevertheless notice whether one was able to give *all* for it, and admitting the discrepancy and weakness can teach one to know God and the courageous spirit that God gives to the humble person (EUD, 368-69, cf. 394-95). He has referred to those who cannot even resolve to devote themselves to the good and begin at once to serve it, but only admire and speak with praise about doing so (EUD, 357-59). Accordingly, one could wonder whether he is speaking, respectively, of the nominal Christian in Christendom, of Bishop Mynster in his pulpit and palace, and of himself hidden behind his books; and more particularly and personally, in the third case, of a weakness of spirit and body, and an inability

---

[62]EUD, 273: "Since I am capable of nothing myself, should I not *desire* the concern and confidence and courage to believe you and in this faith to expect your salvation!" (emphasis added). Cf. 44: let us be honest in our accounting before God, though it is painful, and we may win "the courage to understand that every good and every perfect gift is from above . . . [and] the faith to receive this courage, since it, too, is a good and a perfect gift."

to be known in this and to accept sympathy for it that led him to break his engagement, about which he writes in the *Journal*. But is this the kind of weakness he refers to in his upbuilding discourse?[63] Are his words intended primarily for himself, to caution himself to admit his weakness more openly, to resolve with fuller seriousness and humility to give himself to God, consequently his weakness also, praying God to give *him* courage, to give him a spirit of power and love and self control?[64]

Some scholars have thought that Kierkegaard *is* speaking to and about himself and about this kind of weakness. For example, Kresten Nordentoft, in his provocative study *Kierkegaard's Psychology*, giving one of the few extended discussions of this upbuilding discourse, links it to the analyses of anxiety about evil and about the good in *The Concept of Anxiety*, and of the sin of despairing over one's sin in *The Sickness unto Death*, and all three to certain personal entries in the *Journal*.[65] However, *The Concept of Anxiety* and *The Sickness unto Death* are both indirect works, reduplicated dialectically so that we cannot be sure of the author's intentions, not to add his relationship to what he has written; more significantly, while *Anxiety* was published like "Against Cowardliness" in 1844, and *The Corsair's* attacks were provoked in 1846, *Sickness* did not appear until five years later in 1849.

Kierkegaard does write in his *Journal* about his depression and mentions some physical disability like a twisted spine or impotence, and his unwillingness to be found out and pitied; and he remarks in 1849 that the *Journal* might one day be published: "If someone wanted to publish my journals after my death, it could be done under the title: *The Book of the Judge*" (JP, 6:6380). Other entries from that year and the following one, however, indicate that the judge that he means would be Kierkegaard himself, judging the moral disintegration of Denmark. Only someone who has lived and died as he has could do it. His witness would be the

---

[63]EUD, 373-74, cf. 364-65.

[64]EUD, 368-369, 309, 273.

[65]*Kierkegaard's Psychology*, trans. Bruce Krimmse (Pittsburgh: Duquesne University Press, 1978) esp. 290-307, "The Richard III Complex," drawing especially on CA, 111-54, SUD, 60-67, 110-12, and JP, 4:4599; 5:5913, 6020-21, 6133, 6135; 6:6274, 6325, 6372, 6472, 6500.

judgment.[66] Moreover, what Kierkegaard tells himself in 1849 about his own cowardliness is simply this:

> Pfui, pfui, that my fear of danger, hypochondria, and distrustfulness of God led me to want to make myself out to be far inferior to what I have been given. As if arrogating something to myself were only a matter of defrauding the truth, as if making oneself out to be inferior were not a matter of defrauding God and the truth, and yet it seemed to me to be so humble! O, hypochondria, hypochondria! (JP, 6:6394)

Hypochondria could be a reference to his depression and physical problem; but it need not be understood that way. It could be his concern about his constant exhaustion and need to manage his energies so that he lives to fulfil his goals.[67] In any case, what he emphasizes here is his cowardice in "defrauding God and the truth" while calling it humility; in the discourse he calls for "each one" to test oneself in holding back, to see if this is moved by anger and pride, guilty gloom and isolation that refuses sympathy (EUD, 373-74, 375). If he refers the reader's thoughts to himself as the author, it is to his own maieutic indirection rather than to any private secret. This brings us to the heart of the matter.

Kierkegaard insists that words are used with ethical and religious meaning and truth only if one fulfills them in existence (or at least strives to carry them out, or admits that one has failed), for otherwise one's actions and life disprove them and even show that one does not understand them.[68] But we for our part who read and hear them do not understand them either, nor ourselves in relation to what we understand, unless *we* fulfil them.[69] What matters ethically is their truth and meaning for us, individually.

Thus if we take to heart what Kierkegaard says about maieutic indirection and writing and reading with subjectivity and inwardness, then we ought to acknowledge that what counts is our own relation to what he writes and to the truth that we find in it, so

---

[66]JP, 6:6555, 6609.

[67]JP, 6:6194, 6221, 6232, 6258, 6556, 6664.

[68]See, e.g., JP 3:3506, 3568, 3694, 3748, 3764.

[69]Thus JP, 1:484, 649-13, 656: "truly to apprehend ethical and ethical-religious truth means to reduplicate existentially what is known"; 2:1880; 3:2894: "Action is the true understanding of the law"; 4:4914, cf. EUD, 173; FSE, 28-29.

that our interest in his personal weakness is liable to be an evasion and self-deception.

He warns in his own voice against such "craftiness" (EUD, 332), and his spokesman Climacus declares in the *Postscript* that "If one is inquisitive about [an ethical] thinker's actuality, finds it interesting to know something about it, etc., then one is intellectually censurable, because . . . [in this sphere] the thinker's actuality is a matter of complete indifference," (CUP, 1:325).[70] He means that it is completely indifferent *ethically* to anyone else, whose concern is with one's own task as the only actuality while another's is only a possibility; thus "Woe to him who wants to judge hearts" (CUP, 1:587).

Moreover, when Kierkegaard writes that "as soon as you hear a pronouncement, an exhortation, a sermon, you must say to yourself: Who is the speaker? What is the nature of his life?" (JP, 4:4313), let us notice the reason that he gives for doing this. It is "to protect yourself against falling into the hands of Sophists" of whom Christ says that "You will know them by their fruits" (Matthew 7:15-16); and more particularly, it is "to save yourself from the illusion that Christianity is an objective communication instead of a life of imitation and discipleship." What is the life to which the speaker calls us by his or her own actions and life? Let us understand ourselves in what we understand. We are to *do* as the speaker says, not as he or she does, who only wants to talk about doing it.

Moreover, as Kierkegaard explains elsewhere, these words of Christ are not said "to encourage us to get busy judging one another" (WL, 14), but to encourage each one of us to let love work and bear fruits by which it can be seen in *us*. It is the work of love not to track down hypocrites but boldly to believe in love in others and build it in them, for that makes it recognizable and builds it in us. In other words, we should dare to be not the knower of love in others by its fruits in them, but the one whose love is openly known, or can be; and *now* we will know love, and

---

[70]I thank Howard Hong for constantly bringing forward this passage in meetings whenever such psychobiography was proposed.

be safe from hypocrites (WL 14-16, 236). "The earnest person always lays the stress on himself" (EUD, 340).

Thus, to conclude, reading Kierkegaard's discourse with earnest resolution and humility means concerning ourselves not with his melancholy and with him and his relationship to the truth, but simply with the truth and our own relationship to it. It means concerning ourselves not with *his* cowardliness in failing wholeheartedly to resolve to humble himself to be nothing but a divine instrument, and to ask God for the courage to do this, but with *ours*.

14

Upbuilding as a Propaedeutic for Justice

Robert L. Perkins

Eighteen Upbuilding Discourses is not a typical Kierkegaardian title.[1] It sounds inept, for it suggests some strange combination of the objectivity of arithmetic and the subjectivity and inwardness of a religious and moral psychology. Although Kierkegaard did not create this title, he did parcel out the discourses in six small volumes with titles that announced the number of upbuilding readings the purchaser would find between the covers. One wonders if the volume containing four discourses cost twice that of the volume containing only two. That would be consistent with the objectivity of mathematics. The "upbuilding," however, is qualitatively different from the mathematical. It would be ridiculous to ask if there was twice as much upbuilding in the collection containing four discourses as there is in a book containing only two. Upbuilding has to do with character, subjectivity, and inwardness. This combination of subjectivity and objectivity in the titles of the books accounts for our discomfort.

The complex relation between the inner and the outer, the subjective and the objective, is also characteristic of our lives, and the effort to understand ourselves using those and other distinctions is the major theme of Kierkegaard's authorship. What I propose to examine here is how the inner, the "place" of upbuilding, relates to the outer, our social and political space. The examination initially discovers that the concept of justice is present throughout the authorship from the sermon that closes *Either/Or* to the very end of his life when he published the last of his

---

[1] For the practical interests that created this title see "Historical Introduction." The humorous twist is that there is also a collection of *Sixteen Upbuilding Discourses* (EUD, xxii).

religious discourses, "The Changelessness of God." I then proceed to look at his most remarkable statement of the relation between the religious and the political in "Two Notes."[2] Next I argue that the capacity to rule well resides in the character of the ruler, that is, in the quality of the person's upbuilding or education[3] and that this is excellently provided for in *Eighteen Upbuilding Discourses*. Finally, I attempt to resolve a tension some have found in the relation of the secular, the political, and the upbuilding in Kierkegaard's writings.

Upbuilding and Justice from the "Ultimatum"
to the "Unchangeableness of God"

So central and fundamental is the concept of upbuilding to his authorship that Kierkegaard claims that "the upbuilding is mine" (JP, 6:6461; EUD, Supplement, 483). But that is scarcely apparent in 1843 when he publishes *Two Upbuilding Discourses*, the first of the six volumes, and even less so earlier. First, a bit of historical orientation.

When the first volume of upbuilding discourses appears Kierkegaard is already rather well known around the market town as a leading light in the conservative coterie and as somewhat of an aesthete. He had published a few articles in the newspapers and given a provocative lecture at the Student Union. His views about women,[4] the press, and the National Liberals[5] are at best conven-

---

[2]These texts appear to be part of *On the Point of View for My Work as an Author*, for they appear as a supplement to that work in *Kierkegaard's Writings*. Appearances are deceiving. The arrangement is a holdover from the first publication of these works by Kierkegaard's brother, Peter, in 1859. See PV, xviii.

[3]Plato expressed this same thought in *Republic*, 441-45b.

[4]EPW, 3-5. See also, Julia Watkin, "Serious Jest? Kierkegaard as Young Polemicist in 'Defense' of Women," in *International Kierkegaard Commentary: Early Polemical Writings*, ed. Robert L. Perkins (Macon GA: Mercer University Press, 1999) 7-25. Hereafter, IKC:EPW. *Feminist Interpretations of Søren Kierkegaard*, ed. Céline Léon and Sylvia Walsh (University Park PA: Pennsylvania State University Press, 1997) focuses a number of issues in Kierkegaard's treatment of woman throughout his authorship.

[5]EPW, 3-54, 129-176. See also, Robert L. Perkins, "Power, Politics, and Media Critique: Kierkegaard's First Brush with the Public Press," in IKC:EPW, 27-44. Alastair Hannay's, *Kierkegaard, a Biography* (Cambridge UK: Cambridge University

tional and at worst reprehensible. On 7 September 1838 he publishes a small book on H.C. Andersen, *From the Papers of One Still Living*, but it has the controversial reputation of being so convoluted that probably only he and Andersen ever read the whole thing.[6] His dissertation, *The Concept of Irony with Continual Reference to Socrates*, disgruntles the whole philosophy faculty.[7]

Then comes *Either/Or* I and II. With this huge work, his reputation as a literary giant is guaranteed. Kierkegaard's vision of human society is clear: the common life is divided between those who are single-mindedly self-seeking, self-indulgent, and egocentric, and those who respond dutifully and responsibly to their personal, familial, and civic roles. This much is evident for all to see then and now, but there appears to be something askew with the book. The problem is the final part of the work, the sermon. Why is it there? What is missed if the Parson's sermon is ignored?

Such a selective reading of *Either/Or* edits out a deontological claim for a justice that transcends the temporally and spatially local definitions, Kierkegaard's fundamental view of justice which he never revised or rejected. The title of the sermon is "The Upbuilding that Lies in the Thought that in Relation to God We are Always in the Wrong" (EO, 2:339-54). That thought is not exactly a staple of pop religion. A theological critic could assert that the sermon forecasts the final revelation of a theological reactionary, or worse, iconoclast. Theology aside, a literary critic could suggest that the addition of the discourse destroyed the incisiveness of the title and spoiled the balance between the "either" and the "or." The sermon, by this view, is a clumsy or hasty addition. Such responses ironically support the view

---

Press, 2001) 1-29, offers a historically rich and entertaining review of the disputes.

[6]EPW, 53-102. See also Richard Summers, "Aesthetics, Ethics, and Reality: A Study of *From the Papers of One Still Living*," in IKC:EPW, 45-68, and Bruce H. Kirmmse, "A Rose with Thorns: Hans Christian Andersen's Relation to Kierkegaard," in IKC:EPW, 69-85.

[7]Bruce H. Kirmmse, "Socrates in the Fast Lane: Kierkegaard's *The Concept of Irony* on the University's Velocifère" in *International Kierkegaard Commentary: The Concept of Irony*, ed. Robert L. Perkins (Macon GA: Mercer University Press, 2001) 17-99, esp. 44-82.

defended in *Either/Or*, Part One, that the bourgeois world is ethically smug, holds a complacent view of its religiosity and piety, and has a rather moldy literary taste and duller critical capacity.[8]

Rather, the sermon testifies to the sure hand and genius of an author who has an informed grasp of the literary currents and the wider cultural issues of the time. *Either/Or* is now recognized as an "arabesque novel" and one of the more successful ones.[9] The Parson's sermon calls into question the pompous moral self-satisfaction and self-congratulation of the enlightenment and romantic periods, specifically as manifest in Copenhagen's Golden Age. From the standpoint of ethical reflection the sermon shifts the focus from a Kantian and an Hegelian universalism to a concern for moral psychology, that is, to the consideration of the ethical as that which builds persons up. Theologically the sermon sets the tone of the authorship from the date of its publication to Kierkegaard's death.

Upbuilding is the central theme of the authorship to which every literary technique is subordinated, by which every theological and philosophical concept is judged,[10] and every social arrangement is criticized. No one had previously expanded the upbuilding for such broad uses. The upbuilding is indeed Kierkegaard's in this very special sense.[11] No one would claim that he achieved undiluted truth, that all his concepts are correctly laid out, or that he speaks infallibly, but only that upbuilding was the goal of his effort.

Those with the head and heart capable of reading and understanding the Parson's sermon surmise that the accommodation of Christianity to its social and spiritual environment, which Kierke-

---

[8]David R. Law discusses the status of the sermon in "The Place, Role, and Function of the 'Ultimatum' in *Either/Or, Part II* of Kierkegaard's Pseudonymous Authorship," in *International Kierkegaard Commentary: Either/Or Part II*, ed. Robert L. Perkins (Macon GA: Mercer University Press, 1995) 232-38.

[9]Sylvia Walsh, *Living Poetically: Kierkegaard's Existential Aesthetics* (University Park PA: Pennsylvania State University Press, 1994) 34n.24, 63-64n.1.

[10]Robert L. Perkins, "Kierkegaard, a Kind of Epistemologist," *History of European Ideas* 12 (1990): 7-18.

[11]Robert L. Perkins, "Either/Or/Or: Giving the Parson His Due," in IKC:EO2, 207-31.

gaard later called "Christendom," is radically interrogated and challenged.

Unfortunately, this move from the personal and upbuilding to the questioning of the cultural, social, and political environment, with a view to a just common life, has been the most difficult aspect of Kierkegaard's authorship to grasp.

The sermon suggests that human life is not rounded off in the aesthetic and the ethical; there is a third dimension—the religious. However, Judge William, Kierkegaard's pseudonym for the ethical life in *Either/Or*, has already shown that there are three great allies in the pursuit of happiness: the aesthetic, the ethical, and the religious. The aesthetic and the ethical are taken up into the "higher immediate concentricity" of the religious (EO, 2:57; see also 47, 48, 94). To the extent that persons are able to so structure their lives, they are ethically and religiously justified. To the extent that they fail, they must repent (EO, 2:216-18, 337-41, 247-49). Though repentance is a central part of the Judge's view of religious discipline, his understanding of the religious does not always find us in the wrong. In Judge William's view, the religious transforms our immediate aesthetic egotism into personal, familial and social responsibility as defined by the bourgeois culture of the day. Thus, we are in the right if we conform to those expectations.

Still, it must be emphasized that the Judge is no ordinary moral prig. He expresses a deep pathos and moral sensitivity and a profound sense of temporality. He is perhaps no more ethnocentric than the rest of us; his inwardness conforms to the beliefs and habits of that time and place. But in spite of the rather favorable light in which Kierkegaard casts Judge William, his belief structure and form of life are undercut by the Parson's sermon.[12]

---

[12]It would be somewhat of a misreading to contrast my view of the stages with those of David Gouwens in *Kierkegaard as Religious Thinker* (Cambridge: Cambridge University Press, 1996) 102-103; and George C. Connell, in his "Judge William's Theonomous Ethics," in *Foundations of Kierkegaard's Vision of Community*, ed. George C. Connell and C. Stephen Evans, (Atlantic Highlands NJ and London UK: Humanities Press, 1992) 56-70. More recently Connell has taken a more negative view of Judge William: see his "The Importance of Being Earnest: Coming to Terms with Judge William's Seriousness," in *International Kierkegaard Commentary: Stages on Life's Way*, ed. Robert L. Perkins (Macon GA; Mercer University Press, 2000) 113-48. For a different critical approach to the Judge, see

The sermon develops a more radical view of religion that calls
into question the socialized religious truisms of the Judge and the
compromises that characterize Golden Age Copenhagen, that is,
the context of Kierkegaard's own life and writings. Judge William
tells us no conscious lies, but, being a high-minded and principled
man, he thinks the best of all, including himself, and paints as self-
justificatory a picture of himself and the age as his bourgeois
understanding of the facts permits.

By contrast, the religious, as understood by the Parson, is not
a reflection of the proper manners and social relations characteristic of the respectable bourgeois. Rather, the religious is that
meeting with the divine wherein we find that we are always in the
wrong. The Parson's stark remark emphasizes the difference
between persons and God. Persons have nothing to offer the
divine, a thought Kierkegaard will express through several figures
of speech throughout the writings.[13]

It is not at all clear that anyone at that time recognized that the
Parson's sermon challenges not only the religious self-satisfaction
of Judge William subsequent to repentance, but also his idealized
picture of the social structures and interests that emerge in the
historic development of bourgeois Christendom in the modern
period.

In *Eighteen Upbuilding Discourses* Kierkegaard changes the
figure used by the Parson, being always in the wrong in relation
to God, to the more positive claim that "To Need God is a Human
Being's Highest Perfection" (EUD, 297-326). Such a title is clearly
an assault against every sense of human self-assertion and self-
confidence vis-à-vis the divine. A new kind of character is called
forth, one that "permits no evasion, occasions no self-deception"
(EUD, 309). The struggle between the "first self" and a new
"deeper self" (EUD, 314-15) leads to their reconciliation only
through the victory of the deeper self, the self that, paradoxically,
can do nothing in relation to God.[14]

Ronald L. Hall, *The Human Embrace: The Love of Philosophy and the Philosophy of
Love, Kierkegaard, Cavell, and Nussbaum* (University Park PA: Pennsylvania State
University Press, 2000) 71-81. See also Walsh, *Living Poetically,* 99-125, esp. 123-25.
    [13]For two instances, EUD, 307, 314 and CUP, 1:207-209.
    [14]There are some interesting analogies between the Parson's view that we can

Still it is important to emphasize that the deeper self who must build up himself or herself is a nineteenth century Dane. However, insofar as persons are transformed by appropriating the Parson's sermon, they are a new kind of person and their commitments, goals, and passions will be to some extent incommensurable with their environment. Although Kierkegaard is by no means a religious or Christian reformer (EUD, 142-43), his concept of upbuilding calls for a new form of society founded upon a new kind of person—that is, unless one can demonstrate a complete break between a person's internal psychological constitution and the kind of society a person would desire and support. Upbuilding is not just a personal, private matter; its implications are social and universal. However, this "universal," as noted above, is not the familiar one we meet in Kant or Hegel, the principal objects of Kierkegaard's philosophic criticism. To delineate his own thinking, Kierkegaard coins his own term, the "universally human" (EUD, 143; CUP, 1:73) about which he writes:

> The subject of the single individual appears in every book by the pseudonymous writers, but the price put upon being a single individual, a single individual in the eminent sense, rises. The subject of the single individual appears in every one of my upbuilding books, but there the single individual is what every human being is. This is precisely the dialectic of "the single individual" [changed from the particular]. The single individual can mean the most unique one of all, and it can mean everyone. . . . The point of departure of the pseudonymous writers is continually in the differences—the point of departure in the upbuilding discourses is the universally human. (EUD, supplement, 475-76)

Kierkegaard develops the concept of "the single individual" as a religious concept and struggles to keep it so limited, for he did not want it hijacked by some provincial interest (EUD, xvii-xx, 42-43, TA, 98-99). One major reason for his resistance to a political reading of his thought is that he did not wish to be considered either a supporter of the older establishment (the absolute monarchy and the Danish form of Christendom) or a contributor

---

do nothing in relation to the divine, Socrates' view that he knows nothing really worth knowing, and Luther's *sola fide*.

to the success of the "coming storm," the liberal revolution of 1848–1849.[15] Neither the Christian gospel nor his efforts to revivify its religious authority should be used for mere political or ecclesiastical ends.

Expressions like "the Danish form of Christendom," or "the older establishment," to mention only two historically conditioned concepts, show the contrast between the thought of Judge William and the Parson: how can a religious view both maintain a sense of transcendence and be "of use" in the world without finally being reduced to and measured by that usefulness? Judge William seems to have no problems. The Parson and his author struggle with this issue of the relation of divine expectation and a worldly measure thereof. An analogous relativizing and watering down of justice must also be addressed. This limitation on the ethical-religious thought of Judge William does not completely nullify the validity of his thought, but the Parson's sermon reminds us that every person, politics, and culture remains under divine sanction.

The Parson's warning against the cynicism that can undercut the idealism of youth provides the context of his comment on justice. He writes,

> Justice you will love; justice you will practice early and late. Even if it has no reward, you will practice it. You feel that is has an implicit demand that still must be fulfilled. You will not sink into lethargy and then at some time comprehend that justice did have promises but that you yourself had excluded yourself from them by not doing justice. (EO, 2:344)

For the Parson, the claim of justice is absolute and unconditional, but our participation in its protections and consolations is conditioned by our being just and doing justly.

This theme of the absolute demand of justice in the Parson's sermon reappears in the last discourse Kierkegaard published, "The Changelessness of God" (TM, 283-81).[16] Although, one

---

[15]Kierkegaard's rejection of the interest of the liberal attempt to appropriate his views, in this instance support of civil marriage, is the occasion of "An Open Letter" (COR, 51-59), published in 1851.

[16]Kierkegaard preached this sermon in 1851 during the tumultuous period of the restructuring of the social and political fabric of Denmark and published it on 3 September 1855 in the midst of the [in]famous "Attack on Christendom," only

suspects, most readers would have caught the contrast between the "attack literature," especially *The Moment*, and this discourse, one wonders how many caught the contrast between the tumult of the times and the serenity of the divine.

Speaking about the "terror and the reassurance" of God's changelessness, Kierkegaard writes,

> In a truer sense than the most watchful human justice is said to be present everywhere, he, never seen by any mortal being, is omnipresent, everywhere present, at the least and at the greatest, at what can only figuratively be called an event and at what is the unique event, when a sparrow dies and when the Savior of the human race is born. (TM, 271)

This passage testifies to the orthodox nature of Kierkegaard's understanding of the divine presence, but he extends and intensifies this core Christian belief to make clear its import for the Parson's demand that his listeners (and the rest of us) love and do justice. God's changelessness is usually invoked for purposes of consolation, and that is well and good. However, still insisting on the dichotomy of good and evil (*pace* Nietzsche), Kierkegaard warns the "light-minded" not to presume to forget the demands of justice even if they escape the negative consequences of "their transgressions" and the growing malignancy of their sins as they notice that divine punishment is withheld. That such a person escapes justice in the temporal order of things can be called luck, but it is certainly a trap from the standpoint of eternity. If one neglects justice during one's life, that is, if a person sets oneself against the divine will in time and does not repent, then throughout eternity that person remains in opposition to the divine because God is unchangeable and what occurred in time is unchangeable in eternity (TM, 275-76).

Kierkegaard works clearly within traditional Christian concepts. But he also works within the Socratic tradition of the gadfly and ironist.[17] Acting as a gadfly in the midst of Christendom, he admits that he is not a Christian (an analogy to Socratic ignorance). Kier-

---

two months and one week before he died on 11 November 1855.

[17]TM, 340-47. See Kirmmse's discussion of the connection of Plato and Kierkegaard in his *Kierkegaard in Golden Age Denmark*, 463-66.

kegaard claims his task is "to audit the definition: Christian" (TM, 343), much as Socrates attempted to audit the definitions of justice and many other decisive terms that define the quality of our humanity.

I have shown that Kierkegaard is an engaged author concerned early and late with justice. Although he does not attempt to construct the term politically, sociologically, or even hypothetically as Plato did, Kierkegaard connects the core meaning of justice to a religious view of human relations deeply dependent upon the Christian view of character. The charge could be made that his effort is a mere tip of the hat to justice, pious and platitudinous, but no more. In rebuttal Bruce Kirmmse forcefully writes:

> Only by neglecting social and historical elements has Kierkegaard scholarship missed the point that his entire authorship is informed and guided by his vision of politics and society and that the concluding polemical phase of his authorship must be understood as an expression of the requirements of that vision in the post-1848 world.[18]

The authorship shows Kierkegaard gradually working his critical vision of bourgeois Golden Age of Denmark. What is that vision?

Kierkegaard's Vision of Politics and Society

Kierkegaard reveals the central ideas of his "vision of politics and society" in "Two Notes," where he writes:

> If, however, he (the impatient politician) would kindly be a little patient, I am convinced that he, too, will become aware, even in the brief suggestions communicated in these pages, that the religious is the transfigured rendition of what a politician, provided he actually loves being a human being and loves humankind, has thought in his most blissful moment, even if he will find the religious too lofty and too ideal to be practical. (PV, 103)

This remarkable passage must be read carefully. The contrast between the impatient politician and one who is "a little patient" is primarily a matter of personal formation. As a thought experiment I shall now introduce a phrase, "the patient politician," to

---

[18]Kirmmse, *Kierkegaard in Golden Age Denmark*, 410.

exploit this qualification Kierkegaard provides to qualify his rather negative views of politics. Whether the best that politics can offer is achieved or not is not a matter of the times or the environment but rather is dependent on the character of those who lead in politics, whatever the times and the environment. The quality of the achievement or failure of politics lies in the personal quality of the politician, whether the person is patient or impatient. The weight Kierkegaard assigns to these antithetical personal qualities is a remarkable, perhaps even a laughable approach to political activity and priorities to some readers. A few questions may demonstrate the pertinence of Kierkegaard's recommendations.

First, is there not a difference between the aims and methods of various politicians? That is, would two politicians recommend different or the same policies in the same situation? To be sure, in the same situation different recommendations are often made (Republican, Democratic, or Socialist, for instance). Where there is a difference one must make a distinction.

Second, what is the source of the differences which are so apparent? Do the above differences lie in the personal values of the politicians, their education and experience, their family values or, for short, in fate? The very fact of politics suggests that the differences are the result of a subtle synthesis of our choice of ends and means within a given historic and physical context and are not a matter of fate (SUD, 29-30, 40, 146-47).

Third, are the personal values of politicians (and other folks) a matter of formation, choice, education or, again, fate? Unless one is a very hard determinist, the answer is on the side of human formation and choice. It appears that Plato's question about how one educates the philosophic ruler is back before us.

Fourth, what then would be the basic and preferable qualities or character of the politician, according to Kierkegaard? The brief text from "Two Notes" also makes clear why and how the religious ideal, as understood by Kierkegaard, can drive and direct a politics, dialectically appropriating the limits of the political and the categorical ideality of the religious, understood as the universally human.

However, given "Christendom," its power plays, its establishment, its exercise of self-interest, etc., Kierkegaard realizes that the religious ideal is in itself ambiguous. In response to this complexity, Kierkegaard states the two conditions necessary for a patient politician to create the best that politics can offer, and both are expressed in the core terms of the ethical absolute of Christianity, that is, in terms specific to his own moral and religious environment.[19]

The first condition resulting in a correct character formation of the patient politician is that he or she "loves being a human being," that is, the person has a proper self-love. But more than that it also means loving human existence, what it is to be a human, and this broadening suggests the second condition. The well-formed politician also "loves humankind," (PV, 103) that is, the person loves the neighbor as he or she loves "the dear old self" (Kant). To the extent that these two conditions obtain, a humane politics is possible; to the extent that they are explicitly rejected, rendered nominal, or jingoistic (as in fundamentalism), politics will be rendered both inhumane and irreligious, at least from the standpoint of Christianity.

Fifth, how do we obtain, train, educate, or form such politicians? Quite simply, we train them to be patient. Is that all? That is all we can gather from Kierkegaard's remarks in "Two Notes." But perhaps being patient is a very complex criterion that must be unpacked, like other pithy commands, such as "Love your neighbor as yourself." We are familiar with some of the complexity of the latter instruction. In fairness to Kierkegaard we should examine at least a few of the implications of his complex understanding of patience and seek to apply those to politics insofar as our understanding permits.

---

[19]It is fundamental to the existential "situatedness" of the universally human that Kierkegaard address the local situation. For a parallel instance, it is the responsibility of the Mullahs to address the forms of compromise in the histories of their own cultures, and they are authorized to do so within the terms of their religion.

Ethics and Knowledge in the Moral Psychology
of the Patient Politician:
The Eighteen Upbuilding Discourses
as a Text in Political Leadership

There is a certain grammar (or logic) of patience and impatience. Although primarily a matter of moral psychology, it also has theological and philosophical import. The insights in these several fields are each internally coherent and cohesive and, taken together, they support and reinforce a personal moral excellence and a humane politics. *Eighteen Upbuilding Discourses* makes a singular contribution to understanding the destructive nature of impatience and the upbuilding power and efficacy of patience. More attention is given to this pair of antithetical personal characteristics than to any other moral qualities discussed in the *Eighteen Upbuilding Discourses.*[20] In this section I shall sketch the import of this virtue for political leadership.

In the Parson's sermon a person learns one's place in the universe, that neither a single human being nor humankind is the measure of all things. Rather, the measure is the divine; "God is the criterion" (EUD, 260-61, SUD, 79). Although important, sometimes even terribly important to us personally, our immediate and individual judgment of things and events lacks ultimacy. The object of *Eighteen Upbuilding Discourses* is to aid an individual in understanding and appropriating values that at the same time are both political and social and deeply held personally. As if to challenge the secular view of politics and the anti-Christianity of the Enlightenment and German idealism, Kierkegaard writes polemically:

> Ultimately only the essentially religious can with the help of eternity effect human equality [*Menneske-Lighed*], the godly, the essential, the not-worldly, the true, the only possible human equality; and this is also why—be it said to its glorificaion—the

---

[20]See Andrew C. Burgess, "Patience and Expectancy in Kierkegaard's *Eighteen Upbuilding Discourses, 1843–1844,*" in *Kierkegaard Studies Yearbook 2000,* ed. Niels Jørgen Cappelørn, Hermann Deuser, and Jon Stewart (Berlin: de Gruyter, 2000) 205-23.

essentially religious is the true humanity [Menneskelighed]. (PV, 104)

Such a view of the essentially religious is utterly nonjingoistic, nonauthoritarian while also inclusively ecumenical, qualities that were argued at length in *Concluding Unscientific Postscript to "Philosophical Fragments"* (CUP, 1:129-251, esp. 199).[21]

Given the nature of political relations, patience is central to the development and maintenance of, first, authentic personhood, and, second, political discussions that assume differences. Although certainly no rewrite of Plato's *Republic*, in these discourses Kierkegaard delineates a certain and necessary quality of character of persons who would seek justice within themselves through the development of their capacities and the ordering of their passions as well as in the society through politics.

The patient politician Kierkegaard imagines in "Two Notes" must also be schooled in the grammar of love we find in *Works of Love* so that the person loves the neighbor as one loves "the dear old self." These spiritual conditions being met, social and political transition to a better mundane life would be possible, at least ideally. Although attaining such a worldly goal is not the point of Kierkegaard's authorship (CUP, 1:625-30), it is, at least conceptually, a possibility he recognized and enthused about in "Two Notes" (PV 103-104).

Neighbor love demands equality, that we are to love the person of the highest rank and the person of the lowest rank equally (EUD, 142). This theological egalitarianism has immediate social and political implications. Such externalities are also insignificant for the patient politician. Internal equality is a gift from God that no external historical or sociological circumstance can metaphysically deny and that no political organization or

---

[21]Not to belabor the obvious, this view of "the essentially religious" can include any skeptic and atheist who is not psychologically compulsive to the point of intolerance toward difference. See in this context Robert L. Perkins, "Climacan Politics: Person and Polis in Kierkegaard's *Postscript*," in *International Kierkegaard Commentary: Concluding Unscientific Postscript*, ed. Robert L. Perkins (Macon GA: Mercer University Press, 19970) 33-52, esp. 38-42. Though Perkins does not raise the point, it is clear that Johannes Climacus, the author of *Postscript*, has read and absorbed *Eighteen Upbuilding Discourses*.

economic reform can more than approximately approach (EUD, 143), a point further refined in *Works of Love*.[22] The law of love, loving the neighbor as oneself, and the equality of all persons within the love of God regardless of any and all circumstances, is contrasted in "Two Notes" with the political effort to impose an external equality which he likens to "worldliness against worldliness" and to a "spontaneous combustion" that "has caught on fire" (PV, 104).[23]

In Kierkegaard's view the world and worldliness have never achieved equality in social practice. Worldliness rather is the drill a person puts himself or herself through to be different from others for no other reason than egoism and self-esteem. Worldliness makes distinctions—racial, economic, sexual, educational; any quality will do so long as it is directed to the most gratifying of pleasures, self-congratulation. Such a life plan is the very opposite of that of

> *the prototype* and the relative prototypes normatively formed accordingly, each one separately, managed by their many years of exertion, work, and disinterestedness to become nothing in the world, laughed to scorn, insulted, etc.,—which to a politician must seem the peak of impracticality. (PV, 103)

Such an apparent detachment of even the "relative prototypes" from political effort is clear enough to raise serious questions. There is nothing explicit here about neighbor love, though one must assume that was the motive of all their work and exertion. The politician must reject such a form of life, even the life of the relative prototype. His vocation is different, but is it simply an expression of worldliness? The difficult question then becomes: what is the function of politics in Kierkegaard's thought? Is

---

[22]WL, 49-58, 67-68, 73-77, etc., esp. 136. Ferreira, *Love's Grateful Striving*, contains numerous discussion of these complex issues, 94-98 being the most pertinent here. See also, JP, 1:683. Kierkegaard reports that he read the passage about the king and the charwoman (WL, 135-36) to the king himself (WL, Supplement, 481-82).

[23]The literary history of the works of 1848 is quite complex (PV, xiii, xvi-xix). Given that date it is no wonder Kierkegaard thought there had been a "spontaneous combustion" of "worldliness against worldliness." "Two Notes" was not published until 1859 (PV, xviii-xiv).

political activity directed solely to the exercise of power for purposes of self-aggrandizement and self-congratulation? Or does a patient politics have another end?

The patient politician has a place between the prototype and the relative prototypes, on the one hand, and the purely worldly, on the other. He or she has the right and duty to exercise conscience in politics, just as the king and the charwoman equally do in their very different vocations (WL, 136). The patient politician's conscience is formed by "the religious" which

> is eternity's transfigured rendition of the most beautiful dream of politics. No politics has been able, no politics is able, no worldliness has been able, no worldliness is able to think through or to actualize to the ultimate consequences the idea: human equality, human likeness [*Menneske-Lighed*]. (PV, 103)

This text has been incorrectly read as an expression of Kierkegaard's political passivity, but a careful reading discovers that it is anything but that. Rather, the text is a recognition of the reality of everyday politics. The passage does not inculcate a know-nothing, do-nothing attitude toward political issues and problems any more than it suggests a passivity in undertaking the immediate tasks and necessities that political entities face everyday.

The fact that politics and worldliness have not actualized and cannot actualize "to the ultimate consequences the idea: human equality, human likeness" does not mean that there should be no striving to actualize this ideal at all. The text rather infers that the work of politics must be carried on piecemeal and is never finished. Political acts are not for eternity; policies must be modified as circumstances change. Nor does this text suggest that any politics which has as its aim to actualize the idea of human equality is as good as any other. All political criteria must be brought to bear on any and all political activities and thought: justice, the common good (an ancient term greatly expanded in the modern period), and fairness, to name a few.

The patient politician, then, is one who recognizes the tentativeness and temporary quality of one's work. It will all have to be done again, if not by himself or herself, then by those who come later. But the "true north" of politics will be this "most beautiful dream of politics," human equality and likeness. The beauty of this dream and the recognition that one's work is as temporary and fragile as life itself testifies to the patience of the politician.

Let us now turn to the brief character sketch of the patient politician as opposed to the impatient politician by examining the concepts of patience and impatience as they appear in *Eighteen Upbuilding Discourses* in order to understand the education of the ruler who acts politically on the basis of human equality.

The concept of the universal is basic to the education of the ruler envisioned in "Two Notes." As noted above, Kierkegaard radically shifted the center of gravity of the concept of the single individual by dialectically transforming it so that it comprehends the single individual and the human race (EUD, Supplement, 475-76). Throughout *Eighteen Upbuilding Discourses* Kierkegaard stresses the importance of the universal (EUD, 240, 243, 250), but especially in the discourse, "Think About Your Creator in the Days of Your Youth" (EUD, 233-51; Ecclesiastes 12:1). This text provokes a religious response in the youth through the concept of the Creator as being of ultimate significance, a "concerned truth" that must be inwardly "appropriated" (EUD, 233-34).[24]

Working out the grammar of "Creator" leads the youth to comprehend the universal, and this thought becomes the source of resistance to every vanity and debilitating disease of the soul (EUD, 236-37). By stressing the concept of God that underlies human equality in this discourse about the education of young people, Kierkegaard suggests the basicality of the matching concepts of universality and equality in the character profile of every well-formed person, including (unbeknownst to himself at the time he wrote *Eighteen Upbuilding Discourses*), even the patient ruler. Nesting so early in the person's heart, these related concepts become the foundation of the patient ruler's political values. How does a young person develop into such a ruler?

Everyone has the same initial task: "To Gain One's Soul in Patience" (EUD, 159-75),[25] or as we might say more prosaically, to

---

[24]In the *Concluding Unscientific Postscript to "Philosophical Fragments"* concerned truth will become "subjective truth" and the youth will become the "subjective existing thinker" who "thinks the universal" and "appropriates" it (EUD, 233-34, CUP, 1:77-80).

[25]This discourse and the next, "To Preserve One Soul in Patience," appeal to

become a resourceful, self-directed person. "Soul," as Kierkegaard uses the term, is obviously different from the usual Platonic, Cartesian, or theological notion. His usage is more operational and functional than metaphysical. To speak of gaining one's soul suggests more than an ontological a priori; the soul is an achievement, an end sought and attained. It also makes sense to speak of "gaining oneself."

"Patience" in attaining this end is an art, not in the aesthetic sense, but in the existential connotation of a practice and skill. There is no self-improvement book on the art of patience as there are books introducing drawing or how to improve one's golf game, though both of these activities require the development of disciplined skills. Patience, for instance, must frequently defer to the interests and desires of others. The tedium of such patience may appear as, and actually be, self-denial, and, again like the practice of an art, political patience is a constant and life-long task. As a virtue, art, and task, virtue requires knowledge. How is it taught? Who are the qualified teachers? Perhaps there are none. However, Kierkegaard ironically suggests, contrary to Meno's examples of the teachers of virtue (*Meno*, 89b-94e), all of whom have some valuable arts and skills, that perhaps an impatient person is the best teacher of patience (EUD, 159). Such a person can be a hard master, for it requires patience to put up with obstinacy, complaining, arrogance, or other unpleasant characteristics.

All knowledge requires the appropriation and practice of the skill involved to keep it fresh in mind and developing through experience. The art of carpentry, for instance, relates to the wood, the tools, and the plan. The art of patience is interpersonal; what is "made" by the art is a form of human relation. Patience eschews autonomy, for that suggests independence; patience is the art of relating in such a way that persons are able to maintain their selves, their selfhood, in the relation. The mother does not set out

---

the same text, Luke 21:19. Persons familiar with the so-called Authorized Version's translation, "In your patience possess ye your souls," may be somewhat jarred by the RSV's effort, "By your endurance you will gain your lives," and wonder even more at the NEB's, "By standing firm you will win true life for yourselves."

to learn patience but rather to care for the child. She adapts to the needs and petulance and enjoys the smile and cooing of the child. Incidentally, she learns patience in the relation.

How does patience contribute to a person's gaining a self or soul, that is, to becoming a person? The patient person has cares, and these constitute the attention and activity of the person to being a mother or an educator, two examples Kierkegaard mentions. Such persons submit to "the way it is," in order to be successful. "The mother who wants to have the joy of her child does not wish it to grow up in a hurry but waits patiently through sleepless nights and troubled days" (EUD, 161). Such a woman is "a real mother."

To gain one's soul or to become a self requires one to be a realist, in this instance to understand the child, its difficulties, its strengths, as well as one's own limits and capacities. Reality dictates the terms: the helplessness of the infant, the problems of "the difficult child," the rebelliousness of the adolescent, etc., and the mother submits to those terms for they are the conditions of human development. The mother also must recognize her own capacities and limits within the more intimate social relations such as the family and the wider social relations such as the economic, political, and social structure. Such knowledge is a form of realism, but it is far from a "naïve realism."

Gaining one's soul, in this instance becoming a mother, is rather complex, demanding focus, intelligence, dedication, and strength. Lacking these conditions, the would-be mother may impatiently lapse into "wild, undisciplined outbursts that achieve nothing but only give rise to confusion and harm" (EUD, 161). In a biological and legal sense, she would be no less a mother, but she is less such in the fundamental sense of the child's and her own upbuilding. This circumstance is recognized in common speech when we say of someone, "So and so is not a real mother (or teacher or statesman)."

Upbuilding human relations are not just a matter of passion and sentiment, though these are fundamental to any action. The passions and the sentiments must be disciplined by a cold-eyed realism, the determined focus gained from decided (chosen) ends, and intelligence that matches means to ends.

Likewise for the politician. To become a politician, the person must make the same kind of moves as the would-be mother. Fired by the love of county or country, the patient politician must understand the cultural, political, sociological, and economic realities of "the way it is," choose wisely his or her ends, and pursue them relentlessly with intelligence "through sleepless nights and troubled days." The object of the patient politician is the upbuilding of the county or country; his or her vocation is not an exercise in egoism that would soon manifest itself as impatience and produce "confusion and harm."

Having gained his or her soul, the person's next task is to continue what was so well begun. How does a person, having intelligently focused his or her energies in a certain direction, persist in the self-appointed task of becoming that sort of person?

In the previous discourse on patience, the necessity of knowledge was shown, but the reader had to uncover the word. In the next discourse, "To Preserve One's Soul in Patience," Kierkegaard equates patience with deliberation, saying "they are essentially the same,"[26] an identification that calls into question Kierkegaard's reputation for being an irrationalist (EUD, 187-89). The practice of the virtues requires knowledge, and vice versa, knowledge has import for the practice of the virtues.[27]

The essential identity of patience and deliberation seems odd but is accounted for by the ambiguity of time. There is a certain deceptiveness in time, for it seems that there is always time to deliberate later. The reality is that if we delay deliberation, we will not be able to exercise patience. Rather, not having thought through the matter, when the instance is upon us, we cannot avoid acting impatiently and/or thoughtlessly. The existential and political import of this difficulty about time, generally known as procrastination, surely requires no argument. Still, after stressing that "most crucial issues are decided slowly, not in haste and all at once," Kierkegaard states that patience makes a clear distinction between "tomorrow' and "this very day" (EUD, 200). Politically,

---

[26]Although focused on *Works of Love*, Ferreira's discussion of deliberation is still of great use to readers of this discourse. See her *Love's Grateful Striving*, 13-19.

[27]This claim of an epistemological import of ethical terms was recognized by Kierkegaard as early as the Gilleleie journal (JP, 5:5100, pp. 34-35).

"tomorrow" can be a delusion and clear testimony to the lack of deliberation. "This very day" is the mean between delay and precipitancy

Deliberation may seem useless and unnecessary in the hustle and bustle of everyday life, and besides, all one learns from it is "what one is" (EUD, 188). Deliberation, however, is not idly mulling things over, but is actually a thorough examination of every "little secret" and every "dream in one's soul, this seductive fantasy with which one at times could entertain himself" (EUD, 188). Deliberation is then an encounter with self-deception, escapism, infatuation, and the delusions one entertains about oneself, about others, and the way things are. In deep sympathetic and pathetic irony Kierkegaard writes, "One accomplishes nothing by it [deliberation], achieves nothing, does not amount to anything by it, but simply and solely finds out what one is—which is indeed a very poor and meager observation" (EUD, 188).

Deliberation as Kierkegaard presents it here is Socratism-plus. In addition to the unrelenting intellectualism of the Socratic *elenchus*, Kierkegaardian deliberation is also a sustained effort to examine the import of patience and other virtues for personal integrity, epistemological presence to the world, political wisdom, and the courage to act in a timely manner.

In the person of the patient politician deliberation is internal and personal as well as political. To be sure, he or she is a well-founded person, self-aware, self-critical. Such characteristics are not monologistic. Rather, without the exercise of a deliberative self-choice, one will be the product of one's family values, the sexual and racial stereotypes common in the society, the nationalist pretensions of the political order, the economic prejudices offered by a bought and paid-for system of controlled media, and the staples of "public opinion," which Kierkegaard a short time later dubbed "the crowd" (TA, 85). Such submission to the protocols of the common life propels one into the despair of finitude and necessity (SUD, 35, 37-42) and the despair of weakness which lacks the strength and courage to be a self (SUD, 47-67). Without a courageous choice of the self, one is simply leveled into the mass (TA, 84, 86-96).

The deliberative, well-formed individual is the only basis of politics for Kierkegaard and the only one who can become a patient politician. The basis of the patient politician's rejection of the politics of leveling is "human equality, human likeness." Monologistic politics rejects human equality by its rejection of discourse and dialogue and by its demand for conformity to authority.[28] The patient politician cannot be authoritarian because of his or her common humanity shared with all members of the body politic. Dialogue or the meeting of minds will overcome both leveling and authoritarianism, the two sides of the same counterfeit coin so characteristic of modern politics. Again, both these practices are aesthetic at the personal level and purely private, the expression of a life and a politics compounded of desires, inclinations, and wishes.

Deliberation is also contrary to the "wish."[29] Aesthetic wishing is a special form of escapism and self-pampering, Aladdin being a special hero in that he possessed the "audacity of the child, of the genius, in the wildest wishes" (EO, 1:22). "There is no limit to the wish," and so the wish becomes a byword for impatience; one is never satisfied with what is (EUD,189). By contrast, deliberation helps us comprehend what is, and that bit of realism is the basis of the rational appraisal of the world that enables us to wisely adjust ends and means. Moreover, if we were to gain every wish, we would lose "the best, the holiest, [that is] to be what God has intended him [or her] to be" (EUD, 190). Deliberation is not only pragmatically pertinent but also religiously essential to becoming a self and a patient politician.

Kierkegaard offers a political example of the manner in which ambition, a form of wish or desire, can cause one to lose "the best, the holiest." Self-centered purpose can lead to the loss of the self in great undertakings. Kierkegaard refers to Julius Caesar's "I came, I saw, I conquered" as an instance of such purposes.

---

[28]For a more extensive criticism of the charge of monologism against Kierkegaard, see Martin J. Matuštík, *Postnational Identity: Critical Theory and Existential Philosophy in Habermas, Kierkegaard, and Havel* (New York and London: Guilford Press, 1993) 120-23.

[29]See EO, 1, 43, 50, 52. These texts refer to wishing well, aesthetically, intellectually, and cleverly. Although both texts would come under the category of entertaining fantasies, they are the wishes of the elite, the privileged, and the cultured. There is nothing here for the fishmongers, the roofers, or the convicts.

Suetonius quotes this familiar claim of Caesar and shows its arrogance, its pathetic gaudiness, and its emptiness (EUD, Supplement, 517-18). Kierkegaard is not suggesting that a person should have no cause—"purpose is indeed to be praised"—but only that causes must be very carefully selected else they become an enslaving wish. Such ego enhancing enslavement to great world significant purposes can be the manifestation of the wish, and the result is "impatience" which spells out as the worst excess of personal vanity, political arrogance, and the lust to dominate (EUD, 191).

Of course, the wish also makes for horrendous results in the world, in the present example, for the Gauls. Although a military and political genius, Caesar rejects the fundamental idea of politics, at least as Kierkegaard understands the root of a humane politics, "human equality, human likeness" (PV, 103).

Not having learned of the cares that fill up a life, such as those of the mother, not having learned the patience to deal with what is (EUD, 191), but imposing one's wish on any and all, the impatient person is unprepared to "begin the long battle with an indefatigable enemy, time, and with a multifarious enemy, the world" (EUD, 192). What can fill such a person's life? Conquering many kingdoms is one answer, but there are other forms of the distractions of variety and multiplicity for the less politically dominating persons (EUD 193-94).

Two other instances are locked together. Both great wealth and grinding poverty can be sources of the impatience that destroys the soul. Both the "movers and the shakers" and the "moved and the shaken" learn that "everything is for sale" (EUD, 195). Some purchase distractions ad infinitum but still have nothing of value. Others, not economically successful, suffocate in discouragement and disappointment (EUD, 194-95). Such are some of the destructive ways of impatience.

Patience, grounded in deliberation and bound to the world by care, finds enough to fill a life. Patience presupposes itself; one becomes what one is. In the external world, patience is not just the one thing needful; in that world impatience may be more profitable (EUD, 169). But as we have just seen, Caesar, the movers and the shakers, and the moved and shaken may never possess themselves (EUD, 163-67). But the one who is deliberatively patient realistically deals with the world but puts no claim upon it. What the patient person obtains is himself or herself (EUD, 172). Experiencing no need to dominate others, the self's relations to others are open, honest, nonauthoritarian, and free. Such a person can be patient, and such a person can be a patient politician.

Perhaps the greatest difficulties for a political reading of *Eighteen Upbuilding Discourses* appear in the third discourse we are examining here, "Patience in Expectancy" (EUD, 205-26).

Expectancy is not the same as waiting for the class to begin (or end) or waiting to reach the head of the line and be the next person served by a busy clerk. This is everyday experience, and those who are properly acculturated fall in line. We expect our time will come. All this is well and good, but not quite what Kierkegaard is thinking about in this discourse, for, let us say for argument's sake, this everyday experience is not touched by the eternal (EUD, 208). In contrast to those of us standing in line, Kierkegaard introduces Anna, the prophetess who awaited the Messiah and who staked her hope on this promise which might or might not be fulfilled in her lifetime. The promise was made by the Eternal, and so fulfillment or nonfulfillment is not a matter for temporal concern. Thus she could never be disappointed (EUD, 213-23). Is this just religious fanaticism and/or escapism? Distinctions are called for.

To be sure, persons can be overcome by distress and let themselves "fall to the ground." But the failure of expectancy in this instance is earthly and temporal, and such expectancy can leave one in despair (EUD, 214). In doubt and despair, the problem is not in cognition, for knowledge is indeterminate. But to move from uncertain knowledge to a certain and determined outcome or decision, to let oneself "fall to the ground," invites doubt and despair. That there is no immediate fulfillment of one's hopes disappoints only if one's hopes are temporal and earthly. By contrast, if one's hopes are in the eternal, then the expectancy takes on the character of the eternal. Anna's hopes are founded in the eternal, and so her hopes must be fulfilled whether she lives to see the temporal fulfillment of them or not (EUD, 217). In trustful patience she has set no condition on her expectation. One who has faith in the future fulfillment of a divine promise is concerned with the future in a very different way than other mortals (EUD, 218).

Those who, like Anna, trust a divine promise, do not become impatient. Persons who set goals such as "How much will I be worth five years from now?" can fall into despair because of conditions over which they have no control.

Anna's hope is for fulfillment in time, but her expectancy is in the eternal. Just as persons become like what they love, Anna becomes like what she expects (EUD, 219). She expects to see God's Messiah, but if she does not, God's promise is still fulfilled; the promises of the Divine are unchangeable. Thus, for her the promise is fulfilled even if she does not see it with her eyes. "But true expectancy is such that it pertains to a person essentially and does not leave it up to his [or her] own power to bring about the fulfillment. Therefore, every truly expectant person is in a relationship with God" EUD, 221). Happily, Anna does experience the fulfillment of the promise in her patiently faithful relationship to God. But most do not experience the fulfillment of their expectancy in time. Certainly the patient politician will not, and this suggests difficulties in Kierkegaard's understanding of both upbuilding and politics.

The Impossible Dream of the Patient Politician

Both Anna and the patient politician are exemplars of the single individual, particular individuals in different times and places yet also representative persons who express the universal qualities and potentialities of human being. Both are "moral achievers," for they have been built up by the practice of expectancy and patience. So far all things are alike and equal.

Still there appear to be some disturbing differences between the expectations of the patient politician and Anna, differences that call into question Kierkegaard's view of upbuilding and politics. What are they? The major difference between the two is that one exercises patience in a religious context and the other in the secular world. Anna is cloistered in the temple, witnessing to and praying for the coming of the Messiah. Her expectation is fulfilled; she recognizes an infant as the coming One. Her experience is very religious but unworldly and sectarian; it is utterly lacking in moral and ethical consequence outside the temple and even more inconsequential for social and political life. Figuratively speaking, the presentation in the temple is a universe from the Roman fortification.

However, as Kierkegaard reminds us, "In these times everything is politics" (PV, 103). Kierkegaard understands the political and the fabric of modern life generally as irreligious domains concerned with the aesthetic or worldly, broadly and nonprejudicially conceived. For convinced critics this evaluation joined to the praise he gives Anna gives support to the stereotypical view that Kierkegaard's religious thought is otherworldly and inconsequential for the common life.[30]

Such an inference is as extreme as unfounded. The proper political and social inference is the one Kierkegaard drew long after the publication of *Eighteen Upbuilding Discourses*, that the proper business of the state did not include the supervision of the church and vice versa.[31] Kierkegaard had some concern for these political and social arrangements, but they were not his major ones. However, his political interest is manifest in *Eighteen Upbuilding Discourses*, and it is anything but otherworldly. To obtain a more balanced picture of Kierkegaard's thought, one that will rebut the critics just referred to, we must continue the appraisal of the patient politician who unites the religiously grounded education of *Eighteen Upbuilding Discourses* with the vocation of political leadership.

The patient politician is concerned with the world, its chaos, injustice, and the desperate need of a politics based on patience. The patient politician deals with the neighbor and sometimes with an enemy, and he or she works for justice. This difference especially commends the patient politician to us, for he or she loves and serves justice as the Parson authoritatively commanded.

---

[30]For a typical expression of the charge of otherworldliness in Kierkegaard, see Anthony Rudd, *Kierkegaard and the Limits of the Ethical* (Oxford UK: Clarendon Press, 1993) 166-67. Recent critics of the charge of "otherworldliness" include M. Jamie Ferreira, "Otherworldliness in Kierkegaard's *Works of Love*" and Sylvia Walsh's comment on Ferreira's article in *Philosophical Investigations* 22 (1999): 65-79 and 80-85, respectively.

[31]For a brief review of the complexities of the situation in the political controversies during the writing of the new constitution in 1848–1849, see Kirmmse, *Kierkegaard in Golden Age Denmark*, 73-76. For Kierkegaard's own appraisal of the situation, see TM, 411-12, 574-75.

Thus the critique of Kierkegaard's thought as otherworldly appears to be groundless; his concern is with the immediate, the existential, what is at hand, not constitution writing and the defense of some self-serving institutional arrangement (JP, 4:4181).

The efforts of the patient politician are not futile, although he will apparently never experience a fulfillment like that of Anna who saw her hoped-for Messiah. Perhaps expectancy, in most cases, could be more worldly than Anna's. At best the patient politician will be pleased that city services are working reasonably well and will require no fresh infusion of tax revenue this year. Still, between Anna and the patient politician there are real differences about what constitutes expectation.

Is there any way out of this difficulty short of a *deus ex machina*? Any way out must focus the terms and issues discussed above: the universality of the ethical and the broadened concept of patience that Kierkegaard has introduced into ethical theory and moral psychology. Hopefully these concepts are sufficiently supple to account for the differences between Anna and the patient politician. Still, an incorrect or insufficient answer to this question could jeopardize Kierkegaard's theory of personal formation developed in *Eighteen Upbuilding Discourses*, for it may then appear that only the morally prim and/or religious types could develop from the regime of upbuilding Kierkegaard recommends. First a short recap.

Following Kierkegaard's hint of a distinction between the patient and the impatient politician, I developed a thought experiment featuring the patient politician who is educated by the upbuilding discourses, particularly in the exercise of patience. The examination found that the inward appropriation of patience and its outward expression required a complex array of character traits: It requires self-denial, self-understanding, intelligence, deliberation, tenacity, the capacity to understand the desires, hopes, and fears of others, and the ability to distinguish one's own long-term and short-term ends, to name some of the more obvious features. All this is well and good, but complicated by Kierkegaard's view of politics.

Kierkegaard's pessimism about politics is both philosophically and theologically grounded. Like Kierkegaard, the patient politician would be as far from the politics and religion of Christendom as human imagination can conceive. However, the patient politician has something Kierkegaard did not have: a patient expectancy for the political. Kierkegaard was impatient about the politics he knew, especially when he wrote "Two Notes."[32] At that low point he challenged, we may recall, the politician to "kindly be a little patient" and consider whether "the religious" is not the "transfigured rendition" of what the politician himself has "thought in his most blissful moment" (PV, 103). Ironically, the same gesture also expresses Kierkegaard's own most "blissful" hope for the political: the patient development of a politics guided by the philosophical and theological ideals of human equality, human likeness.

When one turns to *Eighteen Upbuilding Discourses* one finds hope transformed into political struggle, especially the struggle for equality. There are two types of equality discussed in the text, temporal or social equality ("the external") and spiritual equality "before God" (EUD, 142-43). Kierkegaard is interested primarily in the latter and thinks the former, the political and the social, is of secondary importance and "of very little benefit" (EUD, 143). Note, however, that he does not say of no benefit.

We can better understand Kierkegaard's point if we note three grim truths: that what politics and society give they can also take away, that recognition of human equality is hard won and easily lost, and finally, the denial of equality can take many forms, glass ceilings, stereotypical language, and sexual objectification, etc, to use contemporary examples. This is a charitable reading of Kierkegaard's minimizing of the significance of external equality. More critically, it can be said that he was so comfortable with and acculturated to the invidious social inequalities that he did not consider the issues seriously or consistently throughout the authorship.[33]

---

[32]In his article, "Power, Politics, and Media Critique," Perkins suggests the continuity of Kierkegaard's critical views of politics from the beginning of the authorship to this point, 1848. See n. 3 above.

[33]Still Kierkegaard writes in 1849: "Just as Christ tells the rich young ruler to sell all his goods and give to the poor, so one could also speak of the requirement to give all his rank and dignity (that is, the earthly, temporal) to the poor to express equality" (JP, 5:4158).

However, in *Eighteen Upbuilding Discourses* there is a clear recognition that those who seek to appropriate spiritual equality into their patterns of living, that is, to express it in the external world, must struggle against forces and influences that undercut this form of equality in the world. Appropriating Walsh's emendation of the text,[34] Kierkegaard urges a woman

> to fight the good fight with flesh and blood, with principalities and powers, and in the fight to free [her]self for equality before God, whether this battle is more a war of aggression against the differences that want to encumber [her] with worldly favoritism or in a defensive war against the differences that want to make [her] anxious in worldly perdition. (EUD, 143)

It appears, then, that Kierkegaard clearly recognized the importance of social and political conflict at the time he wrote *Eighteen Upbuilding Discourses*. The benefits of political and social equality are minimal and must be continually sustained by reaffirmation of the gift of equality before God. Moreover, the discourses refer constantly to the working out of patience in social encounters of various types, some of which I have mentioned.

Equality before God is then both a gift and an achievement. As a gift, spiritual equality is guaranteed by the character of the giver. As an achievement, the appropriation and expression of God's gift in the external world, that equality must be wrestled away from the "principalities and powers" that have enjoyed privilege and power by the denial of equal rights and privileges for all.

Here is where the patient politician enters the picture. We recall that he or she understands human equality and likeness as the absolute claim of justice, for this person's understanding is theologically anchored in the proper self-love and a love of every human being. These ideals drive his or her social thinking and application in policy decisions. Internally inspired by these ideals, the patient politician must negotiate with the recalcitrant self-interest of persons and the authority of imbedded customs which deny human equality and likeness. These self-serving and other-

---

[34]See Walsh's article, "When That Single Individual Is a Woman," esp. 44-47 in this volume. Walsh reveals the reach of Kierkegaard's analysis when she substitutes feminine nouns and adjectives for his consistent masculine usage.

punishing persons and customs manifest an improper self-love and explicitly reject equality in love for every human being. These rather obvious conditions lie at the bottom of Kierkegaard's criticisms of society and politics, and they engender the unremitting passionate concern of the patient politician.

The startling outcome of the clash of the ideal and the actual in the inner experience of the patient politician is that he or she undertakes to accomplish and express human likeness and equality in the political realm. However, the choice of means must be consistent with ends themselves. The impatient politician uses any means necessary to achieve his or her ends, but in Kierkegaard's view that results only in "a worldly friction of worldliness against worldliness" (PV, 103). Remembering the Creator and the universal implied by that term, and being finely educated in patience, the patient politician attempts to effect political change by non-authoritarian means that require at least an equal participation in an open debate and a maximal restriction of force in enforcement of what most think is for the common good. The patient politician guards the sanctity of inward equality by every means available in a politics of maximal external equality. Kierkegaard did not develop these implications of this thought, but they seem to be consistent with the education in patience confronting political necessity in the world he knew and we all know.

Kierkegaard thought that the patient politician would be eminently impractical in the eyes of the impatient politician (PV, 103), but the patient politician does not despair since he or she has internalized the concepts of human equality and likeness. Such a politician would go about the work of politics and bring a touch of the eternal, the religious, to its task, goals, and means. This is, of course, the kind of politics the world needs.

At this point one can understand the significance of the question previously raised about the differences between the patient politician and Anna due to the different outcomes of their expectations. The simple resolution of that difference lies in our perceptions of what would fulfill their expectations. Anna lived to see her expectation fulfilled in the cloister. The cloister is no privileged place without its challenge to patience. She recognized a baby, and knew that God had fulfilled her expectation.

The patient politician exercises the same virtues as Anna in his vocation and endures the challenges of politics. We tend to think in utopian and totalizing expectations in and for politics, but that is because we are impatient. The patient politician, by contrast, sees the fulfillment of his or her expectation of respect for human equality in the provision of, for instance, safe water in a village that has never had any in a country that could have provided it earlier but did not because of the lack of a sense of justice and equality in the political process. To be sure, his secular success is small potatoes, no "I came, I saw, I conquered," but who wants to say the patient politician's effort is not God's work accomplished by the exercise of a divine virtue, a virtue perpetually exercised on our behalf by the Divine, that is, patience, a.k.a. the forgiveness of sin?

In this essay I have expanded a bare hint from Kierkegaard about patience into a figure, the patient politician, and on that basis have attempted a political reading of *Eighteen Upbuilding Discourses*, a volume most would regard as utterly unpolitical, in order to show how upbuilding is a propaedeutic to justice.

This completed effort is, however, only another beginning for every Kierkegaard reader, for we need to continue to address and to thrash the age-long prejudices that are imbedded in the literature about Kierkegaard's apolitical conservatism, philosophic irrationalism, and asocial individualism. There is much in this article that undermines each of these unfortunate views. Most generally, the very idea of a patient politics rebuts all three of these misunderstandings.

Still there is work to be done, and I see it as the direct application of Kierkegaard's categories in the public arena: a call for reflection, deliberation, and dialogue instead of scapegoating, veiled class and party interests, nationalistic jingoism and fundamentalism in religion and in politics, and the destruction of the natural environment and human well being in the name of a dogmatic economic philosophy that masks a demonic greed. In the ethical sphere we need to continue to urge the cognitive dimension of ethics and the ethical import of knowledge in all spheres of human being, including but not limited to, an intensification of opposition to aestheticism or emotivism and the destructive self-indulgence so prominent in much of pop culture. And each time we appeal to his concept of the individual, we need to express ourselves in such a way as to undercut the unrecognizable readings that concept has received. "That single individual" is one person and all of us together.

Contributors

International Kierkegaard Commentary 5
Eighteen Upbuilding Discourses

THOMAS C. ANDERSON is professor of Philosophy emeritus at Marquette University.

MARTIN ANDIC is associate professor of Philosophy emeritus at the University of Massachusetts.

ANDREW J. BURGESS is associate professor of Philosophy at the University of New Mexico.

RANDALL G. COLTON is assistant professor of Philosophy at Eastern University.

HARVIE FERGUSON is professor of Sociology at Glasgow University.

MICHAEL LOTTI is a teacher at Trinity School at River Ridge in Bloomington, Minnesota.

EDWARD MOONEY is professor emeritus of Philosophy at Sonoma State University in California and Part-time Professor of Philosophy and Religion at Syracuse University.

GEORGE PATTISON is associate professor of Practical Theology on the Theological Faculty at Aarhus University.

ROBERT L. PERKINS is professor emeritus of Philosophy at Stetson University.

DAVID D. POSSEN is a graduate student in the Committee on Social Thought and the Department of Philosophy at the University of Chicago.

M. G. PIETY is assistant professor of Philosophy at Drexel University.

ROBERT C. ROBERTS is professor of Philosophy at Baylor University.

STEVEN SHAKESPEARE is vicar of St. Augustine's in Sheffield and research associate at the Lincoln Theological Institute at the University of Sheffield.

SYLVIA WALSH is scholar in residence at Stetson University.

Previous Volume Consultants

Volume 1. *Early Polemical Writings*
Julia Watkin, University of Tasmania

Volume 2. *The Concept of Irony*
Ronald L. Hall, Stetson University

Title Consultant for *Either/Or* I and II
George Connell, Concordia College

Volume 3. *Either/Or, I*
David Gouwens, Brite Divinity School

Volume 4. *Either/Or, II*
Edward F. Mooney, Sonoma State University

Volume 6. *"Fear and Trembling" and "Repetition"*
Abrahim H. Khan, University of Toronto, *Fear and Trembling*
David Goicoechea, Brock University, *Repetition*

Volume 7. *"Philosophical Fragments" and "Johannes Climacus"*
Lee Barrett, Lancaster Theological Seminary

Volume 8. *The Concept of Anxiety*
Vincent A. McCarthy, St. Joseph's University

Volume 11. *Stages on Life's Way*
Vincent A. McCarthy, St. Joseph's University

Volume 12. *Concluding Unscientific Postscript
to "Philosophical Fragments"*
Merold Westphal, Fordham University

Volume 13. *The Corsair Affair*
Bruce H. Kirmmse, Connecticut College

Volume 14. *Two Ages*
Merold Westphal, Fordham University

Volume 16. *Works of Love*
Lee Barrett, Lancaster Theological Seminary

Volume 19. *The Sickness unto Death*
Louis Dupré, Yale University

Volume 21. *"For Self-Examination" and "Judge for Yourself!"*
David Cain, Mary Washington College

Index